THE HEARSAY RULE

THE HEARSAY RULE

SECOND EDITION

G. Michael Fenner

JAMES L. KOLEY '54 PROFESSOR OF CONSTITUTIONAL LAW
CREIGHTON UNIVERSITY SCHOOL OF LAW

CAROLINA ACADEMIC PRESS
DURHAM, NORTH CAROLINA

Library of Congress Cataloging-in-Publication Data

Fenner, G. Michael.
    The hearsay rule / G. Michael Fenner. — 2nd ed.
        p. cm. Includes bibliographical references and index.
    ISBN 978-1-59460-697-7 (alk. paper)
    1. Evidence, Hearsay—United States. I. Title.
    KF8969.F46 2009
    347.73'64—dc22   2009004925

Carolina Academic Press
700 Kent St.
Durham, NC 27701
Telephone (919) 489-7486
Fax (919) 493-5668
www.cap-press.com

Printed in the United States of America

For Anne

For Hilary, Ben, Tashi, and Alex

And for Yangdon, Kalden, and Lyle

CONTENTS

TABLE OF AUTHORITIES

FOREWORD

Part of my job as a law professor teaching Evidence is to teach hearsay as a tool. My students need to learn to understand hearsay so that they can use this tool to advocate a position, to convince an opponent, first, and a judge, second, and to win. My students need to learn how to manipulate the hearsay rules to serve the ends of their clients. I hope I am a good teacher of manipulation. Part of my job as a lawyer who works with this subject is to take sides, to argue the rules, to persuade. My job as a lawyer with this specialty calls for me to understand these rules and to engage in the manipulation I hope I teach my students.

This book is about those things. It is about how law students, lawyers, and judges can understand and use the hearsay rules. It is about how students can learn these rules right, right from the beginning (for that is so much easier than trying to relearn them later). It is about how students can use these rules in class and on their final exams. It is about how students can manipulate these rules in their clinics, mock trials, internships, and clerkships. This book is about how lawyers can understand the hearsay rules, how lawyers can build a reputation—as in "Hey, here is a lawyer who actually understands this stuff!"— and how lawyers can manipulate the rules in the interests of their clients. It is about how judges can remain faithful to the rule of law while using the rules to see that justice is served. In the process, the book tells nothing but the truth.

* * *

Chapter 1 begins with a fresh look at the principles and values that under- lie the hearsay rule. It presents time-tested and brand-new techniques for rec- ognizing hearsay for, unlike obscenity, sometimes it is not so easy to know it when you see it. Chapter 2 covers the definitional exclusions. Chapters 3, 4, and 5 cover the exceptions in Rule 803, 804, and 805, respectively. Through the first five chapters the topics covered are rather traditional and straightforward for a treatment of the hearsay rule.

Though the organization and much of the content of the first five chapters is very traditional, much of what is in these chapters is not. The key to the exclusions and exceptions is that each has a certain number of foundational facts: The lawyer seeking the admission of hearsay evidence must produce evidence of each of the foundational elements; the lawyer wanting to block admission of hearsay evidence must defeat offering counsel on at least one foundational element. This book takes a foundational approach to hearsay. It breaks out and lists the foundational elements for each exclusion and exception covered in this book. This makes it a handy quick reference. You know exactly what you need to prove or what you need to defeat for each exclusion and exception covered—even when the need arises suddenly, in the heat of battle. Following the foundational elements, is a statement of the values on which each exception is built, which will serve as an interpretative guide to the exception. Following the statement of values, for each exception covered there is a "Use Note" discussing each foundational element and commenting on ways in which each exception, each element, can be used to achieve the student's, lawyer's, or judge's goal. There is the handy, quick reference of the list of foundational elements and the ultimately more helpful detailed discussion, with cases and ideas on the use of each of the foundational elements.

Some other examples of what is new in the first five chapters: Chapter 1 presents new ways of conceptualizing hearsay. The part of Chapter 2 that deals with adoptive admissions presents a whole new way of looking at them, analyzing them, and understanding them—one that seems simpler than the traditional ways of approaching adoptive admissions.

In addition to a very complete treatment of the exclusions and specific exceptions—with foundational elements, the values behind each, and in depth analysis of each foundational element—Chapters 2, 3, and 4 look past the trees of a particular exception and onto how the exception fits into the forest of hearsay. The Use Notes discuss the ways various parts of the hearsay rules interrelate. Surprisingly, this is not commonly addressed in other works, which mostly just talk trees, and not forest. An example of seeing the forest is in the discussion of the former testimony exception. That Use Note begins with a discussion of other ways to get former testimony around the hearsay rule. Students, lawyers, and judges faced with former testimony will see a discussion of eleven ways it might be admissible in spite of the hearsay rule: the former testimony exception and ten other techniques.

Chapter 5 presents the most complete treatment of the residual exception currently available. It includes, for example, a discussion of how that exception can be used to get into evidence an out-of-court statement made by a witness who is testifying—get the out-of-court statement in as substantive evidence of the facts declared and not just as impeachment, even though the out-of-court declarant is a testifying witness. There is offhand reference to this point in some other writings, but there is no analysis and all of the offhand references come to what I think is the wrong conclusion. This is an important point. Take, for example, a criminal case where the prosecutor has a favorable pretrial statement from a witness and the witness takes the stand at trial and tells a different story. Perhaps the witness has had a change of heart out of love or intimidation. Whatever the reason, the witness tells a different story on the stand and the pretrial statement of this available witness does not fit under any of the exclusions in Rule 801(d) or the exceptions in Rule 803 or 804. Chapter 5 discusses how this pretrial statement may be admissible as substantive evidence of the facts declared...even though the declarant is testifying.

The rest of the book—Chapters 6 through 13—is not so traditional in either the topics covered or the content of the coverage. Chapter 6 goes beyond traditional evidence texts and treatises, goes beyond the rules of evidence, and discusses important hearsay exceptions that are found in Rule 32 of the Federal Rules of Civil Procedure and Rule 15 of the Federal Rules of Criminal Procedure.

Chapter 7 is devoted to state of mind evidence. Every out-of-court statement is in some way or another nonhearsay state of mind evidence. That's right: There are ways in which every out-of-court statement is nonhearsay. Sometimes, however, the nonhearsay use of the statement is not relevant. As a result, the statement will be inadmissible as hearsay in its relevant uses and inadmissible as irrelevant in its nonhearsay uses. This chapter makes an important point about the relationship between the hearsay rule and the rules of relevance. It also provides counsel with a way of turning every hearsay problem into a relevance problem. In addition, Chapter 7 gathers together the uses of state of mind evidence and discusses eight ways that such evidence might be used at trial.

Chapter 8 is devoted to the use of opinion evidence—expert and lay opinion—as a way to get around the hearsay rule. Chapter 9 is devoted to miscellaneous other ways around the hearsay rule—judicial notice and the rule of completeness for two examples. Chapters 10, 11, and 12 are devoted to important concepts such as the benefit of applying many exceptions to a single level of hearsay, the problem of multiple levels of hearsay behind a single statement, and the subject of evidence that is inadmissible hearsay to one issue in a case and either nonhearsay or admissible hearsay to another issue in the same case. Each of these chapters is useful to the student, the lawyer, and the judge alike. Chapter 11, for example, discusses how to make underlying levels of hearsay go away. It discusses cases that have found that one or another of the exceptions or exclusions does away with multiple hearsay problems. Under certain exceptions and exclusions, the declarant need not have personal knowledge of the facts declared in the statement and offering counsel need not deal with the hearsay that underlies the statement. Chapter 11 discusses where that has been held to be so, and how to argue that it is so elsewhere.

Chapter 13 deals with the interrelation between the hearsay rule and the competence of witnesses. Among other things, Chapter 13 suggests and discusses ways to stand the hearsay rule on its head and use it affirmatively— ways to use hearsay to get into evidence an out-of-court statement by a witness who was incompetent when the statement was made, is incompetent at the time of trial, or both.

Chapter 14 deals with the Confrontation Clause of the United States constitution, its interrelation with the hearsay rule, and its effect on the admissiblilty of hearsay evidence offered against an accused in a criminal prosecution.

* * *

Hearsay is a tool. Its purpose is to assist the trier of fact in the search for truth by limiting the trier of fact's exposure to unreliable evidence. How effective a tool it is, is open to question. Two things are certain: Hearsay is everywhere, and it either helps you achieve your goal or it stands in your way; either way, it is a tool that must be used to advocate, to win, and to decide. This tool must be mastered by law students, practicing lawyers, and judges alike, and it is for all of them that this book is written.

ACKNOWLEDGMENTS

First and foremost I want to thank my students and my daughter Hilary and her law-school friends for using this material in its early stages and for their unfailing encouragement that I turn it into a book. There are obvious risks associated with going beyond that kind of general thank you and actually naming those who have helped the most. Worse, however, I think, is the kind of arrogance of sole authorship associated with not trying. Some of my current and former students helped me a great deal with the research and writing of this book and they deserve to have their names associated with it. So, here goes:

■ The journey is easy. Starting and stopping are difficult. At the beginning, there was Kathy Ford and, as the manuscript submission date approached, there were Pat Cooper and Vic Padios. (You may have noticed in life the tendency to appreciate most those who've helped you most recently. Pat and Vic, I have told you in person and now I tell you in print that I am immensely appreciative of your help.)

■ In the middle, there was Heather Albertie Garretson (who believes that she wrote the book), Cristy Carbon-Gaul (to whom I said "If you think you are right, convince me," and she did), Josh Dickinson (who helped during the difficult six months when my wife and I were forced to live in Paris), and Shilee Therkelsen Mullin (who allowed me to believe that I wrote the book).

■ Katherine Kimball has been particularly helpful (and cheerfully so) in the preparation of the Second Edition of this book. Though his time on the project was limited, I thank Rob Stark as well.

■ I also want to recognize Dale Cottam, Virginia Albers, and Linda Thompson for their help on my article, Law Professor Reveals Shocking Truth About Hearsay, 62 UMKC L. Rev. 1 (1993).

My thanks to the men and women of the Paris office of Willkie Farr & Gallagher, who gave me a place to plug in and work during the six months of the most wonderful sabbatical anyone could ever have. Particular thanks to Daniel Hurstel for his hospitality and to Jacky Murray for getting my computer up and operating and keeping it working. And to my long-time friend Terry Ferguson for the introduction to Willkie Farr that allowed it to happen.

My two brothers are also lawyers. My brother Gary is a federal judge. My brother Bob is the legal counsel for a federal agency. Each is an inspiration to me, in the law and otherwise. I thank them for that. And I thank my mother and father—Mary Ann and George—for raising the three of us to know the joy of work well done.

One of the great joys in life is having a job where you look forward to coming to work each day. Most law professors have great jobs and, in my experience, most of them realize it. Not as many have as great a place to do the job as I do. For almost all of us on the faculty of the Creighton University School of Law it is true that we fight our battles and then we move on, taking nothing personally, letting nothing go sour and spoil the place where we spend so much of our time. Credit goes to the deans who have set the tone—Rod Shkolnick, Larry Raful, and Pat Borchers—and, even more so, to the faculty who make it happen.

One more thing that makes Creighton such a great place to come to five days a week is the two best faculty secretaries anyone ever had, Joan Hillhouse and Pat Andersen. Pat Andersen—whose main job is to keep us from taking ourselves too seriously—has worked hard on this book, always tirelessly, always with great humor, and always with terrific ideas. Thank you Pat!

Finally, thanks to my family, my wife Anne, and my daughter and son Hilary and Ben. I am blessed with a family of writers. Anne has a book of her own in its second edition with Fairchild Publications. Hilary is a lawyer (Alston and Bird in Atlanta, to King and Spalding in New York City, to Razorfish also in NYC, and now with Levi Strauss & Co. in San Francisco) with a real gift for analysis, synthesization, and composition. Ben is a lawyer as well (Fredericks Peebles & Morgan, an Omaha firm exclusively practicing Native American law).

Special thanks to Anne for her forbearance while I came to the office and worked on this book.

THE HEARSAY RULE

CHAPTER ONE

THE BASIC DEFINITION

I. Introduction to Hearsay

All of the rules of evidence, but for the privilege rules, are aimed at the same single target: the Truth. All but the privilege rules are designed to assist the trier of fact in the search for the truth. The objective of the rules that only relevant evidence is admissible and only competent witnesses may testify is Truth.[1] The objective of Rule 403 — evidence is inadmissible if its probative value is *substantially* outweighed by the danger that the evidence is *unfairly* prejudicial, confuses the issue, or wastes the jury's time — is Truth.[2] Underneath

---

1. Relevance — FED.R.EVID. 401: Evidence that has nothing to do with anything that matters in the case does not assist the trier of fact. Competence — FED.R.EVID. 602: A witness who has no relevant personal knowledge does not assist the trier of fact, but just wastes its time and distracts it from what is important.

2. Evidence is unfairly prejudicial by reason of its tendency to lead the jury to a decision on an improper basis (commonly, though not always, an emotional basis). If its tendency to lead the jury to a decision on an improper basis is stronger than the evidence's probative value, then it does not help (but rather hinders) the jury. If evidence confuses the issue then it makes it more difficult for the jury to keep focused on the real issues, which in turn wastes their time and energy and risks an outcome based on the resolution of false issues. If evidence wastes their time, then, of course, it is of no assistance. Worse than that, however, it too saps their energy, wastes their attention span, and drags them down, dragging the case down with them; it risks leading them astray into consideration of the wasteful evidence, thinking that if someone went to the trouble to put it into the record, it must have some hidden value. *E.g., Old Chief v. United States*, 519 U.S. 172, 180–85 (1997); *United States v. Smithers*, 212 F.3d 306, 316 (6th Cir. 2000) (delay and waste of time); *Blancha v. Raymark Indus.*, 972 F.2d 507, 516 (3d Cir. 1992) (confusion of the issues); *United States v. Brooke*, 4 F.3d 1480, 1485–87 (9th Cir. 1993); *United States v. Hitt*, 981 F.2d 422, 424–25 (9th Cir. 1992) (unfair prejudice); *United States v. King*, 713 F.2d 627, 631 (11th Cir. 1983) (unfair prejudice); *Ballou v. Henri Studios, Inc.*, 656 F.2d 1147, 1153–55 (5th Cir. 1981) (unfair prejudice).

it all, the objective of the hearsay rule is Truth; it is about keeping out evidence that categorically is so unreliable that it does not help us find the truth.[3]

The hearsay rule is a general rule of inadmissibility that expresses a preference for testimony based on firsthand knowledge. We want the real witness to what happened, not someone who was told what happened by the real witness. The hearsay rule is based on the premise that testimony is generally more reliable when it is based on firsthand knowledge than when it is based on second- or third-hand knowledge.[4] It is a rule that must be considered whenever a witness testifies[5] to a prior statement[6] that was made outside of the proceeding at hand.[7]

■ Unreliable: What makes hearsay unreliable is this: At the time the out-of-court statement was made, it was not subject to cross-examination; the trier of fact was not there to observe the out-of-court declarant's demeanor; in most cases the statement was not made under oath and was not surrounded by the solemnity, dignity, and openness of a judicial proceeding.

Cross-Examination: With most hearsay statements, there was no opportunity to cross-examine the out-of-court declarant at the time the declarant made the statement.[8] This means there was no opportunity to contemporaneously test the out-of-court declarant's (1) ability to have perceived (seen, heard, felt, tasted, or smelled) the things stated in the out-of-court assertion; (2) memory; (3) sincerity (as in the practical joke versus the sober truth); and (4) honesty.[9]

---

3. The privilege rules, on the other hand, are designed to protect confidences shared during certain private relationships. Some confidences shared in the context of certain private relationships are not admissible even if, without the evidence, we will not know the truth. FED.R.EVID. 501.

4. At its most basic level it is the difference between these two pieces of testimony: On the one hand, "I saw what happened and here is what I saw." On the other hand, "Someone who said he saw what happened told me what he saw and here is what he told me." The former is the real witness to what happened. The latter is not.

5. The testifying witness is the in-court declarant.

6. The statement is the out-of-court statement.

7. The original declarant is the out-of-court declarant. (As noted below, the in-court declarant and the out-of-court declarant can be the same person. *See* part II(C)(2) of this chapter, below.)

8. There are a few exceptions to this general statement. Some out-of-court hearsay statements were subject to cross-examination at the time they were made and are still hearsay: testimony given in court in a different proceeding, for example. *See* FED.R.EVID. 804(b)(1), the former testimony exception, discussed at Chapter 4(II). In the usual case, however, there was no chance to cross-examine the person who made the out-of-court statement.

9. Cross-examination of the in-court declarant will be available but, if all the in-court declarant has to say is "Hey, I'm only telling you what I heard," it will not be very fruitful.

These things—perception, memory, sincerity, and honesty, sometimes known as the testimonial infirmities—are things that can make testimony unreliable. Cross-examination allows the advocate to probe for these infirmities.

Oath: Most often, the out-of-court statement was not made under oath. The statement may be less reliable because the threats of spiritual and corporal[10] sanctions for lying under oath are not present.

Demeanor Evidence: The lack of demeanor evidence may also make the evidence less reliable. The trier of fact was not present to observe the out-of-court declarant's body language, attitude, intonation, hesitation or certainty, and all of the like things we all rely on day-in and day-out to assess the genuineness and certainty of those with whom we deal.[11]

Pressures Exerted by the Courtroom Setting: Out-of-court declarants may well be less impressed than in-court declarants with the need to be careful and truthful with what they say. In court, witnesses sit in an elevated witness-box, in front of an even further-elevated and robed judge, an armed bailiff, and opposing counsel, with a jury somewhat solemnly lined up off to the side. Just calling where witnesses sit a "box" implies subjugation, as does the imperious position of the judge's bench and black robe. And the in-court testimony is a public airing: It is not a private little telling, perhaps a private lie; it is not an offhand, casual comment to a friend; rather, it is a statement made in public and as part of the public record. The in-court statement is one that can come

---

Even when the out-of-court declarant does testify, there is this danger: over time, and under the influence of others, false statements are " 'apt to harden and become unyielding to the blows of truth.' " California v. Green, 399 U.S. 149, 159 (1970) (citation omitted). "Over a period of time the mind easily traverses the course, 'could it possibly have been X,' to 'it must have been X,' to 'it was X.' [X] emerges as a remembered 'fact.' " I. Daniel Stewart, Jr., *Perception, Memory, and Hearsay: A Criticism of Present Law and the Proposed Rules of Evidence*, 14 UTAH L. REV. 1, 19 (1970).

10. Prosecution for perjury.

11. United States v. Yida, 498 F.3d 945 (9th Cir. 2007) has a good discussion of the value of demeanor evidence. It is "of the utmost importance in the determination of the credibility of a witness." Cross-examination "not infrequently leads a hostile witness to reveal by his demeanor—his tone of voice, the evidence of fear which grips him at the height of cross-examination, or even his defiance—that his evidence is not to be accepted as true, either because of partiality or overzealousness or inaccuracy, as well as outright untruthfulness." *Yida*, 498 F.3d at 951 (multiple quotation marks and citations omitted). Blackstone stressed that cross-examination gives the trier of fact " 'an opportunity of observing the quality, age, education, understanding, behavior, and inclinations of the witness.' 3 William Blackstone, *Commentaries on the Laws of England* 373-74 (1768)." *Yida*, 498 F.3d at 950.

back to haunt you—and that can be the basis for a criminal prosecution for perjury.

The grandeur of most courtrooms, the ceremony and formality of the proceedings, the relative positioning of those involved and their dress, and the courtroom's openness to the public—these things are not accidental. These trappings are designed to impress jurors, witnesses, and even lawyers and judges with the importance of what they are doing and the care they must take while doing it. The whole proceeding is designed, in part, to exert pressure on witnesses—to demand attention and serious consideration.

Fear of Public Speaking: Add to that a general fear of public speaking, which dampens intelligent lying.[12]

■ Inadmissible: What makes hearsay inadmissible is the belief that, categorically, it is too unreliable. We do not trust it, but, really, it is ourselves we do not trust. We do not trust our ability to properly evaluate this kind of evidence.[13] Our goal is to determine the truth and we have decided that as a general rule we will do a better job of determining the truth if we do not use hearsay.

---

12. Far be it from me to argue with John Henry Wigmore, but ... Is cross-examination really "the greatest legal engine ever invented for the discovery of the truth"? 5 JOHN HENRY WIGMORE, EVIDENCE IN TRIALS AT COMMON LAW § 1367 (3d ed. 1940), quoted in California v. Green, 399 U.S. 149, 158 (1970). Perhaps "the greatest legal engine ever invented for the discovery of the truth" has six cylinders: testimony that is sworn, public, in-court, observed by the factfinder, based on firsthand knowledge, and subject to cross-examination. Cross-examination is the final piston turning the engine of truth.

13. The problem is not just that we use lay persons as jurors and do not trust these non-lawyers to understand the dangers of hearsay and to properly evaluate hearsay evidence. The rule against hearsay is not just a rule for jury trials. It applies as well in trials to the court. If jurors were the problem, then "hearsay would be freely admissible in any court where a judge is the trier of fact, and such is not our practice." John MacArthur Maguire, EVIDENCE: COMMON SENSE AND COMMON LAW, at 15 (1947). (For something of a limited exception to this statement, *see* Chapter 11(I), below.) In addition, Professor Herrmann's research into the ancient origins of the hearsay rule show that it was originally developed for use in forums where the trier of fact was a learned, professional judge. Roman, canon, and Jewish law "agreed that hearsay was not to form the basis of a judgment, even when it was a learned judge who evaluated the testimony." Frank R. Hermann, S.J., *The Establishment of a Rule Against Hearsay in Romano-Canonical Procedure*, 36 VA. J. INT'L L. 1, 43 (1995).

> The institution of the jury did not ... create the need for the hearsay rule. The rejection of hearsay is part and parcel of any process of dependable decision making, regardless of who finds the facts. Long before England developed its system of trial by lay jurors under the guidance of a judge, medieval jurists articulated the hearsay rule in a system involving fact finders who were sophisticated professionals.

Id. at 51.

■ **A Preference for the Real Witness:** The hearsay rule expresses the judicial system's preference for the real witness,[14] rather than a witness who heard it from the real witness. You may recall the childhood game, sometimes called "Rumors,"[15] where Person 1 writes something down on a slip of paper, and then whispers it to Person 2; Person 2 then whispers what she heard to Person 3; Person 3 whispers what he heard to Person 4; and so on. If you have played that game, you will recall what became of the original statement by the time it reached, for instance, Person 7. The hearsay rule expresses a preference for the testimony of Person 1. If the issue is, What did Person 1 see?, then the hearsay rule expresses a preference for the testimony of Person 1 (rather than any of the other six persons in the "Rumors" chain). Person 1 is the "real witness" to what she saw; Person 1 is the only one of the seven who is a "real witness"—the only one of the seven who has firsthand knowledge of what was on the piece of paper.

The goal of the hearsay rule is to assist the trier of fact in the search for the truth by driving the lawyers to bring to court, when they can, witnesses who have firsthand knowledge, witnesses whose knowledge has not come through a real-life version of the game of Rumors. The courts that created the common-law hearsay rule, and the committees and legislative bodies that created modern evidence statutes, decided that hearsay evidence is generally unreliable. The rules, therefore, make it generally inadmissible,[16] and then create exceptions where the hearsay is particularly reliable or where there is such a need for it as to outweigh the risk of admitting it.[17]

---

14. *See* part (III)(A)(3) of this chapter, below.

15. A.k.a., telephone.

16. "Hearsay is not admissible except as provided by these rules or by other rules prescribed by the Supreme Court pursuant to statutory authority or by Act of Congress." FED.R.EVID. 802.

17. The guarantee of reliability and the need can be categorical: To varying extents, each individual hearsay exception in Rules 803 and 804 expresses a determination that a particular category of out-of-court statements is reliable or that there is a particular need for that category of evidence or both. The guarantee of reliability can be ad hoc: Rule 807, popularly known as the residual or catchall exception, empowers the judge to admit hearsay evidence if the judge finds the evidence is sufficiently reliable and the need for the evidence is sufficiently great. Under the law, hearsay generally is not reliable, but some subclasses of hearsay are. We would prefer not to have to use less reliable evidence, but sometimes there is not much of a choice; sometimes the only evidence is the out-of-court hearsay statement, and we would prefer to use the hearsay rather than to lose the evidence altogether.

II. The Definition of Hearsay

A. The Definition

Hearsay is:

1. An out-of-court statement (OCS).
2. Offered to prove the truth of the matter asserted (OTOMA).
3. Not fitting within Rule 801(d).[18]

B. The Formula

The hearsay formula is:

> OCS
> + OTOMA
> − 801(d)
> Hearsay

In other words, hearsay includes every out-of-court statement offered to prove the truth of its assertion, except those that fit under 801(d). (Some hearsay is admissible and some is not. Right now, we are only considering this question: Is the evidence hearsay? We are not considering this very different question: Is the evidence admissible hearsay?)

C. An Explanation of the Definition

Here are the pieces of the definition, broken down and briefly explained.

1. A Statement

"'Hearsay' is a statement …"[19] The first and perhaps most important thing to say about "statement" is that the rules enact an assertion-based definition of hearsay. The rule states this: "A '*statement*' is (1) an oral or written *assertion* or (2) nonverbal conduct of a person, if it is intended by the person as an as-

---

18. This is discussed below, in Chapter 2. Rule 801 of the Federal Rules of Evidence contains the definition of the rule. Subpart (d) of Rule 801 lists a small number of kinds of statements that were hearsay at the common law, but are not hearsay—they are excluded from the definition—under the statute.

19. FED.R.EVID. 801(c) (emphasis added).

sertion."[20] The advisory committee's note (part of the legislative history to the rule) states this: "[N]othing is an assertion unless intended to be one."[21] In the end, anything that is intended to assert something is a statement for purposes of the hearsay rule and, of course, everything not intended to assert anything is not a statement. This is true for all out-of-court statements, whether oral, in writing, or by conduct.

■ *Words*: Any assertion made in words—spoken or written—is a statement.[22]

■ *Conduct*: The test for whether conduct is a statement is a simple one: Did the actor intend the conduct to be an assertion? If so, it is a statement and can be hearsay. If not, it is not a statement and cannot be hearsay. At this point, we are not concerned with whether anyone is likely to understand the intended message; we are only concerned with whether a message was intended. Whether conduct is a statement for purposes of the hearsay rule is entirely a function of the intent of the actor. It may sometimes be difficult to decide whether conduct is a statement, but it is always easy to know where to look for the answer: into the mind of the actor.[23]

Assume the following: A truck driver pulls away after having been stopped at a stoplight-controlled intersection. The driver of the car stopped behind the truck wants to prove that the light had turned green, and will testify that the truck pulled away and into the intersection. Opposing counsel makes a hearsay

---

20. Fed.R.Evid. 801(a) (emphasis added).

21. Fed.R.Evid. 801(a) advisory committee's note.

22. *See* Fed.R.Evid. 801(a) advisory committee's note.

23. *See, e.g.*, United States v. Childs, 539 F.3d 552, 559 (6th Cir. 2008) ("A 'declarant' is one who makes a 'statement,' and words qualify as a 'statement' only if they make an 'assertion.'"); People v. Azmudio, 181 P.3d 105, 125 (Cal. 2008) (defendant argued that the victim's out-of-court silence was a "statement" for purposes of the hearsay rule; "'nonverbal conduct'— such as … silence—constitutes a 'statement' under the hearsay rule only if it was 'intended by [the person] as a substitute for oral or written verbal expression;'" nothing suggests the victim "intended her failure to say anything … to be 'a substitute for oral or written verbal expression'").

In Wells v. State, 67 S.W.2d 1020 (Tex. Crim. App. 1902), witnesses testified that the victim's husband assaulted the defendant shortly after the victim had been raped. The court held that this evidence was hearsay because it tended to show that the husband believed that the defendant had raped his wife. This result seems likely to be incorrect under the rules. Whether it is correct or not, the rule is very clear on how we are to decide whether the husband's attack on the defendant was hearsay: Did the husband intend his act of assaulting the defendant to be an assertion? It seems likely that he did not. The burden of showing the actor's intent is on the person seeking the advantage of the hearsay rule: the party opposing the evidence. *See* Chapter 3(I)(D), below and the cross-references there.

objection, arguing that the driver of the car is offering the truck driver's action as an out-of-court assertion that the light had turned green. Whether the truck driver pulling the truck into the intersection is hearsay is entirely dependent on whether the truck driver intended this act to be an assertion. It is not likely that the truck driver intended to make an assertion regarding the color of the light, or, really, anything else; if the truck driver did not intend to make an assertion, then pulling into the intersection was not a statement; if it was not a statement, then it cannot be hearsay.[24]

Take the man who hangs lanterns in the bell tower of the church, in accordance with a prearranged signal to alert confederates of enemy troop movements: "One if by land, and two if by sea." In this context, hanging the lantern is a statement because the lantern hanger intends it to be. If a witness takes the stand and, to prove that troops did come by sea, the witness testifies "A second lamp in the belfry burn[ed],"[25] then the witness's testimony is hearsay. The "second lamp in the belfry" is a statement, because the burning of the lamps was intended to make a statement; it is an out-of-court statement that asserts that the troops are coming by sea; it is offered to prove the truth of the assertion; because, as we will see, it does not fit under any of the definitional exclusions in Rule 801(d), it is hearsay.[26]

If the defendant in a criminal case offers evidence that a third person fled from the scene of the crime, and offers it as evidence that the third person is the guilty party, is the evidence hearsay or not? The answer is in the mind of the actor. Flight is not hearsay unless it is an assertion; it is not an assertion unless the person fleeing intended to make an assertion. Did this third person

---

24. Perhaps the truck was stopped at the red light. A car, driven by Driver C, pulled up behind the truck. As Driver C was pulling up behind the truck, Driver C saw that his car and the truck had a red light. After he pulled in behind the truck, Driver C no longer could see the stoplight. Soon the truck began driving forward, into and across the intersection; Driver C followed the truck into the intersection; Driver C's car was hit by a car coming across the intersection. The question at trial is which of the two drivers in the collision — Driver C or the driver of the other car — had the green light. Driver C will testify that the truck driver pulled into the intersection. From that bit of evidence, Driver C will argue that his light had turned green. Driver C's testimony that the truck driver started her truck up and into the intersection is not hearsay because the truck driver's conduct was not intended to be a statement.

United States v. Astorga-Torres, 682 F.2d 1331, 1335 (9th Cir. 1982) (drug sales were not hearsay because no one intended to make an assertion).

25. Henry Wadsworth Longfellow, *Paul Revere's Ride*, THE COMPLETE POETICAL WORKS OF HENRY WADSWORTH LONGFELLOW 255 (Household ed., Houghton, Miffin & Co. 1902).

26. Regarding the definitional exclusions, see generally Chapter 2, below.

intend to make an assertion when he fled from the scene? Perhaps he intended falsely to throw suspicion off of the defendant and onto himself. If that is the case, then he did intend to make a statement: His intended assertion is the lie "I did it (and not the defendant)." On the other hand, perhaps he is guilty and he was fleeing the scene just to get away. If that is the case, then he probably did not intend to make a statement and he almost certainly did not intend to make the statement "I did it. I am the guilty party." So, did the third person fleeing the scene intend to make a statement? It depends.[27] But, if I am the judge I know where to look for the answer, and if I am the lawyer I know what to argue.

And, by the way, the evidentiary burden of convincing the judge that the evidence is hearsay is on the party who makes the hearsay objection, the party who would keep the evidence out. That party must convince the judge that the actor intended to make an assertion.

■ *Intent*: It is a question of the out-of-court declarant's intention. The rules enact an assertion based definition of hearsay. In the end, anything that is intended to assert something is a statement, while everything that is not intended to assert anything is not a statement. This is true whether the putative statement is oral, written, or by conduct.[28]

---

27. "[I]t is not universally true that a man, who is conscious that he has done a wrong, 'will pursue a certain course not in harmony with the conduct of a man who is conscious of having done an act which is innocent, right and proper;' since it is a matter of common knowledge that men who are entirely innocent do sometimes fly from the scene of a crime through fear of being apprehended as the guilty parties, or from an unwillingness to appear as witnesses. Nor is it true as an accepted axiom of criminal law that 'the wicked flee when no man pursueth, but the righteous are as bold as a lion.'" Alberty v. United States, 162 U.S. 499, 511 (1896).

28. *E.g.*, FED.R.EVID. 801(a) advisory committee's note ("The effect of the definition of 'statement' is to exclude from the operation of the hearsay rule all evidence of conduct, verbal or nonverbal, not intended as an assertion. The key to the definition is that nothing is an assertion unless intended to be one."); Lorraine v. Markel Am. Ins. Co., 241 F.R.D. 534, 563 (D. Md. 2007) ("the hearsay rule ... only applies to intentionally assertive verbal or non-verbal conduct"); United States v. Long, 905 F.2d 1572, 1580 (D.C Cir. 1990) (speaking of "the crucial distinction under rule 801 ... between intentional and unintentional messages...," the court notes that "[o]ne of the principal goals of the hearsay rule is to exclude declarations when their veracity cannot be tested through cross-examination. When a declarant does not intend to communicate anything, however, his sincerity is not in question and the need for cross-examination is sharply diminished. Thus, an unintentional message is presumptively more reliable.").

Assertion: *E.g.*, United States v. Aspinall, 389 F.3d 332, 342 (2d Cir. 2004) (an FBI Agent asked a company for documents containing instructions defendant had given to the company; the company handed over two documents; the conduct of the company is a state-

2. An Out-of-Court Statement

An out-of-court statement is one made at a time and place other than right now in this courtroom. It does not matter if the declarant of the out-of-court statement is in court and available to testify, in court but refuses to testify, or made the statement in some other courtroom. The declarant may be on the stand and repeating his or her own out-of-court statement. The declarant may be dead or missing or otherwise unavailable. When the question is whether we have an out-of-court statement, none of this matters.

That is, if it is an out-of-court assertion offered to prove the truth of the matter asserted and it does not fall within 801(d), then it is hearsay without regard for the current whereabouts or status of the out-of-court declarant. The key is this: (1) Is someone repeating a statement made at a time and place other

---

ment — an assertion that the things on the documents are in fact instructions to the company from the defendant) (citing: "Stevenson v. Commonwealth, 218 Va. 462, 237 S.E.2d 779 (1977) (where a police officer requested that the defendant's wife give him the clothes the defendant had been wearing on the day of a certain homicide, the wife's giving the officer a shirt constituted a nonverbal assertion that defendant wore that shirt on the day of that homicide)."); Graham v. State, 643 S.W.2d 920 (Tex. Crim. App. 1981), *opinion on rehearing*, 643 S.W.2d 925 (Tex. Crim. App. 1983) (police officer asked victim if she knew who shot her and showed her six photos; when he showed her defendant's photo, "[s]he made a shooting motion, cocking her thumb with her finger pointed out," *id.* at 926; this gesture is an assertion for hearsay purposes).

Sometimes the act of standing silent is an assertion. *E.g.*, United States v. Kenyon, 481 F.3d 1054, 1065 (8th Cir. 2008) ("In some circumstances, silence itself can be such a nonverbal assertion."). This is discussed in detail in part III(E) of Chapter 2, below.

Not an assertion: *E.g.*, Florida Conf. Ass'n of Seventh-Day Adventists v. Kyriakides, 151 F. Supp.2d 1223, 1225–26 (C.D. Cal. 2001) (the act of placing the statement on the internet and the act of printing it off of the internet are not hearsay; each is conduct not intended to be an assertion); United States v. Zenni, 492 F. Supp. 464, 469 (E.D. Ky. 1980) (phone calls from bettors, answered by police during raid of illegal gambling establishment, were not assertions and therefore were not hearsay); State v. Stevens, 794 P.2d 38, 43–44 (Wash. Ct. App. 1990) (a witness testified that alleged victims had nightmares in which they cried out "Arne, stop. Arne, don't"; sleep talk is not a statement for hearsay purposes because it is not intended to be an assertion; "[T]he declarant must intend to make the statement in order for it to be hearsay"; the real question here, then, is whether these sleep utterances are relevant and can get past an objection under Rule 403); People v. Davis, 363 N.W.2d 35, 36 (Mich. Ct. App. 1984) (a mother testified that when she asked her daughter about defendant's actions, the daughter burst into tears; "The record ... is void of any indication that the victim intended to make an assertion by her spontaneous act of crying.

than right now in this courtroom? (2) Is the statement offered as evidence of the truth of whatever the statement asserts? (3) Does the statement fit within the definitional exclusions of Rule 801(d)? These three questions are a simple formula for determining whether evidence is hearsay.

Do not make the mistake of thinking that a statement is not hearsay just because the out-of-court declarant and the testifying witness are the same person, or just because the out-of-court declarant is available as a witness and can be called to the stand and cross-examined, or just because the statement was made at another trial. All that matters is whether a testifying witness is testifying to an out-of-court statement, the out-of-court statement is offered to prove the truth of its assertion, and the out-of-court statement does not fit under Rule 801(d).

This is an instance of behavior so patently involuntary that it cannot by any stretch of the imagination be treated as a verbal assertion by the victim …").

Some courts treat some interpreters as "language conduits" and find that their statements are not assertions and, therefore, do not create additional levels of hearsay. These cases are cited below, at chapter 5 (V)(I).

"Various courts have held that the following are not and never will be hearsay: questions, orders, and suggestions." G. Michael Fenner, *Law Professor Reveals Shocking Truth About Hearsay*, 62 UMKC L. REV. 1, 20 (1993) (footnotes omitted). By and large, these courts are saying that these things cannot be hearsay because whether one would characterize them as "statements," they are not intended to assert anything. The better view seems to be the one expressed in Ex parte Hunt, 744 So.2d 851, 857 (Ala. 1999), where the court "conclude[d] that whether a question is a 'statement' for purposes of Rule 801(a) … depends upon the nature of the question, the circumstances surrounding the question, and the fact sought to be proved by offering the question." It depends on whether the question asserts a fact and is being offered to prove the fact asserted—and surely some questions are intended to be assertions, *e.g.*, "*You* are the man who sold those drugs to my daughter, aren't you?" (In *Hunt*, "the questions asked by the caller made no assertion, either expressly or implicitly. They did not state or imply the existence of any facts whatever. Thus the questions were not hearsay.") One case quite properly found a question to be hearsay: "[The] statement, though phrased as a question, seems to have no relevance unless it is being offered to prove the matter asserted." KW Plastics v. United States Can Co., 130 F.Supp.2d 1297, 1299 (M.D. Ala. 2001). *See also* Lexington Ins. Co. v. Western Pa. Hosp., 423 F.3d 318, 330 (3d Cir. 2005) ("[Q]uestions and inquiries are generally *not* hearsay because the declarant does not have the requisite assertive intent, even if the question 'convey[s] an implicit message' or provides information about the declarant's assumptions or beliefs." *Lexington* emphasizes the word "not"; I would emphasize "*generally*."); State v. Craycraft, 889 N.E.2d 1100, (Ohio Com. Pl. 2008) ("True questions or inquiries are incapable of being proved as either true or false; therefore, they cannot be offered to prove the truth of the matter asserted and do not constitute hearsay …").

For more on the definition of statement, *see* Fenner, 62 UMKC L. REV. at 10–21.

3. An Out-of-Court Statement by a Person

Hearsay is defined as a statement by a person.[29] When time is important and the in-court witness testifies, "The clock said 9:30," that is not hearsay.[30] When a blood hound follows a scent, trees a suspect, and stands below the tree barking, and the hound's barking is being offered into evidence to show that the dog was saying, "This is the person whose scent I was following," the testimony that the dog was barking up the tree is not hearsay. Information automatically generated by computer is not hearsay.[31] The postmark on the letter, the time stamp on the fax, the phone company's record of numbers called,[32] the radar gun's report of an automobile's speed—these things are not hearsay even when they are offered to prove the truth of the date, the time, the phone number called, or speed. There is no out-of-court statement by a person.[33]

---

29. Rule 801(a) defines "statement." Rule 801(b) defined "declarant" as "*a person* who makes a statement." (Emphasis added). The rule requires an out-of-court statement by an out-of-court declarant and only a person can be a declarant. United States v. Lamons, 532 F.3d 1251, 1263 (11th Cir. 2008) (regarding phone company billing data generated by computer, "the evidence challenged in this appeal does not contain the statements of human witnesses.").

30. There is no human out-of-court declarant. You might say, "But didn't some person set the clock? And wasn't that person making an out-of-court statement about the correct time as of the time the watch was set? And isn't it quite possible that the person who set the clock intentionally lied about the time, or was playing a joke on someone (who would be blasted awake at 3:00 in the morning instead of 6:00, or had poor eyesight and was mistaken about the time, or read the time off of a clock in one part of the house and on the way to set the clock in question misremembered the time? Every one of the testimonial infirmities could be present in the setting of the clock." I would answer, "Yes." Fenner, *Law Professor Reveals Shocking Truth About Hearsay*, 62 UMKC L. REV. at 24–26. But, still, we do not count the statement of time by the clock to be hearsay. If there is some specific evidence that the time was set incorrectly, bring it on as impeachment. *Lamons*, 532 F.3d at 1263 n.23 ("To be sure, there can be no statements which are wholly machine-generated in the strictest sense; all machines were designed and built by humans. But certain statements involve so little intervention by humans in their generation as to leave no doubt that they are wholly machine-generated for all practical purposes.").

31. *E.g., Lorraine*, 241 F.R.D. 564 ("[A]n electronically generated record [that] is entirely the product of the functioning of a computerized system or process, such as the 're-port' generated when a fax is sent showing the number to which the fax was sent and the time it was received, [is not hearsay.] [T]here is no 'person' involved in the creation of the record, and no 'assertion' being made.") (citing cases holding that computer generated records are not hearsay).

32. *Lamons*, 532 F.3d at 1263–64.

33. *See id.* at 564.

The evidentiary questions raised here are questions of relevance and competence, questions of the validity of scientific evidence, questions of system failure. If there is evidence that the principles upon which the machine operates are sound and that the machine was properly functioning at the time in question, then the information generated by the machine will be accurate. Or, at least, we will presume it is accurate.[34] The burden then falls upon the opponent of the evidence to show that the machine was not functioning properly. If there is evidence that the bloodhound was properly trained and properly handled on the day in question, then the dog's response is automatic, just as is the machine's. If there is evidence of system failure or operator error regarding the timestamp, the radar gun, or the bloodhound, that goes to its relevance or the competence of the witness, not hearsay.

4. Offered to Prove the Truth of the Matter Asserted

Hearsay is defined by the issue to which the evidence is offered. One cannot know whether a statement is hearsay without knowing how it is offered. To decide whether an out-of-court statement is offered to prove the truth of the matter asserted, do these things. First, answer these questions: What is the assertion in the out-of-court statement? What is the issue to which the statement is offered? Second, compare the two answers. Let us say that the assertion in the out-of-court statement is that the plaintiff had the green light. Let us say that the plaintiff offers that statement to prove that he or she had the green light. The assertion in the statement and the issue are the same. The trick is to identify the assertion and the issue.[35]

a. The Assertion

Identifying the matter asserted is easy. The matter asserted is the text of the out-of-court statement. It is whatever is asserted in the out-of-court statement. It is what was said by the out-of-court declarant. A common mistake is to be-

---

34. *See* FED.R.EVID. 301 and 302.
35. "[I]t is by the offer that Rule 801(c) defines hearsay." United States v. Mancillas, 580 F.2d 1301, 1309 (7th Cir. 1978). "'Hearsay is a statement, other than one made by the declarant while testifying at the trial or hearing, offered in evidence to prove the truth of the matter asserted." FED.R.EVID. 801(c). *See also, e.g.,* Anderson v. United States, 417 U.S. 211 220 (1974) (statements introduced "to prove that the statements were made so as to establish a foundation for later showing, through other admissible evidence, that they were false" are not hearsay) (footnotes omitted).

lieve that the assertion is what the attorney offering the evidence asserts as its purpose; this conflates the assertion and the issue; it looks at the lawyer's assertion about the evidence instead the words of the declarant; it is incorrect. The matter asserted is what the declarant asserted in the statement itself. At this point—when identifying the matter asserted—all that is important is the text of the out-of-court statement.

b. The Issue

Identifying the issue should not be that difficult either. The trick here is to identify the issue to which the statement is being offered. It must be an issue in the case at hand (otherwise the statement is irrelevant and inadmissible for that reason). The issues in any case include all of the following:

1. The essential elements of the cause of action (of each cause of action, if there is more than one).
2. The essential elements of any affirmative defense.
3. The essential elements of any counterclaim, or the like.
4. The credibility of each witness.[36]

While the statement may be offered to any issue found on this list, the key to whether the statement is hearsay is the issue to which it actually *is* offered. The issue to which the statement is being offered is determined by the attorney offering the evidence. Identify the issue by identifying why the attorney is offering the evidence.

c. The Assertion and the Issues Compared

This part of the definition—Is the out-of-court statement offered to prove the truth of the matter asserted?—is a function of comparing the assertion in the out-of-court statement with the issue to which it is offered.[37]

---

36. Except for credibility, the issues that are present in the case are, of course, found in the statutes or the case law that are the basis for the cause of action, the defense, or the counterclaim. In many jurisdictions, one good place to find out what the parties have to prove is the pattern jury instructions, many of which list the essential elements of the cause of action or defense that is the subject of the instruction. *See*, for example, Nebraska's book of pattern jury instructions for use in civil cases, NJI2d Civ. (Thomson West), republished annually.

37. The assertion must be of some value to the trier of fact, or it is irrelevant. *See* Fed.R.Evid. 401.

Ask three questions: (1) What is the assertion in the out-of-court statement? (2) What is the issue to which the out-of-court statement is offered? (3) How is this assertion relevant to this issue? The end point is here: Is the statement's value to the issue dependent upon the truth of its assertion, or does the statement have value to the issue without regard to whether its assertion is true or false?

Stated differently: Isolate the fact the lawyer is trying to prove. If the statement tends to prove or disprove the target fact only if the assertion is true, and unless it fits under Rule 801(d), it is hearsay. If this is so, then the statement is offered to prove the truth of the matter asserted in the statement.[38] On the other hand, if the statement tends to prove or disprove the target fact without regard to whether the assertion is true, then the statement is not offered to prove the truth of the matter asserted and then is not hearsay.[39]

To illustrate: Mr. Howell has been murdered. Mrs. Howell is on trial for the murder. At the time of the killing, Mr. and Mrs. Howell were stranded on an island with five other people: Gilligan, the Skipper, Ginger, Mary Ann, and

---

38. If this is true, and if the statement does not fit under one of the definitional exclusions in Rule 801(d), the statement is hearsay.

39. For example, in Garner v. Missouri Dept. of Mental Health, 439 F3d 958 (8th Cir. 2006), the mental health center (Center) fired plaintiff. The superintendent of the Center had been told that plaintiff had received money from a patient's Social Security check. This violates the Center's rules. The superintendent suspended plaintiff and began an investigation which uncovered evidence that plaintiff had been buying items from patients. This too violates the Center's rules. Plaintiff denied the former violation and admitted the latter. *Id.* at 959. Plaintiff was fired "for the latter infraction, rather than for the allegation that triggered the investigation." *Id.* The plaintiff sued alleging race discrimination and unlawful retaliation.

To the issue of why defendant investigated plaintiff (and, presumably to show that race discrimination was not the reason) and over a hearsay objection, a defense witness "testified that two social workers made the Social Security check allegation that caused her to suspend [plaintiff] and order an investigation." *Id.* at 960. Though this testimony reveals that there was an out-of-court conversation between the witness and two social workers, there is no out-of-court statement offered to prove the truth of the matter asserted. Plaintiff has first-hand knowledge that the allegations were made. Plaintiff does not have first-hand knowledge of whether the allegations were true. The fact that allegations were made is relevant to why the investigation was begun. Whether the allegations are true or not is irrelevant to why an investigation was begun. Allegations were made to the testifying witness; she began an investigation; the fact that allegations were made is an *in-court* statement; there is no out-of-court statement offered to prove the truth of the matter asserted.

Likewise, for example, when emails between the defendant and a co-worker are offered to show that a relationship existed between the two and not to prove the truth of any fact asserted in the emails, they are not hearsay. United States v. Siddiqui, 235 F.3d 1318, 1323 (11th Cir. 2000).

the Professor. To prove that Mrs. Howell did in fact kill her husband, the prosecutor calls Mary Ann as a witness. She will testify that on the day of the murder "the Professor came running up to me and said: 'Mrs. Howell just stabbed her husband.'" (1) What is the out-of-court statement? It is the words of the Professor: "Mrs. Howell just stabbed her husband." (The rest of what he said to Mary Ann is an in-court statement.) (2) What is the assertion in the out-of-court statement? "Mrs. Howell just stabbed her husband." (3) What is the issue to which the assertion is offered? Is Mrs. Howell the one who stabbed Mr. Howell? (4) How is this assertion relevant to the issue? Its relevance is dependent on its truth. The assertion is Mrs. Howell did it. The issue is whether Mrs. Howell did it. The assertion and the issue are the same. The out-of-court statement is only relevant if the Professor is making a statement that is sincere and honest and is based on accurate memory and relevant perception. Its relevance is dependent on its truth. The Professor is the one we need to cross-examine. It is an out-of-court statement offered to prove the truth of the matter asserted. It does not fit under any exclusion in Rule 801. It is hearsay.

Now change the facts of the illustration a bit: Gilligan is on trial for the murder. The Professor takes the stand and testifies "I saw Gilligan stab Mr. Howell." (So far there is no hearsay because there is no out-of-court statement.) Now Gilligan's attorney[40] calls Mary Ann to the stand. She will testify that on the day in question "the Professor came running up to me and said: 'Mrs. Howell just stabbed her husband.'" (1) What is the out-of-court statement? "Mrs. Howell just stabbed her husband." (2) What is the assertion? "Mrs. Howell just stabbed her husband." (3) What is the issue to which the assertion is offered? Now it becomes more difficult because the evidence is relevant to two issues. Issue A: Did Gilligan stab Mr. Howell? Issue B: Was the Professor a credible witness when he testified earlier at the trial: "I saw Gilligan stab Mr. Howell"? (4) How is this assertion relevant to each of these issues? Is its relevance dependent on its truth? Issue A: Did Gilligan stab Mr. Howell? The out-of-court statement is that Mrs. Howell stabbed Mr. Howell. This is only relevant to Issue A if it is true. The statement is only relevant if it is sincere and honest and based on a well-remembered perception. Issue B: Impeachment. Should the jury believe the Professor's in-court testimony that he saw Gilligan stab Mr. Howell? Defense counsel offers the out-of-court statement to impeach the Professor's earlier testimony that he saw Gilligan do it. The out-of-court statement is relevant whether it is true or not. The out-

---

40. It is credible that Gilligan might have an attorney: Various additional people did appear on the island from time to time.

of-court statement is relevant because it is a contradictory statement by the same witness. It is relevant as a prior inconsistent statement. The Professor's credibility is weakened just because he has told a contradictory story. It does not matter which version of his story is true and which is not. He is still impeached. His out-of-court statement could just as well have been: "I saw Ginger stab Mr. Howell" or "I saw the Skipper stab him." The out-of-court statement is relevant to Issue B whether it is true or not. Here we have an out-of-court statement that is hearsay to one issue in the case (who did it) and nonhearsay to another issue in the case (the Professor's credibility). If Gilligan's lawyer only offers the evidence to Issue B, the out-of-court statement is not hearsay.[41]

5. *Rule 801(d)*

This part of the basic definition is the subject of Chapter 2. For now, here is the most important thing to know about Rule 801(d): If a party's own statement is offered against him or her, it is not hearsay. For example, in the action styled *A vs. B*, if A offers B's out-of-court statement against B, then Rule 801(d) says the out-of-court statement is *not* hearsay. If one party offers an opposing party's statement against that opposing party, the statement is not hearsay.

III. The Top Ten Approaches to Hearsay

A. The Top Ten Approaches

1. The Formula:

> OCS
> + OTOMA
> − <u>801(d)</u>
> Hearsay

---

41. As stated earlier, it is the issue to which the statement is offered that determines whether it is hearsay. Defense counsel will offer this statement to the issue of the Professor's credibility—to that issue it is not hearsay. Unless it fits under an exception and is thereby admissible hearsay to the issue of who committed the murder, credibility is the only issue to which defense counsel will offer this statement.

What to do when evidence is admissible to one issue in a case and inadmissible to another is the subject of Chapter 12, below.

Hearsay is defined as all out-of-court statements offered to prove the truth of the matter asserted in the out-of-court statement, except for those statements that fit within 801(d). This simple formula determines whether a statement is hearsay.

2. The Manufactured-Evidence Approach:

If the rules of evidence had a slogan it would be "Quality in, quality out."

To some extent, the problem presented by hearsay evidence is that it can be too easy to manufacture. A criminal defendant could, for example, have his pals come into court and testify that someone else told them that she committed the crime in question, and the defendant was not involved in any way. (And, of course, this other person is now dead.)

The hearsay rule has an analogy in the world of business—the world of industry, of manufacturing and fabrication. Look at the trial as a manufacturing process. The manufacturing plant is the courtroom. The product manufactured is the verdict. The raw materials that go into this product are the various pieces of evidence. The quality of our product depends on the quality of our raw materials: to produce a high-quality product, we must use only high-quality raw materials. We do not risk the integrity of the verdict by using raw materials of inferior quality. To this end, we have put into place a set of rules—the rules of evidence—that are designed to insure that we use the highest quality raw materials reasonably available. The rules of evidence govern which raw materials we will accept and which we will reject.[42]

Here is how the hearsay rule helps insure that we use only high-quality raw materials, i.e., high-quality evidence. Almost every bit of material that goes into our finished product was itself manufactured by someone else and was manufactured offsite.[43] One way we insure the quality of the materials presented to the court is by questioning the original manufacturer. To that end, we insist that the original manufacturer deliver the raw materials in person. We want direct testimony from someone with direct knowledge of the original manufacturing process. This is where the hearsay rule comes in: We

---

42. As discussed above, all of the rules of evidence but for the privilege rules are in one way or another intended to aid in the search for the truth. See the Introduction to Hearsay, in Part I of this chapter.

43. Only rarely do we produce any of the raw materials right in the courtroom. Raw materials manufactured in the courtroom would include the spectator who, overcome by the oration of defense counsel, jumps up and confesses to the crime. The only lawyers routinely capable of this are Perry Mason, Ben Matlock, and perhaps Denny Crane before he contracted Mad Cow.

reject the raw material if we cannot question the original manufacturer.[44] We do not use it in our manufacturing process, we do not allow it to go into our product, we look to alternative sources for this raw material. We reject it because we consider the ability to question the original manufacturer to be such an important part of our quality control program that if we are unable to do so we label that raw material hearsay and, with many exceptions, we reject it.

Here is how this works.

■ Take a lawsuit over an intersectional collision where we are trying to prove speed, condition of the road, traffic control devices at the intersection, and the like. A witness to the collision will take the stand and, if allowed to, will testify: "[The plaintiff] had the green light." This is the raw material, and we must decide if we are going to use it in the manufacture of the verdict. Insofar as the hearsay rule is concerned, here is how we decide: We ask who is delivering this raw material. More precisely: Are we receiving this bit of raw material from its original manufacturer, the person with firsthand knowledge of what we want to know? Can we evaluate the quality of the raw material by questioning its original manufacturer?

The raw material here is "[The plaintiff] had the green light." The manufacturer of the information that the plaintiff had the green light is the witness who saw the plaintiff and the color of the light. The manufacturer is the witness who is on the stand delivering this bit of raw material. If we want to investigate the manufacturing of this raw material to see if it is of high enough quality to go into our verdict, the person who manufactured the evidence is the one we want to question, and that is the person on the stand, delivering the evidence. We can question her about her perception, memory, honesty, and sincerity, we can observe her demeanor, she is under oath and subject to the pressures of the courtroom. This raw material does not go into the hearsay bin.

■ If the collision-witness's husband takes the stand to testify: "My wife told me '[The plaintiff] had the green light,'" then there are two steps in the manufacturing process, there are two manufacturers. The collision witness manufactured a raw material we are interested in: "[The plaintiff] had the green light." And her husband, the testifying witness, has added something to that raw material. He has become a second layer in the manufacturing process: What

---

44. We reject it with some exceptions. Regarding the exceptions, see everything following this chapter.

he has manufactured is this: "My wife told me ' …'" The raw material that is of real value to our finished product is "[The plaintiff] had the green light."

To test whether this shipment of raw material delivered by the husband is of sufficient quality to use in the manufacture of our verdict, opposing counsel needs to question each of the two manufacturers: the collision witness and her husband. The latter is on the stand and can be questioned about the part he manufactured: "My wife told me." Is he telling the truth? Could he really hear her? Does he remember accurately? And so forth. That part is not hearsay. The fact that he was told something by his wife is not hearsay. (What she told him is hearsay, but the fact that she told him something is not.) He is the manufacturer of this bit of the raw material and he is on the stand. (The wife is also an original manufacturer of this evidence—whether she spoke to her husband. There can be more than one original manufacturer of a single piece of evidence—a sort of a manufacturing partnership.)

However, standing alone, this bit of raw material that he manufactured—that his wife said something to him—is of no value to the production of our verdict. It adds nothing of value to our product. That part of his testimony, without the rest, is irrelevant. What is of value here is the color of the light. The collision witness is the original manufacturer of that bit of raw material. She is not on the stand. She cannot be questioned about the quality of this raw material. Therefore, we presume that this is not the kind of high quality raw material that we demand for our verdict. We will not risk using this raw material without questioning the original manufacturer. Used for this purpose, the evidence is hearsay. Unless the proponent of this raw material can find some other way to convince the court of its quality by fitting it under an exception to the hearsay rule, then it is inadmissible hearsay.

■ If the collision witness's husband's co-worker takes the stand and testifies, "Her husband said: 'My wife told me "[The plaintiff] had the green light"'"—then the process of manufacturing this bit of raw material was a [*double hearsay*] three layered process. There are three levels in the manufacturing process; there are three manufacturers: (1) The wife has manufactured the raw material that has value to our product: "[The plaintiff] had the green light." (2) The husband added a layer to that raw material: "My wife told me." (3) The co-worker added yet one more layer: "Her husband said."

There were three steps in the manufacture of this bit of raw material. To test the quality of the fact in issue—"[The plaintiff] had the green light"—it is not enough that the coworker is on the stand and can be questioned. All we can get from the coworker is that, "Yes, the husband did tell me that his wife said that." We can test whether the coworker is telling the truth when he says that the husband told him. But we cannot sweat anything out of him regarding the truth about the color of the light, for, in that regard, he only knows what he was told. As a result, the relevant assertion about the color of the light is of insufficient quality to go into our verdict. It is hearsay. In fact, it is double hearsay because there are two layers of manufacturers under the testifying witness, there are two off-the-stand layers: wife to husband; husband to coworker.

It is hearsay and, again, unless the proponent of this raw material can find some other way to convince the court of its quality, that is, unless the proponent of this raw material can make it fit under one of the many exceptions to the hearsay rule, then it is inadmissible hearsay.

■ Let us change the raw material. In the same intersectional collision, the collision witness has testified "[The *plaintiff*] had the *green* light." Now the defendant calls to the stand a friend of the collision witness. If allowed to do so, the friend will testify: "The day after the wreck, my friend said to me '[The *plaintiff*] ran a *red* light.'" Now this bit of raw material goes into our product in two ways.

One issue in this case is the color of the light: The defendant would like to prove that the plaintiff ran a red light, and would like to use the testimony of the friend as the raw material. Another issue in this case is whether to believe the testimony of the collision witness. The defendant would like to prove that the collision witness's in-court testimony about the color of the light was not believable, not credible and, again, would like to use the testimony of the friend as the raw material.

(1) To the issue of who had which light at the time of the collision, the manufacture of the raw material delivered by the friend was a two step process: The collision witness may or may not have seen something (the collision witness is manufacturing plant number one); her friend, the testifying witness, may or may not have heard something (the friend is manufacturing plant number two). To prove the color of the light, there are two levels to the manufacturing process, two different manufacturing plants—the collision witness who saw what happened and the testifying witness who heard what the collision witness said about what happened. The product is hearsay.

Are we receiving this bit of raw material from its original manufacturer? No. Can we evaluate the quality of the raw material by questioning its original manufacturer? No. She is not on the stand.

(2) Another issue in this case is whether the jury should believe the testimony of the collision witness when she testified: "[The *plaintiff*] had the *green* light." To this issue, the raw material is that the day after the wreck the collision wit-

ness told her friend a different story: "The day after the wreck, [she] said to me '[The *plaintiff*] ran a *red* light.'" The collision witness has contradicted herself. The raw material is the prior inconsistent statement. How many manufacturers are we dealing with here? Just one.

Are we receiving this bit of raw material from its original manufacturer? Yes. On the question of the color of the light, there are two manufacturers: the collision witness and the friend. On the question of whether the collision witness made a prior inconsistent statement, there is but one manufacturer: the friend. *Under this theory* of admissibility—the impeachment theory—the raw material that is of value to the verdict is not the color of the light, but what the friend heard the collision witness say about the color of the light. The raw material of value under this theory is the inconsistent statement. Once the collision witness has testified about this critical fact, then the fact that the collision witness made a prior inconsistent statement is valuable raw material. This bit of raw material has been delivered by the original manufacturer, the person who has firsthand knowledge of the making of the inconsistent statement. Because the original manufacturer can be questioned about its quality, it is not hearsay.

When what we want to know and what the testifying witness perceived are the same thing, then the testifying witness is an original manufacturer and the out-of-court statement probably is not hearsay. The question is this one: Did the witness perceive the very thing we want to know, or just what someone said about the thing we want to know?

Is the evidence offered to prove the color of the light or the prior inconsistent statement? To the first issue, the friend's testimony is hearsay; to the second, it is not. "[I]t is by the offer that [the rule] defines hearsay."[45] The defendant is offering this statement to impeach the testifying witness' in-court testimony. By this offer, the evidence is not hearsay. The statement might be inadmissible. Rule 403 might keep it out. But the hearsay rule does not keep it out, for it is offered for a nonhearsay purpose.

3. The Real-Witness Approach:

Many find that "The Real Witness," by Professor James W. McElhaney,[46] presents the most useful way to look at hearsay. It is universally understandable. It

---

45. United States v. Mancillas, 580 F.2d 1301, 1309 (7th Cir. 1978).

46. James W. McElhaney, *The Real Witness*, 74 A.B.A.J. 82 (Nov. 1988), republished by the ABA, as Chapter 42 of a book-compilation of Professor McElhaney's columns: James W. McElhaney, *McElhaney's Litigation*, ch. 42, at 227–30 (1995). Professor McElhaney up-

works well in the middle of each situation where a person is likely to need to be able to spot hearsay: in class; during the final exam or a bar exam; in a settlement conference when you suddenly need to know whether a new piece of evidence is admissible; while preparing a pretrial evidentiary brief or oral argument; during mediation or arbitration; and at trial. This remarkable short piece may be the single best way to understand the first two parts of the hearsay formula:

> OCS
> + OTOMA
> − 801(d)
> Hearsay

The real witness approach may well be the best single way to understand the "out-of-court statement" and the "offered to prove the truth of the matter asserted" parts of the above formula. Other than that, all you have to do is to learn the definitional exclusions from Rule 801(d).

Professor McElhaney asks this simple question: Who are the real witnesses to what we want to know? This requires figuring out two things: (1) What is it—exactly and precisely—that we want to know? (2) Who are the real witnesses? Asking "Who is the real witness?" is another way of asking "Who has personal knowledge of what we want to know?" It is also another way of asking, "Who is the original manufacturer of the evidence?" Here are a few examples of this approach in action.

■ If we want to know the color of the stoplight at a relevant time, then anyone who saw the color of the light at that time is a real witness to the color of the light. The fact to be proved is the color of the light; anyone and everyone who saw it is a "real witness" to the color of the light. Such testimony from such a witness is not hearsay. But someone who only heard about the color of the light is not a "real witness" to its color.

■ If we want to know what an occurrence witness *said* about the color of the stoplight (perhaps to impeach the witness), then anyone who heard what this occurrence witness said is a real witness to what the witness said. The fact in issue here is what the occurrence witness previously said about the color of the light and everyone who heard the occurrence witness say it is a "real witness." The testimony of every such real witness is not hearsay.

---

dated his Real Witness approach in James W. McElhaney, *The Heart of the Matter*, 89 A.B.A.J. 51 (Issue 3, March 2003) (citing THE HEARSAY RULE).

■ If we are trying to show that the defendant shot and killed the victim, then anyone who saw him shoot and kill the victim is a real witness: This kind of eyewitness testimony is not hearsay. Someone who heard rumors that the defendant had killed the victim is not a real witness to who killed the victim. Someone who heard on the news that the defendant confessed is not a real witness: This kind of second- or third- or fourth-hand evidence is hearsay.

■ If we want to know the price of a share of a particular stock on a particular day, then there may not be any "real witness." How does one have actual first-hand knowledge of the price of a share of stock? How does one have this knowledge except by reading some numbers someone has entered into a machine?

If, on the other hand, we want to know what the *Wall Street Journal* stock table said about the price of a share of a particular stock on a particular day, then a copy of the *Wall Street Journal* from the next business day would itself be a real witness, as would anyone who read that stock's price from the *Journal*, and can remember it.

■ If we are trying to prove what was said over the telephone to a 911 operator—not that what was said was true, but just what was said—real witnesses would include: (1) the person who said it to the operator; (2) the operator; (3) anyone who was in the room with the person who made the call and overheard that end of it; (4) if the 911 call was received on a speaker phone, anyone who was in the room with the operator and overheard the incoming part of the phone call; (5) if the police had a wiretap on the phone from which the call was made, any officer listening at the time; (6) a properly authenticated tape-recording of the phone call (either at the 911 center or off of the wiretap); and (7) anyone who has listened to a properly authenticated tape-recording of the phone call. We are trying to prove what was said by the caller. Each of these persons (and the authenticated tape) is a real witness to what was said. There may be competency or credibility problems with those who casually overheard what was said—they may not remember—but there are no hearsay problems. There may be problems with the rule requiring the production of the original[47] when using someone's memory to prove what he or she heard on the tape, but there are no hearsay problems.

If what was said to the 911 operator was a description of someone breaking into a house, and we are trying to prove what the burglar looked like, the operator is no longer a real witness. The tape recording is no longer a

47. FED.R.EVID. 1001, *et seq.*

"real witness." The real witness has to be someone who saw the burglar. And that excludes most everyone in the seven classes of persons and audio tape listed above.

■ Try a document. Imagine an action on a contract to purchase wheels of Wisconsin mild cheddar cheese. The plaintiff is the seller, who alleges that she was ready to deliver. The defendant is the buyer, who argues that the cheese plaintiff tried to deliver was not up to the specifications in the contract. The plaintiff offers the contract into evidence against the defendant.

In this context, is the contract hearsay? No, it is not! There are two reasons why it is not. The least complicated reason is that the contract, properly authenticated to have been signed by the plaintiff and the defendant (or their authorized agents) is excluded from hearsay by Rule 801(d)(2)(A), (C), or (D).[48] It is either the defendant's own statement or that of defendant's agent, offered against the defendant. For that reason alone, it is not hearsay.

The second reason is that *the contract is the real witness*. What do we want to know? The terms of the agreement between the plaintiff and the defendant. Who (or, in this case, what) is the real witness to the terms of the agreement? The agreement itself, the written contract. (The persons who signed the contract are also real witnesses to its terms. Though their testimony might have problems under the parole evidence rule, or they may be incompetent if they do not remember just what the contract said, their testimony would not be hearsay. There often is more than one "real witness.")

■ Professor McElhaney's model really does work and is very much worth getting used to. It works in nearly all situations but this one: Rule 801(d) of the Federal Rules of Evidence defines certain kinds of statements made by persons who are not "real witnesses" as nonhearsay. McElhaney's model does not take Rule 801(d) into account, but then neither do any of the other definitions of hearsay, with the single exception of the formula: Out-of-Court Statement + Offered to Prove the Truth of the Matter Asserted – Rule 801(d) = Hearsay).[49]

---

48. *See* Chapter 2(III)(B), (C), and (D), below.
49. In addition, the real witness approach does not work in this situation: when an out-of-court statement is offered to prove the truth of the matter asserted, the in-court declarant and the out-of-court declarant are the same person, and none of the definitional exclusions apply. ("'Hearsay' is a statement, other than one made by the declarant *while testifying at the trial or hearing*, offered in evidence to prove the truth of the matter asserted." FED.R.EVID. 801(c) (emphasis added).) This includes the situation where a prior inconsistent statement by a testifying witness is inadmissible hearsay if used as substantive evidence and, therefore, is admissible only as impeachment evidence.

4. The Two-Boxes Approach:

Out-Of-Court Statement	Offered To Prove What?
[The text of the out-of-court statement]	[The issues/the elements]
This is the matter asserted in the out-of-court statement.	This is the matter asserted by the lawyer at trial. This is the immediate inference to be drawn.

Pick out the out-of-court statement and put its text in the first box. Figure out the immediate inference to be drawn from the out-of-court statement, that is, figure out the matter asserted by the lawyer, at trial, and put it in the second box. If the two are the same, then—unless the out-of-court statement fits under 801(d)—the out-of-court statement probably is hearsay. If they are different, think it through some more, try other approaches.

5. The Comic-Balloons Approach:

This approach is a way of visualizing whether there is an out-of-court statement. It does not help you tell whether the statement is offered to prove the truth of the matter asserted, but just whether it is an out-of-court statement.

With this approach, keep in mind that the *in-court* statement does not have to be oral: It can be written. The seated stick figure in the witness chair could just as well be a writing—a written statement, a deposition, a police officer's notes, an invoice, medical records, etc. Likewise, the *out-of-court* statement does not have to be oral: It can be written. The stick figure inside the speech balloon could just as well be a writing.

Also keep in mind that the in-court declarant and the out-of-court declarant can be the same person. The seated stick figure and the standing stick fig-

ure can be the same person and the out-of-court statement can still be hearsay.
The statement in double quotation marks is an out-of-court statement even if
the person in the witness chair and the person inside the speech balloon are the
same person.[50]

6. The Plain-Fact-That-the-Words-Were-Spoken Approach:

Is the relationship between the assertion and the issue dependent on the truth
of the words spoken out of court, or is it dependent only on the fact that they
were spoken? If the former is what is important, the out-of-court statement
probably is hearsay. If the latter is what is important, the out-of-court statement probably is not hearsay. If the truth of the out-of-court statement is irrelevant, then the statement probably is not hearsay. If the statement is relevant
to an issue (perhaps the credibility of a testifying witness, to establish an oral
contract, or as evidence of a warning) even if the declarant was lying and the
statement is 100% untrue, then the statement probably is not hearsay. If the
statement is offered only to show that it was said and the truth of its assertion
is irrelevant, then the inability to assess the credibility of the declarant is not
important. You only need to assess the credibility of the in-court declarant,
the person who claims to have heard it. Here, the link between the words
spoken out-of-court and the issues in the case is direct, without having to
travel through the sincerity or belief of the person who spoke the words.

First question: What do we want to know? Is it just that the words were spoken? Second question: What did the testifying witness perceive? That the words
were spoken? If the answer to each question is "Yes," then the out-of-court declaration is not hearsay. Anyone who heard them is an original manufacturer,
is a real witness.

7. The Credibility Approach:

First, a caveat: This approach does not work when the in-court declarant and
the out-of-court declarant are the same person,[51] that is, when the testifying
witness is trying to repeat something he or she said out of court. It only works
when they are not the same person.

The question is, "Whose credibility is important?" If the only person whose
credibility is important is the testifying witness, then the testifying witness's

---

50. *See* part II(C)(2) of this chapter, above.
51. *See* part II(C)(2) of this chapter, above.

credibility can be assessed, it can be attacked, and it can be bolstered. The testifying witness can be cross-examined. The trier of fact can observe the demeanor of the testifying witness. The testifying witness will be under oath (or affirmation). If the only person whose credibility is important is the testifying witness, then the out-of-court statement probably is not hearsay.

Whose credibility is important? At what time? Is it the credibility of the testifying witness? If this is the case, then the out-of-court statement probably is not hearsay. (Keep in mind, however, the caveat that this approach does not work when the in-court declarant was also the out-of-court declarant.) Is it the credibility of some original communicator, at some prior time? If this is the case, then the out-of-court statement probably is hearsay.

If the truth of the out-of-court statement is irrelevant—if the out-of-court statement is relevant even if the out-of-court declarant was lying and the out-of-court statement is 100% untrue—then the out-of-court statement probably is not hearsay. If the out-of-court statement is offered only to show that it was said, and its truth is irrelevant, then the inability to assess the credibility of the out-of-court declarant is not important. You only need assess the credibility of the in-court declarant, the person who claims to have heard it said.

8. The Effect-on-the-Mind-of-the-Hearer Approach:

When the out-of-court statement has relevance when we only consider the effect it had on those who heard (or read) it—not whether the statement was true or not—then the statement is not hearsay. When the statement is offered to show its effect on someone who heard it, then the link between the words spoken out of court and the issues in the case is direct, without having to travel through the sincerity or belief of the person who spoke the words.[52]

A statement of fact that is offered to prove that the person hearing it was on notice of the fact stated often comes into evidence under this approach. Take this example: someone overhears an out-of-court statement by an airplane mechanic to the pilot of a small plane, stating, "I wouldn't take that plane up without first checking that oil leak"; the pilot takes off anyway and the plane goes down. If the mechanic's out-of-court statement is offered as evidence that there was an oil leak, then it is offered to prove the truth of the matter asserted.

---

52. This is discussed at greater length and in greater depth in other places in this Treatise, particularly in Chapter 7.

If the statement is offered as evidence that the pilot was on notice of an oil leak before taking off, then it is not offered to prove the truth of the matter asserted; it is not offered to prove the truth of the oil leak, but only that the pilot was told—correctly or incorrectly; either way, he is on notice—that there was an oil leak. This out-of-court statement has the following effect on the mind of the pilot: It puts the the the pilot on notice.[53]

This is one way of looking at whether the statement is offered to prove the truth of the matter asserted, on the one hand, or only that such a statement was made, on the other. One important caveat here: Make sure that the state of mind of the hearer is relevant. As one court wrote in response to the argument that a statement was admissible as nonhearsay state-of-mind evidence, "if [the testimony about the out-of-court assertion] did not go to the truth of that assertion, to what did it go? ... For testimony to be admissible for any purpose ... it must be relevant."[54]

9. The Words-with-Independent-Legal-Effect Approach, a.k.a. the Verbal-Acts Approach:

If the mere fact that the words were spoken creates, alters, or completes a legal relationship then the statement is not hearsay. If the words spoken out-of-court have a legal effect of their own, they are not hearsay. If the utterance is the issue, not hearsay. Sometimes the words themselves are the issue (or, often more precisely, *an* issue). Sometimes the words themselves are the principal fact in controversy.[55] Examples include:

---

53. This is discussed at greater length and in greater depth in other places in this Treatise, particularly in part II(D) of Chapter 7.

54. United States v. Evans, 216 F.3d 80, 85 (D.C. Cir. 2006). The relationship between nonhearsay state-of-mind evidence and relevance is discussed in part III of Chapter 7, below.

55. "If the significance of an out-of-court statement lies in the fact that the statement was made and not in the truth of the matter asserted, then the statement is not hearsay." Cal-Mat Co. v. United States Dept. of Labor, 364 F.3d 1117, 1124 (9th Cir. 2004). In Garner v. Missouri Dept. of Mental Health, 439 F3d 958 (8th Cir. 2006), which is discussed at length in note 39, above, the court noted that the employer's state of mind is "'of crucial importance in wrongful discharge cases.'" *Id.* at 960. The fact that two social workers told the employer that the fired employee had received money from a patient's social security check, in violation of company policy, is relevant because of it shows why the superintendent began an investigation, and that the reasons were not racial. To the issue of the superintendent's state of mind it does not matter whether the allegations were true or not. *See also, e.g.,* Fields v. J Haynes Waters Builders, Inc. 658 S.E.2d 80, 87 (S.C. 2008) (the words accompanying an ambiguous act may, "regardless of their truth, ... give the act legal significance ...");

■ In a breach of contract action, the terms of a contract;[56]

■ In a defamation action, the allegedly libelous words;[57]

■ In an employment discrimination case, the racially derogatory words that created the hostile work environment;[58]

■ In a tort action for intentional infliction of emotional distress, words used to inflict the distress;[59]

■ In a criminal action, words that are an element of a crime, such as perhaps the crimes of insurance or securities fraud, any crime of solicitation, or a crime where out-of-court words provide motive; or words that are at issue in an affirmative defense to a criminal action, such as words of coercion or entrapment.[60]

These cases involve words that have a legal effect that is not concerned with the out-of-court declarant's memory, perceptions, or honesty. In these cases, the link between the words spoken out of court and the issues in the case is direct, without having to travel through the sincerity of the person who spoke the words or the accuracy of that person's perceptions or memory. This is one way of looking at the question of whether the out-of-court statement is offered to prove the truth of the matter asserted or whether it is just offered to show that it was said.

---

56. Supporting cases are cited at Chapter 7(II)(B), below. If the contract is offered against a party to the lawsuit, who is also a party to the contract, then it is a Rule 801(d) admission, and is not hearsay in any event.

57. Supporting cases are cited at Chapter 7(II)(B), below. These words are not hearsay for a number of other reasons, perhaps most simply because they are not offered to prove the truth of their assertion. In fact, the party offering them maintains they are false. *See, e.g.,* Anderson v. United States, 417 U.S. 221, 219–20 (1974) (statements admitted "to prove that the statements were made so as to establish a foundation for later showing ... they were false" are not offered to prove the truth of the matter asserted and, therefore, cannot be hearsay).

58. Supporting cases are cited at Chapter 7(II)(B), below. Again, the words are not hearsay because they are not offered to prove the truth of the matter asserted but just to show that they were said and the effect that the words had on the employee who heard them.

59. Supporting cases are cited at Chapter 7(II)(B), below.

60. Supporting cases are cited at Chapter 7(II)(B), below.

10.   The Flow-Chart Approach:

Hearsay Flow Chart Number 1: Hearsay or Nonhearsay

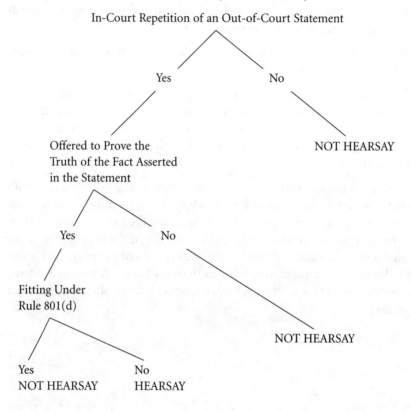

Hearsay Flow Chart Number 2: Hearsay or Nonhearsay—More Detail

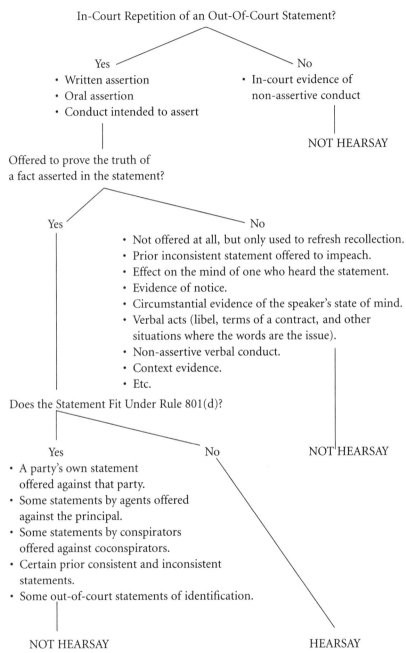

In-Court Repetition of an Out-Of-Court Statement?

Yes
• Written assertion
• Oral assertion
• Conduct intended to assert

No
• In-court evidence of
  non-assertive conduct

NOT HEARSAY

Offered to prove the truth of
a fact asserted in the statement?

Yes

No
• Not offered at all, but only used to refresh recollection.
• Prior inconsistent statement offered to impeach.
• Effect on the mind of one who heard the statement.
• Evidence of notice.
• Circumstantial evidence of the speaker's state of mind.
• Verbal acts (libel, terms of a contract, and other
  situations where the words are the issue).
• Non-assertive verbal conduct.
• Context evidence.
• Etc.

Does the Statement Fit Under Rule 801(d)?

Yes
• A party's own statement
  offered against that party.
• Some statements by agents offered
  against the principal.
• Some statements by conspirators
  offered against coconspirators.
• Certain prior consistent and inconsistent
  statements.
• Some out-of-court statements of identification.

No

NOT HEARSAY

NOT HEARSAY

HEARSAY

Hearsay Flow Chart Number 3: Hearsay—Admissible or Inadmissible?

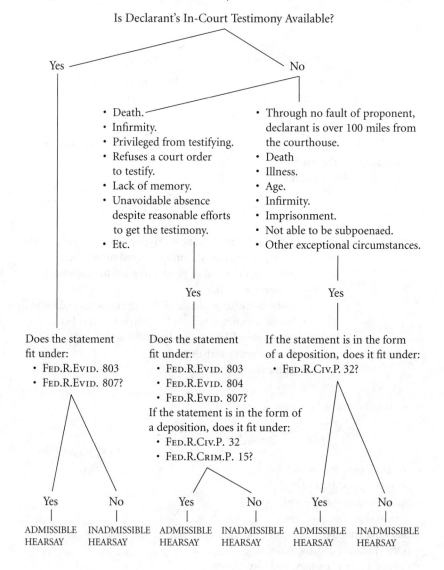

Is Declarant's In-Court Testimony Available?

Yes / No

Yes branch:
- Death.
- Infirmity.
- Privileged from testifying.
- Refuses a court order to testify.
- Lack of memory.
- Unavoidable absence despite reasonable efforts to get the testimony.
- Etc.

No branch:
- Through no fault of proponent, declarant is over 100 miles from the courthouse.
- Death
- Illness.
- Age.
- Infirmity.
- Imprisonment.
- Not able to be subpoenaed.
- Other exceptional circumstances.

Yes   Yes

Does the statement fit under:
- FED.R.EVID. 803
- FED.R.EVID. 807?

Does the statement fit under:
- FED.R.EVID. 803
- FED.R.EVID. 804
- FED.R.EVID. 807?
If the statement is in the form of a deposition, does it fit under:
- FED.R.CIV.P. 32
- FED.R.CRIM.P. 15?

If the statement is in the form of a deposition, does it fit under:
- FED.R.CIV.P. 32?

Yes   No   Yes   No   Yes   No

ADMISSIBLE   INADMISSIBLE   ADMISSIBLE   INADMISSIBLE   ADMISSIBLE   INADMISSIBLE
HEARSAY   HEARSAY   HEARSAY   HEARSAY   HEARSAY   HEARSAY

B. Some Analysis and a Few Caveats

1. Rule 801(d)

Rule 801(d) enacts a number of definitional exclusions from the hearsay rule. It lists a number of out-of-court statements, offered to prove the truth of the matter asserted, that are excluded from the hearsay definition. Except for approach # 1, the ten approaches set out above do not take into account the kinds of statements excluded from the definition of hearsay by subparagraph (d) of Rule 801.

2. Overlap

Many of these approaches overlap. They are set out separately for ease of understanding and accessibility, because they are such frequently encountered subsets, and because different students of the hearsay rule connect with different approaches.[61]

---

61. As an example of this point, see, *e.g.*, Noviello v. City of Boston, 398 F.3d 76 (1st Cir. 2005). This complaint here alleged sexual harassment and retaliation in the workplace. In opposition to the defendant's motion for summary judgment, the plaintiff's affidavit recounted various specific out-of-court statements made by coworkers and characterized by the court as "insult[ing] and taunting." *Id.* at 84. (As one example, she affirmed that a coworker shouted at her that she "was the 'scum of the earth.'" *Id.* at 82.) The defendant objected that the out-of-court statements plaintiff recounted were inadmissible hearsay. The court disagreed. "The insults and taunting that the plaintiff recounts do not create hearsay problems; those statements are not offered for their truth, but, rather, to show that the words were spoken (and, thus, contributed to the hostile work environment)." *Id.* at 84. What matters regarding these statements is that the words were said (not that they were true) and the effect they had on the plaintiff. The in-court declarant (the plaintiff) has first-hand knowledge of both of those things. What the court wrote about a different statement is true here: "[I]ts effect on the plaintiff would be the same regardless of the truth of the matter asserted." *Id.* at 85 n.2.

These are out-of-court statements but they are not offered to prove the truth of the matter asserted (approach # 1), and, in fact, the plaintiff would argue that the words are not true; the in-court declarant is an "original manufacturer" of this evidence (approach # 2); what we want to know is what was said and she is a "real witness" to what we want to know (approach # 3); what matters here is not the truth of the words spoken but that they were spoken at all (approach # 6); it is her credibility that is important (*i.e.*, did she really hear those things) (approach # 7); it is the effect of the words on her mind (not the truth of the words) that is in issue (approach # 8); these words have a legal effect regardless of their truth, the words are the issue (not the truth of the words) (approach # 9).

On the other hand, one of the statements in plaintiff's affidavit—her statement that a coworker had told her that other employees had told him to "stay away" from plaintiff and that plaintiff was "trouble," is hearsay. There are two layers of out-of-court declarants: the

3. Imprecision

Some of these approaches are not very precise. The comic-balloons approach, for example, only helps you determine whether there is an out-of-court statement; it does not answer the question whether the out-of-court statement is hearsay.

4. The Best of the Ten

Of the ten approaches, # 1 (the formula), # 2 (the manufactured-evidence approach), and # 3 (the real-witness approach) are the most universally useful. They are the three approaches to work with the most. They are the three approaches to use as the first line of defense to the question: "Is it hearsay?"

IV. Examples—The Basic Definition Applied

A. Variations from *Shepard v. United States*[62]

1. *Shepard* Example One

Dr. Shepard is on trial for the murder of his wife. One witness for the prosecution is a nurse who cared for the deceased. If allowed, the nurse will testify as follows: "Early on the morning of May 12, Mrs. Shepard said to me: 'Dr. Shepard has poisoned me.'"

(1) *In-Court Statement*: Part of that piece of testimony is an in-court statement. "Early on the morning of May 12, Mrs. Shepard said to me." This is not, and cannot be, hearsay because it is an in-court statement, not an out-of-court

---

coworker who spoke to plaintiff (OCD 1) and the coworkers who had spoken to him (OCD 2). The immediate out-of-court statement is OCD 1's statement to the plaintiff, "Other coworkers said 'stay away' from plaintiff and she is 'trouble.'" The issue here is whether OCD 2 did in fact say these things. The out-of-court statement by OCD 1 is offered to prove the truth of the matter asserted—it is offered to prove that these things were in fact said to OCD 1; the in-court declarant is not an "original manufacturer" of this evidence; she is not a "real witness" to the "stay away" and "trouble" out-of-court statements; what matters here is the truth of the words spoken by OCD 1, and not simply that OCD 1 said them; it is OCD 1's credibility that is important (*i.e.*, did OCD 1 really hear those things) and OCD 1 is on the stand; etc.

62. The first example hereafter is taken from Shepard v. United States, 290 U.S. 96 (1933). The five examples that follow immediately thereafter are based off of this case. Regarding this first example, *see also* Chapter 3(IV)(D)(3), below.

statement. The nurse is the manufacturer of the in-court part of the statement. She is on the stand. The quality of this raw material can be fully tested. So far, the nurse is the real witness. She is the surviving real witness to the fact that Mrs. Shepard said something. (That fact alone is, however, of no consequence to the action and, alone, is inadmissible as irrelevant.) So far, there is no hearsay.

(2) *Out-of-Court Statement*: Part of that piece of testimony is an out-of-court statement: " 'Dr. Shepard has poisoned me.' " The nurse is repeating in court something she heard out of court, thus it is an out-of-court statement. Mrs. Shepard is the manufacturer. She is not on the stand. The nurse—the testifying witness—is not a real witness to the asserted fact that Dr. Shepard had poisoned his wife.

(3) *Assertion*: In general, the assertion is the text of the out-of-court statement. In this specific example, the assertion in the out-of-court statement is "Dr. Shepard has poisoned me."

(4) *Issue*: Did Dr. Shepard poison her?

(5) *Offered to Prove the Truth of the Matter Asserted?*: The out-of-court statement is offered in court to prove that Dr. Shepard poisoned his wife: It is offered to prove the truth of the matter asserted.

The raw material is the evidence that Dr. Shepard poisoned his wife. The wife is the original manufacturer of that raw material, and she is not on the stand. She is not the person delivering the raw material. We cannot question her about its quality. The quality of this raw material cannot be tested to our satisfaction.

The fact in issue here is: Did Dr. Shepard poison her? Who are the real witnesses to that fact? Dr. Shepard certainly is. Mrs. Shepard may or may not have been. Based on what we know, the nurse was not a real witness.[63]

What is the text of the out-of-court statement, that is, what is the matter asserted in the out-of-court statement? "Dr. Shepard poisoned me." Put that in one box. What is it offered to prove, that is, what is the inference to be drawn? Dr. Shepard poisoned her. Put that in the second box. They are the same. The out-of-court statement is hearsay.

Whose credibility is important? That of Mrs. Shepard, the out-of-court declarant. Hearsay.

The effect the statement had on the mind of the person who heard it, the nurse, is irrelevant and the words do not have independent legal effect.

---

63. Given just the text of the nurse's answer—"Mrs. Shepard said to me 'Dr. Shepard has poisoned me.' "—we cannot say that the nurse was a real witness. Her testimony is hearsay.

(6) *801(d)*: This out-of-court statement does not fit within any of the definitional exclusions in Rule 801(d).

(7) *Hearsay*: When paragraphs 3, 4, 5, and 6, immediately above, are combined, this is hearsay: It is an out-of-court statement, offered to prove the truth of the matter asserted, and not covered by Rule 801(d).

2. *Shepard* Example Two

Change the case. Assume that the doctor and his wife died at about the same time and the issue in a probate proceeding is which of them died first. There is evidence the husband died on May 11. The nurse attending Mrs. Shepard takes the stand to testify as follows: "On May 12th, I remember it was the 12th because that is my daughter's birthday and I'd wanted the day off, but couldn't get it. The best I could do was to trade for the early morning shift, the ten-at-night to seven-in-the-morning shift. And I remember when it was midnight because it was her birthday—my daughter's—and I thought of her. Anyway, after midnight, I heard Mrs. Shepard say: 'Dr. Shepard has poisoned me.'"

(1) *In-Court Statement*: Part of that piece of testimony is an in-court statement. The in-court statement is the long, rambling introductory part of the account, beginning with "On May 12th, I remember it was the 12th ..." and ending with "I heard Mr. Shepard say:"

The nurse is the manufacturer of this, the in-court part of the statement. She is on the stand. The quality of this raw material can be fully tested. So far, this is not hearsay. So far, the nurse is the real witness. She is a real witness to the date and why she remembers the date and her problem with getting the day off, and the rest, including the fact that Mrs. Shepard said something.

(2) *Out-of-Court Statement*: The out-of-court statement is "Dr. Shepard has poisoned me." All the rest is an in-court statement.

(3) *Assertion*: "Dr. Shepard has poisoned me."

(4) *Issue*: Was Mrs. Shepard alive on May 12?

(5) *Offered to Prove the Truth of the Matter Asserted?*: This out-of-court statement by Mrs. Shepard is not offered to prove the truth of the matter asserted. This out-of-court statement is not offered to prove that Dr. Shepard poisoned his wife. Instead, it is offered just to show that Mrs. Shepard made a statement, which is evidence she was alive (conclusive evidence, as it happens, if the nurse is believed). This out-of-court statement is not hearsay.

The nurse is a real witness and the original manufacturer of the evidence and she is on the stand and the relevant fact can be fully tested. All that is important here is that Mrs. Shepard said something and said it on the 12th of May. Not hearsay.

(6) *801(d)*: We do not get this far in the analysis, because we already decided it is not hearsay because it is not offered to prove the truth of the matter asserted.

(7) *Nonhearsay*: The key part of the witness's testimony is still an out-of-court statement but it is not offered to prove the truth of the matter asserted. The fact that she spoke is relevant, without regard to the truth of the words she spoke. The issue and the assertion are not the same. The statement is not hearsay.

3. *Shepard* Example Three

Change the case again: On May 12, Mrs. Shepard executed a new will. The issue is whether she had testamentary capacity. The challenger of the May 12 will calls the nurse to the stand to testify that, "On May 12th, just before all of those people came to her room to have her sign the new will, she said: 'Elvis has poisoned me.'"

(1) *In-Court Statement*: The following part of that piece of testimony is an in-court statement: "On May 12th, just before all of those people came to her room to have her sign the new will, she said." This is not hearsay. (Again, however, standing alone it is not relevant either.)

(2) *Out-of-Court Statement*: "Elvis has poisoned me."

(3) *Assertion:* As always, the assertion is the out-of-court statement. Here, it is: "Elvis has poisoned me."

(4) *Issue*: Did Mrs. Shepard have testamentary capacity?

(5) *Offered to Prove the Truth of the Matter Asserted?*: This out-of-court statement is not offered to prove the truth of the matter asserted. No one is trying to prove that Elvis poisoned her. It is offered, instead, just to show that she said it and the fact that she said it is relevant to the issue of her state of mind. (It does not prove that she was incompetent. She could have been joking, but it is relevant circumstantial evidence of her state of mind.)

All we are trying to prove is that Mrs. Shepard uttered these words. The nurse is a "real witness" for this purpose. So long as the raw material is the fact that Mrs. Shepard said "Elvis has poisoned me," the nurse is the manufacturer of this raw material. She is on the stand. The quality of this raw material can be fully tested by questioning the person who is delivering it. Whatever problems one may have with this evidence, it is not hearsay.

(6) *801(d)*: Again, we answered the hearsay question before we got to this part of the definition.

(7) *Nonhearsay*: Part of the nurse's testimony is still an out-of-court statement but it is not offered to prove the truth of the matter asserted.

4. *Shepard* Example Four

Change the case back to the original issue: whether Dr. Shepard killed his wife. There is other evidence that she was poisoned. The prosecutor calls the nurse to the stand. She will testify as follows: "Early in May, just before Mrs. Shepard died, I heard Dr. Shepard on the phone. I was in the hall, walking towards Mrs. Shepard's room, walking past the doctor's den. The door was ajar and I heard him say: 'I've done it. I poisoned her.'"

(1) *In-Court Statement*: The following part of that piece of testimony is an in-court statement: "Early in May, just before Mrs. Shepard died, I heard Dr. Shepard on the phone. I was in the hall, walking towards Mrs. Shepard's room, walking past the doctor's den. The door was ajar and I heard him say."

(2) *Out-of-Court Statement*: "I've done it. I poisoned her."

(3) *Assertion*: The out-of-court statement: "I've done it. I poisoned her."

(4) *Issue*: Did he poison her?

(5) *Offered to Prove the Truth of the Matter Asserted?*: The assertion and the issue are the same. The out-of-court statement is offered to prove the truth of the matter asserted.

(6) *801(d)*: The out-of-court declarant is Dr. Shepard. The out-of-court statement is offered by the prosecutor, against Dr. Shepard. This is a party's own statement offered against him. Therefore, it is not hearsay. Rule 801(d)(2)(A) excludes it from the definition.[64] (Using only the real-witness or the manufactured-evidence approach, this statement would be hearsay. Keep in mind that only the formulaic approach accounts for Rule 801(d).)

(7) *Nonhearsay*: Subsection (d) of Rule 801 excludes it from the definition of hearsay.

5. *Shepard* Example Five

Change the issue to this: Was the nurse who cared for Mrs. Shepard afraid of Dr. Shepard? Late on the morning of May 12th, the nurse pulled a gun and shot Dr. Shepard, and she is on trial for assault with intent to murder. The defendant claims she shot the doctor in self-defense. The defendant's state of

---

64. This is discussed at Chapter 2(III)(B), below.

mind—her fear of the victim—is relevant to one of the elements of the defense of self-defense. It is relevant to whether the defendant-nurse acted reasonably in using this kind of force against the victim. If allowed, the defendant will testify as follows: "Early on the morning of May 12th, Mrs. Shepard said to me: 'Dr. Shepard has poisoned me.'"

(1) *In-Court Statement*: The in-court part of the statement is, "Early on the morning of May 12th, Mrs. Shepard said to me." This is not an out-of-court statement and cannot be hearsay.

(2) *Out-of-Court Statement*: The out-of-court statement is, "'Dr. Shepard has poisoned me.'"

(3) *Assertion*: The assertion is the text of the out-of-court statement: "Dr. Shepard has poisoned me."

(4) *Issue*: Was the nurse afraid of Dr. Shepard?

(5) *Offered to Prove the Truth of the Matter Asserted?*: Here, the out-of-court assertion is not offered to prove the truth of the matter asserted, that Dr. Shepard poisoned his wife. It is offered, instead, to show the effect that the statement had on the listener—the nurse, who is now the defendant. The fact in issue here is: Was the nurse afraid of Dr. Shepard, did she believe him to be a killer? Breaking her fear down further, we want to know whether the nurse heard Mrs. Shepard, whether she believed her, and what effect that had on her. (Perhaps she feared he would kill her to keep her quiet.) The nurse, the testifying witness, is the real witness to what she heard and the effect it had on her. She is the original manufacturer of this raw material, *i.e.*, what she heard and how she felt, and she is the one on the stand delivering the raw material. The raw material can be fully tested by questioning the person delivering it.

Whose credibility is in issue? The nurse's. Do we believe the nurse is telling the truth? Who knows? Whether the testifying witness is telling the truth or not is a question for the trier of fact, not for the trier of law.

(6) *801(d)*: We have already decided that the statement is not hearsay because it is not offered to prove the truth of the matter asserted, so 801(d) does not come into play.

(7) *Nonhearsay*: As explained in subparagraph 5, above, this out-of-court statement is not hearsay.

B. Lee Harvey Oswald

The Warren Commission concluded that President John F. Kennedy was killed by a single assassin, Lee Harvey Oswald, working alone. As the Dallas police were transporting Lee Harvey Oswald from one place to another, he was gunned down by Jack Ruby. This shooting took place live on national television.

Assuming you can lay an appropriate foundation for the television feed, then anyone who was watching that live transmission is a real witness to the shooting of Lee Harvey Oswald. If the raw material needed in a subsequent trial is the identity of the shooter, then anyone watching that live transmission is an original manufacturer. We can put the manufacturer under oath, watch the manufacturer's demeanor, and cross-examine the manufacturer regarding the testimonial infirmities of memory, perception, sincerity, and honesty. All of the pressures exerted by the courtroom are on the manufacturer.[65] If you can authenticate the television feed, everyone watching was a "real witness."

Those who were not watching television but were in the next room when someone who was watching television ran into the room and said "Jack Ruby just shot Oswald on national television," they are not real witnesses to the shooting, they are not the manufacturers of the relevant raw material, but only middlepersons passing it along.

C. "I Want to Discontinue My Insurance Policy"

Through his employer, the deceased had an insurance policy on his life. The policy had a double indemnity clause for accidental death. The employer contributed one-half of the premium, and the employee contributed the other half, which was automatically deducted from his paycheck each month. The policy and the payroll deduction were to continue until either the employment relationship was terminated or the employee notified his employer's personnel manager that he wished to drop the policy (and, of course, discontinue his contributions).

After the policy was in effect for some months, the deceased came into the personnel office and told the manager: "I want to discontinue my group life insurance policy." The personnel manager notified the insurance company, and the policy was rescinded. Soon thereafter, the deceased was killed in an automobile accident.

The beneficiary sought payment under the policy, the insurance company refused to pay, and the beneficiary brought suit. The defense is that the insured had rescinded the policy. At trial, the insurance company offered the testimony

---

65. *See* Chapter 1(I), above.

of the personnel manager that the deceased told him: "I want to discontinue my group life insurance policy." The question is, of course, whether this is hearsay?

If the contract can be rescinded orally through the personnel manager, then, no, it is not hearsay.[66] "Whether [the deceased] in fact subjectively 'wanted' to cancel his coverage is irrelevant."[67] If the insurance contract may be rescinded orally through the personnel manager, then the fact that the deceased spoke these words in this context rescinded the contract. It altered that legal relationship. The words, coupled with the context, have a legal effect of their own, without regard to their subjective truth.[68] The out-of-court statement is not offered to prove the truth of the matter asserted, but only to show that it was said. The personnel manager has the relevant firsthand knowledge. He is a real witness to the operative words of rescission. He is an original manufacturer of the evidence in question.

D. "He Killed My Brother and He'll Kill My Mommie Too"

A husband and wife had two children and then divorced. The mother was awarded custody and then moved in with a man named Caporale. One of the children, a young boy, died and Caporale was suspected of killing him. The other child, a young girl, was placed in foster care and her father sued to obtain custody. This is a child custody case. The following evidence was admitted at trial: The foster mother testified that she told the surviving child she had read in the paper that her mother had married Caporale, and the girl "ran and put her arms around me and her head in my lap and started crying real bad and hard and said, 'He killed my brother and he'll kill my mommie too.'"

The girl's statement to her foster mother is an out-of-court statement, but it is not offered to prove the truth of the matter asserted. It is not offered to

---

66. If the contract cannot be rescinded orally through the personnel manager and there is other evidence of rescission, then "I want to discontinue my ... policy" is irrelevant unless it is offered to prove the truth of the fact asserted. The statement is hearsay because it is offered to prove the truth of its assertion and it does not fit under any of the provisions of Rule 801(d). If there is no other evidence of rescission and the contract cannot be rescinded orally through the personnel manager, then a defense based on rescission cannot win and the case should be dismissed on summary judgment.

67. Freeman v. Metropolitan Life Ins. Co., 468 F.Supp. 1269, 1271 (W.D. Va. 1979).

68. This is approach # 9 (the verbal-acts approach) of The Top Ten Approaches to Hearsay, above. *See also* approaches #s 6 and 7 (plain-fact-that-the-words-were-spoken and the credibility approaches). Of course, and as always, see also the first three approaches: the formula, the real witness, and manufactured evidence.

prove that Caporale killed the young boy. It is not hearsay. It is a nonhearsay statement that circumstantially indicates the girl's state of mind regarding her relationship with her mother's husband, Caporale. It is not being used to prove the truth of the out-of-court assertion, but instead to show the girl's state of mind. The fact that the little girl said this is relevant to the little girl's state of mind, which, in turn, is relevant to the custody issue. Her foster mother is a real witness to whether she said it.

Change the issue. If Caporale is on trial for the murder of the boy, then the foster mother's testimony is hearsay. Her testimony about what the little girl told her is an out-of-court statement, it is offered to prove the truth of the matter asserted, and it does not fit under any of the exclusions in Rule 801(d), so it is hearsay. The assertion in the out-of-court statement is 'Caporale killed the boy.' The issue is, Did Caporale kill the boy? The assertion in the out-of-court statement and the issue are the same.[69] The issue is whether Caporale killed the boy; the testifying witness, the foster mother, is not a real witness to that, she is not the original manufacturer of that piece of raw material.

Change the issue back to who gets custody of the girl, her father or her mother. If Caporale did kill the boy, that would be relevant to who should have custody of the boy's sister. However, in order to make this evidence relevant in the child custody case, we need not offer it for the inference that Caporale killed the young boy. We can offer it for the inference that the young girl has a horrible relationship with the man her mother has married. By itself, that stands as some evidence that she would be better off in the custody of her birth father. Regarding that latter inference, it is not being used to prove the truth of the out-of-court statement, but instead to show the young girl's state of mind. There is a material inference to which this evidence is relevant, and its relevance is not dependent on the truth of the facts reported in the statement.[70]

---

69. *See* approach # 4 (the two-boxes approach) of The Top Ten Approaches to Hearsay, above.

70. This example is Betts v. Betts, 473 P. 2d 403 (Wash. Ct. App. 1970). *Betts* is the child custody case discussed in the main text, not the murder trial. *Betts* is discussed at various places throughout this book.

CHAPTER TWO

THE DEFINITIONAL
EXCLUSIONS

I. The Definitional Exclusions versus the Exceptions—Evidentiary Burdens

II. Nonhearsay Prior Statements by a Witness: Rule 801(d)(1)

A. Prior Inconsistent Statements: Rule 801(d)(1)(A)
1. Text of the Rule
2. Foundational Elements
3. Need + Reliability = 1
4. Use Note

B. Prior Consistent Statements: Rule 801(d)(1)(B)
1. Text of the Rule
2. Foundational Elements
3. Need + Reliability = 1
4. Use Note

C. Statement of Identification of a Person: Rule 801(d)(1)(C)
1. Text of the Rule
2. Foundational Elements
3. Need + Reliability = 1
4. Use Note

III. Nonhearsay "Admissions": Rule 801(d)(2)

A. General Use Note
1. Exclusions, Not Exceptions
2. The Two Sets of Definitional Exclusions
3. Need + Reliability = 1?
4. Using the Out-of-Court Statement Itself to Establish Foundational Elements of These Exclusions

B. A Party's own Statement: 801(d)(2)(A)
1. Text of the Rule
2. Foundational Elements
3. Use Note

C. A Statement by an Agent: 801(d)(2)(D)

I. The Definitional Exclusions versus the Exceptions—Evidentiary Burdens

Before discussing the definitional exclusions from the hearsay rule, note that they are not exceptions. It is important to understand that 801(d) does not create exceptions to the hearsay rule; rather, it excludes certain statements from the rule itself. In a former life—at the common law—these kinds of statements were hearsay but they fit under exceptions. In their present incarnation—under the Federal Rules of Evidence—they are not hearsay in the first place. The definition in the rule very clearly states that they are not hearsay.[1] As one court nicely put it, 801(d) is a "carveout."[2]

It is important to know this, first, because it is true. Lawyers have an obligation to the truth and their success depends on their speaking and writing precisely. Characterizing the exclusions of 801(d) as exceptions is simply wrong. Second, failing to understand this is a mistake that may make a difference that can change the outcome of a case. The evidentiary burden of showing that a statement is hearsay is on the party opposing the admission of the evidence; that is, the party seeking the benefit of the rule against hearsay must show that the evidence is hearsay.[3] In theory, this means that the party opposing admis-

---

1. FED.R.EVID. 801(d) labels them "[s]tatements which are not hearsay." *See also* FED.R.EVID. 806 ("When a *hearsay* statement *or* a statement defined in Rule 801(d)(2)(C), (D), or (E) ...") (emphasis added).

2. DSC Sanitation Mgmt., Inc. v. Occupational Safety & Health Rev. Comm'n, 82 F.3d 812, 815 (8th Cir. 1996). The definition of hearsay in the Federal Rules of Evidence is basically the common-law definition except that these statements have been "carved out." They are now nonhearsay.

The definitional exclusions were the result of a compromise between these two positions: (1) no prior statement of any testifying witness should be hearsay; and (2) when offered to prove the truth of the matter asserted, every prior statement by every witness, testifying or not, should be hearsay (and then, of course, subject to the exceptions). Rules of Evidence: Hearings on H.R. 5463 Before the Committee on the Judiciary, 93 Cong. 7086–87 (1974); JACK B. WEINSTEIN & MARGARET A. BERGER, WEINSTEIN'S EVIDENCE MANUAL ¶ 15.01[01], at 15–3 (student ed. 1987).

3. The evidentiary burden often shifts back and forth. It starts with the proponent of the evidence, who must show that the evidence is relevant and, if it is testimonial evidence, that the witness is competent. Relevance: *e.g.*, FED.R.EVID. 402; DesRosiers v. Moran, 949 F.2d 15, 23 (1st Cir. 1991); United States v. Connors, 825 F.2d 1384, 1390 (9th Cir. 1987); United States v. Short, 790 F.2d 464, 468 (6th Cir. 1986). Competence: *e.g.*, FED.R.EVID. 602; United States v. Davis 792 F.2d 1299, 1304 (5th Cir. 1986) (citing authorities); Miller v. Keating, 754 F.2d 507, 511 (3d Cir. 1985) (competence and the out-of-court declarant of a hearsay statement). Once the proponent shows that the evidence is relevant and competent, it is presumptively admissible; it comes in unless the opponent of the evidence shows that there is some other rule of evidence that excludes it. FED.R.EVID. 402 & 602. If the opponent of the evidence shows that the evidence is hearsay, then the evidentiary burden shifts back to the proponent, who must show that the evidence fits under one or more exceptions to the hearsay rule. *E.g.,* Idaho v. Wright, 497 U.S. 805, 816 (1990) (proponent of evidence presumptively barred by the hearsay rule has the burden of establishing the exception); United States v. Two Shields, 497 F.3d 789, 793 (8th Cir. 2007); United States v. Arnold, 486 F.3d 177, 206 (6th Cir. 2007); American Auto. Accessories, Inc. v. Fishman, 175 F.3d 534, 540 (7th Cir. 1999); United States v. Samaniego, 187 F.3d 1222, 1224 (10th Cir. 1999); Bemis v. Edwards, 45 F.3d 1369, 1373 (9th Cir. 1995). *See also* the cross-references in the next footnote.

sion must show that the evidence (1) is an out-of-court statement, (2) is offered to prove the truth of the matter asserted, and (3) does not fit into one of the definitional exclusions. Once the opponent of the evidence shows these three things, then the evidence is hearsay; it is presumptively inadmissible and the evidentiary burden of showing that it fits under an exception to the rule is on the proponent of the evidence. The party seeking the benefit of an exception must lay the foundation for the exception.[4]

At common law these exclusions were exceptions to the hearsay rule; they were admissible hearsay. Rather than maintain them as exceptions, the drafters of the rules carved them out of the definition of hearsay; now they are not hearsay at all.[5] This was a deliberate change, and there is no legal or practical reason for it except to change the burden of production. To characterize a definitional exclusion as an exception seems to misplace the evidentiary burden. And this misplacement of the burden can change the outcome of a case.

Take a case where the following three things are true. (1) The only evidence of an essential element of plaintiff's case is a statement that was made out of court and is offered to prove the truth of the matter asserted. (2) The statement is only admissible if it was an 801(d)(2)(D) statement by a party opponent's (defendant's) agent. (3) There is not enough evidence to say for sure whether that person was the defendant's agent. The outcome of this case will depend on which party has the evidentiary burden.[6]

---

4. *See* Chapter 3(I)(D) (evidentiary burdens and the foundational elements of the exceptions) and Chapter 6(I)(E)(11) (evidentiary burdens under Rule 32 of the Federal Rules of Civil Procedure).

5. Unless there is a difference in the evidentiary burden, the exclusions should have been left as exceptions and included in either Rule 803 or 804. But they were not. The Advisory Committee that drafted the *proposed* federal rules of evidence classified every out-of-court statement made by any testifying witness as nonhearsay. Had that proposed rule been adopted, the burden on one seeking to take advantage of the hearsay rule would have been to show that there is an out-of-court statement, offered to prove the truth of the matter asserted, and that it is not the statement of a testifying witness. After the proposed rule was announced, there were objections to excluding from the rule all prior statements by testifying witnesses. In response to those objections the rule was changed. As enacted, the statute pulls back from the Committee's more sweeping change. Rules of Evidence: Hearings on H.R. 5463 Before the Committee on the Judiciary, 93 Cong. 7086–87 (1974); JACK B. WEINSTEIN & MARGARET A. BERGER, WEINSTEIN'S EVIDENCE MANUAL ¶ 15.01[01], at 15–3 (student ed. 1987). Now, with this compromise version of the basic definition, the burden on one seeking to take advantage of the hearsay rule is to show that there is an out-of-court statement, offered to prove the truth of the matter asserted, and it does not fit under subpart (d) of Rule 801.

6. The placement of this evidentiary burden may have determined the outcome in American Eagle Ins. Co. v. Thompson, 85 F.3d 327 (8th Cir. 1996). An insurance company

Here is the problem—admittedly a major problem—with the above analysis: The cases do not agree. The cases that say anything about the burden of establishing the foundation for the definitional exclusions treat the exclusions just like they were exceptions. They place the burden on the proponent of the evidence. They do so without any analysis of the point and mostly, if not always, as dicta; without any discussion of why the drafters of the federal rules changed these common-law exceptions into statutory exclusions from the rule itself; without any discussion of the difference between hearsay exceptions and nonhearsay exclusions; without any discussion of why the exclusions are classified as exclusions if they are to be treated exactly like exceptions. They do so without any recognition of the fact that moving classes of statements from the list of exceptions and placing them on a list of exclusions from the definition of hearsay only does one thing of any consequence: It changes the evidentiary burden. They do so incorrectly, in my opinion. These cases simply do not address the question, and they do not address it because they do not notice it.

The most important case of this sort is *Bourjaily v. United States*.[7] The question in *Bourjaily* was whether the evidentiary burden in a criminal case is "beyond a reasonable doubt" or "by a preponderance of the evidence." Having decided that the evidentiary burden does not follow the burden of proof, but

---

brought an action seeking a declaration that Mr. Thompson was not an employee of Arkansas Aircraft, Inc. If he was an employee on the date of a certain accident, then the insurance company was on the hook for the damages caused by the accident. The trial court admitted certain out-of-court statements made to Mrs. Thompson (the in-court declarant) by an insurance agent named Medlock (the out-of-court declarant). The question was whether Medlock was the plaintiff's agent and his statements were admissible under Rule 801(d)(2)(D), as admissions by an agent of a party opponent. The trial court found that Medlock was plaintiff's agent and the statements were admissible. The Court of Appeals reversed. "[Because] Mrs. Thompson failed to meet her burden of establishing the necessary agency relationship, ... the district court erred in admitting Medlock's statements pursuant to Rule 801(d)(2)(D)." *Id.* at 333 (citation omitted). If this evidence had been admissible, then any other errors would seem to have been harmless; it seems that this evidence would have been the tipping point.

If the burden of establishing that a statement is hearsay includes the burden regarding all parts of the definition, including the exclusions, then the Court of Appeals had it backwards and the sentence just quoted should read: "[Because American Eagle] failed to meet [its] burden of establishing [the nonexistence of] the necessary agency relationship, ... the district court [did not err] in admitting Medlock's statements pursuant to Rule 801(d)(2)(D)." *American Eagle* applied the evidentiary burden to the proponent of a definitional exclusion, and did so without comment, let alone explanation.

7. 483 U.S. 171 (1987).

is the same in civil and criminal cases, the Court stated this: "Therefore, we hold that when the preliminary facts relevant to Rule 801(d)(2)(E) are disputed, the offering party must prove them by a preponderance of the evidence."[8] The part about the strength of the evidentiary burden was discussed at length and was essential to the answer to the question before the Court. The part about the placement of the burden is dictum.[9] It is, however, dicta from the Supreme Court of the United States[10] and, as noted above, most Circuits follow the rule.[11]

---

8. *Id.* at 176.

9. It is of course possible that I am trying too hard to accomplish what I think is right and required, but it does seem to me that this part of *Bourjaily* is dictum.

There is another statement from the Supreme Court that, to me, is even more clearly dictum, but which the Sixth Circuit Court of Appeals felt bound to follow: In General Elec. Co. v. Joiner, 522 U.S. 136, 141–42 (1997), the Court addressed the burden on appeal of a trial court's evidentiary ruling under the statutory rules. The Supreme Court offhandedly stated that all evidentiary issues are reviewed on appeal for abuse of discretion. Hearsay was not the issue on appeal in *Joiner*. If, however, *Joiner's* statement about review of evidentiary rulings under the statutory rules is true across the board, then, if a trial court admits hearsay into evidence in violation of the statute's command (ignores the definition or the foundational elements of an exception), the review is for abuse of discretion. Subsequently, in a case that did involve the hearsay rule, the Sixth Circuit stated that it is not clear how trial courts have "discretion" to ignore the statute, "but it is not this court's privilege to 'question why.' Therefore, in disregard of our heretofore well-settled precedent that hearsay evidentiary rulings are reviewed de novo, we shall review the district court's ruling for an abuse of discretion." Trepel v. Roadway Express, Inc., 194 F.3d 708, 717 (6th Cir. 1999) (citation omitted).

Perhaps I am trying too hard. Perhaps the Sixth Circuit did not try hard enough.

10. *See also* Crawford v. Washington, 541 U.S. 36, 56 (2004) (referring to nonhearsay statements by coconspirators as fitting under a "hearsay exception[]") (dictum). "The Federal Rules of Evidence do not treat declarations by coconspirators as an exception to the hearsay rule but as nonhearsay.... The Supreme Court consistently refers to [them] as a 'hearsay exception[].'" United States v. Faulkner, 439 F.3d 1221, 1226 n.1 (10th Cir. 2006) (quoting *Crawford*, 541 U.S. at 56, and citing *Bourjaily*, 483 U.S. passim).

11. *See also, e.g.,* Sea Land Serv., Inc. v. Lozen Int'l, LLC, 285 F.3d 808, 821 (9th Cir. 2002) (statements of an agent) (no discussion; citing cases); United States v. Perez-Ruiz, 353 F.3d 1, 11 (1st Cir. 2003) (statements by co-conspirators) (no discussion; citing a case that states the point without discussion); Gomes v. Rivera Rodriguez, 344 F.3d 103, 116 (1st Cir. 2003) (statement by an agent) (no discussion; citing two cases, one of which does not mention burdens and the other of which states the point without discussion); United States v. Chang, 207 F.3d 1169, 1176 (9th Cir. 2000) (statements by an agent) (quoting a case that states the point without discussion and which, in turn, cites an opinion that says nothing about this burden); Wilkinson v. Carnival Cruise Lines, Inc., 920 F.2d 1560, 1566 (11th Cir. 1991) (statements by agents) (no discussion; citing a number of cases stating the point without discussion); Curtis v. Oklahoma City Pub. Sch. Bd. of Educ., 147 F.3d 1200, 1218 (10th

This change in the evidentiary burden may seem to be unworkable and, there-fore, acceptable. Take admissions by agents: It may not be acceptable to say that anytime a proponent argues that otherwise-hearsay evidence is a nonhearsay ad-mission by an agent, then the opponent must come up with evidence that the de-clarant was not its agent. Perhaps it does not seem acceptable to say that a statement can come in as an admission by an agent when there is no evidence of agency.

About that, first, this is a statute and it is not the Court's job to rewrite it. Second, if this is a problem, it can be handled as follows: The opponent of the evidence shows that the statement is an out-of-court statement that is offered to prove the truth of the matter asserted, and there is no evidence that the de-clarant was an agent of the party against whom the statement is offered. This satisfies the opponent's evidentiary burden-of-production, shifting the bur-den of production to the proponent. Now the proponent must produce some evidence of this foundational element, or lose the point. While the evidentiary *burden of production* shifts to the proponent, the evidentiary *burden-of-per-suasion* stays with the opponent of the evidence, and: (1) if the proponent does not present any evidence of this foundational element, then the opponent has satisfied the evidentiary burden of persuasion and the evidence is hearsay; (2) if the proponent does put on some evidence of this element, then the oppo-nent must put on some counter evidence; then the judge must decide—but the evidentiary burden-of-persuasion remains with the opponent. In other words, the solution to this problem is a presumption—an ad hoc or categorical pre-sumption—that shifts the burden of producing evidence of each element of the exclusion. The presumption shifts the evidentiary burden of production to the proponent but leaves the ultimate evidentiary burden on the opponent of the evidence. Wherever it is permissible from the record to infer that the foun-dational element for a definitional exclusion is present, then, unless the op-ponent shows that things are otherwise, that is the inference to be drawn.[12]

Of what consequence is this? Doesn't this get us right back to treating the ex-clusions just like they were exceptions? No, it does not. There is one difference. The tie still goes to the proponent. Take admissions by an agent for example, and say that it comes down to the scope of the agency. If the statement is offered and the opponent objects that it is hearsay, then the presumption kicks in and

Cir. 1998) (statement by agent) (no discussion; citing case with no discussion which, in turn, cites cases that either have little or nothing to do with the burden or thoughtlessly apply the common law to the statutory rule).

12. *See* "The 'Trustworthiness' Clause—the Burden of Proof" in the Use Note to the public records and reports exception. Chapter 3(VIII)(E).

the proponent must bring forth some evidence of the scope of the agency, or lose the point. If the proponent does that, then the issue is joined and the burden of proving the scope of the agency is on the opponent. If the opponent's evidence outweighs the proponent's, then the evidence stays out; if the proponent's evidence outweighs the opponent's, then the evidence comes in; and if the evidence is in equipoise, and the judge concludes "I cannot tell," then the evidence comes in. The ultimate evidentiary burden is the opponent's and if the evidence is in perfect balance, then the opponent of the evidence has not met that burden.[13]

II. Nonhearsay Prior Statements by a Witness: Rule 801(d)(1)

A. Prior Inconsistent Statements: Rule 801(d)(1)(A)

1. Text of the Rule

> (d) Statements which are not hearsay. A statement is not hearsay if—
> (1) Prior statement by witness. The declarant testifies at the trial or hearing and is subject to cross-examination concerning the statement, and the statement is (A) inconsistent with the declarant's testimony, and was given under oath subject to the penalty of perjury at a trial, hearing, or other proceeding, or in a deposition....

2. Foundational Elements

1. The out-of-court declarant is testifying at the trial or hearing and is subject to cross-examination regarding the out-of-court statement.
2. The statement is inconsistent with the declarant's trial testimony.
3. The statement was "made under oath subject to the penalty of perjury at a trial, hearing, or other proceeding, or in a deposition."

3. Need + Reliability = 1[14]

a. Need

The prior inconsistent statements of a testifying witness are coming in anyway: They are admissible to impeach the inconsistent testimony. If the court al-

---

13. The placement of the burden can, of course, change the outcome of the case. *See American Eagle Ins. Co.*, discussed in note 6, above.

14. *See* Chapter 3(I)(B), below.

lows the evidence to be used to impeach the witness but cannot allow it to be used as substantive evidence of the facts declared in the statement, then the court has to instruct the jury that they may consider the evidence in the one way, but they may not consider it in the other way. This is difficult, if not impossible, for the jury to do. Perhaps it is better just to let the evidence in and let the jury deal with it. This may be a more honest expression of what will happen anyway. Additionally, there will be times when the prior inconsistent statement is valuable—even the most valuable—substantive evidence of the fact declared.[15]

b. Reliability

This definitional exclusion does not apply unless the out-of-court declarant is testifying at the trial and subject to cross-examination. Those things that mitigate the testimonial infirmities—in-court cross-examination, oath, and demeanor evidence, the pressures exerted by the courtroom setting and the fear of public speaking,[16] are all present. The "real witness" and the "original manufacturer" of the evidence is on the stand.[17] Furthermore, this definitional exclusion requires that the out-of-court statement itself has been made under oath.

4. Use Note

■ *Prior Inconsistent Statements Used as Nonhearsay Impeachment Evidence, and not as Substantive Evidence*: If a testifying witness's prior inconsistent statement *does not* meet the foundational requirements set out above,[18] it is still nonhearsay insofar as it is used solely to impeach the witness.[19] If an out-of-court statement is a testifying witness's own statement and is inconsistent with

---

15. Regarding this latter point, see particularly the discussion of the turncoat witness in Chapter 5(V)(E)(2), below.

16. *See* Chapter 1(I), above.

17. *See* Chapter 1(III)(A)(2) & (3), above.

18. A common reason for this would be that the prior statement was not made under oath.

19. *See*, for example, United States v. Williams, 272 F.3d 845, 859 (7th Cir. 2001) where the prosecutor put on a witness who testified that the defendant was involved in the drug deal in question and then, to minimize the damage from the witness's prior inconsistent statement, offered it under Rule 801(d)(1)(A). The Court of Appeals notes that the prosecutor missed the point. Rule 801(d)(1)(A) is irrelevant. The prosecutor is not offering the statement to prove the truth of the matter asserted. The statement is that defendant was not involved in the crime charged. The prosecutor is in fact trying to prove just the opposite. The out-of-court statement is that defendant was not involved. The issue is the credibility of the testifying witness. The text of the statement and the issue to which it is offered are not the same.

the witness's in-court testimony it can be used to impeach that in-court testimony. When used for that purpose only, such an out-of-court statement is not hearsay. It is not offered to prove the truth of what was said out-of-court, but rather to show that what was said out-of-court is different from what was said in-court. The fact that the witness said one thing then and another now is relevant to how much weight the jury should give this testimony. It may indicate many different things: that the witness is dishonest, unobservant, forgetful, confused, a bundle of nerves, or having second thoughts. Whatever the trier of fact makes of it, the fact of self-contradiction reflects on the weight to be given to the witness's testimony.[20]

■ *Prior Inconsistent Statements Used as Nonhearsay Substantive Evidence*: If, however, a testifying witness's prior inconsistent statement *does* meet the foundational requirements set out above, then it is admissible for all purposes. It is admissible to impeach and as substantive evidence of the matter asserted.[21]

Declarant must be testifying at the trial or hearing where the statement is offered and subject to cross-examination regarding the statement.[22] "Ordinarily a witness is regarded as 'subject to cross-examination' when he is placed on the stand, under oath, and responds willingly to questions."[23]

"In applying Rule 801(d)(1)(A), 'inconsistency is not limited to diametrically opposed answers but may be found in evasive answers, inability to recall, silence, or changes of position.'"[24]

---

20. Here is the irony in the fact that such a prior inconsistent statement may not be used to prove the truth of the fact stated therein, but only to impeach the witness and discredit the inconsistent fact stated on the stand. If on the day of the wreck the witness said plaintiff's light was "Green!" and at trial said it was "Red!," the out-of-court statement that it was green may not be used to prove that it was green at the time of the wreck, but it may be used to prove that the witness's in-court testimony that it was red should not be believed.

21. Continuing with the example in the previous footnote, the out-of-court statement may be used as evidence that the witness's in-court testimony that plaintiff had a red light should not be believed and as evidence that in fact the plaintiff had the green light.

22. *E.g.*, United States v. Sadler, 234 F.3d 368, 372 (8th Cir. 2000) ("defendant may not rely on Rule 801(d)(1)" because the declarant "did not testify at the trial and was not subject to cross-examination").

23. United States v. Owens, 484 U.S. 554, 561 (1988). *See also* part II(C)(4) of this chapter, below.

24. United States v. Matlock, 109 F.3d 1313, 1319 (8th Cir. 1997) (citation omitted). *Accord, e.g.*, United States v. Mayberry, 540 F.3d 506, 516 (6th Cir. 2008) (under this exclusion "'limited and vague recall of events, equivocation, and claims of memory loss' can constitute prior inconsistent statements"); United States v. Iglesias, 535 F.3d 150, 159 n.3 (3d Cir. 2008) (this exclusion "'provide[s] a party with desirable protection against the "turncoat witness" who changes his story on the stand and deprives the party calling him of evidence

■ *"[A]t a trial, hearing, or other proceeding, or in a deposition"*: This exclusion requires more than just an inconsistent statement made under oath. The statement must have been made "at a trial, hearing, or other proceeding, or in a deposition."[25] A sworn affidavit that grew out of an investigative interview with the declarant is not a statement made "in conjunction with a 'proceeding.'"[26]

■ *The Oath*: A prior *inconsistent* statement offered as nonhearsay under Rule 801(d)(1)(A) must have been made under oath.[27] As noted below, a prior *consistent* statement offered as nonhearsay under Rule 801(d)(1)(B) need not have been made under oath. Why the difference? The proposed federal rules of evidence did not have the oath provision in either place. Congress added it to 801(d)(1)(A) and, perhaps inadvertently, did not add it to 801(d)(1)(B). Alternatively, perhaps it is that the risk is less with a prior consistent statement because the out-of-court statement is necessarily cumulative. In any event, "[a]s a result, rehabilitative hearsay material is more readily admissible than is impeaching hearsay material."[28]

---

essential to his case'") (citation omitted); United States v. Cisneos-Gutierez, 517 F.3d 751, 757 (5th Cir. 2008) ("[T]he unwilling witness often takes refuge in a failure to remember.") (footnote and multiple quotation marks omitted)); United States v. Gajo, 290 F.3d 922, 931 (7th Cir. 2002) (("[I]n ... the recalcitrant witness, a lack of memory is inconsistent with the [prior] description of specific details."); United States v. Distler , 671 F.3d 954, 958 (6th Cir. 1981) ("[P]artial or vague recollection is inconsistent with total or definite recollection."); State v. Simpson, 945 A.2d 449, 460–61 (Conn. 2008) ("'[T]he testimony of a witness as a whole, or the whole impression or effect of what has been said, must be examined.... Inconsistency in effect, rather than contradiction in express terms, is the test for admitting a witness' prior statement.... [I]nconsistency may be determined from the circumstances and is not limited to cases in which diametrically opposed assertions have been made. *Thus, inconsistencies may be found in changes in position and they may also be found in denial of recollection....'*") (emphasis added in *Simpson*; citations and internal quotation marks omitted in *Simpson*); State v. Caine, 746 N.W.2d 339, 350 (Minn. 2008) ("[F]eigned memory loss is inconsistent with the witness's prior testimony.").

25. FED.R.EVID. 801(d)(1)(A).
26. United States v. Williams, 272 F.3d 845, 859 (7th Cir. 2001).
27. The statement can have been made under oath or adopted under oath. Cisneos-Gutierez, 517 F.3d at 758 (while not under oath the declarant made a statement; while under oath at his plea hearing the declarant adopted the statement as true). United States v. Meza-Urtado, 351 F.3d 301, 304 (7th Cir. 2003) ("In [his prior statements, declarant] admitted that a drug deal was to take place and that he was paid $200 for providing 'protection.' Because these sworn statements were clearly inconsistent with his trial testimony, they were properly received as substantive evidence. And because Farias could have been cross-examined at length about them, no Sixth Amendment Confrontation Clause [sic] is presented.").
28. 4 JACK B. WEINSTEIN & MARGARET A. BERGER, WEINSTEIN'S EVIDENCE 801–32 (1996).

■ *The Confrontation Clause*: Since this exclusion only applies when the out-of-court declarant testifies and is subject to cross-examination, the Confrontation Clause does not limit the admissibility of the statement.[29]

■ *Exclusions versus Exceptions*: This is an exclusion from the definition of hearsay. It is not an exception to the hearsay rule. As discussed elsewhere, there may be a difference.[30]

B. Prior Consistent Statements: Rule 801(d)(1)(B)

1. Text of the Rule

(d) Statements which are not hearsay. A statement is not hearsay if—
(1) Prior statement by witness. The declarant testifies at the trial or hearing and is subject to cross-examination concerning the statement, and the statement is ... (B) consistent with the declarant's testimony and is offered to rebut an express or implied charge against the declarant of recent fabrication or improper influence or motive ...

2. Foundational Elements

1. The out-of-court declarant is testifying at the trial or hearing and is subject to cross-examination regarding the out-of-court statement.

2. The statement is offered to rebut a charge that the declarant has recently made up a lie or been subject to improper influence.

3. The out-of-court statement was made before the event that arguably triggered the lie.[31]

---

29. *See* Chapter 14, below.
30. *See* Chapter 2(I), above.
31. This foundational element is made explicit in Tome v. United States, 513 U.S. 150, 158 (1995), rather than in the text of the rule itself. Often a witness's motive to "fabricate" arises at the time of his or her arrest. There is, however, no "'bright line rule that motive to fabricate necessarily and automatically attaches upon arrest.'" United States v. Drury, 396 F.3d 1303, 1317 (11th Cir. 2005) (citation omitted). In Large v. State, 177 P.3d 807, 819 (Wyo. 2008) the court received testimony from a foster mother and the prosecutor's investigator about the child-witnesses' prior statements of sexual abuse, which prior statements were consistent with the children's trial testimony. Defendant argued "that the children had been influenced to tell false stories about [defendant's] involvement [in their sexual abuse]." Regarding the timing of the statements vis-à-vis the development of the motive to fabricate, defense counsel argued that the children's "motive" to fabricate developed as they spoke with and were influenced by the foster mother and the investigator. The prior consistent statements and the development of the motive were more or less simultaneous. *See*

4. The out-of-court statement is consistent with the declarant's in-court statement.

3. Need + Reliability = 1[32]

a. Need

Every statement covered by this definitional exclusion has at least one non-hearsay use—as a prior consistent statement that rehabilitates the credibility of a witness who has been impeached. Every statement covered by this exclusion is coming in as rehabilitation evidence anyway. If the court allows the evidence to be used to rehabilitate the witness but cannot allow it to be used as substantive evidence of the facts declared in the statement, then the court has to instruct the jury that they may consider the evidence in the one way but they may not consider it in the other way. This is difficult, if not impossible, for the jury to do. Perhaps it is better just to let the evidence in and let the jury deal with it. This may be a more honest expression of what will happen anyway. This supplies the need for a way around the hearsay rule.

b. Reliability

This definitional exclusion does not apply unless the out-of-court declarant is testifying at the trial and subject to cross-examination. As noted above,[33] cross-examination, oath, demeanor evidence, the pressures exerted by the courtroom setting, the fear of public speaking, the preference for the real witness and the original manufacturer of the evidence—all of these are present. There is also this: Since this is a prior statement consistent with the declarant's trial testimony, it will be cumulative of evidence already considered sufficiently reliable to have been admitted into evidence.

4. Use Note

■ *Substantive Evidence versus Credibility Evidence*: Rule 801(d)(1)(B) defines certain prior consistent statements out of the hearsay rule.[34] Even without Rule

---

also State v. Bujan, No. 20060883, 2008 WL 2776682, at *2–4 (Utah 2008) (discussing rule's application to premotive consistent statements only; discussing other ways such statements might be admissible as non-substantive credibility evidence).

32. *See* Chapter 3(I)(B), below.

33. *See* Chapter 2(II)(A)(4), above.

34. Not hearsay: FED.R.EVID. 801(d)(1)(B). *Accord, e.g.,* United States v. Gonzalez, 533 F.3d 1057, 1061 (9th Cir. 2008); United States v. Bercier, 506 F.3d 625, 629 (8th Cir. 2007).

801(d)(1)(B), every statement covered by this rule would have at least one nonhearsay use. All Rule 801(d)(1)(B) evidence is also nonhearsay credibility evidence. That is, it is all post-impeachment rehabilitation evidence.[35] The result of Rule 801(d)(1)(B) is that these out-of-court statements are also admissible as substantive evidence of the facts declared therein. In either case, their admissibility is dependent on their rehabilitative status.[36]

■ *Subject to Cross-Examination*: Declarant must be testifying at the trial or hearing where the statement is offered and subject to cross-examination regarding the statement. "Ordinarily a witness is regarded as 'subject to cross-examination' when he is placed on the stand, under oath, and responds willingly to questions."[37]

■ *The Oath*: A prior *inconsistent* statement offered as nonhearsay under Rule 801(d)(1)(A) must have been made under oath. A prior *consistent* statement offered as nonhearsay under Rule 801(d)(1)(B) need not have been made under oath. This difference is discussed above.[38]

----

35. "When the prior statements are offered for credibility, the question is not governed by Rule 801." United States v. Simonelli, 237 F.3d 19, 27 (1st Cir. 2001) (a prior consistent statement that does not meet the foundational elements of this exclusion and is not admissible as nonhearsay substantive evidence under this rule may be admissible as nonhearsay credibility evidence if it is not offered for its truth, but only to rehabilitate the witness following impeachment with a prior inconsistent statement). *Accord, e.g.,* United States v. Ellis, 121 F.3d 908, 919 (4th Cir. 1997); State v. Bujan, No. 20060883, 2008 WL 2776682, at *2–4 (Utah 2008).

36. Evidence rehabilitating a witness's credibility is generally inadmissible until after the introduction of evidence impeaching the witness's credibility. By the terms of the rule itself, this general rule applies to Rule 801(d)(1)(B) prior consistent statements. *E.g.,* Ross v. Saint Augustine's Coll., 103 F.3d 338 (4th Cir. 1996) (district court violated required sequence; harmless error).

37. *Owens*, 484 U.S. at 561. United States v. Green, 258 F.3d 683, 692 (7th Cir. 2001) (the prior consistent statement need not be introduced during the declarant's testimony but may be introduced through someone else's so long as the declarant is available for cross-examination about the statement some time during the trial) (citing and discussing cases); *Sadler*, 234 F.3d at 372 (defendant may not admit his statement under this rule "because he did not testify at the trial and was not subject to cross-examination, as required by [the rule]"); *Large*, 177 P.3d at 818 ("When evaluating the cross-examination requirement, we [allow] … testimony under W.R.E. 801(d)(1)(B) even when 'counsel for the defense studiously avoided cross-examining most witnesses and deferred his opening statement until after the State had presented its case.' … [Defendant] had an opportunity to cross-examine [the witnesses]…, even though she chose not to take that opportunity [with regard to one] and only briefly cross-examined [the other].") (citation and paragraph break omitted). *See also* part II(C)(4) of this chapter, below.

38. *See* Chapter 2(II)(A)(4), above.

■ *Recent Fabrication or Improper Influence*: The only difficult part of this rule is that the evidence must be offered "to rebut a charge of 'recent fabrication or improper influence or motive.'"[39] Opposing counsel must have suggested that the out-of-court declarant recently made up a lie or was subject to improper influence. Whether opposing counsel has done so is judged against the universe of inferences the jury could possibly draw from the evidence,[40] and not by opposing counsel's stated reason for offering the evidence. The "charge of 'recent fabrication or improper influence or motive'" that activates this exception may come in the evidentiary portion of the trial or during the opening statement.[41]

For example: The defendant is charged with having sexually molested his daughter. At trial, the defendant implies that his daughter made up the allegations of abuse, at the prodding of her mother, after the mother learned that he was going to seek custody of the girl. Any out-of-court statement about abuse that she suffered at the hands of her father, which the girl made prior to the date on which the mother learned the father was going to seek custody, is nonhearsay. It is a nonhearsay, substantively admissible, prior consistent statement under Rule 801(d)(1)(B). It is a statement offered to rebut a charge of improper influence. This line of questioning opens the door for the prosecutor to offer any and all of the girl's prior consistent statements made prior to the time when the alleged motive to lie came into existence.[42]

---

39. *Tome*, 513 U.S. at 157 (quoting Fed.R.Evid. 801(d)(1)(B)). *See, e.g.,* United States v. Griham, 76 Fed. R. Evid. Serv. 761, 764 (11th Cir. 2008) (the prior consistent statement must be "'offered to rebut a specific allegation of recent fabrication, not to rehabilitate credibility that has been generally called into question'") (not selected for publication in the Federal Reporter); United States v. Anderson, 303 F.3d 847, 858–59 (7th Cir. 2002) (particularly valuable on the issue of recent fabrication); State v. Bujan, No. 20060883, 2008 WL 2776682, at *2–4 (Utah 2008) (discussing rule's application to premotive consistent statements only; discussing other ways such statements might be admissible as non-substantive credibility evidence).

40. United States v. Young, 105 F.3d 1, 9 (1st Cir. 1997). *Accord, e.g.,* United States v. Ettinger, 344 F.3d 1149, 1160–61 (11th Cir. 2003) (defense counsel asked witness if he had read any other reports of the incident and implied that he had fabricated his testimony based on other reports; witness denied reading other reports; prior consistent statement deemed admissible nonhearsay); Brown v. State, 671 N.E.2d 401, 408 (Ind. 1996) (all that is required is that the party implied improper motive; question is not whether counsel *intended* to imply fabrication but whether she *did* imply improper motive; question is not counsel's intent but possible inferences jury could make).

41. State v. Quinn, 490 S.E.2d 34, 45 (W. Va. 1997). *See also, e.g., Large,* 177 P.3d at 819 (discussed above, in notes 31 and 37)); State v. Neufeld, 578 N.W.2d 536, 540 (N.D. 1998) (improper motive implied during opening statement and cross-examination).

42. This scenario is, unfortunately, based on far too many cases. *See also, e.g., Large,* 177 P.3d at 819 (discussed above, in notes 31 and 37).

Example No. 2: The defendant is a grocer charged with violating the Food Stamp Act by purchasing stamps for cash rather than exchanging them for food. Defendant claims he no longer owned the store at the time of the crime alleged, but had sold it to a person who is a witness for the government. This government witness testifies that there was no such sale and defendant owned the store at all times. Defense counsel argues that the witness is lying to protect himself from prosecution for this very same crime. In response, the prosecutor offers the witness's prior statement to an insurance agent that the defendant owned the store. The statement was made after the date the defendant says he sold the store and *prior to the date* when the defendant or the witness became aware of this criminal investigation. This is a statement offered to rebut a charge of improper motive.[43]

Example No. 3: A police officer continuously transmitted information to the dispatcher, including information that a man he had spotted had a gun and that, during a footchase, the man threw the gun into a stairwell. As is routinely the case, these transmissions were tape-recorded. At trial, defense counsel asserts that after he found a gun in the stairwell, the officer made up the story about having seen the gun on the defendant and having seen the defendant throw it into the stairwell. The tape recording is admissible nonhearsay: declarant is testifying and subject to cross-examination regarding the statement; it is offered to rebut a charge of recent fabrication; the statement was made prior to the event said to have triggered the fabrication, and the statement is consistent with declarant's in-court statement.[44]

Example No. 4: In a drug-conspiracy trial, two coconspirators testified against the defendant that he, the defendant, was the leader of the conspiracy. "The defense insinuated that the witnesses had planned the story they would tell when they were jointly incarcerated pending trial."[45] In rebuttal, the government offered into evidence portions of one of the witness's grand jury testimony and the other witness's statement made during his interrogation, each of which was

---

43. This scenario is based on United States v. Hebeka, 25 F.3d 287 (6th Cir. 1994).

44. This scenario is based on United States v. Young, 105 F.3d 1 (1st Cir. 1997), which is discussed at Chapter 10(I), below. This prior statement would also have been admissible hearsay under the present sense impression exception, FED.R.EVID. 803(1), probably under the excited utterance exception, FED.R.EVID. 803(2), and, if the proper foundation is laid, as it likely could have been, under the record of a regularly conducted activity and the public records and reports exceptions, FED.R.EVID. 803(6) & (8). *Accord* United States v. Ruiz, 249 F.3d 643, 647–48 (7th Cir. 2001).

45. United States v. Smith, 893 F.2d 1573, 1582 (9th Cir. 1989).

made prior to their incarceration pending trial and was consistent with their trial testimony that the defendant was the leader of the conspiracy. These prior consistent statements are admissible nonhearsay under Rule 801(d)(1)(B).[46]

One lesson to be learned is this: When choosing a defense or a credibility argument, keep one eye on the doors it will open through which your opponent can bring in otherwise undeliverable evidence.[47]

■ *Consistencies*: The trial testimony and the out-of-court statement need not be entirely consistent in order for the statement to fit under this definitional exclusion. It is enough that the statement is "consistent with respect to a fact of central importance to the trial."[48]

■ *Using Unimpeached Parts of a Prior Statement*: For this exclusion to work, the prior consistent statements need "not specifically relate to the subject matter of the statements impeached."[49] If part of an out-of-court statement is used to impeach, other parts of the statement that are consistent might be admissible under this exception to show how serious the inconsistencies are (or, in this case, to show that the inconsistencies are not serious).[50] This means that impeaching a witness with parts of a statement may open the door for the admissibility of other parts of the same statement as nonhearsay substantive evidence of the facts declared.[51]

---

46. This scenario is based on *United States v. Smith*, *supra*.

47. A somewhat frequent 801(d)(1)(B) argument is that post-arrest statements increasing the culpability of others and decreasing one's own are always tainted by a motive to lie. The lie is motivated by a desire to curry favor with the government and obtain a more favorable outcome for one's self. The cases do not impose such a hard and fast rule. Instead, they hold "that statements made after arrest are not automatically and necessarily contaminated by a motive to fabricate in order to curry favor with the government." United States v. Prieto, 232 F.3d 816, 821 (11th Cir. 2000) (discussing cases). There are a number of other reasons that one who has been arrested might "disgorge the details of a crime," such as conscience, confession, remorse and sorrow, and others. *Id.* (the decision is one for the trial court based on the particular circumstances of the individual case).

48. United States v. Vest, 842 F.2d 1319, 1329 (1st Cir. 1988).

49. United States v. Conroy, 424 F.3d 833, 840 (8th Cir. 2005). *See also Ettinger*, 344 F.3d at 1160–61 (the witness did not include the fact in the initial report; the witness did mention it at a subsequent FBI interview; the subsequent mention was admissible under this rule).

50. " '[I]f some portions of a statement made by a witness are used on cross-examination to impeach him, other portions of the statement which are relevant to the subject matter about which he was cross-examined may be introduced in evidence [under this exception] to meet the force of the impeachment.' " Coltrane v. United States, 418 F.2d 1131, 1140 (D.C. Cir. 1969) (quoting Affronti v. United States, 145 F.2d 3, 7 (8th Cir. 1944)).

51. *See also* part III of Chapter 9 discussing the rule of completeness (FED.R.EVID. 106) as a hearsay exception.

■ *Confrontation Clause*: Since this exclusion only applies when the out-of-court declarant testifies and is subject to cross-examination, the Confrontation Clause does not limit the admissibility of the statement.[52]

■ *Exclusions versus Exceptions*: This is an exclusion from the definition of hearsay. It is not an exception to the hearsay rule. As discussed elsewhere, there may be a difference.[53]

C. Statement of Identification of a Person: Rule 801(d)(1)(C)

1. Text of the Rule

> (d) Statements which are not hearsay. A statement is not hearsay if—
> (1) Prior statement by witness. The declarant testifies at the trial or hearing and is subject to cross-examination concerning the statement, and the statement is … (C) one of identification of a person made after perceiving the person …

2. Foundational Elements

1. The out-of-court declarant is testifying at the trial or hearing and is subject to cross-examination regarding the out-of-court statement.[54]

2. The statement is one identifying a person and was made after perceiving the person in question.

3. Need + Reliability = 1[55]

a. Need

At trial, when the witness sits in the box and is asked if the perpetrator is in the courtroom, there may as well be a blinking neon arrow directing attention to the defendant. The in-court identification of the defendant as the perpetrator is suspiciously easy. Partly for that reason, it makes sense to allow into evidence an earlier, generally less guided, less leading (and therefore more

---

52. *See* Chapter 14, below.
53. *See* Chapter 2(I), above.
54. United States v. Sadler, 234 F.3d 368, 372 (8th Cir. 2000) (defendant may not rely on Rule 801(d)(1) "because he did not testify at the trial and was not subject to cross-examination, as required by [the Rule]").
55. *See* Chapter 3(I)(B), below.

credible) identification.[56] This exclusion is not limited to criminal cases, and even in a criminal case the declarant need not be the victim. When the declarant is the victim in a criminal case it seems somewhat artificial to keep from the jury that the victim made an earlier identification of the perpetrator and the absence of such testimony may suggest that there was no prior victim-identification of the accused as the perpetrator.

b. Reliability

The out-of-court declarant must be testifying at the trial or hearing and subject to cross-examination. There will be a chance to test perception, memory, sincerity, and honesty. The out-of-court declarant will be under oath. The trier of fact will get to see the declarant's demeanor. The pressures exerted by the trappings of the courtroom and by the formality and openness of the proceedings therein will be exerted on this declarant. Additionally, the earlier the identification, the less likely it is to be adversely affected by the testimonial infirmities associated with the passage of time: memory loss, the power of self-suggestion as the victim relives the crime, the power of external suggestion during the investigation and the trial preparation, the power of suggestion inherent in the defendant's presence in the courtroom as the one on trial (including the blinking neon arrow from above), and the like.[57]

4. Use Note

■ *Pretrial Identification of a Criminal Suspect:* This definitional exclusion is commonly used to allow into evidence things said at a pretrial (often pre-arrest) identification of a suspect by a victim or a witness.[58] At trial, the victim

---

56. FED.R.EVID. 801(d)(1)(C) advisory committee's note. "The theory is that courtroom identification is so unconvincing as practically to impeach itself." Michael H. Graham, *Handbook of Federal Evidence* § 801.13, at 767–68 (3d ed. 1991). "Statements of prior identifications are admitted as substantive evidence because of 'the generally unsatisfactory and inconclusive nature of courtroom identifications as compared with those made at an earlier time under less suggestive conditions.'" United States v. Lopez, 271 F.3d 472, 485 (3d Cir. 2001) (quoting FED.R.EVID. 801 advisory committee's note).

57. United States v. Lopez, 271 F.3d 472, 485 (3d Cir. 2001), quoted in the immediately preceding footnote.

58. "[E]vidence is generally admitted under 801(d)(1)(C) 'when a witness has identified the defendant in a lineup or photospread, but forgets, or changes, his testimony at trial.' [T]his Rule then permits a third person to testify regarding the previous statements of the eyewitness." *Lopez*, 271 F.3d at 485. The part of that quotation reading "but forgets, or changes, his testimony at trial" could be omitted. The sentence could simply read "[E]vidence is gen-

can testify "At a lineup three days after the crime I pointed to the defendant and said 'That's him. Number three. He did this to me.'" And a police officer who was present at the lineup can testify "At the lineup, three days after the crime, the victim pointed to the defendant and said 'That's him.'" And a second police officer who was present can testify "At the lineup three days after the crime, the victim identified the defendant as the perpetrator." Three different witnesses have testified to this out-of-court statement offered to prove the truth of the assertion and the testimony is not hearsay. The out-of-court declarant in each case is the victim. The declarant is testifying and is subject to cross-examination concerning the out-of-court statement, and the statement is one identifying a person and made after perceiving that person (at the lineup).

■ By the plain language of the rule[59] it applies when a witness simply comes forward and states that he saw a particular individual commit the crime, or saw a particular individual at the time and place of the crime. That is, if a person who is testifying and subject to cross examination witnessed a pedestrian stuck by a car and later that day told a police officer, "The mayor was driving the car," that would be a nonhearsay statement of identification of a person made after perceiving that person.[60] The statement identifies the driver and was made after seeing the driver.

■ *Subject to Cross-Examination*: The out-of-court declarant must be *subject to* cross-examination concerning the out-of-court statement. Sometimes this is a troublesome element of this foundation.

The out-of-court declarant does not have to remember the out-of-court statement or the event. The only requirement is that the out-of-court declarant can be cross-examined, even if only to point out that she does not have a very good memory. The out-of-court declarant can tell a completely different

---

erally admitted under 801(d)(1)(C) 'when a witness has identified the defendant in a lineup or photospread.'" There is no forgetful or turncoat witness requirement.

59. "We interpret the legislatively enacted Federal Rules of Evidence as we would any statute." Daubert v. Merrell Dow Pharms., 509 U.S. 579, 587 (1993) (citing Beech Aircraft Corp. v. Rainey, 488 U.S. 153, 163 (1988)). *Accord, e.g.*, United States v. Weinstock, 863 F.Supp. 1529, 1534 (D. Utah 1994) (rules "interpreted as a statute[,] ... in accordance with [their] plain meaning.")

60. "[V]iewing both the Advisory Committee notes to Rule 801 and our own case law, we see no basis to conclude that [this rule] does not extend to" an identification "that consists of a person coming forward after a crime is committed and saying he saw a particular person at a certain place and time ..." "Any concerns regarding conditions or circumstances that might bear on reliability are matters going to the weight of the evidence, which can be addressed on cross-examination, and should not affect the admissibility of the statement." United States v. Lopez, 271 F.3d at 485 (order of quotation rearranged). *Accord* United States v. Shryock, 342 F.3d 948, 982 (9th Cir. 2003).

story on the stand, denouncing the identification or identifying someone else,[61] for example, so long as she can be cross-examined about why she said one thing before and another now. The cross-examination allows opposing counsel to explore the loss of memory and to explore the inconsistencies between the out-of-court statement and the in-court statement.

If, on the other hand, the out-of-court declarant refuses to testify, then the out-of-court declarant is not subject to cross-examination. "Ordinarily a witness is regarded as 'subject to cross-examination' when he is placed on the stand, under oath, and responds willingly to questions."[62]

This can lead to these two different results. Assume a witness picked the defendant out of a lineup and then was threatened with death if he testified. If the witness refuses to take the stand, the out-of-court statement of identification does not fit under this hearsay exclusion because the witness is not subject to cross-examination. If the witness takes the stand and rejects the lineup identification, then the out-of-court statement of identification does fit under this hearsay exclusion because, among other things, the witness is subject to cross-examination.

■ *Confrontation Clause*: Since this exclusion only applies when the out-of-court declarant testifies and is subject to cross-examination, the Confrontation Clause does not limit the admissibility of the statement.[63]

■ *Exclusions versus Exceptions*: This is an exclusion from the definition of hearsay. It is not an exception to the hearsay rule. As discussed elsewhere, there may be a difference.[64]

III. Nonhearsay "Admissions": Rule 801(d)(2)

A. General Use Note

Keep these four things in mind throughout the following discussion of Rule 801(d)(2):

---

61. At the trial in United States v. Salameh, 152 F.3d 88 (2d Cir. 1998), when the declarant was asked to identify two people allegedly involved in the World Trade Center bombing, he pointed to two of the jurors. The trial court allowed the witness's out-of-court identifications of the defendants to be admitted into evidence. These prior identifications are Rule 801(d)(1)(C) nonhearsay.

62. United States v. Owens, 484 U.S. 554, 561 (1988).

63. *See* Chapter 14, below.

64. *See* Chapter 2(I), above.

1. Exclusions, Not Exceptions

Once again, as with Rule 801(d)(1), note that Rule 801(d)(2) does not create exceptions to the hearsay rule, but definitional exclusions from the rule itself. The kinds of statements defined here are not admissible hearsay. They are nonhearsay (and, if no other rule is violated, they are admissible nonhearsay).

These statements are excluded from the definition of hearsay. They are not listed in the statute as exceptions to the hearsay rule, but are not hearsay in the first place. There were members of the committee who argued that, because of the oath, cross-examination, the opportunity to observe the witness's demeanor, and pressure to tell the truth that is applied by the courtroom setting, every prior statement by a testifying witness should be nonhearsay. There were those who thought that went too far. Rule 801(d)(2) was a compromise.[65]

2. The Two Sets of Definitional Exclusions

There are two sets of definitional exclusions. The definitional exclusions in Rule 801(d)(1) do not apply unless the out-of-court declarant is testifying at the trial or hearing and is subject to cross-examination concerning the out-of-court statement. Those in Rule 801(d)(2) apply without regard to the availability of the out-of-court declarant or the out-of-court declarant's testimony.[66]

3. Need + Reliability = 1?[67]

The definitional exclusions of 801(d)(2) are based more on history and tradition than they are on need or reliability. Some of the statements fitting under these definitional exclusions will, when made, have been statements against the interest of the out-of-court declarant. To the extent that we tend not to make statements against our interests, these statements will tend to be reliable.[68]

---

65. Rules of Evidence: Hearings on H.R. 5463 Before the Committee on the Judiciary, 93 Cong. 7086–87 (1974); JACK B. WEINSTEIN & MARGARET A. BERGER, WEINSTEIN'S EVIDENCE MANUAL ¶15.01[01], at 15–3 (student ed. 1987).

66. This means that the Confrontation Clause is not a problem when admitting evidence under Rule 801(d)(1) and it may or may not be a problem when admitting evidence under Rule 801(d)(2).

67. See Chapter 3(I)(B), below.

68. Pappas v. Middle Earth Condo. Ass'n, 963 F.2d 534, 537 (2d Cir. 1992) (regarding admissions by an agent or employee, "an employee is usually the person best informed about certain acts committed in the course of his employment, and ... while still employed an employee is unlikely to make damaging statements about his employer, unless those statements are true"); United States v. Goldberg, 105 F.3d 770, 775 (1st Cir. 1997) ("[T]he ...

Some of the statements fitting under these definitional exclusions will have been made by a party. The party against whom these statements are offered is almost always in court and, if he or she chooses, can testify and explain the statement. This party will not get far with the complaint that there was no opportunity for self-cross-examination.

Some of the statements fitting under these definitional exclusions will have been made by an agent or a coconspirator of a party. If the statement was made by the party's agent or coconspirator, then the party is likely to have some particular knowledge that he or she can offer by way of explanation. In other words, there will be someone in court who can testify and who can shed some light on the truth and the context of the out-of-court statement. Plus, in the case of an agent or employee that relationship might inhibit the declarant "from making erroneous or underhanded comments."[69]

None of these things, however, is a foundational element of these exclusions. Sometimes some or all of these factors will be present, and pressing towards reliability, but not always. If these were the guarantees of reliability, then they would be foundational elements of the exclusions.

It seems more likely that these statements are excluded from the definition of hearsay out of rough justice, out of a rough sense of fairness: These statements are to various degrees the responsibility of the party against whom they are offered. We are accountable for our own statements, and for certain statements of our employees and coconspirators.

4. Using the Out-of-Court Statement Itself to Establish Foundational Elements of These Exclusions

Under the Rule 801(d)(2) exclusions, when the question for the judge is the authority of one person to speak for another,[70] the existence of an agency or

---

co-conspirator [exclusion from] the hearsay rule makes little sense as a matter of evidence policy. No special guarantee of reliability attends such statements, save to the extent that they resemble declarations against interest."); Guzman v. Abbott Labs, 59 F.Supp.2d 747, 756 (N.D. Ill. 1999) (agent or employee admissions "are presumably reliable in the absence of cross-examination because an agent 'who speaks on any matter within the scope of his agency or employment during the existence of that relationship, is unlikely to make statements damaging to his principal or employer unless those statements are true.'"). *See also* the discussion of need plus reliability accompanying the discussion of the statement against interest exception, Rule 804(b)(3) in part IV of Chapter 4, below.

69. Young v. James Green Mgmt., Inc., 327 F.3d 616, 623 (7th Cir. 2003).

70. This is an amendment to Rule 801(d)(2)(C). It applies to trials commencing after December 1, 1997.

employment relationship or the scope of such a relationship,[71] the existence of a conspiracy or the identity of the coconspirators,[72] the court shall consider the contents of the out-of-court statement, but the contents of the statement alone are not enough.[73] There must be something more.

B. A Party's own Statement: 801(d)(2)(A)

1. Text of the Rule

(d) Statements which are not hearsay. A statement is not hearsay if—

****

(2) Admission by party-opponent. The statement is offered against a party and is (A) the party's own statement, in either an individual or representative capacity ...

2. Foundational Elements

1. The out-of-court statement is a party's own statement—an out-of-court statement by a party to the litigation at hand.

2. The statement is offered against the party who made it.

---

71. This is an amendment to Rule 801(d)(2)(D). It applies to trials commencing after December 1, 1997.

72. This is an amendment to Rule 801(d)(2)(E). It applies to trials commencing after December 1, 1997.

The rule states that "[t]he contents of the statement ... are not alone sufficient to establish ... the [declarant's] participation" in the conspiracy. Fed.R.Evid. 801(d)(2)(E). *But see* United States v. Engler, 521 F.3d 965, 973 (8th Cir. 2008) ("Engler and Gatena ... argue that the district court erred in admitting ... photographic images of text messages sent via cellular telephone to Engler from an unknown person while law enforcement officers were about to execute a search warrant on Engler's residence. They assert that the government failed to show that the unknown declarant ... was a co-conspirator. However, the very content of the text messages establishes by a preponderance of the evidence that the sender was a coconspirator.") (citing a case stating that a coconspirator's statement may be "consider[ed]" to determine that a conspiracy existed, but does not say that a statement by an unknown declarant can, by itself, establish that a conspiracy existed, let alone that the unknown declarant was a coconspirator).

73. Fed.R.Evid. 801(d)(2).

3. Use Note

a. This Exclusion Is Particularly Important

This definitional exclusion comes up all the time, so pay attention. Learn it particularly well. Train yourself to notice it. It appears on most law school exams and in most trials of any significant length.

About an out-of-court statement, ask these two questions: (1) Who made it? (2) Against whom is it offered? If the answer to the first is "The statement was made by a party to this litigation," and the answer to the second is "The statement is being offered into evidence by counsel for an opposing party," then the out-of-court statement is not hearsay. It is this simple:

> OCS
> + Made by a party to this litigation
> + <u>Offered against that party</u>
> Not hearsay.

If plaintiff's counsel offers into evidence an out-of-court statement made by the defendant, it is not hearsay. If defendant's counsel offers into evidence an out-of-court statement made by the plaintiff, it is not hearsay.[74]

b. There Is No "Against Interest" Requirement with This Exclusion

This definitional exclusion and the two that follow do not have an "against interest" requirement. The out-of-court statement does not have to have been against the party's interest when it was made.[75] It does not have to be against

---

74. *E.g.*, United States v. Heppner, 519 F.3d 744, 751 (8th Cir. 2008) (defendant's testimony before the Commodity Futures Trade Commission testimony was "not hearsay when admitted against him"); United States v. Vasilakos, 508 F.3d 401, 406–07 (6th Cir. 2007) ("801(d)(2)(A) establishes that a statement is not hearsay if it 'is offered against a party and is … the party's own statement.'"); United States v. Dennis, 497 F.3d 765, 769 n.1 (7th Cir. 2007) (defendant's post-arrest statements offered against defendant are not hearsay); Thanongsinh v. Board of Educ., 462 F.3d 762, 779 (7th Cir. 2006) (written statements offered against the party who wrote them are not hearsay); United States v. Brown, 459 F.3d 509, 528 n.17 (5th Cir. 2006) (Brown's email offered against Brown is not hearsay); United States v. Tolliver, 454 F.3d 660, 665 (7th Cir. 2006) ("His statements on the tapes [offered against him] constitute admissions by a party-opponent, and, as such, those statements are, by definition, not hearsay...."); United States v. Garza, 435 F.3d 73, 77 (1st Cir. 2006) ("So long as there is a preponderance of evidence indicating that it was Garza's voice on the tapes," the tapes are not hearsay when offered against Garza.); United States v. Siddiqui, 235 F.3d 1318, 1323 (11th Cir. 2000) (a properly authenticated e-mail from the defendant, offered against the defendant, is a nonhearsay statement of a party).

75. *E.g.*, Territory of Guam v. Ojeda, 758 F.2d 403, 408 (9th Cir. 1985) ("[S]tatements

the party's interest when it is offered into evidence (though it usually is, which is why the opposing party is offering it).[76]

c. There Is No "Trustworthiness" Requirement with This Exclusion

Similarly, this definitional exclusion and the two that follow it do not have a trustworthiness requirement.[77]

d. The Rationale for This Exclusion

The rationale for this definitional exclusion from hearsay is threefold: First, parties cannot very well object that they did not have a chance to cross-examine themselves.[78] Second, these declarants are parties and, therefore, will almost always be available to testify. If they can explain away the out-of-court statements, they have the opportunity to take the stand and do so.[79] Third, this exclusion has a long common-law history as an exception; in these rules, a compromise in the committee that drafted the rules resulted in it being changed from an exception to an exclusion.[80]

e. Exclusions versus Exceptions

This is an exclusion from the definition of hearsay. It is not an exception to the hearsay rule. As discussed elsewhere, there may be a difference.[81]

---

need not be incriminating to be admissions."); L.W. ex rel. Whitson v. Knox County Bd. of Educ., 76 Fed. R. Evid. Serv. 796, 798 (E.D. Tenn. 2008) (whether the statement is against the interest of the party it is offered against is irrelevant; all that matters is that it is the party's statement offered against the party).

76. *E.g.*, United States v. Towsend, 206 Fed.Appx. 444, 450 (6th Cir. 2006) (unpublished opinion) ("Notwithstanding the appearance of the word 'admission' in the heading of Rule 801(d)(2), there is no requirement that a party's out-of-court statement be a confession or statement against interest to be admissible against the party in trial.") (citing United States v. McDaniel, 398 F.3d 540, 545 n.2 (6th Cir. 2005)).

77. FED.R.EVID. 801(d)(2) advisory committee's note.

78. *See, e.g.*, Bingham v. State, 987 S.W.2d 54, 57 (Tex. Crim. App. 1999); Commonwealth v. Chmiel, 738 A.2d 406, 420 (Pa. 1998) ("[A] party can hardly complain of his inability to cross-examine himself."); State v. Kennedy, 343 A.2d 783, 788 (N.J. Super. Ct. App. Div. 1975).

79. In addition, since this exclusion is confined to a party's statement, problems of surprise are virtually eliminated. CHRISTOPHER B. MUELLER & LAIRD C. KIRKPATRICK, EVIDENCE §8.27, at 864 n.1 (2d ed. 1999).

80. *See* part III(A)(1) of this chapter, above. This exclusion and the ones following it are "the result of the adversary system rather than satisfaction of the conditions of the hearsay rule." FED.R.EVID. 801(d)(2) advisory committee's note.

81. *See* part I of this chapter, above.

f. The General Use Note

In addition to this Use Note, see the General Use Note, above,[82] which is applicable to all of the admissions.

C. A Statement by an Agent: 801(d)(2)(D)

1. Text of the Rule

> (d) Statements which are not hearsay. A statement is not hearsay if—
>
> ****
>
> (2) Admission by party-opponent. The statement is offered against a party and is ... (D) a statement by the party's agent or servant concerning a matter within the scope of the agency or employment, made during the existence of the relationship ... The contents of the statement shall be considered but are not alone sufficient to establish ... the agency or employment relationship and scope thereof under subdivision (D) ...

2. Foundational Elements

1. At the time the out-of-court statement was made, the declarant must have been an agent or employee of the party against whom the statement is now offered.

2. The out-of-court statement must concern something that was within the scope of the declarant's agency or employment. (The focus here is on the subject of the statement and its relationship to the out-of-court declarant's job, not on the out-of-court declarant's authority to speak for company.)[83]

3. Use Note

a. The Timing of the Statement

The statement must have been made while the declarant was an agent or employee of the party against whom the statement is offered. The declarant need not have been on the job when he or she made the statement. The state-

---

82. *See* part III(A) of this chapter, above.

83. *E.g.*, Young v. James Green Mgmt., Inc., 327 F.3d 616, 622 (7th Cir. 2003) ("The rule simply requires that the statement be made by an individual who is an agent, that the statement be made during the period of the agency, and that the matter be within the subject matter of the agency"). This exclusion is broader than many of the pre-Rule, common-law exceptions. *See, e.g., id.*

ment can have been made at work, over the lunch hour, after work, or on a day off. The time frame for this exclusion is "hired to fired." The statement must have been made between the time when the employment or agency relationship began and ended. This requirement is designed to weed out retributive statements by disgruntled former employees.[84]

b. Things That Are within the Scope of the Agency or Employment

The out-of-court statement must concern a matter within the scope of the declarant's agency or employment. What are the boundaries of what "concern[s] a matter within the scope of [one's] agency or employment?" In that regard, first this: The advisory committee's note states that the history of admissions "calls for generous treatment of this avenue to admissibility."[85] Second, this exclusion can be used for statements by an agent or an employee in an illegal or fraudulent operation. So long as the foundational elements are present, it does not matter that the activity involved is illegal or fraudulent.[86]

Third, the rule requires that the statement "concern[] a matter within the scope of one's employment" This is not synonymous with, and much narrower than, a statement that "relates to one's job." The rule calls for generous treatment of this avenue to admissibility, but not so generous as to include all statements relating to one's job.[87] This is not to say that the em-

---

84. "'[W]hile still employed an employee is unlikely to make damaging statements about his employer, unless those statements are true.'" Smith v. Pathmark Stores, Inc., 485 F.Supp.2d 235, 238 (E.D.N.Y. 2007) (quoting Pappas v. Middle Earth Condo. Assoc., 963 F.2d 534, 537 (2d Cir. 1992). *James Green Mgmt., Inc.*, 327 F.3d at 622 (statements in resignation letter do not fit under this exclusion; declarant "was not speaking as an employee ... when he resigned."); Barsamian v. City of Kingsburg, 76 Fed. R. Evid. Serv. 766, 777 (E.D. Cal. 2008) ("[E]x employees ... are no longer inhibited from making false statements that could harm their former employer.").

85. FED.R.EVID. 801(d)(2) advisory committee's note. *See, e.g.,* Williams v. Pharmacia, Inc., 137 F.3d 944, 950 (7th Cir. 1998) (court expresses reluctance to adopt appellant's more restrictive view of the scope of this exclusion, "especially in light of the Advisory Committee's ... call[] for generous treatment of this avenue of admissibility"). The advisory committee also points out that the common law rule applied to statements "made by the agent acting in the scope of his employment," while Rule 801(d)(2)(D) applies to statements "related to a matter within the scope of the agency or employment." FED.R.EVID. 801(d)(2)(D) advisory committee's note.

86. *E.g.,* Harris v. Itzhaki, 183 F.3d 1043, 1054 n.5 (9th Cir. 1999) (employer instructed employee to act in furtherance of a fraudulent scheme; employee's statements concerning that scheme are admissible against the employer under FRE 801(d)(2)(D)).

87. Simple v. Walgreen Co., 511 F.3d 668, 672 (7th Cir. 2007) (employment discrimination case: declarant was not involved in the employment action, but was consulted about the ap-

ployee must have had direct involvement with the particular subject of the out-of-court statement, but just to say that the employee's job must include some involvement with the general subject matter. "[T]he focus of [this part of] Rule 801(d)(2)(D) is the content of the statement and whether it relates to some aspect of the employer's business within the scope of the employee's activities."[88]

---

pointment, and therefore involved in the process leading up to the action; her statement about the employment decision was within the scope of her employment); Davila v. Corporacion de P. R. Para a la Difusion Publica, 498 F.3d 9, 16–17 (1st Cir. 2007) (unattributed "office gossip" is not admissible under this exclusion); Marra v. Philadelphia Housing Auth., 497 F.3d 286, 298 (3d Cir. 2007) (scope of employment "'extends beyond direct decision-makers'"); Ahlberg v. Chrysler Corp., 481 F.3d 630, (8th Cir. 2007) (statements regarding pickup–truck safety were not within the scope of employment of employees charged with evaluating mini-van safety); Eliserio v. United Steelworkers of Am. Local 310, 398 F.3d 1071, 1078 (8th Cir. 2005) (declarant was a member of the union's executive board; his "statements ... made in regard to a matter of union concern and in the presence of a union steward" qualify as admissions by an agent of the union); Jacklyn v. Schering-Plough Healthcare Prods. Sales Corp., 176 F.3d 921, 928 (6th Cir. 1999) (making a statement while one is an employee versus making a statement that is within the scope of one's employment); Williams, 137 F.3d at 950 (things that "relate to" one's job do not necessarily fall within the scope of one's employment; non-managerial employees making statements about managerial practices were the subjects of the decisions being made, not the ones making them, and the statements were not within the scope of their employment); United States v. Rioux, 97 F.3d 648, 661 (2d Cir. 1996) (statements by "an advisor or other significant participant" in the process qualify); Woodman v. Haemonetics Corp, 51 F.3d 1087, 1094 (1st Cir. 1995) (declarant had no decision making authority, but did participate in the process; her statements about the decision fit under this exclusion); Union Mut. Life Ins. Co. v. Chrysler Corp., 793 F.2d 1, 8–9 (1st Cir. 1986) (declarant wrote a letter that included statements of fact taken from files in his possession and available for his use within the scope of his employment; statements in the letter fit under this exclusion); Wilkinson v. Carnival Cruise Lines, Inc., 920 F.2d 1560, 1566 (11th Cir. 1991) ("[T]he inquiry is whether [declarant] was authorized to act for his principal ... concerning the matter about which he allegedly spoke."); Staheli v. The University of Mississippi, 854 F.2d 121, 127 (5th Cir. 1988) (A statement of a faculty member who "had nothing to do with Dr. Staheli's tenure decision—or with any personnel matter concerning Dr. Staheli ... did not concern a matter within the scope of his agency and was made in his capacity as wiseacre only."); United States v. Portsmouth Paving Corp., 694 F.2d 312, 322 (4th Cir. 1982) ("because part of her job entailed relaying messages from [her boss] to business callers," declarant's statement about what her boss said was within the scope of her employment); Wright v. Farmers Co-Op of Arkansas & Oklahoma, 681 F.2d 549, 552–53 (8th Cir. 1982) (declarant's statement concerning action he was being trained to take fit under this exclusion); Bickerstaff v. Nordstrom, Inc. 48 F.Supp.2d 790, 803 (N.D. Ill. 1999) ("Statements are outside of the scope of the declarant's employment when they concern decisionmaking [sic] processes into which the declarant has no input.").

88. Shuck v. Texaco Refining & Mktg., Inc., 872 P.2d 1247, 1250 (Ariz. Ct. App. 1994).

Fourth, the agent or employee need not be "specifically authorized to speak on [the] subject."[89] The agent specifically authorized to speak on a subject is the subject of the definitional exclusion discussed next, and is an entirely different exclusion than the one discussed here.

c. Agent Defined

"Agent" is defined broadly. While it is partly defined by reference "to general common law principles of agency,"[90] it is not rigidly bound by that definition.[91] That is to say, there need not be an actual, technical "agency" relationship.[92] This approach better achieves the general goals of the rules as a whole. Under this approach, partners are "agents" of other partners even though under the substantive law of agency and employment partners may not be agents or employees of each other.[93] Likewise, because of the government's supervisory role, government informants can be agents or employees of the government.[94] Volunteers also can be agents, for example, a volunteer serving in a governance role in a condominium association can be an agent of the association.[95] And so forth.[96]

---

89. Canatxx Gas Storage Ltd. V. Silverhawk Capital Partners, LLC, 76 Fed. R. Evid. Serv. 500, 514 (S.D. Tex. 2008). *See also* cases cited above in footnote 87.

90. *E.g.*, American Eagle Ins. Co. v. Thompson, 85 F.3d 327, 333 (8th Cir. 1996); Lippay v. Christos, 996 F.2d 1490, 1497 (3d Cir. 1993) ("we apply federal common law rules of agency, rather than ... the agency law of the forum"); United States v. Saks, 964 F.2d 1514, 1523 (5th Cir. 1992).

91. *E.g.*, Lippay, 996 F.2d at 1505 (Becker, J. concurring).

92. "[I]t would be a 'hyper-technical construction of [Rule 801(d)(2)(D)]' to conclude that it does not apply when there is a sufficient supervisory relationship between two individuals, although there is no actual agency relationship between the two." Lippay, 996 F.2d at 1505 (Becker, J. concurring) (quoting United States v. Paxson, 861 F.2d 730 (D.C. Cir. 1988)).

93. United States v. Saks, 964 F.2d 1514, 1523 (5th Cir. 1992).

94. United States v. Reed, 167 F.3d 987, 989 (6th Cir. 1999).

95. EEOC v. Watergate at Landmark Condo., 24 F.3d 635, 640 (4th Cir. 1994).

96. Moore v. Kuka Welding Sys., 171 F.3d 1073, 1081 (6th Cir. 1999) (concerning a matter within the scope of his employment, one of defendant's employees made a statement to a second employee and asked him to relay it to a third; the statement did not concern a matter that would ordinarily be within the scope of the second's employment but, when the first asked the second to relay the statement, he "used him as an agent of the company" and number two's statement to number three fit under this exclusion; employee number three can testify as to what number two said to him); Ryder v. Westinghouse Elec. Corp., 128 F.3d 128, 134 (3d Cir. 1997) (company CEO is an agent or an employee of the company). *See also* Gomes v. Rivera Rodriguez, 344 F.3d 103, 117–18 (1st Cir. 2003) (insufficient evidence the mayor's wife was an agent of the mayor); Carden v. Westinghouse Elec.

Before the statement can be considered in any sense to be the party's—including vicariously, as with a statement by an agent—it does seem that there must be either some element of control or some element of equality. That is, either the party the statement is offered against must have had some control over the declarant (as with a true agency relationship) or the party must be on a more-or-less equal footing with the declarant (as with the partnership relationship). The expert witness's testimony from a previous trial, when offered against the party who called the expert at the previous trial, does not fit under either this definitional exclusion (statement by an agent) or the one discussed next (statement by one authorized to speak for another). An expert witness is not subject to the control of the party with respect to the consultation and testimony the expert is hired to give.[97] An expert witness and the party who hired the expert are not on an equal footing in the enterprise out of which the expert's statement arose.

Contrary to the general rules just discussed, there are cases stating that this exclusion generally does not apply to statements by police officers, law enforcement personnel, and government employees when offered against the government in a criminal trial.[98]

d. The Role of the Statement in Establishing Its Own Foundation

The rule is quite clear on this point: "The contents of the statement shall be considered but are not alone sufficient to establish … the agency or employment relationship and scope thereof."[99]

Corp., 850 F.2d 996, 1002–03 (3d Cir. 1988) (a statement attributed to an unidentified source cannot be an admission by an agent).

97. Kirk v. Raymark Indus., Inc., 61 F.3d 147, 167 (3d Cir. 1995).

98. *E.g.*, United States v. Prevatte, 16 F.3d 767, 779 (7th Cir. 1994); Lippay v. Christos, 996 F.2d 1490, 1497–98 (3d Cir. 1993) (citing cases). The theory here seems to be that the government cannot be bound by its employees. This, however, does not seem to be a hearsay problem. Rather, it is a relevance problem, or a Rule 403 problem, or perhaps a competence problem—anything but a hearsay problem to be solved by a judicial gloss on Rule 801(d)(2)(D).

This rule does not apply in civil cases—belying the justification that the government cannot be bound by its employees. *See* United States v. AT&T, 498 F. Supp. 353, 356–58 (D.D.C. 1980) (officials from various executive agencies deemed agents of party-opponent, the United States, for purposes of Rule 801(d)(2)(D)).

99. FED.R.EVID. 801(d)(2). This is an amendment to Rule 801(d)(2) that will not be found in the oldest publications of the rules. It applies to trials commencing after December 1, 1997. *E.g.*, Sea Land Serv., Inc. v. Lozen Int'l, LLC, 285 F.3d 808, 821 (9th Cir. 2002) (electronic signature on email indicates it was written by a specific person; other admissible evidence indicates he is an employee).

e. Exclusions versus Exceptions

This is an exclusion from the definition of hearsay. It is not an exception to the hearsay rule. As discussed elsewhere, there may be a difference.[100]

f. The General Use Note

In addition to this Use Note, also see the General Use Note, above,[101] which is applicable to all of the admissions.

D. Statement by Person Authorized to Speak: 801(d)(2)(C)

1. Text of the Rule

> (d) Statements which are not hearsay. A statement is not hearsay if—
>
> ****
>
> (2) Admission by party-opponent. The statement is offered against a party and is ... (C) a statement authorized by the party to make a statement concerning the subject ... The contents of the statement shall be considered but are not alone sufficient to establish the declarant's authority under subdivision (C) ...

2. Foundational Elements

1. The out-of-court statement must be offered against a party.
2. The out-of-court statement must have been made "by a person authorized by the party to make a statement concerning the subject."

3. Use Note

a. This Exclusion Is Mostly Subsumed by Another

This definitional exclusion is mostly subsumed by 801(d)(2)(D), the exclusion for statements by an agent, discussed above. Rule 801(d)(2)(D) does not apply unless there is an agency or an employment relationship, while this exclusion does not depend on such a relationship. Even so, almost all cases that fit here, also fit there.[102]

---

100. *See* Chapter 2(I), above.

101. *See* Chapter 2(III)(A), above.

102. For just one example, see Fischer v. Forestwood Co., Inc., 525 F.3d 972, 984 (10th Cir. 2008) (as president of the defendant company, declarant was "'authorized ... to make a statement concerning' hiring and firing," Fed.R.Evid. 801(d)(2)(C), and, when he made

There are exceptional cases that do fit here and not under 801(d)(2)(D). Take, for example, a murder case where the police engaged in a pre-arrest, low-speed "chase" of a car in which the defendant was a passenger. During the chase the police were talking on the phone with the driver of the car they were following. The defendant authorized the driver to make certain statements to the police, and the driver made them. Now, at trial, the driver cannot be found, but the police can produce evidence that the defendant did authorize the driver to make these statements, and a police officer testifies to what she heard the driver say. There may be cases where someone authorizes someone else to make a statement when there is no agency or employment relationship between them and, therefore, 801(d)(2)(D) does not apply, but 801(d)(2)(C) does.[103]

---

the statements, he was acting within the scope of his authority as defendant's agent, FED.R.EVID. 801(d)(2)(D); the fact that declarant was also plaintiff's father has no bearing).

There are contrary cases stating that this exclusion for statements by a person authorized to speak only applies where there was an agency relationship. *E.g.*, Sabel v. Mead Johnson & Co., 737 F.Supp. 135, 138 (D. Mass. 1990); State v. Frustino, 689 P.2d 547, 553 (Ariz. Ct. App. 1984). This is not correct—not unless every authorization to speak creates a Rule 801(d)(2)(D) "agency" relationship. First, there is nothing in the text of the rule supporting such a position. Second, were this true, then this exclusion would be totally subsumed by 801(d)(2)(D), the exclusion for statements by an agent. The authorized-to-speak exclusion would be unnecessary. *E.g.*, Glendale Fed. Bank v. United States, 39 Fed. Cl. 422, 424 (Ct. Fed. Cl. 1997) ("[T]he difference between the 'person authorized' of 801(d)(2)(C) and the 'agent' of 801(d)(2)(D) is not as apparent. We may not treat either FRE 801(d)(2)(C) or (D) as superfluous nor interpret either rule so as to render its companion rule without effect.") The *Sabel* and *Frustino* cases cite WEINSTEIN's EVIDENCE. The cited paragraph from *Weinstein* states that these cases are "[o]rdinarily ... resolved by applying agency doctrine," *see* 4 JACK B. WEINSTEIN & MARGARET A. BERGER, WEINSTEIN'S EVIDENCE ¶801(d)(2)(C)[01], at 801–269 (1996), which is not the same as stating that these cases are dependent upon an agency relationship.

103. The kinds of situations covered by this exclusion include: Reid Bros. Logging Co. v. Ketchikan Pulp Co., 699 F.2d 1292, 1306 (9th Cir.1983) (a report prepared by someone outside the defendant company, at the defendant company's request, is admissible against the defendant as an authorized admission); Lightning Lube, Inc. v. Witco Corp., 4 F.3d 1153, 1198 (3d Cir. 1993) (a party's attorney's statements directly related to the management of the litigation are admissible against the party as authorized admissions); United States v. Duncan, 919 F.2d 981, 987 (5th Cir. 1990) (a declarant-medical provider's records released to an insurance company, with the patient's authorization, are admissible against the patient as an authorized admission); United States v. Sanders, 749 F.2d 195, 199 (5th Cir. 1984) (when offered against the party, a transcription of a party's notes by a person authorized to make the transcription gets around hearsay problems inherent in the transcription as an authorized admission); B-W Acceptance Corp. v. Porter, 568 F.2d 1179, 1183 (5th Cir. 1978) (testimony at a previous trial by a man authorized by B-W to testify

b. Authorized to Make a Statement

The rule states that the declarant must be "authorized ... to make a statement concerning the subject." The authorization may be explicit or it may be implicit.[104] On the question of authorization to speak for another, the rule states that the contents of the out-of-court statement itself "shall be considered," but the out-of-court statement by itself is not enough.[105]

This exclusion applies to persons such as a press agent or a lawyer—some sort of "speaking agent."[106] The identity of the person to whom the communication flows does not determine the application of this exclusion.[107] It does

---

to what he knew, now offered against B-W, is an authorized admission); PG&E v. United States, 73 Fed. Cl. 333, 439–40 (Ct. Fed. Cl. 2006) (Department of Energy (DOE) hired a contractor to write a report for DOE; DOE "authorized" the contractor to make the report and the statements therein), *aff'd in part & rev'd in part*, PG&E v. United States, No. 2007-5046, 2008 WL 3089272 (Fed. Cir. 2008); Glendale Fed. Bank v. United States, 39 Fed. Cl. 422, 424–25 (Ct. Fed. Cl. 1997) (an expert put forward at trial is authorized to speak for the party, and this includes prior deposition testimony of the expert; an expert retained by a party but not put forward at trial is not authorized to speak for the party); Covington v. Sawyer, 458 N.E.2d 465, 469 (Ohio App. 1983) ("A patient whose general practitioner refers her to a specialist for diagnosis and interpretation of specific symptoms, particularly at the patient's own request, authorizes her doctor to discuss her symptoms with the specialist.").

104. State v. Frustino, 689 P.2d 547, 553 (Ariz. Ct. App. 1984). *See* Messner v. Lockheed Martin Energy Sys., Inc., 126 F.Supp.2d 502, 512–13 (E.D. Tenn. 2000) ("'[t]here is a critical difference between making a statement while one is an employee and having the actual or implied authority to make such a statement on behalf of your employer'"; there are no facts on which the court could conclude this declarant was "authorized" to make a statement on this subject (quoting Jacklyn v. Schering-Plough Healthcare Prods. Sales Corp., 176 F.3d 921, 927 (6th Cir. 1999))).

105. This is an amendment to Rule 801(d)(2) that applies to trials commencing after December 1, 1997.

106. *See, e.g.*, Grace United Methodist Church v. City of Cheyenne, 451 F.3d 643, 666 (10th Cir. 2006) (upholding the admission against the church of a statement by a bishop of the church because he "was a 'superintending authority'" and therefore was a representative of a party authorized to speak for the party).

107. Zenith Radio Corp. v. Matsushita Elec. Indus. Co., Ltd., 505 F. Supp. 1190, 1246 (E.D. Pa. 1980) ("The Advisory Committee Notes state that the wording of Rule 801(d)(2)(C) was intended to resolve a division among the circuits as to whether an agent's statements were only admissible if made to a third person, or whether statements to the principal himself or itself could also be authorized admissions.... The Advisory Committee notes to Rule 801(d)(2)(C) make it clear that under that Rule a statement may be an authorized admission even though it was never communicated to a third party."), *aff'd in part, rev'd in part, remanded, sub nom* In Re Japanese Elec. Prods. Antitrust Litig., 723 F.2d 238 (3d Cir. 1983), *rev'd and remanded sub non* Matsushita Elec. Indus. Co. v. Zenith Radio Corp., 475 U.S. 574

not matter whether the declarant makes the statement to a third party or back to the person who authorized the declarant to make the statement. And, of course, by the very terms of the rule, this exclusion only applies when the statement is offered against the party who authorized the statement.

c. The Role of the Statement in Establishing Its Own Foundation

The rule is quite clear on this point: "The contents of the statement shall be considered but are not alone sufficient to establish the declarant's authority" to make the statement.[108]

d. Exclusions versus Exceptions

This is an exclusion from the definition of hearsay. It is not an exception to the hearsay rule. As discussed elsewhere, there may be a difference.[109]

e. The General Use Note

In addition to this Use Note, also see the General Use Note, above,[110] which is applicable to all of the admissions.

E. Adoptive Admission: 801(d)(2)(B)

1. Text of the Rule

> (d) Statements which are not hearsay. A statement is not hearsay if—
>
> ****
>
> (2) Admission by party-opponent. The statement is offered against a party and is ... (B) a statement of which the party has manifested an adoption or belief in its truth ...

2. Foundational Elements—Two Kinds of Adoptive Admissions

There are two kinds of adoptive admissions: (1) those where a party explicitly adopts the statement of another; and (2) those where a party implic-

---

(1986); Kingsley v. Baker/Beech-Nut Corp., 546 F.2d 1136, 1144 (5th Cir. 1977) (the testifying witness overheard the declarant's end of a telephone conversation; this exclusion applies even though we do not know to whom the declarant was speaking).

108. FED.R.EVID. 801(d)(2). This is an amendment to Rule 801(d)(2) that applies to trials commencing after December 1, 1997.

109. *See* Chapter 2(I), above.

110. *See* Chapter 2(III)(A), above.

itly adopts the statement of another. The foundational elements are different for each.

a. Foundational Elements—Explicit Adoptive Admission

Here are the foundational elements of an explicit adoptive admission, one where a party explicitly and unambiguously adopts a statement made by another:

1. The out-of-court statement is offered against a party.

2. The party against whom the statement is offered has explicitly adopted the statement as true, that is, has in some way affirmatively acknowledged the truth of the statement.

b. Foundational Elements—Implicit Adoptive Admission

Here are the foundational elements of an implicit adoptive admission, commonly one where a person is silent in the face of a statement and that silence can be taken to be agreement with or adoption of the statement:

1. The out-of-court statement is offered against a party.

2. The party against whom the statement is offered heard the statement or read it.[111] You cannot be held to have adopted a statement unless you can be held to have heard it or read it.[112]

3. Probable human behavior would be to deny the statement if it was not true.[113]

4. The party did not deny the statement.

---

111. The out-of-court statement need not be oral. It could be American Sign Language or Braille. There are cases finding an adoptive admission based on lack of response to a written communication. In this case, there would have to be some indication that the party received and read the communication. (As far as I know, no one has argued an adoptive admission based on a failure to respond to a smell, a taste, or the feel of something; for a hearsay objection to lie here, the odor, the flavor, or the item felt (as with Braille) would have been intended as a statement.)

112. This element has to do with whether the out-of-court statement registered with the party's senses, not whether the party understood what he or she sensed. The latter is taken care of in element number 5.

113. "The decision in each case calls for an evaluation in terms of probable human behavior." United States v. Hoosier, 542 F.2d 687, 688 (6th Cir. 1976). Regarding this foundational element, the judge's job is to evaluate probable human behavior and the lawyer's job is to affect the judge's evaluation. This is discussed in detail below, in the Use Note.

5. There is no other apparent reason for the lack of denial.[114]

3. Use Note

a. *Explicit Adoptive Admissions*

The first kind of adoptive admission—explicit adoption—is fairly easy to recognize and to deal with. A third party says to the current defendant, "You are the one who robbed that liquor store," and the defendant responds, "Yes, I am." When the defendant said, "Yes, I am," the defendant affirmed the truth of the statement that the defendant *is* "the one who robbed that liquor store." That third-party statement that the defendant "is the one ..." is a nonhearsay adoptive admission—an explicit adoptive admission—offered against the party who adopted it as true.[115]

Explicit adoption involves an affirmative act in the nature of saying "Yes, that's exactly right"; nodding one's head in the affirmative; signaling thumbs up; reading over a statement written out by someone else[116] and then signing it;[117] or not signing it, but saying "Yes, that's right"; responding to someone else's suggestion that a crime be committed, by agreeing to participate;[118] joining in

---

114. Regarding this foundational element, the judge's job is to evaluate the behavior of this particular party in the particular circumstances presented in the case at bar, and the lawyer's job is to affect the judge's evaluation. This is discussed in detail in the Use Note, Chapter 2(III)(E)(c), below.

115. Defendant's statement, "Yes, I am," is a personal admission under Rule 801(d)(2)(A). The third-party's statement, "You are the one ..." is an explicit adoptive admission under Rule 801(d)(2)(B). Neither is hearsay. *E.g.*, United States v. Torres, 519 F.2d 723, 726 n.10 (2d Cir. 1975) (the party's admission takes the other person's statement "out of the hearsay category and gives it the status of an adoptive admission.").

116. It will be written by someone else because if it were written by the party against whom it is offered, then the writing would be a nonhearsay personal admission under Rule 801(d)(2)(A).

117. United States v. Orellana-Blanco, 294 F.3d 1143, 1148 (9th Cir. 2002) ("Ordinarily a signed statement, even if written by another in another's words, would be adopted as the party's own if he signed it, because signing is a manifestation of adopting the statement." In this case, however, defendant's signature was not enough foundation. There was a considerable language barrier, no translator present for substantial parts of the interview, and no showing that the defendant could read the document or that it was read to him).

118. *E.g.*, State v. Laws, 668 S.W.2d 234 (Mo. Ct. App. 1984) (out-of-court declarant suggested illegal way to make money; party offered against agreed to participate) (discussed below, at parts III(F)(3)(g) & (j) of this chapter); State v. Anderson, 409 A.2d 1290 (Me. 1979) (out-of-court declarant suggested robbery; defendant responded with his participation in the planning).

the conversation in a way that corroborates what the third-party speaker has said.[119]

b. Implicit Adoptive Admissions

The second kind of adoptive admission—implicit adoption—can be more difficult. The typical implicit admission comes about when a third party makes a statement and a party adopts it as true by remaining silent, by not protesting the statement, or by not denying its truth in some fashion when a reasonable person would have done so. A third party says to the current defendant "You are the one who robbed that liquor store" and the defendant remains silent. The lack of denial may be the functional equivalent of the oral response, "Yes, that's true." If a reasonable person hearing that kind of accusation would deny it, the defendant did not deny it, and there is no other apparent reason for the lack of denial, then defendant's silence in the face of the accusation will be held to be the equivalent of the oral response, "Yes, that's true."[120]

Less typical is the implicit adoptive admission by conduct. Sometimes a party's conduct adopts a statement made by another. Three people were in the room: an undercover police officer, a second person from whom the officer has been purchasing drugs, and a third person, now the defendant, whom the officer had not seen before. The man the officer had been dealing with told the officer "I can get more rocks of crack from my partner in this operation." The defendant got out of his chair, walked over to a container concealing a stash of crack, and began to open it.[121] By that action, the defendant adopted the "partner" statement made by the second man.[122]

The oral statement standing alone had nothing to do with the defendant. In the face of that particular assertion, a reasonable person would not see a need to deny that he is the partner. Defendant's silence did not adopt the "partner" statement. His conduct, however, did adopt it. In defendant's drug conspiracy trial the statement "I can get more rocks of crack from my partner in this op-

---

119. State v. Anderson, 409 A.2d 1290 (Me. 1979) (in presence and hearing of defendant, out-of-court declarant said to testifying witnesses that "they had to shoot the guy"; later in conversation, defendant said that "when he pulled the trigger he had aimed for the guy's shoulder"; adoptive admission by explicit corroboration).

120. Defendant's "silent assertion" is a nonhearsay personal admission under Rule 801(d)(2)(A). The third-party oral statement is a nonhearsay implicit adoptive admission under Rule 801(d)(2)(B). Neither is hearsay.

121. This scenario is based on the facts of United States v. Beckham, 968 F.2d 47 (D.C. Cir. 1992).

122. Id. at 52.

eration" and the defendant's reaction both are admissible nonhearsay. Defendant's conduct was a statement and is offered against him; therefore, it is a personal admission. The second man's statement, "I can get more rocks of crack from my partner in this operation," is an implied adoptive admission because the defendant implicitly adopted as true that he was the "partner" in the statement.

Sometimes, the adoptive admission comes from a combination of silence and action (or lack of action). There can, of course, be other reasons for silence,[123] and silence is intrinsically ambiguous.[124] In one employment discrimination case, for example, someone (not an agent or an employee of the company) rose at a company meeting and said: "Managers must keep their qualifications up or they can be replaced by a younger person."[125] Company personnel at the meeting did not respond. That silence alone, however, probably was not enough to establish an adoptive admission. One case held, however, that when the company put that unattributed statement into the minutes of the meeting and distributed those minutes, the company adopted the statement. The silence plus the distribution of the unattributed statement in the minutes established an implicit adoptive admission.[126]

Sometimes the adoption comes from the party's possession of a document that is tied to the party in some meaningful way.[127]

---

123. Other reasons are listed and discussed below, in this Use Note.

124. This is discussed below, in this Use Note.

125. Horvath v. Rimtec Corp., 102 F.Supp.2d 219, 223 (D.N.J. 2000).

126. *Id.* See *also* Pekelis v. Transcontinental & W. Air, Inc., 187 F.2d 122, 128 (2d Cir. 1951) ("Even if the principal does not expressly vouch for the agent's statement, if he acts or conducts his business in such a way as to show by implication that he adopted the statement, then such parts of the statement as he acted upon are 'his.' And to that extent the statement is receivable against the principal as an adoptive admission.") (citations and multiple quotation marks omitted); Yuan v. Riveria, 2000 U.S. Dist. Lexis 4483, *13 (S.D.N.Y. 2000) ("[T]he information in the bill is not hearsay because it constitutes an adopted admission: having received a bill demanding payment for services, Ms. Chi would reasonably have been expected to register disagreement if she believed that it misrepresented the services rendered."); Wright-Simmons v. City of Oklahoma City, 155 F.3d 1264, 1268 (10th Cir. 1998) (a two-page report with interview notes attached was provided to the defendant's City Manager who then sought the resignation of the employee who was the subject of the report; the report and the notes are not hearsay; seeking the resignation was an implicit adoption of the report; that the City Manager need not have adopted every fact in the report to have sought the resignation goes to weight, not admissibility); Pilgrim v. Trustees of Tufts Coll., 118 F.3d 864, 870 (1st Cir. 1997) (when he implemented all of the recommendations in a report, defendant implicitly adopted the report's conclusions as true).

127. United States v. Marino, 658 F.2d 1120, 1125 (6th Cir. 1981) ("Though introduction of the airline tickets ... was arguably an attempt to prove the truth of the matter as-

c. A New Way to Look at Adoptive Admissions

There is another way to handle adoptive admissions. This second way is, in general, simpler, it is more consistent with basic hearsay theory, and it explains why an out-of-court admission of fact does not have to be based on personal knowledge of the fact declared.

Take this example involving the murder of Mrs. Shepard.[128] If Mrs. Shepard's nurse says "You killed Mrs. Shepard" and, in response, Dr. Shepard says "Yes, I did," and a third-party witness to the conversation testifies against Dr. Shepard at his trial for murder, then two things happen. First, Dr. Shepard's statement "Yes, I did," is not hearsay. It is his own statement offered against him. As such, it is a personal admission; Rule 801(d)(2)(A) excludes it from the hearsay definition. Second, the statement by the nurse, "You killed Mrs. Shepard," is not hearsay either. Dr. Shepard has explicitly adopted this statement and it is offered against him. It is an adoptive admission and Rule 801(d)(2)(B) excludes it from the definition.

That is the traditional way to look at this adoptive admission problem. Here is another way to look at it. Dr. Shepard's statement—"Yes I did"—is not hearsay because it is a personal admission—his own statement offered against him. The nurse's statement—"You killed Mrs. Shepard"—is not hearsay either because it is not offered to prove the truth of the matter asserted. We are not really concerned with the nurse's honesty or accuracy. Perhaps the nurse made a mistake, perhaps she misinterpreted something she saw. It does not matter for hearsay purposes. All that matters is that Dr. Shepard said "Yes I did (kill Mrs. Shepard)." Whether the nurse lied, whether she based her statement on gossip she picked up on the internet or something she heard on talk radio, whether it was simply a wild guess, is not relevant to the hearsay question. When Dr. Shepard adopted the nurse's statement, the nurse's statement became his. The nurse's statement became the implied clause at the end of Dr. Shepard's statement. "Yes I did (kill Mrs. Shepard)." The only person whose credibility we care about is Dr. Shepard.

---

serted, that is, that the defendants traveled in interstate commerce, this evidence was admissible because the defendants' possession of the tickets and the other documents constituted an adoption."); State v. Draganescu, 755 N.W.2d 57, 80 (Neb. 2008) ("[A] party's possession of a written statement [—an airline ticket—] can be an adoption of what its contents reveal under circumstances that tie the party to the document in a meaningful way.") (citing and discussing cases).

128. This example is based on Shepard v. United States, 290 U.S. 96 (1933), discussed above, particularly at Chapter 1(IV)(A). The point being made here is also discussed at part III(E)(3)(a)–(c) of this chapter.

Dr. Shepard's personal admission standing alone does not have any relevant meaning. It only has full and relevant meaning in the context in which he said it.[129] In that context, there is an implied clause at the end of his response: "Yes I did (kill Mrs. Shepard)." The only thing the nurse's statement does for us is this: It is evidence of the content of the implied clause on the end of Dr. Shepard's sentence. In the final analysis, we don't care whether the nurse knew what she was talking about. All we care about is whether Dr. Shepard knew what he was talking about. The nurse's statement is simply context evidence; it supplies the relevant meaning to Dr. Shepard's admission and it does so even if she was lying, mistaken, or had no knowledge of the subject at all.

Once we take the nurse's statement "You killed Mrs. Shepard" and use it to give meaning to Dr. Shepard's response, the nurse is out of the picture. All that matters is, what did Dr. Shepard say. All we care about is whether we believe Dr. Shepard when he said "Yes I did (kill Mrs. Shepard)."[130] The nurse's statement is not offered to prove that Dr. Shepard killed his wife. Dr. Shepard's statement is offered to prove he killed his wife. The nurse's statement is offered only to help us understand Dr. Shepard's statement.

---

129. The declarant's statements were not admitted for their truth but "for the context they provided for [the coconspirator's] statements." United States v. Schalk, 515 F.3d 768, 775 (7th Cir. 2008). *Accord* United States v. Page, 521 F.3d 101, 106 (1st Cir. 2008) ("Evidence is not inadmissible hearsay if used only for the limited purpose of establishing "background" or "context" information ...") (citing cases).

130. *See* United States v. Jinadu, 98 F.3d 239, 245 (6th Cir. 1996) ("'If the defendant accepts the out-of-court statement as his own, cross-examination of the declarant of the hearsay becomes unnecessary and irrelevant.'") (citation omitted); Lee v. McGaughtry, 892 F.2d 1318, 1324 (7th Cir. 1990); United States v. Jordan 810 F.2d 262, 264 (D.C. Cir. 1987); State v. Gano, 988 P.2d 1153, 1162 (Haw. 1999) ("'The party becomes the declarant, and the statement of the other person becomes the party's.'") (quoting State v. Carlson, 808 P.2d 1002, 1005–06 (Or. 1991)); State v. Cotten, 879 P.2d 971, 983 (Wash. 1994) ("An adoptive admission is attributed to the defendant and becomes the defendant's own words.")); State v. Hoffman, 828 P.2d 805, 809 (Haw. 1992) ("[The] declarant's accusatory or incriminating statements are not admitted to prove the truth of matters asserted. Such statements are admissible because they lay the foundation to show what the defendant acquiesced or admitted to by adoption."); United States v. Finley, 708 F.Supp. 906, 911 (N.D. Ill. 1989) ("The declarant of an adoptive admission is the one who adopts it as his own statement[.]"); People v. Silva, 754 P.2d 1070, 1080 (Cal. 1988) ("once the defendant has expressly or impliedly adopted the statements of another, the statements become *his own admissions* ... Being deemed the defendant's own admissions, we are no longer concerned with the veracity or credibility of the original declarant.").

Dr. Shepard is the real witness.[131] Dr. Shepard is the manufacturer of the raw material we need for this trial.[132] It is Dr. Shepard's forthrightness, his ability to have perceived and remembered the events in question, his honesty that concerns us. Dr. Shepard is the one we need to cross-examine regarding the statement "Yes I did (kill Mrs. Shepard)."

Another example: Assume that the out-of-court declarant and the defendant are sister and brother. In the presence of the defendant and others, a few months before the explosion that is the gravamen of the criminal prosecution against her brother, the sister said: "A revolution is coming and my brother is an important part of it. He's going to be using his skills with explosives to further the cause." The evidence is that her brother heard the statement and remained silent. If the prosecutor can convince the judge that the brother's silence was an adoptive admission, then the party's statement is his silence, which is held to adopt the truth of what his sister has said. The adoptive admission gives text to the party's silence. The adoptive admission turns what a nonparty has said into a non-hearsay admission by a party. His silence becomes an assertion. His silence becomes, "Yes, that is true. (A revolution is coming and [I am] an important part of it. [I'm] going to be using [my] skills with explosives to further the cause.)" The whole point of the adoptive admission exclusion is that it takes a nonparty's out-of-court statement and turns it into a party's admission.

Once the silence becomes "Yes, that is true. (A revolution is coming and [I am] an important part of it. [I'm] going to be using [my] skills with explosives to further the cause.)," then we no longer care about the credibility of the third-party speaker, but just the credibility of the person who silently communicated.[133]

In the *Mahlandt*[134] case the question was whether a wolf named Sophie bit a child. Mr. Poos was the wolf's handler. The defendant's are Poos and the company for which he handles the wolf. A witness will testify that Poos said, "Sophie bit a child." One of two things must be true: either Poos has personal knowledge that Sophie bit a child, or he does not. And the truth is that it does not really matter which. (In the actual case it was clear that Poos was no where near the scene and he did not have personal knowledge. He had to be basing what he said on what a third party told him.)

---

131. *See* Chapter 1(III)(A)(3).
132. *See* Chapter 1(III)(A)(2).
133. *But see* note 189 and accompanying text, below in this chapter.
134. Mahlandt v. Wild Canid Survival & Research Ctr., Inc., 588 F.2d 626, 630–31 (8th Cir. 1978). *See* the discussion of *Mahlandt* in part III(G)(2) of this chapter, below.

Change the evidence. If the witness would testify that she heard a third party say to Poos, "Sophie bit a child," and Poos either said "Yes," as an explicit adoptive admission, or said "No," as an implicit adoptive admission. The third party's statement is only offered to give content to Poos's admission; it is not offered to prove the truth of the matter asserted; it is not hearsay. Surely the result is no different when, instead of saying "Yes" or remaining silent, Poos says "Sophie bit a child."[135]

----

135. Consider also this hypothetical based on United States v. Torres, 519 F.2d 723 (2d Cir. 1975). A witness will testify that she overheard a conversation between the defendant and a third party. The third party said: "You still owe $16,000 for those drugs." The defendant replied "Yes, I know." It does not matter what kind of trial it is. It could be a criminal trial for the purchase of illegal drugs, a suit by an insurance company to recover a payment made, or a child custody case. All that matters is that this evidence is relevant when offered against the defendant.

Defendant's statement, "Yes, I know," is not hearsay. It is a party's own statement offered against him. The third party's statement, "You still owe $16,000 for those drugs," is not hearsay either. It is not offered to prove the truth of its assertion. The defendant said "Yes, I know." This raises the question "Yes, I know" what? To give meaning to defendant's statement, we must refer to the third-party's statement. We refer to it not for its truth, but because it supplies the critical content of defendant's admission. Defendant's response has an implied clause on the end. "Yes, I know (I still owe $16,000 for those drugs)." In this context, "Yes, I know" fully, though in part impliedly, expresses exactly the same message as "Yes, I know that I still owe $16,000 for those drugs." The defendant's statement is not hearsay, as it is a party's own statement offered against him. The third party's statement is not hearsay, as it is not offered to prove the truth of the matter asserted, but to give content to the defendant's admission. The only assertion offered *for its truth* is defendant's.

Accord United States v. Page, 521 F.3d 101, 106 (1st Cir. 2008) ("Evidence is not inadmissible hearsay if used only for the limited purpose of establishing "background" or "context" information …") (citing cases); United States v. Zizzo, 120 F.3d 1338 (7th Cir. 1997) (a former member of a conspiracy who became a cooperating government witness had conversations with others who were still members of the conspiracy; what the cooperating witness and the other parties said were admissible under the exclusion for coconspirators' statements, *id.* at 1348; the cooperating witness's statements were nonhearsay "context" evidence admitted not for their truth "but rather to give context to the" nonhearsay statements of the coconspirators, *id.*).

See also Chapter 2(III)(G) and at the discussion of *Cole v. State* in Chapter 7(II)(D), below.

Some courts take a contrary position. For example, the Honorable Edward R. Becker (whose writings on the subject of the rules of evidence are among the very best) has written:

> Under the Federal Rules of Evidence, admissions under Rule 801(d)(2) are non-hearsay, rather than hearsay admitted under an exception. As a result, hearsay within an admission is not strictly within the terms of Rule 805, governing "hearsay included within hearsay." We think, nevertheless, that internal hearsay in a state-

As a result of looking at admission in this way, an admission of fact cures preceding levels of hearsay.[136]

d. Impeachment of the Third Party Who Made the Statement the Litigation Party Has Adopted

Introducing an adoptive admission does not open the door for impeachment of the person who made the statement that the party adopted. The declarant is the party who adopted the third-party statement. The third party's credibility is not in issue. The third party could have been making a wild guess, basing the statement on mistaken information, or intending a lie or bad joke. For purposes of the hearsay rule, it does not matter. The statement has become the party's own; the party is the declarant; the party is the real witness, the original manufacturer of the evidence; the party's statement is the only one that must be true; our only concern is with the credibility of the party who has adopted the statement.[137]

e. Ambiguous Responses Are Not a Basis for an Adoptive Admission

Be on the lookout for the problem of the ambiguous response. As a general rule, an ambiguous response cannot be the basis for an adoptive admission. If we cannot tell whether the party's response is an adoption or a denial

---

ment which comes into evidence as an admission must be subjected to an independent analysis to determine whether or not it would survive a hearsay objection in its own right.

Zenith Radio Corp., 505 F.Supp. at 1266. This case involved the admissibility of a chart that clearly was not based on the personal knowledge of the declarant who prepared it. Using the analysis I propose, this chart should have been excluded either because the person who prepared it was incompetent (*see* Chapter 13(I)(C), below) or because the chart does not admit the facts on the chart, but only that someone said these things to the person who prepared the chart. *See also* United States v. Dotson, 821 F.2d 1034, 1035 (5th Cir. 1987) (preceding levels of hearsay must be considered when dealing with Rule 801(d) nonhearsay statements, here the exclusion for prior consistent statements.)

136. As a general rule, if there are multiple layers of hearsay behind an out-of-court statement, then for the final out-of-court statement to be admissible there must be an exclusion or an exception for each of the underlying hearsay statements upon which the final statement is based. This general rule does not apply to admissions. This is discussed below, at part G. of this Use Note.

137. *See* the text following note 4, above in this chapter. For these same reasons, even if the defendant is unable to confront the third party, the Confrontation Clause does not bar the admission of the statement. *See* Chapter 14, below.

(or something else altogether), then we cannot say that it is an adoption.[138] Some courts have held that silence is inherently ambiguous and courts should be reluctant to find an admission in a party's silence.[139]

f. Other (Non-Adoptive) Reasons for the Lack of a Denial

The third foundational element of the implicit adoptive admission is that probable human behavior would be to deny the statement if it was not true. The fifth foundational element is that there was no other apparent reason for the lack of denial. The former requires that the judge consider general human behavior. The latter requires that the judge consider the probable behavior of the particular party in the context of the event. Is there something about this person or the circumstances of the particular event that provides another reason for the silence?[140]

---

138. The ambiguity in question here is not the ambiguity of the third person's statement, but the ambiguity of the party's response. The ambiguity of the statement setting up the response is discussed at part III(E)(3)(f) of this chapter, below. Regarding the ambiguous response, *see, e.g., Gano*, 988 P.2d at 1163 (head or body movements may be ambiguous, calling for a closer examination); Romano v. State, 909 P.2d 92, 107 (Okla. Crim. App. 1995) (in response to question from investigator, defendant trembled and dropped his head; this was too ambiguous to constitute adoption); State v. Beckett, 383 N.W.2d 66, 69 (Iowa Ct. App. 1985) (defendant nodded his head in response to a statement; the nod was too ambiguous; the witness did not testify whether the defendant's "head nod was affirmative or negative…, aggressive or slight"); Village of New Hope v. Duplessie, 231 N.W.2d 548, 551–53 (Minn. 1975) (defendant's nodding his head and laughing in the face of an incriminating statement was equivocal and therefore not an adoptive admission). *But see* United States v. Tocco, 135 F.3d 116, 128 (2d Cir. 1998) (the innocent ordinarily deny involvement in a crime; the "silence or *other ambiguous conduct* [of one so accused] is admissible as an adoptive admission …") (citation omitted; emphasis added); Dant v. Commonwealth, 258 S.W.3d 12, 18 (Ky. 2008) (accused of abusing the accuser's seven-month-old daughter, defendant "replied that he was tired of working forty hours a week to support a child that was not his;" this "indicated he understood [the] accusation and chose not to deny it even though it was made 'under circumstances that would normally call for his denial'"; his statement is admissible as an adoptive admission).

139. *E.g.*, United States v. Hale, 422 U.S. 171, 176 (1975) ("In most circumstances silence is so ambiguous that it is of little probative force."); United States v. Coppola, 526 F.2d 764, 769 n.2 (10th Cir. 1975) ("A trial court should be most reluctant to credit mere silence—inherently ambiguous—as 'conduct' sufficient for adoption of an inculpatory statement."); Commonwealth v. Babbitt, 723 N.E.2d 17, 22 (Mass. 2000); State v. Hoffman, 828 P.2d 805, 810 (Haw. 1992).

140. "What is natural for one person may not be natural for another. There are persons possessed of such dignity and pride that they would treat with silent contempt a dishonest accusation." Commonwealth v. Dravecz, 227 A.2d 904, 906 (Pa. 1967) (Musmanno,

These two points—probable human reaction and this party's probable re-action—can be argued as a matter of law and as a matter of fact. First, the party's lawyer can argue to the trier of law that there is something about this particular situation or this particular person that either makes this silence am-biguous or defines it as something other than assent.

Second, if the trier of law disagrees and the out-of-court statement is admit-ted as a nonhearsay adoptive admission, then the party's lawyer can argue these points to the trier of fact. The lawyer can take the same argument made to the judge, and make it to the jury. The lawyer can argue to the jury that there is something about this particular situation or this particular person that defines the silence as something other than assent. The lawyer gets a second crack at convincing some-one that her client's silence did not mean assent to the out-of-court statement.

The fifth foundational element asks whether there are other reasons for the silence, for the lack of denial. Other reasons may include:

The right to remain silent: A party who remains silent while, for example, being questioned by the police may be exercising the constitutional right to remain silent.[141]

J.). *Accord* State v. Forbes, 953 A.2d 433, 436 (N.H. 2008) ("[T]he possible motivations for a person's silence in the face of an untruthful accusation are numerous.") (listing many of them); Weinbender v. Commonwealth, 398 S.E.2d 106, 107–08 (Va. Ct. App. 1990) ("'The personal makeup of the speaker, e.g., young child, or his relationship to the party or the event e.g., bystander, may be such as to make it unreasonable to expect a denial.'" (quoting E. Cleary, McCormick On Evidence § 270, at 800–01 (3d ed. 1984))).

141. *E.g.*, Doyle v. Ohio, 426 U.S. 610, 617 (1976) (not a hearsay case, but stating that "[s]ilence in the wake of [Miranda] warnings may be nothing more than the arrestee's ex-ercise of these Miranda rights. Thus, every post-arrest silence is insolubly ambiguous be-cause of what the State is required to advise the person arrested."); United States v. Lafferty, 503 F.3d 293, 307 (3d Cir. 2007) (defendant who invokes her Fifth Amendment right to re-main silent cannot be penalized for doing so by using her silence as an adoptive admission); United States v. Schaff, 948 F.2d 501, 505 (9th Cir. 1991) (post-arrest silence may not be used as evidence that the defendant adopted the statement of another); United States v. Flecha, 539 F.2d 874, 877 (2d Cir. 1976) ("many arrested persons know, without benefit of warnings, that silence is usually golden"); Commonwealth v. MacKenzie, 597 N.E.2d 1037, 1043 n.8 (Mass. 1992) (defendant's silence when advised of his rights in a custodial inter-rogation "is 'insolubly ambiguous'"). Additionally, note that as a matter of constitutional law the prosecutor cannot comment on the defendant's failure to take the stand. Carter v. Kentucky, 450 U.S. 288, 297–98 (1981); Griffin v. California, 380 U.S. 609, 615 (1965) (the Constitution "forbids either comment by the prosecution on the accused's silence or in-structions by the court that such silence is evidence of guilt"). The jury cannot draw an ad-verse inference from a defendant's exercise of his or her constitutional right to remain silent. Portuoudo v. Agard, 529 U.S. 61, 67 (2000); *Carter*, 450 U.S. at 300.

The silent denial: Silence in the face of an accusation can be the best form of denial.[142]

Distractions or other duties: The non-responding party may be otherwise engaged. "[T]he situation after the accident was one of confusion, and [the non-responding party] was busy rendering aid to plaintiff."[143]

Shock: The non-responding party may have been so startled by the accusatory statement, surrounding events, or both, that words would not come.[144]

Long, complex statements: The length and complexity of the statement may account for the lack of response.[145]

Ambiguous statements: The ambiguity of the out-of-court statement may allow various interpretations, some of which do not call for denial. Without sufficient context, for example, what does it mean that a party did not respond

---

142. In his funeral oration on Roscoe Conkling, Robert G. Ingersoll said:
"He was maligned, misrepresented and misunderstood, but he would not answer. He was as silent then as he is now—and his silence, better than any form of speech, refuted every charge." George Bernard Shaw said: "Silence is the most perfect expression of scorn." The immortal Abraham Lincoln summed up his philosophy on this subject in characteristic form: "If I should read much less answer, all the attacks made upon me this shop might as well be closed for any other business."
Dravecz, 227 A.2d at 906 n.1. "There are persons possessed of such dignity and pride that they would treat with silent contempt a dishonest accusation. Are they to be punished for refusing to dignify with a denial what they regard as wholly false and reprehensible?" *Id.*

143. Klever v. Elliot, 320 P.2d 263, 265 (Or. 1958). *Accord, e.g.,* Forbes, 953 A.2d at 436 (silence may be a result of "'inattention or perplexity'" (quoting *Babbitt*, 723 N.E.2d at 22)); Beck v. Dye, 92 P.2d 1113, 1118 (Wash. 1939) (at the time the bystanders' statements were made, appellant was not concerned with laying blame for the accident, but with getting medical assistance for the woman unconscious in the street; "It was the legal, as well as the moral, duty of appellant to render the required assistance, and he was not called upon to enter into a verbal combat with every bystander, at the risk of having his silence [taken as an admission].").

144. "It may be desirable and dramatic for the wrongly accused person to shout: 'I am innocent!' but not everybody responds spontaneously to stimuli. The accusation may be so startling that the accused is benumbed into speechlessness. There are persons so sensitive and hurt so easily, that they swallow their tongue in the face of overwhelming injustice." *Dravecz*, 227 A.2d at 906. *Accord, e.g.,* Arpan v. United States, 260 F.2d 649, 657 (8th Cir. 1958) (the non-responding party was "depressed or withdrawn into himself, in a 'state of shock' [and] under the influence of liquor"); State v. Clark, 175 P.3d 1006, 1011 (Or. Ct. App. 2008) (discussing the issue from *Arpan*).

145. *Gano*, 988 P.2d 1167 ("little assurance that he adopted, as his own admission, every detail of the lengthy conversation"); *Dravecz*, 227 A. at 908 (the statement was a long one; it could have contained averments with which the defendant agreed and averments with which he disagreed) (Musmanno, J.).

to the out-of-court statement "You did it," or was it "*You* did it?" or "You *did* it?" or "You did *it?*" or "*You* **did** *it!*" And, for that matter, what is "it"?[146]

The bother of responding: Sometimes a person just does not take the trouble to respond. Perhaps lack of a response to an unsolicited letter or phone call or to an accusation hurled at you as you walk down the sidewalk, may mean nothing more than "Go away," "How dare you," "When did society begin this slide downhill?" "I'm not getting involved in this," or "Why bother, no one believes me anyway."[147]

Exasperation: Perhaps the lack of response is out of a sense of frustration or exasperation with the declarant—surely we all have relatives, friends, or coworkers who bring this out in us—or the situation.[148] Sometimes it is clear from the way the statement is phrased, clear from the facts in general, that a denial would be meaningless or futile.[149]

Relationship peculiarities: There may be facts about the relationship between the speaker and the one who remained silent.[150] Which of us hasn't received a silent denial from a loved one?

The degree of the non-responding party's involvement in the situation: Without "some tie on the part of the [non-responding party] to the setting or the events of the making of the statement"[151] there may be no reason to reply.

---

146. *Forbes*, 953 A.2d at 437 (statements to which there was no response were "suppositious and equivocal"); State v. Carlson, 808 P.2d 1002 (Or. 1991) (en banc). The subject here is the ambiguous statement setting up the response. The ambiguous response is discussed above, at part III(E)(3)(e) of this chapter, above.

147. *E.g., Klever*, 320 P.2d at 265 ("[E]ven if Elliott heard the remark and had opportunity to reply, he was under no obligation to enter into a debate over liability, particularly with one who was not involved in the accident nor an eyewitness, and whose opinions must have been based only upon inference.").

148. Perhaps the non-responding party knows that the out-of-court declarant, to the party's great frustration, is someone who is constantly exaggerating or lying. *See, e.g.*, State v. Carlson, 808 P.2d 1002, 1010 (Or. 1991) (defendant testified he did not reply because "he did not see any benefit in arguing with an irrational, mentally ill and angry woman.").

149. *Forbes*, 953 A.2d at 437.

150. *Weinbender*, 398 S.E.2d at 107 (The speaker's "'relationship to the party or the event e.g., bystander, may be such as to make it unreasonable to expect a denial.'" (quoting E. CLEARY, McCORMICK ON EVIDENCE § 270, at 800–01 (3d ed. 1984))). These special facts may be based on cultural factors. *Gano*, 988 P.2d at 1168 ("The record also does not reflect whether, in a cultural context, at this meeting between two Filipino families, an innocent defendant would be induced to respond to [statements] offers made by a family member …").

151. *Arpan*, 260 F.2d at 656 (a passerby overhearing strangers talking about him could hardly be expected to stop and set the record straight or risk his silence being treated as an

Rhetorical statements: Sometimes the statement simply does not call for a response.[152]

Inability to hear the statement: Of course there must be sufficient foundational evidence that the non-responding party heard the statement.[153]

Inability to understand the statement: Perhaps, for example, the out-of-court statement was in French or American Sign Language, or it involved complex math, science, or other ideas. In such a case, there would have to be some evidence that the party understood French, American Sign Language, or the complex ideas involved.[154]

g. An Employee's Adoption used against an Employer

If the statement was adopted by an employee of a party, then under Rule 801(d)(2)(B), it becomes her admission; if it concerned a matter within the scope of her employment, then under Rule 801(d)(2)(D), her adoption becomes an admission by an employee and vicariously admissible against the employer.[155]

h. Exclusions versus Exceptions

This is an exclusion from the definition of hearsay. It is not an exception to the hearsay rule. As discussed elsewhere, there may be a difference.[156]

i. The General Use Note

In addition to this Use Note, also see the General Use Note, above,[157] which is applicable to all of the admissions.

---

adoptive admission by him); *Forbes*, 953 A.2d at 436 ("[T]he statement in question was not directed at the defendant ...").

152. Perhaps it was a rhetorical question, irony, or a joke. Perhaps when you put the statement in the context of the whole conversation it was a joke and everyone understood it was a joke.

153. *E.g.*, Carr v. Deeds 453 F.3d 593, 607 (4th Cir. 2006).

154. *E.g.*, *Id.* at 607 (there must be sufficient foundational evidence that the non-responding party "heard, understood, and acquiesced in the statement"); United States v. Sears, 663 F.2d 896, 905 (9th Cir. 1981) (party was not wearing her hearing aids, which made communication with her difficult; adoptive admission nonetheless); *Gano*, 988 P.2d at 1168 (the statement alleged to have been adopted was in Tagalog, which was not defendant's first language). Here, foundational elements number two and five overlap.

155. Sea Land Serv., Inc. v. Lozen Int'l, LLC, 285 F.3d 808, 821 (9th Cir. 2002).

156. *See* Chapter 2(I), above.

157. *See* Chapter 2(III)(A), above.

F. Admission by a Coconspirator: 801(d)(2)(E)

1. Text of the Rule

(d) Statements which are not hearsay. A statement is not hearsay if—

****

(2) Admission by party-opponent. The statement is offered against a party and is ... (E) a statement by a coconspirator of a party during the course and in furtherance of the conspiracy. The contents of the statement shall be considered but are not alone sufficient to establish ... the existence of the conspiracy and the participation therein of the declarant and the party against whom the statement is offered under subdivision (E).

2. Foundational Elements

1. The out-of-court statement is offered against a party.

2. A conspiracy existed.

3. The declarant and the party against whom the evidence is offered were both members of the conspiracy.

4. The statement was made during the course of the conspiracy.

5. The statement was made in furtherance of the conspiracy.

3. Use Note

a. The First Foundational Element: The Statement is Offered against a Party

As with all of the exclusions in Rule 801(d)(2), the out-of-court statement must be offered against a party who is to one degree or another to be held accountable for the statement.

b. The Second Foundational Element: A Conspiracy Existed

The second and third foundational elements are not really separate. Proof of the third element—that the out-of-court declarant and the party were members of a conspiracy—also proves the second element—that a conspiracy existed. They are separated here for ease of understanding. Sometimes it is clear that the out-of-court declarant and the party had an association, and the key question is whether it was a conspiracy; and sometimes it is clear that there was a conspiracy, and the key question is whether the out-of-court declarant or the party was a member of the conspiracy. Counsel may be able to challenge an out-of-court statement on either of these two points.

c. The Third Foundational Element: The Party against Whom the Statement Is Offered and the Declarant Were Both Members of the Conspiracy

Mueller and Kirkpatrick's treatise, *Evidence*, explains the second element of the foundation as follows: "The exception requires a conspiracy involving the speaker and the party against whom the statement is offered. Proving that the latter participated in a conspiracy involves at least showing that he knew of the venture and intended to associate with it, and neither knowledge nor association alone is sufficient."[158]

First, there must be evidence of a conspiracy (which repeats the second element, above). Second, there must be evidence that the out-of-court declarant was a member of the conspiracy.[159] Among other things, this means that while knowledge of the exact identity of the declarant is not required[160] there must be enough evidence to support a conclusion that the declarant was a member of the particular conspiracy. Third, there must be evidence that the party was a member of this same conspiracy.[161] We need not know the singular identity of the declarant,[162] but only that the declarant was a member of the conspiracy. The key to this exclusion is not identity, but participation in the conspiracy. The declarant's identity can be relevant to the critical question of whether he or she was a member of the conspiracy.[163]

---

158. CHRISTOPHER B. MUELLER & LAIRD C. KIRKPATRICK, EVIDENCE § 8.33, at 797 (3d ed. 2003).

159. "A defendant's membership in a conspiracy is presumed to continue until he withdraws from the conspiracy by affirmative action." In order to establish withdrawal or abandonment, the defendant must show that he acted to "defeat or disavow the purpose of the conspiracy." "Mere cessation" of conduct in furtherance of the conspiracy is insufficient to make this showing.
United States v. Nelson, 530 F.Supp.2d 719, 725 (D. Md. 2008) (citations to Fourth Circuit Court of Appeals cases omitted).

160. United States v. Bolivar, 532 F.3d 599, 604 (7th Cir. 2008).

161. *E.g.*, United States v. Payne, 437 F.3d 540, 544–46 (6th Cir. 2006).

162. United States v. Arias, 252 F.3d 973, 977 (8th Cir. 2001).

163. In United States v. Mouzin, 785 F.2d 682 (9th Cir. 1986), the trial court had let a ledger into evidence as a nonhearsay statement by a coconspirator. The government argued

Finally, "[i]t is immaterial that the other person in the conversation ... was not a coconspirator but a government informant."[164] The critical inquiry concerns the declarant, not the person to whom the declarant was speaking.

d. The Fourth Foundational Element: The Statement Was Made During the Conspiracy

The key to this fourth foundational element—whether the statement was made during the course of the conspiracy—is this: When did the conspiracy begin and when did it end?[165] Any of the following may arguably end the conspiracy:

(a) Completion of the conspiracy.[166]

(b) Arrest.[167] Arrest may end the conspiracy, but only for the arrested conspirator. Things said by unarrested coconspirators may still fit under this exclusion. This is so even when those statements are made to an already arrested conspirator.[168] Furthermore, arrest does not necessarily end the conspiracy

---

that the ledger was a record of a large cocaine operation. There was no evidence of the identity of the ledger's author. The ledger was found at the residence of the defendant, who was a member of the conspiracy and whose fingerprints were on the ledger. From that, the trial court concluded that the author was a coconspirator with the defendant. The court of appeals reversed. Without more information about the identity of the declarant, it cannot be established that the declarant and the party against whom the evidence is offered were both members of the conspiracy. This summary of *Mouzin* is taken from United States v. Smith, 893 F.2d 1573, 1577–78 (9th Cir. 1990).

164. *E.g.*, United States v. Aviles-Colon, 536 F.3d 1, 15 (1st Cir. 2008) (brackets in original) (the testimony must simply meet the rule's foundational elements, and this is not one of them).

165. Was the statement made "during the active life of the conspiracy." United States v. Smith, 520 F.2d 1245, 1247 (8th Cir. 1975).

166. *E.g.*, Jones v. State, 940 A.2d 1, 11 (Del. 2007) ("statements made after the robbery but before the proceeds were divided are made in furtherance of the conspiracy") (multiple and internal quotation marks omitted); State v. Jones, 873 P.2d 122, 130 (Idaho 1994) (murder for hire; conspiracy not complete until final payment made). Statements made to cover up an otherwise completed conspiracy are discussed below in this Use Note.

167. United States v. Palow, 777 F.2d 52, 57 (1st Cir. 1985); United States v. Poitierr, 623 F.2d 1017, 1020 (5th Cir. 1980); United States v. Smith, 520 F.2d 1245, 1247 (8th Cir. 1975) (joint enterprise ended when coconspirators apprehended and separately searched); State v. Darby, 599 P.2d 821 (Ariz. Ct. App. 1979) (this conspiracy was defeated when defendant was arrested; statement by coconspirator made after defeat of conspiracy, not during its pendency). United States v. Harris, 542 F.2d 1283, 1301 (7th Cir. 1976) (arrest or incarceration of conspirator may constitute withdrawal, "but it does not as a matter of law").

168. *E.g.*, United States v. Emuegbunam, 268 F.3d 377, 396 (6th Cir. 2001) (statements by an arrested conspirator, to coconspirators still capable of executing the conspiracy fit this exclusion even when the declarant acted "under the direction and surveillance of gov-

even for the arrested conspirator; even an arrested conspirator can continue to pursue the objectives of the conspiracy.[169]

(c) Indictment.[170]

(d) Confession. Again, confession may end the conspiracy for the one making the confession and the conspiracy may continue for other conspirators.[171]

(e) The division of the property that was the subject of the conspiracy.[172]

(f) Resignation from the conspiracy of either the out-of-court declarant[173] or the party against whom the out-of-court statement is offered.[174]

(g) Becoming a cooperating government witness (which, perhaps, is an informal resignation from the conspiracy).[175]

---

ernment agents to obtain evidence against the coconspirators.") (citing cases; multiple quotation marks omitted); United States v. Zarnes, 33 F.3d 1454, 1468 (7th Cir. 1994) (to withdraw from conspiracy, arrested conspirator has to do more than simply cease activity; the conspirator must also, for example, "make a clean breast to authorities" or communicate abandonment in a manner calculated to reach coconspirators; this declarant's "incarceration, by itself, did not establish that she withdrew from the [conspiracy]) (citing cases).

169. United States v. Townley, 472 F.3d 1267, 1274–75 (10th Cir. 2007) ("[A]lthough these conversations took place after Appellant's arrest, the conversations reflect [his] intent to continue pursuing the conspiracy's objectives.").

170. Though not every indictment necessarily ends the conspiracy. United States v. Carmine Persico, 832 F.2d 705 (2d Cir. 1987).

171. State v. Caudill, 706 P.2d 456, 459 (Idaho 1985) (crime completed, out-of-court declarant confessed).

172. State v. Yslas, 676 P.2d 1118, 1122 (Ariz. 1984).

173. United States v. Zizzo, 120 F.3d 1338, 1348 (7th Cir. 1997) (when the statement was made, the declarant was no longer a member of conspiracy, but instead a cooperating government agent).

174. *See, e.g.,* United States v. Hubbard, 22 F.3d 1410 (7th Cir. 1994) (good discussion of withdrawal; coconspirator must take affirmative actions to show withdrawal); United States v. Zarnes, 33 F.3d 1454, 1468 (7th Cir. 1994) (*see* note 168, above); United States v. Harris, 542 F.2d 1283, 1301 (7th Cir. 1976) (arrest or incarceration of conspirator may constitute withdrawal, "but it does not as a matter of law").

175. *Emuegbunam,* 268 F.3d at 396 (*see* note 168, above); United States v. Pratt, 239 F.3d 640, 644 (4th Cir. 2001) (harmless error); *Zizzo,* 120 F.3d at 1348. *See also* United States v. Monteleone, 257 F.3d 210, 221–22 (2d Cir. 2001) ("Membership in a criminal conspiracy and rendering services to the government as an informant are not necessarily mutually exclusive roles.... We draw a distinction between a co-conspirator who exchanges information with the government while still pursuing the conspiracy's criminal objectives, and one whose conduct as a 'co-conspirator' is shaped and directed by the desire of the government.").

(h) Making an exculpatory statement to the police that inculpates a coconspirator.[176]

(i) Anything and everything else that is relevant.

In this regard, it is clear that the conspiracy can exist even though it becomes impossible for it to succeed. Impossibility of completion does not automatically terminate the conspiracy.[177]

e. The Fifth Foundational Element: The Statement Was Made in Furtherance of the Conspiracy

The plain meaning of the rule requires something more than just conversation among coconspirators or a conspirator's statement to a third party: It requires that the statement be made in furtherance of the conspiracy. "The requirement that a co-conspirator's statement be in furtherance of the conspiracy is not to be construed too strictly lest the purpose of the exception be defeated.... [B]ut on the other hand, mere idle conversation ... is not considered in furtherance of a conspiracy."[178] The key is the intention of the declarant.[179] A statement "'need not have been made exclusively, or even primarily, to further the conspiracy.' Rather the only question is whether 'some reasonable basis' exists for concluding that [the statement was] intended to move the conspiracy closer to its objectives."[180]

---

176. *E.g.*, United States v. Perez-Ruiz, 353 F.3d 1, 11 (1st Cir. 2003); United States v. Smith, 520 F.2d 1245, 1247 (8th Cir. 1975).

177. United States v. Jiminez Recio, 537 U.S. 270, 274–77 (2003) (citing cases and authorities).

178. United States v. Green, 180 F.3d 216, 223 (5th Cir. 1999) (internal quotation marks and citations omitted).

179. "When inquiring whether a statement was made 'in furtherance of' a conspiracy, we do not focus on its actual effect in advancing the goals of the conspiracy, but on the declarant's intent in making the statement." United States v. Perez, 989 F.2d 1574, 1578 (10th Cir. 1993) (multiple quotation marks omitted).

180. *Zizzo*, 120 F.3d at 1353 (citation omitted). "A statement is made in furtherance of a conspiracy if it was intended to promote conspiratorial objectives; it need not actually further the conspiracy." United States v. Salgado, 250 F.3d 438, 449 (6th Cir. 2001). Additional examples of statements made in furtherance of the conspiracy can be found in the following: United States v. Aviles-Colon, 536 F.3d 1, 15, 16 (1st Cir. 2008) ("informing coconspirators of the activities of the conspiracy's members"; attempting to kill a member of a rival conspiracy); United States v. Rodriguez, 525 F.3d 85, 101 (1st Cir. 2008) (coconspirators explaining to others the defendant's role in the local drug marketplace "were in essence ... steering business toward [defendant] and advancing the objective of the drug ring"); United States v. Schalk, 515 F.3d 768 (7th Cir. 2008) (discussing "sup-

One oft-cited case discusses the "in furtherance" question as follows: Such statements can include "statements made to recruit potential coconspirators, statements seeking to control damage to an ongoing conspiracy, statements made to keep coconspirators advised as to the progress of the conspiracy, and statements made in an attempt to conceal the criminal objectives of the conspiracy. Narrative declarations, mere 'idle chatter,' and superfluous casual conversations, however, are not [included]."[181]

---

ply, demand, transportation, and finances," *id.* at 775; "Documents that [are] 'tools of the drug trade,'" *id.* at 777); United States v. Thompson, 449 F.3d 267, 273 (1st Cir. 2006) (statement that two coconspirators "no longer intended to deal directly with one another"); United States v. Gardner, 447 F.3d 558, 560 (8th Cir. 2006) (statements "concerning their distribution of drugs or their efforts to recruit other conspirators"); *Payne,* 437 F.3d at 546 (concealing ongoing conspiracy); United States v. Miles, 290 F.3d 1341, 1351 (11th Cir. 2002) (recruiting new members and explaining the conspiracy to them; statements need "only further the interests of the conspiracy in some way."); United States v. Phillips, 219 F.3d 404, 420 (5th Cir. 2000) (conspirator's "attempt[] to explain to her daughter the nature of the conspiracy in an effort to exact sympathy so that the scheme could remain a secret ..."); United States v. Bowman, 215 F.3d 951, 960–61 (9th Cir. 2000) (statement made to keep coconspirator informed, enlist her help, and enable her to help conduct the conspiracy and evade capture); United States v. Curry, 187 F.3d 762, 766 (7th Cir. 1999) ("recruiting statements"); United States v. Cordova, 157 F.3d 587, 598 (8th Cir. 1998) ("'in furtherance'... broadly construed ..."); United States v. Shores, 33 F.3d 438, 443 (4th Cir. 1994) (statement intended to promote, whether it succeeds or not) (citing numerous cases). Regarding statements such as those made "to recruit potential coconspirators," remember that this is not the only foundational element. In addition, for example, the statement must have been made in the course of a conspiracy, raising the question When did the conspiracy actually begin? *See* foundational element number three, above.

Examples of statements that were not made in furtherance of the conspiracy can be found in the following: United States v. Cazares, 521 F.3d 991, 999 (8th Cir. 2008) (though "'in furtherance of the conspiracy' [is interpreted] broadly, 'a statement that simply informs the listener of the declarant's criminal activities is not made in furtherance of the conspiracy.'") (citations omitted); United States v. Williams, 272 F.3d 845, 860 (7th Cir. 2001) (conspirator's "admissions to law enforcement that the money was 'drug money'"); *Salgado,* 250 F.3d 449 ("Mere 'idle chatter' or conversations which further the speaker's own individual objectives rather than the objective of the conspiracy are not made in furtherance of the conspiracy.").

181. United States v. Doerr, 886 F.2d 944, 951 (7th Cir. 1989) (citation omitted). *See also* cases cited in the preceding footnote.

f. Statements Made before the Coconspirator on Trial Entered into the Conspiracy

The definitional exclusion for coconspirator statements applies to statements made by the conspirators before the party at trial—the party against whom the statement is offered—entered into the conspiracy. "[A] late-joining conspirator takes the conspiracy as he finds it."[182]

g. Statements Made while Covering-Up the Crime

Some statements made while covering up the conspiracy will fit under this exclusion? In this context, there are three kinds of cover-ups. First, there is the cover-up or concealment of the conspiracy that occurs while the conspiracy is ongoing. Where the concealment is in furtherance of the conspiracy, this definitional exclusion applies just as it would to any other part of the conspiracy.[183]

Second, there is the cover-up that was included in the original plans for the conspiracy. The initial crime and the post-crime cover-up may each be a piece of the same conspiracy. Here, any statement from the outset to the completion of the cover-up is a statement made during the existence of the conspiracy.[184]

Third, there is the cover-up that occurs after the central purposes of the conspiracy have either failed or been achieved and that was not part of the

---

182. United States v. Goldberg, 105 F.3d 770, 775 (1st Cir. 1997) ("[I]nsofar as hearsay is concerned[,] a late-joining conspirator takes the conspiracy as he finds it."). *Accord* United States v. Seguro-Gallegos, 41 F.3d 1266 (9th Cir. 1994) (citing cases) (such statements not admissible to show defendant's participation in conspiracy).

183. *E.g., Payne*, 437 F.3d at 546 ("Statements designed to conceal an ongoing conspiracy are made in furtherance of the conspiracy for purposes of Rule 801(d)(2)(E)."); United States v. DiDomenico, 78 F.3d 294, 303–04 (7th Cir. 1996) (statements designed to prevent conspiracy from collapsing are made in furtherance of the conspiracy, but not statements designed to cover-up finished conspiracy); United States v. Pecora, 798 F.2d 614, 630–31 (3d Cir. 1986).

184. Grunewald v. United States, 353 U.S. 391, 404 (1957) (where there is "an express original agreement among the conspirators to continue to act in concert in order to cover up, for their own self-protection, traces of the crime after its commission," this exclusion applies to the cover-up just as it would to any other part of the conspiracy; the question here concerned when the conspiracy ended for purposes of application of statute of limitations rather than hearsay rule); Blecha v. People, 962 P.2d 931, 938 (Colo. 1998). *See also,* Lutwak v. United States, 344 U.S. 604, 616 (1953) (no evidence the conspiracy included an agreement to conceal it after it was otherwise completed).

original conspiracy agreement. Under the federal rules statements made in furtherance of this kind of cover-up only fit under this exclusion when offered against coconspirators in the new and separate cover-up conspiracy.[185] A conspiracy to cover-up is not presumed. There must be evidence of each foundational element of the exclusion.[186]

There is some authority for the proposition that statements made in furtherance of a second conspiracy—perhaps a conspiracy to cover-up a previous conspiracy—will not fit under this exclusion when the only crime charged is the first conspiracy. These courts hold that in order for evidence of the second conspiracy to be admissible under this exclusion it must be part of the crime charged.[187] This seems unwarrantedly narrow. None of the other ex-

---

185. *Payne*, 437 F.3d at 547 n.4 ("It is crucial that the conspiracy be ongoing, as 'statements regarding concealment that are made after the objects of the conspiracy have been completed are not made in furtherance of the conspiracy.'") (quoting United States v. Martinez, 430 F.3d 317, 327 (6th Cir. 2005) (citing Krulewitch v. United States, 336 U.S. 440 (1949)); United States v. Shores, 33 F.3d 438, 443 (4th Cir. 1994).

186. *Lutwak*, 344 U.S. 616–17 (conspiracy to cover-up not assumed, but must be evidenced); *Krulewitch*, 336 U.S. at 443–445 (conspiracy to cover-up cannot be implied from original conspiracy); Villafranca v. People, 573 P.2d 540, 542 (Colo. 1978).

This is not the rule in some other jurisdictions. State v. Daniels, 636 N.E.2d 336, 342–43 (Ohio App. 1993) (citations omitted), for example, states:

A conspiracy to commit a crime does not necessarily end with the commission of the crime. For this reason, "a declaration of a conspirator, made subsequent to the actual commission of the crime, may be admissible against any co-conspirator if it was made while the conspirators were still concerned with the concealment of their criminal conduct or their identity."

… The theory for the admission of evidence of the acts and declarations of a co-conspirator made after the crime charged has been committed is that "persons who conspire to commit a crime, and who do commit a crime, are as much concerned, after the crime, with their freedom from apprehension, as they were concerned, before the crime, with its commission; the conspiracy to commit the crime devolves after the commission thereof into a conspiracy to avoid arrest and implication."

This seems to presume a conspiracy to cover-up. *See also* State v. Gondor, No. 90-P-2260, 1992 Ohio App. Lexis 6219, *17 (1992) (unpublished opinion) (exclusion applies to statements "made 'during the course and in furtherance of the conspiracy' or the coverup which follows").

187. This exclusion's "dependence on agency principles makes the scope of the conspiracy critical. [A conspiracy] and a conspiracy to conceal an earlier, completed conspiracy, are two different conspiracies, like two different firms, and statements made in furtherance of the second, the cover-up conspiracy, are therefore not admissible in evidence to demonstrate participation in or the acts of the first conspiracy." *DiDomenico*, 78 F.3d at 303–04.

clusions requires that the statement have been made in connection with the matter on trial. The other admissions do not require that the statement somehow be part of the crime charged. The better view—the view more consistent with the general purposes of the rules and with the way in which the rules generally are interpreted—is that this is a definitional exclusion like all of the others. It has foundational elements. When those foundational elements are present, the exclusion applies. None of the foundational elements for this exclusion has anything to do with the statement being part of the crime charged. Therefore, the rule does not require any such thing. The better view is that,

> the designation of a declaration as non-hearsay under Rule 801(d)(2)(E) is neither count-specific nor conspiracy-specific. Subject to relevancy and similar considerations, out-of-court statements of a declarant co-conspirator, if made during and in furtherance of a conspiracy, are admissible for the truth of the matter asserted, regardless of whether the conspiracy furthered is charged or uncharged, and regardless of whether it is identical to or different from the crime that the statements are offered to prove.[188]

The foundational elements that are stated in the rule must, of course, be shown. For example, the person against whom the statement is offered at trial must have been a member of the conspiracy charged and the one in which the statement was made.[189]

h. Other Ways to Get Coconspirator Statements into Evidence

Do not forget that the Rule 801(d)(2)(e) exclusion is not the only way to get a coconspirator's statement around the hearsay rule. As with all other Rule 801(d) statements, all of the other exclusions and all of the exceptions are on the table. Because a statement was made by a coconspirator does not mean it must stand or fall under the coconspirator exclusion. Here are some examples of other more or less common ways a coconspirator's statement might get around the hearsay rule.

---

188. United States v. Lara, 181 F.3d 183, 196 (1st Cir. 1999) (citations omitted).

189. *See, e.g.,* United States v. Murphy, 193 F.3d 1, 6 (1st Cir. 1999) ("The distinction matters: statements made solely in the course of the former [conspiracy] would not be admissible against Murphy under the co-conspirator exception because (according to the government) Murphy never became a member of that conspiracy.").

There are cases wherein a trial court let a statement in as a coconspirator admission and the appellate court held that was error but not reversible because the statement was admissible under the statement against interest

(a) *Statement against Interest*: One other way around the hearsay rule, which particularly applies to coconspirator statements, is the statement against interest exception. *State v. Helmick*,[190] held that the trial court erred in admitting a statement under the coconspirator exclusion, but the error was not reversible because the statement was admissible under the statement against interest exception.[191]

(b) *Excited Utterance*: *United States v. Vazquez*,[192] held that statements made by a codefendant were not admissible under the coconspiracy exclusion, but were admissible under the excited utterance exception.[193]

(c) *Nonhearsay Statement Offered against Party-Declarant*: In *United States. v. Taylor*,[194] a statement that may not have been admissible as a nonhearsay coconspirator statement was admissible as a nonhearsay personal admission: It was a party's own statement offered against the party.[195]

(d) *Adoptive Admission*: Some out-of-court statements by coconspirators, made in the presence of the party against whom they are offered will be admissible as explicit or implicit adoptive admissions.[196] In *State v. Laws*,[197] a statement was not admissible under the coconspirator's exclusion, because there was no independent evidence—no evidence other than the out-of-court statement itself—that the conspiracy had begun that early. The out-of-court declarant said he knew a way of making money "real easy" by robbing and killing old

---

190. 495 S.E.2d 262 (W. Va. Ct. App. 1997).

191. Fed.R.Evid. 804(b)(3). *See also, e.g.*, United States v. Watson, 525 F.3d 583, 587 (7th Cir. 2008) ("[A] statement that implicates the declarant in a larger conspiracy tends to subject the declarant to criminal liability and thus is a statement against interest … because a member of a conspiracy is liable for any co-conspirator's act committed in furtherance of the conspiracy.");

192. 857 F.2d 857 (1st Cir. 1988).

193. Fed.R.Evid. 803(2).

194. 802 F.2d 1108 (9th Cir. 1986).

195. Fed.R.Evid. 801(d)(2)(A). *See also* Lutwak v. United States, 344 U.S. 604, 618 (1953) (conspirator declarations not in furtherance of conspiracy and, therefore, not admissible against coconspirator, may be admissible against declarant).

196. Fed.R.Evid. 801(d)(2)(B). *See, e.g.*, State v. Opsahl, 513 N.W.2d 249, 254 (Minn. 1994) (certain conversations in presence of defendant need not be admitted under coconspiracy exclusion because properly admitted as adoptive admissions; court incorrectly labeled the exclusion as an exception).

197. 668 S.W.2d 234 (Mo. Ct. App. 1984).

people. The defendant agreed to participate. By agreeing to participate, he explicitly adopted the out-of-court declarant's admission. The out-of-court statement was admissible as an explicit adoptive admission.[198]

(e) *Context Evidence*: In *United States v. Zizzo*,[199] out-of-court statements by a former member of a conspiracy were admitted as "context" evidence. The former conspirator, Rainone, became a cooperating government witness. While cooperating, he had conversations with other members of the conspiracy. The government attempted to introduce these conversations: what Rainone said and what the other parties to the conversations said. The statements by the other parties to the conversations were admissible nonhearsay admissions by coconspirators.[200] Rainone's statements were admissible, nonhearsay "context" evidence: "[They] were not admitted for their truth but rather to give context to the conspirators' ends of the conversations."[201]

i. *Using the Text of the Statement Itself to Prove the Foundational Elements*

The rule is quite clear on this point: Two of the foundational elements cannot be established using the out-of-court statement itself. To prove the existence of a conspiracy or participation therein by the out-of-court declarant and the party against whom the statement is offered, the contents of the out-of-court statement "shall be considered." The statement alone, however, is not enough to establish either of these two foundational elements.[202]

---

198. *Id.* at 239. *State v. Laws* is also discussed at part III(F)(3)(j) of this chapter, below. Rule 801(d)(2)(B) is discussed at Chapter 2(III)(E), above. It seems that this statement should also have been admissible under the coconspirator's-statement definitional exclusion. This aspect of this case is discussed elsewhere in this Use Note, above.

199. 120 F.3d 1338 (7th Cir. 1997).

200. The other parties to the conversations were not parties to this action. They were unindicted coconspirators. Their statements — their parts of the conversations — were admitted under the definitional exclusion for coconspirators' statements. The court erroneously labeled this exclusion as an exception. *Id.* at 1348.

201. *Id.* at 1348. The trial court gave a limiting instruction that the members of the jury were not to use Rainone's statements to prove the truth of any matter they asserted. *Id.*

202. FED.R.EVID. 801(d)(2). This is an amendment to Rule 801(d)(2) that will not be found in older publications of the rules. It applies to trials commencing after December 1, 1997. *But see* United States v. Engler, 521 F.3d 965, 973 (8th Cir. 2008) ("The very content of the text messages establishes by a preponderance of the evidence that the sender was a coconspirator.");

In *State v. Laws*,[203] there is an interesting application of this aspect of the rule. It involves the statement that begins the conspiracy. In front of the defendant and the testifying witness, the out-of-court declarant said that he knew a way of making money "real easy" by robbing and killing old people. The court stated that though there was plenty of subsequent evidence of a conspiracy, this out-of-court statement was the only evidence that the conspiracy existed at this particular time. The statement that began the conspiracy is the only evidence that it began this early, and the statement itself is not enough to establish this definitional exclusion.[204] The court went on, however, to find that because the defendant agreed to go along with the scheme, he explicitly adopted the out-of-court declaration and it was admissible as a nonhearsay adoptive admission.[205]

The *Laws* case seems overly restrictive. The rule requires is some independent evidence of a conspiracy and the party's participation. There was plenty of other evidence of both. There is no rule requiring that corroborating evidence preexist the statement. The fact that the evidence post-dates the making of the statement in question does not mean it cannot corroborate the existence of the conspiracy and the defendant's participation therein as of the time that statement was made. Also, if the defendant adopted the out-of-court statement by going along with the scheme, as *Laws* said he did, isn't that enough independent evidence? The out-of-court statement itself shall be considered, says the rule, when deciding whether there was a conspiracy, but the out of court statement alone is not enough. But surely the out-of-court statement followed by the defendant agreeing to go along is enough.

j. The Substantive Law of Conspiracy versus the Law of Evidence

The substantive law of criminal conspiracy has no application to this evidentiary rule of hearsay exclusion. The fact that the out-of-court declarant is not named as a defendant does not bar the use of this hearsay exclusion.[206] The fact a con-

---

203. 668 S.W.2d 234 (Mo. Ct. App. 1984). *State v. Laws* is also discussed at part III(F)(3)(g) of this chapter, above.

204. *Id.* at 238–39. Though this court did not allow this conspiracy-beginning declaration to establish the foundation for its own admission, it did allow this same statement to be used to establish the foundation for the admission for coconspirator statements made later. *Id.* at 239.

205. *Id.* The rule regarding nonhearsay adoptive admissions is Rule 801(d)(2)(B), discussed at Chapter 2(III)(E), above.

206. *E.g.*, United States v. Nixon, 418 U.S. 683, 701 (1974); Champagne Metals v. Ken-Mac Metals, Inc, 458 F.3d 1073, 1081 n.5 (10th Cir. 2006); State v. Tonelli, 749 N.W.2d 689, 691–92 (Iowa 2008).

spiracy has not been charged does not bar the use of this exclusion.[207] The fact that a conpspiracy cannot be charged—perhaps, for example, because the statute of limitations has run—does not bar the use of this exclusion.[208] Just like all of the other exclusions and exceptions, this exclusion has certain foundational elements and, when each is present, the statement is not hearsay.

k. Civil Conspiracies

Though most of the coconspirator-statement cases are criminal, this exclusion applies to civil conspiracies as well as criminal.[209]

l. Conditional Admission, Subject to a Motion to Strike

One other important point about the coconspirator exclusion is that it may be conditionally admitted by the court, subject to a later motion to strike.[210] This is the case throughout the law of evidence, but it seems to happen sufficiently frequently here so as to warrant pointing it out here.

m. Exclusions versus Exceptions

This rule regarding coconspirator statements is an exclusion from the definition of hearsay. It is not an exception to the hearsay rule. As discussed elsewhere, there may be a difference.[211]

---

207. Senate Comm. On Judiciary, Fed. Rules of Evidence, S.Rep. No. 1277, 93d Cong., 2d Sess., p. 26 (1974); 1974 U.S. Code Cong. & Admin. News 7051, 7073 ("While the rule refers to a coconspirator, it ... is meant to carry forward the universally accepted doctrine that a joint venturer is considered as a coconspirator for the purposes of this rule even though no conspiracy has been charged.").

208. State v. Jones, 873 P.2d 122, 130–31 (Idaho 1993) (citing cases). "'[I]t makes no difference whether the declarant or any other partner in crime could actually be tried, convicted and punished for the crime of conspiracy.'" Id. at 131 (quoting United States v. Gil, 604 F.2d 546, 549 (7th Cir. 1979)).

209. Tonelli, 749 N.W.2d at 692 ("The teaching of cases from other jurisdictions and legal commentators is that the rule of evidence regarding statements of coconspirators applies in civil as well as criminal settings.") (citing cases and commentators).

210. E.g., United States v. Aviles-Colon, 536 F.3d 1, 14, (1st Cir. 2008); United States v. Urena, 27 F.3d 1487 (10th Cir. 1994); United States v. Tracy, 12 F.3d 1186 (2d Cir. 1993). This happens when evidence of one or more of the foundational elements will not be introduced until after the statement is offered.

211. See Chapter 2(I), above.

n. The General Use Note

In addition to this Use Note, also see the General Use Note, above,[212] which is applicable to all of the admissions.

G. Rule 801(d)(2) Admissions Need Not Be Based on Personal Knowledge[213]

As a general rule, if there are multiple layers of hearsay behind an out-of-court statement, then for the final out-of-court statement to be admissible there must be an exclusion or an exception for each of the underlying hearsay statements upon which the final statement is based. There are a number of cases that hold that this is not the case when the final out-of-court statement is a Rule 801(d)(2) admission.[214] To the hearsay rule, it does not matter whether the persons making admissions are describing events they personally witnessed or simply passing on things they were told by someone else. If the final out-

---

212. *See* Chapter 2(III)(A), above.

213. For discussion of and cross-reference to other discussions of personal knowledge and the hearsay rule, *see* Chapter 13, below. *See also* Chapter 11.

214. Mahlandt v. Wild Canid Survival & Research Ctr., Inc., 588 F.2d 626, 630–31 (8th Cir. 1978), is one of the premiere cases taking this position—one of the first and one of the best. It is discussed in a number of places in this book. *See particularly* Chapter 13(II)(A). *Accord, e.g.,* Grace United Methodist Church v. City of Cheyenne, 451 F.3d 643, 667 (10th Cir. 2005) ("[A]n admission of a party opponent may be introduced in evidence even though the declarant lacked personal knowledge of the matter asserted."); Lexington Ins. Co. v. Western Pa. Hosp., 423 F.3d 318, 330 n.7 (3d Cir. 2005) ("Although we do not know how this employee gathered the information … or whether he or she had personal knowledge supporting the information, these are not requirements for admissibility [of admissions by agents].") (citation omitted); Sea Land Serv., Inc. v. Lozen Int'l, LLC, 285 F.3d 808, 821 (9th Cir. 2002) (a statement adopted by an employee of a party and concerning a matter within the scope of her employment becomes a nonhearsay admission by an employee); United States v. Saccoccia, 58 F.3d 754, 782 (1st Cir. 1995) (coconspirator admissions are admissible "without a showing of personal knowledge"); United States v. Goins, 11 F.3d 441, 444 (4th Cir. 1993) (citing cases); Brookover v. Mary Hitchcock Mem'l Hosp., 893 F.2d 411, 418 (1st Cir. 1990) (citing cases and discussing the issue); Donlin v. Aramark Corp., 162 F.R.D. 149, 150 (D. Utah 1995); Grace v. Keystone Shipping Co., 805 F.Supp. 436, 443–44 (E.D. Tex. 1992); Ruszcyk v. Secretary of Pub. Safety, 517 N.E.2d 152, 155 (Mass. 1988) ("Rule 403, rather than … Rule 801(d)(2)(D), is the appropriate vehicle for consideration of the firsthand knowledge issue.") (citing cases); State v. Worthen, 765 P.2d 839, 848 (Utah 1988); Rutherford v. State, 605 P.2d 16, 24–25 (Alaska 1979) ("the majority view …"); Metropolitan Dade County v. Yearby, 580 So.2d 186, 189 (Fla. App. 1991) (calling this "the clear majority rule throughout the country" and citing cases).

of-court statement is a Rule 801(d)(2) admission of fact, then, even if the out-of-court declarant did not have personal knowledge of the fact admitted, the statement is not barred by the hearsay rule.

Let us say that there is a chain of five out-of-court statements: unknown declarant makes a statement to a passerby (no. 1) about a nearby delivery truck; passerby repeats the statement to a police officer (no. 2); the police officer repeats it to a newspaper reporter (no. 3); the reporter tells to a vice president of the company whose truck it is (no. 4), a vice president whose duties include overseeing the fleet of deliver trucks; the vice president tells someone in his regular golf foursome (no. 5). The company that owns the truck is the defendant. The testifying witness is the vice president's friend from the foursome. The friend has been called to testify against the defendant company. The friend is asked to tell the court what the vice president said to him about the accident and the testimony is offered to prove the truth of the factual assertions in the vice president's statement. The *final* out-of-court statement (no. 5) in this chain of declarations is a Rule 801(d)(2) admission. For purposes of the hearsay rule the fact that the *final*[215] out-of-court statement is an 801(d)(2) admission means that it is irrelevant that the vice president did not have personal knowledge of the facts asserted in his statement. That means that there are no multiple hearsay problems, that Rule 805[216] does not apply here, and that insofar as the hearsay rule is concerned we need not look behind the last statement in this chain—the admission. We do not need to concern ourselves with the fact that statements 1 through 4 were also hearsay.

This scenario really raises three separate questions. Many courts have trouble with this issue because they do not separate out the three questions. Many

---

215. The word "final" is italicized twice in this paragraph from the main text to highlight the fact that the 801(d)(2) admission must be the final out-of-court declaration in the chain. An admission cures preceding levels of hearsay but it does not cure succeeding levels. Let me add a fifth level of out-of-court statement to the delivery truck scenario from the text. The vice president of the company goes home and tells (no. 4) his wife and the next day his wife tells (no. 5) a member of her golf foursome. The friend from the wife's foursome is the testifying witness. The statement from the vice president to his wife cures preceding levels of hearsay but it does not cure the succeeding level; it does not cure out-of-court statement no. 5; the wife to her friend is still hearsay and, unless an exception can be found for that statement this evidence is inadmissible hearsay. *See, e.g.,* Bennett v. Saint-Gobain Corp., 507 F.3d 23, 28–29 (1st Cir. 2007); Burns v. Board of County Comm'rs of Jackson County, 330 F.3d 1275, 1284 n.5 (10th Cir. 2003).

216. "Hearsay within hearsay is not excluded under the hearsay rule if each part of the combined statements conforms with an exception to the hearsay rule provided in these rules." FED.R.EVID. 805. Regarding multiple levels of hearsay, *see* particularly Chapter 11, below.

lawyers get into trouble because they fail to make all three objections. One question is whether Rule 805, the double hearsay rule applies: "Hearsay within hearsay is not excluded under the hearsay rule if each part of the combined statements conforms with an exception to the hearsay rule provided in these rules."[217] A second question is whether Rule 602, the personal knowledge rule applies: "A witness may not testify to a matter unless evidence is introduced sufficient to support a finding that the witness has personal knowledge of the matter."[218] The third question is whether Rule 403 keeps the evidence out—whether the probative value of the evidence is substantially outweighed by the danger of unfair prejudice. The relationship between admissions and personal knowledge cannot be understood without dealing with each of these rules.

One's initial reaction to the testimony of the golfing buddy may be that this testimony is not admissible. From there, it is easy to jump to the conclusion that it is inadmissible hearsay, for hearsay is what it looks most like. It might well be that this initial reaction is right, but that the hearsay rule is not the reason the statement is inadmissible. It may be that it is Rule 602 (lack of personal knowledge) or Rule 403 (very low probative value and very high danger of unfair prejudice) that keeps it out.

There are three objections to be made: Rule 805, double hearsay; Rule 602, lack of personal knowledge; and Rule 403, the probative value of the evidence is substantially outweighed by the danger of unfair prejudice. These are separate objections. Making one of these objections is not enough to raise and preserve all three issues. A hearsay objection, for example, is not enough to preserve either a personal knowledge or a 403 problem for appeal. To preserve all three issues, an attorney must make all three objections.[219]

1. Rule 805 and Double Hearsay

When an admission is the final statement in a chain of hearsay statements, there is no Rule 805 multiple-level hearsay problem. An admission cures all underlying or preceding levels of hearsay. The reason is that the admission of fact adopts all of the statements that preceded it. This was discussed above, with the discussion of adoptive admissions.[220] One example given there involved the death of Dr. Shepard's wife. To recap, Mrs. Shepard's nurse says to

---

217. FED.R.EVID. 805.

218. FED.R.EVID. 602.

219. *See* FED.R.EVID. 103(a)(1) (to preserve an objection for appeal, counsel must state the specific grounds of the objection).

220. This discussion is at part III(E)(3)(c) of this chapter, above.

Dr. Shepard, "You killed Mrs. Shepard." The doctor replies, "Yes, I did." This was overheard by a third party who is testifying against Dr. Shepard at his trial for the murder of his wife. Dr. Shepard's statement is a personal admission—his own statement offered against him—and is not hearsay. He explicitly adopted the nurse's statement, "You killed Mrs. Shepard," and is not hearsay either.

That is the traditional way to look at this particular adoptive admission problem. The other way of looking at it—the way that shows why Rule 805 does not apply here—recognizes that "Yes I did" is not hearsay because it is a personal admission and "You killed Mrs. Shepard" is not hearsay either because it is not offered to prove the truth of the matter asserted. It is only offered because it gives content to, supplies the meaning of, Dr. Shepard's admission. When Dr. Shepard adopted the nurse's statement, the nurse's statement became his. The only person whose credibility we care about is Dr. Shepard.

Once we take the nurse's statement "You killed Mrs. Shepard" and use it only to give meaning to Dr. Shepard's response, then the nurse falls out of the picture. The only statement we care about is Dr. Shepard's. It does not matter whether we believe the nurse was telling the truth or had personal knowledge. We do not care if she was making a wild guess. All we care about is whether we believe Dr. Shepard when he said "Yes I did (kill Mrs. Shepard)."[221] We do not offer the nurse's statement to prove the truth of the fact it asserts; we offer the doctor's reply to prove the truth. There is no double hearsay problem. The adoptive admission turns what a nonparty has said into a nonhearsay admission by a party. There is only one out-of-court de-

---

221. *See* United States v. Jinadu, 98 F.3d 239, 245 (6th Cir. 1996) ("'If the defendant accepts the out-of-court statement as his own, cross-examination of the declarant ... becomes unnecessary and irrelevant.'"); Lee v. McCaughtry, 892 F.2d 1318, 1324 (7th Cir. 1990); United States v. Jordan 810 F.2d 262, 264 (D.C. Cir. 1987); State v. Gano, 988 P.2d 1153, 1162 (Haw. 1999) ("'The party becomes the declarant, and the statement of the other person becomes the party's.'" (quoting State v. Carlson, 808 P.2d 1002, 1005–06 (Or. 1991)); State v. Cotten, 879 P.2d 971, 983 (Wash. 1994) ("An adoptive admission is attributed to the defendant and becomes the defendant's own words.")); State v. Hoffman, 828 P.2d 805, 809 (Haw. 1992) (the out-of-court "statements are admissible because they lay the foundation to show what the defendant acquiesced or admitted to by adoption."); United States v. Finley, 708 F.Supp. 906, 911 (N.D. Ill. 1989) ("The declarant of an adoptive admission is the one who adopts it as his own statement[.]"); People v. Silva, 754 P.2d 1070, 1080 (Cal. 1988) ("[O]nce the defendant has expressly or impliedly adopted the statements of another, the statements become *his own* admissions ... Being deemed the defendant's own admissions, we are no longer concerned with the veracity or credibility of the original declarant.").

clarant of concern. The whole point of the adoptive admission exclusion is that it takes a non-party's out-of-court statement and turns it into a party's admission.

This analysis is exactly the same even if the nurse did not have personal knowledge of who killed Mrs. Shepard, or even how she died. The analysis is no different if there was a chain of two, three, or ten out-of-court declarants who relayed the information until it finally reached the nurse.

And the analysis is no different if Dr. Shepard made a silent admission, said "Yes I did" or said "Yes, I killed my wife." His assertion is an admission—either an implicit or explicit adoptive admission or a personal admission—and the statements preceding it in the chain do not matter to the hearsay rule.

The admission cures preceding levels of hearsay—and Rule 805's general requirements regarding layered hearsay does not apply—when the out-of-court admission is the final link in the hearsay chain and when it admits a relevant fact—that is, the statement does not just admit that someone told me something about a relevant fact; it admits the truth of the relevant fact itself. Consider, once again, the *Mahlandt* case.[222]

The issue is whether Sophie the wolf bit a child. Whether the out-of-court admission is the final link in the chain is the difference between the witness testifying, "I heard Mr. Poos say 'Sophie bit a child,'" on the one hand, and the witness testifying "My neighbor told me that he heard Mr. Poos say 'Sophie bit a child,'" on the other. When the witness testifies, "I heard Mr. Poos say 'Sophie bit a child,'" the witness is testifying to Poos' own statement. Here, Poos' own statement is the final link in the chain of hearsay. The testifying witness has firsthand knowledge of the admission. The testifying witness is a real witness to the admission. When, however, the witness testifies, "My neighbor told me that he heard Mr. Poos say 'Sophie bit a child,'" the witness is not testifying to Poos's own statement. The admission is not the final link in the chain of hearsay. Whether the admission was made is dependent upon a subsequent out-of-court statement. The testifying witness is not a real witness to the admission, but only to the fact that someone said there had been an admission. The admission only cures layers of hearsay that precede the admission.

Additionally, the admission must admit a relevant fact. This is the difference between the witness testifying, "Mr. Poos said, 'Sophie bit a child'" and testifying "Mr. Poos said, 'Someone told me that Sophie bit a child.'" In the first statement, Poos adopted the truth of the wolf bite. In the second statement, Poos

---

222. *See* the discussion of the *Mahlandt* case in part III(E)(3)(c) of this chapter, above.

did not adopt the truth of the wolf bite, but only the truth that someone else told him it happened.[223]

Admissions of fact cure all preceding levels of hearsay[224] because, in the end, there is only one declarant, and that is the party making the admission. There are not multiple levels of statements, just one. There are not multiple levels of declarants, just one. There are not multiple levels of hearsay: In fact, since the final statement is excluded from the hearsay rule as an admission, there is not even one level of hearsay.

2. Rule 602 and Personal Knowledge

Rule 805 is not a problem, but what about Rule 602? Does it require that the proponent of an admission show that the person making the admission had personal knowledge of the matter admitted? First, the fact that the double hearsay rule does not apply to admissions does not mean that the rule requiring personal knowledge does not apply either. The hearsay objection and the lack of personal knowledge objection are two separate objections, based on two separate rules, and each must be considered separately. Making one of these two objections is not enough to raise or preserve both issues. A hearsay objection (or a multiple hearsay objection) is not a "specific" objection[225] for purposes of raising the issue of lack of personal knowledge,[226] and vice versa.

So, what about admissions and Rule 602? To better stake out the field to which the question applies, let us assume for a moment that Rule 602 does

---

223. *Accord, e.g.,* Schering Corp. v. Pfizer Inc. 189 F.3d 218, 239 (2d Cir. 1999) ("a party admission containing hearsay is admissible where ... the admission draws inferences from the underlying hearsay and thus 'manifests an adoption or belief in its truth.' A party admission may, however, be inadmissible when it merely repeats hearsay and thus fails to concede its underlying trustworthiness.") (citation to rule omitted); Pittman v. Grayson, 149 F.3d 111, 124 (2d Cir. 1998) (the declarant, a party's agent, made an admission of fact and immediately said she did not have personal knowledge but was just repeating what she had been told; inadmissible because of the level of hearsay behind the agent's statement).

224. Some courts take a contrary position. *See, e.g.,* footnote 135, above.

225. Absent plain error, appellant cannot complain that evidence was erroneously admitted unless appellant lodged a specific objection with the trial court. Fed.R.Evid. 103(a)(1).

226. United States v. Nnanyererugo, 39 F.3d 1205, 1208 (D.C. Cir. 1994) ("[A]ppellant's contemporaneous hearsay objection at trial was insufficient to constitute an objection based on the witness' personal knowledge. These objections are denominated separately in the Federal Rules of Evidence, see FED. R. EVID. 602 (personal knowledge); FED. R. EVID. 801 et seq. (hearsay).... We do not think that every hearsay objection ... logically implies an objection based on lack of personal knowledge ...").

apply to admissions, and it requires that the person making the admission have personal knowledge of the matter admitted. If that is so, then it is reasonable to apply a presumption that the person making an admission of fact does have personal knowledge of the fact admitted. If the admission is "Yes I did (kill Mrs. Shepard)" it is reasonable to presume that Dr. Shepard had personal knowledge of the fact admitted, *i.e.*, that he did kill Mrs. Shepard.

Change the illustration to fit the facts of *Mahlandt v. Wild Canid Survival & Research Center, Inc.*[227] *Mahlandt* involved an alleged mauling of a child by a wolf named "Sophie." Kenneth Poos, who was both a defendant and an agent of another defendant, made this out-of-court statement: "Sophie bit a child."[228] Where the admission is "Sophie bit a child" it is reasonable to presume that Mr. Poos had personal knowledge of the fact admitted, *i.e.*, that Sophie bit a child. (On the other hand, if the out-of-court statement is "I heard that Sophie bit a child," then it is not reasonable to presume that he has personal knowledge of the bite, but only reasonable to presume that he has personal knowledge of a hearsay statement.) If Sophie's owner or caretaker states that "Sophie bit a child," we can presume from that very statement that the owner or caretaker had sufficient personal knowledge. Traditional interpretations of Rule 602 and traditional hearsay both support engaging this presumption.[229]

Where are we so far? First, regarding Rule 805, double hearsay is not a problem when the admission is an admission of fact and is the final statement in

---

227. 588 F.2d 626 (8th Cir. 1978). This case is also discussed at Chapter 13(II)(A).

228. The Eighth Circuit held that the hearsay-within-hearsay rule from Rule 805 does not require looking behind a party's out-of-court admission of fact. The court does not have to inquire into how Poos knew: whether he had personal knowledge or someone told him is irrelevant. The Eighth Circuit held that an admission cures preceding levels of hearsay and allowed the statement as against Poos under Rule 801(d)(2)(A) (personal admission), and as against his employer under Rule 801(d)(2)(D) (admission by an agent). We need not know where Poos got his information or how he came to his particular conclusion. If his statement was based on what he was told by someone else, we need not find an exception to the hearsay rule for the underlying first-level of hearsay. According to *Mahlandt*, hearsay analysis starts from the point where Poos made his admission.

229. Regarding Rule 602, see Chapter 13(I)(A), below. Regarding hearsay theory, some of the statements fitting under these definitional exclusions will, when they were made, have been statements against the interest of the out-of-court declarant. Not all of them, but enough of them to engage the presumption. Sometimes they are directly against the interest of the declarant; sometimes they are against the interest of the declarant's employer or principal and, thereby, against the declarant's interest in continued employment. Traditional hearsay theory holds that we tend not to make statements against our interest unless we know what we are talking about, unless we have all of the firsthand knowledge we feel we need. *See* Chapter 4(IV)(C)(2).

the chain of statements. Second, regarding Rule 602, we can presume that the party making the admission has personal knowledge. That leaves us with this question: When there is evidence that the person who made the alleged admission did not have personal knowledge, is there any way to get around Rule 602's requirement that all witnesses have personal knowledge of the matters about which they testify?[230]

The cases holding that there is no firsthand knowledge requirement for admissions generally support their conclusion in two ways: they note that there is no firsthand knowledge requirement written into the rule; and they nod to the advisory committee's note to Rule 801(d)(2).[231]

■ The statement that there is no firsthand knowledge requirement *written into* the rule is of course correct, but it begs the question. None of the exclusions or exceptions specifically mentions a firsthand knowledge requirement, and yet others require that an out-of-court declarant stating a fact have personal knowledge of the fact. The requirement that witnesses have firsthand knowledge is, however, written into Rule 602. It is stated there as a rule of general application, a requirement attached to all witnesses.[232] And the statement that out-of-court declarants are in effect witnesses is written into the very beginning of the legislative history of Rule 806.[233] Likewise, on the face of Rule 801(d)(2) there is no limitation on the use of seriously and unfairly prejudicial evidence of low probative value. There isn't even any requirement written

---

230. State v. Morant, 701 A.2d 1, 8 (Conn. 1997) ("Rule 601 'reflects a strong presumption in favor of witness competency.' Borawick v. Shay, 68 F.3d 597, 601 (2d Cir. 1995); United States v. Khoury, 901 F.2d 948, 966 (11th Cir. 1990); United States v. Bloome, 773 F.Supp. 545, 546 (E.D.N.Y. 1991)"). Rule 601 states that "[e]very person is competent to be a witness except as otherwise provided in these rules." Rule 602 qualifies that general rule. Rule 602 is part of the "except as otherwise provided." It "otherwise provide[s]" that witnesses must be shown to have personal knowledge. The advisory committee's note to Rule 806 makes it clear that "[t]he declarant of a hearsay statement which is admitted in evidence is in effect a witness." As does the advisory committee's note to Rule 803: "In a hearsay situation, the [out-of-court] declarant is, of course, a witness, and neither this rule nor Rule 804 dispenses with the requirement of firsthand knowledge.... See Rule 602." Therefore the personal knowledge rule from Rule 602 applies to the out-of-court declarant.

231. For example: "We are impressed by the fact that there is no requirement of personal knowledge in the Rule. The Notes of the Advisory Committee are a strong indication that such a requirement was knowingly and purposefully omitted." Brookover v. Mary Hitchcock Memorial Hosp., 893 F.2d 411, 417 (1st Cir. 1990).

232. "A witness may not testify to a matter unless evidence is introduced sufficient to support a finding that the witness has personal knowledge of the matter." FED.R.EVID. 602.

233. "The declarant of a hearsay statement which is admitted in evidence is in effect a witness." FED.R.EVID. 806 advisory committee's note.

into the rule that the out-of-court statement be relevant. But no one argues that those rules do not apply to 801(d)(2) admissions.

Regarding what is or is not written into the rule, the proper way of looking at this would be to say these two things: (1) There is nothing written into Rule 801(d)(2) that excuses it from the general rule requiring personal knowledge. (2) There is nothing written into Rule 602 that creates an admissions exception to the personal knowledge requirement.[234]

■ The statement that the advisory committee's note strongly indicates "that [the personal knowledge] requirement was knowingly and purposefully omitted"[235] is also incorrect. What the advisory committee's note states is this: "The

---

234. There is no limitation on the use of expert-opinion evidence (*see* FED.R.EVID. 701, *et seq.*) written into Rule 801(d)(2) either, and no limitation on the use of character evidence (*see* FED.R.EVID. 404, 405, 608, and 609), and there is nothing in Rule 801(d)(2) that requires that the out-of-court statements be relevant (*see* FED.R.EVID. 401, *et seq.*), but all of these limitations apply to Rule 801(d)(2) admissions.

One more argument that will not work here is the one that says we can excuse 801(d) "admissions" from the requirement that declarants have personal knowledge because declarants do not make statements that they know to be against their interest unless they are satisfied they have all of the personal knowledge they need and the statements are true. The problem with this argument is at least two-fold. First, Rule 801(d) admissions are not really admissions in the sense that the declarant is admitting something against his or her interest. There is no requirement that Rule 801(d)(2) statements be against the declarant's interest. An 801(d)(2) admission can be solidly in the best interest of the declarant as of the time the statement was made. (The statement against interest exception in Rule 804 requires that the out-of-court statement be against the declarant's interest at the time it was made and that the out-of-court declarant knew it was against his or her interest, and yet we do not exempt statements against interest from the general requirement that the declarant had personal knowledge. *E.g.*, United States v. Lang, 589 F.2d 92, 97–98 (2d Cir. 1978).)

The second argument is this. Even if the first argument were meritorious, how would that get around the fact that the statute requires otherwise?

One could also argue that the rules exempt admissions from the personal knowledge requirement "because it is disingenuous for a party to claim that a statement that he himself made is unreliable." United States v. Lindemann, 85 F.3d 1232, 1238 (7th Cir. 1996). Again, two problems: First, not all 801(d)(2) admissions are made by the party against whom they are offered. Second, regarding admissions that are made by the party against whom they are offered, what rule of logic leads from the premise that "it is disingenuous for a party to claim that a statement that he himself made is unreliable" to the conclusion that when a party is a witness, he or she need not have personal knowledge? What rule of statutory construction leads from the premise that "it is disingenuous for a party to claim that a statement that he himself made is unreliable" to the conclusion that somehow this otherwise generally applicable personal-knowledge part of the statute does not apply here?

235. Or, as United States v. Goins, 11 F.3d 441, 444 (4th Cir. 1993) puts it: "The Advisory Committee's Notes to Rule 801(d)(2) ... confirm that the foundational requirements

freedom which admissions have enjoyed from technical demands of searching for an assurance of trustworthiness in some against-interest circumstance, and from the restrictive influences of the opinion rule and the rule requiring first-hand knowledge, when taken with the apparently prevalent satisfaction with the results, calls for generous treatment of this avenue to admissibility."[236] This is a part of a discussion of whether or not admissions are trustworthy and, therefore, should be excluded from the definition of hearsay. It is not a discussion of levels of hearsay underlying an admission. The committee's statement is a recognition of how admissions were treated at common law. Based in part on this recognition, the committee concludes that the common law considered admissions trustworthy.

The committee also states that "generous treatment of this avenue to admissibility" is called for. This is not, however, a statement that Rule 602 does not apply to admissions, any more than it is a statement that Rule 402's requirement that evidence be relevant does not apply to admissions. "Generous treatment" is one thing. Ignoring otherwise applicable rules of evidence is completely another. Otherwise, we might as well conclude that the call for "generous treatment" means that admissions are not subject to the subsequent remedial measures rule,[237] the rules regarding opinion evidence,[238] other-crimes evidence,[239] and privileges.[240] In fact, there is no basis to conclude that 801(d)(2)'s various kinds of admissions are excused from Rule 602's personal knowledge requirement, any more than there is to conclude that they are excused from any of the other rules of evidence. There is no basis for doing so unless one is willing to simply read the common-law into the statute, even though the words of the statute do not support such a reading and, really, neither does the legislative history.

When courts conclude that the advisory committee's notes are a strong indication that the omission of the firsthand knowledge requirement was knowing and purposeful, they are basing their conclusion on a faulty major premise, *i.e.*, that the requirement was omitted. It was not omitted. It is in Rule 602. Had the personal knowledge requirement been omitted, then the note to Rule 602 would be a strong indication that it had been "knowingly and purpose-

---

of Rule 602 do not apply to statements admissible as non-hearsay admissions under Rule 801(d)(2)."

236. Fed.R.Evid. 801(d)(2) advisory committee's note.
237. Fed.R.Evid. 407.
238. Fed.R.Evid. 701–704.
239. Fed.R.Evid. 404, 412–415.
240. Fed.R.Evid. 501.

fully omitted." But that is not the case, and the inference we should draw, based on Rule 602, is this: Since 801(d)(2) is silent on the subject, then the firsthand knowledge requirement "knowingly and purposefully" was not omitted from 801(d)(2). As noted, some jurisdictions have read the personal knowledge requirement out of admissions. Those courts have done so by reading the common law rule into the statute. There is no justification for this in the statute itself.

The double hearsay rule does not apply, but the personal knowledge rule does.[241] That is, the personal knowledge rule applies when the opponent of the evidence can overcome the presumption that the person making the admission did have personal knowledge. Personal knowledge is required of all witnesses. It can be presumed, but a proven lack of personal knowledge cannot be ignored.

3. Rule 403 and Low Probative Value Substantially Outweighed by the Danger of Unfair Prejudice

With the golf-buddy example from above, when you know that you have a statement from an unidentified bystander to a passerby to a police officer to a company vice president to his golfing buddies, the real problem may be that the probative value of the information diminishes each time the statement is passed to another declarant; by the time the statement passes through so many declarants its probative value is quite low.[242] Add the fact that the testifying witness is stating that he was told this by a vice president of the company. That might give the statement a certain gravitas that it does not deserve—it might render it unfairly prejudicial. In the end, the probative value of the evidence may be substantially outweighed by the danger of unfair prejudice. Rule 403

---

241. Gross v. Burggraf Const. Co., 53 F.3d 1531, 1541–43 (10th Cir. 1995) ("Rule 801(d)(2)(A) merely indicates that the a party's own admission is not hearsay. It does not eliminate the requirement of Rule 602 of the Federal Rules of Evidence that '[a] witness may not testify to a matter unless evidence is introduced sufficient to support a finding that the witness has personal knowledge of the matter …'").

242. This will be understood immediately by anyone who has played the game "telephone," a.k.a. "rumors." In this decidedly low-tech game, which may not be familiar to today's high-tech students, someone writes something on a piece of paper and gives it to person number 1; number. 1 whispers the information on the paper to number 2; number 2 whispers it to number 3; and on and on until number 6, say, is whispering it to number 7. Person number 7 states aloud what was whispered by number 6 and number 1 reads what is on the piece of paper. What was originally written and what is said by number 7 are always—or, at least from my experience, were always—quite different.

is often the rule that ought to be argued against the admission of many-layered hearsay.[243]

IV. Additional Examples of Various Applications of the Hearsay Definition

A. "I Give to You [but Mostly] You Give to Me, Love Forever True," Plus Half-a-Million in Cash and Some Lovely Jewelry

1. The Facts

Over the course of several years, Mr. Kritzik gave over a half a million dollars and some jewelry to Ms. Harris. Either Kritzik had to pay gift taxes on these transactions, or Harris had to pay income taxes. Neither one paid.

Harris is on trial for willful evasion of her income tax obligation. She offers into evidence several letters she received from Kritzik. In one letter, for example, Kritzik conveyed his love for Harris and told her that "so far as the things I give you are concerned—let me say that I get as great if not even greater pleasure in giving than you get in receiving.... I love giving things to you and to see you happy and enjoying them." Kritzik sent a letter to his insurance company, with a copy to Harris, stating that certain jewelry had been "given to Ms. Lynette Harris as a gift."[244] On the government's side, there was some evidence that Kritzik treated Harris as an employee and that these things may have been employee compensation. Everyone seems to agree she was one of his mistresses.

Harris takes the stand in her own defense and offers the letters. Are they hearsay or not? As always, whether they are hearsay or not depends on why they are offered: to what issues are they relevant? In this case, there are two related issues, two related elements of the government's proof, which bear on whether these letters are hearsay: (1) Were these transactions in fact in the nature of gifts or income? "[T]he donor's intent is the 'critical consideration' in

---

243. "Although relevant, evidence may be excluded if its probative value is *substantially* outweighed by the danger of *unfair* prejudice …." FED.R.EVID. 403 (emphasis added). *E.g.,* United States v. Dennis, 497 F.3d 765, 769 n.1 (7th Cir. 2007) (defendant's post-arrest statements offered against defendant are not hearsay; other rules, however, may of course render the statements inadmissible—Rule 403 for example).

244. United States v. Harris, 942 F.2d 1125, 1130 (7th Cir. 1991) (quoting trial exhibits).

distinguishing between gifts and income."[245] (2) Did Harris "willfully" violate the tax statute in question? Regarding this question, of course, the donee's—Harris'—intent is the critical consideration.

2. The First Issue: Kritzik's Intent

To the issue of Kritzik's (the donor's) intent, is this evidence hearsay? (Again, for now the question is not whether it is admissible, for there is admissible hearsay and inadmissible hearsay, but whether it is hearsay.) Let us try a variety of approaches to this question.

■ What do we want to know? We want to know Kritzik's intent when he gave Ms. Harris the money and the jewelry—his actual intent. What is the evidence? The evidence is letters Kritzik had written, one to Ms. Harris, saying that he enjoys giving her gifts, and one to his insurance company, saying that he had given Ms. Harris some jewelry. There is no one testifying to firsthand knowledge of Kritzik's intent, just someone offering into evidence out-of-court statements of Kritzik's intent. We want to know his intent; the letters are offered into evidence to show what he said about his intent; the letters are out-of-court statements offered to prove the truth of the intent asserted therein; Kritzik is not a party opponent, so the letters are not Rule 801(d)(2) admissions. The letters are hearsay.

■ Are we concerned with the truth of the words spoken, or only with the fact that they were said? To the issue of Kritzik's intent, we are concerned with their truth: The issue is whether he intended these things to be gifts. The statements are that he intended these things to be gifts. The question is whether the out-of-court declarant was telling the truth. Hearsay.

■ Whose credibility is in question, and at what time? What matters is Kritzik's credibility at the time he wrote the letters. His credibility at the time he wrote the letters is all important to the issue of what his intent had been and continued to be when he gave money to Harris. As to the issue of Kritzik's intent in this whole matter, who do you want to cross-examine? Kritzik. But Kritzik is not the testifying witness. The letter, the out-of-court statement, is the "witness." The person testifying and subject to cross-examination is Harris. Probably hearsay.

■ Do the words of the letter have independent legal effect, so that they are offered only to show that they were said, not to show some subjective truth? No. If Harris could testify that Kritzik handed her some money and, along with the money, handed her a note that read: "This is a gift from me to you.

---

245. *Id.*, at 1134.

Let me say that I get as great if not even greater pleasure in giving than you do in receiving. I love giving things to you and to see you happy and enjoying them," then the words would have independent legal effect. They would not be hearsay. In that context, the subjective truth of Kritzik's out-of-court statement would be irrelevant: It is the fact that he made the statement, in the context of handing over the money, which creates the gift. But this is not the case here. The statements in these letters do not create the gifts, but reflect on them.

■ Who is the real witness to Kritzik's intent? Kritzik. Kritzik is the real witness. Harris is the testifying witness, and the evidence is the letter, the out-of-court statement. The real witness is not testifying. His out-of-court statement is being offered into evidence. Hearsay.

■ Who manufactured the raw material, the letters? Kritzik. To fully assess the quality of this raw material, Kritzik is the person we need to question. Hearsay.

3. The Second Issue: Harris's Intent

Now, regarding the second issue, the issue of Harris's (the donee's) intent, is this evidence hearsay?

■ This is state of mind evidence: Kritzik's letters are offered for the effect they had on Harris' state of mind. Their value is not dependent on whether Kritzik was telling the truth. Their value is dependent only on the effect they had on Harris, only on what Harris thought about them. The ultimate question here is not Kritzik's intent, but Harris's belief about Kritzik's intent. Harris is the real witness. The out-of-court statement is not hearsay.

■ What do we want to know? What effect these letters had on Harris. What did the testifying witness (Harris) perceive? The effect these letters had on her. Used in this way, the letters are not hearsay.

■ Whose credibility is important, and at what time? Harris's credibility is important, her credibility when she testified that these letters led her to conclude that the money and jewelry from Kritzik were gifts (and not income).

Who do we want to cross-examine? Harris. We want to know what Harris thought and why, and we can ask her because she is the testifying witness. Again, to this second issue, the letters are not hearsay.

■ This out-of-court statement is offered to show its effect on the mind of the hearer. This is a classic type of nonhearsay state-of-mind evidence.

■ Who is the real witness to the effect these letters had on Harris? Harris. What do we want to know? Harris's belief. Who is the real witness to Harris's belief? Harris. Who is the testifying witness? Harris. Not hearsay.

■ Who manufactured this raw material? The raw material here is the effect these letters had on Harris. Harris manufactured this raw material. Harris is the testifying witness. The quality of the raw material can be fully tested. Not hearsay.[246]

4. What to Do with Evidence That Is Hearsay to One Issue and Nonhearsay to Another?

This aspect of *United States v. Harris* is discussed elsewhere.[247]

B. Auto Accident Examples

Take these variations in an auto-accident negligence case:

■ If we want to know the color of the stoplight at the corner where the auto accident occurred, anyone who saw the color of the light at the relevant time is a real witness. If such a person takes the stand and testifies to the color of that light, that testimony is not hearsay, for that person is a real witness to the color of the light. We are satisfied that we can adequately test the quality of this bit of raw material because the testifying witness is the manufacturer of the evidence. What do we want to know? The color of the light. Who are the real witnesses to the color of the light? Anyone and everyone who saw the color of the light. Who are the witnesses who have personal knowledge of the color of the light? Anyone and everyone who saw it. Who are the manufacturers of this evidence (the original manufacturers)? Same answer.

■ If we want to know the color of the light and a third-party witness takes the stand to testify that someone else told him the light was a certain color,

---

246. Here is how the Seventh Circuit Court of Appeals put it:

   These letters were hearsay if offered for the truth of the matters asserted—
   that Kritzik did in fact love Harris, enjoyed giving her things, wanted to take care
   of her financial security, and gave her ... gift[s]. But the letters were not hearsay
   for the purpose of showing what Harris believed, because her belief does not depend on the actual truth of the matters asserted in the letters. Even if Kritzik were
   lying, the letters could have caused Harris to believe in good faith that the things
   he gave her were intended as gifts. This good faith belief, in turn, would preclude
   any finding of willfulness on her part.

Id. (citations omitted). The Seventh Circuit, citing *United States v. Harris*, later summed up the point as follows: "An out of court statement that is offered to show its effect on the hearer's state of mind is not hearsay." United States v. Hanson, 994 F.2d 403, 406 (7th Cir. 1993).

247. *See* Chapter 12, below.

this testifying witness is not a real witness to the color of the light. We are not satisfied that we can adequately test the quality of this bit of raw material because the testifying witness is not the manufacturer.

What do we want to know? The color of the light. Who are the real witnesses to the color of the light? They are not those who were told about it later. Those who were told about it are not the manufacturers of the color-of-the-light raw material. At best, they are simply middlepersons who took raw material from the manufacturer and passed it along to someone else.

■ Assume a witness told an investigator at the scene that the plaintiff had run the red light and testifies at the trial that she saw that the plaintiff had the green light. If we want to know whether this witness has given inconsistent versions of the color of the light, then anyone who heard her tell the investigator (including the investigator, as well as anyone else who overheard) is a "real witness." What we want to know is what she said, and anyone who heard her say it is a real witness to what she said.

What do we want to know? Whether the testifying witness made this prior inconsistent statement. Who are the real witnesses to whether she made this statement? Anyone and everyone who heard her say it. Who are the witnesses who have personal knowledge of whether she made the statement? Anyone and everyone who heard.

The relevant raw material is what the woman said—not the color of the light, though that certainly is important in the trial for other reasons. For purposes of impeachment by prior inconsistent statement, however, what matters is just that the witness made this prior inconsistent statement. The testifying witness who heard her make the prior statement is the manufacturer of this bit of raw material.

■ If we want to know the color of the light and the defendant calls a third-party witness who will testify that the plaintiff had told him that he (the plaintiff) had run the red light, is this hearsay? No. Part of the rule defining hearsay excludes this kind of statement from the definition. Rule 801(d)(2) excludes a party's own statement offered against him or her.

Who manufactured the evidence regarding the color of the light? The plaintiff did, and the testifying witness did not. Who is the real witness to the color of the light? The plaintiff is, and the testifying witness is not. The manufactured evidence and real witness approaches do not work here because this statement fits under one of the Rule 801(d) definitional exclusions. Under Rule 801(d)(2), all we need is a real witness to the party's own statement, offering it against the party-declarant.

■ To come at it from a different angle, anyone who saw the color of the light is a real witness to the color of the light. Anyone who overheard the conversation is a real witness to the conversation. Anyone who did not see the color of the light, but was told its color by someone else, is not a real witness to the color of the light. Anyone who did not hear the conversation, but was told about it by someone else, is not a real witness to the conversation. Anyone who did not see the color of the light but did overhear the conversation is a real witness to the conversation, but not a real witness to the color of the light. A person who was on the scene of the accident and saw the color of the light and overheard the conversation, is a real witness both to the conversation and to the event described in the conversation.

When the question is "What was the color of the light?," then (except for the exclusions in Rule 801(d)) the hearsay definition calls for someone who was a real witness of the color of the light. It calls for an original manufacturer of that raw material—"an" original manufacturer, for there can be more than one manufacturer, more than one source for this raw material. When the question is "Did the witness make a prior statement and, if so, what did she say?," then (except for the exclusions in Rule 801(d)) the hearsay definition calls for someone who was a real witness to the prior statement. It calls for an original manufacturer of that raw material.

When there are two questions, both alive in the same case—"What was the color of the light?" and "Did the witness make a prior statement and, if so, what did she say?"—then there will be people who are real witnesses to neither. There may also be people who are real witnesses to one, but not the other. There may be people who are real witnesses to both. The hearsay rule has to do with sorting out the testimony of these witnesses into hearsay and nonhearsay.

CHAPTER THREE

RULE 803, SELECTED EXCEPTIONS

     7. A Series of Exciting Events (the Rolling Exciting-Event) or a Subsequent Related Event Triggering Excitement Anew

     8. Often an Out-of-Court Statement Will Be Both a Present Sense Impression and an Excited Utterance

     9. The Excited Utterance and the Child Witness

IV. State of Mind or Statement of Then-Existing Mental, Emotional, or Physical Condition: Rule 803(3)

  A. Text of the Rule

  B. Foundational Elements

  C. Need + Reliability = 1

    1. Need

    2. Reliability

  D. Use Note

    1. The Breadth of the Exception

    2. The "No Elaboration" Rule

    3. A Statement That Looks to the Past

    4. A Statement That Looks to the Future

    5. The Out-of-Court Statement Must Reflect the Declarant's Own State of Mind

    6. The Out-of-Court Statement Must Be a Direct Statement of the Declarant's State of Mind

    7. Just Because an Out-of-Court Statement Fits under This Exception Does Not Mean It Is Admissible into Evidence

    8. State of Mind Evidence That Is Not Hearsay in the First Place

    9. The State of Mind Exception and the Excited Utterance and Present Sense Impression Exceptions

    10. The Intertwining of the Admissible and the Inadmissible: Redaction and Rule 403

V. Statements for Purposes of Medical Diagnosis or Treatment: Rule 803(4)

  A. Text of the Rule

  B. Foundational Elements

  C. Need + Reliability = 1

    1. Need

    2. Reliability

  D. Use Note

    1. The Person to Whom the Statement Was Made

    2. The Person by Whom the Statement Was Made

    3. The Reason the Statement Is Made

    4. Statements Regarding Mental Health

    5. The Content of the Statement

I. Introduction to the Exceptions Generally, and Rule 803 in Particular

"[W]hen the choice is between evidence which is less than best and no evidence at all, only clear folly would dictate an across-the-board policy of doing without."[1]

A. Exceptions: A Brief History

The hearsay rule began its life as a pretty clear rule: every out-of-court statement offered to prove the truth of the matter asserted was hearsay. Most hearsay was inadmissible.[2] It was simple (certainly as compared with today's version of the rule[3]), but too severe. It kept out too much valuable evidence.

---

1. FED.R.EVID. art. VIII advisory committee's introductory note. And, of course, the theory behind the hearsay rule is that hearsay evidence is "less than best." *See* Chapter 1(I), above.

2. *See* Paul S. Milich, *Hearsay Antinomies: The Case for Abolishing the Rule and Starting Over*, 71 OR. L. REV. 723, 741–46 (1992).

3. "The basic rule against hearsay, of course, is riddled with exceptions developed over

Sometimes hearsay is more credible than nonhearsay.[4] Sometimes hearsay is less credible than nonhearsay, but not all that much less, and the cost of producing nonhearsay evidence is too high.[5] Sometimes hearsay is the only evidence available.[6] Sometimes it just does not seem fair to exclude the hearsay evidence.[7]

For these reasons and more, cracks began to appear in the rigid rule of the common-law.[8] This was the beginning of the end. Today's rule has the clarity of badly shattered safety-glass.[9]

---

three centuries." State v. Roberts, 448 U.S. 56, 62 (1980). *Accord* G. Michael Fenner, *Law Professor Reveals Shocking Truth About Hearsay*, 62 UMKC L. Rev. 1, 9–10 (1993).

4. *See, e.g.*, White v. Illinois, 502 U.S. 346, 355 (1992) ("[T]he evidentiary rationale for permitting hearsay testimony regarding spontaneous declarations and statements made in the course of receiving medical care is that such out-of-court declarations are made in contexts that provide substantial guarantees of their trustworthiness.... [and the] factors that contribute to the statements' reliability cannot be recaptured even by later in-court testimony.").

5. *See*, for example, the text accompanying note 17 in Chapter 4, below.

6. Rule 804 only applies if the declarant's in-court testimony is not available. Fed.R.Evid. 804. In some of those cases, there will not be any evidence of the point other than the out-of-court statement. Rule 803(16) covers statements in ancient documents; part of the point of this exception is that often the ancient document will be the only evidence of the ancient event. *See* part XI of this chapter, below. No one is likely to remember the exact closing price of a particular stock on a particular day three and a half years ago, so we have an exception for market reports and commercial publications. *See* part XII of this chapter, below.

7. *See*, for example, the discussions of nonhearsay admissions, at Chapter 2(III)(A)(3), above, and the exception that applies when, among other things, a party kills a witness to keep the witness from testifying, at Chapter 4(VII), below.

8. "Even before the hearsay rule was fully established, courts began finding specific situations in which hearsay should be admitted." Paul S. Milich, *Hearsay Antinomies: The Case for Abolishing the Rule and Starting Over*, 71 Or. L. Rev. 723, 745 (1992).

9. "The basic rule against hearsay, of course, is riddled with exceptions developed over three centuries." *Roberts*, 448 U.S. at 62. There are eight definitional exclusions in Rule 801(d). (*See* Chapter 2.) There are 23 exceptions in Rule 803 (*see* Chapter 3) and five in Rule 804 (*see* Chapter 4). Rule 807 invites the court to create new exceptions. (*See* Chapter 5.) The Federal Rules of Civil and Criminal Procedure create important exceptions for depositions. (*See* Chapter 6.) The opinion-evidence rules can be used to get around hearsay inadmissibility. (*See* Chapter 8.) Judicial notice can be a way around the hearsay rule. (*See* Chapter 9(IV).) Various state courts continue to create common-law exceptions.

The statute states the general rule that hearsay *is not* admissible unless it fits under an exception. Fed.R.Evid. 802. There are so many ways around today's hearsay rule that it is fair to say that Rule 802 turns the truth on its head. The truth is that hearsay *is* admissible, except in the minority of cases where there is no exception.

B. N + R = 1: The Shared Theoretical Basis for Each Exception

Hearsay exceptions are based mostly on one or both of two things: the system's need for the evidence (N) and the reliability of the evidence (R).[10] Rules 803 and 804 create categorical exceptions; they remove the barrier of the hearsay rule from categories of hearsay evidence; they do so on the basis of some combination of the need for the category of evidence and its reliability.[11] Rule 807 creates an ad hoc exception; it allows the court to create exceptions on the facts of individual cases for individual uses of hearsay evidence; courts are directed to make these ad hoc decisions based on the particular need for and reliability of the evidence in question.

Professor Irving Younger once said—and, in a loose sort of way, he was right—that the exceptions can be thought of as follows: The greater the general need for a category of evidence, the more likely there is to be an exception. The greater the general reliability of a category of evidence, the more likely there is to be an exception. As need increases, we require less reliability, and as reliability increases, we require less need. Exceptions tend to be created based

---

10. As already noted, there is sometimes a third reason: sometimes it just does not seem fair to exclude the hearsay. As long ago as 1947, Professor Maguire identified three motives behind the creation of exceptions. His first motive was reliability, his second was necessity, and his third was adversary practice. John MacArthur Maguire, Evidence: Common Sense and Common Law 130, 132, 140 (1947). Some of what I characterize as the "doesn't seem fair to keep the evidence out" fits under Maguire's third reason.

11. *E.g.*, United States v. Williams, 571 F.2d 344, 350 (6th Cir. 1978) ("The touchstone for admission of evidence as an exception to the hearsay rule has been the existence of circumstances which attest to its trustworthiness."); Dallas County v. Commercial Union Assurance Co., 286 F.2d 388, 397–98 (5th Cir. 1961) ("necessary and trustworthy."); State v. Letterman, 616 P.2d 505, 508 (Or. Ct. App. 1980) (two requirements common to most, if not all, exceptions: circumstantial guarantees of trustworthiness; need for the evidence), *superceded by statute*, Oregon Evidence Code, Or.Rev.Stat. §40 (2007), *as stated in* State v. Rodreguiez-Castillo, 151 P.3d 931 (Or.Ct.App. 2007); John MacArthur Maguire, Evidence: Common Sense and Common Law, at 130, 132, 140 (1947); V John Henry Wigmore, Evidence §§1420–22 (2d ed. 1923) (trustworthiness and necessity). *See also* Idaho v. Wright, 497 U.S. 805, 820 (1990) (various exceptions are based on circumstantial guarantees of trustworthiness that existed when the statement was made).

It is important to keep in mind that considerations of reliability or trustworthiness go into *creation of the category*. Unless a particular exception includes it as an element, the trustworthiness of the out-of-court statement is not a separate requirement for *application of the exception*. It goes instead to the credibility of the evidence.

on an inversely proportional relationship between need and reliability: Need + Reliability = 1.[12]

Understanding that hearsay exceptions are somehow based on need and reliability is useful in a number of ways. Most importantly, knowing the rationale supporting an exception helps us when we have to interpret it, and apply it to a new situation.[13] For this reason, this book's discussion of each exception in Rules 803, 804, and 807 will include a discussion of the need (N) for and the reliability (R) of the evidence. It will be under the heading "N + R = 1."

C. The Foundational Elements, the Evidentiary Burden, and the Decision Maker

Each hearsay exception has some number of foundational elements.[14] Each is a statutory rule stating that if the foundational elements are satisfied, then the hearsay rule does not keep the evidence out. The foundational elements are the keys that unlock each exception. If the attorney offering hearsay evidence can establish each of the foundational elements of any one exception, then the

---

12. *See also* I. Daniel Stewart, Jr., *Perception, Memory, and Hearsay: A Criticism of Present Law and the Proposed Rules of Evidence*, 1970 UTAH L. REV. 1, 23 (1970).

The availability of the out-of-court declarant's in-court testimony is irrelevant to the 803 exceptions, whereas 804 exceptions require the unavailability of the declarant's in-court testimony. It is that unavailability that establishes the need for the 804 exceptions. In theory, then, less reliability is required for the 804 exceptions; there are those who believe that the 804 exceptions generally produce less reliable evidence than do those in Rule 803. *E.g.*, 5 JOSEPH M. MCLAUGHLIN & JACK B. WEINSTEIN, WEINSTEIN'S FEDERAL EVIDENCE § 804.02 (2d ed. 1999) ("[T]he drafters of the Federal Rules of Evidence considered the categories of evidence listed in Rule 804 less inherently trustworthy than those set forth in Rule 803.").

13. *See, e.g.*, United States v. Gabe, 237 F.3d 954, 958 (8th Cir. 2001) (the guarantee of reliability for the exception is used to set the boundaries within which a child abuse victim's statement to a physician, identifying the perpetrator, will fit under the medial diagnosis or treatment exception); Costantino v. Herzog, 203 F.3d 164, 170–71 (2d Cir. 2000) (using the rationale behind the exception "to 'make law'" regarding whether information published in new media is covered by the learned treatise exception).

The Federal Rules of Evidence is, after all, a statute. "Those who write statutes seek to solve human problems. Fidelity to their aims requires us to approach an interpretive problem not as if it were a purely logical game, like a Rubik's Cube, but as an effort to divine human intent that underlies the statute. Here that effort calls not for an appeal to canons, but for an analysis of language, structure, history, and purpose." J.E.M. Ag Supply, Inc. v. Pioneer Hi-Bred Int'l, Inc., 534 U.S. 124, 156 (2001) (Breyer, J. dissenting).

14. For example, the present sense impression exception (Rule 803(1)) has two foundational elements. *See* Chapter 3(II)(B), below. The recorded recollection exception (Rule 803(5)) has five. *See* Chapter 3(VI)(B), below.

hearsay rule no longer bars the admission of the statement. If an attorney opposing admission can convince the judge that there is insufficient evidence of
at least one foundational element of each exception presented, then the hearsay
rule does bar admission of the statement.[15]

The burden of establishing the foundational elements of the hearsay exceptions is on the party offering the evidence; offering counsel must convince
the judge that each of the foundational elements is present for at least one exception.[16] While the party opposing the admission of hearsay evidence does
not have the evidentiary burden, as a practical matter opposing counsel must
be prepared to argue that one or more of the foundational elements has not been
established.

---

15. If the foundation is laid for an exception, then the hearsay rule is not a bar to admission. United States v. Cardascia, 951 F.2d 474, 487 (2d Cir. 1991).

The abstract merits of the hearsay exception are irrelevant to the court's job. It is not for
the judge to say whether an exception is desirable. Except for the few exceptions that specifically state on their face that the judge should consider whether the evidence is trustworthy—
Rule 803(6), 803(7), 803(8), 804(b)(3), 807—it is not for the judge to decide whether a particular out-of-court statement is trustworthy. The legislature has made that decision. The
legislature has decided that certain categories of evidence are admissible over a hearsay objection.

Whether the foundational elements of an exception are established is a question of law—
for the trier of law. Whether the evidence is credible (trustworthy) is a question of fact—
for the trier of fact. E.g., Jewell v. CSX Transp. Inc., 135 F.3d 361, 365–66 (6th Cir. 1998).
It is irrelevant that the in-court declarant is an interested party. The in-court declarant's
"motivation as a witness presents a straightforward credibility question." United States v.
Ruiz, 249 F.3d 643, 647 (7th Cir. 2001). When witnesses testify to out-of-court statements
that are in their own best interest, it is no different than when they testify to physically observable facts that are in their best interest. Id. (self-interest and lack of corroboration goes
to "the weight owed to this evidence but did not bar its admission.").

On a related matter, regarding trustworthiness versus credibility, see Chapter 5(V)(E)(2),
below, and see also part VIII(E)(4)(a) of this chapter, below.

16. E.g., Garcia-Martinez v. City and County of Denver, 392 F.3d 1187, 1193 (10th Cir.
2004); Pittsburgh Press Club v. United States, 579 F.2d 751, 757–60 (3d Cir. 1978); United
States v. Bartelho, 129 F.3d 663, 670 (1st Cir. 1997) ("A party who seeks admission of hearsay
evidence bears the burden of proving each element of the exception that he asserts."); Zenith
Radio Corp. v. Matsushita Elec. Indus. Co., 505 F. Supp. 1190, 1236 (E.D. Pa. 1980), aff'd
in part, rev'd in part, remanded, sub nom In Re Japanese Elec. Prods. Antitrust Litigation, 723
F.2d 238 (3d Cir. 1983), rev'd and remanded sub non Matsushita Elec. Ind. Co. v. Zenith Radio
Corp., 475 U.S. 574 (1986) (burden of laying foundation for hearsay exceptions is on the
party seeking admission of the evidence) (citing cases); State v. Stonaker, 945 P.2d 573, 578
(Or. Ct. App. 1997) (proponent must show hearsay evidence fits under an exception); Blecha
v. People, 962 P.2d 931, 940 (Colo. 1998). See also Chapter 2(I), above; note 183 and accompanying test in Chapter 4; and Chapter 6(I)(E)(11).

Whether or not the foundation for an exception has been satisfied is a question of law—a question for the judge, not the jury.[17] If the only problem with the admissibility of a particular out-of-court statement is the hearsay rule and the judge decides the foundation for at least one exception is present, then the out-of-court statement is admissible. If it is admissible, then the jury may consider the statement. The jury will decide whether they believe the statement and what weight, if any, to give it. Once again—because it is so important—the key to each hearsay exception is its foundational elements.

D. Rule 803's Exceptions versus Rule 804's: The Availability of the Live, Firsthand, In-Court Testimony of the Out-of-Court Declarant

In the Federal Rules of Evidence, the direct exceptions to the hearsay rule are found in three rules: Rules 803, 804, and 807. Rules 803 and 804 create more-or-less-specific exceptions for categories of evidence: excited utterances, business records, former testimony, and the like. These exceptions are categorical. Rule 807 creates a residual exception that guides the judge to create additional exceptions in individual situations, based on particular facts.

Among the things Rule 803 and 804 exceptions have in common is that they are the categorical exceptions. The difference between 803 and 804 exceptions has to do with the availability of the in-court testimony of the out-of-court declarant. Under Rule 803 the present availability of the testimony of the out-of-court declarant is *never* an issue—it simply is of no consequence. Regarding each and all of the exceptions in Rule 803, it does not matter if the out-of-court declarant is alive or dead, ready, willing, and able to testify, or incompetent, singing like a bird or invoking the Fifth Amendment, in the

---

17. United States v. Mobley, 421 F.2d 345, 348 (5th Cir. 1970), involved the hearsay exception for statements under belief of impending death, FED.R.EVID. 804(b)(2). One foundational element for this exception is that, at the time he made the out-of-court statement, the declarant must have believed that he was about to die. The judge allowed the out-of-court statement in question to be admitted into evidence, but first instructed the jury that "unless they found that the declarant knew of his impending death, they should not consider the contents of the statement." This is error. Whether evidence is admissible and, therefore, within the box of evidence the jury may consider, is a question of law to be answered by the trier of law. Whether evidence is true and how much weight it should be given are questions of fact to be answered by the trier of fact. The judge in *Mobley* instructed the jury to revisit, and to re-answer, the question of law. The judge has asked the jury to perform a judicial function. The judge has violated the separation of the functions of the trier of law and the trier of fact.

courtroom or absent from the hearing.[18] Under Rule 804, the present availability of the testimony of the out-of-court declarant is *always* an issue, as the unavailability of the declarant's in-court testimony is a foundational element of each and every exception in Rule 804.[19]

II. Present Sense Impression: Rule 803(1)

A. Text of the Rule

The following are not excluded by the hearsay rule, even though the declarant is available as a witness:

(1) Present sense impression. A statement describing or explaining an event or condition made while the declarant was perceiving the event or condition, or immediately thereafter.

B. Foundational Elements

1. The out-of-court statement must have been made while the declarant was perceiving an event or a condition, or *immediately* thereafter.

2. The out-of-court statement must describe or explain the thing being perceived.

C. Need + Reliability = 1

1. Need

Categorical need for the out-of-court statements covered by the present sense impression exception is almost nonexistent.[20] This is a Rule 803 excep-

---

18. *See* Chapter 3(I), below.

In criminal prosecutions the availability of the out-of-court declarant may be an issue of great consequence under the Confrontation Clause. The fact that an out-of-court declarant's in-court testimony is unavailable may mean that the declarant's out-of-court statement is barred from the trial as a matter of constitutional law. Regarding the Confrontation Clause, see Chapter 14, below.

19. This is clear from the face of each rule. *See also, e.g.,* Lorraine v. Markel Am. Ins. Co., 241 F.R.D. 534, 568 (D. Md. 2007) ("Rule 803 contains twenty-three separate hearsay exceptions. At first glance they may seem like they have nothing in common, but they do. All twenty-three are admissible regardless of whether the declarant is available to testify, distinguishing them from the five exceptions in Rule 804, each of which is inapplicable unless the declarant is unavailable, as defined by any of the five methods identified in Rule 804(a).").

20. In some situations the declarant will be ready, willing, and able to provide the same

tion and, therefore, it applies whether the live testimony of the declarant is available or unavailable. This category of evidence is considered so reliable that need is not a factor in the creation of the exception.

2. Reliability

The first part of Chapter 1 of this book talks about the testimonial infirmities—the things that can make testimony unreliable. The list includes faulty perception, bad memory, lack of sincerity, dishonesty, and ambiguity. Cross-examination, which provides an advocate with a way to probe for these infirmities, only works well when the person with the relevant firsthand knowledge is the one subjected to the cross-examination.

The theory behind this hearsay exception is that spontaneity deals with these testimonial infirmities. Spontaneity replaces cross-examination. There was no time for insincerity or outright dishonesty, each of which is a conscious act. There was no time for memory to have faded[21] or been influenced. There was no time for the declarant to replay the event over and over again in his or her mind, with all of the shading of the story that come with each replay. The exception applies to anything seen, heard, felt, touched, or smelled, no matter how drab, dull, or commonplace, no matter how forgettable. Spontaneity is the only guarantee of reliability. The statement is reliable because it is unreasoned, unstudied, and unpremeditated. It is reflexive.[22]

In addition, spontaneity tends to lead to proximity. Quite often, the testifying witness who heard the out-of-court statement was near the scene and has some relevant firsthand knowledge of his or her own. This is not always so,

---

evidence live and in person on the witness stand and there is no need for the exception. In other situations the declarant's in-court testimony will be unavailable and without this exception the evidence will be lost, there will be evidence of the fact in question other than the present sense impression, but getting that other evidence is expensive and time consuming, or, without this exception, the out-of-court statement will be admissible only as an impeaching prior-inconsistent statement and the party seeking to take advantage of this evidence needs it as substantive evidence.

21. In saying this, I do realize that there has, by the time the trial comes around, been time for the testifying witness's memory of the out-of-court statement to have faded.

22. *E.g.*, United States v. Green, 541 F.3d 176, 180–81 (8th Cir. 2008) (citing and discussing cases); Ross v. St. Augustine's Coll., 103 F.3d 338, 342 (4th Cir. 1996) ("[T]he 'substantial contemporaneity of event and statement negate the likelihood of deliberate or conscious misrepresentation.'") (quoting FED.R.EVID. 803 advisory committee's note); United States v. Peacock, 654 F.2d 339, 350 (5th Cir. 1981), *modified on other grounds,* 686 F.2d 356 (5th Cir. 1982) ("There was no time ... to consciously manipulate the truth.").

but in many cases, the testifying witness will have some relevant firsthand knowledge of the declarant's ability to have perceived the event and of some parts of the event itself. The testifying witness can be cross-examined with respect to these things.[23]

Of course, none of this is necessarily true. First, it does not take any time at all to formulate the response, "No, you don't look fat" or "I am *not* drunk." Second, the testifying witness need not have been anywhere near the scene described by the out-of-court declarant.[24] In such a case, it is pretty easy for those

---

23. *E.g.*, McCormick on Evidence § 271, at 474 (John W. Strong gen. ed., 4th ed. 1992); Edmund Morgan, *A Suggested Classification of Utterances Admissible as Res Gestae*, 31 Yale L.J. 229, 236 (1922); James Bradley Thayer, *Bedingfield's Case—Declarations as a Part of the Res Gesta*, 15 Am. L. Rev. 71, 107 (1881). In the usual case, there will be an opportunity for a more meaningful cross-examination than there would be with many of the other exceptions. Take, for example, the self-authenticating business record, where there is no one to cross examine, *see* part VII(D)(3(b) of this chapter, below, or the public report introduced by a custodian who had absolutely no knowledge of any of the facts reported thereon, *see* part VII(E)(2) of this chapter, below.

24. Consider the following: On May 3, 1963, in Birmingham, Alabama, two African American men, A.G. Gaston and David Vann, were talking on the phone. Outside of Gaston's office, the Birmingham Fire Department was breaking up a demonstration by training fire hoses on the demonstrators. They were using special equipment designed for long-range fire fighting that increases water pressure by forcing water from two hoses through a single nozzle. Gaston said to Vann: "They've turned the fire hoses on a little black girl. And they're rolling that girl right down the middle of the street." Taylor Branch, Parting the Waters: America in the King Years 1954–63 759 (1988). Gaston's statement of what he saw was a present sense impression: he described the event while he was perceiving it. Had there been litigation, Vann's testimony as to what Gaston said to him over the phone would be admissible to prove the truth of the facts asserted in Gaston's statement, admissible under the present sense impression.

E.g., United States v. Ruiz, 249 F.3d 643, 647 (7th Cir. 2001) (over his radio, one police officer described to a second what he was seeing; this exception allowed the second to testify to what he was told); United States v. Portsmouth Paving Corp., 694 F.2d 312, 323 (4th Cir. 1982) (Remington was on the phone with the defendant; he hung up and described the conversation to the testifying witness; defendant's statements to Remington are non-hearsay statements of a party offered against that party, and Remington's statements to the testifying witness are admissible present sense impressions); State v. Jones, 532 A.2d 169 (Md. 1987) (one trucker speaking to another over a CB radio described a high-speed automobile chase as he was seeing it; a state trooper overheard the radio transmission; to prove facts regarding the chase, the trooper was allowed to testify to what he heard; the truck driver's out-of-court statement was admissible as a present sense impression; no one knew the identity of either trucker); Booth v. State, 508 A.2d 976 (Md. 1986) (witness's testimony to what declarant said to him over the phone admissible as a present sense impression).

with something to hide to simply and completely fabricate a description of where they are and what they are doing at the moment. Consider the following phone conversations. "I can't come in today. I am not feeling well." "No, I'm not at the casino. I'm at the office." "I am in Chicago," and the crime with which the declarant is charged was committed within the hour in New Orleans. While there is no time for memory to have faded, there is plenty of time for a reasoned, studied, and premeditated lie.[25]

This exception extends far beyond its guarantee of reliability.

D. Use Note

Because the theoretical guarantee of reliability for this exception is so often so spurious, courts must pay particular attention to the element of immediacy or spontaneity (as if even that really guaranteed reliability).[26]

The present sense impression can also be in writing, in which case the "testifying witness" is a piece of paper with no relevant firsthand knowledge. *E.g.*, Michaels v. Michaels, 767 F.2d 1185, 1201 (7th Cir. 1985) (witness to event sent telex "immediately" after event; telex accepted in evidence as a present sense impression).

25. "The rationale ... is that spontaneous utterances, especially in emotional circumstances, are unlikely to be fabricated, because fabrication requires an opportunity for conscious reflection. As with much of the folk psychology of evidence, it is difficult to take this rationale entirely seriously, since people are entirely capable of spontaneous lies in emotional circumstances. 'Old and **new studies agree** that less than one second is required to fabricate a lie.' Douglas D. McFarland, 'Present Sense Impressions Cannot Live in the Past,' 28 *Fla. St. U. L. Rev.* 907, 916 (2001)." Lust v. Sealy, Inc., 383 F. 3d 580, 588 (7th Cir. 2004) "There is no more facile a method of creating favorable evidence than writing a self-exculpatory note." *Id.*

There are contrary views. *See, e.g.,* John E.B. Myers *et al., Children as Victims and Witnesses in the Criminal Trial Process: Hearsay Exceptions: Adjusting the Ratio of Intuition to Psychological Science,* 65 LAW & CONTEMP. PROB. 3, 8 (2002) (citing studies that suggest "lying may be a difficult task, particularly when individuals are not prepared to lie or are required to deceive regarding important issues" and concluding that lying may be more difficult under stressful circumstances).

26. Take, for example, Lust v. Sealy, Inc., 383 F.3d 580 (7th Cir. 2004), an employment discrimination action. Defendant offered into evidence exculpatory memoranda written by the supervisor who had passed the plaintiff over for promotion. Some statements therein had the appearance of present sense impressions. The court of appeals stated that the declarant "was hardly under emotional pressure when he was writing these memos, and *their length, lucidity, and self-congratulatory tone all refute any inference of spontaneity.*" *Id.* at 588 (emphasis added). *Accord* Davila v. Corporacion de P. R. Para la Difusion Publica, 498 F.3d 9, 16–17 (1st Cir. 2007) (insufficient foundation because the offering party did not offer any "facts regarding the temporal relationship between" the

Many statements that fit under this exception also fit under the excited utterance exception or the exception for statements of then-existing mental, emotional, or physical condition, or both.[27] This exception is best understood by
comparing and contrasting it with the excited utterance exception. The rest of
the Use Note for the present sense impression exception has been combined with
the Use Note for the excited utterance exception.[28]

III. Excited Utterance: Rule 803(2)

A. Text of the Rule

The following are not excluded by the hearsay rule, even though
the declarant is available as a witness:

****

(2) Excited utterance. A statement relating to a startling event or condition made while the declarant was under the stress of excitement
caused by the event or condition.

---

occurrence and the out-of-court statement); United States v. Shoup, 476 F.3d 38, 42 (1st
Cir. 2007) (precise contemporaneity is not required since in many cases it is not possible) (citing Fed.R.Evid. 803(1) advisory committee's note); Schindler v. Joseph C. Seiler
& Synthes Spine Co., 474 F.3d 1008, 1012 (7th Cir. 2007) (because the statement "was a
calculated narration" and counsel did not satisfy the evidentiary burden to show immediacy, the exception does not apply); United States v. Gil, 58 F.3d 1414, 1422 (9th Cir. 1995)
(police officers who are "note takers" can testify to statements made by surveillance officers because the statements fall under the present sense impression exception); Canatxx
Gas Storage Ltd. v. Silverhawk Capital Partners, LLC, 76 Fed. R. Serv. (Callaghan) 500,
517 (S.D. Tex. 2008) (admitting an email summarizing a phone conversation typed as
soon as the conversation was over); Woolford v. Rest. Concepts, II, LLC, 2008 U.S. Dist.
LEXIS 5187, *15 (S.D. Ga. Jan. 23, 2008) (while the customer's complaints to the server
about the food were present sense impressions, the server's later relay of the complaints
to the manager were not; the former fits under a hearsay exception, and the latter does
not; the testimony is inadmissible).

27. At least one state—Nebraska—adopted a version of the federal rules of evidence but
did not include the present sense impression exception. *See* Neb.Rev.Stat. § 27-803 (Reissue 1995). Many statements that would otherwise fit under the present sense impression
exception will still be excepted from the operation of the hearsay rule by other exceptions,
particularly the excited utterance or state of mind exceptions.

28. *See particularly* part III(D) of this chapter, below.

B. Foundational Elements

1. There was a sufficiently startling event.

2. The out-of-court declarant was sufficiently startled by this event—startled into a mental state where reflection and reasoning are blocked.

3. The out-of-court statement was made while the declarant remained under the stress of the excitement caused by the event—made while declarant's reflection and reasoning continued to be blocked by the effect of the triggering event.

4. The out-of-court statement must relate to the startling event.

C. Need + Reliability = 1

1. Need

As with the present sense impression exception, categorical need is almost nonexistent. As this is a Rule 803 exception, it is available even if the declarant is a fully responsive, testifying witness. The exception is pretty much entirely based on reliability.[29]

2. Reliability

The first and principal guarantee of reliability is the lack of capacity to fabricate.[30] This exception takes the present sense impression and carries it out beyond the immediate time of the event. It extends it for as long as the startled witness stays sufficiently startled so as to lack the capacity to fabricate.

Lying is a conscious act, a product of controlled thought. If a declarant is in a state just enough this-side-of-shock to allow coherent speech, then the theory is that whatever the declarant says will be reflexive—unthinking. If the out-of-court statement is about something other than the startling event, that indicates it might have been a product of conscious thought rather than a reflexive reaction. Therefore, the exception requires three things: a triggering event sufficiently startling to the declarant that it blocked his or her ability to fabricate, a statement made during the duration of that stress, and a statement related to the startling event.

---

29. On some facts there will be a need for this evidence—as discussed in part II(C) of this chapter—and sometimes there will not. The exception was not created out of need.

30. It is not the lack of time to fabricate, which is the supposed guarantee of reliability for the present sense impression exception, but the lack of capacity.

If the statement is unthinking, it cannot be a conscious act; if it is not a conscious act, it cannot be a lie. It may not be accurate. The out-of-court declarant may have been mistaken. The shock may have interfered with the declarant's observation or memory.[31] But the statement will not be a lie.[32] And if it is true that stress greatly reduces the chances the declarant was lying, then the in-court testimony of this same witness would tend to be less reliable than the hearsay statement because the declarant (now the testifying witness) now has the ability to lie.[33]

The second part to the guarantee of reliability has to do with perception and memory. *Perception*: The declarant must have been startled by the triggering event; that tends to mean that the declarant was near the event and perceived at least some of it. *Memory*: The statement must have been made while the declarant was under the continuing stress of the triggering event; that tends to mean that the declaration and the event will be close together in time;[34] that means less time to forget and reduces the chance of faulty memory.

---

31. There is, in fact, considerable evidence that shock does interfere with observation and memory. *See, e.g.*, I. Daniel Stewart, Jr., *Perception, Memory, and Hearsay: A Criticism of Present Law and the Proposed Rules of Evidence*, 1970 UTAH L. REV. 1, 19 (1970) ("Excitement, a factor evidence law relies upon as a warrant for trustworthiness, produces a significant degree of error, sometimes of the most bizarre type.").

Regarding these potential problems with this exception, one appellate court has said this: "Whatever the abstract merits of such concerns, it is not for the trial court, or for us, to determine the desirability of the exception." State v. Stonaker, 945 P.2d 573, 579 (Or. Ct. App. 1997).

32. Professor Christopher Mueller put the lie to this guarantee of reliability when he wondered what father would tell his daughter "'trust what you're told an excited man said,'... because 'excited men don't lie'"? Christopher B. Mueller, *Post-Modern Hearsay Reform: The Importance of Complexity*, 76 MINN. L. REV. 367, 375 (1992).

In the case of children, at least one court seems to have said that children—in the case in question, a four-year-old—generally lack the ability to fabricate. People In Interest of O.E.P., 654 P.2d 312 (Colo. 1982). Where that court got the idea that children, even four-year-old children, lack the ability to fabricate is anyone's guess. Studies have shown just the opposite. Research at the Robert Wood Johnson Medical School has shown that 70 percent of guilty three-year-olds lied about peeking at a toy after an adult told them not to peek and then left the room. WEBSTER RIGGS, JR. M.D., THE YOU YOU DON'T KNOW 29 (Prometheus Books 1997). In any event, the end result of this approach is to allow the statement and the triggering event to be much farther apart.

33. White v. Illinois, 502 U.S. 346, 355–56 (1992); MCCORMICK ON EVIDENCE, § 272 (John W. Strong gen. ed., 4th ed. 1992).

34. This is not necessarily the case. There are excited utterances that are made months after the triggering event. *See* part III(D)(9) of this chapter, below. *See also* part III(D)(4) of this chapter, below.

D. Use Note

1. The Unidentified Onlooker As Out-of-Court Declarant

Whether we know the identity of the out-of-court declarant is irrelevant, so long as we can establish the foundation for the exception.[35]

The following testimony about the color of the traffic light would be both a present sense impression and an excited utterance: "A man who was cross-ing the street and was almost hit by the car—he was crying and shaking. As the car tore into the baby carriage he screamed 'He ran the red light.' The man wandered off in a daze. I do not know who he was."[36]

2. Self-Serving Statements

It does not matter if the out-of-court statement was self-serving.[37] When spoken hurriedly, loudly, and excitedly, and in reference to the driver of the

---

35. *E.g.*, Parker v. State, 778 A.2d 1096, 1105 (Md. 2001) (unnamed declarants who witnessed a shooting); State v. Jones, 532 A.2d 169, 172 (Md. 1987) (*see supra*, note 24). The party offering the statement must show that the declarant had personal knowledge of facts contained in the statement (FED.R.EVID. 805; *see* Chapter 13 and *see also* Chapter 11, below), but, as in the cases just cited, may be able to do that without knowing just who the declarant was.

36. The hearsay rule is not a bar the admission of such a statement. In a prosecution of the driver of the car for negligent homicide, the Confrontation Clause is likely to bar the admission of the statement. Regarding the latter, see Chapter 14, below.

37. A self-serving statement is one that serves the speakers own interest, often in such a way as might give the speaker reason to disregard the truth or the interest of others. MER-RIAM-WEBSTER'S COLLEGIATE DICTIONARY, CD-ROM (Zane Pub. Co. 1996). It does not mat-ter, then, that the facts declared in the out-of-court statement promote the interest of the declarant or the party offering the statement, or both. Further, it does not matter that the facts declared perfectly suit the interests of the out-of-court declarant and are just what the declarant would have said if he or she had lied. United States v. Ruiz, 249 F.3d 643, 647 (7th Cir. 2001) (opposing counsel argued that the statement did not qualify as a present sense impression because the in-court declarant "was not a disinterested party"; the in-court declarant's "motivation as a witness presents a straightforward credibility question"). *See* Mashburn v. Wright, 420 S.E.2d 379 (Ga. Ct. App. 1992) (in an action to recover the value of a certificate of deposit in deceased's name and found among his possessions, plain-tiff testified that deceased handed him the certificate and stated "this is yours, I want you to have it," *id.* at 380, it will "mature in February" and we will go to the bank then and have it signed over; deceased said he would keep possession of the certificate because he had a safe place to keep it; the court admitted these "uncorroborated and self-serving" statements, *id.* at 381, under Georgia's residual exception; that the testifying witness stands to gain from the statements goes to credibility, not admissibility, *id.*)

truck that just smashed in the side of the declarant's car, the following out-of-court statement fits under the excited utterance exception: "He was going way too fast and ran right through the red light." This statement was completely self-serving when it was made[38] and it is completely self-serving when it is offered into evidence on behalf of the declarant.[39] So long as the accident was startling enough, the declarant was sufficiently startled by the accident and made the statement while so startled, and the statement relates to the event, it is an excited utterance—and the hearsay rule does not care that it was and still is totally self-serving. Counsel can argue to the jury that they should not believe the statement because it was so completely self-serving, but the statement is not inadmissible hearsay. Whether the in-court declarant is telling the truth about having heard the out-of-court statement "presents a straight credibility question."[40]

3. Laying the Foundation for the Statement with the Statement Itself

The party offering a hearsay statement as a present sense impression or an excited utterance must put on evidence of each foundational element. The foundational evidence can be supplied by the out-of-court statement itself. Independent corroborating evidence is not a requirement for admission under these exceptions.[41] This is the generally prevailing rule in

---

As discussed in footnote 15 of this chapter, above, the abstract merits of the hearsay exception are irrelevant to the court's job. The court's job is simply to apply the exceptions using the foundational elements in the statute. Regarding admissibility versus credibility, *see* part (I)(C) of this chapter, above. Regarding trustworthiness versus credibility, *see* Chapter 5(V)(E)(2), below; *see also* part VIII(E)(4)(a) of this chapter, below.)

38. It is self-serving in that it places blame elsewhere. This is so even if the out-of-court declarant did not have litigation in mind at the time.

39. This is not a Rule 801(b) nonhearsay admission by a party-opponent. It is a party's own statement but it is not offered against that party. Rather, the statement is offered by the declarant-party.

40. United States v. Ruiz, 249 F.3d 643, 647 (7th Cir. 2001). Regarding the weight of the evidence versus its admissibility, *see particularly* part (I)(C) of this chapter, above. Regarding trustworthiness versus credibility, *see* Chapter 5(V)(E)(2), below; *see also* part VIII(E)(4)(a) of this chapter, below.

41. Corroboration would tend to make the evidence more trustworthy, but trustworthiness is not a foundational element. The trial judge is not asked to decide whether a present sense impression is trustworthy, but only whether (1) the statement was made while the declarant was perceiving an event or immediately thereafter and (2) the statement describes or explains the thing being perceived. The theory behind the exceptions is that if the foundational elements are present then the statement is sufficiently reliable and it is not inadmissible hearsay. If there is something about this particular present sense impression

the courts,[42] commentators tend to agree,[43] and the advisory committee's note calls this the prevalent practice.[44]

4. The Keys to the Excited Utterance Exception: The Particular Event and the Individual Declarant

Though the amount of time that has elapsed between the triggering event and the out-of-court statement is a relevant fact, it is not the key fact. The key to this entire exception is the lack of *capacity* to fabricate, not the lack of *time* to fabricate.[45] Stress works on different people in different ways. The lock on

---

that makes it less reliable than others, that is a question for the jury. It goes to weight, not admissibility. Regarding admissibility versus credibility, *see particularly* Chapter 3(I)(C), above. Regarding trustworthiness versus credibility, *see* Chapter 5(V)(E)(2), above; *see also* Chapter 3(VIII)(E)(4)(a), below.

Requiring corroboration confuses admissibility with weight; it rewrites the rule, adding to a third foundational element—trustworthiness—to the two stated in the rule; and it ignores the fact that when the drafters of the rules of evidence wanted to include trustworthiness as a separate foundational element—trustworthiness through, among other things, corroboration—they knew how to come right out and say it on the face of the rule. (*See* Rules 803(6), 803(7), 803(8), 804(b)(3), and 807.) The abstract merits of the hearsay exception are irrelevant to the court's job. The legislature has made that decision. The judge's job is simply to apply the exception or not, depending on the foundational elements written into the statute have been established. *See supra*, note 15.

42. United States v. Brown, 254 F.3d 454, 459 (3d Cir. 2001) (citing cases); People v. Barrett, 749 N.W.2d 797, 804 (Mich. 2008) ("the excited utterance exception ... does not require that a startling event or condition be established solely with evidence independent of an out-of-court statement before the out-of-court statement may be admitted."); Parker v. State, 778 A.2d 1096, 1105 (Md. 2001) (contents of statements and surrounding circumstances established the foundation for excited utterances by unnamed declarants); Warren v. State, 774 A.2d 246, 252 (Del. 2001) ("[I]ndependent corroboration ... is not a prerequisite for admission under the present sense impression exception. In some cases, corroborating evidence may be required to determine whether the declarant made the statement at the time of the triggering event or whether the declarant actually perceived the triggering event.") (citing cases and commentators); People v. Hendrickson, 586 N.W.2d 906, 912–14 (Mich. 1998) (Boyle, J. concurring) (citing cases and commentators); State v. Jones, 532 A.2d 169, 173 (Md. 1997) (*see supra*, note 24); Booth v. State, 508 A.2d 976, 984 (Md. 1986) (corroboration may be required to prove a foundational element in a particular case, but it is not required in all cases—it is not a foundational element); State v. Flesher, 286 N.W.2d 215, 218 (Iowa 1979).

43. *Brown*, 254 F.3d at 459 (citing commentators).

44. *Id.* (citing FED.R.EVID. 803(2) advisory committee's note).

45. *E.g.*, United States v. Wesela, 223 F.3d 656, 663 (7th Cir. 2000) ("The timing of the statement is important but not controlling."). *See also supra* part III(D)(9) of this chapter ("The Excited Utterance and the Child Witness"); State v. Smith, 909 P.2d 236, 240 (Utah

this exception has two tumblers: (1) How much stress did the particular triggering event cause the particular declarant? (2) How long would this stress
have stilled this declarant's capacity to reflect and fabricate—or, breaking the
latter into two questions, how does this particular declarant react to stress generally and how did he or she react to this stressful event in particular?[46]

1995) (justification for exception disappears as emotional excitement of declarant subsides
and capacity for reflection revives; though utterance and event need not be contemporaneous,
proximity is a factor to consider); State v. Plant, 461 N.W.2d 253, 264 (Neb. 1990) ("[T]ime
lapse is not dispositive"); People In Interest of O.E.P., 654 P.2d 312, 318 (Colo. 1982) (this
exception "finds its source primarily in 'the lack of capacity to fabricate rather than the lack
of time to fabricate.'" (quoting Rule 803(2) advisory committee's note); lapse of time does
not "nullif[y] the admissibility of this evidence under the excited utterance exception"). See
also infra, text preceding note 101. But see, e.g., Bemis v. Edwards, 45 F.3d 1369, 1372 (9th
Cir. 1995) ("[I]n order to qualify under [the excited utterance] exception, an out-of-court
statement must be nearly contemporaneous with the incident described and made with little chance for reflection.") (emphasis added) (Bemis is discussed in depth at Chapter 13(I)(D),
below).
    46. The facts to be considered in laying the foundation for this exception are as varied
as the situations in which persons are startled. Common kinds of considerations include the
following: The situation "sounded pretty bad"; the declarant "sounded very upset"; the declarant "spoke quickly, was out of breath, and sounded scared and nervous"; and the declarant "was visibly distraught[,] ... crying and her hands were shaking"; the time lapse
between the triggering event and the statements was short; and the statements "were not made
in response to suggestive questioning." United States v. Phelps, 168 F.3d 1048, 1055 (8th
Cir. 1999) (combining facts regarding two different statements; each quotation is from this
page of this case). E.g., United States v. McPike, 512 F.3d 1052, 1055 (8th Cir. 2008) (the
government did not identify a startling event; that declarant "she was 'crying' and 'hysterical'" when she made the statement is not enough.); United States v. Lawrence, 349 F.3d
109, 119 (3d Cir. 2003) (fact that declarant, in the hospital paralyzed from the neck down
from being shot, waited until he was speaking to a family member the day after the shooting to say who shot him suggest this declaration was a product of deliberation, not an excited utterance); Simmons v. United States, 945 A.2d 1183, 1187 (D.C. 2008) (Declarant had
just seen a man get shot. He was "in a state of considerable distress—pacing back and forth,
mumbling to himself, and looking and acting so patently 'scared and upset' that [the testifying witness] was moved to ask this total stranger whether he was 'okay.' This ... establish[ed] that the gentleman was in the requisite state of nervous excitement."); State v. Buda,
949 A.2d 761, 773 (N.J. 2008) (the declarant child was beaten earlier in the day; when his
mother saw him, the result was "screaming and a dash to the emergency room and ... a
two-week hospitalization"; the "sobbing, emotional child [made the statement] in a strange
and frightening place—a hospital emergency room—to ... a person previously unknown
to the child." While the time between the bearing and the statement is significant, the court
"must assess ... the quality and nature of that period. [Here,] the time elapsed was not of
a kind likely to allow this child to deliberate and, thus, fabricate the statement.... [T]he
circumstances of this incident and the mental and physical condition of the declarant did

That time itself is not the key is borne out on the face of the rule and in the principal guarantee of reliability. By its terms, the rule requires an out-of-court statement made while *the* declarant was under the stress of the triggering event.[47] The principal guarantee of reliability is that *this* continuing stress diminishes *this* person's capacity to fabricate.[48] Each startling, disgusting, and threatening event produces a different amount of mind-numbing stress. Each witness to and each victim of every such event reacts differently to that mind numbing stress. It is a combination of the particular event and the individual declarant.[49] The more stressful the event, the longer the stress is likely to affect a declarant. The more susceptible this declarant is to stress, perhaps taking into account factors such as age,[50] maturity, and the like, the longer the stress is

---

not permit the disqualifying opportunity to deliberate or fabricate."); State v. Lopez, 974 So.2d 340, 345 (Fla. 2008) (declarant, who had been abducted at gunpoint, was "nervous, shaken, and speaking rapidly"); State v. Bergevine, 942 A.2d 974, 979 (R.I. 2008) (declarant had just witnessed the sexual molestation of his daughter and "appeared to be '[e]motionally traumatized,' breathing quickly, at times crying and 'repeating the same words over and over again.[.]'"); State v. Graham, 941 A.2d 848, 859 (R.I. 2008) (A police officer, testified that declarant "was 'very upset, her eyes were very wide open, she was in a very excited state.' [H]er torso, hands, and face were covered in blood. [S]he 'calm[ed] down after a period of time'" and immediately made the statement in question. "Even though she may have 'calmed down' to some extent, it is clear that [she] still was covered in her husband's blood and she made her statements ... shortly after she found her husband's wounded body.").

47. *Wesela*, 223 F.3d at 663 ("All that [this] exception requires is that the statement be made contemporaneously with the excitement resulting from the event, not necessarily with the event itself.") (multiple and internal quotation marks omitted; citing cases).

48. *See* part III(C)(2) of this chapter, above.

49. *See also infra*, test preceding note 102.

The Understatement Award for 2008 goes to People v. Barrett, 747 N.W.2d 797, 804 (Mich. 2008):

Bartel's statement to her neighbor that defendant was chasing her with an ax; her statements to the 911 operator that defendant had kicked the door down, beaten her, tried to strangle her, and threatened her with a hatchet; and her similar statements to the responding police officer, as corroborated by the neighbor's observation that Bartel was hysterical and crying, the transcript of the 911 call in which the operator advised Bartel to calm down and gain control of her breathing, the first responding officer's observation that Bartel was so agitated that she could not sit down and that she had been crying, the hatchet in the house, a 12-inch hole in one of the doors, the marks on her shoulders and arm, and the cut on the inside of her mouth, all support that hers were excited utterances pertaining to a startling event or condition.

50. Some courts, for example, are of the opinion that, as a general, stress remains with children longer than with adults.*See* part III(D)(9) of this chapter, below.

likely to affect this declarant. It is incorrect, then, to say that the excited utterance exception has any direct requirement of immediacy; immediacy is a factor only to the extent that the stress of an exciting event abates over time.[51]

In *United States v. Napier*,[52] a woman was shown a photograph in a newspaper.[53] This startled her and led her to exclaim that the man pictured was the person who, approximately eight weeks ago, had beaten her nearly to death. Newspaper photographs are not necessarily startling and there was nothing inherently startling in this particular newspaper photograph. Viewing this photograph, however, did sufficiently startle this declarant, and the exception applied to her statement.[54] Each application of this exception depends upon its own particular facts and circumstances and requires inquiring into the nature of the particular event and the particular declarant.

5. An Excited Utterance Provided in Response to Questioning

Whether an excited utterance is exclaimed impulsively or provided in response to questioning is not determinative of its status as an excited utterance. Instead, this is just one of the many factors to consider when deciding whether,

---

51. *E.g.*, United States v. McPike, 512 F.3d 1052, 1055 (8th Cir. 2008) ("consider, among other factors, the lapse of time …"); United States v. Kenyon, 481 F.3d 1054, 1062 (8th Cir. 2007) (consider, among other things, the time lapse between event and statement "and whether the declarant's stress or excitement was continuous from the time of the event until the time of the statements"); Morgan v. Foretich, 846 F.2d 941, 947 (4th Cir. 1998) (lapse of time, declarant's age, declarant's physical and mental state, the characteristics of the event, the subject matter of the statements); MacDonald v. B.M.D. Golf Assocs., 813 A.2d 488, 491 (N.H. 2002) (" '[C]ontemporaneity is a factor [but] it is by no means controlling, and such things as the nature of the event, the victim's state of mind, and all other circumstances are important considerations.' ") (citation omitted); State v. Smith, 909 P.2d 236, 240 (Utah 1995) ("consider the likely effects of the declarant's age, the declarant's physical and mental condition, the circumstances and nature of the startling event, the subject matter of the statement, and the time lapse between the event and the utterance."); State v. Chapin, 826 P.2d 194, 198 (Wash. 1992) (Generally, "as the time between the event and the statement lengthens, the opportunity for reflective thought arises and the danger of fabrication increases. The longer the time interval, the greater the need for proof that the declarant did not actually engage in reflective thought.…"); State v. Carlson, 808 P.2d 1002 (Or. 1991) (relational concept "cannot be determined without focusing on the event's effect on the declarant"). *But see, e.g., Bemis*, 45 F.3d at 1372 (discussed in depth at Chapter 13(I)(D), below).

52. 518 F.2d 316 (9th Cir. 1975).

53. United States v. Napier, 518 F.2d 316, 317 (9th Cir. 1975).

54. *Id.* at 318.

the statement was made while the declarant was still under the stress of the excitement of the event.[55]

6. Two Differences between the Present Sense Impression Exception and the Excited Utterance Exception

Keep in mind two differences between the present sense impression exception and the excited utterance exception: The first difference is the element of *immediacy*. The time lapse between the triggering event and the out-of-court statement can be much longer under the excited utterance exception, than is allowed under the present sense impression exception. The second difference is that the present sense impression must *describe* the thing being perceived; the excited utterance exception need only *relate to* the startling event.

a. Immediacy

A present sense impression must be made "while the declarant was perceiving the event or condition, or immediately thereafter."[56] This pretty much involves someone saying it while seeing it. Because an event can be over faster than the declarant can formulate and speak the words, the rule allows the statement to be made "immediately thereafter." That means, however, pretty much as soon as it is possible to get the words out.[57] It is the timing that matters here and not the nature of the event or the susceptibility of the declarant.

An excited utterance must be made while the declarant is still under the

---

55. United States v. Marrowbone, 211 F.3d 452, 454–55 (8th Cir. 2000) (one factor to consider); Territory of Guam v. Cepeda, 69 F.3d 369, 372 (9th Cir. 1995) (that the statements was in response to a police inquiry is but one factor to consider on the question of whether the statement was the product of stress and excitement) (citing cases); MacDonald v. B.M.D. Golf Assocs., 813 A.2d 488, 491 (N.H. 2002) ("That the declarant may have been responding to a question does not prevent his statement from being spontaneous."); Parker v. State, 778 A.2d 1096, 1106 (Md. 2001); People v. Brown, 517 N.E.2d 515, 519–20 (N.Y. 1987) (the fact that the "emergency room statements were given in reply to the deliberate questions of a police officer" does not preclude their admission as excited utterances; it is but one factor to consider "in determining whether the statements were made under the continuing influence of the stress and excitement" of the triggering event).

56. Fed.R.Evid. 803 (1). *See, e.g.*, United States v. Green, 541 F.3d 176, 181–82 (8th Cir. 2008) (canvassing and discussing cases regarding the timing requirement for a present sense impression).

57. *See supra*, note 26, for cases supporting this point. The almost reflexive nature of the present sense impression is its guarantee of reliability. *See* part II(C)(2) of this chapter, above. The guarantee of reliability is relevant to defining the outer edges of the exception. *See* part I(B) of this chapter, above.

stress of the excitement caused by the triggering event, however long that lasts.[58] This allows for a greater lapse of time between event and statement than does the present sense impression exception.[59]

Cases routinely apply the excited utterance exception to time lapses measured in minutes, often measured in hours, and sometimes, though rarely, measured in days, weeks, or, in at least one case, months.[60] It depends on the continuity of the stress from the time of the triggering event to the time of the out-of-court statement, which, in turn, often depends on the nature of the stressful event and the nature of the individual declarant.[61]

b. *"Describing the Thing Being Perceived" versus "Relating to the Startling Event"*

A present sense impression must "describe" the triggering event. An excited utterance must "relate to" the triggering event.[62] The second is a looser stan-

---

58. This is discussed above, at part III(D)(4) of this chapter.

59. "[T]he present sense impression exception requires that the statement be made contemporaneously, or almost contemporaneously, with the event that prompted it. The excited utterance exception, on the other hand, requires only that the statement be made contemporaneously with the excitement resulting from the event, not necessarily with the event itself." United States v. Moore, 791 F.2d 566, 572 n.4 (7th Cir. 1986). *See also* Christopher B. Mueller & Laird C. Kirkpatrick, Evidence § 8.36, at 911 (2d ed. 1999) ("Other things being equal, the more quickly a statement follows the occasion, the more likely it is to be a spontaneous reaction. Statements during or immediately after an exciting occurrence have smooth sledding, but it is the exception for present sense impressions to which immediacy is indispensable, not the excited utterance exception."); Fed.R.Evid. 803 (1) and (2) advisory committee's note (most significant practical difference between these two exceptions lies in time lapse between event and statement; present sense impression exception recognizes that precise contemporaneity often is not possible, and allows "slight lapse of time" between triggering event and statement; excited utterance exception applies for duration of state of excitement).
     One court has said that it is possible for a statement to be made "immediately" after an event, so the present sense impression exception applies, and yet long enough after the event for the stress of the excitement to have dissipated, so the excited utterance exception does not apply. United States v. Ferber, 966 F.Supp. 90, 99 (D. Mass. 1997). This seems wrong. *Ferber* recognizes "a possible inconsistency" in its ruling, but explains it away. Contrary to what the court stated, the inconsistency seems real, and insurmountable. The kind of immediacy required for the present sense impression exception does not allow for the kind of time it takes to come down from the kind of excitement required for an excited utterance.

60. *See* part III(D)(9) of this chapter, below.

61. *See* part III(D)(4) of this chapter, above.

62. If someone standing nearby is startled by an explosion and immediately says something about someone he saw running from the scene of the blast, then the statement will fit under both of these exceptions. If he goes on to say something about how he slipped

dard. Take another look at *Betts v. Betts*.[63] This is a child custody case. The child's birth father was trying to get custody from the child's birth mother. The child's foster mother testified that she told the child her birth mother had married a man named Caporale. The foster mother testified that the child "ran and put her arms around me and her head in my lap and started crying real bad and hard and said, 'He killed my brother and he'll kill my mommie too.' "[64] This out-of-court statement is a nonhearsay statement that circumstantially indicates the girl's state of mind regarding her relationship with her mother (her custodial parent) and Caporale. It is not being used for the truth of the out-of-court assertion, but to show the girl's state of mind.[65] The testifying witness, the foster mother, is a real witness to the girl's state of mind, to the fact that the girl made this statement. And in the child custody action the child's state of mind is relevant. Whose credibility is at issue? Since the fact that the girl made this statement is relevant to her state of mind, all we need to know is whether the girl did make the statement and it is the foster mother's credibility that is at stake—she is the one who says the girl did make the statement.

Change the nature of the case. Make it a damage action; say that either Caporale has been acquitted of murdering the young boy or the prosecutor has refused to file charges, and the boy's natural father has brought a wrongful death action against Caporale. Now the issue issue to which the out-of-court statement is relevant is whether Caporale killed her brother, and the out-of-court statement is that he did kill her brother. It is an out-of-court statement offered to prove the truth of the matter asserted and it does not fit under a Rule 801(d) definitional exclusion. Bingo! Now it is hearsay. And the next question is whether it is admissible hearsay, that is, does it fit under an exception to the hearsay rule? Consider the present sense impression exception and the excited utterance exception.

Present sense impression: A present sense impression must describe or explain the event being perceived. The "event" the girl perceived was her foster mother telling her that her mother had married Caporale. The out-of-court statement does not describe or explain that event. It was evoked by the event, but it does not describe or explain the event. Instead, it describes an earlier and quite different event: the death of her brother. Even though the statement was made

---

and fell on mayonnaise in a grocery store, that part of his statement does not fit under either exception.

63. 473 P.2d 403 (Wash. Ct. App. 1970). This case is discussed throughout this book, first and particularly at Chapter 1(IV)(F).

64. Betts v. Betts, 473 P.2d 403, 407 (Wash. Ct. App. 1970).

65. *Id.* at 407–08.

immediately after the triggering event, it does not fit under the present sense impression exception because it does not "describe" the triggering event.

Excited Utterance: The statement does, however, fit under the excited utterance exception. There was a startling event—the foster mother telling the child of her mother's marriage to Caporale. The out-of-court declarant was startled by the event—this child was startled by her foster mother's statement. The out-of-court statement made while the declarant was startled—the child made the out-of-court statement while she was in the grip of this emotional reaction to the news. The out-of-court statement related to the startling event— the startling event was the foster mother telling the child that her natural mother had married Caporale; the out-of-court statement was that Caporale had killed her brother and would kill her mother too; the statement does relate to the startling event.[66] This out of court statement fits under the excited utterance exception. It is admissible hearsay. If there is no other evidentiary or constitutional problem, it is admissible evidence.[67]

Here is another example of this difference between these two exceptions. This is a slip and fall case in which a customer was startled when she saw another customer fall. While still startled, she said: "I told them to clean it up about two hours ago...."[68] While the statement does not *describe* an event being perceived and, therefore, cannot fit under the present sense impression exception, it is *related to* the event being perceived and, therefore, can fit under the excited utterance exception.[69]

---

66. *But see, e.g., Bemis*, 45 F.3d at 1372, which states that "in order to qualify under [the excited utterance] exception, an out-of-court statement must be nearly contemporaneous *with the incident described* and made with little chance for reflection." *Id.* at 1372 (emphasis added). *Bemis* is discussed in depth at Chapter 13(I)(D), below. Taken literally, this seems to make every excited utterance a present sense impression. Rule 803(2) becomes the excited present-sense-impression exception and is subsumed into Rule 803(1). This really does away with the excited utterance exception.

67. You might be saying to yourself, "Wait a minute! We cannot find against a defendant based on this evidence. How do we know, for example, that the little girl knows what she is talking about?" The question here is not whether the little girl is competent, *i.e.*, has the requisite personal knowledge; it is not whether the Confrontation Clause renders the evidence inadmissible; the question is not whether there is enough evidence to convict or whether there is even enough evidence to get the case to the jury. The only question here is whether the hearsay rule bars the admission of the evidence—is it inadmissible hearsay. The answer to that question is "No."

68. David v. Pueblo Supermarket of St. Thomas, 740 F.2d 230, 234 (3d Cir. 1984).

69. Even though the out-of-court statement addresses something that happened "about two hours" before the startling event, it nonetheless relates to the startling event.

7. A Series of Exciting Events (the Rolling Exciting-Event) or a Subsequent Related Event Triggering Excitement Anew

The event that triggers an excited utterance need not be the primary focus of the excited utterance. The two only need be related. The statement can, for example, look back beyond the triggering event, so long as it does relate to the triggering event. In *Betts v. Betts*, also discussed just above,[70] the foster mother told the girl that the girl's mother had married a man named Caporale. Startled by the news, the little girl exclaimed, "He killed my brother and he'll kill my mommie too." The startling event that triggered the excited utterance was the news of the girl's mother's marriage to this particular man; the excited utterance expressed the girl's fear that this man would kill her mother and it expressed part of the basis for this fear—he had killed her brother. The triggering event is not the primary focus of the statement. The statement looks back beyond the triggering event. The statement is, however, "related to" the triggering event and should fit under this exception.[71]

In *United States v. Napier*,[72] the defendant was on trial for crimes in connection with having beaten a woman nearly to death. The beating left the victim unable to comprehend the significance of the oath and, therefore, incompetent to testify.[73] Approximately eight weeks after the beating, the victim saw a photo in the newspaper. "[H]er 'immediate reaction was one of great distress and horror and upset.'"[74] She pointed at the photo and said, "'He killed me, he killed me.'"[75]

The event that triggered the excited utterance was seeing the photo. The event on trial is the beating. They are not the same and, in fact, they took place eight weeks or so apart. Nonetheless, offering counsel can law the foundation for the excited utterance exception: (1) seeing the photo is the startling event, (2) the declarant's immediate reaction of great distress, horror, and upset shows that she was startled by the event, (3) her statement was made while the startling event continued to block reflection and reasoning, and (4) the statement,

---

70. This case is discussed throughout this book, including just above in part III(D)(6)(b) of this chapter. *See particularly* Chapter 1(IV)(F).

71. *See* United States v. Jahagirdar, 466 F.3d 149, 155 (1st Cir. 2006) ("continued or renewed insecurities"). *But see, e.g.,* Bemis v. Edwards, 45 F.3d 1369, 1372 (9th Cir. 1995) (discussed in depth at Chapter 13(I)(D), below).

72. 518 F.2d 316 (9th Cir. 1975).

73. Regarding the admissibility of an out-of-court statement made by a person who would not have been competent to testify, *see* Chapter 13, below.

74. United States v. Napier, 518 F.2d 316, 317 (9th Cir. 1975) (quoting testimony from the victim's sister).

75. *Id.*

"He killed me" relates to the startling event.[76] (It also relates to an earlier event, the event on trial, but that does not change its nature as an excited utterance: the foundation for the exception has been satisfied.)

As a variation of this point, exciting events sometimes roll by in series and whether or not the excited utterance exception applies may depend on which of the exciting events is selected as the triggering event. In one such case the complainant and her boyfriend were driving home in a car when the boyfriend hit her a number of times.[77] When they arrived home, the complainant played back a message on her answering machine that turned out to be a holiday greeting from a male friend of hers. This angered the defendant, who got out his gun case and opened it. She ran to a neighbor's and called 911. The trial court kept the 911 tape out. The trial judge held that the complainant's statements on the tape were not an excited utterance because of the period of reflection between the startling event and the out-of-court statement. The court of appeals reversed. "[W]e conclude that, although the complainant was no longer

---

76. This is an example of what one case called "continued or renewed insecurities." *Jahagirdar*, 466 F.3d at 155. *See also* United States v. Beverly, 369 F.3d 516, 540 (6th Cir. 2004) (shown a photograph taken during a bank robbery, defendant's wife said, "oh, my God, that looks like Johnny," her husband; "viewing the photo was a startling event"); People v. Garcia, 826 P.2d 1259, 1264 (Colo. 1992) (after seeing his mother in a casket and as he was leaving the funeral home with his grandfather, declarant said "Daddy did it"; after seeing his mother's photo at his grandfather's home, approximately one week after her stabbing, he said "Mama crying, mama and daddy fighting, mama bleeding"); In re Troy P., 842 P.2d 742, 746–47 (N.M. 1992) (imminent return to father's house caused child to become upset and state "[t]hat boy touches me"; startling event was imminent return and statement related thereto; this court refers to this as "rekindled excitement"); State v. Carlson, 808 P.2d 1004 (Or. 1991) (defendant's lie that marks on arm were from working on car caused declarant to become upset, break in, and yell "You liar, you got them from shooting up in the bedroom with all your stupid friends"; excited utterance); State v. Owens, 899 P.2d 833 (Wash. Ct. App. 1995) (family investigated child's deteriorating health; cause remained undiagnosed despite visits to numerous medical personnel until one doctor investigated possibility of abuse; the day he saw this doctor, the boy "hysterically" told his mother defendant had molested him; medical examination was startling event, statements were made while under stress of startling event, and statements relate to startling event; excited utterance); Bayne v. State, 632 A.2d 476 (Md. Ct. Spec. App. 1993) (excited utterance about prior happening may be admissible under excited utterance exception if subsequent startling event relates directly or indirectly to prior event; admissibility absent such relationship left for latter case); People v. Ojeda, 745 P.2d 274 (Colo. Ct. App. 1987) (excited utterance by victim of attempted sexual assault identified defendant as assailant and reported suspicious questions defendant had asked her five months before; both statements qualify as excited utterances).

77. State v. Stonaker, 945 P.2d 573 (Or. Ct. App. 1997).

under the stress of excitement caused by the alleged assault when she made the 9-1-1 call, she was under the stress of excitement caused by the gun case incident throughout the call."[78]

8. Often an Out-of-Court Statement Will Be Both a Present Sense Impression and an Excited Utterance

When a declarant witnesses an exciting event and describes the event as it is happening, the out-of-court statement may fit under both the present sense impression and the excited utterance exceptions. When the in-court witness testifies, "I heard someone scream, 'The truck is running the light,' and then I saw the truck hit that little car," the out-of-court part of that statement is a present sense impression (statement made while perceiving event and describes event being perceived) and it is an excited utterance (startling event, declarant startled by it, statement made while declarant was under the stress of that excitement, and statement relates to startling event).

Take this example: Homeowner wakes to the sound of breaking glass, calls 911, and describes to the 911 operator a burglary in progress and the burglar. What the homeowner said to the 911 operator is a present sense impression and, no doubt, also an excited utterance.[79]

---

78. *Id.* at 579. *See also* State v. Pepin, 940 A.2d 221, 227 (N.H. 2007) ("[H]ours after the beating stopped," the victim made a statement to police regarding the beating; she contacted police after she was able to flee her home. "'[T]here is no requirement that the crime be the startling event.' In this case, the victim was still under the stress of excitement caused by the beating, her flight from the defendant and her decision to leave her baby behind, and these were the 'startling or shocking' events giving rise to her statements on the 911 call.") (citation omitted); Newbill v. State, 884 N.E.2d. 383, 387–89 (Ind. App. 2008) (a sexual assault occurred between 2:00 and 3:00 a.m.; defendant left the victim in a bedroom with her son while he apparently stayed in the next room between her and the door to the residence; she later heard another person outside the bedroom and pleaded with him to take her home; he told her to lock herself in the room until he returned; he returned and took her home before 7:00 a.m.; she put her son to bed; a third-person who had been told what had happened called the victim, urged her to call the police, and then called the police herself; not long after 7:00, just as the victim was about to call the police, the 911 dispatcher called her; the recording of the 911 call was admissible as an excited utterance; the statement was made over four hours after the assault but within the hour of the captivity; though the court simply recites the facts and affirms use of the exception, one way to look at this is that there was either one long and continuous startling event or a series of startling events).

79. *See, e.g.,* State v. Bergevine, 942 A.2d 974, 979 (R.I. 2008) ("statements to the 911 operator were ... both present sense impressions and excited utterances"). *See also* Bemis v. Edwards, 45 F.3d 1369, 1372 (9th Cir. 1995). *Bemis* incorrectly treats the admissibility of

Take this more complicated example: Husband is standing at the window, watching a beating being administered in the next-door yard; Wife is on the phone with Daughter. As Husband is watching the beating, he describes what he is seeing to Wife; as Wife is hearing what Husband is saying, she relays this information to Daughter. Husband is very agitated by what he is seeing, and Wife is very agitated by what she is hearing. At trial, what happened during the beating is relevant to an issue.[80] The plaintiff calls Daughter to the stand to have her testify to what she heard.

There is, of course, double hearsay here.[81] In chronological order, the first level is Husband's statement to Wife, and the second level is Wife's statement to Daughter. Each statement is admissible. Husband's statement to Wife is a present sense impression; he is stating aloud his visual perception while perceiving it. If it can be established that he was sufficiently excited by what he was seeing, then his statement to Wife is also an excited utterance. Wife's statement to Daughter is also a present sense impression; she is stating aloud her aural perception while perceiving it. If it can be established that she was sufficiently excited by the event—excited by what she was being told, by the way her husband was telling it, etc.—then her statement is also an excited utterance.[82]

---

a tape recording of a 911 call as a double hearsay problem. *Bemis* states that the tape recording of the call is one level of hearsay and the statement by the homeowner is another. This is not so; there is only one level of hearsay. The only out-of-court declarant is the homeowner; the only out-of-court statement is the statement made over the phone by the homeowner; the tape recording is not a separate declarant or a separate out-of-court statement. All that is required here is proper authentication of the tape recording and a hearsay exception for the homeowner's out-of-court statement. This is one mistake made in *Bemis*. For two others, *see supra*, note 66, and *infra*, note 82. *Bemis* is discussed in depth at Chapter 13(I)(D), below.

80. Perhaps the plaintiff is the party injured by the beating, the defendant is a police officer who allegedly beat him, and the action is a civil rights action against the police officer and the city brought under 42 U.S.C. § 1983.

81. *See* Chapter 11, below.

82. *But see Bemis*, at 1373, citing FED.R.EVID. 602 for the proposition that the out-of-court declarant must be making the statement based on personal knowledge, and holding that this kind of contemporaneous relay of knowledge from the one who saw the fight, to the one on the phone at the scene, to the one on the other end of the phone call does not fit the exception because the one on the phone at the scene does not have personal knowledge of the fight. This misapplies the personal knowledge requirement. Continuing with the example from the text, Husband has personal knowledge of the facts in his statement: "I see X, Y, and Z." Wife has personal knowledge of the facts in her statement: "I heard X, Y, and Z." Unless the court is amending the rule, adding a foundational element not found in its text, each out-of-court statement should fit under the present sense impression exception. Each out-of-court declarant is describing something while perceiving it, which is all the

Perhaps Husband and Wife have since died or disappeared. Perhaps Husband has testified about what he saw, and Wife about what she heard, and Daughter's testimony is offered on top of that. Insofar as the hearsay rule is concerned, it does not matter. Because these are Rule 803 exceptions, whether the in-court testimony of the out-of-court declarant is available or not is irrelevant.

9. The Excited Utterance and the Child Witness

Many excited utterances are made within minutes of the triggering event (just beyond the time that would qualify the statement as a present sense impression). Some are made hours,[83] days, and sometimes even weeks or months later.[84]

It is difficult to see how the capacity to fabricate is suppressed for all of those weeks or months.[85] It is difficult to see how the influence of playing the situation over again and again in one's mind, for weeks or months, does not alter the perception of the triggering event. It is difficult to see how we can factor out weeks and months of living with the situation and, even without discussing the triggering event, perhaps being around and listening to doctors, relatives, and others who may have a personal or professional stake in the situation.[86]

In most of the cases allowing an "excited utterance" made weeks or months after the triggering event, the declarant is a child who either is alleged to have been abused or was a witness to a brutally violent crime, and the abuse or other crime is the subject of the out-of-court statement.[87] It is one thing to

---

rule requires. The first is describing the beating, while perceiving it, and the second is describing what the first is saying, while perceiving it. There are two levels of hearsay, each separately fitting under this one exception. *Bemis* is discussed in depth at Chapter 13(I)(D), below.

83. United States v. Jahagirdar, 466 F.3d 149, 155 (1st Cir. 2006) ("Although '[t]he time lapse in most excited utterance cases is usually a few seconds, or a few minutes,' there are exceptions stretching into hours.") (citation omitted); State v. Timmons, 178 P.3d 644, 651 (Idaho Ct. App. 2007) ("Idaho's appellate courts have upheld the admission of statements as excited utterances, when made by young children, even when several hours have passed since the event.").

84. *But see, e.g., Bemis*, at 1372 (discussed in depth at Chapter 13(I)(D), below).

85. Unless, perhaps, the victim is just emerging from some sort of dissociative state.

86. What is not difficult to see is that we abhor child abusers and we would like to see all of them in jail and so we take the rules of evidence that stand in the way of that goal and we bend them and stretch them, sometimes until they break. G. Michael Fenner, *Law Professor Reveals Shocking Truth About Hearsay*, 62 UMKC L.Rev. 1, 64–70 (1993).

87. United States v. Wesela, 223 F.3d 656, 663 (7th Cir. 2000); Wright v. State, 249 S.W.3d 133, 139 (Ark. 2007) ("[T]he trend [in Arkansas] has been toward expansion of that time interval.... [T]he more liberal cases appear to be cases in which the declarant has been a child."). A child or someone with the mind of a child: *e.g.,* Cole v. State, 818 S.W.2d

tearfully announce an assault soon after it occurs, it is another to announce it weeks later.[88] Cases applying the excited utterance exception to a statement made so long after the triggering event, seem to be making credibility[89] and policy decisions[90] (this child seems to be telling the truth and we do not have much other evidence[91] and do not want the defendant to get away with this crime) rather than legal decisions (the proponent of the evidence has shown each foundational element of the exception).

In cases where the witness is a child who has been the victim of or a witness to a violent crime, excited utterance cases tend to relax the requirement that the declarant continue to be under the stress of the excitement of the triggering event.[92] Examples:

■ *One day*: In a first-degree statutory rape trial, the out-of-court statement of the five-and-one-half-year-old victim, made "at least 20 hours" after the "startling" event, was an excited utterance.[93]

---

573 (Ark. 1991) (twenty-three-year-old rape victim with mental capacity of six-year-old, made statement a day after the rape).

Using this exception, and others, as a way to get in an out-of-court statement made by a declarant who would be incompetent to testify if called as a witness, is discussed below, in Chapter 13. Regarding this matter, *see also* G. Michael Fenner, *Law Professor Reveals Shocking Truth About Hearsay*, 62 UMKC L. Rev. 1, 38, 64–70 (1993).

88. If there is an aura of reliability, it is still difficult, in the facts of many of these cases, to find the foundational elements of the excited utterance exception. And, of course, saying a statement is reliable and saying it fits under an exception are two different things.

89. Credibility decisions are, of course, for the trier of fact and not for the trier of law. This is the general rule. *See* part (I)(C) of this chapter, above. There are exceptions. One exception is the rare case where a witness is incredible as a matter of law. Another is where the admissibility of evidence depends in part on credibility and, therefore, the trier of law must make a credibility decision. This latter point is discussed below, at Chapter 5(V)(E)(2) (the residual exception and the turncoat witness); *see also* part (VIII)(E)(4)(a) of this chapter, below.

90. Regarding abusing the rules of evidence in service of public policy, *see* Chapter 5(V)(F) and *see also* Chapter 5(V)(G), both below.

91. This is the perfect situation for consideration of the residual exception, Fed.R.Evid. 807. *See* Chapter 5, below. It is a lousy situation for the application of the excited utterance exception.

92. *See* United States v. Jahagirdar, 466 F.3d 149, 155 (1st Cir. 2006) ("Although '[t]he time lapse in most excited utterance cases is usually a few seconds, or a few minutes, there are exceptions stretching into hours. But these cases involve … continuing physical pain after beatings or shootings, continued or renewed insecurity, or … *young children who were sexually abused*.") (citations omitted, emphasis added).

93. State v. Woodward, 646 P.2d 135 (Wash. Ct. App. 1982), *superceded by statute*, Wash.Rev.Codex § 9A.44.120 (2006), *as recognized in* State v. Rameriz, 730 P.2d 98, 102–03

■ *Two days*: In a trial for second degree murder of his 18-month-old step-son and first degree assault and child abuse of his four-year-old stepson, a statement by defendant's four-year-old daughter, made two days after she witnessed the "startling" event, was an excited utterance.[94]

■ *Three days*: In a trial for sexual assault, the 10-year-old victim's out-of-court statement, made three days after the "startling" event, was an excited utterance.[95]

■ *One week*: In a trial for felony murder resulting from a rape-homicide, the out-of-court statement of a three-and-one-half-year-old eyewitness, made one week after the "startling" event, was an excited utterance.[96]

■ *Two months*: In a proceeding to restrict a sex-abuser father's right to visitation with his minor children, the out-of-court statement of one of the child-

---

(Wash. Ct. App. 1986). *Accord* Cole v. State, 818 S.W.2d 573 (Ark. 1991) (a twenty-three-year-old rape victim with mental capacity of six-year-old, made the statement a day after the rape).

94. State v. Plant, 461 N.W.2d 253 (Neb. 1990). State v. Galvan, 297 N.W.2d 344 (Iowa 1980) is an interesting case because of the age of the child (two years old), the nature of the statements (acting out), and the timing of the statements (two days and then five months after the triggering event). A man was bound, beaten, and stabbed. He died and defendant was convicted of first-degree murder. At his trial, his ex-wife was allowed to testify that their two-year-old daughter had been out with the defendant on the night of the murder. Two days after the murder, the daughter, in behavior that was unusual for her, took "a belt from her mother's robe and bound her own hands with it. Then she made several gestures as if beating her own chest." *Id.* at 346. The ex-wife was also allowed to testify that five months after the murder, the same daughter had an adverse reaction to a television cartoon. In the cartoon a mouse was shown tied up and this "caused the daughter to cry." *Id.* The Iowa Supreme Court found each instance to be assertive conduct and hearsay. It found the first statement admissible under a common-law "res gestae" exception. "The passage of two days, especially for so young a child, leaves it close enough to the transaction so that the trial court could have" concluded fabrication was unlikely. *Id.* at 347. The second statement, however, was too remote in time; its admission was error and the error was reversible.

The court noted that the two-year-old out-of-court declarant would not have been competent to take the stand. "[A]dmissibility in such cases," however, "does not turn on the competence of the child to take the oath, but on the spontaneity of the utterance or act described." *Id.* at 347. *See* Chapter 13 for a discussion of using hearsay exceptions to get into evidence out-of-court statements by persons who were, at the time the statement was made, or are, at the time the statement is offered, incompetent to testify in court.

95. State v. Padilla, 329 N.W.2d 263 (Wis. 1982). The court recognized that more time elapsed between the triggering event and the out-of-court statement in this case than in other excited utterance cases, but this does not matter "because spontaneity and stress are the keys" and, for young victims of sexual assault, stress may be present even some time after triggering event. *Id.* at 266–67.

96. People v. Lovett, 272 N.W.2d 126 (Mich. Ct. App. 1976).

victims, made "approximately two months" after the "startling" event, was an excited utterance.[97]

■ *Three months*: One-hundred-plus years ago, a court affirmed the admission of a child's statement to her mother, made three months after the triggering event.[98]

All of these cases involve crimes of violence perpetrated on or witnessed by children, and in most cases fairly young children. Most involve child abuse and the victim's statements about that abuse. Some stretch the excited utterance exception to its very limit (and perhaps beyond). Underlying this is, of course, the system's desire to protect children—our desire put child abusers in jail, to keep children from having to confront their abusers (and, necessarily then, not allowing accused abusers to confront their complaining witness), and to prevent the cross-examination of children who have already been traumatized quite enough.[99] We are making substantive policy decisions, rather than interpreting evidence rules.[100]

---

97. *In re* Marriage of Theis, 460 N.E.2d 912, 917 (Ill. App. Ct. 1984). *But see* State v. Galvan, 297 N.W.2d 344 (Iowa 1980), discussed *supra*, note 94, holds that a child-witness's out-of-court statement made five months after a murder is too remote in time and does not fit under a hearsay exception.

98. People v. Gage, 28 N.W. 835, 836–37 (Mich. 1886).

99. Society's compelling interest in protecting children is discussed below, at Chapter 5(V)(F) & (G) (the residual exception and the child-abuse cases).

The Confrontation Clause may render all such statements inadmissible at the criminal trial of the alleged abuser except those where the defendant previously had or at trial has a chance to confront the child-witness. It is also possible, however, that, like all other constitutional rights, the right of confrontation is not an absolute right and that, like all other constitutional rights, the law can allow evidence against the defendant in a criminal case in a situation where the defendant cannot confront the witness if the state can show that it has a compelling reason for doing so and that doing so is necessary to achieve that compelling goal. Though I do not bet on this happening, it would align the right of confrontation with other constitutional rights, such as free speech, free exercise, equal protection, and due process. And in other areas of constitutional law the two most commonly used and cited compelling state interests are national security and protecting children. Regarding the Confrontation Clause, see Chapter 14.

100. The pressure created to do this sort of thing is discussed below, at Chapter 5(IV)(B). The better, more direct and more honest way of dealing with this kind of evidence is to see if the statement in question can satisfy the foundational elements of the residual exception in Rule 807. The use of that exception in this situation is discussed below, at Chapter 5(V)(G).

In Morgan v. Foretich, 846 F.2d 941 (4th Cir. 1988), the court notes that the four-year-old girl reporting sexual abuse to her mother was discussing activities about which a child of this age would have too little knowledge to fabricate. Her "tender years greatly reduce

The larger lesson to be learned from these cases is this: Though the amount of time that has elapsed between the triggering event and the out-of-court statement is a relevant fact, it is not the key fact. As discussed above, the key to this particular exception is the lack of capacity to fabricate, not the lack of time to fabricate.[101] Stress works on different people, in different ways. The key is how much stress the particular triggering event caused the particular declarant, and how the particular declarant reacts to stress generally and reacted to this stressful event in particular.[102]

IV. State of Mind or Statement of Then-Existing Mental, Emotional, or Physical Condition: Rule 803(3)

A. Text of the Rule

> The following are not excluded by the hearsay rule, even though the declarant is available as a witness:
>
> ****
>
> (3) Then existing mental, emotional, or physical condition. A statement of the declarant's then existing state of mind, emotion, sensation, or physical condition (such as intent, plan, motive, design, mental feeling, pain, and bodily health), but not including a statement of memory or belief to prove the fact remembered or believed unless it relates to the execution, revocation, identification, or terms of declarant's will.

B. Foundational Elements

1. The out-of-court statement must be a statement of the declarant's own

    a. state of mind,

---

the likelihood that reflection and fabrication were involved." *Id.* at 948. Unless the fact that the girl is so young leads to the conclusion that the shock or near-shock of the assault lasts longer, this statement is irrelevant to the foundational elements of this hearsay exception. It would be more relevant to a discussion of why this evidence is admissible under the residual exception of Rule 807.

101. *E.g.* People In Interest of O.E.P., 654 P.2d 312, 318 (Colo. 1982) (quoting FED.R.EVID. 803(2) advisory committee's note).

102. *See generally* part III(D)(4) of this chapter, above.

b. emotion,

c. sensation, or

d. physical condition.

2. The statement must reflect a state of mind, emotion, sensation, or physical condition existing at the time the statement is made.

3. Forward and Backward Looking Statements:

a. Forward Looking: When it is used as evidence of future conduct, the statement is admissible only as evidence of the declarant's future conduct, not as evidence of the future conduct of another.[103]

b. Backward Looking: Rule 803(3) itself states that but for one particular kind of backward looking statement this hearsay exception does not "includ[e] statement[s] of memory or belief to prove the fact remembered or believed." The one kind of backward looking statement allowed by the terms of this exception is a statement of the out-of-court declarant's own state of mind, emotion, sensation, or physical condition, which "relates to the execution, revocation, identification, or terms of declarant's will."

C. Need + Reliability = 1

1. Need

The statements included under this exception are present sense impressions.[104] This really is a specialized application of the present sense impression exception. The underlying need for the exception is the same here as there. Sometimes there is great need for the evidence in the out-of-court declaration and sometimes there is little or none.[105]

---

103. This limitation comes not so much from the text of the rule, as from the legislative history in the House Judiciary Committee and the interpretive case law. *See* part IV(D)(6) of this chapter, below, for a discussion of this part of the rule.

104. Every statement included under the state of mind exception is a present sense impression with the exception of some "statement[s] of memory or belief ... relat[ing] to the execution, revocation, identification, or terms of declarant's will." FED.R.EVID. 803(3). Including these kinds of statements of memory or belief within the exception "represents an *ad hoc* judgment ... resting on practical grounds of necessity and expediency rather than logic." *Id.* advisory committee's note. *See also* part IV(D)(10) of this chapter, below.

105. *See* part II(C)(1) of this chapter, above.

2. Reliability

The guarantee of reliability for the state of mind exception is the same as that for the present sense impression exception: the lack of time to fabricate and the lack of time for memory to deteriorate.[106] It is said that the spontaneity of these statements overcomes potential problems with faulty perception, bad memory, lack of sincerity, dishonesty, and ambiguity. Because the sensations perceived are one's own, "'there is ordinarily no possibility of erroneous perception.'"[107]

Hearsay theory is that lying is a conscious act that requires time.[108] Remove the time, prevent the lie. If a statement about an impression is made contemporaneously with the forming of the impression, the time element is removed and the chance that it is a lie is greatly decreased. A present sense impression will tend to be sincere, including a present sense impression in the form of a statement of a presently existing state of mind.

This exception is so broad, however, that the guarantee of reliability seems to break down. First, it is undoubtedly possible for a person to plan in advance to lie about a present sense impression. A person trying to get out of attending a dinner party might decide to call the host and say, "I have a horrible headache." A person intending to commit suicide but wanting to make a case against suicide so that his family will be able to collect on his life insurance policy might tell people, "I've never been happier or more content." A husband who is having an affair might tell his wife, "I love you." A thief wanting an alibi for a crime she intends to commit later that evening might decide to tell a group of people, "I'm exhausted.[109] I'm goin' straight home and get right into bed."[110] There are all kinds of reasons to plan out in advance to lie about how you feel.

---

106. *See* part II(C)(2) of this chapter, above.

107. Horton v. Allen, 370 F.3d 75, 85 (1st Cir. 2004) (reliable because spontaneous and therefore probably sincere); Schering Corp. v. Pfizer, Inc. 189 F.3d 218, 233 (2d Cir. 1999) (quoting Laurence H. Tribe, *Triangulating Hearsay*, 87 Harv. L. Rev. 957, 965 (1974)). In addition, since the out-of-court statement must be a statement of a presently existing state of mind, then, unless it is written hearsay, the testifying witness must have been there to hear the statement. The testifying witness must have been on the scene when the statement was made and may have some relevant personal knowledge of his or her own.

108. Regarding the time it takes to lie, *see* note 27, above in this chapter.

109. This part of the statement fits under the present sense impression and the state of mind exceptions, Rules 803(1) and 803(3), respectively.

110. This part of the statement fits under the state of mind exception. It is a statement of a present state of mind, a present intention to do something in the future.

Second, this exception includes statements of a present intention to do something in the future.[111] We often give careful thought to our intentions before we
express them. Such statements can be long thought out, with plenty of time to
decide to lie about it. Using the same situations as in the previous paragraph, but
with statements of a present state of mind regarding future actions, if the dinner
party is next week, the invitee might call and say, "I won't be able to come. I am
going to Chicago on business." The person intending to cover up his suicide might
say, "Next month I am going to Paris to visit my daughter." The philandering
husband might call his wife and say, "I have to stay late at the hospital to clear up
some paperwork." The thief establishing an alibi might plan ahead to tell a group
of people "I'm exhausted. I'm goin' straight home and get right into bed."

The statements covered by this exception are not necessarily made without
time to fabricate.[112] Some statements of "[t]hen existing mental, emotional,
or physical condition" will be honest. Some will not be. It seems that more
often than not these statements will be honest statements but that is only because more often than not people tell the truth. Most people who say "I have
a headache" have no reason to lie. "I'm exhausted. I'm going straight home."
"I have to stay late at the hospital to clear up some paperwork." "I love you."
"I am afraid." Most of the time when people say these things they are being
honest. But the general tendency to speak the truth is not the guarantee of reliability upon which the hearsay exceptions are based. The general tendency
to speak the truth applies to every out-of-court statement. The hearsay exceptions take categories of statements and look for something more—overpowering stress, prior cross examination, business pressures toward honesty.
I do not find that "something more" in this category of statements.[113]

D. Use Note

1. The Breadth of the Exception

This exception includes statements of then-existing sensations, such as cold
or hot, hunger, exhaustion, and pain shooting down the left arm, headache,

---

111. *See* part IV(D)(4) of this chapter, below.

112. *See* many of the cases cited and discussed in the Use Note, part IV(D) of this chapter, below. *See particularly* the text and footnotes around note 136, below in this chapter.

113. The same might of course be said about the present sense impression exception,
so why don't I say this there too? Reliability problems are particularly up front in this exception, in part because of its use as the vehicle for getting into evidence statements of an
intention to do something in the future. *See* part IV(D)(4) of this chapter, below.

backache, or sore feet. It includes a statement of the then-existing sensation of the smell of burning hair, the taste of crème caramel, or the feel of a tightly knotted shoulder muscle. A contemporaneous statement of the sound of the whistle of an approaching train, the beeping of a backing truck, or the crunch of car wheels on a gravel road. This exception includes statements of presently felt emotions, such as joy, fear, mental or emotional pressure, suspicion or mistrust, anxiety, affection or estrangement, love or hate, and remorse. It includes "I am pregnant," "I am not pregnant," or "I am confused." "This water is rancid." "This coffee is scalding hot." "The beer is skunked, the wine is corked, and I am thirsty."[114] This exception includes a parent's statement of then-existing state of mind while standing in the doorway looking at the van that has just pulled up to transport the daughter on her first date.[115]

---

114. United States v. Samaniego, 345 F.3d 1280, 1282 (11th Cir. 2003) ("An apology is evidence of a then-existing state of mind or emotion: remorse."); Ross v. St. Augustine's Coll., 103 F.3d 338, 341 n.1 (4th Cir. 1996) (a witness's testimony that the plaintiff had "'started complaining of mediastinum pains'"); United States v. Alzanki, 54 F.3d 994, 1008 (1st Cir. 1995) (declarant's statement that she was "afraid, hungry, exhausted"); Lorraine v. Markel Am. Ins. Co., 241 F.R.D. 534, 566 n.45 (D. Md. 2007) (when offered to prove the declarant felt good, the out-of-court statement "'I feel good'... is hearsay, but" fits under the state of mind exception); Pierce v. State, 705 N.E.2d 173, 176 (Ind. 1998) (statements of declarant's then-existing anxiety regarding her relationship with the defendant); Sherrell v. State, 622 So. 2d 1233, 1236 (Miss. 1993) (deceased's statement that she intended to ask defendant to move out); Nielsen v. Nielsen, 462 P.2d 512, 516 (Idaho 1969) (the "testimony of various witnesses regarding the intent of the donors in the establishment of the trust"); People v. Rowland, 841 P.2d 897, 912 (Cal. 1992) (victim's statement on the evening of the her alleged rape and murder that "'she better get herself home because she had a headache and she had to work in the morning"); State v. Poehnelt, 722 P.2d 304, 320 (Ariz. Ct. App. 1985) (police officer's testimony that the allegedly abused child told him she was hungry and cold).

As you may have noticed, many of these statements will also be present sense impressions, and some will also be excited utterances. This exception and the present sense impression are closely related. This is discussed at part IV(D)(10) of this chapter, below.

115. It is not entirely clear how far this part of this exception reaches. The Oxford English Dictionary's first definition of sensation states: "1. An operation of any of the senses; a ... state of consciousness consequent on and related to a particular condition of some portion of the bodily organism, or a particular impression received by one of the organs of sense. Now commonly in more precise use, restricted to the subjective element in any operation of one of the senses, a physical 'feeling' considered apart from the resulting 'perception' of an object.... b. In generalized use: The operation or function of the senses; 'perception by means of the senses[.]'" IX THE OXFORD ENGLISH DICTIONARY 456 (1933). This definition seems split on whether "sensation" is a synonym for "perception" (see part b), or has a narrower meaning (see part 1), and, if it has a narrower meaning, just what that meaning is. Perhaps, then, sensation has to do with the feeling of cold rather than the state

It also includes statements of a present intention to do something in the future—statements that are more a product of active thought than of spontaneous physical or emotional reaction. This can include an intention to go somewhere, to hurry to get there, to see some particular person (but not that other person's intention to see the declarant[116]), and to fire a gun. It can include a statement of an intention to order a product or pay a bill, to follow or ignore a doctor's advice, or to rat out a friend or keep your lips zipped.[117]

2. The "No Elaboration" Rule

a. In General

This exception covers an out-of-court statement of a state of mind, emotion, sensation, or physical condition, but not an accompanying statement of the underlying reasons for that state of mind, emotion, sensation, or physical condition.[118] Take these three variations on an out-of-court statement:

---

of cold: "I feel cold," versus "It is cold." "I see an old blue van," versus "It is an old blue van." That, however, seems a rather silly parsing of meaning, and one not relevant to the reasons for the hearsay rule. It is an awfully arbitrary way to draw the line between what is admissible under the exception and what is not. Perhaps this part of the discussion is itself irrelevant because all of these statements would qualify as present sense impressions, admissible under Rule 803(1). (The discussion certainly remains relevant in states that enacted the state of mind exception but not the present sense impression exception. *See, e.g.*, Neb. Rev. Stat. §27–803 (Reissue 1995).)

116. *See* part IV(D)(6) of this chapter, below.

117. *See* part IV(D)(4) of this chapter, below.

118. *E.g.*, Apanovitch v. Houk, 466 F.3d 460, 487 (6th Cir. 2006) ("[A] witness may testify that someone expressed to them fear of someone or something, but they may not testify as to that person's explanations of *why* they were afraid.") (citing cases); McInnis v. Fairfield Cmtys., Inc., 458 F.3d 1129, 1143 (10th Cir. 2006) (testifying witness may not "'relate any of the declarant's statements as to why [the declarant] held the particular state of mind, or what [the declarant] might have believed that would have induced the state of mind.'") (citation omitted); United States v. Duran Samaniego, 345 F.3d 1280, 1282, 1283 (11th Cir. 2003) ("[a]n apology is evidence of a then-existing state of mind," but why declarant was sorry is an inadmissible, is a backward looking elaboration); United States v. Alzanki, 54 F.3d 994, 1008 (1st Cir. 1995) (the witness can testify that the declarant said she was afraid, hungry, and exhausted, but not to her "more expansive statements elaborating upon the underlying reasons for [this] state of mind"); United States v. Fontenot, 14 F.3d 1364, 1371 (9th Cir. 1994) (the witness may not testify to declarant's statements as to why he or she held the state of mind or what induced the state of mind); United States v. Joe, 8 F.3d 1488, 1493 (10th Cir. 1993) (*see* note 120, below); United States v. Liu, 960 F.2d 449, 452 (5th Cir. 1992) (defendant conspired with known government agents whom he believed to be corrupt; he offered a witness's testimony that at a relevant time defendant told her he was

■ First: "I am afraid because my husband has threatened to kill me." "I am afraid" fits under this exception. "[B]ecause my husband has threatened to kill me" does not. The latter is a statement of memory or belief offered to prove the fact remembered or believed, and therefore inadmissible by the very terms of Rule 803(3).[119]

■ Second: "I am afraid of my husband because he has threatened to kill me." "I am afraid of my husband" fits under this exception. "[B]ecause he has threatened to kill me" does not.[120] Again, the latter is a statement of memory or belief offered to prove the fact remembered or believed, and therefore inadmissible by the very terms of Rule 803(3).

---

fearful for his life, afraid of what certain government agents would do to him if he did not play along with them; the part of his statement expressing his fear fits under this exception, but the part expressing the reason for his fear does not); United States v. Emmert, 829 F.2d 805, 810 (9th Cir. 1987) (quoted in the next footnote); United States v. Mazloum, 563 F.Supp.2d 779, 782 (N.D. Ohio 2008) ("[A] declarant's statement that she was scared would be admissible, while the declarant's statement explaining that defendant raped her would not be admissible."); Bennett v. Yoshina, 98 F.Supp.2d 1139, 1155–56 (D. Haw. 2000) ("a legislator's intent to support a bill and ... feeling of being 'impressed' by certain testimony are admissible" but not the reasons for the intent or impression); Fomby v. Popwell, 695 So. 2d 628, 632 (Ala. Ct. App. 1996) (Fomby's declaration of mental anguish fits, but his declaration of the cause of that anguish does not).

But see United States v. Newell, 315 F.3d 510, 523 (5th Cir. 2002) ("[T]he rumors comment was a statement of memory or belief used to show why Cooper was confused and confronted Gianakos, and was not used to prove the truth of the rumors.").

This does not seem to be the rule in North Carolina. In State v. Smith, 588 S.E.2d 453 (N.C. 2003), a witness testified that the victim had told her that it was "spooky" when she was home alone during the day, as sometimes a blue van would drive by, hesitate, and turn and leave; that it was "spooky" was a statement of her then existing state of mind or emotion; "[t]he activity of the blue van was a factor contributing to [the] discomfort." Id. at 457. "[W]here such statements 'serve ... to demonstrate the basis for the [victim's] emotions,' [they] will be admitted under Rule 803(3)." Id. (citation omitted). This is contrary to the rule in other jurisdictions and, it seems, to the plain language of the rule itself as this part of the declarant's statement clearly seems to be "a statement of memory or belief [offered] to prove the fact remembered or believed...." N.C. Gen. Stat. §8C-1, Rule 803(3) (2008).

119. United States v. Emmert, 829 F.2d 805, 810 (9th Cir. 1987) ("'[T]he text of the rule ... must be understood to narrowly limit those admissible statements to declarations of condition—"I'm scared"—and not belief—"I'm scared because Galkin threatened me."'" (quoting United States v. Cohen, 631 F.2d 1223, 1225 (5th Cir. 1980)). See also parts IV(D)(3) and (5) of this chapter, below.

120. United States v. Joe, 8 F.3d 1488, 1493 (10th Cir. 1993) ("Ms. Joe's statement that she was afraid of her husband was admissible under Rule 803(3)," but her statement of her belief he would kill her was not).

■ Third: "I am afraid that my husband will kill me." The state of mind—"I am afraid"—fits under this exception. The elaboration—"that my husband will kill me"—does not fit under the exception.[121] "[T]hat my husband will kill me" does not fit under the exception for two reasons: first, it violates the no elaboration rule; second, it is a statement of the declarant's belief regarding someone else's intention to do something in the future and, as such, it clashes with part of the third foundational element of this exception—"When it is used as evidence of future conduct, the statement is admissible only as evidence of the declarant's future conduct, not as evidence of the future conduct of another."[122]

It may well be that the "elaboration" part of each of these statements will be admissible. Depending on the facts, there may be an argument that the elaboration is not hearsay in the first place or that it fits under some other exception, but it does not fit under the state of mind exception. "[T]he state of mind exception does not permit the witness to relate any of the declarant's statements as to why he held that particular state of mind, or what he might have believed that would have induced the state of mind."[123]

b. Damages, but Not Proximate Cause

In the garden-variety personal injury action, the state of mind exception provides a way around the hearsay rule for the injured party's statements about his or her pain, but not for statements about the cause of the pain. In other words, it provides a way around the hearsay rule regarding the issue of damages—"I have a terrible headache" But it does not provide a way around the hearsay rule regarding the issue of proximate cause—"I hit my head on an I-beam at work." The latter is not covered by the exception for two reasons: it looks to the past[124] and it is an elaboration. That this evidence is admissible to the issue of damages, but not proximate cause, is a specialized application of the "no elaboration" rule.

A husband may come home from work and say to his wife: "I hit my head on an I-beam at work and have a terrible headache." Applying Rule 803(3), the part of the statement that does not fit under the exception is redacted; here is how the statement would look: "I ~~hit my head on an I-beam at work and~~ have a terrible headache." Damages, but not proximate cause. If the statement is

---

121. *Joe*, 8 F.3d at 1493.
122. Part IV(B)(3) of this chapter, above. *See also* part IV((D)(6) of this chapter, below.
123. United States v. Liu, 960 F.2d 449, 452 (5th Cir. 1992) (citation omitted).
124. *See* part 3 of this Use Note, below.

hearsay and no other exception can be found for the redacted part, that part is inadmissible.[125]

c. The Difficult "No Elaboration" Cases

The "no elaboration" rule can be tricky. For example, while elaboration of the underlying reason for the state of mind is not covered by this exception, a statement of a present intention to do something in the future is, and this might include some of what could be thought of as "elaboration."

Consider this case. Hughes was on trial for his alleged role in a drug conspiracy operated out of El Chubasco Bar. Hughes argued that he was not a dealer, courier, bookkeeper, or broker—not a part of the conspiracy—but just an addict who, in exchange for heroin, did handyman work at the bar. Hughes called a witness who was prepared to testify that she and Hughes had had numerous conversations in which he told her that he intended to go to El Chubasco to purchase drugs. This, Hughes argued, was evidence that explained why Hughes was so often at the headquarters of the conspiracy: He was doing handyman work in exchange for personal-use drugs.[126]

The trial court allowed the witness to tell the jury that Hughes had said he intended to go to the bar, but not what Hughes had said about why he was going. The trial court ruled that the former fit under the state of mind exception, but the latter did not. The Court of Appeals found this to be error (though harmless error). Rule 803(3) includes a statement of an intention to do something in the future, and the witness was testifying that Hughes had told her of his intention to do something in the future. The trial judge, however, had drawn a distinction between "where" and "why," allowing the witness to testify to what Hughes said about where he was going, but not about why he was going there.[127] The rule, however, contains no such distinction. Hughes' statement of his "intent to go to the El Chubasco to procure drugs was admissible under Federal Rule of Evidence 803(3) because it was offered to show Hughes' then existing state of mind...,"[128]

What we see here is not an elaboration on why Hughes was in a state of mind, but Hughes expressing a state of mind to go somewhere and do some-

---

125. "In damage suits for personal injuries, declarations by the patient to bystanders or physicians are evidence of sufferings or symptoms, but are not received to prove the acts, the external circumstances through which the injuries came about." Shepard v. United States, 290 U.S. 96, 105 (1933) (citation omitted).

126. United States v. Hughes, 970 F.2d 227 (7th Cir. 1992).

127. *Id.* at 233.

128. *Id.* at 234.

thing. It is all his own statement of his own state of mind. It is not his own statement of his own state of mind, offered with an explanation for that state of mind—"I am afraid [declarant's own state of mind] that my wife will kill me [explanation]." It is not his own statement of his own state of mind accompanied by a statement of someone else's state of mind—"I am going to J.B. Big Boy's [declarant's state of mind regarding his future actions] and Angelo will be there [declarant's state of mind regarding someone else's future actions]."[129]

A second way in which the no-elaboration rule can be a problem is illustrated as follows. The cause of action involves insurance fraud. The husband took out a large insurance policy on his own life. The allegation is that his daughter from a first marriage was to be listed as the beneficiary, but that his second wife bribed the insurance agent to make her the beneficiary instead and then had her husband murdered. The out-of-court statements in question are several statements made by the husband that he was *afraid* that his *wife was planning to kill him.* Is all or part of each statement admissible?

Rule 803(3) analysis leads to the conclusion that his statement of fear would be admissible, but his statement of why he was afraid would not. However, Rule 803 does not apply here at all. These statements are not hearsay in the first place. The fact that he would say these things—just that he would say them, whether true or not, whether he believed them or not—makes it less likely that he would take out a large policy on his life, naming his second wife as the beneficiary. The issue to which these statements were offered was whether there was fraud in the naming of the second wife as the deceased's beneficiary or whether the deceased intended to name her the beneficiary. Whether she was plotting to kill him is not the issue; the statement is not offered for the truth of the matter asserted and thus is not hearsay. Whether or not it is true that she was plotting to kill him, the fact that he would say it is relevant to whether he would take out a large life insurance policy with her as the beneficiary. These are nonhearsay out-of-court statements circumstantially indicating the declarant's state of mind.[130] So, the tricky part here is that some statements that

---

129. This is based on United States v. Pheaster, 544 F.2d 353 (9th Cir. 1976). *See* part IV(D)(6) of this chapter, below.

130. This hypothetical is based on United States v. Hartmann, 958 F.2d 774 (7th Cir. 1992). In *Hartmann,* the court held that the entire out-of-court statement fit under the state of mind exception to the hearsay rule. That analysis runs afoul of the "no elaboration" part of this exception. A more appropriate way of reaching the same conclusion is that this evidence is not hearsay in the first place. *See also,* part IV(D)(9) of this chapter and Chapter 7(II)(C), below, and the variation on the *Shepard* case discussed at Chapter 1(III)(C), above.

would seem to be inadmissible under 803(3)'s no elaboration rule, simply are not hearsay in the first place. Rule 803(3) does not apply because the evidence is not hearsay. The "no elaboration" rule does not apply because the evidence is not hearsay.[131]

3. A Statement That Looks to the Past

The out-of-court statement must declare a state of mind, emotion, sensation, or physical condition existing at the time the out-of-court statement is made. The statement and the state of mind must be contemporaneous. The statement cannot be backward looking, remembering a state of mind, emotion, sensation, or physical condition experienced in the past.[132] This exception does not include what are sometimes called "reflective pronouncements."

---

131. *Accord, e.g.*, State v. Martin, 458 So. 2d 454 (La. 1984), discussed at part IV(D)(3) of this chapter, below.

132. "Declarations of intention, casting light upon the future, have been sharply distinguished from declarations of memory, pointing backwards to the past. There would be an end, or nearly that, to the rule against hearsay if the distinction were ignored." Shepard v. United States, 290 U.S. 96, 105–06 (1933). *See also, e.g.*, United States v. Cardascia, 951 F.2d 474, 487 (2d Cir. 1991) (prosecution for bank fraud; after federal auditors "descended" upon the bank, defendant wrote a letter of resignation from the bank, stating his disagreement with the loans that became gravamen of criminal charge; the letter was a statement of memory offered to prove the fact remembered; it does not fit under Rule 803(3)); State v. Langley, 711 So.2d 651 (La. 1998), *rev'd on other grounds*, 958 So. 2d 1160 (La. 2007), *cert. denied*, Louisiana v. Langley, 128 S.Ct. 493 (2007). (criminal defendant wanted to introduce, as state of mind evidence, portions of a videotaped interview with a psychiatrist; court held that tape not offered to prove then-existing state of mind, but state of mind at time of killing, two years earlier; sometimes state of mind evidence may look backwards to prove continuity of that state of mind, but there must be some showing of continuity); People v. Reynoso, 534 N.E.2d 30, 31 (N.Y. App. 1988) ("While such declarations may be received to show the declarant's state of mind at the time the statement was made, they are not admissible to establish the truth of past facts contained in them.").

In United States v. Newell, 315 F.3d 510 (5th Cir. 2002), the prosecutor offered some notes under the state of mind exception. The notes said things such as, "Kim … caused me confusion by telling me 'I want to do things right, pay my taxes, etc.' so I found it difficult to accept that perhaps things were not being 'done right.'" *Id.* at 522. Leaving aside the question of how much of this is inadmissible elaboration, the court let the notes in; responding to the fact that this is a backward looking expression of a fact remembered, the court stated that although the declarant "could not identify the specific date on which she wrote the notes, she testified that she authored them when the events were still 'fresh in her mind,'" *id.* at 523, and, therefore, they fit under this exception. The problem with this is that the specific date on which the declarant wrote the notes is irrelevant to this exception. To the extent that this is a statement of her state of mind, it is "a statement of memory or belief

There is an important distinction here between these two things: First, an out-of-court statement of a *previously existing* state of mind offered to prove a *previously existing* state of mind. When the out-of-court statement "I *was* furious" is offered to prove that the declarant was furious at a time before the declarant made the statement, then the statement does not fit under this exception. It is a reflective pronouncement—backward looking, remembering an emotion experienced in the past.

Second, an out-of-court statement of a *presently existing* state of mind used to prove a *previously existing* state of mind. When the out-of-court statement "I *am* furious" is offered as evidence that the declarant was also furious at a particular time before the declarant made the statement, then the statement does fit under this exception. The statement is not backward looking. The trier of fact is being asked to make certain backward looking inferences from the statement, but the statement itself is a statement of a then existing state of mind. The later statement may not be relevant to the previous state of mind, or it may not survive Rule 403 analysis, but it is not inadmissible hearsay.[133]

I am also distinguishing between a statement of a *previously existing state of mind* and a statement of a *past event offered as circumstantial evidence of a state of mind* that existed at the time the statement was made. In *State v. Mar-*

---

to prove the fact remembered or believed" and specifically excluded from the exception by its plain language. FED.R.EVID. 803(3). A declarant might sometimes make a statement of a currently existing state of mind but express it unartfully using the past tense. There was no evidence that was what happened here.

133. If the question is the declarant's state of mind at 5:00 a.m., then a declaration of a state of mind made at 5:01 a.m. is likely to be relevant. Likewise, a declaration of state of mind made at 5:45 a.m. may be relevant to the declarant's state of mind 45 minutes earlier. Two hours later? It all depends on the rest of the facts. The point is that sometimes a statement of a present state of mind is relevant to prove a past state of mind; sometimes a jury can take a statement of a present existing state of mind and infer backwards therefrom. Such a statement is *relevant to* a previously existing state of mind, but it is not a *statement of* a previously existing state of mind. E.g., United States v. Ponticelli, 622 F.2d 985, 991 (9th Cir. 1980), *overruled on other grounds*, United States v. De Bright, 730 F.2d 1155, 1259–60 (9th Cir. 1989) (regarding a backward looking statement, "[w]here state of mind itself is in issue, the court must determine if the declarant's state of mind at the time of the declaration is relevant to the declarant's state of mind at the time at issue."); *Langley*, 711 So. 2d 651 (sometimes state of mind evidence may look backwards to prove continuity of that state of mind, but there must be some showing of continuity). *See also In re* Estate of Spiegelglass, 137 A.2d 440, 445 (N.J. Super. Ct. App. Div. 1958) (this will contest case asks the question "whether testimony as to declarations of a person disclosing his then state of mind, is admissible to show a prior state of mind," and answers it yes).

tin,[134] the defendant was on trial for the murder of his wife. A fact critical to this analysis is that he pled self-defense. A witness testified that the wife said that if she ever tried to leave her husband, he would kill her. This was admissible as nonhearsay, state of mind evidence. It was not offered to prove the truth of the matter asserted—that he would kill her if she tried to leave—but rather as circumstantial evidence of her state of mind—fear of the defendant.[135] The question then becomes whether the circumstantially indicated state of mind is relevant?[136] It is relevant to her fear of the defendant, which is relevant to rebut the defendant's defense that she was the first aggressor.

4. A Statement That Looks to the Future

This exception includes a statement of a presently existing state of mind that expresses an intention to do something in the future.[137] The declaration

---

134. 458 So. 2d 454 (La. 1984).

135. State v. Martin, 458 So. 2d 454, 460–61 (La. 1984). This point is discussed in detail at part IV(D)(9) of this chapter, and at Chapter 7(II)(C), below.

136. "The fact that the statement is offered for a nonhearsay purpose does not alone make the statement admissible; the general requirement of relevance must also be met before the out of court statement is admissible evidence." *Martin*, 458 So. 2d at 461. Regarding state of mind evidence and the issue of relevance, *see* Chapter 7(II), below.

137. Mutual Life Ins. Co. v. Hillmon, 145 U.S. 285, 295–96 (1892) (intention to travel to a certain place) (the advisory committee's note to Rule 803(3) states that "[t]he rule of Mutual Life Ins. Co. v. Hillmon ... allowing evidence of intention as tending to prove the doing of the act intended, is ... left undisturbed.") (*Hillmon* is discussed in the text following this footnote); Allen v. Sybase, Inc. 468 F.3d 642, 659 (10th Cir. 2006) ("Rule 803(3) permits an out-of-court statement regarding a declarant's then-existing state of mind where the statement serves as evidence of the declarant's intent to perform an act."); United States v. Best, 219 F.3d 192, 198 (2d Cir. 2000) (an intention to speak with a specific person and ask him to see that a certain thing is done); *Hartmann*, 958 F.2d at 784 (a nonparty declarant's statement of intention "to carry out the 'juice loan scam was admissible'" as evidence that he did in fact carry out the plan); United States v. Badalamenti, 794 F.2d 821, 825 (2d Cir. 1986) (an informant's statement "that he was going to meet Venuti at 5:00 at the Cafe Borgia to obtain a sample of heroin" was admissible as evidence that he did each of the things stated); United States v. Pheaster, 544 F.2d 353, 374–80 (9th Cir. 1976) (long discussion, citing cases; affirming admission of the deceased's statement, "that he was going to meet Angelo at Sambo's North at 9:30 P.M. to 'pick up a pound of marijuana which Angelo had promised him for free,'" *id.* at 375); United States v. Alfonso, 66 F.Supp.2d 261, 267 (D.P.R. 1999) (testimony that the declarant stated that "once he gets out [of jail] he will attempt a second mission to assassinate Castro because his sole mission in life is to kill Castro"); Figgins v. Cochrane, 942 A.2d 736, 753 (Md. 2008) ("[E]vidence of a 'forward-looking' state of mind is admissible ... to show that the declarant ... subsequently acted in accord with his or her stated intention."); State v. Coffey, 389 S.E.2d 48, 59 (N.C. 1990) (the vic-

and the state of mind must be contemporaneous with each other, but they need not be—will not be—contemporaneous with the intended action.

Mutual Life Insurance Co. v. Hillmon[138] is the seminal case regarding this aspect of this exception. Two men disappeared, skeletal remains were found near Crooked Creek, Colorado, and the in-court battle was over the identity of the skeleton. A number of large policies had recently been taken out insuring Mr. Hillmon. His wife claimed the remains were Mr. Hillmon and made a claim against the insurance companies. The companies claimed that the remains were those of the other man who had disappeared, Mr. Walters, and refused to pay. Mrs. Hillmon sued.

The companies argued that Walters had been misled into traveling off with Hillmon, who killed him and left him to be found so Hillmon's faux-widow could claim that her husband was dead, collect the insurance, meet up with him, and live happily ever after on the insurance money. As part of their proof that the remains found at Crooked Creek were those of Walters, the companies wanted to prove that Walters had gone to Crooked Creek. They offered into evidence letters he had written to his fiancée, wherein he stated that he and Mr. Hillmon intended to travel together to Crooked Creek. The Supreme Court found the letters admissible under the common-law predecessor to Rule 803(3). It is a two step process. First, the letters were admissible evidence of Walters' state of mind—his intention—as it existed when he wrote them. Second, his state of mind when he wrote the letters was relevant to what he did a few weeks later. (The fact that the letters also indicate that Mr. Hillmon is going was not discussed by the Court.[139])

A next logical question is just how far out into the future can this exception extend? The answer is not found in the hearsay rules, but in the relevancy rules. This hearsay exception does not have a time limitation. The foundational elements for this exception can be satisfied if the intended act follows the statement of intention by a day or a decade. There is no time limit for the exception. There will be other evidentiary issues, however, if the time between

---

tim's statement that she planned to go fishing "with a nice gray-haired man"); People v. Nunez, 698 P.2d 1376, 1378 (Colo. 1984) (regarding the sale of heroin, declarant's statement to undercover officer that he would call his "connect" allowed as evidence that he did call his "connect"); Johnson v. Skelly Oil, Co., 288 N.W.2d 493, 494 (S.D. 1980) (declarant was driving from her home to the post office when she was injured; to the issue of whether she was injured while on the job, her husband "was allowed to testify that before she left for work [she] told him: 'I have to stop at the post office to mail these letters that I brought home [from work] on Friday.'").

138. 145 U.S. 285 (1892). Regarding *Hillmon*, *see also* Chapter 7(II)(F), below.

139. This is discussed below, in parts 5 and 6 of this Use Note.

the statement and the act intended is too long. A statement of an intention to do something too far out into the future might be either irrelevant or so lacking in probative value as to create Rule 403 problems.[140]

5. The Out-of-Court Statement Must Reflect the Declarant's Own State of Mind

The out-of-court statement is admissible hearsay under Rule 803(3) when used as evidence of declarant's own state of mind, including a state of mind (an intention) to do something in the future. It is not admissible hearsay under Rule 803(3) when it is used as evidence of what someone else did at a future time. Here is how this is so.

On its face the exception excludes most "statement[s] of memory or *belief* to prove the fact[s] remembered or *believed*."[141] What, then, is a statement of

---

140. In State v. East, 481 S.E.2d 652 (N.C. 1997), "the victim's state of mind regarding her intention not to give defendant the money" was relevant to whether or not she did give him money, which, in turn, "was relevant to the issue of defendant's motive for murder." *Id.* at 662. "The fact that the statement was made some time before the estimated time of the murders is irrelevant.... 'Rule 803(3) does not contain a requirement that the declarant's statement must be closely related in time to the future act intended.'" *Id.* If counsel believes that too much time elapsed between the statement and the intended act, the objection has to be something other than hearsay—and the objections to make are the Rule 401 and 403 objections. Likewise, in State v. Taylor, 420 S.E.2d 414 (N.C. 1992), the court noted that the appellant argued "that the victim's statement was not close enough in time to the actual future event to be admissible under this exception to the hearsay rule." *Id.* at 422. The court held that Rule 803(3) has no time requirement, so this objection cannot be proper. The court stated that the only requirement is that the statement "be relevant under Rule 401." *Id.* at 423. I add this: The probative value of the evidence must not be substantially outweighed by the danger of unfair prejudice, waste of time, or confusion of the issues under Rule 403. *Accord* United States v. Hogan, 886 F.2d 1497, 1512 (7th Cir. 1989) ("[S]tatements [of intention] derive reliability and probative value from their nexus to the act itself."); People v. Griffin, 93 P.3d 344, 371 (Cal. 2004) (Defendant was on trial for the murder of his 12-year-old stepdaughter during a sexual assault. The had previously stated that she intended to confront defendant if his fondling of her continued. Her "statement fell within the state-of-mind exception, specifically to prove [declarant's] future conduct in confronting defendant prior to the murder in accordance with the intent expressed in her statement."). *See also* United States v. Ponticelli, 622 F.2d 985, 991 (9th Cir. 1980), *overruled on other grounds,* United States v. De Bright, 730 F.2d 1155, 1259–60 (9th Cir. 1989) (in the context of a backward looking statement the court wrote, "[w]here state of mind itself is in issue, the court must determine if the declarant's state of mind at the time of the declaration is relevant to the declarant's state of mind at the time at issue.').

141. FED.R.EVID. 803(3) (emphasis added). *Accord, e.g.,* United States v. Quinones, 511 F.3d 289, 311–12 (2d Cir. 2007) ("Defendants are correct that Rule 803(3) does not permit

belief and how is it different from a statement of intention? The difference between the two starts with the fact that this exception's exclusion of "statement[s]
of memory or belief" does not mean to give both "memory" and "belief" a
backward looking meaning. Were that the case, then "belief" would be subsumed
by "memory"; it would be redundant.

The difference is, rather, that statements of "then existing state of mind,
emotion, sensation, or physical condition" have long been held to include a
declarant's statements of his or her own intention to do something in the future, but not statements of the declarants' belief that someone else will do
something in the future.[142] This is the distinction between memory and belief.

---

statements of memory or belief to be admitted for their truth. But where, as in this case, a
district court plainly instructs the jury that the out-of-court statements cannot be considered for their truth, no hearsay concern arises requiring a rule exception."); Allen v. Sybase,
Inc. 468 F.3d 642, 659 (10th Cir. 2006) (statements of "memory or belief to prove the fact
remembered or believed" are not admissible under Rule 803(3); the statements in question
here "spoke not to then-existing state of mind, but spoke to a past act, and more than that,
to an act by some one not the speaker.") (multiple and internal quotation marks omitted)
Boyce v. Eggers, 513 F.Supp.2d 139, 143 (D. N.J. 2007) ("Eggers's statement was not a statement of her then-existing state of mind.... Beppel testified that Eggers came to the police
station to file a harassment complaint three days after her last encounter with Plaintiffs.
Further, Beppel testified that Eggers was motivated by a continuing course of conduct that
had been 'ongoing for some time.' Therefore, any indication that she felt harassed is better
characterized as a memory of how she had felt in the past, rather than of her then-existing
state of mind as she sat in the police station that Monday morning.") (citations to the record
omitted).

142. The statement must reflect the declarant's own state of mind, not that of another.
Also, if it is a statement of intention, it must be the declarant's own intention, not that of
another. United States v. Joe, 8 F.3d 1488, 1493 (10th Cir. 1993) (out-of court statement
by wife that she was afraid of her husband because she thought he might try to kill her;
afraid of husband, admissible; because he might try to kill her, inadmissible—violates no
elaboration rule and, in so far as it reflects a future course of conduct, it reflects future
course of conduct of another, not declarant).

In United States v. Natson, 469 F.Supp.2d 1243 (M.D. Ga. 2006), the defendant was on
trial for killing the mother of his unborn child as a way of eliminating problems associated
with the pregnancy. The government's theory of the case required that it prove that the defendant knew the victim was pregnant. The out-of-court statement was the victim's statement to "her mother that she [was] going to talk to the Defendant about obtaining military
benefits for herself and her unborn child. This statement was clearly made as part of [de-
clarant's] plan in dealing with her pregnancy and how it would involve the Defendant. It is
a statement of her then existing state of mind ... [and fits] under Rule 803(3)." Id. at 1249.
Her entire statement was a statement of her state of mind regarding her intention. This is
just a statement about the future conduct of the declarant, and not a statement about the
future conduct of another—defendant included. Regarding a second statement, Natson

The statement of intention allowed under this exception is a statement internal to the declarant. "I am going to Crooked Creek next week." A statement of belief concerns facts external to the declarant. "I am going to Crooked Creek next week and Hillmon is coming with me." "I am going to Crooked Creek next week" is a statement of the declarant's own intention or state of mind and is admissible hearsay under Rule 803(3). "Hillmon is coming with me" is a statement of belief—a belief in Hillmon's intention. As a statement of belief, this exception does not apply.[143] As used in this rule, "belief" seems to have to do with a state of mind that is offered to evidence the future circumstances of another.

Writing for the Court in *Shepard v. United States*,[144] Justice Cardozo pointed out that "[d]eclarations of intention, casting light upon the future, have been sharply distinguished from declarations of memory, pointing backwards to the past."[145] The rule also sharply distinguishes between declarations of inten-

---

states that the victim's statement to a third party that "Defendant was 'tripp'n' about the baby' does not fit under the state of mind exception because it is not declarant's statement of her own state of mind, but her statement of someone else's state of mind." *Id.*

This is the general, but not exclusive, rule in federal court. The legislative history of the state of mind exception to the hearsay rule, that it, "the report of the House Judiciary Committee[,] states that it intended Rule 803(3) to 'be construed ... to render statements of intent by a declarant admissible only to prove his future conduct, not the future conduct of another person.' H.R. REP. NO. 93-650, at 13–14 (1973), *reprinted in* 1974 U.S.C.C.A.N. 7051, 7075, 7087." Coy v. Renico, 414 F.Supp.2d 744, 768 (E.D. Mich. 2006). Regarding this legislative history, see also part IV(D)(6) of Chapter 3.

Coy canvasses federal and state court decisions on this issue, draws the above conclusion regarding federal courts, and concludes that state courts are much more generous when it comes to admitting such a statement to prove a nondeclarant's future conduct. The "overwhelming majority of" state courts to consider the issue "have allowed introduction of [such] statements to establish the future conduct of a nondeclarant...." *Coy*, 414 F.Supp.2d at 769.

One more thing about the *Natson* case discussed above in this footnote. Under Rule 803(3) the court allowed the testifying witness to relate a phone conversation with the deceased wherein the deceased said that "she was ... with the Defendant, that they were stopped to get gas, that they were on their way to get her a car in Columbus, that she had to be back ... by 7:00 A.M. for work, that she had her "stuff" with her so she could go [directly] to work...." *Natson*, 469 F.Supp.2d at 1249. There is some question as to whether the part of this statement where the victim said "she was presently with the Defendant" fits under the state of mind exception, but the question is irrelevant because that part of the statement fits under the present sense impression exception. *Id.*

143. *See generally* Glen Weissenberger, *Hearsay Puzzles: An Essay on Federal Evidence Rule 803(3)*, 64 TEMPLE L. REV. 145, 154, *et seq.* (1991).

144. 290 U.S. 96 (1933).

145. Shepard v. United States, 290 U.S. 96, 105–06 (1933).

tion used to cast light upon the declarant's own future conduct and declarations of intention used to cast light upon the future conduct of another.

Consider this out-of-court statement by Walters: "I am going to visit Hillmon." Walters turns up murdered and Hillmon is on trial. To the issue of Hillmon's opportunity to have committed the murder, will a witness be allowed to testify, "The day Walters was killed, I heard him say, 'I am going to visit Hillmon.'" There are two ways of looking at this. First, the entire statement is a *direct expression of the victim's intention* to do something in the future: to visit Hillman. Second, part of the statement is an *indirect expression of someone else's intention* or action. Whether the statement is admissible in whole or in part depends on what it is being offered to prove. If it is being offered to prove opportunity (*i.e.*, that Hillmon and Walters did meet, giving Hillmon the opportunity to kill Walters) then the statement is an expression of the declarant's own intention and it is also an expression of someone else's intention. In one of its uses (evidence of what Walters did), the statement fits under the exception; in the other (evidence of what Hillmon did), it does not.[146]

If counsel is trying to prove what Hillmon did on the day in question, then the appropriate thing to do here is either to redact the statement[147] or to apply Rule 403.[148] If the entire statement is admitted, grant a limiting instruction.[149] As with so many hearsay questions, the answer to this one depends upon taking a careful look at the issue to which the out-of-court statement is being offered, and if there is more than one, apply Rule 403.

In any event, the forward looking statement must be a statement of the declarant's own state of mind, emotion, sensation, or physical condition, offered to prove the declarant's intention. To the extent that the statement is a statement of someone else's state of mind, offered to prove that other person's intention, it is a "belief" and does not fit under this exception.[150]

---

146. If this is correct, then the point made here is, in part, at least, exactly the same as that made in the Use Note preceding this one, *i.e.*, part IV(D)(5) of this chapter.

147. Redact the inadmissible part and, if there is anything of value left, let in what is left. Regarding redaction, *see* Chapter 12(I), below.

148. Does the danger of unfair prejudice regarding the inadmissible issue—Johnson's intention—substantially outweigh the probative value to the admissible issue—the declarant's intention?

149. Instruct the jury that they may consider the evidence to the issue of the declarant's (the victim's) intention, but they may not consider it to the issue of Jan Johnson's intention. Regarding limiting instructions, *see* Chapter 8(I)(D)(4)(g) and Chapter 12(IV), both below.

150. *E.g.*, Deravin v. Kerik, 2007 U.S. Dist. LEXIS 24696, *35 (S.D.N.Y. 2007) ("Because Meringolo is the declarant, not Kerik, Meringolo's statements about Kerik's state of

6. The Out-of-Court Statement Must Be a Direct Statement of the Declarant's State of Mind

The out-of-court statement must more or less directly state the declarant's state of mind, emotion, sensation, or physical condition. This exception does not cover, for example, a statement from which the lawyer can argue and the trier of fact can infer the declarant's state of mind, emotion, sensation, or physical condition.

Here is an example. A young girl asked her babysitter not to let her mother return her to her father. When asked why, the young girl said: "Because my father gets drunk and he thinks I'm his wife." The father was on trial for aggravated sexual abuse. The prosecutor offered the babysitter's testimony regarding her conversation with the young girl, arguing it fit under Rule 803(3) because the young girl's statements showed her then-existing fear of her father. The court disagreed.[151]

The first part of the statement does not express fear, but just says don't let my mother send me back to be with my father; the second part is a statement of memory, offered to prove the thing remembered. I would add this—fear may be a reasonable inference to be drawn from this exchange, and, in fact, it may be an unavoidable inference, but the statement is not a statement of that emotion (fear). It is a statement of something else from which that emotion (fear) can be inferred; that is why it does not fit under this exception.[152]

The point here goes hand in glove with one of the points made above—the no-elaboration rule. This exception covers the statement of the state of mind,

---

mind" do not fit under Rule 803(3).); Figgins v. Cochrane, 942 A.2d 736, 753 (Md. 2008) ("[E]vidence of a 'forward-looking' state of mind is admissible only to show that the declarant, *not the hearer*, subsequently acted in accord with his or her stated intention.") (emphasis in original).

151. United States v. Tome, 61 F.3d 1446 (10th Cir. 1995), *on remand from* United States v. Tome, 513 U.S. 150 (1995).

152. This does not mean that the young girl's statement will be inadmissible hearsay, but just that it will not fit under the state of mind exception to the hearsay rule. Depending on the rest of the facts, the prosecutor might be able to lay the foundation for the exception for excited utterances or statements for purposes of medical diagnosis or treatment. If the issue is custody, there is a way to offer the child's statements so that they are not hearsay in the first place—they are not offered to prove the truth of the matter asserted but just to show that they were said; the fact that she said this is circumstantial evidence of her state of mind regarding her father; her state of mind regarding her father is relevant to her best interest and the question of her custody. The point, worth making again and again, is that the inability to establish the foundational elements of any one exception does not necessarily mean that the evidence is inadmissible hearsay. Keep thinking. Keep trying. *See generally* Chapter 10, below.

but does not cover an accompanying elaboration of the underlying reasons for the state of mind.[153]

7. Just Because an Out-of-Court Statement Fits under This Exception Does Not Mean It Is Admissible into Evidence

As with every other exception to the hearsay rule (but more frequently with this exception than some of the others), just because the statement fits under the exception does not mean it is admissible. For one thing, the declarant's state of mind must be relevant in the case at bar.[154] For another, the declarant must be competent.[155]

8. State of Mind Evidence That Is Not Hearsay in the First Place

Watch out for statements that almost fit under this exception, but come up short and, for that matter, statements that do fit under this exception, but do not need to because they are not hearsay in the first place—statements that are not offered to prove the truth of the matter asserted, but just to show that they were said. Here are two examples:

(1) *Effect on the mind of the hearer:* The first is a statement offered to show the effect it had on the mind of someone who heard it. It is not offered to prove the truth of any fact it asserts.[156] The defendant is charged with driving the get-

---

153. *See* part IV(D)(2) of this chapter, above.

154. This issue is discussed in detail and relevant cases are presented at Chapter 7(III)(D), below. *See, e.g.,* United States v. Udey, 748 F.2d 1231, 1243 (8th Cir. 1984) (defendant, arrested for harboring a fugitive, made a post-arrest statement that he had planned to negotiate the surrender of the fugitive in a week; if the statement was offered to prove defendant's state of mind on the day of the arrest it fell under Rule 803(3), but was irrelevant; if it was offered to prove his state of mind on the day the harboring began, it is backward looking and not admissible under Rule 803(3); either way it is inadmissible); Prather v. Prather, 650 F.2d 88, 90 (5th Cir. 1981) (plaintiff offered two witnesses to testify as to the plaintiff's understanding of an oral contract; appellate court ruled that the testimony was either irrelevant or backward looking and, as such, inadmissible hearsay; either way it is inadmissible).

155. As a general rule, that there must be some showing that the out-of-court declarant was competent. This is the topic of Chapter 13, below. Unlike relevance, this problem is less likely to come up when dealing with the state of mind exception because each out-of-court statement reflects the state of mind of the out-of-court declarant whether that declarant was competent or not. In other words, state of mind has to do with what the out-of-court declarant believed or thought, not with whether that belief was based on personal knowledge or in any way rational.

156. This point is discussed in detail at Chapter 7(II)(D). See the discussion and the cases found there.

away car. The defense is duress. The defendant testifies that two men with guns jumped in his car, one said "Drive! Get us out of here or I'll kill you!" Hearsay 101 is that the out-of-court statement must be offered to prove the truth of the matter asserted. The statement is "drive or I'll kill you;" it is not being offered to prove the truth of its assertion, *i.e.*, that the declarant would have killed the driver. Instead, it is offered to show that it was said and the effect that had on the driver. This statement is relevant to duress whether it is true or not.

(2) *Circumstantial evidence of the state of mind of the speaker.* The second is the out-of-court statement that is not offered to prove that its assertion is true, but rather as circumstantial evidence of declarant.[157] On trial for the murder of his wife, the defendant asserts that he killed her in self-defense. A witness testified that the wife had told her that if she ever tried to leave her husband, he would kill her. Here is the argument that this is nonhearsay state of mind evidence. The prosecutor is not offering this evidence to prove the truth of the matter asserted, *i.e.*, that the defendant would try to kill his wife if she ever tried to leave him. Rather, the prosecutor is offering this as circumstantial evidence of declarant's (deceased wife's) state of mind, *i.e.*, fear of defendant. And her fearful state of mind is relevant to rebut the defense that she was the first aggressor.[158]

The prosecutor has come up with a use of the statement that is not hearsay because it is not being offered to prove the truth of the matter asserted.[159] If there is one relevant nonhearsay use then the evidence is not excluded by the hearsay rule.[160] While one could argue that her fear makes it *more* likely she was the first aggressor—a preemptive strike—the point here is that the jury can decide what inferences are to be drawn from this circumstantial evidence of state of mind.

Since this statement is admissible to the issue of her state of mind but not as direct evidence of the fact that he would try to kill her, then it will have to survive the test of Rule 403 before it will be allowed into evidence.[161] If the evidence survives Rule 403 and is admitted, then the defendant is entitled to a limiting jury-instruction, if he wants one.[162]

---

157. This issue is discussed in detail and relevant cases are presented at Chapter 7(III)(C), below.

158. This example is taken from State v. Martin, 458 So. 2d 454 (La. 1984).

159. A statement's hearsay status is determined by the issue to which the evidence is offered. *See* Chapter 1(II)(C)(3).

160. Regarding the relevance of statements circumstantially indicating the state of mind of the declarant, *see particularly* Chapter 7(III)(B).

161. Regarding Rule 403, *see* Chapter 7(III)(C) and Chapter 12(III), below. *See also* Chapter 8(I)(D)(4)(b), and Chapter 11(V), below.

162. Regarding limiting instructions, *see* Chapter 8(I)(D)(4)(g) and Chapter 12(IV), below.

There can be reasons to argue that a statement is not hearsay rather than arguing it is admissible hearsay. It may be easier to convince the judge that the statement is not hearsay than to convince the judge it is admissible hearsay. Also, there may be a difference in which party has the evidentiary burden and, therefore, which party wins the issue if the judge cannot be convinced.[163]

9. The State of Mind Exception and the Excited Utterance and Present Sense Impression Exceptions

The out-of-court statement, "I am coughing up blood," is a present sense impression and fits under Rule 803(1). It may also be an excited utterance that fits under Rule 803(2). It is also a statement of a then existing sensation or physical condition and fits under Rule 803(3). Most 803(3) statements are also 803(1) statements.[164] The state of mind exception is in large part a specialized application of the present sense impression exception.[165] When considering one of them, consider the other as well. Often all of the first three exceptions in Rule 803—present sense impression, excited utterance, and state of mind—will apply to the same out-of-court statement. Because a good argument under three exceptions is more persuasive, more difficult for a judge to ignore, than a good argument under just one exception, keep this relationship in mind.

10. The Intertwining of the Admissible and the Inadmissible: Redaction and Rule 403

As noted throughout the discussion of this exception, many hearsay expressions of state of mind intertwine statements of past, present, and future state of mind, statements of the declarant's own state of mind and the state of mind of

---

163. The *opponent* of the evidence has the evidentiary burden of showing that the evidence *is hearsay*. Once it is shown to be hearsay, the *proponent* of the evidence has the evidentiary burden of showing that it *fits under an exception*. That this difference seems to exist and that it can determine the outcome of the case is discussed at Chapter 2(I), above.

164. Perhaps all 803(3) statements also fit under 803(1). Rule 803(1) applies to statements "describing or explaining an event or a condition made while the declarant was perceiving the event or condition, or immediately thereafter." FED.R.EVID. 803(1). Whether all 803(3) statements fit under 803(1) may depend on the definition of "condition." Is love a condition? If so, then "I love you" not only fits under 803(3), but also under 803(1).

165. FED.R.EVID. 803(3) advisory committee's note.

another, state of mind and elaboration—intertwining statements that fit under 803(3) with those that do not. In these cases, follow these steps: (1) Look for another hearsay exception that applies to the rest of the statement.[166] (2) If there is not another exception, try to redact the statement—redact out the inadmissible part and then let in the rest.[167] (3) If the statement cannot be redacted turn to Rule 403—does the danger of unfair prejudice from the inadmissible part substantially outweigh the probative value of the admissible part?[168] If the evidence fails the Rule 403 test, the whole statement is out; if it passes, it all comes in and counsel opposing admission is entitled to a limiting instruction.

V. Statements for Purposes of Medical Diagnosis or Treatment: Rule 803(4)

A. Text of the Rule

The following are not excluded by the hearsay rule, even though the declarant is available as a witness:

****

(4) Statements for purposes of medical diagnosis or treatment. Statements made for purposes of medical diagnosis or treatment and describing medical history, or past or present symptoms, pain, or sensations, or the inception or general character of the cause or external source thereof insofar as reasonably pertinent to diagnosis or treatment.

B. Foundational Elements

1. The declarant believed that the out-of-court statement would result in medical diagnosis or treatment. This element inquires into the declarant's mind.

2. A doctor would reasonably rely upon the out-of-court statement in diagnosing or treating a patient. This element inquires into a reasonable doctor's mind.

---

166. *See* Chapter 10.
167. Regarding redaction, *see* Chapter 12(I), below.
168. Fed.R.Evid. 403. *See* Chapter 12, below.

Keep in mind that this is a Rule 803 exception. This means that the availability of the declarant's in-court testimony is of no consequence.

C. Need + Reliability = 1

1. Need

This is a Rule 803 exception. As with many of the Rule 803 exceptions, there is no categorical need.[169] This exception is pretty much entirely based on reliability.

2. Reliability

First, and foremost, we do not lie to those we believe will make us well for, if we do, we will not get well. The principal guarantee of reliability is that only the truth will make you well.[170] Second, physicians make life and death decisions based on these statements. If the information is reliable enough for life or death decisions, then it is reliable enough for legal decisions.[171]

There is, however, one aspect of this exception that erodes that guarantee of reliability. In the law, there are two kinds of doctors: There is the treating physician—the doctor who treats the patient. There is the testifying physician—a doctor who is hired to make a diagnosis and testify as an expert witness at the trial, but not to treat the patient. The exception applies to both treating and testifying physicians. Hearsay theory is that our overpowering motivation when we visit the doctor is to get well and, therefore, we tell the truth. When we hire a doctor just to testify, that doctor is not going to make us well. That doctor might help make us rich, or help us get even with some-

---

169. In this regard, see the discussion of "Need" under Rule 803(1), the present sense impression exception.

170. White v. Illinois, 502 U.S. 346, 356 (1992) ("declarant knows that a false statement may cause misdiagnosis or mistreatment"); United States v. Pacheco, 154 F.3d 1236, 1240 (10th Cir. 1998) ("because a patient's medical care depends on the accuracy of the information she provides, the patient has a selfish motive to be truthful") (citing cases); Meaney v. United States, 112 F.2d 538, 540 (2d Cir. 1940) ("treatment will in part depend upon what he says").

171. United States v. Iron Shell, 633 F.2d 77, 84 (8th Cir. 1980) (physicians make "life and death decisions ... in reliance on such facts and as such [they] should have sufficient trustworthiness to be admissible in a court of law"); Duke v. American Olean Tile Co., 400 N.W.2d 677, 685 (Mich. Ct. App. 1986) (if "reliable enough to serve as a basis for medical diagnosis," then reliable enough to be admissible around the hearsay rule).

one we believe has wronged us, but isn't on board to make us well. This link between truth telling and wellness does not apply to the testifying physician. The only thing riding on the patient telling the truth is to the testifying physician is the verdict.[172]

D. Use Note

1. The Person to Whom the Statement Was Made

The out-of-court statement need not be made to a doctor or nurse; it need not be made to someone with medical training of any kind.[173] The key is the

---

172. That the guarantee of reliability breaks down when the physician is hired only to testify raises this question: Why is the testifying physician included in the exception? Because the link between truth telling and wellness is is missing, the common-law exception did not include "statements to a physician consulted only for the purpose of enabling him to testify." FED.R.EVID. 803(4) advisory committee's note. The Federal Rules of Evidence extends the exception to cover both treating and testifying physicians. *E.g.*, United States v. Kappell, 418 F.3d 550, 555 (6th Cir. 2005) (exception covers statements "made to non-treating persons who provide a diagnosis").

The common law drew a distinction between treating and testifying physicians. The hearsay exception that allowed a patient's statements to a doctor to come in as substantive evidence only applied when the doctor was a treating physician. Physicians retained solely to testify were allowed to state their expert opinions, just like any other expert witness. Once they testified to their opinions, they were allowed to state the basis for their opinions, sometimes including what the patient had told them. What the patient had told them was, however, not admissible as substantive evidence of the patient's assertions, but only as credibility evidence in support of the credibility of the doctor's opinion: basis evidence. The jury was instructed that they must only consider this basis evidence when deciding how much weight, if any, to give to the doctors' testimony, and not as substantive evidence of the facts the patients told them. The drafters of the federal rules believed that this was asking the jury to make a distinction they were not likely to be able to make. *Id* at 556. The advisory committee decided to keep the exception for treating physicians, saw that handling the testimony of the treating physician differently from that of the testifying physician resulted in asking the jury to do something it is unlikely to be able to do, and decided to apply the same rules to both kinds of physicians, treating and testifying. The half of the exception for treating physicians pulled along with it the half of the exception that is for testifying physicians.

173. *E.g.*, FED.R.EVID. 803(4) advisory committee's note ("[T]he statement need not have been made to a physician. Statements to hospital attendants, ambulance drivers, or even members of the family might be included."); United States v. Kappell, 418 F.3d 550, 556–57 (6th Cir. 2005); Danaipour v. McLarey, 386 F.3d 289, 297 (1st Cir. 2004) ("The plain language of the rule does not require the statements to be made by the patients, or even to a physician."); United States v. Yazzie, 59 F.3d 807, 813 (9th Cir. 1995) ("The plain language of the Rule does not limit its application to patient-declarants."); Davignon v. Clemmey, 322 F.3d 1, 8 n.3 (1st Cir. 2003) (statement need not be made to a licensed physician; state-

purpose of the statement and not the person to whom it was made. This exception is broad enough to encompass statements made to almost anyone. As noted, the exception includes statements to treating physicians and also to physicians hired just to provide diagnosis and testimony.[174] This exception can include an injured child's statement to her father, an ill husband's statement to his wife, and an accident victim's statement to a complete stranger who happens on the scene. All that matters is that the declarant believes the statement will assist in diagnosis or treatment[175] and that a reasonable doctor would find the statement pertinent to diagnosis or treatment.

The identity of the listener is irrelevant except to the extent, if any, that it is evidence of the declarant's expectation that the statement will result in diagnosis or treatment.[176] Why is the listener's identity not "[t]he critical in-

---

ment to social worker admitted); United States v. Cucuzzella, 66 M.J. 57, 60 (C.A.A.F. 2008) (statements made to nonmedical personnel as long as they are made for the purpose of seeking treatment").

174. *See* part V(C)(2) of this chapter, above. The out-of-court statement can be made to a doctor who was hired only to diagnose, and not to treat—the so-called "testifying physician," who will not come within 10 miles of treating the witness, but is expected to make a good witness at the upcoming trial.

175. "[N]ot every statement to a physician is rendered admissible. The motive of the declarant must be for treatment or diagnosis." Grundberg v. Upjohn Co., 137 F.R.D. 365, 369 (D. Utah 1991). *Accord, e.g.*, Territory of Guam v. Ignacio, 10 F.3d 608, 613 (9th Cir. 1993) ("Thus, a child victim's statements about the identity of the perpetrator are admissible under the medical treatment exception *when they are made for the purposes of medical diagnosis and treatment.*") (emphasis in original).

In some child-abuse cases "courts have refused to admit parental statements to medical doctors who diagnosed physical abuse. [T]hose cases are based on the theory that a parent who abuses his or her own child may harbor a strong motive to mislead the doctor. *See, e.g.*, United States v. Yazzie, 59 F.3d 807, 813 (9th Cir. 1995)." *Davignon*, 322 F.3d at 8 n.3. The rule-based rational for these evidentiary rulings would be the judge's conclusion that the statements, though made to a physician, were not really made for purposes of diagnosis or treatment but to exonerate the declarant.

176. When, for example, a child made a statement about a medical problem to his mother, the identity of the listener is relevant to the child's expectation. When a person badly injured in an automobile accident makes a statement to the EMT ministering to the declarant at the scene, the identity of the listener is relevant to the declarant's expectation. In the case of a child declarant, the foundational element that the declarant believe the statement will assist in diagnosis or treatment requires that the child be sufficiently mature to have some notion of, or at least some feeling for, diagnosis or treatment and the relationship between that and the statement. This might not ever be a problem when the statement is made to the child's primary caregiver, but it may be a problem when the statement is made to one who is a stranger to the child.

quiry?"[177] First, because of the plain language of the rule: the key to every hearsay exception is its foundational elements; here there are only two; the identity, the ability, or the intention of the *listener* is not one of them.[178] Second, because of the guarantee of reliability that supports this exception: we tell the truth when the diagnosis or treatment of our illness depends on it. This guarantee of reliability is totally focused on the mind of the declarant, on the declarant's expectation.[179]

---

177. "The critical inquiry is whether such statements are 'made for purposes of medical diagnosis or treatment' and are 'reasonably pertinent to diagnosis or treatment.' Fed. R. Evid. 803(4)." United States v. George, 960 F.2d 97, 99 (9th Cir. 1992).

178. This is supported by the advisory committee's note to Rule 803(4). *See George*, supra note 177. It really is that simple: Those are the two and only foundational elements. Other questions of admissibility are handled under other rules, Rule 403 for example.

179. In some cases there is language indicating that the out-of-court statement must have been made to a medical professional capable of diagnosis or treatment. For the most part, this seems to be a sloppy way of saying that on the facts of the case involved there is insufficient evidence that the declarant thought the statement would result in diagnosis or treatment; but, if the out-of-court statement had been made to someone capable of diagnosis or treatment that might have been enough to turn the evidentiary tide. Such statements are either that, *i.e.*, unartful, or they are simply wrong.

For example, in the context of this exception, the Ninth Circuit has stated the following: "It is astonishing, however, to have the state contend that Proctor, a social worker, was engaged in medical diagnosis or treatment." Webb v. Lewis, 44 F.3d 1387, 1390 (9th Cir. 1994).This seems to be an unartful way of supporting its finding that there was insufficient evidence the declarant thought her statement would result in diagnosis or treatment; but, if the person to whom the statement was made had been engaged in diagnosis or treatment, that might have been enough. Tellingly, the next paragraph of this opinion states, "There is not the slightest indication in Heather's conduct that she is a patient seeking or needing treatment." *Id.* at 1391. *See also* United States v. Kappell, 418 F.3d 550, 556 (6th Cir. 2005) (to the issue of whether statements to a psychotherapist fit under this exception, "[t]he critical inquiry ... is whether [the therapist] undertook her interviews for the primary purpose of medical diagnosis, rather than for some other purpose, such as determining whether to notify state authorities of suspected abuse[,] deciding whether a protective order was necessary to ensure the children's safety ... or obtaining evidence") (paragraph break and citations omitted); the court found that this therapist's motivation was diagnosis and allowed the statement) (author's note: the "critical inquiry" should focus on the out-of-court declarant— the person making the out-of-court statement—and not the in-court declarant—the person to whom the out-of-court statement is made); United States v. Tome, 61 F.3d 1446, 1451 (9th Cir. 1995) (this court got it right—"the test for admissibility ... is 'whether the subject matter of the statements is reasonably pertinent to diagnosis or treatment'"—and in the next breath got it wrong—that the statements "could not have been for the 'purpose[] of medical diagnosis or treatment'" because the person to whom they were made did not treat or diagnose the declarant); Ring v. Erikson, 983 F.2d 818, 820 (8th Cir. 1992) (exception does not apply because there was no evidence the declarant knew she was talk-

2. The Person by Whom the Statement Was Made

The declarant need not be the patient—need not be the person who is experiencing the symptoms to be diagnosed or treated. In other words, the statement need not refer to the declarant's own symptoms.[180]

---

ing to a doctor) (author's note: this is not the test); State v. J.C.E., 767 P.2d 309, 313 (Mont. 1988), *overruled in part on other grounds*, State v. S.T.M., 75 P.3d 1257 (Mont. 2003) (statement to a social worker inadmissible because it was to a social worker) (author's note: the court should have focused on the belief of the declarant rather than the education of the listener).

180. Danaipour v. McLarey, 386 F.3d 289, 297 (1st Cir. 2004) ("The plain language of the rule does not require the statements to be made by the patients, or even to a physician."); United States v. Yazzie, 59 F.3d 807, 813 (9th Cir. 1995) (need not be a statement by the patient); McKenna v. St. Joseph Hosp., 557 A.2d 854, 857–58 (R.I. 1989) (finding a bystander's statement within the exception; the fact that "the statement does not refer to the declarant's physical condition is not controlling"); Benson v. Shuler Drilling Co., 871 S.W.2d 552, 556 (Ark. 1994) (statements relating to someone else's symptoms are admissible if they were made for purposes of diagnosis or treatment and a reasonable physician would rely upon the information for purposes of diagnosis or treatment).

Some cases hold that statements by young children or about the physical condition of someone other than the declarant him- or herself must possess extra indicia of trustworthiness, over and above the foundational elements. For example, *McKenna*, in the first paragraph of this footnote, states that "[t]he crucial factor is that the statement was made to promote the efficient delivery of emergency medical services *and was accompanied by indicia of truthfulness.*" *McKenna*, 557 A.2d at 858 (emphasis added). There is no basis for doing this, no basis in the statute for adding on the requirement that the statement be accompanied by indicia of truthfulness. The Federal Rules of Evidence is a statute. The statute rejects an ad hoc approach to the admission of statements for purposes of diagnosis and treatment and instead adopts a categorical approach. There are two foundational elements. When these two foundational elements are present, the statement fits under the exception. Trustworthiness is not one of the foundational elements. There is no more basis for saying that the judge has independent power to judge the trustworthiness of a medical diagnosis or treatment statement, than for saying that the judge had independent power to judge the trustworthiness of a present sense impression, an excited utterance, or a statement in a work authenticated as a learned treatise. Where the drafters of the statute wanted the judge to be able to take an ad hoc approach to the trustworthiness of evidence, they specifically wrote that kind of discretion into the rule. For example, the exception for records of regularly conducted activities lists the foundational elements and then adds this: "unless the source of information or the method or circumstances of preparation indicate lack of trustworthiness." FED.R.EVID. 803(6). (Other exceptions that include such a "trustworthiness" clause are FED.R.EVID. 803(7), 803(8), 804(b)(3), 807.) There is no such clause in the exception for statements for purposes of medical diagnosis or treatment. And there is no authority for the courts to write such a clause into the rule.

If a court has a problem with the trustworthiness of a statement that otherwise fits the

Take this example. A child makes a statement to his mother, expecting that she will use the information either to treat him herself or to see that someone else treats him. The mother repeats the statement to the ambulance driver, with either of the same two expectations. The ambulance driver repeats the statement to the doctor, expecting that the information will be used to treat the child. If the information in the thrice-repeated statement is the sort of thing that doctors reasonably rely upon when they diagnose or treat patients, then each of the three out-of-court statements fits under this exception.[181] A doctor would reasonably rely on such information when diagnosing or treating and each declarant along the line believed the statement would result in medical diagnosis or treatment. Those are the two, and only two, foundational elements.

Take this second example. A mother sees her son injured. She calls for an ambulance and tells the EMT what she saw and the EMT tells a nurse, who tells a doctor. There is no patient-statement anywhere in this chain. If each statement—mom to EMT; EMT to nurse; nurse to doctor—was made with diagnosis or treatment in mind, then as much of each statement as a doctor would reasonably rely on when diagnosing or treating fits under this exception.

Take this third example. A declarant sees a complete stranger injured and makes a statement to someone else, thinking the statement will result in treatment for the injured person. In that situation, any part of the statement a doctor would reasonably rely upon when diagnosing or treating fits under this exception.[182]

---

exception, it is not a hearsay problem. It is either a Rule 403 problem (for the trier of law) or a credibility problem (for the trier of fact). In this regard, see note 187, below, and its accompanying text.

One case has stated that before a child's statement identifying his or her abuser will be admissible under this exception, the person to whom the statement is made must specifically discuss with the child why it is important to diagnosis and treatment that the child tell the truth. United States v. Sumner, 204 F.3d 1182, 1185 (8th Cir. 2000) (citing cases). In some cases this may be warranted under the foundational element that the statement must have been made for purposes of diagnosis or treatment. It may help establish that element. This is different from adding trustworthiness on as an additional foundational element. Regarding children, compare United States v. Barrett, 8 F.3d 1296, 1300 (8th Cir. 1993) (where the declarant is a very young child, there must be evidence the child understood the physician's role), with Virgin Islands v. Morris, 191 F.R.D. 82, 86 (D.V.I. 1999) ("There is no presumption that a child is any less aware that visiting a doctor is for the purpose of seeking medical treatment.").

181. This is an example of triple hearsay that is admissible because there is an exception for each level and, in this case, the exception for each level happens to be the same one. *See* Chapter 11, below.

182. In McKenna v. St. Joseph Hosp., 557 A.2d 854 (R.I. 1989), an unidentified by-

The original declarant can be the person who is injured or ill, someone closely related to, and presumably deeply concerned about the well being of, the person who is ill or injured,[183] or a stranger to the person who is ill or injured. Again, there are only two foundational elements. They are listed above. The identity of the declarant is not one of them.[184] The identity of the declarant is only relevant to hearsay rule the extent it is evidence of the purpose of the speech—"made for purposes of medical diagnosis or treat-

---

stander made statements to rescue personnel, who repeated the statement to hospital emergency-room staff. Both levels of hearsay were admissible under this exception. "[T]he fact that the statement does not refer to the declarant's physical condition is not controlling." *Id.* at 858. *See also Yazzie, supra,* note 180 (similar); *Wilson,* 939 F.2d at 272 (similar); *In re Wheeler,* 408 N.E.2d 424, 428 (Ill. App. Ct. 1980) ("[this] exception ... allows a treating physician to state information obtained either from the patient or from outside sources for purposes of diagnosis and treatment"; the statement here was inadmissible because of the then applicable Illinois rule that excluded statements to physicians consulted for diagnosis but not treatment). *But see* Field v. Trigg County Hosp., Inc., 386 F.3d 729 (6th Cir. 2004) (statements by a consulting physician to a treating physician do not fit under this exception; "exception ... applies only to statements made by the one actually seeking or receiving medical treatment"); Stull v. Fuqua Indus., Inc., 906 F.2d 1271, 1274 (8th Cir. 1990) (the declarant must be the one seeking treatment or, in some instances, someone with a special relationship to the person seeking treatment).

There are cases holding that the only statements that fit under this exception are those flowing towards the person expected to provide medical diagnosis or treatment, and not those flowing back towards the patient. *E.g., Field,* 386 F.3d at 736; Bombard v. Fort Wayne Newspapers, 92 F.3d 560, 564 (7th Cir. 1996) (a physician's statements back to the patient did not fit under this exception, *id.* at 564); Bulthuis v. Rexall Corp., 789 F.2d 1315, 1316 (9th Cir. 1985).

183. Lovejoy v. United States, 92 F.3d 628, 632 (8th Cir. 1996) (statements by patient's mother); *Yazzie,* 59 F.3d at 813 (statements by patient's parents); Wilson v. Zapata Off-Shore Co., 939 F.2d 260, 272 (5th Cir. 1991) (statements by patient's sister); Stull v. Fuqua Indus., Inc., 906 F.2d 1271, 1274 (8th Cir. 1990) (declarant can be someone with a special relationship to the person seeking treatment).

184. *See* part V(B) of this chapter, above. There may be other objections to the statement, other than hearsay. It is possible that the identity of the declarant could be relevant to the admissibility of the statement in the face of an objection other than the hearsay objection. Historically, this exception is built upon the premise that we tell the doctor the truth when our own good health or the good health of a loved one depends on the truth. As the declarant's relationship to the person being diagnosed or treated becomes less close, there may be less pressure to tell the truth. The foundational elements of this exception do not take that into account but under Rule 403 the court can exclude such a statement when the probative value is substantially outweighed by the danger of unfair prejudice or the danger that the jury will be mislead thereby. One can imagine a case where the identity of the declarant and the relationship between the declarant and the patient would factor into the Rule 403 decision. Regarding Rule 403, *see also* the cross references in note 187, below.

ment...."[185] Outside of the hearsay rule, the identity of the declarant may be relevant to a Rule 403 objection.[186] One factor that will *sometimes* affect the probative value of the evidence is the relationship between the declarant and the person who is the subject of the statement. Not every Good Samaritan statement will be low in probative value, but some may, and it may be a factor appropriate for the trial judge to consider. And in some cases, the statement's low probative value may be substantially outweighed by the danger of unfair prejudice, confusion of the issues, or waste of time.[187]

3. The Reason the Statement Is Made

The declarant must believe that the statement will result in medical diagnosis or treatment.[188] The declarant must believe either that the person to whom the statement is made will provide medical diagnosis or treatment or that the person to whom it is made will pass the information on to someone who will provide medical diagnosis or treatment. Sometimes—though not often—this is the piece of the puzzle that is missing.

Some statements to doctors—even statements regarding the cause of injuries the doctor is treating—are not made for purposes of diagnosis or treatment. If a father on trial for crimes involving the abuse of his child offers statements he made to the child's treating physician, a judge might conclude

---

185. FED.R.EVID. 803(4). Perhaps, for example, a judge might more easily be persuaded that the child's mother is more likely to be seeking diagnosis or treatment than is a complete stranger.

186. FED.R.EVID. 403.

187. If a court has a problem with the trustworthiness of a statement that otherwise fits the exception, it is not a hearsay problem. It is either a Rule 403 problem (for the trier of law) or a credibility problem (for the trier of fact). Regarding Rule 403, see, *e.g.*, Benson, 871 S.W.2d at 556 (as the relationship between the declarant and the patient becomes more remote, the statement can become less reliable; it can become so unreliable as to be inadmissible under Rule 403.); State v. Ochoa, 576 So.2d 854, 856–57 (Fla. 1991) (the child's age and other circumstances ordinarily go to the weight of the evidence, not its admissibility; if it is shown that a particular statement fits under the exception but is not reliable, the court may be able to keep it out under Rule 403). Regarding Rule 403, *see* Chapter 7(III)(C), Chapter 11(V), and Chapter 12(II), below. *See also* Chapter 1(II)(C)(3), above, and Chapter 8(I)(D)(4)(b), below.

188. "Here the subjective state of mind of the declarant is a key factor ... [J]udgments on this element [of the exception] ... may ... hinge on ... inferences drawn from the context presented." United States v. Cucuzzella, 66 M.J. 57, 60 (C.A.A.F. 2008) (paragraph break omitted).

that the father made the statements to cover his crime rather than to get the best possible medical treatment for his child.[189]

In one case a prisoner was ordered to see the prison psychologist. The prisoner did not believe that he had any reason to see the psychologist. The statements he made to the psychologist were not made for purposes of diagnosis or treatment. He simply went because he was ordered to do so and he had no choice in the matter.[190] Again, the key is the reason the statements were made.

4. Statements Regarding Mental Health

Statements made for purposes of diagnosis or treatment of a psychological condition or mental illness fit under this exception.[191] The exception applies to "medical diagnosis or treatment." A person consults a psychologist for "diagnosis or treatment," so that part of the exception is satisfied, and the question becomes What is the meaning of "medical."

The first definition of "medical" in the Oxford English Dictionary is "[p]ertaining or related to the healing art or its professors. Also, in a narrower sense, Pertaining or related to 'medicine' as distinguished from surgery, obstetrics,

---

189.   *A parent's statement to a doctor identifying the assailant in a child molestation case must be treated as suspect. Indeed, one of the most bitter ironies of these cases is that the perpetrators are usually parents or relatives who are supposed to act in the child's best interest. See* Judy Yun, *Note, A Comprehensive Approach to Child Hearsay Statements,* 83 Col. L. Rev. 1745 (1983)…. [A] parent or guardian's motive for casting blame may or may not be in the child's best interest or for the purpose of medical diagnosis. For example, a parent might misidentify the assailant in an effort to protect the other spouse, to avoid reprisal from the other spouse, to avoid having suspicion cast upon him or her, or to incriminate falsely the other spouse for personal motives.
United States v. Yazzie, 59 F.3d 807, 813 (9th Cir. 1995).
See also United States v. Cucuzzella, 66 M.J. 57, 61 (C.A.A.F. 2008) (courts must be particularly careful "where the mental health diagnosis and treatment is offered in the context of marital counseling. In such context, declarants may well have mixed motives as well as ulterior motives behind their words.").
190.   United States v. Matta-Ballesteros, 71 F.3d 754, 767 (9th Cir. 1995).
191.   First, as noted above in previous text, a statement covered by this exception can be made to anyone—psychiatrist, psychologist, social worker, or anyone else, for that matter—so long as it is made for purposes of medical diagnosis or treatment and is reasonably pertinent thereto. The fact that a statement was made to a mental health professional does not disqualify it from this exception.

etc."[192] There are two definitions, one narrow and one broad; the narrow definition excludes surgeons and obstetricians and this exception clearly covers statements to surgeon and obstetricians; therefore, this exception does not adopt the narrow definition. The exception must adopt the broad definition; the broad definition includes mental health professionals; therefore, the exception covers statements to made for the purpose of the diagnosis and treatment of mental ailments.[193]

---

192. VI OXFORD ENGLISH DICTIONARY 293 (1933).

193. More recently, the Merriam Webster Collegiate Dictionary defines medical as "of, relating to, or concerned with physicians or the practice of medicine." It defines medicine as "the science and art dealing with the maintenance of health and the prevention, alleviation, or cure of disease." And it defines disease as "a condition of the living animal or plant body that impairs normal functioning." MERRIAM WEBSTER COLLEGIATE DICTIONARY (CD ed. Zane Pub., Inc. 1997). Mental health professionals certainly are engaged in "the science and art of dealing with the maintenance of health and the prevention, alleviation, or cure of" "condition[s] that impair[] normal functioning." The ordinary meaning of the word "medical" seems to include mental health professionals, and not just medical doctors.

The cases generally agree. See Willingham v. Crooke, 412 F.3d 553, 562 (4th Cir. 2005) (statements regarding physical injuries and emotional trauma); United States v. Kappell, 418 F.3d 550, 556 (6th Cir. 2005) ("statements ... to a psychotherapist"); Davignon v. Clemmey, 322 F.3d 1, 8 n.3 (1st Cir. 2003) ("statements ... to social workers ..."); Morgan v. Foretich, 846 F.2d 941, 949–50 (4th Cir. 1988) (statements to a psychologist hired to diagnose and testify, not to treat); United States v. Lechoco, 542 F.2d 84, 89 n.6 (D.C. Cir. 1976) (statements to a psychiatrist); Whitfield v. Pathmark Stores, Inc., 1999 U.S. Dist. LEXIS 7096, *9, (D. Del. Apr. 9, 1999) ("a psychiatrist, a psychologist or a licensed clinical social worker trained in psychotherapy [consulted] for treatment of mental health issues.") (footnote omitted); State v. Pettrey, 549 S.E.2d 323, 334 (W. Va. 2001) (statements to "a social worker, counselor, or psychologist," trained in play therapy who treats a child abuse victim with play therapy "); Gohring v. State, 967 S.W.2d 459, 461 (Tex. App. 1998) ("a drama therapist working under the supervision of a licensed psychologist for the purpose of providing psychological treatment").

But see State v. White, 507 N.W.2d 654 (Neb. App. 1993). Under a rule virtually identical to the federal rule, the Nebraska Court of Appeals held that this exception does not apply where a sexual assault victim is sent to a psychiatrist hired to diagnose and testify, not to treat; such a rule "could lead to a standard operating procedure in which any sexual assault victim is sent to a psychiatrist to tell his or her story so that the psychiatrist can then retell the victim's story to the jury and thereby bolster the credibility of the victim's story by virtue of the psychiatrist's expert, professional status." Id. at 658. The court does not explain how it arrives at this holding in the face of the plain language of the statutory rule of evidence, or how it limits this to psychiatrists hired to diagnose and testify, and not other medical doctors hired to diagnose and testify, or how the "problem" it is trying to address is any different than any other time a person with an injury and a lawsuit is sent to yet another doctor to tell his or her story yet again. The real problem this court had with the evidence is not a hearsay problem. Rather, it is a problem best addressed under the rules regarding rel-

This means that statements made for purposes of diagnosis or treatment of mental-health problems are covered by this exception, so long as the things said are reasonably related to mental-health diagnosis and treatment. The obvious problem raised here is that virtually everything the client says to the mental health professional is "reasonably pertinent to diagnosis or treatment."[194] This hearsay exception is limited only by the declarant's ability to get a mental health professional to take him or her on as a client. While this is a problem, it is not a hearsay problem. Rather, it is one dealt with in one of four ways: (1) argue that the evidence is irrelevant;[195] (2) argue that the probative value of the evidence is substantially outweighed by the danger of unfair prejudice, waste of time, or confusion of the issues, and inadmissible under Rule 403;[196] (3) argue that the declarant of the hearsay statement is incompetent;[197]

---

evance (including Rule 403) competence, and credibility. *See* the text following this footnote.

194. FED.R.EVID. 803(4). "Generally, all statements made to psychiatrists or psychologists, regardless of content, are relevant to diagnosis or treatment since experts in the field view everything relating to the patient as relevant to the patient's personality." State v. Schreuder, 726 P.2d 1215, 1224 (Utah 1986). *See also* United States v. Cucuzzella, at note 196, below.

195. FED.R.EVID. 401 & 402.

196. If the trial judge concludes, for example, that the declarant has hired a psychologist simply so he could make statements to the psychologist and then get those statements admitted into evidence under the medical diagnosis or treatment exception, then the trial judge may be able to say that the probative value of the statements could be substantially outweighed by the danger of unfair prejudice, and exclude the statements under Rule 403. FED.R.EVID. 403. One court has said that courts must be particularly careful "where the mental health diagnosis and treatment is offered in the context of marital counseling. In such context, declarants may well have mixed motives as well as ulterior motives behind their words. So too, the reliability of the statements at issue may be clouded by emotional distress." United States v. Cucuzzella, 66 M.J. 57, 61 (C.A.A.F. 2008).

Regarding Rule 403, *see* the cross references *supra*, note 187. The trial judge must be careful, however, not to make a credibility decision. That is, the judge must not exclude the psychologist's testimony just because the trial judge does not think the declarant was credible. Credibility is a decision for the trier of fact, not the trier of law. For a discussion of the division of responsibility between the trier of law and the trier of fact, see the following: Regarding admissibility versus credibility, *see* part (I)(C) of this chapter, above. Regarding trustworthiness versus credibility, *see* Chapter 5(V)(E)(2), below; *see also* part VIII(E)(4)(a) of this chapter, above.

197. There may be cases where the problem that sent the declarant to the mental health professional so impairs the declarant's powers of perception or memory that the declarant is not competent to be a witness. FED.R.EVID. 601 & 602. The declarant is, of course, a witness for purposes of application of the rules of evidence. *See* note 198, immediately below.

or (4) engage in a vigorous cross-examination and argue that the evidence is not credible.[198]

5. The Content of the Statement

This exception is limited to information that is "reasonably pertinent to diagnosis or treatment."[199] Some information clearly is pertinent to diagnosis or treatment, and can be presumed to be so.[200] Some clearly is not, and will not fit under this exception. Sometimes it is not clear one way or the other, and the proponent of the evidence will have to present expert testimony that the information is reasonably pertinent to diagnosis or treatment. This foundational testimony will usually come from a physician who is already testifying for the party offering the evidence.[201]

The statement need only be reasonably pertinent to diagnosis or treatment. It need not determine or change the diagnosis or the treatment. Determining

---

198. "The declarant of a hearsay statement which is admitted in evidence is in effect a witness. His credibility should in fairness be subject to impeachment and support as though he had in fact testified." FED.R.EVID. 806 advisory committee's note. Admissibility decisions are for the trier of law and credibility decisions are, for the most part, for the trier of fact. Regarding admissibility versus credibility, *see* part (I)(C) of this chapter, above. Regarding trustworthiness versus credibility, *see* Chapter 5(V)(E)(2), below, and *see also* part VIII(E)(4)(a) of this chapter, below; *see also* part (VIII)(E)(4)(a) of this chapter, below.

199. FED.R.EVID. 803(4).

200. *E.g.*, Willingham v. Crooke, 412 F.3d 553, 562 (4th Cir. 2005) (declarant's out-of-court statement that a gun was pointed at her was relevant to her diagnosis and treatment as her emotional trauma stemmed in part from having the gun pointed at her).

201. Cook v. Hoppin, 783 F.2d 684, 690 (7th Cir. 1986) ("The test ... is whether such statements are of the type reasonably pertinent to a physician in providing treatment. In determining which statements are relevant to diagnosis or treatment, each case must be examined on its own facts, and in making such a judgment much will depend on the treating physician's own analysis.") (citation omitted); Brown v. Seaboard Airline and R.R., 434 F.2d 1101, 1103 (5th Cir. 1970) ("the doctor ... testified that this particular history, how plaintiff got under the train, was not necessary for the purpose of treatment"; statement inadmissible); Virgin Islands v. Morris, 191 F.R.D. 82, 86 (D.V.I. 1999) ("Having examined many rape victims over the years, Dr. Reid's testimony supports the conclusion that the information she gathered was relevant, routinely obtained in child sexual abuse cases, and relied upon for treatment and diagnosis."); Zito v. City of N.Y., 857 N.Y.S.2d 575, 577 (N.Y. App. Div. 2008) ("[I]t was error to admit into evidence the statement, contained in the history portion of the plaintiff's hospital records, that the bullet entered through the front of his body. [T]he record does not establish whether the statement was germane to either diagnosis or treatment ..."); Goldade v. State, 674 P.2d 721, 726 (Wyo. 1983) ("[T]he court must rely upon the view of the treating physician or the views of other medical service personnel with respect to what facts are pertinent to diagnosis and treatment.").

what you do not need to treat is an important step in determining what you do need to treat; statements eliminating other causes or symptoms can be relevant to diagnosing the true cause and planning the correct treatment.[202]

Many of the arguments in this area are over statements that assign fault or blame.[203] It may be reasonably pertinent to diagnosis or treatment that the other car was traveling at 60 miles per hour, but not that it ran a stop sign.[204] It may be pertinent to diagnosis or treatment whether the person who sexually assaulted the victim was her father or a complete stranger, but generally not which complete stranger.[205] It may be reasonably pertinent to diagnosis or

202. United States v. Iron Shell, 633 F.2d 77, 84 (8th Cir. 1980) ("Discovering what is not injured is equally as pertinent to treatment and diagnosis as finding what is injured.").

203. *Cook*, 783 F.2d at 690 (by its terms, this exception does not apply to statements of fault that are not reasonably pertinent to diagnosis or treatment); *Iron Shell*, 633 F.2d at 84; *Goldade*, 674 P.2d at 725 (the general rule is that statements attributing fault are not admissible).

204. An accident victim says to an ambulance attendant, "This big blue car came out of nowhere, doin' at least 60. It ran the red light and slammed into the car I was in, right on the side where I was sitting." A doctor might find it relevant to diagnosis or treatment that the other car was "big" and going "at least 60" miles per hour and that it hit on Passenger's side of the car. There is a direct relationship between the size and speed of the car that hit the declarant's car and the declarant's injuries. It would, however, probably be irrelevant to the doctor's diagnosis or treatment that the car was "blue" or that it "ran the red light." Therefore, the statement admitted under this exception will have to be redacted and might end up looking like this: "This big ~~blue~~ car ~~came out of nowhere,~~ doin' at least 60 miles. It ~~ran the red light and~~ slammed into the car I was in, right on the side where I was sitting." This entire statement has "liability value": "blue car," "came out of nowhere," "ran the red light," and "doin' at least 60," assuming all of these things are in dispute. Only part of the statement has "medical value." Unless another exception applies—the whole statement might, for example, fit under the excited utterance exception—then the part of the statement that does not have medical value must be redacted. *See also* the cases and cross references *infra*, note 208.

205. *E.g.*, United States v. Peneaux, 432 F.3d 882, 893 (8th Cir. 2005) (statement that abuser is member of victim's immediate household is reasonable pertinent to diagnosis or treatment); Territory of Guam v. Ignacio, 10 F.3d 608, 613 (9th Cir. 1993) (identity of perpetrator admissible when reasonably pertinent to diagnosis or treatment); United States v. Joe, 8 F.3d 1488, 1494–95 (10th Cir. 1993) (the identity of a sexual assailant is reasonably pertinent to treatment of an adult or child victim because the doctor must be attentive to treating the victim's emotional and psychological injuries, which often depend on the identity of the abuser; whether the doctor takes steps to have a child victim removed from the home or advise an adult victim to leave the home and seek shelter will depend on the identity of the perpetrator); Goldade, 674 P.2d at 726 (injuries inflicted are more than just bruises on a child's body; they are also scars on a child's mind; the latter may vary depending on the perpetrator's relationship to the child; also, the victim cannot be effectively treated

treatment that the victim was shot, but not that he was shot by a white man, six-feet two-inches tall, wearing glasses just like the defendant's.[206] It may be reasonably pertinent to diagnosis or treatment that the injured party fell down a flight of stairs, but not whether the tripped on loose carpet, his or her own shoelace, or was tripped by someone else.[207]

Quite often, part of a hearsay statement will be relevant to diagnosis or treatment, and part will not. In that case, admit the part that is reasonably pertinent and, if no other exception applies to the part that is not, then redact it. Admit the admissible parts and keep out the rest.[208] If the statement cannot be redacted, apply a Rule 403 analysis.[209]

6. The Timing of the Facts Stated

This exception is not limited to statements of present facts (present symptoms, for example). The out-of-court statement can relate to facts that existed in the past (symptoms, for example, that were experienced yesterday, last week, or a year ago).[210] "Right after I was hit in the head, this headache began building. It peaked that evening, lasted for three days, then went away." "Two years ago, I shared drug needles." "I fell last week, onto my left side, and when I woke up the next morning, I could hardly move my left arm and it has hurt

---

if she is sent back to her abuser and it is important for this part of the treatment to know the identity of the assailant.). *See also* United States v. Renville, 779 F.2d 430, 438 (8th Cir. 1985) (a doctor's legally imposed duty not to return an abused child to the perpetrator makes the identity of the perpetrator relevant to the duty of the doctor, but does not alone make it relevant to medical diagnosis or treatment) (author's note: while that legal duty does not make the information relevant to diagnosis or treatment, the treatment of the child by not sending the child back to the abuser does).

206. United States v. Narciso, 446 F.Supp. 252, 289 (E.D. Mich.1977).

207. *See, e.g.*, Rock v. Huffco Gas & Oil Co., 922 F.2d 272, 278 (5th Cir. 1991).

208. Willingham v. Crooke, 412 F.3d 553, 562 (4th Cir. 2005) (part of statement admissible and part inadmissible); Ramrattan v. Burger King Corp, 656 F.Supp. 522, 530 (D. Md. 1987) ("Statements ... concerning who ran the red light or the fault of the parties are not pertinent to diagnosis or treatment. Accordingly, they are inadmissible and must be redacted prior to introducing the records at trial."); United States v. Nick, 604 F.2d 1199 (9th Cir. 1979). Regarding redaction, *see* Chapter 12(I), below.

209. Regarding Rule 403, see *supra*, note 187 and the cross references therein.

210. On its face, the rule applies to "[s]tatements ... describing medical *history*, or *past* or present *symptoms*, pain, or sensations, or *the inception* or general character of the cause or external source thereof...." FED.R.EVID. 803(4) (emphasis added). *Accord, e.g.*, United States v. Iron Shell, 633 F.2d 77, 83 (8th Cir. 1980) ("[T]he rule adopted an expansive approach by allowing statements concerning past symptoms and those which related to the cause of the injury.").

since" This is in contrast to Rule 803(3), the exception for statements of *then-existing* mental, emotional, or physical condition.[211]

7. Admissibility of the Statement as Nonhearsay Basis Evidence

When an out-of-court diagnosis or treatment statement is offered to prove the truth of assertions in the statement, it is hearsay.[212] If an expert witness forms an opinion based in part on the statement, then the statement may be admissible as nonhearsay basis evidence. It is not offered for the truth of its assertions but only so the trier of fact can understand and evaluate the basis for the expert's opinion, and thereby understand and evaluate the opinion itself. Whether and when this argument will work is discussed at length elsewhere in this book.[213]

VI. Recorded Recollection: Rule 803(5)

A. Text of the Rule

The following are not excluded by the hearsay rule, even though the declarant is available as a witness:

****

(5) Recorded recollection. A memorandum or record concerning a matter about which a witness once had knowledge but now has insufficient recollection to enable the witness to testify fully and accurately, shown to have been made or adopted by the witness when the matter was fresh in the witness's memory and to reflect that knowledge correctly. If admitted, the memorandum or record may be read into evidence but may not itself be received as an exhibit unless offered by an adverse party.

B. Foundational Elements

1. The out-of-court statement must be recorded somewhere, in some way. It can be written down, typed up, recorded on tape, entered onto a hard

---

211. If you are struggling to use Rule 803(4) to get in a statement of a then-presently-existing condition, Rules 803(1), present sense impression, and 803(3), then existing state of mind, may be easier ways to get the job done.

212. It is hearsay unless, of course, it is some form of "admission" and defined as non-hearsay in Fed.R.Evid. 801(d)(2). *See* Chapter 2(III), above.

213. *See* Chapter 8(I)(D)(4), below.

drive, painted on the side of a barn, or impressed in someone else's memory.

2. The statement must have been made or adopted by the testifying witness.

3. At the time the testifying witness made or adopted the statement, she must have had knowledge of the matter recorded and that knowledge must have been fresh in her memory.

4. At the time of the trial, the testifying witness must no longer have sufficient memory of the matter recorded to allow her to testify fully or accurately. All that is required is some impairment of memory.[214]

5. At trial, the witness must remember that the record is accurate. That is, while the witness does not remember the facts recorded, she does remember that the record is accurate.

6. Those are the foundational elements, and then there is this restriction on the use that can be made of the record: "[It] may be read into evidence but may not itself be received as an exhibit unless offered by an adverse party."[215]

C. Why Not Let the Paper or Other Record into Evidence?

The rule ends as follows: "the memorandum or record may be read into evidence but may not itself be received as an exhibit unless offered by an adverse party."[216] Why not admit the record as an exhibit? *Viva voce* evidence is not

---

214. Commonwealth v. Nolan, 694 N.E.2d 350, 353 (Mass. 1998) (the witness' inability to remember some of the details recorded in the statement is enough).

Rush v. Illinois Cent. R.R. Co., 399 F.3d 705, 719 (6th Cir. 2005) (the out-of-court declarant "provided detailed and lengthy testimony at trial regarding the events prior to, during, and immediately following the accident. It therefore would be erroneous to conclude that [he] had 'insufficient memory to testify about the matters' in the interview transcript. Indeed, [appellee] concedes in its brief that [the declarant] had sufficient memory of the accident.... Accordingly, the past recollection recorded exception [does not apply]."); United States v. Reyes, 239 F.R.D. 591, 600 (N.D. Cal. 2006) ("Notwithstanding Reyes' observation that the statements he seeks were made about two years ago, he has made no showing that the [out-of-court declarants] ... would be unable to remember what they said. The mere passage of time does not make a statement admissible as a past recollection; to hold otherwise would swallow the rule entirely—*all* hearsay involves a prior out-of-court statement.").

215. Fed.R.Evid. 803(5).

216. Research Sys. Corp. v. IPOS Publicite, 276 F.3d 914, 923 (7th Cir. 2002) (party did not try to read the memorandum of past recollection into the record but, using this exception, offered the memo itself; the trial court excluded the evidence; the court of appeals affirmed, noting that the party offering the evidence "sought to introduce the memorandum as substantive exhibits, something the rule explicitly prohibits").

physically in the jury room; it is not transcribed and given to the jury. Exhibits are physically present in the jury room. If a record of the forgetful witness's recollection were received as an exhibit, that recollection would be in the jury room—physically present—while the jurors deliberated. Its presence would give the recorded recollection more significance than it deserves. It would make the evidence easier for the jury to remember, and perhaps more prominent than it would otherwise be.[217] Second, if (as some suggest) there is a tendency to believe more readily things we read than things we hear, then giving the jury a written record would make it more likely the jury would find it credible.[218]

Sending the recorded recollection into the jury room as an exhibit would give an advantage to evidence from a witness who has forgotten as opposed to evidence from a witness who remembers. This we do not want to do.[219]

D. Need + Reliability = 1

1. Need

The witness has forgotten something relevant. The witness has forgotten some or all of the things recorded. Without this exception, remembrances will be lost.

2. Reliability

The person who made or adopted the record must be a witness at the trial or hearing where testimony from the record is offered, the witness must have present personal knowledge that the record is true, and someone must estab-

---

In this regard, this exception is very much like the learned treatise exception discussed in part XIII of this chapter, below.

217. Corbett v. State, 746 A.2d 954, 965 (Md. Ct. Spec. App. 2000) (out of concern that the jury might place more weight on the past recollection recorded testimony than on other live witness testimony).

218. McCormick, on the other hand, states that the rule that the record itself cannot be received into evidence, but just read into evidence, comes from the fact that this exception "sprang by cellular division" from the practice of using a writing to refresh recollection. Since the latter writing is not allowed in evidence, courts got started not allowing the former into evidence either. CHARLES T. MCCORMICK, HANDBOOK OF THE LAW OF EVIDENCE §278, at 593 (1954).

219. In a related vein, this exception gets the record itself around the hearsay bar. It does not necessarily get everything on the record into evidence. E.g., Rosario v. City of Chicago, 2008 U.S. Dist. LEXIS 40562, *6 (N.D. Ill. May 15, 2008) (Regarding past recollection recorded, "[e]ven though a document itself may come within an exception to the hearsay rule, statements within the documents must themselves qualify either as hearsay exceptions or as nonhearsay. And in that regard Rule 403 is always a relevant consideration.").

lish that the record was made or adopted while the events recorded were fresh in the mind of the declarant.[220] The witnesses (sometimes there will be more than one) who establish these foundational elements will have some present recollection of events surrounding the matter recorded in the statements. These witnesses will be in court and under oath; opposing counsel can test their competence, memory, and honesty on cross-examination; and the jury can observe their demeanor. To the extent that the reliability of the witnesses who vouch for the recorded statement can be tested, the truth of the statement itself can be tested.[221]

E. Use Note

1. Past Recollection Recorded versus Present Recollection Refreshed

The nonhearsay use of a statement to refresh or revive a witness's memory and the hearsay exception for past recollection recorded are often confused with each other or blended together as though they were one thing.[222] "[I]t is

---

220. Other exceptions refer to the out-of-declarant as the declarant. This exception refers to the out-of-court declarant, that is, the person who made or adopted the statement, as "a witness"; in context, this clearly means a witness at the trial or hearing at which the statement is being offered. The declarant's in-court testimony about the event must be unavailable by reason of lack of memory, but the declarant—the person who made or adopted the statement—must be available and testifying. The foundational elements require the in-court testimony of the person who made the statement or adopted it as true.

221. *E.g.*, Parker v. Reda, 327 F.3d 211, 215 (2d Cir. 2003) (declarant is "available for cross examination on … the reliability of the document: his capacity for observation, his general credibility, his narrative abilities, and the circumstances under which [this document and others like it are] ordinarily prepared"); United States v. Porter, 986 F.2d 1014, 1017 (6th Cir. 1992) ("declarant is actually on the witness stand and subject to evaluation by the finder of fact").

In some more unusual cases, either the declarant's testimony at some earlier hearing or circumstantial evidence will be used to establish the truth of the statement. This is discussed at part VI(E)(5) of this chapter, below.

222. "Because they both arise from the common seedbed of failed memory and because of their hauntingly parallel verbal rhythms and grammatical structures, there is a beguiling temptation to overanalogize Present Recollection Revived and Past Recollection Recorded. It is a temptation, however, that must be resisted." Baker v. State, 371 A.2d 699, 702 (Md. Ct. Spec. App. 1977). *See* McCormick, *supra* note 218. Perhaps they never fully separated at birth.

Parliament Ins. Co. v. Hanson, 676 F.2d 1069 (5th Cir. 1982), is an example of this confusion. The appellant argued that it should have been allowed to use certain notes to refresh the recollection of one of its witnesses. The court of appeals held that "the district court was acting within its discretion in *excluding the notes,* because of the lack of reliabil-

important to keep clear the distinctions between the doctrine of present recollection refreshed ... and that of past recollection recorded."[223]

Present recollection refreshed is a litigation technique that revives witnesses' memories, restoring what had been forgotten and allowing the witnesses to testify to their own refreshed observations, from their own refreshed memories. If an out-of-court statement is used to refresh recollection, it simply helps the witness remember and then it disappears. There is no hearsay because there is no out-of-court statement *offered into evidence*. Past recollection recorded, on the other hand, allows an out-of-court hearsay-statement to come into evidence (albeit only to be read into evidence) to prove facts contained in the statement.[224]

---

ity surrounding them." *Id.* at 1074 (emphasis added). The problem is that the notes were not excluded from evidence; they were never offered into evidence. The witness's present recollection refreshed is what was offered into and excluded from evidence.

Given the final clause of the *Parliament Ins. Co.* quotation, perhaps the court affirmed on the theory that the notes were too unreliable to be used to refresh recollection. The problem with this is that it still confuses these two techniques: A thing used to refresh recollection does not have to be reliable; it just has to refresh otherwise-lost recollection. Perhaps the court was saying that the witness was lying when he stated that these notes did refresh his recollection and was really reading from them. Unless the trial court is saying that the witness was lying as a matter of law, then this is a jury question. The witness who claims that his recollection has been refreshed can be cross-examined. His credibility can be explored, including his memory and his honesty in stating that it has been refreshed. *See* United States v. Johnson, 495 F.2d 1097, 1102 (5th Cir. 1974); Nees v. SEC, 414 F.2d 211, 218 (9th Cir. 1969) ("ample opportunity to examine the documents, and question the witnesses with respect to them"); O'Quinn v. United States, 411 F.2d 78, 80 (10th Cir. 1969) (appellant had the opportunity and the material necessary to challenge the recollection of the witness).

See also United States v. Humphrey, 279 F.3d 372, 377 n.3 (6th Cir. 2002) (court was correct in refusing to admit the document into evidence; offered as substantive evidence it is hearsay and does not fit under the past recollection recorded exception; offered for the limited purpose of refreshing recollection, the document would not be introduced into evidence).

223. Butler v. State, 667 A.2d 999, 1002–03 (Md. Ct. Spec. App. 1995). *See, e.g.,* Fraser v. Goodale, 342 F.3d 1032, 1037 (9th Cir. 2003) (regarding the contents of plaintiff's diary and how the information therein might be admissible into evidence, the court wrote of this logical progression, "Fraser could testify to all the relevant portions of the diary from her personal knowledge. Fed. R. Evid. 602. If she forgets the **exact dates** or the **details** of the events, she may be able to use the diary to refresh her recollection. Fed. R. Evid. 612.... If the diary fails to refresh her recollection, she might still be able to read the diary into evidence as a recorded recollection under Fed. R. Evid. 803(5).").

224. *E.g., Humphrey*, 279 F.3d at 377 n.3 (as substantive evidence of the facts contained therein the document is inadmissible hearsay and as a writing used to refresh recollection

This is the critical difference between the two: (1) Present recollection re-freshed—the evidence received is the testifying witness's revived firsthand mem-ory; there is no out-of-court statement offered into evidence; therefore, the evidence cannot be hearsay. (2) Past recollection recorded—the evidence re-ceived is the recorded recollection; there is an out-of-court statement offered into evidence and therefore, the evidence can be hearsay. When attorneys argue that they are refreshing recollection, the court must satisfy itself that the witness is using the material to refresh recollection and not simply testifying from the material.[225]

---

the document is not be offered into evidence); Nees v. SEC, 414 F.2d 211, 218 (9th Cir. 1969) (with present recollection refreshed "it is the testimony, not the document stimulat-ing recall that is offered as evidence"); United States v. Riccardi, 174 F.2d 883, 886 (3d Cir. 1949) ("The primary difference between the two classifications is the ability of the witness to testify from present knowledge: where the witness's memory is revived, and he presently recollects the facts and swears to them, he is obviously in a different position from the wit-ness who cannot directly state the facts from present memory and who must ask the court to accept a writing for the truth of its contents because he is willing to swear, for one rea-son or another, that its contents are true;" with present recollection refreshed, the present memory is the evidence, not the writing that stimulated present memory); Jewett v. United States, 15 F.2d 955, 956 (9th Cir. 1926) (present recollection refreshed "awaken[s] a slum-bering recollection of an event"); State v. Ballew 667 N.E.2d 369, 379 (Ohio 1996) (when refreshing recollection with a statement, "a party may not read the statement aloud, have the witness read it aloud, or otherwise place it before the jury."); Thomas v. State, 766 So.2d 860, 903 (Ala. Crim. App. 1998) (with present recollection refreshed, "'[n]ot only is the writ-ing not offered to prove the truth of the matter asserted, it is not offered as evidence at all. It is the refreshed recollection of the witness ... that is the evidence.'") (citation omitted); Baker, 371 A.2d at 702–04 ("Notwithstanding the surface similarity between the two phe-nomena, the difference between them could not be more basic. *It is the difference between evidence and non-evidence.* [With present recollection refreshed,] the only source of evi-dence is the testimony of the witness.... The stimulus may have jogged the witness's dor-mant memory, but the stimulus itself is not received in evidence. [W]hen a writing of some sort is ... used to stir the embers of cooling memory, the writing need not be that of the forgetful witness himself, need not have been adopted by him, need not have been made contemporaneously with or shortly after the incident in question, and need not even be necessarily accurate. The competence of the writing is not in issue for the writing is not of-fered as evidence but is only used as a memory aid.") (emphasis in original; footnote and paragraph break omitted).

225. *E.g.*, United States v. Socony-Vacuum Oil Co., 310 U.S. 150, 234 (1940) ("[T]here would be error where under the pretext of refreshing a witness's recollection, the prior tes-timony was introduced as evidence."); Imperial Meat Co. v. Untied States, 316 F.2d 435, 437 (10th Cir. 1963); Delaney v. United States, 77 F.2d 916, 917 (3d Cir. 1935) ("While a witness may use memoranda made by another to refresh his memory so as to enable him to testify from his own recollection, he may not testify directly from those memoranda."); Jewett, 15 F.2d at 956 ("The witnesses were unable to testify without having in their hands

2. Present Recollection Refreshed

Examples of uses of the present-recollection-refreshed technique of promoting recall include a doctor who is testifying about a patient's injuries refreshing his recollection with his medical report[226] and a police officer testifying about an arrest refreshing her recollection with her own report or with a police report prepared by a second officer involved in the same arrest.[227] In a securities fraud case witnesses against the defendant refreshed their recollection by reading memoranda prepared by an SEC investigator, including the investigator's personal marginal notes.[228] During a several month long investigation, Treasury Agents made daily notes; these daily notes were transferred to larger papers to get them in order; progress reports were typed off of the larger paper; after the investigation was completed, each Government witness prepared summary statements from his progress reports. The witnesses used these summary statements to refresh their recollection while testifying.[229]

> Not only may the writing to be used as a memory aid fall short of the rigorous standards [required to satisfy the recorded recollection exception], the memory aid itself need not even be a writing. What may it be? It may be anything. It may be a line from Kipling or the dolorous refrain of "The Tennessee Waltz"; a whiff of hickory smoke; the running of the fingers across a swatch of corduroy; the sweet carbonation of a chocolate soda; the sight of a faded snapshot in a long-neglected album. All that is required is that it may trigger the Proustian moment. It may be anything which produces the desired testimonial prelude, "It all comes back to me now."

  ****

---

the copied data to which they could refer for facts which they could not remember; they had no independent recollection thereof."); State v. York, 489 S.E.2d 380, 385 (N.C. 1997) ("Where the testimony of the witness purports to be from his refreshed memory but is *clearly* a mere recitation of the refreshing memorandum, such testimony is not admissible as present recollection refreshed …") (multiple quotation marks omitted).

  226. Dexheimer v. Indus. Comm'n., 559 N.E.2d 1034, 1036 (Ill. Ct. App. 1990).

  227. Baker v. State, 371 A.2d 699 (Md. Ct. Spec. App. 1977).

  228. Nees v. SEC, 414 F.2d 211, 217–18 (9th Cir. 1969) (this was a pretrial examination of these memoranda). Similarly, *e.g.*, in a suit over the revocation of a McDonald's franchise, court appointed investigators testified and refreshed their recollection with their reports and photographs they had taken. Dayan v. McDonald's Corp., 466 N.E.2d 958, 971 (Ill. App. Ct. 1984).

  229. *O'Quinn*, 411 F.2d at 79. *See also Imperial Meat Co.*, 316 F.2d at 437 (compilations of notations made by investigators).

[The process of refreshing recollection could proceed as follows:]
"Your honor, I am pleased to present to the court Miss Rosa Ponselle
who will now sing 'Celeste Aida' for the witness, for that is what was
playing on the night the burglar came through the window.' [sic][230]

This technique may be used whenever witnesses' recollections are incomplete.
The witnesses do not have to testify that there are things they have forgotten,
or even realize they have forgotten anything. Even witnesses who believe they
have total recall might remember additional facts if their memories are jogged.[231]

Two caveats about refreshing recollection—First, whenever counsel hands
material to a testifying witness to refresh recollection, opposing counsel has a
right to review the material and to use it in cross-examination.[232] Second, refreshing recollection with privileged material may waive the privilege.[233] The

---

230. *Baker*, 371 A.2d at 704–05, 706 (footnotes omitted). *Accord, e.g.*, United States v.
Rappy, 157 F.2d 964, 967 (2d Cir. 1946) ("Anything may in fact revive a memory: a song,
a scent, a photograph, an allusion, even a past statement known to be false.") (L. Hand,
J.); *Jewett*, 15 F.2d 956 ("[I]t is quite immaterial by what means the memory is quickened;
it may be a song, or a face, or a newspaper item, or a writing of some character.").

231. McCormick on Evidence §9, at 17 (John W. Strong, gen. ed., 5th ed. 1999).
On one side, the risk is that witnesses will forget important facts unless reminded. On
the other, the risk is that witnesses may mistakenly think they remember a fact just because
they see it in a statement. Refreshing recollection seems particularly suited to control by
judicial discretion rather than bright-line rule. *Id.*

232. Fed.R.Evid. 612 (if a witness uses a writing to refresh recollection while testifying,
an adverse party is entitled to have the writing produced at the hearing, to inspect it, and
to cross-examine from it; if a witness uses a writing before testifying, to refresh recollection
for purposes of testifying, the court has the discretion to order the writing produced and
allow inspection and cross-examination therefrom); Socony-Vacuum Oil Co., 310 U.S. at
233. *See also* Fed.R.Evid. 613(a) ("In examining a witness concerning a prior statement
made by the witness ... the statement need not be shown nor its contents disclosed to the
witness at that time, but on request the same shall be shown or disclosed to opposing counsel.").

233. Alexander v. FBI, 198 F.R.D. 306, 319 (D.D.C. 2000) (the attorney client privilege
is "undermined by" Rule 612, which states that "if a witness uses a writing to refresh memory for the purpose of testifying during the testimony, the 'adverse party is entitled to have
the writing produced at the hearing, to inspect it, to cross-examine the witness thereon,
and to introduce in evidence those portions which relate to the testimony of the witness'"
(quoting Fed.R.Evid. 612)); Redvanly v. Nynex Corp., 152 F.R.D. 460, 469–70 (S.D.N.Y.
1993) (discussing the potential for conflict between Rule 612 and the work-product rule
and finding that in this case material used to refresh recollection before testifying should be
turned over even if it was work product); City of Denison v. Grisham, 716 S.W.2d 121, 123
(Tex. App. 1986) ("[U]se of a writing to refresh the memory of a witness while he is testifying waives both attorney-client privilege and work-product protection of the document ...").

point is that there are two sides to this coin: Be careful about refreshing recollection with material you do not want opposing counsel to see. Always ask
to see anything your opponent uses to refresh a witness's recollection.

Finally, as opposing counsel, be alert for a witness who isn't really using the
material to refresh recollection but is simply testifying from the material. Object.[234] Ask for permission to take the document from the witness, preventing
the witness from simply testifying from the material and forcing the witness to
testify from refreshed recollection. Make the point that the witness does not really remember and either ask that some or all of the witness's testimony be
stricken from the record or argue the witness's credibility in closing (or both).

3. A Past Recollection That Was Recorded by Someone Other Than the In-Court Witness

This exception covers a memorandum or record "shown to have been made
or adopted by the witness." The testifying witness need not have made the
record.[235] Here is an example of how "adopted by" might look at trial. A witness might testify, "My mother and I saw the whole thing, but it was a long
time ago. I really don't remember much about it now. I do remember that just
after we saw it, mom wrote down what she saw and she had me read it and I
remember thinking, 'Boy, she really got that right.' She wrote it just as I remembered it." And then the mother's statement is produced, marked for identification, authenticated, and read to the jury.[236]

---

234. *See supra*, note 225 and accompanying text.

235. United States v. Williams, 571 F.2d 344, 348 (6th Cir. 1978) ("'When the verify-
ing witness has not prepared the report, but merely examined it and found it to be accurate, he has adopted the report, and it is therefore admissible.'") (citation to legislative
history omitted).

236. In Cunningham v. State, 944 P.2d 261 (Nev. 1997), the court held that the past
recollection recorded exception applied when the defendant made a statement in front of
a man known as "Oldtimer" and a man named Wright. Oldtimer took notes of the conversation and sent them in a letter to a homicide detective. The detective took the letter to
Wright and asked Wright to sign the letter if it accurately reflected his memory of what the
defendant had told him. Wright did sign the letter. At trial, Wright could not remember
the conversation but testified that the Oldtimer letter was accurate and that he, Wright,
adopted it as his own. The past recollection recorded exception applied.

In a related kind of case, when someone perceives an event and reports it to another
"who records the statement, both must ordinarily testify to establish [the foundation for
this exception]. The person who witnessed the event must testify to the accuracy of his oral
report to the person who recorded the statement. The recorder must also testify to the accuracy of his transcription." United States v. Schoenborn, 4 F.3d 1424, 1427–28 (7th Cir. 1993).

4. The Record Must Have Been Made while the Event Was Fresh in the Witness's Memory

The out-of-court statement must have been made or adopted while the event was fresh in the witness's memory. The record does not have to have been made at the time of or immediately after the event. The passage of time is not the critical inquiry; freshness of memory is. The freshness of a witness's memory will depend on the particular event and the particular witness. There is no bright-line rule regarding the time it takes for memory to spoil.[237]

5. Showing that the Record Correctly Reflects the Witness's Past Knowledge

The memorandum or record must be "shown ... to reflect the testifying witness's knowledge correctly." There seem to be three ways this can be done. First, and most often, the declarant takes the stand and testifies that the statement is accurate.[238] "I wrote down what happened, I remember what I wrote was accurate, this [Exhibit A] is what I wrote."   Second, counsel may be able to use the declarant's testimony from a previous trial or hearing. Changing the facts of an actual case just a bit, here is an example. On the night of a murder, a witness to the murder made a statement to the police. She identified the defendant as the shooter. When the witness "testified before the grand jury, her statement to the police was read and she affirmed that it was true."[239] At defendant's trial,

---

237. *E.g.*, Parker v. Reda, 327 F.3d 211, 214 (2d Cir. 2003) (statement dated the day of the incident); United States v. Smith, 197 F.3d 225, 231 (6th Cir. 1999) ("Contemporaneousness is not required ..."; the event was still fresh in the witness's memory when she made her statement 15 months later); United States v. Senak, 527 F.2d 129, 141 (7th Cir. 1975) (the recorded recollection was admissible even though it was made three years after the event recorded); Abney v. Commonwealth, 657 S.E.2d 796, 801 (Va. Ct. App. 2008) ("Given the nature of the events set forth," the court upholds the trial court's decision that a statement made 10 months after the event recorded was made while the event was fresh in the declarant's memory); Morse v. Colombo, 819 N.Y.S.2d 162, 164 (N.Y. App. Div. 2d 2006) (A statement made two years after the declarant witnessed the fact recorded is not a statement made while the event was fresh in the declarant's memory).

238. Parker v. Reda, 327 F.3d 211, 214 (2d Cir. 2003) (declarant's testimony that statement is accurate; statement signed by declarant and dated the day of the event recorded).

239. Carey v. United States, 647 A.2d 56, 57 (D.C. 1994). In *Casey*, the witness "testified at trial that she had no present memory of the events, ... her memory was not refreshed by reviewing her grand jury testimony or her police statement[,] ... the statement she gave to the police was accurate[,] and ... she testified truthfully at the grand jury proceeding." *Id.* at 58.

the witness testifies that she does not remember what happened on the night of the murder. The statement may be read into the record under this exception to the hearsay rule.[240] Part of that foundation was laid at her appearance before the grand jury when she testified then that the statement to the police was hers and was the truth, and part at the trial at which the statement was offered when she testified that she did not remember the event.

Third, the accuracy of the statement may be established by circumstantial evidence.[241] It may be enough if the declarant testifies that she does not remember this particular statement, but she knows it is accurate because it is her habit or routine practice to record this kind of thing accurately (or to check it for accuracy, in the case of an adopted statement).[242] "At the extreme, it is even sufficient if the individual testifies to recognizing her signature on the statement and believes the statement is correct because she would not have signed it if she had not believed it true at the time."[243] In one case, the declarant testified that when she made the statement she was "screwed up" on drugs and, "although she tried to tell the truth in the statement, she was not sure she had done so."[244] Nonetheless, the court found sufficient circumstantial evidence to justify admitting the statement as past recollection recorded. It was very detailed and internally consistent; it was made soon after the events recorded; it was made under penalty of perjury; and the declarant had heavily edited the statement, initialed each change, and signed each page.[245]

---

240. It is "[a] memorandum or record concerning a matter about which a witness once had knowledge but now has insufficient recollection to enable the witness to testify fully and accurately, shown to have been made or adopted by the witness when the matter was fresh in the witness's memory and to reflect that knowledge correctly." FED.R.EVID. 803(5).

241. United States v. Porter, 986 F.2d 1014, 1017 (6th Cir. 1993) ("Rule 803(5) does not specify any particular method of establishing the knowledge of the declarant nor the accuracy of the statement. It is not a sine qua non of admissibility that the witness actually vouch for the accuracy of the written memorandum."); State v. Marcy, 680 A.2d 76, 80 (Vt. 1996); State v. Alvarado, 949 P.2d 831, 836 (Wash. Ct. App. 1998) ("[T]he requirement that a recorded recollection accurately reflect the witness's knowledge may be satisfied without the witness's direct testimony of accuracy at trial."), review denied, 960 P.2d 937 (Wash. 1988). See also Parker v. Reda, 327 F.3d 211, 214 (2d Cir. 2003) (in addition to declarant's signature on the statement and his testimony that the statement is accurate, the statement is dated the day of the incident).

242. Johnson v. State, 967 S.W.2d 410, 416 (Tex. Crim. App. 1998) (citation omitted).

243. Id. at 416.

244. United States v. Porter, 986 F.2d 1014, 1017 (6th Cir. 1993).

245. Id. (Furthermore, the trial judge, "who had full opportunity to view the witness's demeanor and evaluate her testimony, determined that ... in attempting to distance herself from [her earlier statement she] was being 'disingenuous' and 'evasive,' and was acting either out of her recently professed desire to marry the defendant or out of fear of the defendant.").

6. Statements Recorded in Memory, Rather Than on Paper

The recorded recollection need not be written. It can, of course, be an audio recording. It also can be recorded in someone else's mind. In one case, for example, the alleged victim testified that she did not remember details of what the defendant had done to her. She did, however, remember that she had told the details to the investigating police officer, and that she had told him the truth. The officer testified to the details as reported to him by the victim. Over defendant's hearsay objection, the trial court admitted the officer's testimony as past recollection recorded. The past recollection was that of the victim. The record of her past knowledge was in the memory of the officer.[246] Each foundational element is satisfied just as surely as it would have been had the record been written down in the back of a bible, a letter to a newborn child, or an affidavit bedecked with ribbons, seals, and rhinestones.

7. A Re-Recording of Original Notes

The fact that the recorded recollection is not from the declarant's original notes, but rather from a report prepared from those notes does not render the recollection inadmissible under this exception.[247]

8. Foreign Records as Past Recollection Recorded

The fact that the record was made in another country does not affect admissibility under this exception.[248] This is a hearsay exception and, therefore,

---

See also People v. Speed, 731 N.E.2d 1276, 1279 (Ill. App. Ct. 2000) (the statement was not admissible under this exception because the declarant could not vouch for the accuracy of the statement and there was not sufficient other evidence to support its accuracy); State v. Sua, 987 P.2d 959, 973 (Haw. 1999) (Declarant "wrote the statement himself, indicating that he 'once had knowledge' of the information contained therein. [He] signed the statement, thereby adopting it as his own. Inasmuch as the statement was made less than a month after the incident, we may fairly infer that it was given when the events were still 'fresh in his memory.' Finally, [the declarant] testified at trial that he was unable to remember writing the statement. Under these circumstances, the foundational requirements of [a state rule identical Federal Rule 803(5)] were met.").

246. People v. Guardado, 47 Cal. Rptr. 2d 81, 83 (Cal. Ct. App. 1995). *Accord* Flynn v. State, 702 N.E.2d 741, 744 (Ind. Ct. App. 1998) (testimony of two police officers about what declarant told them admitted as declarant's past recollection recorded).

247. Dayan v. McDonald's Corp., 466 N.E.2d 958, 970–71 (Ill App. Ct. 1984).

248. *Id.* at 968–71. *See also*, the following parts of this chapter: VII(D)(6) (foreign business records), VIII(E)(6) (foreign public records and reports), and XI(D)(6) (foreign ancient documents).

a question of foundational elements and there is nothing in these foundational elements requiring that the record be a domestic record.

VII. Records (and Absence of Records) of a Regularly Conducted Activity: Rules 803(6) & (7)

A. Text of the Rules

The following are not excluded by the hearsay rule, even though the declarant is available as a witness:

****

(6) Records of regularly conducted activity. A memorandum, report, record, or data compilation, in any form,[249] of acts, events, conditions, opinions, or diagnoses, made at or near the time by, or from information transmitted by, a person with knowledge, if kept in the course of a regularly conducted business activity, and if it was the regular practice of that business activity to make the memorandum, report, record, or data compilation, all as shown by the testimony of the custodian or other qualified witness or by certification that complies with Rule 902(11), Rule 902(12), or a statute permitting certification, unless the source of information or the method or circumstances of preparation indicate lack of trustworthiness. The term "business" as used in this paragraph includes business, institution, association, profession, occupation, and calling of every kind, whether or not conducted for profit.[250]

(7) Absence of entry in records kept in accordance with the provisions of paragraph (6). Evidence that a matter is not included in the

---

249. This can include tape recordings of telephone conversations to the extent that the statements thereon were made in the regular course of the out-of-court declarant's business. United States v. Davis, 170 F.3d 617, 626–27 (6th Cir. 1999). In the case of a business that records its calls, employee statements made in the regular course of business can fit under this exception but other-party statements not made in the regular course of the other party's business cannot.

250. The words "or by certification that complies with Rule 902(11), Rule 902(12), or a statute permitting certification" are an amendment to Rule 803(6), effective December 1, 2000.

memoranda, reports, records, or data compilations, in any form, kept in accordance with the provisions of paragraph (6), to prove the nonoccurrence or nonexistence of the matter, if the matter was of a kind of which a memorandum, report, record, or data compilation was regularly made and preserved, unless the sources of information or other circumstances indicate lack of trustworthiness.

B. Foundational Elements

1. The out-of-court statement must be a record (or an absence of an entry in a record) that was made in the course of a regularly conducted business activity.[251] The out-of-court declarant is the key here—the out-of-court statement needs to be made as part of his or her business. (But, as noted under the third foundational element, below, the person actually making the record need not necessarily have firsthand knowledge of what he or she is recording.) Business is broadly defined in the rule and does not need to be for profit.

2. The record must have been made at or near the time of the event recorded; in other words, made while memory was fresh.

3. The record must have been made by someone who either: (a) had personal knowledge of what is recorded, or (b) based the record on information provided by someone who both had personal knowledge and provided the information in the regular course of the particular activity involved.[252]

4. Those are the foundational elements, and then there is a trustworthiness clause: "unless the source of information or the method or circumstances of preparation indicate lack of trustworthiness." This allows the judge to

---

251. The Nebraska exception for records of a regularly conducted activity is different from the federal rule. The federal exception includes records "of acts, events, conditions, opinions, or diagnoses." The Nebraska exception includes records "of acts, events, or conditions, other than opinions or diagnoses." NEB.EVID.R. 803(5) & (6), NEB. REV. STAT. §§ 27-803(5) & (6) (Reissue 1995). A record of a regularly conducted activity in the form of an opinion or a diagnosis can fit under the federal exception, but cannot fit under the Nebraska exception. Nebraska took the approach it did in part so the safeguards of cross-examination would apply to opinions and diagnoses.

252. The rule requires that these first three foundational elements be "shown by the testimony of the custodian or other qualified witness, or by certification that complies with Rule 902(11), Rule 902(12), or a statute permitting certification...." FED.R.EVID. 803(6).

keep the evidence out, even if the foundational elements are satisfied, if the judge is sufficiently suspicious of the evidence.[253]

C. Need + Reliability = 1

1. Need

With regard to many of the documents covered by this exception, there will not be anyone who has a current memory of the details recorded. Who today remembers what a doctor billed a particular patient three years ago, the exact balances in all savings accounts at a given bank on a given day, or the specifications of the front-wheel struts on a 1978 Honda "Gold Wing" motorcycle? Who today remembers exactly which Oscars were won by the movie *Titanic* (or why)?

2. Reliability

These records tend to be reliable because they are regularly kept and both the business and someone's job depend on them being kept and being kept accurately.[254] These records are important to the business, so the business is going to build in safeguards. And there is this: If business relies on these records, why shouldn't the law?

It is not just that these kinds of records are considered generally accurate. It is that, in this situation, the hearsay is often more accurate than a later personal

---

253. Regarding the foundation generally, and a textbook example of how to lay the foundation, see, *e.g.*, United States v. Ary, 518 F.3d 775, 786–87 (10th Cir. 2008); Thanongsinh v. Bd. of Educ., 462 F.3d 762, 776–79 (7th Cir. 2006).

254. Palmer v. Hoffman, 318 U.S. 109, 115 (1943) ("methods systematically employed for the conduct of the business as a business"); United States v. LeShore, 543 F.3d 935, 942 (7th Cir. 2008) (that the infrequently compiled record was regularly verified indicates reliability); United States v. Ary, 518 F.3d 775, 786 (10th Cir. 2008) (business incentives to keep accurate records); *Thanongsinh*, 462 F.3d at 776; Parker v. Reda, 327 F.3d 211, 214–15 (2d Cir. 2003) (quoting FED.R.EVID. 803(6) advisory committee's note); United States v. Wells, 262 F.3d 455, 462 (5th Cir. 2001) (reliability "'supplied by systematic checking, by regularity and continuity which produce habits of precision, by actual experience of business in relying on them, or by duty to make an accurate record as part of a continuing job or occupation.'") (quoting FED.R.EVID. 803(6) advisory committee's note); Certain Underwriters at Lloyd's v. Sinkovich, 232 F.3d 200, 205 (4th Cir. 2000) (the "routine and habitual patterns of creation of business records" promote reliability); United States v. Baker, 693 F.2d 183, 188 (D.C. Cir. 1982) ("[B]usiness records have a high degree of accuracy because the nation's business demands it, because the records are customarily checked for correctness, and because recordkeepers are trained in habits of precision.").

recollection. If you were the trier of fact in a lawsuit that turned on the exact date a vision-blocking hedge was removed from defendant's front yard on a particular summer-weekday three years ago, would you rather have the testimony of someone who saw the hedge come down or the business record of the landscape company that cut it down and hauled it off? It is not just that the hearsay is reliable, but that so often it is more reliable than present memory.[255]

The trustworthiness clause—the final clause of this exception, which states that even if the rest of the foundation is satisfied the exception does not apply if "the sources of information or other circumstances indicate lack of trustworthiness"—also goes a long way to promote reliability. If there is a problem with the trustworthiness of the particular record, including the record keeper, the trial judge has the discretion to deny the exception.

D. Use Note

1. Made in the Course of a Regularly Conducted Business Activity (by a Person Acting in the Regular Course of his or her Business)

The record must have been made in the course of a regularly conducted business activity.[256] Four points are particularly important here.

First, and important because it comes up so often, a document prepared to exculpate the declarant in the event there is litigation is generally not a document prepared in the ordinary course of business.[257]

---

255. As long ago as 1947, Professor Maguire identified eight guarantees of reliability behind this particular exception:

> (a) regularity of practice in making business entries, (b) the occasional fact that the entrant was under oath, (c) contemporaneousness of the entries with acts or observations recorded, (d) connected occurrences to prove the truth and precision of the record, (e) the frequent fact that entries in question formed part of a series of connected items, (f) the entrant's inclination to perform his duty correctly, and the risks to him of incorrect performance, (g) the fact that the entrant had no personal interest to misstate what he did or saw, and (h) the fact that the entrant had peculiar personal knowledge from having done the recorded act or make the recorded observation.

John MacArthur Maguire, Evidence: Common Sense and Common Law, at 131 (1947).

256. *E.g.,* Noffle v. Perez, 178 P.3d 1141, 1147 (Alaska 2008) ("[A] business record can come from any business, including a doctor's office, a hospital, or the Social Security Administration;" the record here was "communication between medical doctors and the Social Security Disability Determination Unit") (footnote omitted).

257. *E.g., Palmer,* 318 U.S. at 111–15; Lust v. Sealy, Inc. 383 F.3d 580, 588 (7th Cir. 2004) ("They were business records in ... *a* literal sense, of being documents created for a

Second, "made in the course of a regularly conducted business activity" means that the declarant who makes the records must be acting in the regular course of his or her business. Sometimes a business requires that its customers provide the business with certain information. It is the regular practice of the business to have the customer fill certain forms, but filling in such forms is not the regular practice of the customer, the declarant.[258] The critical inquiry is the one into the out-of-court declarant's regular practice.

---

business purpose—namely to create evidence of nonliability! ... [But they] were not created as a part of the regular record-keeping processes of the [defendant].... Their only purpose was to create evidence for use in [plaintiff]'s anticipated lawsuit, and that purpose disqualifies them from admission as business records."); Hertz v. Luzenac Am., Inc., 370 F.3d 1014, 1020 (10th Cir. 2004) (factors that can be considered under the "trustworthiness clause" include "(1) the business significance of the document outside the litigation context, (2) the level of experience of the preparer in creating such documents, and (3) the neutrality of the preparer"); *Certain Underwriters at Lloyd's*, 232 F.3d at 205 ("Litigants cannot evade [this] trustworthiness requirement ... by simply hiring an outside party to investigate an accident and then arguing that the report is a business record because the investigator regularly prepares such reports as part of his business."); United States v. Blackburn, 992 F.2d 666, 670 (7th Cir. 1993) (a document is not trustworthy when it "is created for a particular use that lies outside the business's usual operations—especially when that use involves litigation"); State v. Sweet, 949 A.2d 809, 817–18 (N.J. 2008) (admitting as business records "ampoule testing certificates and ... breath testing instrument inspection certificates ... [as evidence the] Breathalyzer® ... was in good working order"); Dawn VV v. State, 850 N.Y.S.2d 246, 248 (N.Y. App. Div. 2008) (hospital employees "were under a business duty to report incidents to the Department of Health, ... but not to local police;" report to local police inadmissible) (citation omitted).

258. For example, when there is an unauthorized withdrawal from a customer's bank account the money withdrawn will be credited back to the account, but only after the customer fills out an affidavit affirming that he or she neither withdrew the funds nor authorized the withdrawal. This is the bank's regular procedure. The affidavit does not fit under this exception. While it was in the regular course of the *bank's* business to require the affidavit, the focus here is on the declarant and such an affirmation was not part of the regular course of the *declarant's* business. Stahl v. State, 686 N.E.2d 89 (Ind. 1997). On this point, the text of the rule is less than clear as a matter of syntax. The advisory committee explained, however, that such a statement might "qualify as a regular entry except that the person who furnished the information was not acting in the routine of the business." Fed.R.Evid. 805 advisory committee's note. Also, the guarantee of reliability for this exception depends on the regularity of the declarant's action; the guarantee of reliability is not present unless the statement was made as part of out-of-court declarant's regular business activity. *See* part VII(C)(2) of this chapter, above, and *Stahl v. State, supra. See also, e.g.,* State v. Reynolds, 746 N.W.2d 837, 842 (Iowa 2008) (though relied on by the bank, certain reports from the Federal Reserve were inadmissible because there was no evidence the declarant from the Federal Reserve satisfied the foundational elements of this exception).

Furthermore at least one case states that it is not enough that declarants regularly make

Third, the guarantee of reliability for a business record is not that the documents are *frequently prepared*, but that they are *regularly prepared*. Regular is not a synonym for frequent. "Regular" stresses conformity to a pattern.[259] The pattern need not repeat frequently in order to repeat regularly. The statement must have been made in the regular course of a business activity. The occasion to make a record can arise infrequently; so long as the record is made in the regular course of the business when the (infrequent) occasion does arise, this foundational element of this exception is satisfied. It may be unusual that anyone fails to pay the company in question for services rendered, but if it is the regular course of business for this company to make a record every time someone does fail to pay, then such a record can fit under this exception. It may be unusual that anyone calls in to the company in question to compliment it about the high quality of one of its products, or to complain about a defect, but if it is the regular course of business for this company to make a record every time someone does make such a call, then such a record can fit under this exception.[260] The frequency with which such records are made may, however, be

---

the kind of record as part of how they do their jobs. There must be some evidence they have a business duty to make this kind of record—the employer must require the record keeping. United States v. Ferber, 966 F.Supp. 90, 98 (D. Mass. 1997) (otherwise most any document pertaining to company business and found within company files would fit under the exception and could be gotten around the hearsay rule even when offered by the company on its own behalf). Other cases stating the declarant must have a business duty to make the statement simply include the point as dicta in a foundational-elements list. *See* State v. Carroll, 36 S.W.3d 854, 867 (Tenn. Crim. App. 1999); Rabovsky v. Commonwealth, 973 S.W.2d 6, 10 (Ky. 1998). This is not a necessary interpretation of the rule. The text of the rule requires that the statement be made "in the course of a regularly conducted business activity" and that "it was the regular practice of that business activity to make [such a report]." FED.R.EVID. 803(6). The key word here is "practice," not duty. Neither the rule nor the advisory committee's note mentions a "business duty" to make the record. As far back as at least 1944, the English version of this exception tended to emphasize a duty to make the record, while the American version tended to emphasize "made in the ordinary course of the business without regard to the existence of any special duty in reference to it." JOHN JAY McKELVEY, HANDBOOK OF THE LAW OF EVIDENCE §247, at 455 (1944).

259. MERRIAM-WEBSTER'S COLLEGIATE DICTIONARY, CD-ROM (Zane Pub. Co. 1996).

260. *Palmer,* 318 U.S. at 113–15 (The fact that a company regularly records "its employees' versions of their accidents does not put those statements in the class of records made 'in the regular course' of the business ... If it did, ... [a]ny business by installing a regular system for recording and preserving its version of accidents for which it was potentially liable could qualify those reports under the Act. The result would be that the Act would cover any system of recording events or occurrences provided it was 'regular' and though it had little or nothing to do with the management or operation of the business as such.... '[R]egular course' of business must find its meaning in the inherent nature of the

relevant to whether a record is untrustworthy and therefore ineligible for this exception. This is discussed below.[261]

Fourth, it is worth noting that this exception specifically includes records of "opinions[] or diagnoses."[262]

2. Information Automatically Gathered and Retained by Computer

The rule states that the record must be made by someone who has personal knowledge or who makes the entry based on information provided by someone who has personal knowledge.[263] Many modern business records are made by computers, not persons.[264] Take, for example, a record of calls made from a particular phone. The information in question is gathered and entered into a computer's memory by the computer itself. The cases hold that where information is automatically stored in the computer and retained in the ordinary course of business, it is a business record and a printout of this information fits under this exception.[265]

---

business in question and in the methods systematically employed for the conduct of the business as a business.") (paragraph breaks omitted).

261. Part 5 of this Use Note, below.

262. FED.R.EVID.803(6). *Accord, e.g.,* Sosna v. Binnington, 321 F.3d 742, 747 (8th Cir. 2003) (dismissing the argument "that the statement ... was solely the opinion of the pathologist," the court quoted the rule and held that "the opinions of the pathologist contained in his autopsy report fit comfortably within Rule 803(6)'s confines"); Shelton v. Consumer Prods. Safety Comm'n, 277 F.3d 998, 1010 (8th Cir. 2002) (laboratory test reports as business records).

263. At least one court has characterized this part of the foundation as "arguably the most important element." Boca Investerings P'ship v. United States, 128 F.Supp.2d 16, 19 (D.C.D.C. 2000), *rev'd on other grounds,* 314 F.3d 625 (D.C. Cir. 2003) (testimony that it "would be unlikely" the writing was made by someone who did not have personal knowledge is insufficiently certain to satisfy this element of the foundation; if the author of the document is not "reasonably certain," the court cannot have confidence that the document is sufficiently trustworthy).

264. "'[I]t is immaterial that the business record is maintained in a computer rather than in company books.'" United States v. DeGeorgia, 420 F.2d 889, 891–93 n.11 (9th Cir. 1969) (citation omitted) (quoted in United States v. Bennett, 363 F.3d 947, 954 (9th Cir. 2004)).

265. United States v. Salgado, 250 F.3d 438, 452 (6th Cir. 2001) (citing cases). Furthermore, the party offering the computer printout "is not required to present expert testimony as to the mechanical accuracy of the computer where it presented evidence that the computer was sufficiently accurate that the company relied upon it in conducting its business." *Id.*

Though this record was not *made* by a computer, it is of course true that the exception applies to "business record[s] maintained in a computer" just as it does to records maintained

3. The Sponsoring Witness

a. Establishing the Foundation with the Live Testimony of a Sponsoring Witness

The rule states that the foundation must be established "by the testimony of the custodian or other qualified witness, or by certification that complies with Rule 902(11), Rule 902(12), or a statute permitting certification...."[266] As with every exception to the hearsay rule, the sponsoring witness for a business record must be someone who has personal knowledge of the foundational facts.[267] The sponsoring witness does not have to be the person who prepared the record being offered, or even someone who has direct personal knowledge of the specific record being offered.[268] It can be anyone who has first-hand knowledge of the routine record-keeping practices of the business activity in question. It can be anyone who has personal knowledge that (1) the regular practice of this

---

"in company books." Sea Land Serv. v. Lozen Int'l, LLC, 285 F.3d 808, 819 (9th Cir. 2002). So long as the specific foundational elements are established, then unless the format in which the records are kept "indicate[s] lack of trustworthiness," the format in which they are kept is irrelevant to this exception. *See also* State v. Draganescu, 755 N.W.2d 57, 79 (Neb. 2008) ("Computerized printouts that are merely the visual counterparts to routine electronic business records are usually hearsay, but they can be admissible under the business records exception.")

266. FED.R.EVID. 803(6). As discussed below, this is not altogether true: some documents are self authenticating. *See* part VII(D)(3)(b) of this chapter, immediately below.

267. United States v. Riley, 236 F.3d 982, 984–85 (8th Cir. 2001) (it may be possible for a police officer to have the personal knowledge of the foundational facts necessary to qualify a state crime lab report under the business records exception, but the two police officers who testified here did not have the requisite personal knowledge). *See also* United States v. Dickerson, 248 F.3d 1036, 1048 (11th Cir. 2001) (the trial court abused its discretion when it admitted business records under Rule 803(6) without the testimony of the custodian or other qualified witness to authenticate the records). *See, e.g.,* United States v. Ary, 518 F.3d 775, 786 (10th Cir. 2008) (thorough example).

268. *E.g., Salgado,* 250 F.3d at 451–52 ("'Rule 803(6) does not require that the custodian personally gather, input, and compile the information memorialized in a business record.'") (citation omitted); State v. Mubita, 188 P.3d 867, 880–81 (Idaho 2008) (after a long discussion of the practice of medicine today versus the practice of medicine at the time of the creation of the exception, when fewer scientific tests were conducted and more were conducted, processed, and interpreted in the office of the treating physician, holding that "[i]t is not necessary to examine the person who actually created the record so long as it is produced by one who has the custody of the record as a regular part of [the person's] work or has supervision of its creation.") (multiple quotation marks and citations omitted; emphasis deleted).

particular business entity (2) is that such records are made at or near the time of the event recorded and (3) are made by someone who either has personal knowledge of the fact recorded or bases the record on information provided in the regular course of the business by someone who has personal knowledge.

In fact, quite often the sponsoring witness is someone who has no personal knowledge of the particular record being offered into evidence. Someone who has worked in a doctor's office for two years may be able to sponsor a five-year-old medical bill from that office, even though he or she has never seen that particular bill before. Someone—scientist or secretary—who has worked in a crime lab for one year may be able to sponsor a four-year-old report from that crime lab, even though he or she has no direct personal knowledge of how things were handled in the lab four years ago. Someone who has personal knowledge of the current record keeping practices in the office of a paper company may be able to sponsor a record from that office that was prepared years before he or she joined the company. If the witness testifies to personal knowledge of the usual practice today, then the court will presume that the same practice was followed in times past. Absent evidence to rebut the presumption—absent evidence that the testimony regarding today's routine is incorrect, that today's routine was not the routine when the record was made, or that the routine was not followed in this particular instance—the exception has been established.[269]

---

269. *E.g.,* United States v. LeShore, 543 F.3d 935, 942 (7th Cir. 2008) (witness did not compile the record but had personal knowledge of how it was compiled); Dyno Constr. Co. v. McWane, Inc. 198 F.3d 567, 575–76 (7th Cir. 1999) ("To be an 'other qualified witness,' it is not necessary that the person laying the foundation for the introduction of the business record have personal knowledge of their preparation.") (citing and discussing cases); United States v. Parsee, 178 F.3d 374, 380 (5th Cir. 1999) (employee of New Orleans subsidiary allowed to testify to regular practice of Houston subsidiary of same rental car company when that employee could testify that, nationwide, all subsidiaries of this company generated and maintained their records in the same manner and that he was familiar with the practice in the New Orleans office); *Zenith Radio Corp.,* 505 F.Supp. at 1236 (no need to produce or even identify specific individual upon whose firsthand knowledge out-of-court statement based; enough to show such is regular practice of business or activity in question); Nash v. State, 754 N.E.2d 1021, 1026 (Ind. Ct. App. 2001) ("[E]ntries in business records are rebuttably presumed to have been made by a person with personal knowledge of the entry and a duty to record the information."); Second Med., P.C. v. Auto One Ins. Co., 857 N.Y.S.2d 898, 901 (N.Y. Civ. Ct. 2008) ("The witness need not have made the record or even be familiar with the record. It is not even required that the witness be a current or former employee of the business that created the record." The witness only needs to show enough "familiarity with the … record keeping procedures of the business that created the record '… that he [can] state that the record he received was made in the regular

b. Establishing the Foundation without the Live Testimony of a Sponsoring Witness

The rule states that the foundation must be "shown by the testimony of the custodian or other qualified witness or by certification that complies with Rule 902(11), Rule 902(12), or a statute permitting certification."[270] This really is not altogether true. What the rule really requires is that documents that need to be authenticated as records of regularly conducted activities must be authenticated in one or more of these ways. Sometimes, neither a sponsoring witness nor a certification is needed.[271] Some documents offered under this exception will contain within themselves circumstantial evidence of the foundational elements of this hearsay exception. Some documents are self-authenticating.[272]

Take, for example, a cancelled check produced by a bank. Its cancellation marks will be self-authenticating. In addition, the look of the check and the fact that someone can affirm that it was found in the bank files where such a check would be if authentic may be enough to establish the elements of the record of a regularly conducted activity exception to the hearsay rule.[273]

---

course of [that] business, that it was in the regular course of [the] business to make the record and that the record was made contemporaneously with [the events recorded therein]' ...") (multiple citations omitted).

270. FED.R.EVID. 803(6).

271. FED.R.EVID. 902.

272. Because we believe that the Federal Rules of Evidence favor a flexible approach, see Rule 102, and in the absence of a clear indication to the contrary in the Advisory Committee Note, we opt for the view that the testimony of the custodian or other qualified witness is not a sine qua non of admissibility in the occasional case where the requirements for qualification as a business record can be met by documentary evidence, affidavits, or admissions of the parties, *i.e.*, by circumstantial evidence, or by a combination of direct and circumstantial evidence. *Zenith Radio Corp.*, 505 F.Supp. at 1236.

273. Regarding the admissibility of a cancelled check, to prove the information included on the cancellation marks (here the "Paid" stamp on the back), the defendant in Richter & Phillips Jewelers & Distribs., Inc. v. Dolly Toy Co. (*In re* Richter & Phillips & Distribs., Inc.), 31 Bankr. 512 (Bankr. S.D. Ohio 1983), argued "that a representative from the bank in question should have been available to testify and be cross-examined as to what the stamp on the check means and whether it was placed on the check in the course of regularly conducted business, and that, in the absence of such representative, the Rule 803(6) business records exception to the hearsay rule is not applicable." *Id.* at 514 n.1. The court disagreed, finding that the cancelled check was self-authenticating and that the document itself and the surrounding circumstances meet the burden of establishing the foundation for this exception. No sponsoring witness was necessary. *See also, e.g., Zenith Radio Corp.*, 505 F.Supp. at 1236.

This is somewhat akin to judicial notice of the foundational elements: It is common knowledge that the check canceling marks on the back of a check are placed there in the regular course of business, that they are placed thereon in a timely fashion, and that a date incorporated into the cancellation will be the correct date of cancellation, and that these marks are placed there either by a person with personal knowledge of what he or she is doing or by a machine programmed by a person with such personal knowledge.

This is also somewhat akin to a presumption, a burden-of-production shifting presumption. Show the court the cancelled check and the court will assume the cancellation marks are business records unless those opposing admission put on evidence to overcome the presumption.[274]

Additionally, sometimes a sponsoring witness is not necessary because the opposing party has admitted that the record is a business record—in discovery, perhaps, by admitting that the document is what it purports to be, and what it purports to be is a business record.[275]

As a variation of laying the foundation without a sponsoring witness, there are cases where the foundation for the business records exception has been laid by an affidavit, which is itself hearsay. In *FSLIC v. Griffin*,[276] for example, an affidavit of a bank Vice President who was a custodian of documents established that the documents were kept in the regular course of a business activity, that they were prepared in a timely fashion, and that the personal knowledge requirement was satisfied. The court referred to this as "a business records af-

---

274. Ground v. State, 702 N.E.2d 728, 730 (Ind. Ct. App. 1998) ("Absent rebuttal evidence to the contrary, it may be presumed that someone with personal knowledge prepared the challenged … documents."). *See also* CHARLES T. McCORMICK, HANDBOOK OF THE LAW OF EVIDENCE § 286, at 602 (1954) (if there is evidence that it was someone's job to make a record based on either his or her own personal knowledge or the personal knowledge of someone who had a business duty to report to the declarant, then, absent rebuttal evidence, it will be presumed that this particular declarant did so).

275. *E.g.*, United States v. Garth, 540 F.3d 766, 778 (8th Cir. 2008) ("Garth argues that the tax documents were inadmissible hearsay. By stipulating that the records were business records, Garth has necessarily forfeited this argument because business records are admissible under the hearsay exception."). Thanongsinh v. Bd. of Educ., 462 F.3d 762, 778–79 (7th Cir. 2006) is an interesting example. There was no sponsoring witness so the court scoured the record and found two things. First, the opposing party admitted in discovery that the record was what it purports to be, and what it purports to be is a business record. Second, the opposing party relied on a record substantially similar in all respects, thereby conceding the accuracy of the record in question.

276. 935 F.2d 691 (5th Cir. 1991).

fidavit."[277] The result was that there was a sponsoring witness for the underlying business record, but that sponsoring witness's evidence was presented by an affidavit. It may be that it is the regular practice of this business to have someone with the required knowledge make such affidavits at or near the time of the event recorded (*i.e.*, the locating of the records), but that begs the question. The affidavit is hearsay—an out of court statement that is offered to prove the truth of the matter asserted and does not fit fitting under a definitional exclusion. There has to be an exception for the affidavit—and to get it under the business records exception there must be a sponsoring witness to establish the foundational elements for the affidavit. So it goes.

This does not mean, by the way, that a testifying sponsoring witness is never necessary and that the foundation for the record can always be laid by affidavit or certification. The general rule is still "that hearsay does not establish the foundation for admission of otherwise inadmissible hearsay documents."[278] It does mean that some business records are self-authenticating, sometimes a court can take judicial notice that such a record is authentic, and sometimes (*i.e.*, when the foundation is laid by a hearsay affidavit) courts get it wrong.

4. Multiple Levels of Hearsay

The record of a regularly conducted activity exception often involves multiple levels of hearsay.[279] Quite often, these records contain much more than the firsthand, personal observations of the declarant who made the record.

The third foundational element listed above states that the record must be made by someone who either (a) had personal knowledge of what is recorded, or (b) based the record on information provided by someone who both had personal knowledge and provided the information in the regular course of the particular activity involved. The latter part of that requirement means nothing more than this: if there are two or more layers of hearsay, it may be possible to apply this exception to each layer.

Multiple hearsay problems demand that there be multiple exceptions or multiple applications of the same exception. Specifically allowing the record to be

277. FSLIC v. Griffin, 935 F.2d 691, 702 (5th Cir. 1991).

278. Pannoni v. Bd. of Trs., 90 P.3d 438, 446–47 (Mont. 2004) (plaintiff offered a four letters as business records and attempted to establish the foundation for the exception with "a written certification prepared by the custodian of [the] records," which certification parroted the language of the rule; the court refused to allow the hearsay certification to establish the foundation for the hearsay exception).

279. *See* Chapter 11, below.

based on information provided by someone who had personal knowledge and provided the information in the regular course of the activity involved is an express statement that multiple applications of this same exception may be used to deal with layers of hearsay within a business record. Other exceptions might also work.[280] This part of the foundation does not require that each level of hearsay within a business record be handled under the business record exception. It simply states it as an available, but not an exclusive, remedy to layered hearsay.[281]

There are, however, a number of jurisdictions that have held that in certain circumstances the business records exception does away with the need to deal separately with hearsay incorporated into the business record.[282]

---

280. For example, in the regular course of business the right person, might make a timely record of a statement that was itself an excited utterance or a statement for purposes of medical diagnosis or treatment. *See generally* Chapter 11, below.

281. *E.g.*, United States v. Ary, 518 F.3d 775, 786 (10th Cir. 2008) (final declarant's sources also had a business duty to report); United States v. Vigneau, 187 F.3d 70, 75–76 (1st Cir. 1999) ("despite its language," this exception does not apply to hearsay statements within a business record unless they were made in the regular course of the business or another exception applies); United States v. Baker, 693 F.2d 183, 188 (D.C. Cir. 1982) (if every "participant in the chain producing the record [is] acting in the regular course of business, the multiple hearsay is excused by Rule 803(6). However, if the source of the information is an outsider," another exception or exclusion must apply.); Koch Indus., Inc. and Subsidiaries v. United States, 564 F.Supp.2d 1276, 1292 (D. Kan. 2008) ("If both the source and the recorder of the information, as well as every other participant in the chain producing the record, are acting in the regular course of business, the multiple hearsay is excused by Rule 803(6). However, if the source of the information is an outsider, as in the facts before us, Rule 803(6) does not, by itself, permit the admission of the business record. The outsider's statement must fall within another hearsay exception to be admissible....").

282. In Amtrust, Inc. v. Larson, 388 F.3d 594, 599 (8th Cir. 2004), the court found that the "trustworthiness clause" of the public records and reports exception replaces the usual requirement that underlying levels of hearsay must have their own exclusion or exception. The proponent of the evidence need not establish an exclusion or exception for underlying levels of hearsay. Rather, the burden shifts to the opponent of the evidence to show that it is not trustworthy; that there are underlying levels of hearsay may be relevant to that trustworthiness decision. There is no apparent reason why that reasoning would not apply to this "trustworthiness clause" exception as well.

In Air and Land Forwarders, Inc. v. United States, 172 F.3d 1338 (F.C. 1999), the court noted that other circuits "have generally held that a document prepared by a third party is properly admitted as part of the business entity's records if the business integrated the document into its records and relied upon it," *id.* at 1342, and if "other circumstances indicat[e] the trustworthiness of the document," *id.* at 1343. (Citing and discussing cases from other circuits). *Accord* United States v. Grant, 56 M.J. 410, 414 (C.A.A.F. 2002) (citing cases, including *Air and Land Forwarders*). These cases involve "documents" incorporated into a

5. The "Trustworthiness" Clause

a. Judicial Discretion to Exclude the Evidence If It Seems Untrustworthy

This exception contains a "trustworthiness" clause stating, "unless the source of information or the method or circumstances of preparation indicate lack of trustworthiness." This is one of the exceptions that gives the trial judge considerable discretionary power to exclude the evidence even though the proponent is otherwise able to satisfy the foundational elements.[283]

It is important here to keep in mind that "trustworthiness" is not the same as "credibility." The trustworthiness decision is for the trier of law; the credibility decision is for the trier of fact. The judge must be careful not to usurp the function of the jury by deciding that the statement is not trustworthy because the judge does not believe it is true. Say, for example, the business record contradicts other evidence and the judge believes that the other evidence is true and, therefore, not the business record. This is not a trustworthiness decision left in the hands of the judge; it is a credibility decision left in the hands of the jury.[284]

As discussed above, business records need not be frequently prepared, just regularly prepared.[285] The rule requires regularity. The frequency with which particular records are made may, however, be relevant to whether the records

---

business record; they do not involve oral statements incorporated into business records. On their facts, these cases generally deal with incorporation of information business to business but their conclusions do not seem so limited. The reasoning of these courts boils down to this: incorporating businesses rely on the accuracy of the incorporated records. That may be so but it is no reason to rewrite this exception and to ignore Rule 805. I rely on the accuracy of what my spouse tells me. That does not mean I can incorporate it into my recorded recollection and get it into evidence under Rule 803(5).

283. Sometimes this foundational element and others overlap. *See* Boca Investerings P'ship v. United States, 128 F.Supp.2d 16, 21 (D. D.C. 2000), *rev'd on other grounds*, 314 F.3d 625 (D.C. Cir. 2003) (if it is not "reasonably certain" who authored a document, then the court cannot say it was made by someone who had personal knowledge and cannot have confidence that it is sufficiently trustworthy). *And see supra*, note 257 regarding the overlap between the requirement that the document be prepared in the regular course of business and the trustworthiness clause.

284. Regarding admissibility versus credibility, *see* part (I)(C) of this chapter, above. Regarding trustworthiness versus credibility, *see* Chapter 5(V)(E)(2), below; *see also* part VIII(E)(4)(a) of this chapter, below.

285. *See supra* part VII(D)(1) of this chapter.

are trustworthy. There may be things about the frequency with which such records are made that make them more trustworthy. A system set up for frequent record keeping may be more reliable than one set up for infrequent record keeping, but then again it may not. Trustworthiness decisions are ad hoc.

As a general rule, the closer preparation of the record is to the core of the business, the more likely it is to be trustworthy and, of course, the further away the preparation is from the heart of the business, the less likely it is to be trustworthy. In the usual case, documents prepared in anticipation of litigation are considered untrustworthy and therefore inadmissible as business records.[286] Again, however, trustworthiness decisions are ad hoc.

Other factors the judge might consider (and, therefore, the lawyer might argue) are discussed elsewhere in this book.[287]

b. The "Trustworthiness" Clause and the Burden of Proof

The burden of establishing the foundational elements of an exception is on the party seeking the advantage of the exception, the party offering the evidence. That party does not, however, have to affirmatively demonstrate the trustworthiness of each record offered under this hearsay exception. The other foundational elements establish categorical trustworthiness — presumptive trustworthiness. The burden of demonstrating that a particular business record or report is not trustworthy is on the party opposing admission, the party arguing that the exception does not apply.[288]

---

286. See the cases cited *supra*, note 257.

287. *See* part VIII(E)(4)(a) of this chapter, below.

288. *E.g.*, Shelton v. Consumer Prods. Safety Comm'n, 277 F.3d 998, 1010 (8th Cir. 2002) ("[O]nce the offering party has met its burden of establishing the foundational requirements of the business records exception, the burden shifts to the party opposing admission to prove inadmissibility by establishing sufficient indicia of untrustworthiness." Same rule here as with public records and reports exception); United States v. Loyola-Dominguez, 125 F.3d 1315, 1318 (9th Cir. 1997) (public records exception; "presumed trustworthy"; opponent's burden to show otherwise); Bank of Lexington & Trust Co., 959 F.2d 606, 609 (6th Cir. 1992) ("[P]arty opposing admission … must prove that the report is not trustworthy."); Moss v. Ole S. Real Estate, Inc., 933 F.2d 1300, 1305 (5th Cir. 1991); Ellis v. Int'l Playtex, Inc., 745 F.2d 292, 301 (4th Cir. 1984) (public records and reports exception; because most government investigations employ well accepted means of gathering, analyzing, and reporting data, it makes practical sense to place the "lack of trustworthiness" burden on the party opposing admission, rather than to require the proponent to reinvent the wheel each time such a report is offered; it makes sense to presume trustworthiness); United States v. Davis, 826 F.Supp. 617, 624 (D.R.I. 1993) (public records and reports; once the rest of the foundation is established the document is presumed to fit

6. Foreign Records of Regularly Conducted Activities

This exception is not limited to domestic records of regularly conducted activities, but also applies to foreign records of regularly conducted activities.[289] Regarding the authentication of foreign records, see the Foreign Records of Regularly Conducted Activity Act[290] and Federal Rule of Evidence 902(12), entitled "Certified foreign records of regularly conducted activity."

7. The Absence of an Entry and the Hearsay Rule

Rule 803(7) enacts an exception for the admission of the fact of the absence of an entry in a record of a regularly conducted activity. This exception is largely, if not entirely, unnecessary. Hearsay is an out-of-court statement. A "statement" is an "oral or written assertion."[291] "[N]othing is an assertion unless intended to be one."[292] Absent the most unusual circumstances, the lack of an entry is not an oral or written assertion and no one intends the lack of a recording

---

under the exception and the burden is on the opponent to "demonstrate untrustworthiness.").

This means one of two things: (1) trustworthiness is a foundational element, but once the proponent of the evidence proves the other foundational elements, then trustworthiness is presumed and the evidentiary burden on the point is shifted to the party opposing the evidence, or (2) trustworthiness is not a foundational element at all.

But see Chadwell v. Koch Ref. Co., 251 F.3d 727 (8th Cir. 2001), which seems to misplace this burden. *Chadwell* states that even if the notes in question "do warrant the Rule 803(6) exception as records kept during the course of the regular business activity of a union steward, there is no evidence to indicate that the source of the information guarantees trustworthiness as required by Rule 803(6)." *Id.* at 732. I would say that if the proponent establishes the rest of the foundational elements, the ones listed as the first three in the list in part VII(B) of this chapter, then that is evidence of trustworthiness and it is up to the party opposing admission to show that the statement is not trustworthy. This *Chadwell* court avoided discussing whether the foundational elements were satisfied by stating that in any case the evidence did not fit under the exception because there was no evidence of trustworthiness. This is only proper on backwards day and, in the law, it never is backwards day. The court incorrectly used the trustworthiness clause as an escape hatch.

289. *See, e.g.,* United States v. Wilson, 249 F.3d 366, 376 (5th Cir. 2001) (records from foreign bank). *See also* the following parts of this chapter: VI(E)(8) (foreign past recollection recorded), VIII(E)(6) (foreign public records and reports), and XI(D)(6) (foreign ancient documents).

290. 18 U.S.C. § 3505 (2001).

291. Fed.R.Evid. 801(a)(1). *See* the discussion of conduct as hearsay in Chapter 1.

292. Fed.R.Evid. 801(a) advisory committee's note.

or entry to be a statement. In the normal course, then the lack of an entry is not hearsay in the first place.[293]

Say the person in the company who is in charge of keeping such records is told by someone with knowledge and with a duty to report, "I was wrong. There was no fire." The record keeper does not think, "Okay. I will assert that there was no fire by not making an entry in the record that there was a fire." All we have here is testimony is that no entry was found and that is an in-court statement, based on personal knowledge. No one is offering an out-of-court statement; there is no hearsay. Absence of an entry almost never fits within the definition of hearsay.[294]

---

293. *See, e.g.*, People v. Zamudio, 181 P.3d 105, 125 (Cal. 2008) (defendant argued that the victim's out-of-court silence regarding anything being missing or having been taken was a "statement" for purposes of the hearsay rule; "'nonverbal conduct'—such as a person's silence—constitutes a 'statement' under the hearsay rule only if it was 'intended by [the person] as a substitute for oral or written verbal expression;'" nothing suggests the victim "intended her failure to say anything ... to be 'a substitute for oral or written verbal expression'"). As a geneal rule, the lack of an entry is not "intended ... to be 'a substitute for oral or written verbal expression.'" *Id.*

There is the rare case where the absence of an entry is intended as an assertion. Say that a man (the out-of-court declarant) is positioned in the bell tower of the church. He takes with him two lanterns. By prearrangement, he will light two lanterns if the British are coming by sea, he will light one lantern if the British are coming by land, and he will light no lantern if the British are not coming. If a witness offers to testify that he looked at the bell tower and no lantern was lit and that is offered to prove that at that moment the British were not coming, that lack of an "entry" would be hearsay. But, of course, this is not a case of a regularly conducted activity so this exception would not apply anyway. (If you had evidence that the watcher in the bell tower was alert and watching, the witness's testimony that there was no lantern would be a present sense impression: the out-of-court declaration was made while the declarant was perceiving the event (no British) and the out-of-court statement describes the thing being perceived (no British).

294. The counter argument is that the out-of-court statement is the book or the computer file, or whatever was consulted in the search for the entry. It is as if the witness testified, "The book said 'There is no such entry.'" The testifying witness is offering his recollection of the book into evidence to prove the lack of an entry. This is no different from offering his recollection of the book into evidence to prove the presence of an entry. That is the argument, but it is not a good one. Still, there is no assertion by an out-of-court declarant. The argument that there is an implied assertion does not work unless that there was an out-of-court act that the actor intended to be an assertion. Here there is no such intention.

VIII. Public Records and Reports: Rule 803(8)

A. Text of the Rule

The following are not excluded by the hearsay rule, even though the declarant is available as a witness:

****

(8) Public records or reports. Records, reports, statements, or data compilations, in any form, of public offices or agencies, setting forth (A) the activities of the office or agency, or (B) matters observed pursuant to duty imposed by law as to which matters there was a duty to report, excluding, however, in criminal cases matters observed by police officers and other law enforcement personnel, or (C) in civil actions and proceedings and against the Government in criminal cases, factual findings resulting from an investigation made pursuant to authority granted by law, unless the sources of information or other circumstances indicate lack of trustworthiness.

B. Foundational Elements

1. The out-of-court statement must be a public record or report.

2. It must set forth one of the following three kinds of things:

    (a) The activities of the office or agency that prepared the report.[295]

    (b) Matters the agency had a legal duty to observe and a legal duty to report upon (unless it is a criminal case and the record in question is a police report; this protects defendant's confrontation rights).[296]

    (c) Factual findings resulting from an investigation made pursuant to authority granted by law. This includes factually based conclusions or opinions.[297] This part of the exception only applies in civil actions

---

295. FED.R.EVID. 803(8)(A).

296. FED.R.EVID. 803(8)(B).

297. FED.R.EVID. 803(8)(C). *E.g.*, Beech Aircraft Corp. v. Rainey, 488 U.S. 153, 170 (1988) ("As long as the conclusion is based on a factual investigation and satisfies the Rule's trustworthiness requirement, it should be admissible along with other portions of the report."). This exception does not cover findings of fact by courts. Herrick v. Garvey, 298 F.3d 1184, 1192 (10th Cir. 2002) ("Rule 803(8) was not intended to allow the admission of findings of fact by courts. Rule 803(8) is limited to investigations: 'A judge in a civil trial is not an investigator, rather a judge.'"); United States v. Jones, 29 F.3d 1549, 1554 (11th Cir. 1994); Nipper v. Snipes, 7 F.3d 415, 417 (4th Cir. 1993) ("does not apply to judicial find-

and when the evidence is offered against the government in criminal actions. It is not available for the government to use against the defendant in a criminal action.[298]

3. And then there is a "trustworthiness" clause. The record or report is admissible unless the evidence does not seem trustworthy. Once the foundation for the exception is established the court can still decide that the evidence does not seem trustworthy and sustain the hearsay objection.

C. A Variation of This Rule That Is Worth Considering

The version of this rule enacted in at least one state is worth considering for general adoption. It adds as a foundational element to the exception pre-trial notice of an intention to use the exception.[299] Public records, reports, and data compilations can be so far removed from the case at hand that opposing counsel should not, and cannot, be expected to anticipate their use or even know of their existence. Without notice, it may not be possible for opposing counsel to be prepared for the use of such a report at trial.[300] Requiring this kind of notice seems fair and efficient; it makes sense.

D. Need + Reliability = 1

1. Need

The need for the exception is that the declarant who prepared the "[r]ecord[], report[], statement[], or data compilation[]" is unlikely to have any present firsthand knowledge of the information contained therein. Without this exception, that evidence will not be available from this source.

---

ings of fact"). It does apply to findings of fact by administrative agencies. Davignon v. Hodgson, 524 F.3d 91, 113 (1st Cir. 2008); Goldsmith v. Bagby Elevator Co., 513 F.3d 1261, 1288 (11th Cir. 2008) (an EEOC "'finding of intentional racial discrimination … is a finding of fact. Rule 803(8)(c) explicitly makes such evaluative reports admissible, regardless whether they contain factual opinions or conclusions.'"); Young v. James Green Mgmt., Inc., 327 F.3d 616, 624 (7th Cir. 2003) ("As a general proposition, administrative findings regarding claims of discrimination may be admitted under Rule 803(8)(C).").

298. There is no such limitation under some state rules, including Nebraska's. Neb.Evid.R. 803(7), Neb. Rev. Stat. §27-803(7) (Reissue 1995).

299. Neb.Evid.R. 803(7), Neb. Rev. Stat. §27-803(7) (Reissue 1995).

300. I imagine that the public records and reports storage depot is the building into which the Lost Ark of the Covenant was placed at the end of the Steven Spielberg movie *Raiders of the Lost Ark.*

Additionally, this exception includes factual findings resulting from an investigation made pursuant to authority granted by law. A litigant who wants to present evidence of the cause of an airplane crash is not likely to be able to go out and reconduct the investigation that has already been conducted by the National Transportation Safety Board. That evidence will be lost without an exception. And even if the litigant could redo the whole investigation, wouldn't it be a horrible waste of resources to require the litigant to do so? And after the litigant had reconducted the investigation, would we really rather have the results of the investigation conducted by the litigant's people or the results of the one conducted by independent government investigators?

If the evidence is not available anywhere else, it will be lost to the trier of fact. If it is available elsewhere but only at great expense, then it will be lost to the trier of fact except when at least one party to a lawsuit can afford the great expense.[301]

2. Reliability

Reliability comes from three things. First, searching the record and finding the entry in question will almost always be more reliable than having a public official testify from memory about the facts recorded. about the entry. Second, the record is reliable enough to use in court because it is generally assumed that public officials perform their jobs properly and, therefore, that public records can be trusted.[302] Third, there is a bit of a feeling that these records are, after all, the public record. If they are good enough to constitute the public record, they are good enough to be used in court.[303] The guarantee

---

301. *E.g.*, United States v. Enterline, 894 F.2d 287, 288 (8th Cir. 1990) (were computer records not admissible as public records to prove particular cars had been *reported* stolen, "the difficulty of proving that simple fact would be enormous.").

302. FED.R.EVID. 803(8) advisory committee's note; Coleman v. Home Depot, Inc., 306 F.3d 1333, 1341 (3d Cir. 2002); Melville v. Am. Home Assurance Co., 443 F.Supp. 1064, 1112 (E.D.Pa. 1997) ("[P]ublic records or reports, by virtue of their being based on legal duty and authority, contain sufficient circumstantial guarantees of trustworthiness to justify their use at trial."); Gross v. King David Bistro, Inc., 84 F.Supp.2d 675, 677 (D. Md. 2000) ("the general reliability of public agencies in conducting their investigations and the absence of a motive other than informing the public."); Easterling v. Weedman, 922 S.W.2d 735, 743 (Ark. Ct. App. 1996) ("[T]he law deems the reports from governmental offices concerning their regularly conducted and recorded activities to be trustworthy statements of what was done in the public interest.").

303. To the extent that public officials, even when doing their duties properly, often rely upon hearsay rather than, or in addition to, personal knowledge, that is a multiple hearsay problem. A brief discussion of this problem, and a cross-reference to a more detailed discussion, are in the Use Note, part VIII(E) of this chapter, below.

of reliability here is quite similar to that for the business records exception, discussed above.

The final clause of this exception states, "unless the sources of information or other circumstances indicate lack of trustworthiness." If there is a problem with the particular record, including a problem with the particular record keeper, the trial judge has the discretion to deny the exception.[304] This provides additional protection against unreliable records.

E. Use Note

1. Establishing the Foundation with Certified Copies of the Record

Generally, one does not need the live testimony of a sponsoring witness in order to establish the foundation for this exception. A certified copy of the public record or report is enough.[305]

2. Multiple Levels of Hearsay

This is another exception that commonly presents problems with multiple levels of hearsay. It is often the case that public employees do not have personal knowledge of the things they record, the things they report on, the things they include in data compilations. The Seventh Circuit Court of Appeals has stated that if we apply the general rules regarding hearsay within hearsay and require an exception for each level of hearsay behind the public record or re-

---

304. The "trustworthiness" clause is "ample provision for escape if sufficient negative factors are present." FED.R.EVID. 803(8) advisory committee's note. The "trustworthiness" clause is discussed further at part VIII(E)(4) of this chapter, below.

305. FED.R.EVID. 902 and 903, particularly 902(4). "The difference in operation between [the business records exception and the public records exception] is that [the former] requires the testimony of the custodian or other qualified witness, while [the latter] does not require any foundational testimony." United States v. Doyle, 130 F.3d 523, 546 (2d Cir. 1997) (citations and internal quotation marks omitted). *See also, e.g.,* Hughes v. United States, 953 F.2d 531, 540 (9th Cir. 1992); United States v. Aikins, 923 F.2d 650, 656 (9th Cir. 1990). Some public records are presumptively what they purport to be. Rockwell v. State, 176 P.3d 14, 24–25 (Alaska Ct. App. 2008) (a "passport and the stamps placed in his passport by foreign government officials when he entered the foreign country ... fall within the public records exception to the hearsay rule ...").

Regarding the authentication of official records of a foreign country, in addition to FED.R.EVID. 901–903 (particularly 902(3)), see FED.R.CIV.PRO. 44(a)(2) and FED.R.CRIM.PRO. 27. *See also, e.g.,* United States v. Squillacote, 221 F.3d 542, 562 (4th Cir. 2000).

port, that will make this exception "essentially useless."[306] It concluded that the proponent of a public record or report need not deal with layers of hearsay contained within the report.[307] In the eyes of this appellate court, Rule 805[308] does not apply to Rule 803(8).

The Eighth Circuit has come to the same place. A party argued that a public record contained hearsay within hearsay; the official preparing the record did not have firsthand knowledge of the facts recorded. The court stated that the rule provides that "public records are admissible 'unless the sources of information or other circumstances indicate lack of trustworthiness.' "[309] As regards the hearsay rule, this assumes admissibility of the public record or report unless the opponent of admission can "prove the report's untrustworthiness."[310] In the Eighth Circuit, the public record or report exception does away with double hearsay problems unless the opponent of the evidence can convince the court that the layers of hearsay make the particular report untrustworthy.[311]

---

306. *In re* Oil Spill by the Amoco Cadiz, 954 F.2d 1279, 1308 (7th Cir. 1992).

307. We recognize that some courts treat Rule 803(8) as avoiding only the first-level hearsay problem—that is, as excusing the presence of the documents' authors. If the statements would be hearsay even were the author present in court, then Rule 803(8) does not apply, on this view. Nothing in either the text or the history of Rule 803(8) supports an approach that would make the rule essentially useless—for the bureaucrat who fills out a governmental form usually incorporates information furnished by others. Rule 803(8) has a long common law history behind it ... that allow[s] the introduction of [public records that are based on information furnished by others]. The Advisory Committee's notes endorse cases of this kind and this subsection of Rule 803 was enacted without change or comment by Congress. Courts that treat 803(8) as limited to the first-level hearsay problem rely on a negative implication of Rule 805, which says that "hearsay included within hearsay is not excluded ... if each part of the combined statements conforms with an exception to the hearsay rule provided in these rules." Rule 805 does not say (or even imply) that none of the other exceptions deals with more than a single level. Rule 803(8) is a multi-level exception, in the footsteps of its common law precursors.
In re *Oil Spill by the Amoco Cadiz*, 954 F.2d at 1308 (citations—including citations to contrary cases from other jurisdictions—omitted).

308. FED.R.EVID. 805. The idea that certain hearsay exceptions cleanse underlying layers of hearsay is discussed further in Chapter 11(IV), below, and the cross-references found therein.

309. Amtrust, Inc. v. Larson, 388 F.3d 594, 599 (8th Cir. 2004).

310. *Id.* ("The rule assumes admissibility in the first instance but with ample provision for escape if sufficient negative factors are present. The burden is on the party opposing admission to prove the report's untrustworthiness.") (internal quotation marks and citations omitted).

311. There is no apparent reason to treat differently any of the other exceptions that contain a "trustworthiness clause." One can argue that in the Eighth Circuit underlying lev-

Other courts seem to disagree. One court found that "statements by third persons … are not admissible under this exception merely because they appear within public records."[312] This could, however, mean nothing more than that this exception does not automatically turn every third-party statement recorded in a public report into admissible hearsay. The exception covers three things within a public report. Two of them—records of the activities of the office and factual findings resulting from investigations made pursuant to authority granted by law—do not cover third-party hearsay statements recorded on the report. Perhaps all these cases are saying is that the exception's inclusion of matters the agency had a legal duty to observe and report upon does not allow the admission of each and every third-party hearsay statement the public employee happens to record in the report—not that the report must be based on the personal knowledge of the reporter, just that the third-party hearsay statements recorded do not necessarily come in.

3. Records Prepared by Private Parties and Filed with Public Agencies

This exception does not apply to records prepared by private entities and simply filed with public agencies.[313] This is so even if the law requires the pri-

---

els of hearsay are not a problem whenever any exception with a "trustworthiness clause" applies.

312. United States v. Mackey, 117 F.3d 24, 28–29 (1st Cir. 1997) ("In line with the advisory committee note…, decisions in this and other circuits squarely hold that hearsay statements by third persons … are not admissible under this exception merely because they appear within public records. This is the [familiar] 'hearsay within hearsay' problem." Id. 28–29 (citation omitted)). See also, e.g., Lewis v. Velez, 149 F.R.D. 474, 487 (S.D.N.Y. 1993) ("[A]ny double hearsay contained in a [Rule 803(8)] report is admissible only if each level of hearsay qualifies independently for a hearsay exception.).

313. Marsee v. United States Tobacco Co., 866 F.2d 319, 325 (10th Cir. 1989) (reports prepared by non-public officials who participated in and based their reports on papers and speeches at a government-agency sponsored conference are not admissible under this exception); John McShain, Inc. v. Cessna Aircraft Co., 563 F.2d 632, 635–36 (3d Cir. 1977) (accident reports filed with the National Transportation Safety Board on accidents in which Cessna landing-gear gave way contained statements filed by pilots, witnesses, and government investigators; statements by pilots and witnesses who had no duty to observe and report are not covered by this exception; statements by government investigators often contained statements from witnesses, creating unresolved double hearsay problems); Easterling v. Weedman, 922 S.W.2d 735, 743 (Ark. Ct. App. 1996) ("Private parties may not bootstrap what amounts to hearsay about private conduct merely by getting a private report of that conduct filed … in a public office…."); Fiberboard Corp. v. Pool, 813 S.W.2d 658, 676 (Tex.

vate party to prepare and file the report.[314] The exception does, however, apply to "statements of non-governmental parties who act as agents for the government under a duty imposed by law."[315] The line seems to be drawn at the difference between " 'a genuine official duty' and 'a mere penal responsibility.' "[316]

4. The "Trustworthiness" Clause

a. Judicial Discretion to Exclude If the Evidence Seems Untrustworthy

This is another of the exceptions that contains a "trustworthiness" clause: "unless the sources of information or other circumstances indicate lack of trustworthiness."[317] This gives the trial judge considerable discretionary power to exclude the evidence even though the proponent is otherwise able to satisfy the foundational elements.[318]

App. 1991) ("Documents prepared by private individuals and filed with a governmental agency are not official documents as contemplated by Rule 803(8).").

Such a report may, of course, fit under another exception such as the business records exception. Missing one exception does not foreclose using another. *See* Chapter 5(V)(A), below.

314. United States v. Doyle, 130 F.3d 523, 546 (2d Cir. 1997) ("[W]e doubt that a legal 'request' for filing records with a government agency would alone qualify the records for the hearsay exception without some showing that the records were reliable, such as a showing that the private party was acting as an agent of the government."); State, ex rel. McDougall v. Johnson, 891 P.2d 871, 876 (Ariz. Ct. App. 1994); R.R. Comm'n of Tex. v. Rio Grande Valley Gas Co., 683 S.W.2d 783, 788 (Tex. App. 1985) (this exception applies "only when the documents are prepared by public officials or employees under their supervision in the performance of their official duties").

315. *Doyle*, 130 F.3d at 546 ("*See, e.g.,* United States v. Meyer, 113 F.2d 387, 397–98 (7th Cir. 1940) (map prepared by engineer for the government from information furnished by persons under his supervision admissible as government record) (cited by Advisory Committee Note to Rule 803)." *Id.* at 546–47). *Accord* United States v. Lykes Bros. Steamship Co., 432 F.2d 1076, 1079–80 (5th Cir. 1970) ("[T]he duty to prepare the report can be delegated, under government regulations, to an independent agency or to a foreign government without the report losing its character, when submitted through the appropriate United States agency, as a report of a 'department or agency of the United States.'"); *Fiberboard Corp.*, 813 S.W.2d at 676 (exception applies to government agents acting under a duty imposed by law, but not to persons who are "under contract" with government, but are not public officials or employees).

316. *Doyle*, 130 F.3d at 546 (quoting 5 WIGMORE, EVIDENCE § 1633a (Chadbourn rev. 1974)).

317. FED.R.EVID. 803(8).

318. *E.g., Young*, 327 F.3d at 623 (Although "[a]s a general proposition, administrative findings regarding claims of discrimination may be admitted under Rule 803(8)(C)," the findings here were not sufficiently trustworthy).

In this regard, keep these two points in mind. First, though the distinction may at times be a subtle one, there is a difference between trustworthiness and credibility.[319] Whether the report is credible has to do with whether the jury believes it. Whether it is untrustworthy has to do with whether the method of preparation leaves the report unreliable. Second, the inability to cross-examine the investigator is not a sufficient reason by itself to exclude the report from this exception.[320]

Regarding untrustworthiness, courts seem to be looking at four things: bias, expertise, memory, and thoroughness. Were either those who prepared the report or those from whom the information was obtained biased?[321] Did the re-

---

319. "When considering whether a report is trustworthy, the court should not consider whether the report is credible, but rather should consider whether the report is reliable. '[T]he trial court is to determine primarily whether the report was compiled or prepared in a way that indicates that its conclusions can be relied upon.'" Union Pac. R.R. Co. v. Kirby Inland Marine, Inc., 296 F.3d 671 (8th Cir. 2002) (citing and then quoting Moss v. Ole S. Real Estate, Inc., 933 F.2d 1300, 1306–07 (5th Cir. 1991)). Regarding trustworthiness versus credibility, *see* Chapter 5(V)(E)(2), below. On a related point, regarding admissibility versus credibility, *see* part (I)(C) of this chapter, above.

320. Distaff, Inc. v. Springfield Contracting Corp., 984 F.2d 108, 112 (4th Cir. 1993) ("Although there may be many reasons for finding a report untrustworthy, it is clear that the inability ... to cross-examine the author on the conclusions in the report is not a reason for exclusion.") (citing MICHAEL GRAHAM, FEDERAL PRACTICE AND PROCEDURE § 6759 (1992)).

321. FED.R.EVID. 803(8) advisory committee's note ("motivation problems"); Hertz v. Luzenac Am., Inc., 370 F.3d 1014, 1020 (10th Cir. 2004) (re record of a regularly conducted activity, neutrality of the preparer). *See generally* Lust v. Sealy, Inc. 383 F. 3d 580, 588 (6th Cir. 2004) (reason records were prepared as a factor under the trustworthiness clause of the exception for records of regularly conducted activity).

Prepared in Anticipation of Litigation: "By bias the courts and the Advisory Committee refer principally to reports compiled in anticipation of litigation." Gentile v. County of Suffolk, 129 F.R.D. 435, 457 (E.D.N.Y. 1990), *aff'd*, 926 F.2d 142 (2d Cir. 1991). *Accord, e.g.,*; Coleman v. Home Depot, Inc., 306 F.3d 1333, 1342 (3d Cir. 2002); Pierce v. Atchison Topeka, Santa Fe Ry., 110 F.3d 431, 444 (7th Cir. 1997) (business record).

Personal Interest—Pecuniary, Penal, or Psychological: E.g., United States v. Spano, 421 F.3d 599, 604 (7th Cir. 2005) (the officials who prepared the report are the ones who were under investigation—now on trial—for various crimes arising out of their attempts to defraud the city; "The [trustworthiness] provision is tailor-made for a case in which the records are controlled by the defendants themselves rather than by clerks assumed to be disinterested."); United States v. Jackson-Randolph, 282 F.3d 369, 381 (6th Cir. 2002) (report offered by defendant was based on information from a person "intimately involved in the defrauding scheme" and later charged as a co-defendant); Faries v. Atlas Truck Body Mfg. Co., 797 F.2d 619, 623 (8th Cir. 1986) (report based almost entirely on the statements of biased eyewitnesses); Lewis v. Valez, 149 F.R.D. 474, 488–89 (S.D.N.Y. 1993) (prison guards made report of incident knowing civil rights action likely to be filed against them, over the

port require some kind of special skill or expertise and, if so, did those who prepared the report have the needed skill or expertise?[322] Are there facts present that may have influenced the memories of those involved? For example, was the investigation started too long after the event being investigated? Or did too much time elapse between the conclusion of the investigation and the preparation of the report?[323] And the fourth consideration is the thoroughness of both the investigation and the report.[324]

---

incident reported; affected by desire to exculpate themselves and relieve themselves or employer of liability).

Institutional or political bias: E.g., *Coleman*, 306 F.3d at 1342 ("'suspect motivation [such as] an institutional or political bias'" with which the final report is consistent); Pearce v. E.F. Hutton Group, Inc., 653 F. Supp. 810, 814 (D.D.C. 1987) ("Given the obviously political nature of Congress, it is questionable whether any report by a committee or subcommittee of that body could be admitted under rule 803(8)(C) against a private party.... [T]oo great a danger that political considerations might affect the findings of such a report.") (paragraph breaks omitted).

322. *Skill and Experience of the Investigator*: FED.R.EVID. 803(8) advisory committee's note ("the special skill or expertise of the official"); E.g., Young, 327 F.3d at 624 (untrustworthy: investigator testified erroneously); *Coleman*, 306 F.3d at 1342; Baker v. Elcona Homes Corp., 588 F.2d 551, 558 (6th Cir. 1978) (investigator possessed special skill and experience); Fraley v. Rockwell Int'l Corp., 470 F. Supp. 1264, 1267 (S.D. Ohio 1979) (untrustworthy: "prepared by an inexperienced investigator in a highly complex field of investigation") (quoted at Beech Aircraft Corp. v. Rainey, 488 U.S. 153, 168 n.11 (1988)). *See also* United States v. Jackson-Randolph, 282 F.3d 369, 381 (6th Cir. 2002) (report offered by defendant was based on information from a person "intimately involved in the defrauding scheme" and later charged as a co-defendant); *Zenith Radio Corp.*, 505 F.Supp. at 1147 (if the report offers expert opinion, look at the extent to which the rules regarding expert opinion are satisfied).

323. *Time Between Event and Investigation*: FED.R.EVID. 803(8) advisory committee's note ("The timeliness of the investigation."); *Bank of Lexington & Trust Co.*, 959 F.2d at 617 ("time between the acts or events ... the agency is investigating and the start of the investigation," not the time it takes to complete a thorough investigation). *Coleman*, 306 F.3d at 1342; *Baker*, 588 F.2d 558 (the investigation was begun immediately after the accident; the report was not issued for two months, but the investigation continued during that time).

Time Between Investigation and Preparation of Report: Likewise, with the right facts, the lapse of time between the conclusion of the investigation and the preparation of the report could be a factor in the report's trustworthiness.

324. *A Hearing*: A hearing is not required. It is simply one factor that may be relevant. FED.R.EVID. 803(8) advisory committee's note ("[W]hether a hearing was held and the level at which [it was] conducted."); *Coleman*, 306 F.3d at 1342; *Bank of Lexington & Trust Co.*, 959 F.2d at 617; *Baker*, 588 F.2d at 558.

Procedural Safeguards: Guerra v. N.E. Indep. Sch. Dist., 496 F.3d 415, 419 (5th Cir. 2007) ("the EEOC letter was created under questionable conditions—the EEOC investigators initially determined that NEISD had not discriminated against Guerra but later, fol-

b. The Evidentiary Burden Regarding Trustworthiness

The burden of establishing the foundational elements of an exception is on the party seeking the advantage of the exception, the party offering the evidence. That party does not, however, have to affirmatively demonstrate the trustworthiness of each public record or report offered under this hearsay exception. The other foundational elements establish categorical trustworthiness—presumptive trustworthiness—and the burden of demonstrating that a particular public record or report is not trustworthy is on the party opposing admission, the party arguing that the exception does not apply.[325]

---

lowing complaints by Guerra to a member of Congress, reopened the file and reversed their decision without any new evidence."); United States v. Orozco 590 F.2d 789, 794 (9th Cir. 1979) (the procedures in place to help catch mistakes was an indication that the report in question was trustworthy); *Zenith Radio Corp.*, 505 F.Supp. at 1147 (if there was a hearing, the extent to which appropriate safeguards were used, including compliance with agency rules and procedures and the extent to which the findings come from "proceedings pervaded by receipt of substantial amounts of material which would not be admissible in evidence").

The Pervasiveness of Evidence that would be Inadmissible in Court: Miller v. Field, 35 F.3d 1088, 1091 (6th Cir. 1994) (factual findings based on inadmissible hearsay found untrustworthy); *Zenith Radio Corp.*, 505 F.Supp. at 1147 ("The extent to which the agency findings are based upon or are the product of proceedings pervaded by receipt of substantial amounts of material which would not be admissible in evidence").

Thoroughness of the Procedures and the Report Generally: *Jackson-Randolph*, 282 F.3d at 381 (report offered by defendant was based on information from a person "intimately involved in the defrauding scheme" and later charged as a co-defendant); *Guerra*, 496 F.3d at 419 (*see Guerra, supra*, this note); *Faries*, 797 F.2d at 623 (report based almost entirely on the statements of biased eyewitnesses deemed untrustworthy); Matthews v. Ashland Chem., Inc., 770 F.2d 1303, 1310 (5th Cir. 1985) (investigatory report can be excluded where no thorough investigation was conducted); Reedy v. White Consol. Ind., Inc., 890 F.Supp. 1417, 1452 (N.D. Iowa 1995) ("trustworthy, in light of the nature of the proceedings and thoroughness of the findings and conclusions offered"); *Zenith Radio Corp.*, 505 F.Supp. at 1147 ("The extent to which the findings are based upon findings of another investigative body or tribunal which is itself vulnerable as the result of trustworthiness evaluation.").

Interim Reports: Smith v. Isuzu Motors Ltd., 137 F.3d 859, 862 (5th Cir. 1998) (though not a "trustworthiness" case, *Smith* does state "that interim agency reports or preliminary memoranda do not satisfy Rule 803(8)(C)'s requirements"); *Zenith Radio Corp.*, 505 F.Supp. at 1147 (the finality of the findings is a factor).

325. The evidentiary burden regarding the trustworthiness clause is discussed above, at part VII(D)(5)(b) of this chapter. The general evidentiary burden regarding the exceptions is discussed above, at part (I)(C) of this chapter.

5. Introducing the Entire Investigatory File

By its terms, the rule applies to reports setting forth the activities of the office or agency, to matters the agency had a legal duty to report upon, and factual findings resulting from an investigation made pursuant to authority granted by law. This exception only applies to the parts of a report doing one or more of those three things, nothing more.[326]

Under Rule 106, the rule of completeness, opposing counsel may be able to introduce parts of the file that do not fit under this exception. This may be true even if the other parts of the document are otherwise inadmissible hearsay.[327]

6. Reports Prepared by State, Local, and Foreign Governments

This exception includes public records and reports prepared by state and local jurisdictions in the United States,[328] and those prepared by foreign governments and their local jurisdictions.[329] There may be particular trustwor-

---

326. Moss v. Ole S. Real Estate, Inc., 933 F.2d 1300, 1310 (5th Cir. 1991) (if a government agency makes an investigation pursuant to authority granted by law, part (C) of this exception "by its terms allows only the introduction of the report setting forth factual findings; there is no provision for requiring the admission of an entire investigatory file."); John McShain, Inc. v. Cessna Aircraft Co., 563 F.2d 632, 635–36 (3d Cir. 1977) (National Transportation Safety Board report on accidents in which Cessna landing-gear gave way contained statements filed by pilots and by witnesses; to this extent, the report is inadmissible hearsay).

327. This aspect of Rule 106 is discussed at Chapter 9(III).

328. "The rule makes no distinction between federal and nonfederal offices and agencies." Fed.R.Evid. 803(8) advisory committee's note.

329. E.g., Mike's Train House, Inc. v. Lionel, L.L.C., 472 F.3d 398, 412 (6th Cir. 2006) (notices of arrest, complaint, investigative reports, and indictments all from Korea) (citing many cases); In re Oil Spill by the Amoco Cadiz, 954 F.2d 1279 (7th Cir. 1992) (documents of the Republic of France and local jurisdictions therein); FAA v. Landy, 705 F.2d 624, 633 (2d Cir. 1983) (a telexed report from the German government to the FAA and incorporated in the FAA's report was admissible as a public record and report); United States v. Regner, 677 F.2d 754 (9th Cir. 1982) (documents of state-run Hungarian taxicab company); United States v. Grady, 544 F.2d 598, 604 (2d Cir. 1976) (Irish police records); Morgan Guar. Trust Co. v. Hellenic Lines Ltd., 621 F. Supp. 198, 217 (S.D.N.Y. 1985) (Greek public documents); Melridge, Inc. v. Heublein, 125 B.R. 825, 829 (D. Or. 1991) (Swiss police reports).

See also United States v. Lykes Bros. Steamship Co., 432 F.2d 1076, 1079–80 (5th Cir. 1970) (report prepared by Korena officials; "[T]he duty to prepare the report can be delegated, under government regulations, to an independent agency or to a foreign government without the report losing its character, when submitted through the appropriate United States agency, as a report of a 'department or agency of the United States.'").

Regarding the authentication of foreign records, see also the following parts of this chap-

thiness problems with some foreign public records,[330] but the rule makes no distinction based on the home jurisdiction of the office or agency.

7. Police Reports

Part (B) of this exception covers records and reports of "matters observed pursuant to duty imposed by law as to which matters there was a duty to report...."[331] This part of this exception applies in civil cases. It does not apply in criminal cases when the out-of-court declarant is a police officer or other law enforcement personnel, and this is so whether the evidence is offered by the government or the defendant.[332] Part (C) of this exception covers factual findings resulting from an investigation made pursuant to authority granted by law."[333] This part of the exception applies in civil cases.[334] It does not apply in criminal cases where the evidence is offered by the government, but it does apply where the evidence is offered by the defendant.[335]

Two reasons have been offered for treating police reports differently. First, "observations by police officers at the scene of a crime or the apprehension of the defendant are not as reliable as observations by public officials in other cases because of the adversarial nature of the confrontation between the police and the defendants in criminal cases."[336] The police have an interest in the outcome. Second, allowing police reports into evidence at a criminal trial interferes with an accused's right to confrontation.[337] Whatever the rationale, some parts of police reports are sometimes excluded from this particular exception in criminal cases.

Some courts have read this exclusion narrowly. As just noted, one reason these reports are not admitted in this situation is to keep out police officers' observations at the scene of a crime because they are made in an adversarial

---

ter: VI(E)(8) (foreign past recollection recorded), VII(D)(6) (foreign business records), and XI(D)(6) (foreign ancient documents).

330. *See* United States v. Garland, 991 F.2d 328, 335 (6th Cir. 1993).
331. FED.R.EVID. 803(8)(B).
332. *Id.*
333. FED.R.EVID. 803(8)(C).
334. *E.g.,* Baker v. Elcona Homes Corp., 588 F.2d 551, 556 (6th Cir. 1978).
335. *Id.*
336. FED.R.EVID. 803(8) advisory committee's note.
337. United States v. Owens, 484 U.S. 554 (1988). This rationale does not apply, of course, if the police officer in question can be called to the stand and cross-examined (*i.e.,* confronted). Regarding the constitutional right to confront witnesses, see Chapter 14, below.

setting and, therefore, are not sufficiently trustworthy. Some courts hold that this exclusion does not apply when the matter is observed and recorded by a police officer in a non-adversarial setting. For example, when a police officer makes a report of the vehicle identification number of an automobile reported stolen and that report is offered to prove that the automobile in question was reported stolen, some courts would hold that this exclusion does not apply.[338] There is a better way to handle this situation, better than simply ignoring the plain meaning of the rule. The better way is to recognize that even if this report does not fit under the public record and reports exception, it may fit under the present sense impression and business records exceptions, and perhaps others.[339]

8. Near-Miss Evidence—Documents That Just Miss Fitting under This Exception and Fit under Some Other Exception

What about the line between public records and, for example, records of a regularly conducted activity? There is no line. What about the line between public records and, for example, past recollection recorded? Again, there is no line. Each exception is separate and distinct, each with its own foundational elements. A statement either fits under an exception or it does not. If it does not fit under one exception, it may fit under another. In fact, that a statement does not fit under one exception is pretty much irrelevant to whether it fits under any other.[340] This is the problem of "near miss" evidence: Can evidence that just barely misses qualifying for admission under one exception, be admitted under another?

For example, if a statement qualifies for the public record or report exception in every way except that it is offered against the defendant in a criminal case, can it still be received into evidence against the defendant in this criminal case if it satisfies all of the elements of some other exception, the exceptions for present sense impressions or records of a regularly conducted activity, for example? The answer is yes, the police report inadmissible under the public records and reports exception can still be ad-

---

338. United States v. Enterline, 894 F.2d 287, 290–91 (8th Cir. 1990) (discussing cases); United States v. Wilmer, 799 F.2d 495, 500–01 (9th Cir. 1986) (citing cases; noting rejection of more literal and restrictive interpretation from United States v. Oates, 560 F.2d 45 (2d Cir. 1977)).

339. *See* the next part of this Use Note, immediately below in the main text.

340. The exception, I suppose, would be when two exceptions have a common foundational element.

missible under another exception.[341] This matter is discussed at length later in this book.[342]

IX. Absence of Public Record or Entry: Rule 803(10)

A. Text of the Rule

The following are not excluded by the hearsay rule, even though the declarant is available as a witness:

****

(10) Absence of public record or entry. To prove the absence of a record, report, statement, or data compilation, in any form, or the nonoccurrence or nonexistence of a matter of which a record, report, statement, or data compilation, in any form, was regularly made and preserved by a public office or agency, evidence in the form of a certification in accordance with Rule 902, or testimony, that diligent search failed to disclose the record, report, statement, or data compilation, or entry.

B. Foundational Elements

1. There must be evidence that the public official or agency in question regularly made and preserved such records or entries.

2. There must be either testimony or a Rule 902(4) certification that a diligent search failed to uncover such a record or such an entry.

---

341. For example, when a police officer, in the regular course of his or her job as a police officer, enters vehicle license numbers into a computer, as the vehicles cross the border, then, under the narrow construction of this exclusion discussed in the text, above, the computer record may fit under the public records and reports exception. Even if it does not, it is a present sense impression under FED.R.EVID. 803(1); it probably is a business record under FED.R.EVID. 803(6); it may be a recorded recollection under FED.R.EVID. 803(5). Couple that with the rule that because a statement almost fits under one exception, but not quite, does not mean it cannot fit under other exceptions. A near miss under one exception does not rule out other exceptions. *See* Chapter 5(V)(A) & (B), below.

342. *See* Chapter 5(V)(A) and Chapter 10(I), below.

C. Need + Reliability = 1

1. Need

The truth is that this exception will only rarely, and perhaps never, be necessary because the absence of an entry may never be hearsay. As explained in the Use Note, below, there is no out-of-court statement.

The theory behind the exception is that the non-entry implies an assertion of non-occurrence. The person not making the entry is the out-of-court declarant. How often will that declarant remember that he or she did not make that particular entry? Almost never.

Additionally, we do not want government officials out of the office and in court testifying—even if only to testify that they do not recall—every time a litigant needs to show an absence of a public record. We want them back in their public office, working for the public.[343]

2. Reliability

Searching the record and failing to find the entry in question will almost always be more reliable than having a public official testify from personal knowledge about whether a particular entry was or was not made. This is so in part because, except in the most extraordinary case, the witness will not have personal knowledge that no such record was ever made. Even if one witness will testify "I remember that I never made such an entry" and another witness will testify "I did a thorough search of the record yesterday and there is no such entry," isn't the latter more reliable?

In addition, we believe that public officials tend to perform their jobs properly and, therefore, the public records tend to be reliable. Even if the work of some public officials is not reliable, the records themselves are, after all, the public record. If they are good enough to constitute the public record, they are good enough to be used in court.[344]

D. Use Note

■ If in the normal course an event would be recorded in the public record if it had occurred and it is not recorded, then that is evidence that it did not

---

343. *See* part VIII(D)(1) of this chapter, above.
344. *See* part VIII(D)(2) of this chapter, above.

occur. This exception applies when the records custodian certifies that there is no such entry, or a witness takes the stand and testifies that he or she searched the public record and there was no such entry.[345]

Except in the most extraordinary case, however, this exception is not necessary. A "statement" is an "oral or written assertion."[346] "[N]othing is an assertion unless intended to be one."[347] Absent the most unusual circumstances, the lack of an entry is not an oral or written assertion, or an assertion of any kind, for that matter. No one intends the lack of a recording or entry to be a statement. In the normal course, the lack of an entry is not hearsay in the first place.

Say the public official who is in charge of such things is told by someone with knowledge and with a duty to report, "There was no fire." The record keeper does not think, "Okay. I will assert that there was no fire by *not noting* in the record that there *was* a fire." The record keeper who does not make a record is not intending to assert anything.

All we have here is testimony that no entry was found and that is an in-court statement, based on personal knowledge. There is no underlying hearsay statement. Absence of an entry simply does not fit within the definition of hearsay.[348]

---

345. "From such a statement, the factfinder may infer that an event that normally would be reflected in the public record did not occur." United States v. Pinto-Mejia, 720 F.2d 248, 257 (2d Cir. 1983). *See*, for example, United States v. Hale, 978 F.2d 1016 (8th Cir. 1992) (affidavit by Bureau of Alcohol, Tobacco and Firearms specialist that diligent search located no record of defendant applying to register weapon).

346. FED.R.EVID. 801(a)(1). *See* the discussion of conduct as hearsay in Chapter 1.

347. FED.R.EVID. 801(a) advisory committee's note.

348. This is discussed further at part VII(D)(7) of this chapter. See that discussion. The counter argument would be that the out-of-court statement is the book or the computer file, or whatever was consulted in the search for the entry. It is as if the witness testified, "The book said 'There is no such entry.'" The testifying witness is offering his recollection of the book into evidence to prove the lack of an entry. This is no different from offering his recollection of the book into evidence to prove the presence of an entry. That is the argument, but it is not a good one. Any way you look at it there is no assertion by an out-of-court declarant. The argument that there is an implied assertion is based on the fact that there was an out-of-court act that the actor intended to be an assertion. Here there is no such intention. *See, e.g.*, People v. Zamudio, 181 P.3d 105, 125 (Cal. 2008) (defendant argued that the victim's out-of-court silence regarding anything being missing or having been taken was a "statement" for purposes of the hearsay rule; " 'nonverbal conduct' — such as a person's silence — constitutes a 'statement' under the hearsay rule only if it was 'intended by [the person] as a substitute for oral or written verbal expression;' " nothing suggests the victim "intended her failure to say anything … to be 'a substitute for oral or written verbal expression'"). As a general rule, the lack of an entry is not "intended … to be a 'substitute for oral or written verbal expression.' " *Id.*

The hearsay rule does not render the evidence inadmissible; if absence of an entry is relevant and there is no other evidence rule that keeps it out, absence of an entry is admissible.

■ An out-of-court statement that draws conclusions from the absence of a record or entry does not fit under this exception. For example, an affidavit regarding a search of FBI records stating that the defendant in a criminal case " 'has failed to perform a given act or that he does not enjoy a certain status' "[349] would not fit under this exception. All that fits under this exception is testimony that the records were searched and the entry in question was not found.[350] The affidavit quoted above in this paragraph would have been admissible hearsay if, instead of stating that the defendant had not performed a given act, it had stated that the relevant records had been searched and there was no entry stating that the defendant had performed the given act and no entry that the defendant enjoyed the certain status in question. Inferences to be made from the absence of records are to be made by the trier of fact.

In addition to hearsay problems, in the usual case witnesses may only testify (or the affiant may only affirm) that they searched the records and the entry in question was not found because this is all they are competent to say, this is the extent of their personal knowledge.[351]

X. Statements in Documents Affecting an Interest in Property: Rule 803(15)

A. Text of the Rule

The following are not excluded by the hearsay rule, even though the declarant is available as a witness:

****

(15) Statements in documents affecting an interest in property. A statement contained in a document purporting to establish or affect an interest in property if the matter stated was relevant to the pur-

---

349. LaRouche v. Webster, 175 F.R.D. 452, 456 (S.D.N.Y. 1996) (plaintiffs sought injunctive and declaratory relief from FBI's allegedly unconstitutional investigation of them; defendants moved for summary judgment and filed supporting affidavits regarding absence of public records of such investigation) (quoting United States v. Yakobov, 712 F.2d 20, 26 (2d Cir. 1983)).
350. *LaRouche*, 175 F.R.D. at 456.
351. Fed.R.Evid. 602.

pose of the document, unless dealings with the property since the document was made have been inconsistent with the truth of the statement or the purport of the document.

B. Foundational Elements

1. The statement must be "contained in a document purporting to establish or affect an interest in property."
2. The statement must be "relevant to the purpose of the document."
3. There must not be subsequent inconsistent dealings with the property in question.

C. Need + Reliability = 1

1. Need

This is a Rule 803 exception. As with many of the Rule 803 exceptions, there is no categorical need. Sometimes there will be great need because there will not be any other evidence of a party's claim to an interest in property.[352] Sometimes there will be almost no need because there will be other more probative evidence of the party's claim to an interest in property. This exception is not based on need.[353]

2. Reliability

Citing the advisory committee's note to Rule 803(15), one federal court stated that the statements covered by this exception tend to be reliable because the documents in which they appear "are executed in relation to serious and carefully planned transactions, and [because of] the financial stake in the transaction, plus [third-party] reliance upon the truth of statements...."[354] This is

---

352. The advisory committee's note states that "[t]he age of the document is of no significance, though in practical application the document will most often be an ancient one." FED.R.EVID. 803(15) advisory committee's note. This, however, does not establish a need for this exception for when this particular need is present, the document would fit under the ancient documents exception and this particular exception would not be needed.

353. In this regard, see the discussion of "Need" under Rule 803(1), the present sense impression exception.

354. Compton v. Davis Oil Co., 607 F.Supp. 1221, 1229 (D. Wyo. 1985). *Accord* United States v. Weinstock, 863 F.Supp. 1529, 1533 (D. Utah 1994); Madden v. State, 799 S.W.2d 683, 689 (Tex. Crim. App. 1990), *rev'd on other grounds*, Turro v. State, 837 S.W.2d 232 (Tex. 1992).

okay so far as it goes. The use of the word "execute," however, seems to antic-ipate a more formal document than many that are covered by the exception: there is no requirement that the document be executed, that the financial stake be large, or that the document have been prepared in anticipation of third-party reliance. The exception far outstrips this guarantee of reliability.

The out-of-court statement must be "relevant to the purpose of the docu-ment." This is a bit of a trustworthiness check. In one case,[355] the statement was in a document that purported to be a "will." The document contained a lengthy statement implicating the defendant in a crime. A two-page narrative about her husband's participation in the crime in question was surrounded by, on the front end, a sentence stating that this was the declarant's will and, on the back end, a sentence stating that anything she owned should "please go to my mother and family." This court found this statement inadmissible because, "whether or not [this statement] purports to establish or affect an interest in property, the lengthy description of the crime is not a matter germane to the purpose of the document."[356] This element of the rule gives the court some flexibility.

The statement must be in a document. This generally means that it must be in writing. *Weinstein's Evidence* states that this "eliminates the danger of inac-curacy of transmission."[357]

The statement will not fit under this exception if "dealings with the prop-erty since [the making of] the document ... have been inconsistent with the truth of the statement or the purport of the document."[358] This will keep out some statements that would otherwise be admissible under this exception.[359] Things change, and we often note these changes in documents — diaries; letters to loved ones or to our attorneys; affidavits; and the like. The real test of change, however, is behavior. If the declarant's behavior after making the statement is inconsistent with the statement, then that belies the truth of the statement, renders it less reliable, and leaves it inadmissible.

---

355. People v. Burton, 441 N.W.2d 87 (Mich. Ct. App. 1989).

356. *Id.* at 89 (the court so held in the face of the argument that the description of the crime was "relevant to the purpose of the document ... as [her] explanation for excluding her husband from the 'purported' will."

357. 4 JACK B. WEINSTEIN & MARGARET A. BERGER, WEINSTEIN'S EVIDENCE ¶ 803(15)[01], at 803-346 (1996).

358. FED.R.EVID. 803(15).

359. United States v. Alexander, 1989 U.S. Dist. LEXIS 17812 (W.D. Mich. 1989) (state-ments in a quit claim deed did not fit under this exception because "subsequent dealings with the property [were] inconsistent with the truth of the proffered statement or purport of the document").

D. Use Note

1. The Kinds of Documents Covered by This Exception—In General

The statement must be contained in a document "purporting to establish or affect an interest in property." This requires a particular format: the statement must be in a document, that is to say, for the most part, it must be in writing. The first definition for document in Black's Law Dictionary is, "[s]omething tangible on which words, symbols, or marks are recorded." The second definition is, "[t]he deeds, agreements, title papers, letters, receipts, and other written instruments used to prove a fact."[360]

It must be in a document "purporting to establish or affect an interest in property." This is very fact specific and must be decided on a case by case basis. Later in this Use Note, there are examples of the kinds of documents some of the cases have found to fit within this exception. First, however, there is something to be said about the nature of the document. The advisory committee's note mentions "[d]ispositive documents," such as deeds, and it only mentions dispositive documents.[361] There is nothing in the rule, however, that limits its application to dispositive documents. From the face of the rule, the document in which the statement is contained must simply be "a document," any kind of document, so long as it is "a document purporting to establish or affect an interest in property."

> [N]othing in the wording of Rule 803(15) requires a dispositive document. The statement in the notes of the Advisory Committee is correct as far as it goes, however it cannot be taken as a limitation on the types of documents to which Rule 803(15) applies. For example, an affidavit accompanying a notice of the death of a joint tenant "affects an interest in property," but is not dispositive. Matters allied to interests in real or personal property, that relate to the property may affect an interest in it but not be dispositive.[362]

---

360. BLACK'S LAW DICTIONARY 498 (7th ed. 1999). *Accord* III OXFORD ENGLISH DICTIONARY 573 (1978) ("4. Something written, inscribed, etc., which furnishes evidence or information upon any subject as a manuscript, title-deed, tomb-stone, coin, picture, etc."); MERRIAM-WEBSTER'S COLLEGIATE DICTIONARY, CD-ROM (Zane Pub. Co. 1996) ("2 a: a writing conveying information.").

361. FED.R.EVID. 803(15) advisory committee's note.

362. *Weinstock*, 863 F.Supp. 1532 (the court goes on to note that there are several cases from other federal and state courts that interpret exactly the same rule and that do not require that the statement be in a dispositive document).

This exception applies to statements in documents that "establish" or "affect" an interest in property. "Establish" or "affect." These are two different words with two different meanings. Each was purposefully and knowingly included in the rule, and the rule must be interpreted so as to give meaning to each. Dispositive documents "establish" an interest in property. Documents like the letters and notes at issue here "affect" an interest in property.

> [This hearsay exception] is an Act of Congress and should be interpreted as a statute. Therefore, [it] should be interpreted in accord with its plain meaning. The term "affects" an interest in property must be given its ordinary meaning. Also, the term "affect" must be given a meaning in addition to the word "establish" in the rule, with respect to an interest in property.[363]

When the definition of document is combined with the use of the words "establish or affect," and the rules of statutory interpretation are taken into account, it all seems to lead inevitably to the conclusion that the document in which the statement is found does not have to be a dispositive document such as a deed.[364]

2. The Kinds of Documents Covered by This Exception—Examples

This exception applies to everything from statements in deeds[365] or contracts,[366] to statements in affidavits, a handwritten list of weapons owned by the declarant, including their serial numbers, and a "state court judgment [that] affected an interest in property."[367] In one case involving an affidavit,

---

363. *Weinstock*, 863 F.Supp. at 1534. "We interpret the legislatively enacted Federal Rules of Evidence as we would any statute," Daubert v. Merrell Dow Pharms., 509 U.S. 579, 587 (1993) (citing Beech Aircraft Corp. v. Rainey, 488 U.S. 153, 163 (1988)).

364. *But see* Stahl v. State, 686 N.E.2d 89, 93 (Ind. 1997) (the document here does not fit under the exception because it bears none of the indicia of reliability the rule assumes; "[I]t is neither ancient nor dispositive"); McGuire v. Walker, 423 S.E.2d 617, 618 (W. Va. 1992) ("'This exception ... is limited to title documents, such as deeds.'" (quoting 2 Mc-CORMICK ON EVIDENCE § 323, at 361 (John W. Strong, gen. ed., 4th ed. 1992))).

365. *Weinstock*, 863 F.Supp. at 1532 n.2 (recitals in deeds; citing cases); Maui Land & Pineapple Co. v. Infiesto, 879 P.2d 507, 511 (Haw. 1994) (recitals in a deed that are relevant to the purpose of the deed); McGuire v. Walker, 423 S.E.2d 617, 618 (W. Va. 1992).

366. Ryan v. Illinois, 1999 U.S. Dist. LEXIS 1095, *9 (N.D. Ill. 1999) ("the promissory note from Fast Motor Service to Cosmopolitan Bank" is admissible under Rule 803(15); it is a statement in a contract affecting an interest in property).

367. United States v. Boulware, 384 F.3d 794, 807 (9th Cir. 2004), *vacated*, 128 S.Ct. 1168 (2008) ("The Federal Rules of Evidence are an act of Congress, and we must therefore interpret Rule 803(15) as we would a statute, in accordance with its plain meaning.") (citation omitted).

the affiant declared that he was "the legal and beneficial owner of 35,000 shares of … stock." The affidavit was "a document purporting to establish or affect an interest in property," the statement about the ownership of the stock was "relevant to the purpose of the document," and there had not been subsequent inconsistent dealings with the property in question. It was admissible under this exception.[368] In the aforementioned list-of-weapons case, a state court held that a handwritten list found among the declarant's personal papers, after his death, listing his weapons and their serial numbers, was admissible as evidence of exactly what weapons the defendant had stolen from the declarant.[369]

XI. Statements in Ancient Documents: Rule 803(16)

A. Text of the Rule

The following are not excluded by the hearsay rule, even though the declarant is available as a witness:

---

368. *Weinstock*, 863 F.Supp. 1529. *But see* Star Rentals, Inc. v. Seeberg Constr. Co. 730 P.2d 573, 575 (Or. Ct. App. 1986) (based on its 1986 conclusion that the federal rule had been interpreted as being "'limited to title documents such as deeds,'" the court refused to apply this exception to an affidavit (quoting E. CLEARY, McCORMICK ON EVIDENCE 905 (3d ed. 1984))).

369. *Madden*, 799 S.W.2d at 689 (the point for which *Madden* is cited here was reaffirmed in Guidry v. State, 9 S.W.3d 133, 147 (Tex. Crim. App. 1999).) *See additionally* T.C.M. v. United States, 93-2 U.S. Tax Cas. (CCH) P50, 583 (D. Ariz.1993) (settlement documents regarding the sale of the subject property, escrow instructions regarding the sale of the subject property, and the addendum to the escrow instructions are admissible under Rule 803(15)); Broad. Music, Inc. v. Airhead Corp., 1990 U.S. Dist. LEXIS 19382, *5 (E.D. Va Dec. 27, 1990) (a certificate of registration of a copyright admissible under Rule 803(15)); Walters v. Illinois Farmers Ins. Co., 1988 U.S. Dist. LEXIS 17512, *25 (N.D. Ind. May 26, 1988) (tax records and bankruptcy petition appear to be admissible under Rule 803(15)); Guidry v. State, 9 S.W.3d 133, 146 (Tex. Crim. App. 1999) (a "Trial Inventory and Appraisement" filed in state court in a divorce proceeding and listing a particular Jeep as property of the husband and wife was admissible under Rule 803(15) as evidence that the husband had a property interest in Jeep); Harris v. State, 846 S.W.2d 960, 963 (Tex. App. 1993) ("the manufacturer's certificate of origin from General Motors Corporation," used to prove the Vehicle Identification Number of a particular vehicle, is admissible under Rule 803(15)); Compton v. WMV Enters., 679 S.W.2d 668, 671 (Tex. App. 1984) ("statements made in deeds, leases, mortgages"). *See also* State v. Kelly, 1984 Ohio App. LEXIS 9387, *4–5 (Ohio Ct. App. Feb. 16, 1984) (the vehicle registration papers "might" be admissible under Rule 803(15), but the police officer's testimony as to the contents of the papers is inadmissible under the rule requiring the production of the original).

****

(16) Statements in ancient documents. Statements in a document in existence twenty years or more the authenticity of which is established.

B. Foundational Elements

1. The document is 20 years old or older.[370]
2. The document is authenticated, that is, it is shown to be what it purports to be. For example, it was found where you would expect such a document to be found.

C. Need + Reliability = 1

1. Need

The need for the exception is that the evidence is 20 years old or older. There is not likely to be much in the way of present memory, present firsthand knowledge, of the facts recorded. Whatever present memory there is, is likely to be quite flawed.

2. Reliability

General reliability is non-existent. The theory behind the reliability of ancient documents is that "age affords assurance that the writing antedates the present controversy"[371] and, therefore, the document was not "tailored to prove a point in the present controversy."[372] That is the theory, but it is not always the truth. Allow me to speculate that there are documents in the files of cigarette companies and their lawyers that were prepared well over 20 years ago and that were prepared in anticipation of exactly the kind of litigation that may be filed against the companies today—anticipated in all regards but for the name of the plaintiff. Especially today when science makes it so much easier to estab-

---

370. Nebraska's rule requires that the document be 30 years old or older. Neb. Evid. R. 803(15).

371. Fed.R.Evid. 803(16) advisory committee's note.

372. Kraft, Inc. v. United States, 30 Fed. Cl. 739, 762 (Fed. Cl. 1994) (taxpayer suit to recover disallowed business losses; Accounting Acquisition Cards admitted for proof of matters asserted, *i.e.*, corporate histories of acquired companies, mergers, liquidations, transfers of assets; opponent stipulated to authenticity).

lish the link between present symptoms and past causes, some controversies linger for 20 years or more.

In most cases, however, the age requirement for the document does provide assurance that the statement was not tailored for the controversy. Even this, however, does very little to assure the documents' reliability. There is no requirement that the subject of the document be a serious matter, one about which an author might tend to be careful. There is no requirement that the document be more than musing or speculation. There is no requirement that the author be unbiased by factors that are irrelevant to the age of the document. There is no requirement that the document be any different than any hearsay document that is inadmissible—except that it be old and authentic. Whatever the document in question, keep it in the right place long enough and it becomes an ancient document. It does not, of course, become any more reliable than it was the day before, just older.[373]

As a general rule, the reliability component of the hearsay exceptions has to do with some reason to find the category of evidence at hand inherently reliable. When the ancient-document cases speak of reliability, they do not speak of any inherent reliability of this kind of second-hand evidence, but only of its reliability as compared to that of firsthand evidence that might be available. After 20 years, either there will be no witnesses left or their memories will not be accurate. Time and memory-lapse do go hand in hand. This does not, of course, make ancient documents reliable. It only makes them the only evidence available. This is an exception based solely on need.[374]

Some old documents will be reliable, and some will not be. As a category of evidence, the need is seen to be so great that reliability is hardly factored

---

373. *See* United States v. Hajda, 135 F.3d 439, 443–44 (7th Cir. 1998) (witness statements over 20 years old as ancient documents); Gonzalez v. Digital Equip. Corp., 8 F.Supp.2d 194, 201 (E.D.N.Y. 1998) (admitting a document under the residual exception, the court notes that the document would not be any more relevant or persuasive were it "ancient"). Nineteen years and 364 days later, it is inadmissible hearsay; one more day and it is admissible hearsay.

374. *E.g.*, Dallas County v. Commercial Union Assurance Co., 286 F.2d 388, 396 (5th Cir. 1961) ("[I]t seems impossible that the testimony of any witness would have been as accurate and as reliable as the statement of facts in the contemporary newspaper article."); Compton v. Davis Oil Co., 607 F.Supp. 1221, 1228 (D. Wyo. 1985) ("Statements in such ancient documents are admissible due to a rule of necessity as well as to the reliability of such evidence in comparison to any other form of available evidence."). The lapse of time brings an inevitable loss of memory. This makes current testimony by witnesses with firsthand knowledge unreliable. It does not, however, make the ancient document reliable.

into the equation. Absent a complete lack of trustworthiness as a matter of law, these concerns bear on the weight to be given to the evidence, not on the admissibility of the evidence.[375] Once age and authenticity are established, the exception is established.[376]

D. Use Note

1. The Increasing Importance of This Exception

In the beginning, the ancient documents exception was a much different animal than it is today. The ancient documents exception is coming to play a more and more important role in modern tort litigation. The exception developed at a time when injuries were not traced to ancient torts. If you woke up one morning in 1900 with a headache, and remembered that yesterday you had been hit on the head at work, you traced the headache to the hit on the head. If you woke up one morning in 1900 coughing up blood, you did not trace it to building materials used 50 years previously by your 19th Century building contractor. We lacked the science necessary to trace many of our injuries to any cause, let alone an ancient one, and we did not have the literacy or the storage required for the creation and preservation of the range of documents created and stored today. We were only able to create short temporal links between torts and symptoms.[377]

Today we can link present symptoms to long-ago causes. We now recognize all kinds of health hazards that cause diseases that can take decades to become symptomatic. There can be all kinds of relevant ancient documents in toxic-tort cases involving groundwater pollution, asbestos, cigarettes, and the like. In civil and criminal child-abuse cases where the allegations involve abuse inflicted over 20 years ago and just now recovered from memory, a just discovered, properly authenticated diary from 20 years ago will be an ancient document. Advances in storage technologies allow more information to be

---

375. Threadgill v. Armstrong World Indus., 928 F.2d 1366, 1376 (3d Cir. 1991). There may, of course, be nonhearsay admissibility issues such as Rule 403 or witness incompetence.

376. This is, at least, the way the Rule 803(16) reads. Some courts read a trustworthiness requirement into the rule. This is discussed further below, in the Use Note in part XI(D)(2) of this chapter, below.

377. Even the medieval version of the hearsay rule had "various exceptions ... for establishing facts beyond anyone's memory." Frank R. Hermann, S.J., *The Establishment of a Rule Against Hearsay in Romano-Canonical Procedure*, 36 Va. J. Int'l L. 1, 47 (1995). The United States Supreme Court recognized a kind of ancient documents exception as early as the 1800s. Fulkerson v. Holmes, 117 U.S. 389, 396–97 (1886) (deed); McGuire v. Blount, 199 U.S. 142, 144–45 (1905) (public and proprietary records).

saved for longer, and advances in our ability to search for, retrieve, and organize this material make it ever easier to find.

Couple that with this—statutes of limitations are being rolled back to allow toxic-tort litigation based on exposure over 20 years before and civil and criminal actions based on sexual-abuse that occurred over 20 years before.[378] And some jurisdictions are beginning to excuse some of the hearsay exceptions, including this one, from the restrictiveness of Rule 805's rule on the admissibility of hearsay within hearsay.[379]

This kind of application of the exception was undreamt of at the time the common law was developing the ancient documents exception. There was not much of a guarantee of reliability, but then it was a rather meager little exception. Today, with the expansion of the exception to include more recent documents,[380] advances in science allowing us to link diseases to ancient causes, extensions of the time in which actions can be filed, and advances in information storage and retrieval, we have a much more important exception. The ancient documents exception, with one of the weakest categorical guarantees of reliability for any of the exceptions, seems destined to play a more and more important role in modern tort litigation.

2. Old Age and Authenticity Alone Establish This Exception, without Any Special Regard for Trustworthiness

By its terms, this exception has just two foundational elements and they ask these two questions: (1) Has the document been shown to be old enough? (2) Is the document authentic? The latter is a function of satisfying Rule 901(b)(8): "Evidence that a document or data compilation, in any form, (A) is in such condition as to create no suspicion concerning its authenticity, (B) was in a place

---

378. See authorities cited and discussed at G. Michael Fenner, *Law Professor Reveals Shocking Truth About Hearsay*, 62 UMKC L. Rev. 1, 30–32 (1993). *See also, e.g.*, Reichhold Chems., Inc. v. Textron, Inc., 888 F.Supp. 1116, 1130 n.15 (N.D. Fla. 1995) (toxic tort; documents from defendant's files at least 50 years old and authentic).

379. *See generally* Chapter 11(IV), below. *See particularly* Gregg Kettles, *Ancient Documents and the Rule Against Multiple Hearsay*, 39 Santa Clara L. Rev. 719, 723 (1999).

A seminal case for the ancient documents exception involved the admission into evidence of an old newspaper article. Dallas County v. Commercial Union Assurance Co., 286 F. 2d 388 (5th Cir. 1961) (fifty-eight-year-old newspaper article about lightening striking church steeple). It is unlikely that the newspaper reporter had firsthand knowledge of the facts reported.

380. Recall that the relevant age has been reduced from the common law's 30 years, to the rule's 20 years.

where it, if authentic, would likely be, and (C) has been in existence 20 years or more at the time it is offered."[381] For example:

> In Threadgill v. Armstrong World Industries, Mrs. Threadgill sued a laundry list of asbestos companies for the death of her husband. During the trial, plaintiff's counsel offered into evidence approximately 6,000 documents tending to indicate that the manufacturer of the asbestos knew as early as the 1930s of the health hazards of asbestos and tried to conceal them. The documents were offered under the ancient documents exception. The Third Circuit Court of Appeals held that the documents were admissible under the ancient documents exception. Regarding this exception, the only questions for the trial judge are: (1) Were the documents in question what they purported to be? and (2) Do they purport to have been in existence twenty years or more?[382]

Some of the hearsay exceptions include a specific reference to trustworthiness, empowering judges to consider whether the evidence is trustworthy and to deny the exception if it is not.[383] Trustworthiness is not a separate consideration, not a foundational element, under this exception, and to read a trustworthiness requirement into the exception is a mistake. Problems with such ancient documents that lead some judges to attach trustworthiness as a separate hearsay-exception consideration can be dealt with in another way, without violating the plain language of the statute. If the document is sufficiently untrustworthy, then it will be inadmissible under Rule 403.[384]

Since the only two foundational elements for the exception are old age and authenticity, a stipulation to authenticity satisfies one-half of the foundation.[385] All that is left for the proponent to establish that the statement is 20 years old or older and it is admissible hearsay.

---

381. Fed.R.Evid. 901(b)(8).

382. G. Michael Fenner, *Law Professor Reveals Shocking Truth About Hearsay*, 62 UMKC L. Rev. 1, 30–31 (1993) (footnotes omitted) (discussing Threadgill v. Armstrong World Indus., 928 F.2d 1366 (3d Cir. 1991)); Matuszewski v. Pancoast, 526 N.E.2d 80 (Ohio Ct. App. 1987); and United States v. Koziy, 728 F.2d 1314 (11th Cir. 1984).

383. *See supra*, note 15, and *infra*, note 387, below.

384. Fed.R.Evid. 403. The risk of unfair prejudice and jury confusion, will substantially outweigh the document's probative value. *See* part 8 of this Use Note, below.

385. *See, e.g.*, Kraft, Inc. v. United States, 30 Fed. Cl. 739, 761–62 (1994) (Accounting Acquisition Cards admitted for proof of matters asserted, *i.e.*, corporate histories of acquired companies, mergers, liquidations, transfers of assets; authenticity part of foundation satisfied when opponent stipulated Cards were "authentic documents").

There is this caveat to the trustworthiness discussion. While Rule 803(16) does not require trustworthiness, some courts have read a trustworthiness requirement into the rule. For example, one state-court case held that the exception "carries the qualification that the document itself or its contents not be suspicious with regard to its genuineness and reliability."[386] Since there is at least one court that does find trustworthiness to be a foundational element, the argument that a particular ancient document is inadmissible hearsay because it is not trustworthy is one that may be available in opposition to the exception and may need to be anticipated in support of the exception. There may be times the proponent of an ancient document will want to remove all doubt and get something on the record regarding trustworthiness.[387]

---

386. Moore v. Goode, 375 S.E.2d 549, 558 (W. Va. 1988). Presumably the burden of showing that the document is not trustworthy is on the party opposing admission. *See* the text accompanying note 308, above in this chapter, and the cross-reference in note 308 itself.

387. Trustworthiness is not an element of this exception. Cases that say otherwise really mistake trustworthiness for authentication. They turn to one subpart of the authentication rules, FED.R.EVID. 901(b)(8), which provides, "by way of illustration only, and not by way of limitation, the following" example of one way a document may be authenticated: "Evidence that a document or data compilation, in any form, (A) is in such condition as to create no suspicion concerning its authenticity, (B) was in a place where it, if authentic, would likely be, and (C) has been in existence 20 years or more at the time it is offered." The "suspicion" referred to here is "'suspicion concerning [the document's] authenticity.'" United States v. Demjanjuk, 367 F.3d 623, 630 (6th Cir. 2004) (quoting FED.R.EVID. 901(b)(8)). "[T]hat suspicion goes not to the content of the document, but rather to whether the document is what it purports to be." *Demjanjuk*, 367 F.3d at 631 (citing without quotation marks United States v. Kairys, 782 F.2d 1374, 1379 (7th Cir. 1986), which makes the same statement). Suspicion regarding the contents of an authenticated document go to the weight of the evidence. *Id.*

Documents that are authenticated as ancient documents under Rule 901(b)(8) "automatically fall within the ancient documents exception to the hearsay rule." Fagiola v. Nat'l Gypsum Co. AC & S, Inc., 906 F.2d 53, 58 (2d Cir. 1990). The converse, however, is not true. Because all 901(b)(8) documents are 803(16) documents, does not mean that all 803(16) documents have to be 901(b)(8) documents. *See* Dartez v. Fiberboard Corp., 765 F.2d 456, 464 (5th Cir. 1985) ("Ancient documents are *most frequently* authenticated under the provisions of Rule 901(b)(8)") (emphasis added). There are several ways ancient documents might be authenticated; the ancient documents exception does not require any one particular method of authentication, and none of the other methods requires a showing of trustworthiness. *See, e.g.*, FED.R.EVID. 901(a), 901(b)(4), 901(b)(7), 902(3), 902(5), and 902(6); United States v. Koziy, 728 F.2d 1314 (11th Cir. 1984) (regarding foreign public document). Taking the premise that all 901(b)(8) documents are 803(16) documents and drawing the conclusion that all 803(16) documents must be 901(b)(8) documents is like knowing that all persons are featherless bipeds and concluding that therefore all featherless bipeds are persons.

The exception has two foundational elements and trustworthiness is not one of them.

3. Nonhearsay Admissions and Ancient Documents

When ancient documents are discovered from an opponent's files, there may be two other obvious ways to get them around the hearsay rule. First, they may be nonhearsay statements by an agent of a party, offered against that party.[388] Second, they may also fit under the hearsay exception for records of a regularly conducted activity.[389] In any particular situation, there may be an advantage to using either the definitional exclusion or the other exception, or to using all three.[390]

4. Undated Documents

The ancient document need not bear a date. At least one court has said it is enough if the document is found filed with other documents bearing a date over twenty years old.[391]

5. Photographs and Other Such Ancient "Documents"

This exception is not limited to written documents. It applies to photographs[392] and other kinds of non-written documents.

6. Foreign Ancient Documents

The ancient document need not be from this country.[393]

> [In one case,] ancient birth, death, and marriage certificates from Czechoslovakia were allowed to prove that twelve persons living in Czechoslovakia were the heirs of the deceased. [In another,] Ukrainian police employment forms were used to establish that the defendant

---

When the drafters of the rules wished to include trustworthiness as an element of an exception, they had no trouble saying so. FED.R.EVID. 803(6), (7), and (8), 804(b)(3), and 807.

388. FED.R.EVID. 801(d)(2)(D). *See* Chapter 2(III)(B), (C), & (D), above.

389. FED.R.EVID. 803(6). *See* part VII of this chapter, above.

390. *See generally* Chapter 10, below, regarding applying multiple exceptions, and Chapter 11(IV), below, and the cross-references therein, regarding jurisdictions in which admissions cure preceding levels of hearsay.

391. United States v. Osyp Firishchak, 468 F.3d 1015, 1022 (7th Cir. 2006); Kath v. Burlington N. R.R., 441 N.W.2d 569 (Minn. Ct. App. 1989).

392. De Weerth v. Baldinger, 658 F.Supp. 688, 695 n.12 (S.D.N.Y. 1987).

393. United States v. Stelmokas, 100 F.3d 302, 304, 311–13 (3d Cir. 1996) (documents obtained from Lithuanian archives, regarding Nazi occupation, properly admitted in citi-

was hostile to the United States and defendant's citizenship was re-voked. The defendant objected that the documents were forgeries, ir-relevant, immaterial and hearsay. The court admitted them under the ancient documents exception.[394]

7. Multiple Levels of Hearsay

Often, ancient documents are not based on firsthand knowledge. They will present multiple-level hearsay problems. Documents pulled from the files of one party or discovered from the files of an opposing party may have been pre-pared by someone who did not have firsthand knowledge of the things recorded.[395] Old newspaper articles may be based on what someone told the reporter, and not on the reporter's firsthand observation.[396] Often, these doc-uments will present multiple-level hearsay problems.

---

zenship revocation proceeding as evidence defendant "advocated, assisted, participated, and acquiesced in the murder and persecution of Jews and other unarmed civilians" (quo-tation at 304)); United States v. Koziy, 728 F.2d 1314, 1317 (11th Cir. 1984) (an anmel-dung, an abmeldung, and an inimical list; the first two are Ukrainian police documents, and the third is a list prepared by the commission that regulated the immigration of WWII refugees into the United States; citizenship revocation for Holocaust crimes). *See also* the following parts of this chapter: VI(E)(8) (foreign past recollection recorded), VII(D)(6) (foreign business records), and VIII(E)(6) (foreign public records and reports).

394. G. Michael Fenner, *Law Professor Reveals Shocking Truth About Hearsay*, 62 UMKC L. Rev. 1, 30–31 (1993) (footnotes omitted) (discussing, first, Matuszewski v. Pancoast, 526 N.E.2d 80 (Ohio Ct. App. 1987); and, second, United States v. Koziy, 728 F.2d 1314 (11th Cir. 1984)).

395. This was probably the situation in the following cases, for example: Horne v. Owens-Corning Fiberglass Corp., 4 F.3d 276, 283 (4th Cir. 1993) (interoffice memoranda from Owens-Corning files and excerpts from National Insulation Manufacturers Associa-tion brochures admitted as ancient documents); Ohio v. Lawler, 1999 Ohio App. LEXIS 5998 (Ohio Ct. App. Dec. 15, 1999) (a 1977 presentence investigation report was received as an ancient document at the 1998 hearing wherein the appellant was adjudged a sexual predator).

396. This was probably the situation in the seminal case for this exception, the case cited by the advisory committee as an example of why we should have such an exception, Dal-las County v. Commercial Union Assurance Co., 286 F.2d 388 (5th Cir. 1961) (old news-paper article reporting lightning struck steeple of church, admitted as ancient document to prove truth of that lightening strike). *See* Fed.R.Evid. 803(16) advisory committee's note. *See also* Catellus Dev. Corp. v. L.D. McFarland Co., 1993 U.S. Dist. LEXIS 14124 (D. Ore-gon May 14, 1993) (motion for summary judgment denied; forty-two year-old newspaper article, reporting then-14-year-old creosote spill, probably not admissible to prove spill re-ported).

If you are trying to use this exception and your opponent has objected to hearsay within the ancient document, then you may want to argue that the ancient document exception cures problems with hearsay within the ancient document.[397] The argument would be in the nature of that adopted in by the Seventh Circuit, regarding the public records and reports exception.[398] The common-law history of this rule allows the introduction of ancient documents that are based on information others furnished to the author. The Advisory Committee's note endorses at least one case of this kind—an old newspaper article likely based on what the newspaper reporter was told, rather than first-hand knowledge.[399] If multi-level hearsay problems must be dealt with before this exception can be used, that makes the exception essentially useless. Rule 803(16), the argument would conclude, "is a multi-level exception, in the footsteps of its common law precursors."[400]

8. Ancient Documents and Rule 403

Since ancient documents can vary so greatly in their apparent trustworthiness, and since in most jurisdictions trustworthiness has nothing to do with whether the document fits under this exception to the hearsay rule, Rule 403 may come into play here somewhat more often than it does with regard to other exceptions. A document that has been authenticated and is sufficiently old may be inadmissible under Rule 403; its probative value may be substantially outweighed by the danger of unfair prejudice, confusion of the issues, or waste of time.[401]

---

397. If the document is a Rule 801 admission, you may also want to argue that admissions cure preceding levels of hearsay. *See* Chapter 2(III)(G), above.

398. The case is In re *Oil Spill by the Amoco Cadiz, supra,* notes 306–07 and accompanying text. The Seventh Circuit itself has, however, held that when an ancient document contains underlying layers of hearsay there must be an exception for each layer. United States v. Hajda, 135 F.3d 439, 444 (7th Cir. 1998) ("If the [ancient] document contains more than one level of hearsay, an appropriate exception must be found for each level."). *See also* Hicks v. Charles Pfizer & Co., 466 F. Supp. 2d 799, 807 (E.D. Tex. 2005) (adopting *Hajda*'s approach, harmonizing Rule 803(16) and Rule 805).

399. "See Dallas County v. Commercial Union Assurances Co., 286 F.2d 388 (5th Cir. 1961), upholding admissibility of 58-year-old newspaper story." FED.R.EVID. 803(16) advisory committee's note.

400. This argument paraphrases and quotes the argument presented at In re *Oil Spill by the Amoco Cadiz, supra,* notes 306–07 and accompanying text. *See also* Chapter 11, below.

401. FED.R.EVID. 403; Wetherill v. Univ. of Chicago, 565 F.Supp. 1553, 1563 (N.D. Ill. 1983) (an ancient document was inadmissible under Rule 403; the document's probative value was weak because there were so many unanswered questions surrounding the document; we

XII. Market Reports, Commercial Publications: Rule 803(17)

A. Text of the Rule

The following are not excluded by the hearsay rule, even though the declarant is available as a witness:

****

(17) Market reports, commercial publications. Market quotations, tabulations, lists, directories, or other published compilations, generally used and relied upon by the public or by persons in particular occupations.

B. Foundational Elements

1. The out-of-court statement must be a market quotation, tabulation, list, directory, or other published compilation.

2. The out-of-court statement must be generally used and relied upon by either the general public or persons in a particular occupation.

C. Need + Reliability = 1

1. Need

What was the barometric air pressure on a particular day two years ago? What was last year's NADA Blue Book list-price for a 1987 Mercedes Benz 300D, fully loaded and in excellent shape? In December of 1995, what was the address of the Paris office of Willkie Farr & Gallagher? If it is important in today's trial to know any of these things, how are you going to prove it? The kinds of facts covered by this exception tend to be the kinds of facts people do not keep in long-term memory.

---

do not know who wrote it or the basis for the comments therein; admitting the document risks substantial prejudice and confusion of the issues and its probative value is low). As discussed above, at part XI(D)(6) of this chapter, the ancient document can be foreign in origin. It is easy to imagine a foreign document that is found where it is supposed to be and is 20 or more years old, but is so untrustworthy that any probative value is substantially outweighed by the danger of unfair prejudice.

2. Reliability

These documents must be generally used and relied upon: This is one of the foundational elements. This is the guarantee of reliability. These kinds of documents would not survive in the market place—would not be generally used and relied upon for long—if they were not reasonably reliable.

D. Use Note

■ *Examples*: Examples include: Wall Street Journal stock tables; phone books; price lists; the National Automobile Dealers Association's "Blue Book," listing the market value of used cars;[402] books used by dealers or collectors to value antiques, stamps, coins, clocks, and collectibles in general; mercantile credit reports; weather reports; perhaps opinion polls; certain information in almanacs;[403] and so forth and so on.

Many of the items that fit under this exception will be admissible in a second way. Courts may be able to take judicial notice of the facts declared in the report or compilation.[404]

■ *The World Wide Web*: Query: What about market quotations, lists, directories, and the like found on the world-wide-web? As noted above, one reason for the market-reports, commercial-publications exception is that these things tend to be reliable; they tend to be reliable because business relies on them and they would not survive in the market place if they were not reasonably reliable. Anyone can throw anything on the web.

If the same company produces both a traditional 803(17) document and a web entry, and one is a mechanical reproduction of the other, then there will not be a problem.

If that is not the case, quality control may be lacking regarding information on the web. It is true that the second of the foundational elements will tend to take care of this problem. It requires that either the general public or persons in a particular occupation must rely on the report or list. The general public is, however, capable of relying on some fairly far-out reports. Perhaps the answer is that the second foundational element takes care of a lot

---

402. *E.g.*, *In re* Roberts, 210 B.R. 325, 330 (Bankr. N.D. Iowa 1997).
403. *See* the discussion of then-trial-lawyer Abraham Lincoln's trial use of an almanac, Chapter 9(IV), below.
404. This is discussed below, at Chapter 9(IV), below.

of the problem presented here, and the rest of the problem is not a hearsay problem, but is instead a matter of relevance and credibility. If the information is too far-out, it is inadmissible under Rule 403[405] (or perhaps even Rule 402[406]); absent that, the evidence is admissible, and its weight is subject to argument.

XIII. Learned Treatises: Rule 803(18)

A. Text of the Rule

The following are not excluded by the hearsay rule, even though the declarant is available as a witness:

****

(18) Learned treatises. To the extent called to the attention of an expert witness upon cross-examination or relied upon by the expert witness in direct examination, statements contained in published treatises, periodicals, or pamphlets on a subject of history, medicine, or other science or art, established as a reliable authority by the testimony or admission of the witness or by other expert testimony or by judicial notice. If admitted, the statements may be read into evidence but may not be received as exhibits.

B. Foundational Elements

1. The exception is limited to certain specific topics and certain specific sources. The out-of-court statement must be on a subject of history, medicine, or other science or art, and it must be from a treatise, periodical, or pamphlet.

2. The out-of-court statement must either be relied upon by an expert witness in direct examination or called to the attention of an expert witness on cross-examination.

3. The treatise, periodical, or pamphlet must be established as reliable by testimony or admission of the witness or by other expert testimony or by judicial notice.

---

405. FED.R.EVID. 403.
406. FED.R.EVID. 402.

4. Though not a foundational element, the statements may be read into evidence but the text will not be received as an exhibit.

C. Need + Reliability = 1

1. Need

On the one hand, expert evidence read from a treatise, periodical, or pamphlet is generally less persuasive than testimony from an expert witness. On the other hand, it is always less expensive. Some parties, some cases, cannot afford the more expensive alternative of expert witnesses. Given the economics of the practice of law, there are cases that could not be presented without this method of proof, without this exception to the hearsay rule.[407]

In addition, without this exception, some of these same statements from learned treatises would be admissible as credibility evidence, either to impeach an expert witness on cross-examination or to rehabilitate the witness on redirect. Were the treatise evidence only admissible as credibility evidence, then the trial court would have to give an instruction that the jury could consider the statements as evidence of credibility, but not as evidence of the truth of the facts asserted. There is a certain dishonesty in such an instruction. First, how can the statement impeach a qualified expert if it is not credible as substantive evidence of the fact declared? And, second, we instruct the jury as just noted, but do we really expect them to comply? This exception allows the evidence in as both credibility and substantive evidence, it does away with the need for the instruction, and it more honestly conforms the law to reality.[408]

2. Reliability

The reliability of this evidence is provided by the foundational element that requires that the statement be established as reliable either by expert testimony or judicial notice. If the expert testifying that the text is reliable is wrong, opposing counsel can bring that out in further examination of that expert or in the testimony of another expert, or with the use of another, properly qualified learned treatise. Furthermore, " 'authors of treatises have no bias in any particular case [and] they are acutely aware that their material will be read and eval-

---

407. At least to some extent, then, this exception increases the access of the poor to the justice system.

408. Regarding limiting instructions, *see* Chapter 8(I)(D)(4)(g) and Chapter 12(IV).

uated by others in their field, and accordingly feel a strong pressure to be accurate."[409]

D. Use Note

■ *"Treatises, Periodicals, or Pamphlets":* Quoting the rule, it applies to "statements contained in published treatises, periodicals, or pamphlets."[410] This statement of the scope of the exception harkens back to an earlier time when learned information was disseminated in books, magazines, and other printed material that was filed on shelves and held in hands. Today, learned information also comes in the form of videotapes of lectures by the giants in a field. It comes on CD Rom. It comes through the computer. The rule's statement of the scope of the exception seems a bit limited in light of the ways in which information is transmitted today. Some courts have found that some of these new formats for the transmission of information are contemporary variants of published treatises, periodicals, and pamphlets and, therefore, may be considered under the learned treatise exception.[411]

■ *Relied Upon by an Expert in Direct Examination:* This exception includes treatises relied upon by experts in direct examination.[412] A testifying expert

---

409. *In re* Welding Fume Prods. Liab. Litig., 534 F.Supp.2d 761, 765 (N.D. Ohio 2008) (italics omitted) (quoting 2 McCORMICK ON EVIDENCE § 321 (6th ed. 2006)).

As regards authors of treatises having no bias in a particular case, I dispute that claim. We all have biases. Regarding the subject of this treatise, for example, my bias is towards more admissible evidence, rather than less. It is also the case that many treatises are written by authors whose research is funded by interested parties and those authors may be biased—consciously or not. In addition, some treatises are actually written with litigation in mind. *See* In re *Welding Fume Products Liability Litigation, supra,* this note.

410. This includes the traditional kinds of learned treatises, "'[a] treatise, periodical, or pamphlet on a subject of history, medicine, or other science or art ... if it has been established as a reliable authority by the testimony of the expert who relied upon it or to whose attention it was called.'" Fisher v. United States, 78 Fed. Cl. 710, 713–14 (Fed. Cl. 2007) (quoting Matthew Bender 1-6 FED. EVID. PRACTICE GUIDE § 6.06(18)). In spite of its title, "learned treatises," it also includes many other things (periodicals and pamphlets) "established as ... reliable authority." For example, see Paulos v. Covenant Transp. Inc., 86 P.3d 752, 755–56 (Ut. Ct. App. 2004), which canvases cases admitting "safety codes" under the learned treatise exception.

411. Costantino v. Herzog, 203 F.3d 164, 171 (2d Cir. 2000) (videotape used to educate physicians).

412. FED.R.EVID. 803(18). For this part of the foundation, it makes no difference that the treatise is brought up on redirect examination. Caruolo v. John Crane, Inc., 226 F.2d 46, 55 (2d Cir. 2000).

can rely upon a study even when the expert does not agree with its conclusions.[413] The expert need not be relying on the study in its entirety.

■ *The Case Cannot be Tried Using Books Alone*: The authoritativeness of the treatise may be established by expert testimony or judicial notice.[414] Judicial notice that the treatise is authoritative is not enough, by itself, to render the information contained in the treatise admissible under this exception. The treatise must be relied upon by an expert during direct examination or called to the attention of an expert upon cross-examination. The advisory committee was concerned that a treatise might be "misunderstood and misapplied without expert assistance and supervision."[415] The case cannot be tried by books alone, not using this exception, at least.[416]

■ *When Admitting the Treatise on Cross-Examination the Expert must be an Expert in a Relevant Field*: Again, the out-of-court statement must be relied upon by an expert witness in direct examination or called to the attention of an expert on cross-examination. The rule requires a testifying expert because the rule's drafters believed that a treatise might be "misunderstood and misapplied without expert assistance and supervision."[417] To mitigate that risk, when a learned treatise is introduced on cross-examination of an expert, it must be an expert in the relevant field—one who can "explain and assist."[418]

■ *The Evidence May Be Read into the Record*: The evidence in question may be read into the record, but this exception cannot be used to admit the trea-

---

413. *Caruolo*, 226 F.2d at 55.

414. In Schneider v. Revici, 817 F.2d 987, 991 (2d Cir. 1987), the court stated that the rule "explicitly requires that … a proper foundation as to the authoritativeness of the text must be laid by an expert witness." The rule does not require this. In fact, the rule allows the authoritativeness of the text to be established by judicial notice. In addition to judicial notice, the text must be either relied upon by an expert on direct examination or "called to the attention of an expert" on cross-examination, but "called to the attention of an expert" is a long way from established as authoritative by an expert. FED.R.EVID. 803(18).

415. FED.R.EVID. 803(18) advisory committee's notes.

416. United States v. Turner, 104 F.3d 217, 221 (8th Cir. 1997) ("[Rule] 803(18) provides that the portions of the text may be read only to the extent that it is called to the attention of an expert witness or relied upon by the expert witness in direct examination").

417. FED.R.EVID. 803(18) advisory committee's note.

418. Warren v. Medlantic Health Group Inc., 936 A.2d 733, 747 (D.C. 2007) (Dr. Warren did not rely on the treatise during his direct examination; it was called to his attention on cross, and he is an expert in some areas of medicine, but not an expert in the area of medicine that is the subject of the part of the treatise offered into evidence; treatise inadmissible hearsay.).

tise itself into evidence as an exhibit.[419] To allow the treatise to be available to the jury in their deliberations would give undue emphasis to this particular evidence.[420] Letting the learned treatise go to the jury room is error.[421] Some parts of learned treatises do not lend themselves to being "read into the record" in any literal sense of "reading." This evidence may be shown to and discussed with the jury.[422]

---

419. The evidence is, of course, admissible as substantive evidence. That is the point of the hearsay exception. It is just that it is only admissible as viva voce evidence, not as documentary evidence. "If admitted, the statements may be read into evidence but may not be received as exhibits." FED.R.EVID. 803(18). *Fisher*, 78 Fed. Cl. at 714 ("'When statements from a learned treatise are admitted into evidence, they may be read to the finder of fact, but the statements themselves may not be admitted as documentary evidence unless they are admissible under some other exception to … the hearsay rule.'") (quoting Matthew Bender 1-6 FED. EVID. PRACTICE GUIDE §6.06(18)).

As the court stated in Ward v. United States, 838 F.2d 182, 187 (6th Cir. 1988):

The plaintiffs contend that the district court erred when it read and relied on [learned treatises] in establishing the applicable standard of care.… Although Federal Rule of Evidence 803(18) precludes learned treatises from being received as exhibits, the Rule provides that treatises can be read into evidence. It appears that plaintiffs' counsel has confused the concept of not being received as exhibits with not being received as evidence.

420. *See* part VI(C) of this chapter, above, regarding past recollection recorded and explaining why the record may be read into evidence but not received as an exhibit.

421. *E.g.*, Graham v. Wyeth Labs., 906 F.2d 1399, 1414 (10th Cir. 1990); Dartez v. Fiberboard Corp., 765 F.2d 456, 465 (5th Cir. 1985) Garbinicius v. Boston Edison Co., 621 F.2d 1171, 1175 (1st Cir. 1980) (harmless error).

422. For example, the videotape in Costantino v. Herzog, 203 F.3d 164 (2d Cir. 2000). One court has suggested that there may be occasions when the learned treatise, or part of it, can be received as an exhibit: "It is not altogether clear to us how a chart can 'be read into evidence,' and good sense would seem to favor its admission into evidence [as an exhibit]." United States v. Mangan, 575 F.2d 32, 48 (2d Cir. 1978). As long as the material can be shown to and discussed with the jury, then, in the face of the clear language of the rule, it should not be received as an exhibit.

Rule 804 Exceptions

        2. Reliability
   D. Use Note
        1. The Motivation behind Procuring Unavailability
        2. The Subject Matter of the Statement
        3. The Exception Is Not Available to the Wrongdoing Party
        4. Unavailability Procured by the Wrongdoing of a Coconspirator
        5. Arguing This Exception in the Hearing of the Jury
        6. Action Outside of the Rule As Literally Interpreted
        7. The Burden of Establishing that the Party Against Whom the Evidence Is Offered Engaged or Acquiesced in Wrongdoing

I. In-Court Testimony Unavailable: Rule 804(a)

A. Text of the Rule

Rule 804. Hearsay Exceptions; Declarant Unavailable

(a) Definition of unavailability. "Unavailability as a witness" includes situations in which the declarant—

(1) is exempted by ruling of the court on the ground of privilege from testifying concerning the subject matter of the declarant's statement; or

(2) persists in refusing to testify concerning the subject matter of the declarant's statement despite an order of the court to do so; or

(3) testifies to a lack of memory of the subject matter of the declarant's statement; or

(4) is unable to be present or to testify at the hearing because of death or then existing physical or mental illness or infirmity; or

(5) is absent from the hearing and the proponent of statement has been unable to procure the declarant's attendance (or in the case of a hearsay exception under subdivision (b)(2), (3), or (4), the declarant's attendance or testimony) by process or other reasonable means.

A declarant is not unavailable as a witness if exemption, refusal, claim of lack of memory, inability, or absence is due to the procurement or wrongdoing of the proponent of a statement for the purpose of preventing the witness from attending or testifying.

B. Who or What Must Be Unavailable?

There are five hearsay exceptions in Rule 804.[1] The first foundational element of each is that the in-court testimony of the out-of-court declarant must be unavailable.[2] Rule 804 is labeled "Hearsay Exceptions; Declarant Unavailable." That label is incorrect and misleading. The unavailability of the out-of-court declarant is not the key to this exception. The out-of-court declarant can be available, in the courtroom, and on the witness stand: Declarants trigger Rule 804 unavailability when they invoke a privilege or, despite a court order to do so, simply refuse to testify. In fact, the declarant can be testifying as fully and completely as possible and, still, the testimony can be unavailable: they can trigger Rule 804 unavailability by testifying to a complete lack of memory regarding the subject matter of the out-of-court statement. The key is the unavailability of the *testimony* of the out-of-court declarant, not the unavailability of the declarant to testify.

■ If the declarant's in-court testimony is *available*, then the Rule 804 exceptions *do not apply*. There is also authority for the proposition that if the declarant's deposition testimony can be taken for use at trial, then the Rule 804 exceptions do not apply[3] (except perhaps to get the deposition itself admitted).

■ If the declarant's in-court testimony is *unavailable*, then a Rule 804 exception *may apply*. If the declarant's in-court testimony is unavailable and that unavailability is not "due to the procurement or wrongdoing of the proponent of the statement for the purpose of preventing the witness from attending or testifying,"[4] then this first foundational element of each Rule 804 exceptions is satisfied.

The burden of establishing unavailability is, of course, on the proponent of the hearsay statement.[5]

---

1. FED.R.EVID. 804(b)(1)–(4) & (6). Rule 804(b)(5) was a residual exception and is now part of the somewhat newer FED.R.EVID. 807.

2. The other foundational elements of each of these five exceptions are listed below, as each exception is discussed separately.

3. Grace United Methodist Church v. City of Cheyenne, 451 F.3d 643, 665 n.11 (10th Cir. 2005) ("a deposed declarant such as Bishop Brown can never be 'unavailable' for purposes of an exception under Rule 804(b)(3)."). See particularly Chapter 6 regarding depositions and the hearsay rule.

4. FED.R.EVID. 804(a).

5. *See, e.g.*, Garcia-Martinez v. City and County of Denver, 392 F.3d 1187, 1193 (10th Cir. 2004).

C. Unavailability Defined

■ So long as the unavailability was neither procured by nor a result of the wrongdoing of the party seeking to take advantage of the exception,[6] the declarant's in-court testimony is unavailable in situations that include any of the following:

(a) *Privilege*: The court upholds the out-of-court declarant's assertion of a testimonial privilege. This includes any of the evidentiary privileges[7] and the constitutional privilege against self-incrimination.[8] It is not enough that a declarant invokes a privilege and, as a result, is not called to testify. The witness must be exempted from testifying by a ruling of the court.[9]

---

6. In *Garcia-Martinez*, the plaintiff, an illegal alien, left the country to avoid arrest and deportation. At trial, his attorney offered his deposition under Rule 804(b)(1) and Rule 32 of the Federal Rules of Civil Procedure. Plaintiff argued that "[h]is absence was due to exigent circumstances beyond his control, the court should find him 'unavailable' under [Rule 804(b)(1)]". 392 F.3d at 1193. The court noted that the burden of proving unavailability is on the party offering the evidence and held that this plaintiff had not met that burden. He voluntarily left the country and voluntarily failed to return for trial. He did not show that he was unable to return, perhaps on a temporary visa, or that he was unable to testify via video conferencing or other alternative means. "The sponsor of a declarant's former testimony may not create the condition of unavailability and then benefit therefrom.'" *Id.* at 1192 (quoting United States v. Kimball, 15 F.3d 54, 55–56 (5th Cir. 1994) (in *Garcia-Martinez* quotation begins with "[t]"; in *Kimball* it begins with "T").

The government's refusal to displace a witness's privilege against self-incrimination by granting the witness use immunity is not unavailability "procured by, [or] a result of the wrongdoing of, the party seeking to take advantage of the exception." This is so even when other witnesses have been granted such immunity. United States v. Dolah, 245 F.3d 98, 102 (2d Cir. 2001) ("[A] witness who invokes the privilege against self-incrimination is 'unavailable' within the meaning of Rule 804(b) even though the Government has the power to displace the witness's privilege with a grant of use immunity.").

7. FED.R.EVID. 501.

8. "In general, a person who properly invokes his Fifth Amendment privilege [against self-incrimination], leaving others powerless to compel his testimony, is considered to be unavailable to others for purposes of Rule 804." United States v. Peterson, 100 F.3d 7, 13 (2d Cir. 1996). One invoking the privilege against self-incrimination "has made himself unavailable to any other party, but he is not unavailable to himself." *Peterson*, 100 F.3d at 13. *Accord* United States v. Tietjen, 264 F.3d 391, 413 (4th Cir. 2001); United States v. Kimball, 15 F.3d 54, 55–56 (5th Cir. 1994) ("The sponsor of a declarant's former testimony may not create the condition of unavailability and then benefit therefrom.").

9. "'[A] ruling by the judge is required, which clearly implies that an actual claim of privilege must be made.'" United States v. Udey, 748 F.2d 1231, 1243 (8th Cir. 1984) (quoting FED.R.EVID. 804(a)(1) advisory committee's note). In *Udey* defendant offered his own

(b) *Refusal to Comply with a Court Order to Testify*: Testimony is unavailable if the declarant refuses to testify in the face of a court order commanding the declarant to do so. This part of the definition includes any witness who refuses to testify for any reason, whatever the witness's motivation: fear, loyalty, love, stubbornness, ignorance.... In some cases this picks up where the first part of the definition leaves off, *i.e.*, when a declarant called as a witness asserts a privilege, the privilege is denied, and the declarant is ordered to testify, but still refuses.[10]

(c) *Lack of Memory*: The out-of-court declarant testifies, but testifies to a lack of memory of the subject matter of the out-of-court statement. [11]

(d) *Death or Infirmity*: The out-of-court declarant has died or is unable to testify because of the effects of a disabling physical or mental infirmity.[12]

---

post-arrest statements as declarations against interest, arguing that Rule 804's unavailability requirement was satisfied by his Fifth Amendment privilege not to testify. The court disagreed, noting, among other things, that there was no actual claim of privilege during trial, and no ruling by trial court. *Id.*

10. *See, e.g.*, United States v. Jackson-Randolph, 282 F.3d 369, 381 (6th Cir. 2002) (declarant's testimony was unavailable "both because of her attorney's indication that if she were called ... she would invoke her Fifth Amendment privilege ... and her physician's statement [regarding her] impaired ... ability to understand what was happening").

11. In this regard, unavailability of direct testimony is contrasted unavailability for cross-examination. "Ordinarily a witness is regarded as 'subject to cross-examination' when he is placed on the stand, under oath, and responds willingly to questions." United States v. Owens, 484 U.S. 554, 561 (1988). This includes a witness who willingly responds to cross-examination stating that he does not remember.

12. "The fear, nervousness or excitement that renders the child unable to testify in court, though it may be quite normal for someone his age, may fall within the scope of the term 'mental ... infirmity' as that term is used in Rule 804(a)(4)." Virgin Islands v. Riley, 754 F. Supp. 61, 64 (D.V.I. 1991) (finding the child's in-court testimony unavailable and allowing his videotaped deposition to be used as former testimony). *See also, e.g.*, Finizie v. Principi, 69 Fed.Appx. 571, 573 (3d Cir. 2003) ("We require the party seeking to introduce hearsay testimony based on medical unavailability to provide objective medical support for its claim that a witness is ill or infirm."); United States v. McGuire, 307 F.3d 1192, 1205 (9th Cir. 2002) (courts consider "factors such as the nature of the infirmity, the expected time of recovery, the reliability of the evidence concerning the infirmity, and other special circumstances."); Jackson-Randolph, 282 F.3d at 381 (*see* note 10, above).

The disability need not be permanent. If the disability is neither permanent nor long-term the trial court must decide whether to allow the hearsay evidence in or to grant a continuance so the declarant can testify in person. *E.g.*, *McGuire*, 307 F.3d at 1205. In United States v. Faison, 679 F.2d 292, 297 (3d Cir. 1982), the question before the court was the trial judge's discretion in granting an adjournment for witnesses unavailable due to illness:

[A] judge must consider all relevant circumstances, including: the importance
of the absent witness for the case; the nature and extent of cross-examination in
the earlier testimony; the nature of the illness; the expected time of recovery; the

(e) *Reasonable efforts to secure declarant's testimony failed*: Testimony is unavailable if, despite having made reasonable efforts to do so, the proponent of the statement has been unable to get the declarant into the courtroom and unable to secure the declarant's testimony in some other way, such as by deposition.[13] (The unavailable-by-deposition requirement is true for all Rule 804 exceptions but for the former testimony exception, Rule 804(b)(1); the proponent need not take the declarant's deposition if the proponent has qualifying former testimony.)

Inability to get the declarant into the courtroom may include that the declarant cannot be located;[14] cannot be extradited and refuses to appear voluntarily; or is beyond the range of the court's subpoena power[15] and refuses to appear voluntarily.

---

reliability of the evidence of the probable duration of the illness; and any special circumstances counseling against delay. It is essential for appellate review that the district judge elaborate his considerations and explain his reasons for admitting prior testimony rather than granting a reasonable continuance.

Additionally, the court might consider the number of witnesses and attorneys involved and whether or not they have traveled long distances to the trial. *McGuire*, 307 F.3d at 1205.

13. United States v. Yida, 498 F.3d 945, 950–59 (9th Cir. 2007) contains a long and valuable discussion of what constitutes "reasonable efforts" to secure the declarant's testimony at the trial in the context of the government's offer of the former testimony of a deported alien. United States v. Samaniego, 345 F.3d 1280, 1283 (11th Cir. 2003) (as a foreign national outside the United States, the declarant was beyond the subpoena power of the court; his family in Panama tried to locate him to get him to come to trial but could not find him); United States v. Pena-Gutierrez, 222 F.3d 1080, 1088 (9th Cir. 1999) ("[T]he government had [the witness'] address in Mexico ... [and] asserted no basis for believing [he] would not respond to a request to return to the United States to testify. Although good faith and reasonableness are terms that demand fact-intensive, case-by-case analysis, not rigid rules, the government's failure to make any effort to contact Macias-Limon when it had his address in hand was per se unreasonable."); Ayala v. Aggressive Towing and Transp., Inc., 661 S.E.2d 480, 483 (Va. 2008) (at time of trial, declarant was incarcerated; defendants failed to designate declarant as a witness on the scheduling order and did not "timely supplement[] their discovery disclosures; defendants' waived their right to call declarant as a live witness and thereby "failed to use reasonable diligence in seeking to obtain [his] live testimony....").

14. United States v. Chapman, 345 F.3d 630, 632 (8th Cir. 2003) ("Since Mr. Barron was a fugitive from justice at the time of trial," his testimony was unavailable.); Commonwealth v. Robinson, 888 N.E.2d 926, 930 (Mass. 2008) (detailing state trooper's attempts to find declarant).

15. *Samaniego*, 345 F.3d at 1283. *See generally* FED.R.CIV.P. 45(b) (federal-court service of subpoena in civil cases); FED.R.CRIM.P. 17(e)(1) (federal-court service of subpoena in criminal cases). *See also* miscellaneous federal statutes with application to particular kinds of cases: WEINSTEIN'S EVIDENCE cites, "*e.g.*, 15 U.S.C.A. §23 (service in antitrust actions); 38

(f) *Five Categorical Examples*: The rule states the five categorical examples of unavailability just discussed. The world, of course, is not so clearly divided, so these are only examples. There are situations that overlap into all or parts of one or more of the categories. For example, a child declarant was unavoidably absent when he "'froze' and would not even stand or communicate to take the oath."[16] Perhaps the example fits into the second category—"persists in refusing to testify ... despite an order of the court to do so." Perhaps, however, the court would not have to order the child to testify and this example fits into the fourth category—unable to testify because of a then existing physical or mental illness or infirmity. Perhaps this hypothetical frozen child does not readily fit into any of the five categories. Since the categories are not all inclusive, the child does not have to.

There are also situations where the declarant's in-court testimony is unavailable even though the facts do not fit neatly into any of the five categorical examples. For example, undue financial burden: if a fact witness in a civil action is in Nepal and it would cost $4,000 to get the witness into the courtroom, and if the maximum value of the cause of action is $10,000, the undue financial burden makes the witness unavailable.[17]

■ Once in the courtroom, of course, the declarant could either testify to present firsthand knowledge, doing away with the need for the out-of-court statement, or establish the foundation for another part of the definition of unavailability by, for example, refusing to testify or testifying to a lack of memory.

II. Former Testimony Exception: Rule 804(b)(1)

A. Text of the Rule

> (b) Hearsay exceptions. The following are not excluded by the hearsay rule if the declarant is unavailable[18] as a witness:
>
> (1) Former testimony. Testimony given as a witness at another hearing of the same or different proceeding, or in a deposition taken in compliance with law in the course of the same or another proceed-

---

U.S.C.A. §784(a)-(h) (service in action on war risk insurance)." 4 JACK B. WEINSTEIN & MARGARET A. BERGER, WEINSTEIN'S EVIDENCE ¶804(a)[1], at 804–57 n.58 (1996).

16. Bockting v. State, 847 P.2d 1364, 1366 n.4 (Nev. 1993).

17. This witness-in-Nepal example might fit under the category of "unavoidable absence," but the absence does not really seem to be unavoidable, just too expensive.

18. *See* part I of this chapter, above.

ing, if the party against whom the testimony is now offered, or, in a civil action or proceeding, a predecessor in interest, had an opportunity and similar motive to develop the testimony by direct, cross or redirect examination.

B. The Three Principal Versions of the Former Testimony Exception and the Foundational Elements of Each

All versions of the former testimony exception are about these five things: (1) testimonial unavailability; (2) identity of parties; (3) a statement made under oath; (4) the opportunity to cross-examine the declarant; and (5) the motivation to cross.

There are three versions of this exception. Starting with the one that lets in the least amount of hearsay evidence and ending with the one that lets in the most, they are: (1) the federal rule that applies in criminal cases; (2) the federal rule that applies in civil cases; and (3) the proposed federal rule, which was changed by Congress before being enacted into law, but became the rule is some states' statutes.[19]

1. Criminal Cases under the Federal Rules of Evidence

Foundational elements:

1. As with all Rule 804 exceptions, the out-of-court declarant's in-court testimony must be unavailable.[20]

2. The out-of-court statement must have been made under oath at a prior legal proceeding—some kind of hearing or a deposition—in the same or a different case.

3. The party *against whom* the hearsay statement is offered must have been a party to the former proceeding. In federal criminal cases, Rule 804(b)(1) *does not* require that both parties to the second action have been parties in the first action; just the party against whom the evidence is offered in the second action.

4. Both of the following must be satisfied:

   (a) *Opportunity*: At the former proceeding, the party against whom the hearsay is now offered must have had an opportunity to question the

---

19. NEB.EVID.R. 804(2)(a), NEB. REV. STAT. §27-804(2)(a) (Reissue 1995).
20. *See* part I of this chapter, above.

declarant (by direct, cross, or redirect examination). Actual questioning is not required, just the opportunity.

(b) *Motive*: The party against whom the hearsay is offered must have been similarly motivated to cross-examine the declarant at the proceeding where the former testimony was taken as at the proceeding where it is offered.

2. Civil Cases under the Federal Rules of Evidence

Foundational elements:

1. The declarant's in-court testimony must be unavailable.

2. The statement must have been made under oath at a prior legal proceeding — a trial, some kind of hearing, or a deposition — in the same or a different case.

3. Either the party against whom the statement is now offered or a predecessor in interest of that party must have been a party to the former proceeding. (In federal-civil cases, the rule requires less identity of parties than in the situation described above.)

4. Both of the following must be satisfied:

   (a) *Opportunity*: At the former proceeding, this party or its predecessor in interest must have had an opportunity to question the out-of-court declarant.

   (b) *Motive*: The party or predecessor-in-interest's motivation to question the witness must be similar in each proceeding.

3. The Proposed Federal Rules, Which Are the Rules Adopted in Some States

Foundational elements:

1. The declarant's in-court testimony must be unavailable.

2. The statement must have been made under oath at a prior legal proceeding — a trial, some kind of hearing, or a deposition — in the same or a different case.

3. Both of the following must be satisfied:

   (a) *Opportunity*: Someone in the first proceeding (anyone, not just a party to the second proceeding or a predecessor in interest of such a party) must have had an opportunity to question the out-of-court declarant; and

(b) *Motive*: The party against whom the statement is offered and someone who had an opportunity to examine the witness in the first proceeding must have a sufficiently similar motive to examine the declarant.

C. The Difference in the Three Variations in the Rule Summed Up in Three Sentences

First, the federal rule that is applicable in criminal cases requires absolute
identity of parties. Second, the federal rule that is applicable in civil cases requires substantial identity of parties (same party or predecessor in interest or,
in some courts, a mutuality[21] or community of interest[22]). Third, the proposed
federal rule that has been adopted in some states and is applicable in all cases
(civil and criminal), requires identity of interest.[23]

D. Need + Reliability = 1

1. Need

The need for this evidence is found in the exception's first foundational element: The declarant's in-court testimony must be unavailable. Unless another exception applies, then this evidence is lost. If there is no other exception
and there is no other evidence of the point, then the point is lost.

2. Reliability

Reliability comes from the fact that someone similarly motivated to examine the witness and expose problems with the testimony had an opportunity
to do so with the witness under oath.

E. Use Note

1. Other Ways to Get Former Testimony around the Hearsay Rule

There are many ways to get former testimony around a hearsay objection.[24]

---

21. *See* part II(E)(2)(b) of this chapter, below.
22. *See* part II(E)(2)(c) of this chapter, below.
23. Not identity of parties; identity of interests. Under this version, the identity of the
party is only relevant if it helps define the "interests" involved.
24. This is not unique to former testimony, but it may be particularly true with former
testimony, and particularly worth considering here.

a. A Great Deal of Former Testimony Is Not Hearsay in the First Place

Lots of former testimony is not hearsay in the first place. For example:

■ *Admissions—Rule 801(d)(2)*: If the former testimony is the testimony of a party offered against that party, it is a nonhearsay personal admission. If it is the testimony of an employee of a party, acting within the scope of his or her employment, and now offered against the employer, it is a nonhearsay admission by an employee.[25]

■ *Prior Inconsistent Statement Under Oath. Offered As Substantive Evidence—Rule 801(d)(1)(A)*: If the declarant is testifying and subject to cross-examination at the trial or hearing where the former testimony is being offered and the former testimony was given under oath and is inconsistent with the declarant's in-court testimony, then the former testimony is not hearsay.[26]

■ *Prior Consistent Statement Offered to Rebut a Charge of Recent Fabrication—Rule 801(d)(1)(B)*: If the foundation set out in part II(B) of Chapter 2 can be laid, then the former testimony can be a nonhearsay prior consistent statement offered to rebut a charge of recent fabrication.[27]

■ *Statement of Identification of a Person—Rule 801(d)(1)(C)*: If the declarant is testifying at the trial or hearing where the former testimony is being offered and is subject to cross-examination concerning that testimony, and the former testimony is a statement that identifies a person, made after perceiving that person, then the statement is not hearsay.[28]

■ *Prior Inconsistent Statements Offered to Impeach, not to Prove the Truth of the Matter Asserted*: Sometimes former testimony will be used to impeach the same witness's inconsistent testimony at the current subsequent trial or hearing. When it is offered as credibility evidence only, then it is not offered to prove the truth of the matter asserted, and, therefore, is not hearsay in the first place.[29]

■ *Statements Used to Refresh Recollection and not to Prove the Truth of the Matter Asserted*: Sometimes former testimony is used to refresh a testifying witness's recollection. In this case the prior statement is not offered into evidence; since it is not offered into evidence, it cannot be offered to prove the truth

---

25. FED.R.EVID. 801(d)(2). *See* Chapter 2(III), above.
26. *See* Chapter 2(II)(A), above.
27. *See* Chapter 2(II)(B), above.
28. *See* Chapter 2(II)(C)(4), above.
29. *See* Chapter 2(II)(A)(4)(a), above.

of the matter asserted; since it is not offered to prove the truth of the matter asserted, it cannot be hearsay.[30]

b. A Great Deal of Former Testimony Fits under Other Hearsay Exceptions

If the former testimony is hearsay, then it may fit under one or more of the exceptions to the hearsay rule.

■ *Statements in a Deposition Taken in the Same Case—Rule 32 of the Federal Rules of Civil Procedure:* If the hearsay testimony is in the form of a deposition taken in the same case, then one of the premier ways to get it around the hearsay rule is Rule 32 of the Federal Rules of Civil Procedure. For example, if your trial is in the federal courthouse in Grand Rapids, Michigan, and your expert witness lives, works, and, at the time of the trial, is in Detroit, which is more than 100 miles away, then the expert's deposition may be used in lieu of his or her live testimony.[31]

■ *Various Other Exceptions:* Former testimony may also fit under various other exceptions. Testimony within a deposition can be a dying declaration,[32] a statement against interest,[33] a statement of a then existing mental or physical sensation,[34] or any number of other things that fit under various hearsay exceptions.

c. Do Not Give Up on Former Testimony Just Because the Former Testimony Exception Does Not Work

The particular point here is this: Just because an out-of-court declaration is in the form of "testimony" does not mean that the only avenue of admissibility is the former testimony exception. There are many ways to get testimonial declarations around the bar of the hearsay rule; the former testimony exception is only one of them. Each exception and exclusion is a discrete way around the hearsay rule; all you need is one and you are around the hearsay rule;

---

30. *See* Chapter 3(VI)(E)(1) & (2), above.

31. *See* Chapter 6(I), below. "As a practical matter the primary impact of [Rule] 804(b)(1), with respect to depositions, is only in those cases where the deposition was taken in a proceeding different from the one in which it is being offered as evidence." James W. Moore, MOORE'S FEDERAL PRACTICE § 804.04[1], VII-262 (2d ed. 1996).

32. *See* part III of this chapter, below.

33. *See* part IV of this chapter, below.

34. *See* Chapter 3(IV), above.

don't get stuck on the former testimony exception. Consider all reasonably applicable ways around your potential hearsay problem.[35]

2. Predecessor in Interest

a. Predecessor in Interest

Predecessor is defined as: "One who goes or has gone before; the correlative of 'successor.'"[36] Successor in interest is defined as:

> One who follows another in ownership or control of property. In order to be a "successor in interest", a party must continue to retain the same rights as original owner, without change in ownership and there must be change in form only and not in substance, and [a] transferee is not a "successor in interest." In case of corporations, the term ordinarily indicates statutory succession as, for instance, when corporation changes its name but retains same property.[37]

Interest is defined as: "The most general term that can be employed to denote a right, claim, title, or legal share in something."[38]

In the context of the former testimony exception, examples of predecessors in interest include a former holder of a property interest in the property that is the subject of litigation. Assume the following: an eminent domain action where the question is the value of a parcel of land; a former owner of the land in question had been involved in litigation some years ago and some of the witnesses who testified in that action disparaged the value of the land; in the current action, the state offers that testimony from that prior proceeding. The former owner is a predecessor in interest. If each of the other foundational elements of the exception is satisfied—unavailability; oath; opportunity and sufficiently similar motive to examine the witness—then that former testimony fits under this exception as against the current owner.

A former owner of a specific animal—family pet, show dog, genetically-altered lab rat, rodeo horse, circus lion—is a predecessor in interest of the current owner. This might matter if, for example, the animal is the subject of a personal injury action. If so, and if the rest of the foundational elements are established, then testimony given at a trial while the animal was owned by its

---

35. This is the subject of Chapter 10, below.
36. BLACK'S LAW DICTIONARY 1431–32 (6th ed. 1990).
37. *Id.* at 1431–32.
38. *Id.* at 812.

former owner can be offered against the current owner, under the former testimony exception. This is true no matter who gave the former testimony, so long as the former owner had sufficient opportunity to examine those witnesses and was similarly motivated to do so. If the rest of the foundation is in place and there is no other evidentiary problem preventing admission, the former testimony comes in.

The heirs who are continuing the deceased's personal injury action are successors in interest to the deceased; the deceased is predecessor in interest to the heirs.

A former holder of a note that is being sued upon is the predecessor in interest of the current holder of the note.

It is the functional equivalent of buying a company where, unless other arrangements are made, you buy its assets and its liabilities. Successors in interest "buy into" their predecessor's decisions regarding whether and how to examine witnesses in a former, sufficiently-related proceeding.

b. Mutuality of Interest

One commentator defines the predecessor-in-interest relationship as a privity relationship and then provides examples as follows: "'[T]here are privies in estate, as donor and donee, lessor and lessee, and joint tenants; privies in blood, as heir and ancestor, and co-parceners; privies in representation, as executor and testator, administrator and intestate; privies in law, where the law, without privity of blood or estate, casts the land upon another, as by escheat.'"[39] This expands the concept of "predecessor in interest" by including not only successive relationships but also mutual relationships.

c. Community of Interest

Some courts go even farther, and loosely interpret the words "predecessor in interest" as including both the strict predecessor in interest plus those who have a sufficient "community of interest." *Lloyd v. American Export Lines, Inc.*[40] is a leading case behind this interpretation of the rule. It serves as an example of the kind of facts that raise the community of interests issue. Alvarez and

---

39. MOORE, *supra* note 31, §804.04[2] (quoting Metropolitan St. Ry. v. Gumby, 99 F. 192, 198 (2d Cir. 1900) (without reference in *Moore's*, *Gumby* in turn quoted "19 Am. & Eng. Enc. Law, 156")).

40. 580 F.2d 1179 (3d Cir. 1978).

Lloyd, fellow crewmembers of the SS Export Commerce, were in a violent fight. Lloyd sued the ship's owner (Owner) for compensation for injuries suffered in the fight, Owner joined Alvarez as a third-party defendant, and Alvarez counterclaimed against Owner for his injuries sustained in the fight. Lloyd did not proceed with his case, but Alvarez did, and Alvarez's counterclaim went to trial. At trial, Alvarez testified to his version of the fight. For Lloyd's version, Owner offered a transcript of Lloyd's testimony at a Coast Guard hearing that had been held for the purpose of determining whether Lloyd's merchant mariner's document should have been suspended or revoked as a result of charges brought against him for the fight with Alvarez.

The court held that this former testimony was admissible against Alvarez, who was not a party to the Coast Guard hearing. It came down to this foundational element: "[W]hether the Coast Guard investigating officer was Alvarez' predecessor in interest."[41]

> While we do not endorse an extravagant interpretation of who or what constitutes a "predecessor in interest," we prefer one that is realistically generous over one that is formalistically grudging. We believe that what has been described as "the practical and expedient view" expresses the congressional intention: "if it appears that in the former suit a party having a like motive to cross-examine about the same matters as the present party would have, was accorded an adequate opportunity for such examination, the testimony may be received against the present party." Under these circumstances, the previous party ... is, in the final analysis, a predecessor in interest to the present party.[42]

Under this interpretation, "predecessor in interest" and "similar motive to develop the testimony" become redundant. This is nothing more than a judicial rewrite of enacted Rule 804(b)(1)[43] that changes it into proposed Rule

---

41. Lloyd v. American Export Lines, Inc., 580 F.2d 1179, 1186 (3d Cir. 1978).

42. *Id.* at 1187 (citation omitted). The Fourth Circuit's interpretation of the predecessor-in-interest relationship goes beyond changing it into a mutuality-of-interest or privity relationship. *E.g.,* Supermarket of Marlinton, Inc. v. Meadow Gold Dairies, Inc., 71 F.3d 119, 128 (4th Cir. 1995) ("even if privity was a concern in the analysis...."); Horne v. Owens-Corning Fiberglass Corp., 4 F.3d 276, 283 (4th Cir. 1993) ("[P]rivity is not the gravamen of the analysis."); Hynix Semiconductor Inc. v. Rambus Inc., 250 F.R.D. 452, 458 (N.D. Cal. 2008) ("The modern test does not require privity ... [but rather] '[a] previous party having like motive to develop the testimony about the same material facts ...'").

43. In a civil case, either the party against whom the statement is offered or a predecessor in interest to the party against whom the statement is offered must have had an opportunity and been appropriately motivated to develop the former testimony. FED.R.EVID.

804(b)(1).[44] It is as though Congress had not intentionally changed the proposed rule before enacting it into law.[45]

3. Opportunity to Examine the Witness

"Opportunity under 804(b)(1) means more than naked opportunity."[46] Most of the cases that make statements like the one just quoted confuse the two foundational elements of opportunity and motivation. What most of these cases really seem to mean is that opportunity to examine the witness is not the only foundational element. There must be a confluence of opportunity, "naked" or otherwise, and sufficiently similar motivation.

Consider, for example, *Pearl v. Keystone Consolidated Industries, Inc.,*[47] where a party received plenty of notice of a deposition and, though able to attend, chose not to do so. That party had sufficient "opportunity" to examine the witness deposed. She had her own reasons for choosing not to attend the deposition. That does not change the fact that she had the opportunity to attend and therefore the opportunity to examine the witness. A decision not to show up *is* a decision to forgo examination of the witness. Pearl's choice not to attend may

---

804(b)(1). Define a predecessor in interest as anyone appropriately motivated to examine the witness and this rule becomes the proposed rule described in the next footnote.

44. Someone in the first proceeding—without limitation to the party against whom the statement is now offered or that party's predecessor in interest—must have had an opportunity and been appropriately motivated to develop the former testimony. Proposed Fed.R.Evid. 804(b)(1).

45. Compare and contrast parts II(B)(1) & (2) of this chapter with part II(B)(3) of this chapter, all above.

Lloyd is not the only case to do this. *See* Clay v. Johns-Manville Sales Corp, 722 F.2d 1289, 1295 (6th Cir. 1982). *But see, e.g., Lloyd,* 580 F.2d at 1190 (Stern, D.J. concurring) ("I believe that this analysis is contrary to the Rule's clear language and is foreclosed by its legislative history."); Acme Printing Ink Co. v. Menard, Inc., 812 F.Supp. 1498, 1525–26 (E.D. Wisc. 1992).

Regarding this very exception to the hearsay rule, though not regarding these interpretations of "predecessor in interest," the Supreme Court has said: "Nothing in the language of Rule 804(b)(1) suggests that a court may admit former testimony absent satisfaction of each of the Rule's elements.... When Congress enacted the prohibition against admission of hearsay in Rule 802, it ... presumably made a judgment as to what hearsay may come into evidence and what may not. To respect its determination, we must enforce the words that it enacted." United States v. Salerno, 505 U.S. 317, 323 (1992). The community of interest interpretation of "predecessor in interest," and perhaps even the mutuality of interest interpretation, do not seem to square with this statement from the Supreme Court.

46. United States v. Taplin, 954 F.2d 1256, 1258 (6th Cir. 1992).

47. 884 F.2d 1047 (7th Cir. 1989).

be relevant to another foundational element—motive to examine the witness, for example. She may not have attended because she had no interest in examining this witness—but that really is not relevant to the element at hand: She had an opportunity to examine the witness.

On the other hand, opportunity to examine the witness is not established by "naked" presence at or invitation to attend the proceeding.[48] The nature of the proceeding must be such that full examination of the witness is allowed, and the presiding officer must in fact have allowed full examination. Presence at a hastily called proceeding may not have left enough time to prepare to fully examine witnesses. Other kinds of surprise may affect this element of opportunity. For example, if counsel is present at a proceeding involving a co-party of his client and is unexpectedly asked by the judge if he wishes to ask a witness any questions, that may not be a sufficient opportunity to examine the witness.[49] It takes more than presence by fortuity.[50]

Regarding grand jury proceedings, this element of the former testimony exception leads to this result: Since defense counsel is not allowed into the grand jury room, this exception can cover grand jury testimony when offered by the defendant against the prosecutor, but never when offered by the prosecutor against the defendant.[51] (Grand jury testimony may, however, fit under the residual exception.[52])

---

48. "The opportunity to develop testimony offered at another proceeding is not established by presence alone." *Taplin*, 954 F.2d at 1258.

49. "The mere fact that Taplin's attorney was in the courtroom during Bailey's suppression testimony and was asked by the presiding judge if he had any questions, is not proof that Taplin was prepared for a full and thorough cross-examination of the witness." *Taplin*, 954 F.2d at 1258.

50. *See Taplin*, 954 F.2d at 1259 ("The dissent agrees with the standard set forth here but argues that Taplin's presence was no fortuity.").

51. For example, *see* United States v. Omar, 104 F.3d 519, 522 (1st Cir. 1997):

[The] hearsay exception for prior testimony does extend, where all its conditions are met, to grand jury testimony taken at the government's behest and later offered against it in a criminal trial. A grand jury proceeding can be regarded as a "hearing," especially in the context of a rule that applies as well to depositions. And—assuming "an opportunity and similar motive to develop the testimony"—the rationale for an exception to the hearsay rule is made out, namely, that the party against whom the testimony is now offered earlier had the opportunity and similar motive to discredit the testimony, and so did then whatever it would do now if the declarant were on the stand.

See also United States v. Salerno, 505 U.S. 317 (1992).

52. *See* Chapter 5(V)(B), below.

4. Similarly Motivated to Examine the Witness

Someone at the first proceeding[53] must have had motivation to examine the witness similar to the motivation of the party against whom the statement is now being offered. This looks into the mind of the party against whom the hearsay is offered and the minds of the parties to the first proceeding. It asks whether there was a party in the first proceeding whose interest in developing the testimony of the declarant was sufficiently similar to the interest of the party against whom the statement is now offered. This is an attempt to ensure that the cross-examination performed the first time is sufficiently similar to the one that would have been performed this time.[54] If a party to the first proceeding had the opportunity to cross-examine the witness and was sufficiently similarly motivated, then, in theory, at least, the cross-examination that party wants now would have been performed then.

> The Second Circuit has ... developed a two-part test for determining "similar motive" under Rule 804(b)(1): "whether the questioner is on the same side of the same issue at both proceedings, ... [and] whether the questioner had a substantially similar interest in asserting that side of the issue." ... Under that test, the similar-motive inquiry under Rule 804(b)(1) requires scrutiny of the factual and procedural context of each proceeding to determine both the issue in dispute and the intensity of interest in developing the particular issue by the party against whom the disputed testimony is offered.[55]

One's motivation to examine witnesses can depend on many things:

(a) *No Motive to Cross-Examine in the First Proceeding*: Sometimes—for whatever reason—the party against whom the evidence is offered in the second proceeding had *no* significant motive to cross-examine in the first proceeding. Lack of a significant motive in the first proceeding certainly can be

---

53. Just who that someone is depends on which version of the rule applies. In federal criminal actions it is the party against whom the statement is offered. In federal civil actions it is the party against whom the statement is offered or a predecessor in interest of that party. Under the proposed federal rules, which is the version adopted in some states, it is anyone similarly motivated to cross examine. *See, supra*, parts II(B) and (C) of this chapter.

54. *See, e.g.*, United States v. Miles, 290 F.3d 1341, 1353 (11th Cir. 2002) ("Because similar motive does not mean identical motive, this inquiry is inherently factual, depending in part on the similarity of the underlying issues and on the context of the questioning.").

55. United States v. Bartelho, 129 F.3d 663, 670 (1st Cir. 1997), quoting United States v. DiNapoli, 8 F.3d 909, 912 (2d Cir. 1993) (en banc).

lack of a similar motive.[56] Presumably, however, this exception could be used against one with no motive to cross-examine at the first proceeding and no motive to cross-examine at the proceeding at hand, the motive being similar in each case: None.

(b) *The Nature of the Proceedings*: Regarding similar motivation to examine the witness, the nature of the two proceedings may be a determining factor. Take, for example, an intersectional collision resulting in what appeared to be only minor damage. One driver is ticketed and half-heartedly defends against that criminal charge—perhaps after dashed hopes that the officer who issued the ticket would not show up in court. She is convicted. Then the other driver unexpectedly dies, allegedly as a result of that collision, and a million-dollar wrongful death action is filed against the driver who half-heartedly defended (and lost) the traffic-ticket case. On these facts, the defendant was less motivated to examine witnesses in the first trial than she is in the second—as such, her motivation may not be sufficiently similar.[57]

Even when the issues do not change, the motive to examine the witness at the deposition may be entirely different than that at the trial. This might be the case with the deposition of an expert where the purpose is to gather information and not to challenge the expert or to test his theory or methodology.[58] In

---

56. *E.g.,* Hannah v. City of Overland, 795 F.2d 1385, 1390–91 (8th Cir. 1986) (the deposition testimony posed so little danger to the State as to have been insignificant; thus the State did not have any significant motive to cross-examine, let alone a similar motive); United States v. Wilson, 36 F.Supp.2d 1177, 1183–84 (N.D. Cal. 1999) (regarding similar motivation, defense counsel in a criminal case "has a motive to conduct an exhaustive, probing examination" of the prosecution's chief witness; in the deposition offered here, it is clear that defense counsel had no such motive; the goal of this examination "was to gain information to resolve a civil forfeiture case and to aid pre-indictment negotiations, not to fully probe the credibility of [the witness]"; this conclusion is supported by evidence that counsel believed this deposition was not meant to be admitted at a trial against his client).
57. *See, e.g.,* United States v. DiNapoli, 8 F.3d 909, 912 (2d Cir. 1993):

If a fact is critical to a cause of action at a second proceeding but the same fact was only peripherally related to a different cause of action at a first proceeding, no one would claim that the questioner had a similar motive at both proceedings to show that the fact had been established (or disproved). This is the same principle that holds collateral estoppel inapplicable when a small amount is at stake in a first proceeding and a large amount is at stake in a second proceeding, even though a party took the same side of the same issue at both proceedings.

58. *See, e.g.,* Polozie v. United States, 835 F.Supp. 68, 72 (D. Conn. 1993):

In deposing [the expert witness], the defendant's motive was to gather information and, generally, to learn as much as it could about [the expert's] opinions and their bases. It was not the defendant's motive at that point to test [the expert's]

this situation, motivation is different because the party's objectives are different. This is not a mere difference in tactics,[59] but rather a difference in motivation resulting from a difference in objective.

Similarly, sometimes in criminal cases a defendant has quite a different motivation regarding witness examination at preliminary proceedings, as opposed to witness examination at the trial.[60] In the former proceeding, she may want to keep her defenses and the rest of her strategy hidden from the prosecutor. She will, of course, not want to do that in the latter proceeding.

(c) *The Burdens of Proof in the Two Proceedings:* Sometimes, in some proceedings, the burden of proof can be so low that it affects the motivation of the party who has the burden.[61]

(d) *The Stage of the Development of the Legal Theories:* If depositions are taken and then the legal theories of one party or another change, that can, of course, create new and different motives for witness-examination. Say that after certain depositions are taken, the plaintiff amends the petition to add a new cause of action for intentional infliction of emotional distress, or the defendant amends the answer to add the affirmative defense of assumption of the risk. Unless anticipated at the depositions, developments such as these certainly suggest new lines of questioning. A lawyer not motivated to ask about intentional infliction of emotional distress at the deposition (and, in fact, perhaps, steering clear of the topic so as to avoid suggesting the cause of action to opposing counsel), is motivated to ask about it after the petition is amended to make it as a cause of action.[62]

---

methodology or to challenge his skill, credibility, and confidence in his own assessments. The defendant's motive for cross-examination at trial was entirely different.

As always, however, when dealing with former testimony in the form of a deposition, keep in mind the liberal admissibility provided for in Rule 32 of the Federal Rules of Civil Procedure. Rule 32 leaves little for the former testimony exception to do regarding depositions. *See* Chapter 6, below.

59. In this regard, see the discussion of "new counsel or new tactics," in paragraph (i) of this part of this chapter, below.

60. *See, e.g.,* Rodriguez v. State, 711 P.2d 410, 414 (Wyo. 1985) (sometimes defense counsel did not have a similar motive to cross-examine the witness at the preliminary hearing and sometimes defense counsel does).

61. *DiNapoli,* 8 F.3d at 913 ("[B]ecause of the low burden of proof at the grand jury stage, even the prosecutor's status as an 'opponent' of the testimony does not necessarily create a motive to challenge the testimony that is similar to the motive at trial.").

62. To the extent that "the question is whether the issues are substantially similar such that the incentive to develop testimony is similar in the two proceedings," *Taplin,* 954 F.2d at 1259 n.1, then changing the issues certainly can change one's motive to cross-examine.

(e) *The Stage of the Factual Investigation*: When a deposition is taken and new information is subsequently uncovered about the deponent's character or competence, or about what the witness knew or did not know, that can change the motivation for witness-examination. If you had no idea the first time that you could destroy this witness's credibility, your strategy might be to go easy on the cross-examination and downplay the importance of the witness. If you later come into possession of information that leads you to believe you can destroy this witness's credibility, you might decide to play the witness up as much more important to your opponent's case and then go after the witness. In any event, new facts can change one's motivation regarding witness-examination.[63]

(f) *The Identity of the Persons Involved and What Specifically Motivates Them as Individuals*: If we adopt a mutuality of interest or community of interest definition of predecessor in interest, as discussed above, then the identity of the parties may become relevant. The question here is, What kinds of things motivate the person who had the first opportunity to examine the witness versus what kinds of things motivate the person against whom the former testimony is being offered? If the case is about a few thousand dollars and the party who had the first opportunity to question the witness was Bill Gates, and the party against whom the former testimony is now being offered is a law student already struggling under the burden of large educational loans, the motivation of the former and the latter may not be sufficiently similar.

(g) *The Degree of the Identity of the Issues*: Though somewhat overlapping with some of the factors set out above, it goes without saying that dissimilar issues result in dissimilar motivation as regards witness-examination.[64]

United States v. Carson, 455 F.3d 336, 377–80 (D.C. Cir. 2006) (government's legal theory changed in the meantime, which radically changed its motive to cross-examine). *See also, e.g.,* Kirk v. Raymark Indus., Inc. 61 F.3d 147, 166 (3d Cir. 1995) (the district court made no findings regarding opportunity or motive to cross-examine and the appellate court finds nothing in the record to support opportunity or motive).

63. *See, e.g., DiNapoli,* 8 F.3d at 913 ("Frequently the grand jury inquiry will be conducted at a time when an investigation is ongoing. In such circumstances, there is an important public interest in not disclosing prematurely the existence of surveillance techniques such as wiretaps or undercover operations, or the identity of cooperating witnesses."). *But see* Flonnery v. State, 893 A.2d 507, 534 (Del. 2006) (though the opponent of the former testimony evidence had no opportunity to cross examine the declarant regarding crimes committed after the former testimony, there was no need for such cross-examination because the opponent did have the opportunity to put that subsequent evidence before the jury and to argue it, and, in this case, that was enough).

64. *See, e.g.,* Hoppe v. G.D. Searle & Co., 779 F.Supp. 1413, 1417 (S.D.N.Y. 1991) (the plaintiff here and in the prior proceeding were exposed to the product in question for dif-

(h) *Subsequent Scientific or Similar Advances:* Scientific or other similar advances in the time between the original testimony and its offer into evidence at a subsequent proceeding may radically alter a party's motive to develop the testimony. There may, for example, have been scientific advances that would provide whole new ways to discredit the expert.[65]

(i) *New Counsel or New Tactics:* When the party against whom the former testimony is offered was a party in the former proceeding, the fact that the party has changed his tactics, changed his counsel, or both, is not enough to create a dissimilar motivation regarding examination of witnesses.[66]

---

ferent periods of time and, because of product deterioration, this changes the defendant's motive regarding cross-examination of these medical doctors; the defendant here may advance unusual facts regarding this particular plaintiff and causation, and this changes defendant's motive regarding cross-examination of these medical doctors).

And, of course, the converse is equally true: That the issues are similar is evidence of similar motivation.

65. *See, e.g., Hoppe,* 779 F.Supp. at 1417 ("Searle asserts that current scientific and medical literature provides material that Searle would have used to challenge these experts' credibility, but could not because the information was not yet available.").

66. *See, e.g.,* United States v. Avants, 367 F.3d 433, 444 (5th Cir. 2004) ("a change in strategy 'does not mean [a] ... changed motive....'" (quoting trial court)); United States v. Bartelho, 129 F.3d 663, 670, n.9 (1st Cir. 1997) (a tactical decision not to develop particular testimony does not constitute lack of opportunity or dissimilar motive); United States v. Tannehill, 49 F.3d 1049, 1057 (5th Cir. 1995) (One of seven defendants in his first trial, appellant's tactic "was to 'disappear into the woodwork and hope for the best.'" The only defendant in his retrial he had a new lawyer and a new defense theory. When testimony from the first trial was offered against him at the second, he argued his motivation regarding cross-examination was now quite different. The held that disappearing into the woodwork was a trial tactic. "Although [his] trial strategy may have changed..., his motive for cross-examination was the same ..."); Polozie v. United States, 835 F.Supp. 68, 72 (D. Conn. 1993) ; State v. Ayers, 468 A.2d 606, 608 (Me. 1983) (appellant's confession was admitted at her first trial and her trial strategy was to testify, admit the killing, and try to justify it; the confession was suppressed at her retrial and her strategy was to refrain from testifying and attack the State's case by suggesting others had committed the crime; the testimony of a co-defendant from the first trial was admitted at the retrial over her argument that with her confession suppressed at the second trial, her motive to examine the witness was not sufficiently similar; the court affirmed, holding that the former testimony "her guilt or innocence of that crime was the identical issue of both trials").

It is no surprise that sometimes the distinction between motivation and tactics is not so clear. In United States v. Franklin, 235 F.Supp. 909 (D.D.C. 1964), the government offered former testimony and cited to cases where the former testimony was from witnesses testifying for the government and adverse to the defendants; in those cases the defendants were strongly motivated to conduct vigorous cross-examination. In the case at bar the for-

(j) *Grand Jury Testimony*: "[T]he inquiry as to similar motive must be fact specific, and the grand jury context will sometimes, but not invariably, present circumstances that demonstrate the prosecutor's lack of a similar motive. We accept neither the Government's view that the prosecutor's motives at the grand jury and at trial are almost always dissimilar, nor the opposing view, apparently held by the District of Columbia Circuit, that the prosecutor's motives in both proceedings are always similar."[67]

(k) *A Conflict of Interest*: Consider, for example, a criminal trial with multiple defendants, where one of the defendants had the requisite opportunity and motive to examine a witness in a former proceeding. If that defendant has potentially conflicting interests with other defendants in the current trial, then that may make that motive dissimilar as regards the other defendants.[68]

(l) *Other Considerations*: Evidence of whether the motivation to examine the witness at the first proceeding is sufficiently similar to motivation at the second proceeding may come from the actual first examination itself. A thorough examination of the witness at the first proceeding, touching on all subjects relevant at the second proceeding, may be evidence of sufficiently similar motivation.[69] Likewise, an examination in a manner consistent with the na-

---

mer testimony was the testimony of codefendants testifying on their own behalf; the declarants were not adverse to each other; the defendant against whom the testimony is now offered was not strongly motivated not to conduct a vigorous cross-examination in the first proceeding lest "the impeachment of the others ... undermine[] his own assertion of innocence." *Id.* at 914.

67. *Di Napoli*, 8 F.3d at 914 (citing United States v. Miller, 904 F.2d 65, 68 (D.C. Cir. 1990) ("[A]s several circuits have recognized, the government had the same motive and opportunity to question [the witness] when it brought him before the grand jury as it does at trial. Before the grand jury and at trial, [the witness's] testimony was to be directed to the same issue—the guilt or innocence of [the defendants]." (citations omitted)). *See also, e.g.,* United States v. Salerno, 505 U.S. 317 (1992); United States v. Omar, 104 F.3d 519, 522 (1st Cir. 1997) (as quoted at length in note 51, above).

Grand-jury testimony may be admissible at trial, against the government, under the former testimony exception. Other ways to get in grand jury testimony, including possible ways to get it in against the defendant, are discussed at some length at Chapter 5(V)(B), below.

68. Zenith Radio Corp. v. Matsushita Elec. Indus. Co., 505 F. Supp. 1190, 1292 (E.D. Pa. 1980), *aff'd in part, rev'd in part, remanded, sub nom* In re Japanese Elec. Prods. Antitrust Litig., 723 F.2d 238 (3d Cir. 1983), *rev'd and remanded sub non* Matsushita Elec. Indus. Co. v. Zenith Radio Corp., 475 U.S. 574 (1986).

69. *E.g.,* Scroggins v. Norris, 77 F.3d 1107 (8th Cir. 1996). *Scroggins* actually seems to substitute "extent of cross-examination" for "motive to cross-examine:"

[Appellant contends] he did not have a similar motive to develop the testimony

ture of the first proceeding, but "in a manner totally inconsistent with the goals of examination at trial,"[70] may be evidence of a dissimilar motive.

5. Grand Jury Testimony Summarized

If the in-court testimony of the grand jury witness is unavailable,[71] the former testimony exception may be able to be used by the defendant to introduce grand jury testimony against the prosecution. The prosecution had an opportunity to examine the witness presented to the grand jury[72] and sometimes the prosecution had a sufficiently similar motive to examine the witnesses presented to the grand jury.[73]

The former testimony exception cannot be used by the prosecution to introduce grand jury testimony against the defendant. Since defense counsel is not allowed into the grand jury room, defense counsel never has the opportunity to examine grand jury witnesses. Since defense counsel never has the opportunity to examine grand jury witnesses, this exception can never be used to introduce grand jury testimony against the defendant in a criminal case.[74]

Grand jury testimony may be admissible under the residual exception.[75]

---

at the suppression hearing as he would have had at trial. We find Appellant's cross-examination was sufficient to ensure that the testimony bears the adequate indicia of reliability. [T]he inquiry at the suppression hearing ... went beyond issues relevant to the suppression of the [evidence]. Appellant questioned [the witness] about the events leading up to Appellant's arrest as well as his prior involvement with Appellant in legitimate business transactions. His cross-examination also explored issues touching on [the witness's] credibility including prior bad acts and promises of leniency.

Id. at 1108.

70. *See also*, notes 56, 57, and 58, and accompanying text, above.

71. *See* part (I) of this chapter, above.

72. *See* part (II)(E)(3) of this chapter, above.

73. *See* part (II)(E)(4) of this chapter, above.

74. This is so under the rule, see part (II)(E)(3) of this chapter, above, and under the Confrontation Clause, see Chapter 14, below.

75. *See* Chapter 5(V)(B), below. In fact, grand jury testimony may be offered against the defendant under any hearsay exception that applies. Sometimes the residual exception might apply. Presumably a witness before a grand jury could make a statement against interest (Fed.R.Evid. 804(b)(3), part IV of this chapter, above) or, if sufficiently startled during the proceeding, an excited utterance (Fed.R.Evid. 803(2), Chapter 3(III), above). It is just that the former testimony exception will not work if the evidence is offered against the accused.

6. The Confrontation Clause

Evidence that is admissible under the federal rules version of this exception is also admissible under the Confrontation Clause. The in-court testimony of the witness must be unavailable and the criminal defendant must have been a party to the prior proceeding and must have had the opportunity and a similar motive to cross examine (*i.e.*, to confront) the witness. When the exception is covered, the Confrontation Clause is as well.[76]

III. Statements under Belief of Impending Death: Rule 804(b)(2)

A. Text of the Rule

(b) Hearsay exceptions. The following are not excluded by the hearsay rule if the declarant is unavailable as a witness:

****

(2) Statement under belief or impending death. In a prosecution for homicide or in a civil action or proceeding, a statement made by a declarant while believing that the declarant's death was imminent, concerning the cause or circumstances of what the declarant believed to be impending death.

B. Foundational Elements

1. As with all Rule 804 exceptions, the out-of-court declarant's in-court testimony must be unavailable.[77]

2. When the declarant made the statement, the declarant must have believed he or she was about to die. (As in the Use Note, the declarant need not be dead at the time of the trial. Declarant's testimony must be unavailable, but it need not be unavailable on account of death.[78])

---

76. Crawford v. Washington, 541 U.S. 36, 68 (2004) ("Where testimonial evidence is at issue, however, the Sixth Amendment demands what the common law required [and the federal rule still requires]: unavailability and a prior opportunity for cross-examination."); United States v. Avants, 367 F.3d 433, 445 (5th Cir. 2004).

77. *See* part I of this chapter, above.

78. *See* part III(D)(1) of this chapter, below.

3. The out-of-court statement must concern the cause or the circumstances of what the declarant believed to be his or her imminent death.

4. The case in which the out-of-court statement is offered must be either a civil case or a prosecution for homicide. (This fourth foundational element was not part of the proposed federal rule of evidence. Congress adopted this change before enacting the rules into law. This is not a foundational element in some states whose rules are based on the proposed rules.[79])

C. Need + Reliability = 1

1. Need

The need for this evidence is that often when a person thinks he or she is about to die, that person goes ahead and dies. Without this exception or the coincidence of some other exception,[80] when the out-of-court declarant does die, the evidence is lost.

Second, even if the out-of-court declarant does not die, this is a Rule 804 exception. Therefore, one of the foundational elements is the unavailability of the declarant's in-court testimony. Therefore, whether the declarant dies or not, without some exception to the hearsay rule the testimony will be lost.

2. Reliability

The guarantee of reliability for this exception is the tendency in our culture for people to tell the truth when they are conscious of their own impending death. One can argue whether such a tendency is the general rule, and whether it exists among members of certain cultural groups whose statements will be admitted under this exception. Nonetheless, if this exception is founded on anything, it is founded upon the belief "that no one 'who is going into the presence of his Maker will do so with a lie upon his lips.'"[81]

---

79. Nebraska, for example, adopted the proposed federal rule as follows: "A statement made by a declarant while believing that his death was imminent, concerning the cause or circumstances of what he believed to be his impending death." NEB.EVID.R. 804(2)(b), NEB. REV. STAT. § 27-804(2)(b) (Reissue 1995). There is no limitation on the kind of case in which the exception is available.

80. For example, a dying declaration that is also an excited utterance.

81. Commonwealth v. Smith, 314 A.2d 224, 225 (Pa. 1973) (quoting Luch, L.J., Regina v. Osman, 15 Cox C.C. 1, 3 (Eng. 1881)). *Accord* Idaho v. Wright, 497 U.S. 805, 820 (1990) (parts of same quotation; same case cited); State v. Shatterfield, 457 S.E.2d 440, 447 (W. Va. 1995); Berry v. State, 611 So.2d 924, 927 (Miss. 1992) ("[T]he dying declaration exception

The religious aspects of this exception aside, two other indicia or reliability have been suggested. One is that the sudden knowledge of impending death may cause such stress as to suppress the kind of conscious reflection needed to form the lie.[82] The other is that the person who truly believes that he or she is about to die "will not personally benefit from lying."[83]

The guarantee of reliability here has to do with deliberate fabrication. It does not deal with the testimonial infirmities of faulty memory and faulty perception.[84] Statements under belief of impending death present particular occasion for these latter infirmities. As discussed below,[85] however, these problems may not be hearsay problems as much as they are relevance and competence problems.

D. Use Note

1. Unavailability—By Death or Otherwise

Though, at the time the out-of-court declarant made the statement the declarant must have believed he or she was about to die, the declarant need not be dead at the time of the trial. Declarant's testimony must be unavailable, but any of the unavailabilities listed in Rule 804 will do, death or otherwise.[86]

---

found its traditional justification in the once near universal view that no man would meet his maker with a lie on his lips. We live in more secular times, still the dying declaration is regarded 'a firmly rooted hearsay exception.'"); State v. Jordan, 5 S.E.2d 156, 160 (N.C. 1939) ("[A]t the point of death, ... every hope of this world is gone; ... every motive to falsehood is silenced, and the mind is induced by the most powerful considerations to speak the truth. A situation so solemn, and so awful, is considered by the law as creating an obligation equal to that which is imposed by a positive oath administered in a court of justice." (citations and multiple quotation marks omitted)).

On the other hand, "some folks carry grudges to their graves and may not be adverse to exercising them with their dying breath." JOHN MACARTHUR MAGUIRE, EVIDENCE: COMMON SENSE AND COMMON LAW, at 133 (1947). See also United States v. Thevis, 84 F.R.D. 57, 63 (N.D. Ga. 1979) ("More realistically, the dying declaration is admitted, because of compelling need for the statement rather than any inherent trustworthiness.").

82. This would be the same guarantee of reliability as that associated with the excited utterance exception. See Chapter 3, part III(C)(2), above.

83. State v. Shatterfield, 457 S.E.2d 440, 447 (W. Va. 1995).

84. Regarding the testimonial infirmities, see Chapter 1(I), above. "[A]nybody will agree that the victim of a deadly accident or a murderous assault is often not the best observer of what happened." JOHN MACARTHUR MAGUIRE, EVIDENCE: COMMON SENSE AND COMMON LAW, at 133 (1947).

85. See part III(D)(5) of this chapter, below.

86. In North Carolina, "declarant must have died from the cause of circumstances on which he commented." N.C. Gen. Stat. §8C-1, Rule 804(b)(2) (2007), advisory commit-

If declarant has died, the cause of the actual death need not be related to the cause of the anticipated death.[87] If we have a shooting victim who believes he or she is about to die and makes a statement about the circumstances of the shooting, but recovers from the gunshot wound only to be run over and killed while crossing the street, then that declarant's in-court testimony is unavailable for purposes of this exception.[88]

---

tee note. *See, e.g.,* State v. Bodden, 661 S.E.2d 23, 28 (N.C. 2008). There is no such requirement on the face of the rule (federal or North Carolina). This foundational element comes from the legislative history, and it seems to be an odd and, in light of the guarantee of reliability (fear of death at the time the statement was made) unnecessary interpretation.

87. United States v. Tolliver, 61 F.3d 1189, 1204 n.17 (5th Cir. 1995), *vacated on other grounds,* Sterling v. United States, 516 U.S. 1105 (1996).

88. *Tolliver* is instructive. There was a shooting. Some people were killed, and some were shot but survived. Those who survived the shooting included a Mr. Carr, a Mr. White, and a Mr. Elwood. At the hospital, while Carr and White waited to go into surgery, they were interviewed by detectives. On trial for many crimes, including murder and assault in connection with these shootings, the defendants offered transcripts of Carr's and White's pre-surgery interviews into evidence. Upon the prosecutor's hearsay objection, the trial court excluded the transcripts. On appeal, the defendants argued, among other things, that the statements should have been admitted under the hearsay exception for statement under belief of impending death.

Regarding Carr's statement, the appellate court noted it was not admissible under this exception because his in-court testimony was available: Carr survived and, in fact, he testified at the trial. *Tolliver,* 61 F.3d at 1204. A foundational element—the unavailability of declarant's testimony—was missing..

Regarding White's statement, he too survived the shooting, but he "died prior to the trial of causes unrelated to the shootings, and [his testimony] was therefore unavailable." *Id.* at 1204 n.17. Though the unavailability part of the Rule 804 foundation was satisfied, the exception for statements under belief of impending death was not used at the trial and the record did not contain the rest of the foundation for the exception. "[W]e ... do not know whether he spoke with belief of impending death." *Id.* at 1204. The point, however, is that the belief-of-impending-death element of the foundation could be present even though the declarant did not die from the wound in question (and, in fact, could have been present even if he had not died at all).

Defendants also argued that the district court acted inconsistently when it accepted the prosecutor's offer of yet a third pre-surgery statement, while rejecting defendants' offers of two pre-surgery statements. The statement received upon prosecutor's offer was one by a defendant by the name of Elwood. "First," states the court of appeals, "Elwood's statement, by definition, is an admission of a party opponent and therefore not hearsay. Fed. R. Evid. 801(d)(2). Second, even if Elwood's statement could be considered hearsay, no objection was ever made to its admission." *Tolliver,* 61 F.3d at 1204.

Regarding the various kinds of unavailability, *see* part I of this chapter, above.

If anything makes these statements reliable, it is the belief that death is imminent, not actual death itself. Whether the declarant actually dies or not is irrelevant, except for whatever impact it may have on the judge's decision regarding whether the declarant believed death was imminent.

This, by the way, is why this exception is properly called the "statement under belief of impending death" exception, not the "dying declaration" exception. Use Note—Do not call this the "dying declaration" exception, not even in your own mind. It can lead to this kind of erroneous thinking: "Well, dying-declaration doesn't apply because he's not dead."

2. The Imminence of Expected Death

It is not enough that the declarant believed the condition was terminal and, in the end, would lead to death. The declarant must have believed that death was near at hand. The cases tend to state that the declarant must believe death is imminent and inevitable.[89] The Alaska Supreme Court seems to have a more

---

89. "There must be 'a settled hopeless expectation' that death is near at hand, and what is said must have been spoken in the hush of its impending presence." Shepard v. United States, 290 U.S. 96, 100 (1933) (citation omitted). "The [declarant] must have spoken with the consciousness of a swift and certain doom." *Id. Accord* United States v. Lawrence, 349 F.3d 109, 117 (3d Cir. 2003) (exception inapplicable; declarant's "medical treatment was rigorous and undertaken with the expectation that he would survive[, he] was never told by medical staff or police that he was going to die[,] doctors had been discussing the care he would need following his release from the hospital[, and he] appeared on the way to recovery"); Sternhagen v. Dow Co., 108 F.Supp.2d 1113, 1118 (D. Mont. 1999) (exception inapplicable; declarant stated he expected to live another three to six months, continued to work in a limited way, and stated his plans to attempt more work if his condition improved, which statements do not "support a belief in 'imminent' death"; declarant took a trip to a religious shrine to "receive healing," which does not indicate "a 'settled hopeless expectation' that death was near at hand"); State v. Bodden, 661 S.E.2d 23, 28 (N.C. 2008) (responding to defendant's argument that at the time of his 911 call the declarant did not believe he was in danger of imminent death, the court stated that, "about three and a half minutes after the victim called 911, he told his mother that he was going to die. [He] had been shot five times and was bleeding. He was taken to the hospital, received medical treatment in the emergency room, and later died the same day. The[se] circumstances ... support the requirements for admission of a dying declaration."); Collins v. State, 294 P. 625, 627 (Ariz. 1930) ("It is indispensable that the declarant, at the time the declaration is made, be laboring under the influence of impending death. It is not enough that he be fatally ill or that dissolution be imminent, if he be not conscious thereof."); McLean v. State, 16 Ala. 672 (1849) ("The law certainly requires that to render dying declarations admissible, they must be made under a sense of impending death; for it is this sense of his danger that gives to the declaration a sanction considered equivalent to an oath.").

enlightened view, one fully supportable under the rule. "[T]o require that the declarant have abandoned all hope of recovery is overly demanding. In light of modern medical science it is rare indeed that all hope of recovery is abandoned, yet a victim may be aware of the probability that his death is impending...."[90] All the rule requires is enough awareness of a great enough probability to "give adequate assurance of the trustworthiness."[91]

3. Evidence of a Belief in the Imminence of Death

The following may be evidence of whether or not declarants believe their death is imminent:

(a) The declarant's direct statements on the subject—positive or negative.[92]

(b) The declarant's indirect statements on the subject.[93]

(c) The nature of the illness or the wound.[94]

---

90. Johnson v. State, 579 P.2d 20, 25 (Alaska 1978) (footnote omitted).

91. *Id. But see* State v. St. Clair, 282 P.2d 323, 325 (Utah 1955) ("The guarantee of trustworthiness [is] in the idea that the approach of death induces a state of mind in the declarant free from any worldly motives to falsify and a fear of the consequences of deception.... The true test should be whether the declarant at the time of the declaration so fully expected to die from an existing affliction that he had in fact abandoned all hope of recovery.") (footnote omitted).

92. State v. Scholl, 661 A.2d 55, 59 (R.I. 1995) ("First, the declarant's state of mind can be directly proved by his or her express language."); Commonwealth v. Key, 407 N.E.2d 327, 332 (Mass. 1980) (when a police officer told the declarant he was dying, he replied "That's what I thought."); Commonwealth v. Smith, 314 A.2d 224, 226 (Pa. 1973) (deceased expressed repeated concern about amount of blood he had lost, said he had been severely butchered, and told police he did not think he would make it); Hall v. Commonwealth, 403 S.E.2d 362, 366 (Va. Ct. App. 1991) (shot on Christmas Eve, declarant "told his wife he would not see Christmas and that she ... would have to carry on without him"); Hayes v. Texas, 740 S.W.2d 887, 889 (Tex. App. 1987) (relevant that out-of-court declarant "stated several times that he thought he was going to die and was afraid of dying").

Even here, however, where a declarant makes optimistic statements "a person who knows he is about to die will characteristically respond so as 'to comfort the people around him' and to spare their sensibilities." *Key*, 407 N.E.2d at 332. Expressions sounding of hope, then, under the right circumstances, might actually be consistent with hopelessness.

93. In Connor v. State, 171 A.2d 699, 703 (Md. 1961), the out-of-court declarant had been run over by a car. The fact that "she had called for a priest before making her declaration" was evidence that she believed in the imminence of her own death. The out-of-court declarant also made an "anguished entreaty that someone take care of the baby." *Id.* *Accord* State v. St. Clair, 282 P.2d 323, 325 (Utah 1955) (take care of your brother); *Hall*, 403 S.E.2d at 366 (though declarant "was not a religious person [he] asked to speak with a minister and told the minister that he wished to be saved").

94. *E.g.*, Mattox v. United States, 146 U.S. 140, 151 (1892); State v. Ferguson, 581

(d) The direction declarant's condition was taking. Was the declarant's condition improving at the time of the statement, or worsening?[95]

(e) The kind of weapon that inflicted a wound. Small caliber derringer fired from some distance, versus shotgun from close-range.[96]

(f) Statements others have made to the out-of-court declarant about his condition, including, of course, statements by medical personnel.[97]

(g) Declarant's knowledge of the injuries of others involved in the same incident.[98]

(h) Opinion evidence as to the declarant's feeling, attitude, or belief, perhaps through the testimony of an attending physician.[99]

(i) The activity of those around the declarant. That is, not just their statements, but their body language. For example, if an attending physician is engaging in life saving measures and the declarant is sufficiently knowledgeable to appreciate that the steps being taken are a sign of the extreme gravity of his or her condition.[100]

N.W.2d 824, 832 (Minn. 1998) (shot in the stomach, bleeding profusely, fading in and out of consciousness, died within hours of making the statement); Wells v. Commonwealth, 892 S.W.2d 299, 302 (Ky. 1995) (the statements "were made within minutes of the stabbing and while the knife was still imbedded in [declarant's] back"); People v. Arnett, 214 N.W. 231, 234 (Mich. 1927) ("Some wounds certify death.").

95. People v. Nieves, 492 N.E.2d 109, 114 (N.Y. Ct. App. 1986) (insufficient evidence of belief of impending death; "when [declarant] spoke her condition was improving, or at least stabilizing"); People v. Parney, 296 N.W.2d 568, 574 (Mich. Ct. App. 1979) (declarant, in the hospital for a shotgun wound to the neck, had said she would never go home from the hospital; by the time she made the declaration, however, her condition was improving, she asked about being taken outside in a wheelchair, and she asked about suing defendant because she would never be able to work again; subsequently, while still in the hospital, she choked to death on a piece of food).

96. Smith, 314 A.2d at 226 (must consider weapon that wounded out-of-court declarant, here, large-bladed knife).

97. Scholl, 661 A.2d at 60 ("A dying declarant's state of mind may also be inferred when the declarant hears statements regarding his or her medical condition."); Key, 407 N.E.2d at 332 (police officer, doctor, and nurse each told out-of-court declarant of his imminent death).

98. Key, 407 N.E.2d at 332 (the declarant "could see the injuries of ... the other victim, who lay five feet away from him in the emergency room," that similar medical procedures were being performed on each of them, and, eventually, that the other victim died).

99. United States v. Mobley, 421 F.2d 345, 347–48 (5th Cir. 1970); Key, 497 N.E.2d at 332 (opinion evidence from witness who has observed declarant's condition and attitude is valuable aid).

100. Smith, 314 A.2d at 226 ("The deceased was a physician and could appreciate the gravity of the procedures resorted to by the attending physicians.").

(j) The receipt of a sacrament of impending death, such as The Last Rites, or perhaps the waiving off of such a sacrament.

All this foundational element requires is enough evidence to convince the judge that the declarant did believe that he or she was about to die.[101]

4. The Statement Must Relate to the Cause or Circumstances of the Anticipated Death

Not every statement made under belief of impending death is admissible under this exception. The statement must relate to the cause or circumstances of the anticipated impending death.[102] Only the parts of the statement that relate to the cause or circumstances of the impending death are admissible under this exception. If there is more to the statement than the part relating to impending death, then rest of the statement will have to fit under another exception or be redacted out.[103]

---

101. *See additionally, e.g.*, State v. Shatterfield, 457 S.E.2d 440, 450 (W. Va. 1995) ("Is Moore's suicide note a dying declaration? Clearly, there was evidence that Moore wrote the suicide note with the belief that he was facing imminent death because he killed himself soon after writing the note.").

102. "A statement describing ... matters previously inhaled, injected, or ingested fits the exception if the speaker is explaining the predicament that brought him to what seems to be death's door." CHRISTOPHER B. MUELLER & LAIRD C. KIRKPATRICK, EVIDENCE PRACTICE UNDER THE RULES §8.71, at 1317 (2d ed. 1999). An example of a statement that does relate to the cause and circumstances of the impending death: Bucky Moore was a witness for the prosecution in a first-degree murder trial. Defense counsel aggressively cross-examined Moore, suggesting that Moore was in fact the real killer. Thereafter, Moore committed suicide. He left the following suicide note: "'I didn't kill Harper and I won't do time for something that I didn't do. I'm sorry but I just can't take the presure [sic] of going through a trial. Good-by [sic]. [Signed] Bucky Moore. Tell Teresa [Bucky's girlfriend] I loved he [sic] more than any thing in the world.'" State v. Satterfield, 457 S.E.2d 440, 447 (W. Va. 1995). The State offered the note into evidence and the trial judge let it in pursuant to the hearsay exception for statements under belief of impending death. "[T]he suicide note explained why Moore killed himself thereby explaining the cause or circumstances of his death." *Id.* at 513.

An example of a statement that does not relate to the cause or circumstances of the impending death: The deceased made deathbed statements expressing his love and affection for his family. These statements were offered to the issue of damages and under the belief-of-impending-death exception. Because they do not relate to the cause or circumstances of his death, they were inadmissible. Ferguson v. Williams, 399 S.E.2d 389, 395 (N.C. Ct. App. 1991). They were held inadmissible under the exception for statements under belief of impending death. They should, perhaps, have been admissible under the state of mind exception, FED.R.EVID 803(3).

103. Regarding redaction, *see* Chapter 12(I), below.

5. The Competence and Confusion of the Declarant and the Danger of Unfair Prejudice Associated with the Statement

Beware of the following two problems that often arise in regard to a certain kind of statement under belief of impending death. First, sometimes, statements are made by a near-dead victim of a crime to an investigating police officer and the statements consist of a one-word response from the victim, repeated in response to each question. The victim's response to each question is exactly the same and it is either yes or no, or some less-coherent variation of one of the two. Say the victim is near the edge of consciousness and the officer is asking, and the victim answering, as follows:

"Do you realize you are dying?"

"Ah huh."

"Do you know who did this to you?"

"Ah huh."

"Was it Steve?"

"Ah huh."

"Did your ex-boyfriend do this?"

"Ah huh."

"Was it Steve?"

"Ah huh."

"It was dark. Are you sure you actually saw him and recognized him?"

"Ah huh."

Then the declarant lapses into a coma, and dies.[104]

The second common problem is this: The guarantee of reliability for this exception addresses deliberate fabrication. It does not address faulty memory or faulty perception.[105] Take, for example, *Soles v. State*,[106] where two men were in a car, driving away from the scene of the crime. As they drove away, a "shot was fired from a point down the road to their rear and Clifford Long was

---

104. The interrogation above is based on the facts in State v. Jacob, 494 N.W.2d 109 (Neb. 1993). An out-of-court statement made in response to leading questions can fit under this exception. Leading questions, by themselves, do not disable this exception. *See, e.g.,* Connor v. State, 171 A.2d 699, 705 (Md. 1961).

105. *See* Chapter 1(I).

106. 119 So. 791 (Fla. 1929).

wounded in the back of the head. He died as a result of that wound." Carl Soles was charged with murder and convicted of manslaughter. Long's father testified that his son had told him "Carl Soles shot me."[107] In the face of a hearsay objection, the court allowed the father's testimony as a statement under belief of impending death.

Problems such as these two, however, are not hearsay problems as much as they are competency and Rule 403 problems. At some point, situations like these present defense counsel with two good arguments.

(1) *Competency*: In both examples there is insufficient showing that the out-of-court declarant is competent.[108] Counsel can get these statements around the hearsay rule, but how can counsel show that this out-of-court declarant was competent, *i.e.*, had the personal knowledge that Rule 602 requires of a witness?[109] In the first situation—the interrogation—competency problems may be able to be taken care of at the investigative stage. If the declarant is competent, the officer could just ask a question or two that shows the declarant is making distinctions and judgments. The officer could ask a question or two that get a different answer. In the above example, ask at least one question that gets a negative answer. It is up to the investigating officer to show that the declarant is not just flying away on automatic pilot.[110] In the second situation—*Soles v.*

107. Soles v. State, 119 So. 791, 791 (Fla. 1929).

108. The out-of-court declarant is, in effect, a witness. FED.R.EVID. 806 advisory committee's note. As such, the out-of-court declarant must be shown to be competent. FED.R.EVID. 602. This is discussed further in Chapter 13, below.

109. *See also* FED.R.EVID. 806 advisory committee's note, which begins: "The declarant of a hearsay statement which is admitted into evidence is in effect a witness." People v. Garcia, 826 P.2d 1259, 1264 (Colo. 1992) ("Before a court may admit a hearsay statement under the excited utterance exception, there must be enough direct or circumstantial evidence to allow the jury to infer that the declarant had an opportunity to observe the event that is the subject of the declarant's statement.").

110. As was done here:

Officer Barksdale questioned Hopper [the dying victim of a shooting] at approximately 4:30 a.m. on August 3, 1989. Barksdale asked if Hopper knew what had happened to her, if she knew she had been shot, and if she knew who shot her. Hopper responded by nodding her head affirmatively. Barksdale then proceeded to ask Hopper if it was Jacob who shot her, to which she nodded her head yes. Hopper was asked if there was anyone else with Jacob, to which she moved her head back and forth indicating no. Hopper responded affirmatively when asked whether she was shot with a gun, whether she crawled under the bed after Jacob shot her, and whether there were a lot of shots fired. Barksdale asked Hopper if she called on the telephone; Hopper paused for a moment and shrugged her shoulders.... Barksdale testified that Hopper appeared alert and conscious dur-

State—the real problem wasn't the hearsay rule but the question of whether (and how) Clifford Long knew who shot him in the back of the head, from back down the road. The circumstantial evidence suggests that the deceased was not looking and did not see.[111]

(2) *Rule 403*: The probative value of the declaration is substantially outweighed by the danger of unfair prejudice. The less coherent the witness, the less probative the statement, and the more subject to the influence of the investigating officer, the less probative the statement. In the example of the dying woman who answered "Ah huh" to each of the police officer's questions, the prejudice stems from the fact that these are final murmurs from the lips of the dying woman. The unfairness comes from both the high emotional content inherent in this context (and suggesting a verdict on an emotional basis[112]) and, circling back to competency, the danger that we really do not know what she is saying or whether she knows what she is saying. As the out-of-court statement climbs up the speculation ladder, it climbs down the probative value ladder. At some point the probative value of the evidence is so low that it is substantially outweighed by the danger of unfair prejudice and Rule 403 keeps it out.

The victims statements described above do fit under the exception for statement under belief of impending death because all of the foundational elements are present. There comes a point, however, where both the declarant's condition and the evidence regarding the declarant's personal knowledge of the facts

---

ing his questioning. In the view of the anesthesiologist, Hopper was cognizant at 4:35 a.m. on August 3, the medications given to Hopper do not affect cognition, and the anesthetic administered to her does not affect memory. The anesthesiologist also opined that he has found that patients given morphine are often more cooperative and better able to understand questioning once the pain is relieved. *Jacob*, 494 N.W.2d at 116. This case presents the bare minimum amount of evidence that it is the victim's statement being admitted here and not just the investigating officer essentially talking to himself. There was one question answered in the negative and one with a shrug. As for the rest, all of the facts were in the questions and each of the answers was exactly the same. A few more test questions would have been reassuring.

111. There was some other evidence that Soles might have been the shooter, but, in so far as the appellate court's opinion reveals, not much. There is no evidence that the deceased knew who shot him except that he said it was Soles. But the point of Rule 602 is that declarants must be shown to have personal knowledge of the facts to which they testify. Saying a thing does not necessarily establish personal knowledge of that thing. Were it otherwise, there would be no need for a personal knowledge requirement as all witnesses would automatically have personal knowledge of everything in their testimony.

112. *See* Fed.R.Evid. 403 advisory committee's note.

in his statement ("Ah huh." "Carl Soles shot me.") raises other evidentiary problems. These problems may not be glossed over simply by saying "It's not inadmissible hearsay."

As noted, there is a theoretical guarantee against deliberate fabrication. There is, however, no categorical guarantee regarding faulty memory and faulty perception. Since this hearsay exception does not take these two factors into account, they must be dealt with in some other way—perhaps most obviously the rules regarding competency of witnesses, the witnesses in question being out-of-court declarants, and with Rule 403.

6. The Confrontation Clause

Under the Confrontation Clause, the general rule is that testimonial hearsay statements offered against the accused in a criminal case are inadmissible unless the accused has, or has had, an opportunity to cross-examine the declarant. The one exception to this general rule may be testimonial statements made under belief of impending death. In *Crawford v. Washington*, the Supreme Court stated that while it did not need to decide the question in that case, the Confrontation Clause may "incorporate[] an exception for testimonial dying declarations."[113]

IV. Statements Against Interest: Rule 804(b)(3)

A. Text of the Rule

(b) Hearsay exception. The following are not excluded by the hearsay rule if the declarant is unavailable as a witness:

****

(3) Statement against interest. A statement which was at the time of its making so far contrary to the declarant's pecuniary or proprietary interest, or so far tended to subject the declarant to civil or criminal liability, or to render invalid a claim by the declarant against

---

113. Crawford v. Washington, 541 U.S. 36, 56 (2004). As explained in Chapter 14, below, the Confrontation Clause meant to constitutionalize the pre-ratification common law of confrontation, which included an exception for statements under belief of impending death. *See* Chapter 14.

another, that a reasonable person in the declarant's position would not have made the statement unless believing it to be true. A statement tending to expose the declarant to criminal liability and offered to exculpate the accused is not admissible unless corroborating circumstances clearly indicate the trustworthiness of the statement.

B. Foundational Elements

1. As with all Rule 804 exceptions, the out-of-court declarant's in-court testimony must be unavailable.[114]

2. At the time the out-of-court statement was made, it must have been sufficiently against the declarant's interest "that a reasonable person in the declarant's position would not have made the statement unless believing it to be true."

3. At the time the out-of court statement was made, the declarant must have known it was against her interest.

4. In a criminal trial, if the defense offers an out-of-court statement that tends to exonerate the defendant and lay the guilt on the out-of-court declarant, there must be "corroborating circumstances clearly indicat[ing] the trustworthiness of the statement."[115]

C. Need + Reliability = 1

1. Need

This is a Rule 804 exception so the declarant's in-court testimony must be unavailable. Thus, without this exception or the coincidence of another, we will lose what this declarant has to add to the case.

2. Reliability

The theory behind the reliability of statements against interest is this: We do not make statements against our interest unless we have assured ourselves both that we know of what we speak and that we know it to be true. If the declar-

---

114. *See* part I of this chapter, above.
115. Fed.R.Evid. 804(b)(3). Why this is so is discussed below at part IV(D)(4) of this chapter.

ant has enough confidence in the facts asserted to make this statement against his or her interest, then it is reliable enough to get around the hearsay rule.[116]

D. Use Note

1. Timing—"Against Interest" and "Declarant's Knowledge" Are Judged as of the Time the Statement was Made

The out-of-court declarant's interest and knowledge are judged as of the time the out-of-court statement was made, not as of the time of trial (or any other time). The exception is premised on the notion that people do not say things that are against their interest—that will cost them money, property, or time in jail—unless they are convinced that what they are saying is true. It follows that at the time she made the statement the out-of-court declarant must have known that the statement was against her interest.[117]

2. The Extent to Which the Statement Must Be Against the Declarant's Interest

Declarant's interests are defined by the three Ps—pecuniary, proprietary, and penal. The statement must have been against the declarant's pecuniary interest (*i.e.*, it could cost declarant money), proprietary interest (*i.e.*, it could cause declarant to lose property), or penal interest (*i.e.*, it could be used to convict declarant of a crime). That is, it must be the kind of statement that would subject the declarant to civil or criminal liability.

---

116. "[R]easonable people, even reasonable people who are not especially honest, tend not to make self-inculpatory statements unless they believe them to be true." Williamson v. United States, 512 U.S. 594, 599 (1994). "Most people would not say that they knocked over a bank, spit on a policeman, or shoved their mother if it wasn't true." United States v. Watson, 525 F.3d 583, 586 (7th Cir. 2008).

117. Fed.R.Evid. 804(b)(3) ("A statement which was *at the time of its making ...*") (emphasis added). *Accord, e.g.*, United States v. Andreas, 216 F.3d 645, 662 (7th Cir. 2000); United States v. Innamorati, 996 F.2d 456, 475 (1st Cir. 1993); United States v. One Star, 979 F.2d 1319, 1323 n.6 (8th Cir. 1992) (holding that appellant's argument that the statement was not against declarant's penal interest because at the time of the trial he was serving consecutive prison sentences for kidnapping and rape might work except that here the crimes for which declarant was convicted had not been committed *at the time he made the statement*); United States v. Richards, 967 F.2d 1189, 1194 (8th Cir. 1992); Bernard S. Jefferson, *Declarations Against Interest: An Exception to the Hearsay Rule*, 58 Harv. L. Rev. 1, 17 (1944) ("It is not the fact that the declaration is against interest but the awareness of that fact by the declarant which gives the statement significance.").

Whether the statement is against interest is judged by the reasonable person standard. The statement must be sufficiently against the out-of-court declarant's interest "that *a reasonable person* in the declarant's position would not have made the statement unless"[118] he or she believed it was true.[119]

That the declarant made the statement to a confidante—to a person he does not believe will share the information in any way that will lead to declarant's

---

118. FED.R.EVID. 804(b)(3).

119. *Id.* United States v. Westry, 524 F.3d. 1198, 1214 (11th Cir. 2008) presents an interesting and common issue. In *Westry*, the speaker and the listener had such a close relationship that "it would appear that [the speaker] would not have believed his statements would subject him to criminal liability." *Id.* at 1214. The court stated that the test is whether the statement "'so far tend[s] to subject the declarant to criminal liability that a reasonable man in his position would not have made the statement unless he believed it to be true.'" *Id.* The question is whether "a reasonable man would falsely admit to [this] serious crime, knowing there was a chance, albeit slight, that the admission could be used to subject him to severe penalties." *Id.* at 1215. *Accord, e.g., Williamson,* 512 U.S. at 604 (parts of the statement were clearly against declarant's interest and other parts were not (and may have been in his interest in a lighter sentence); a reasonable person in his position would not have said some of these things without knowing them true, but would have said others; the lower courts failed to make the required fact-based inquiry into which parts of the statement fit under the exception and which do not); United States v. Watson, 525 F.3d 583, 587 (7th Cir. 2008) ("[A] statement that implicates the declarant in a larger conspiracy tends to subject the declarant to criminal liability and thus is a statement against interest ... because a member of a conspiracy is liable for any co-conspirator's act committed in furtherance of the conspiracy."); United States v. Loggins, 486 F.3d 977, 981 (7th Cir. 2007) (co-defendant's lawyer's statement at sentencing hearing that tended to exonerate defendant was not a statement against the lawyer's interest; it "did not implicate him nor could it subject him to criminal liability"); United States v. Shryock, 342 F.3d 948, 981 (9th Cir. 2003) ("[T]he statement at issue must be 'examined in context, to see whether as a matter of common sense the portion at issue was against interest and would not have been made by a reasonable person unless he believed it to be true.'" (citation omitted)); United States v. Fowlie, 24 F.3d 1059, 1068 (9th Cir. 1994) (regarding a federal crime, a reasonable person would not believe a statement to be against his interest if he did not intend ever to be present in the United States again and knew he was not subject to extradition); United States v. Lang, 589 F.2d 92, 97 (2d Cir. 1978) ("[I]n United States v. Barrett, 539 F.2d 244, 249–51 (1st Cir. 1976), the court found that the reliability of an inculpatory hearsay statement made to an acquaintance during a card game was not impugned because the declarant 'might not so readily have perceived the disserving character of what was said nor have expected his words to be repeated to the police.'"); United States v. Satterfield, 572 F.2d 687, 691 n.1 (9th Cir. 1978) ("a reasonable person in [declarant's] position, not [declarant] himself"); United States v. Bagley, 537 U.S. 162, 165 (5th Cir. 1976) ("The fact that the statement was made to a friend and cellmate has no relevance to the determination whether the statement was against the declarant's penal interest." It is enough if there is "a chance, even if slight, that this admission could be used" against the speaker's penal interest.).

prosecution—is not determinative. In fact, as a general rule it is not even relevant. The distinction here is between believing that the statement *will be* used against you and knowing that it *could be* used against you. The latter—knowing it is possible—is the key. All that matters is that the statement would have probative value adverse to declarant's pecuniary, proprietary, or penal interest in litigation where the declarant is a party.[120]

Furthermore, the against-interest nature of the statement need not be apparent from text alone. Context can be important.[121]

All of that said, there are plenty of cases that, at first glance, seem to suggest that the test is not what the reasonable person would have known about the statement's potential to subject him or her to liability, but what the actual declarant would have known. There are, for example, cases that hold that a statement by a declarant who, by reason of a mental disability, did not understand that a statement could be used against him, does not fit under this exception.[122]

---

120. United States v. Alverez, 584 F.2d 694, 699–700 (5th Cir. 1978); United States v. Thomas, 571 F.2d 285, 288 (5th Cir. 1978); United States v. Fujii, 152 F.Supp.2d 942, 945 (N.D. Ill. 2000) (a statement is against interest "if it would be probative in a trial against the declarant").

121. *Williamson*, 512 U.S. at 603–04 ("[T]his question can only be answered in light of all the surrounding circumstances. [T]his can be a fact-intensive inquiry ..."); *Watson*, 525 F.3d at 587 ("[W]e must be mindful of the context in which a statement is made."); *Alvarez*, 584 F.2d at 699 (the exception is not limited to "direct confessions of guilt"; in context, these statements tended to subject the declarant to criminal liability because they indicate an insider's knowledge of the crime); United States v. Barone, 114 F.3d 1284, 1297 (1st Cir. 1997) ("These statements ... inculpate [declarant] in criminal acts and conspiracies with others to commit criminal acts. Moreover, to the extent that the statements implicate Limoli in the Patriarca Family and its activities, they demonstrate 'an insider's knowledge' of a criminal enterprise and its criminal activities, which is sufficiently against Limoli's penal interest to come within the exception." (citations omitted)); United States v. Barrett, 539 F.2d 244, 250–53 (1st Cir. 1976) (the context in which the statements were made makes them less clearly disserving, but not so much so as to take them out from under this exception; in context, declarant's statements indicate an insider's knowledge of the crime); United States v. Cole, 488 F.Supp.2d 792, 811 (N.D. Iowa 2007) (Offering party "asserts that the hearsay statement is corroborated by three hearers ... [U]ntil and unless the court is better informed of the circumstances in which each of the witnesses heard the hearsay confession and, indeed, better informed about those witnesses, it cannot assess the trustworthiness of the alleged hearsay confession to determine its admissibility."); State v. Matusky, 682 A.2d 694, 479–80 (Md. 1996) (in addition to all relevant information regarding the declarant, the court must carefully consider all relevant circumstances surrounding the making of the statement).

122. Dawn VV. v. State, 850 N.Y.S.2d 246, 248 (2008) (While this is a "reasonable person standard," the declarant must have the mental capacity to be "aware or ... understand that the statement was harmful to him.").

There are various ways of reconciling this apparent deviation from the general rule. The first is that the rule requires "that a reasonable person in the declarant's position." It can be argued that the declaration by a person with a mental disability must be judged against reasonable persons with such a disability. The second way to handle this—and perhaps the one most suited to the declarant with the mental disability—is to recognize that the problem is not a hearsay problem at all. The problem is competence. The declarant of an out-of-court statement is a witness. The rules are quite clear on that.[123] If an out-of-court declarant was not competent, his or her out-of-court statement is inadmissible.

A third way to handle this—one that loops back a bit to the first way—is to recognize that the guarantee of reliability is based on the declarant's belief when the statement was made that the statement was against his or her interest.

> However, because of the unavailability of the declarant and other problems of proof, the party urging this exception is not required to prove the actual state of mind of the declarant but must prove sufficient surrounding facts from which the trial judge may inferentially determine what the state of mind of a reasonable person would have been under the same or similar circumstances.[124]

There is, in effect, a presumption that the declarant would have behaved as a reasonable person. That presumption applies unless and until the opponent of the evidence rebuts it. The opponent of the evidence must show that the declarant *did not know* that the statement *could* be used against the declarant's interest. It is not enough to show that the declarant *did not believe* that the statement *would* be sued against his or her interest.

3. A Statement Partly Against the Declarant's Interest and Partly in the Declarant's Interest

The exception for statements against interest only applies to those parts of a narrative which actually were against the interest of the declarant. The "statement" in "statement against interest" does not refer to the entire narrative but

---

123. Fed.R.Evid. 806 advisory committee's note.

124. *Matusky*, 682 A.2d at 700 n.6 (quoting State v. Standifur, 526 A.2d 955, 962 (Md. 1987) (a reasonable person in the declarant's circumstances, and not a hypothetical person of reasonable intelligence or sobriety, *Standifur*, 526 A.2d at 959–60; the judge may have to determine whether a reasonable person under the influence of drugs would have understood the statement was disserving)).

to the individual parts of the narrative and only those individual parts that are against interest fit under this exception. Even if the narrative is predominately self-incriminating, this exception does not apply to self-exculpatory parts of the narrative.[125] For purposes of this exception, a mixed narrative must be redacted.[126] Only the self-incriminating parts will fit under this exception.

There may be other ways around the hearsay rule for the non-self-incriminating parts of the narrative. First of all, reconsider whether or not the statement was against interest when made. Take a new and harder look at the context of the statement.[127] Second, a statement that does not fit under the statement

---

125. *Williamson*, 512 U.S. at 598–602.

United States v. Wexler, 522 F.3d 194, 203 (2d Cir. 2008) draws the distinction between statements that incriminate both the declarant and another in a common criminal endeavor, on the one hand, as opposed to statements that implicate the declarant in a criminal endeavor and the other in a separate criminal endeavor, one in which the declarant was not involved, on the other hand. In the former case the entire statement is self-inculpatory and covered by the exception; if the rest of the foundation is laid, the entire statement is admissible hearsay. In the latter case, the non self-inculpatory parts of the statement must be redacted, they do not fit under the exception and, unless there is another exception, they are inadmissible hearsay. (The rest of the statement is admissible hearsay. It may no longer be relevant in the trial of the other person, but the rest of the statement is not barred by the hearsay rule.) *Wexler* characterizes *Williamson, supra*, as involving the latter situation, where the non self-inculpatory parts of the statement are not covered by this statement, and characterizes itself as the former, where the entire statement is covered by the exception. In addition, Wexler finds that the entire statement is not hearsay in the first place: It is a nonhearsay coconspirator admission. *See* Chapter 2(III)(F), above.

State v. Dotson, 254 S.W.3d 378, 394 (Tenn. 2008) is an interesting case. "[P]ractically caught red-handed" defendant confessed to the crime and then claimed he was unarmed, "a fact that might lessen his culpability." The court held that the entire statement was predominately self-serving, confession and all.

Watson, 525 F.3d at 586, states that the exception does not apply to the "neutral" parts of a statement, just the self-inculpatory parts.

The problem of the mixed statement, part covered by an exception and part not, is discussed generally in Chapter 11, below.

126. Regarding redaction, *see* Chapter 12(I), below.

127. *Compare* United States v. Tocco, 200 F.3d 401, 415 (6th Cir. 2000) (declarant made statements to his son implicating others in a conspiracy; the defendant argued that the statements were not adverse to the declarant's own penal interest because they were about others; in context, the declarant "linked himself to the others in the conspiracy, and were therefore against his own penal interest.") *and* Barrett, 539 F.2d at 252 (a statement exculpating another and inculpating someone else yet again was against the declarant's interest because it "strengthened the impression that he had an insider's knowledge of the crimes") *with* United States v. Costa, 31 F.3d 1073, 1079 (11th Cir. 1994) (during a custodial interrogation, declarant was told that he was facing life in prison and that if he provided sub-

against interest exception may not be hearsay at all. It may be nonhearsay admissions by a coconspirator, for example. Third, the statement may be admissible under any of the other exceptions, including the residual exception.[128] The non-self-incriminating parts may be admissible, it is just that they do not qualify for this particular exception to the hearsay rule.

Sometimes the same statement within a narrative will have aspects that are against declarant's interest and aspects that are in declarant's interest. Perhaps, for example, a declarant was involved in a crime and was double-crossed by others involved. If that declarant makes a statement implicating the others involved, it might be against his or her penal interest because it shows insider knowledge of the crime. At the same time, the statement might be in the declarant's interest in revenge. Sometimes declarants confess to one crime as a way of absolving themselves of another, more serious crime. In this situation, the trial court will have to make a determination as to whether this in- and against-interest statement within the narrative was predominately in the declarant's interest or against it.[129] The guarantee of trustworthiness is that persons do not make statements against their penal interest unless they believe them to be true. If the predominate motivation for the statement was revenge or any

---

stantial assistance the United States Attorney would help him; in response, he implicated the defendants; for this, and other reasons, a reasonable person in declarant's position might well have been motivated to misrepresent the role of others in the crime and viewed the statement implicating others to be in his interest, not against it) *and* Stephens, Inc. v. Geldermann, Inc., 962 F.2d 808, 812 (8th Cir. 1992) (while negotiating a settlement of a claim resulting from his fraudulent acts, the declarant made statements implicating the another man as his coconspirator; because he could have been trying to improve his position in the negotiation by shifting attention to another, the statements implicating the other man were not against the declarant's interest).

128. *Williamson*, 512 U.S. at 604 n.*.

129. *E.g.*, *Watson*, 525 F.3d at 588 (declarant was indicating that a problem within the conspiracy was the fault of a different conspirator; a "key situation" where a statement is both against and in a declarant's interest is when "a codefendant is shifting blame away from himself and onto others"); United States v. Chapman, 345 F.3d 630, 632 (8th Cir. 2003) ("'[A] statement admitting guilt and implicating another person, made while in custody, may well be motivated by a desire to curry favor with the authorities and hence fail to qualify as against interest'" so that it cannot be admitted against the third party that it implicates." (citations omitted)); United States v. Evans, 635 F.2d 1124, 1126 (4th Cir. 1980) (a defendant charged with bank robbery proffered a witness to testify that when he saw the defendant with lots of money the defendant told him that he had gotten the money from a bank robber whom he had hidden for a few days; though this was a confession to a crime, it was not really against defendant's interest because "the principal ... function of the statement is to support a defense against a charge of a more serious crime").

other self-serving motivation, then the guarantee of trustworthiness is not there, and the statement should not be admissible under this exception. Given the guarantee of reliability, the predominating interest should control.

4. Corroboration

■ *Exculpating the Accused in a Criminal Case*: When a statement against interest is used to exculpate the accused in a criminal case, there must be "corroborating circumstances" clearly indicating the trustworthiness of the statement.[130]

■ *Why Require Corroboration Here?*: This is a Rule 804 exception, and the out-of-court declarant's testimony must be unavailable. This leads to two possible situations, each of which this part of the rule tries to guard against.

First, it may be too easy for the defendant to put on witnesses who will testify that they heard someone else confess to having committed the crime. The fear is that it is too easy for a defendant to lay the blame on an out-of-court declarant who is not there to defend himself. The defendant can do this by taking the stand or having his friends take the stand to testify that an unavailable out-of-court declarant admitted he committed the crime. Corroboration helps keep the defendant in a criminal case from bringing in a lot of lying witnesses who all say: "I heard [the recently deceased] Mr. Smith say that he committed the crime, not the defendant."

Second, it may be too easy for third persons to make out-of-court statements inculpating themselves and exculpating the defendant and then, at the defendant's trial, make their testimony unavailable by claiming the privilege against self-incrimination. All that's left are the declarants' out-of-court statements against interest.[131] The privilege shields the statements from "the fires of cross-examination."[132] The fear is that the defendant will get a lying friend to make a number of out-of-court statements like the following: "I did it. I am the guilty party." Then, when this friend is called to the stand, he invokes the

---

130. The relevant portion of the rule reads as follows: "A statement tending to expose the declarant to criminal liability and offered to exculpate the accused is not admissible unless corroborating circumstances clearly indicate the trustworthiness of the statement." FED.R.EVID. 804(b)(3). "[T]here is no question but that Congress meant to preclude reception of exculpatory hearsay statements against penal interest unless accompanied by circumstances solidly indicating trustworthiness." *Barrett*, 539 F.2d at 253.

131. United States v. Mackey, 117 F.3d 24, 29 (1st Cir. 1997).

132. United States v. Amerson, 185 F.3d 676, 691 (7th Cir. 1999) (Posner, C.J., dissenting).

privilege against self-incrimination. That makes his testimony unavailable, and, from the lips of those who heard his uncorroborated, uncross-examinable out-of-court statements, they would be admissible as statements against his interest. The corroboration requirement helps keep this from happening.

On the other hand, every hearsay exception applies in situations where the declarant's live testimony is unavailable. (Rule 804 applies only when the testimony is unavailable. Rule 803 applies whether it is available or unavailable.) And yet not every hearsay exception has a corroboration requirement. I think the reason for this difference is that the keepers of the rules feel that the friends and relatives of defendants in criminal cases are, as a class, particularly untrustworthy.[133]

■ *What Is Corroboration?*: There must be some evidence that the out-of-court statement is "trustworthy." First, judges are not being asked to perform the jury's function and decide whether they find the statement to be true. The difference between "truth" and "trustworthiness" is subtle.[134] It is clear, however, that in our daily lives we treat things as trustworthy without knowing if they are true. We trust all kinds of advisors, for example, without having concluded that what they are telling us is "Truth." It is much the same here. For example, if circumstances indicate the out-of-court declarant had a motive either to tell the truth or to misrepresent the facts, the rule does not require that the judge decide whether the statement is in fact true or not true. Rather, the judge decides whether the statement is sufficiently trustworthy to allow the truth-finder to see it.

What the drafters of this rule of evidence were worried about here, what this rules is trying to protect against, is lying in-court witnesses who testify on behalf of their accused friends and testify to exculpating statements made by unavailable out-of-court declarants. We don't trust criminal defendants and we don't trust their friends. Judges perform a kind of "screener" function. As

---

133. This also explains why one of the factors to consider in determining whether corroborating circumstances are present is this: "the relationship between the declarant and the accused." American Auto. Accessories, Inc. v. Fishman, 175 F.3d 534, 541 (7th Cir. 1999). *See also* United States v. Jones, 124 F.3d 781, 786 (6th Cir. 1997) ("statements from a declarant attempting to exculpate a defendant with whom the declarant has a close relationship must be closely scrutinized"; here there was a father-son relationship between the defendant and the declarant); United States v. Butler, 71 F.3d 243, 253 (7th Cir. 1995) (one gang member may lie to benefit another); United States v. Bobo, 994 F.2d 524, 528 (8th Cir. 1993) (the trustworthiness of the statement is diminished because the declarant is the brother of the accused).

134. Judge Posner stated it this way: "not necessarily true, but ... sufficiently worthy of belief to have value as evidence despite the impossibility of subjecting the declarant to the fires of cross-examination." *Amerson*, 185 F.3d at 691 (Posner, C.J. dissenting).

a matter of policy, we ask them to screen out the ones whose claims to have heard exculpating out-of-court statements are not backed by anything but their own word. Judges are deciding whether circumstances indicate that the statement sufficiently trustworthy to pass along to the jury.[135]

Second, corroboration of the trustworthiness of the statement does not require, or even ask for, independent evidence of the truth of the facts asserted

---

135. United States v. Jackson, 540 F.3d 578, 589 (7th Cir. 2008) (some factors to consider are declarant's relationship to defendant, whether the statement was voluntary and Mirandized, and "whether there is any evidence the statement was made to curry favor with authorities") (citing cases); United States v. Cole, 525 F.3d 656, 660–61 (8th Cir. 2008) (wife's statement that certain guns were hers was inadmissible; "corroborating circumstances did not clearly indicate the trustworthiness of [her] statements;" the statements exculpated her husband, she had expressed her concern "about protecting others from criminal liability," and, as regards a separate crime, she "demonstrated ... a willingness to subject herself to criminal liability to shield others"); United States v. Ironi, 525 F.3d 683, 687 (8th Cir. 2008) (declarant's contradictory statements, including at his own plea hearing, shows that the statement in question is not trustworthy); *Mackey*, 117 F.3d at 29 (though not unrealistically severe, this requirement "go[es] beyond minimal corroboration."); United States v. Hall, 165 F.3d 1095, 1112 (7th Cir. 1999) (that the statement includes facts known only to the perpetrator can be a corroborating circumstance indicating trustworthiness); *Bobo*, 994 F.2d at 528 (consider any motive to misrepresent, the general character of the declarant, whether others heard the statement, whether the statement was spontaneous, the timing of the statement, and the relationship between the witness and the declarant); United States v. Sarmiento-Perez, 633 F.2d 1092, 1102 (5th Cir. 1981) (corroborating circumstances indicate that the statement is not trustworthy; it was not a "spontaneous declaration made to friends and confederates, but a custodial confession, given under potentially coercive circumstances" including declarant's interest in currying favor with the police and mitigating his culpability by implicating others, "the enmity often generated in a conspiracy gone awry, [and] the desire for revenge, all [of which] might lead an arrestee-declarant to misrepresent or to exaggerate the role of others in the criminal enterprise"; "declarant was allowed to plead guilty to but one of the five counts upon which he was indicted"; this declarant and a reasonable person in his position "might well have viewed the statement ... to be in his interest rather than against it"); Davis v. State, 872 S.W.2d 743, 749 (Tx. Crim. App. 1994) (declarant's opportunity to have committed the crime).

The rule's requirement that the judge consider whether "corroborating circumstances clearly indicate the trustworthiness of the statement" could be taken to mean that the judge is only to consider corroborating evidence and not undermining evidence. If, however, there is a large amount of undermining evidence and a small amount of corroborating evidence, then the corroborating evidence does not "clearly indicate trustworthiness"—whether corroborating evidence clearly indicates trustworthiness can only be determined in light of any undermining evidence. *Davis*, 872 S.W.2d at 748 ("[T]he prevailing view is that evidence corroborating the statement as well as evidence undermining its reliability should be considered."). *See* United States v. Silverstein, 732 F.2d 1338, 1347 (7th Cir. 1984) ("probably" the judge may consider circumstances that undermine trustworthiness).

in the hearsay statement. If the hearsay statement is that the shooter fled the scene in a dark blue SUV, corroboration does not require other independent evidence that the shooter fled in a dark blue SUV.

Third, there are cases that say that the corroboration can come from the out-of-court statement itself. It does not necessarily have to be external to the statement, though it most often is.[136] Given the reasons for the corroboration requirement this makes sense. If the judge is convinced that the out-of-court statement contains details known to the judge but not otherwise known to the testifying witness that would be a corroborating circumstance.

Fourth, circumstances must corroborate the trustworthiness of the specific part of the statement for which the evidence is being offered. It is not enough that some of the statement is corroborated, that is, corroboration of collateral facts is not enough.[137]

■ *What Must Be Corroborated?*: "It is the hearsay statement of the declarant, and not the testimony of the witness on the stand, that must be corroborated. The witness on the stand is under oath and subject to cross-examination, and can be tested for credibility by the usual procedures. Thus, the testimony of the witness at trial is not subject to the corroboration requirement."[138]

■ *Corroboration when the Statement Is Offered in Civil Cases or to* Inculpate *the Accused in a Criminal Case*: The text of the rule requires corroborat-

---

136. That is most often is, see note 142, above. That it need not be, *see United States v. Hall*, in that same footnote.

137. *Mackey*, 117 F.3d at 29 (bank-robbery defendant tried to explain his new-found wealth as gambling winnings and offered a bookie's out-of-court statement regarding defendant's large winnings; there was plenty of corroboration that defendant placed bets with this bookie but no corroboration of large winnings; there was general corroboration but no corroboration of the "specific, 'essential' assertions" for which defendant offered the statement).

138. State v. Hammons, 597 So.2d 990, 997 n.5 (La. 1992). *Accord* United States v. Barone, 114 F.3d 1284, 1300–01 (1st Cir. 1997) (defendant argued that corroboration was missing because the in-court witness was not credible; corroboration is about the trustworthiness of the out-of-court statement, and not about the credibility of the in-court declarant; the latter is a jury question; an important factor that goes into whether the out-of-court statement was self-serving is whether it shifted the blame off of the declarant; "corroborated" is synonymous with "trustworthy"); United States v. Fujii, 152 F.Supp.2d 942, 945 (N.D. Ill. 2000) (the government argued that corroboration was missing because there is evidence contradicting the facts asserted in the statement; "[t]he government misapprehends the nature of the corroboration requirement"; it does not have to do with independent evidence of the truth or untruth of the fact asserted, but with the circumstances in which the statement was made; quoting *Barone*, above).

ing circumstances when (and only when) a statement tending to expose the declarant to criminal liability is offered to *exculpate* the accused.[139] Some courts have extended this requirement and held that corroborating circumstances are also required when a statement tending to expose the declarant to criminal liability is offered to *inculpate* the accused.[140] One of those same courts has also held that the corroborating circumstances are also required when a statement

---

139. FED.R.EVID. 804(b)(3). Where the declarant and another are tried jointly, the statement can inculpate the declarant-defendant and exculpate another defendant. United States v. Cole, 525 F.3d 656, 660–61 (8th Cir. 2008) (husband and wife tried jointly; husband offered wife's out-of-court statement that the guns in question were hers; statement inadmissible because "corroborating circumstances did not clearly indicate the trustworthiness of [her] statements").

140. Am. Auto. Accessories, Inc. v. Fishman, 175 F.3d 534, 541 (7th Cir. 1999) (the United States Supreme Court explicitly left this question unanswered in *Williamson*, 512 U.S. at 603; this rule was the Seventh Circuit's pre-*Williamson* rule; "best to continue to utilize a unitary standard for applying Rule 804(b)(3) to statements offered both to exculpate and inculpate a third party"); *Barone*, 114 F.3d 1300 n.10 ("By its terms, Rule 804(b)(3) requires corroboration only for [exculpatory] statements.... Nevertheless, a number of courts have interpreted [the rule] to require corroboration whether the statement inculpates or exculpates the accused. *See* United States v. Mendoza, 85 F.3d 1347, 1351 (8th Cir. 1996); United States v. Thomas, 62 F.3d 1332, 1337 (11th Cir. 1995); United States v. Casamento, 887 F.2d 1141, 1170 (2d Cir. 1989); United States v. Boyce, 849 F.2d 833, 836 (3d Cir. 1988); United States v. Alvarez, 584 F.2d 694, 701 (5th Cir. 1978). Although this court has not expressly extended the corroboration requirement to statements that inculpate the accused we have applied the rule as if corroboration were required." (some citations omitted)); United States v. Taggart, 944 F.2d 837, 840 (11th Cir. 1991).

The Second Circuit Court of Appeals has explained this as a function of pre-*Crawford* Confrontation Clause jurisprudence. United States v. Wexler, 522 F.3d 194, 202 (2d Cir. 2008) (referencing Crawford v. Washington, 541 U.S. 36 (2004)). Prior to *Crawford*, admission of a statement by an unavailable out-of-court declarant did not violate the Confrontation Clause if the statement came with "particularized guarantees of trustworthiness" or fit under a "firmly rooted" hearsay exception. The cases requiring corroboration for the admission of an inculpatory statement were those courts' way of insuring that there were "particularized guarantees of trustworthiness." This "confusion arose" out of an attempt to solve a constitutional problem with a rule of evidence. *Wexler*, 522 F.3d at 202. After *Crawford*, the Confrontation Clause itself establishes the rules for the introduction of an inculpatory statement by an unavailable declarant; it no longer shoves the problem off onto the rules of evidence; whether there are "particularized guarantees of trustworthiness" no longer is the test; there is no longer any need for courts to add this particular corroboration requirement onto the statutory rule. *Accord* United States v. Nutter, 22 M.J. 727, 731 (U.S. Army Ct. of Mil. Rev. 1986) ("We agree that statements against penal interest which are offered to inculpate an accused must be accompanied by circumstances which indicate the trustworthiness of the statement, but only because the [Confrontation Clause of the United States] Constitution requires indications of the trustworthiness of any state-

against interest is offered in a civil case.[141] Thus, at least one court has said that the corroborating circumstances requirement applies to every statement offered under the statement against interest exception to the hearsay rule.

Given both the text of this exception and the reasons the corroboration requirement is in the exception,[142] these are not necessary interpretations of this exception. These interpretations tie the hands of the trial court by rigidly extending the category of relevant evidence kept from the jury, No matter how sound the evidence seems to the trial court, it cannot be admitted under this exception unless this additional foundational element is satisfied. This narrowing of the exception seems not just unnecessary, but also unwise.[143]

V. A Comparison: Statements by a Party Opponent versus Statements Against Interest

Nonhearsay: Statements by a Party Opponent, Rule 801(d)(2)(A)	Hearsay Exception: Statement against Interest, Rule 804(b)(3)
1 Declarant must be a party, a representative of a party, or a coconspirator of a party.	1 Declarant's identity does not matter. Declarant need not be a party or in any way associated with a party.

---

ment which is offered against an accused without affording him an opportunity to confront the declarant.").

Regarding the Confrontation Clause, see Chapter 14, below.

141. *Am. Auto. Accessories, Inc.*, 175 F.3d at 541.

142. This is discussed just above, in this chapter, in part 4 of this Use Note.

143. "With broad civil discovery available to uncover where declarant's interests lie, there seems no need to go against the plain language of the RULE in this way. It [keeps] out too much relevant evidence ..." John R. Schmertz, 24 FEDERAL RULES OF EVIDENCE NEWS 99–116 (West Group 1999). *See also* Chapter 5(V)(A)(3)(b) discussing FED.R.EVID. 102 ("These rules shall be construed to secure ... elimination of unjustifiable expense and delay, and promotion of growth and development of the law of evidence to the end that the truth may be ascertained and proceedings justly determined.")

In this regard, see Mike's Train House, Inc. v. Lionel, L.L.C., 472 F.3d 398, 412 (6th Cir. 2006) (witness statements and interrogation transcripts from a Korean criminal investigation are admissible under Rule 804(b)(3)).

2 It makes no difference whether or not the declarant's testimony is available. (And it may not be, *e.g.*, when the admission was by an agent.)

3 It is irrelevant whether the statement was against declarant's interest or self-serving. All that matters is that it is a party's statement and is offered against the party who made it.

4 It is irrelevant whether or not declarant believed that the statement was against his or her interest.

5 At common law, qualifying an out-of-court statement as an admission got it around more than just the hearsay rule—the following did not apply to admissions: rules requiring personal knowledge (codified as Rules 602 and 805); rules restricting opinion evidence (codified as Rule 701); the rule requiring original documents (codified as Rule 1007). At least one Circuit continues the rule that, if a statement qualifies as an admission, that overrides any problem otherwise caused by lack of personal knowledge (overrides multiple hearsay problems).[144]

2 This exception to the hearsay rule only applies when the declarant's testimony is unavailable.

3 The statement must have been against declarant's interest at the time it was made. Declarant's interest is judged as of the time the statement was made.

4 Declarant must have known or should have known that the statement was against his interest. "[A] reasonable person in the declarant's position would not have made the statement unless believing it to be true." Rule 804(b)(3).

5 Rules 601, 701, and 1007 do apply to statements against interest. For example, either the statement must concern a matter about which declarant had firsthand knowledge or the double hearsay problem (Rule 805) must be dealt with.

---

144. *See* Chapter 11, below.

6 The application of the rule on admissions is mechanical. If it is a party's own statement offered against him or her, then it is not hearsay. The court is not left with much discretion.

6 The exception for statements against interest gives the court more discretion. Is declarant's testimony unavailable? Was the statement against declarant's interest at the time declarant said it? Did declarant realize it was against his or her interest? Should declarant have realized that it was against his or her interest? Did declarant have firsthand knowledge? Etc. These are all questions the judge must answer.

7 This is a definitional exclusion. The argument for admission is that evidence is not hearsay. If relevant, this evidence is presumed to be admissible. It is admissible until it is shown to be inadmissible. The burden may be on those who would keep the evidence out.[145]

7 This is an exception. The argument for the admission of this statement into evidence is that it is hearsay, but it should be admitted anyway. This evidence is presumed inadmissible, because it is hearsay. The burden is on those who want the evidence admitted.

VI. Statement of Personal or Family History: Rule 804(b)(4)

A. Text of the Rule

(b) Hearsay exception. The following are not excluded by the hearsay rule if the declarant is unavailable as a witness:

****

(4) Statement of personal or family history. (A) A statement concerning the declarant's own birth, adoption, marriage, divorce, legit-

---

145. *See* Chapter 2(I), above.

imacy, relationship by blood, adoption, or marriage, ancestry, or other similar fact of personal or family history, even though declarant had no means of acquiring personal knowledge of the matter stated; or (B) a statement concerning the foregoing matters, and death also, of another person, if the declarant was related to the other by blood, adoption, or marriage or was so intimately associated with the other's family as to be likely to have accurate information concerning the matter declared.

B. Foundational Elements

There are two exceptions here. One covers a declarant's statement about him- or herself. The other covers declarant's statement about someone else.

Declarant's statement about him- or herself:

1. As with all Rule 804 exceptions, the out-of-court declarant's in-court testimony must be unavailable.[146]

2. The out-of-court statement must be a statement of fact.[147]

3. The fact stated must concern the declarant's own personal or family history ("birth, adoption, marriage, divorce, legitimacy, relationship by blood, adoption, or marriage, ancestry, or other similar fact of personal or family history").[148]

Declarant's statement about someone else:

1. Unavailability: The declarant's in-court testimony must be unavailable.

2. The out-of-court statement must be a statement of fact.[149]

3. The fact stated must be a statement of the personal or family history (as above) of either someone to whom the declarant is related by blood, adoption, or marriage, or someone with whose family the declarant is so intimately associated that the declarant is likely to have accurate information concerning the thing declared.

---

146. *See* part I of this chapter, above.

147. It must be "[a] statement concerning the declarant's own birth, adoption, marriage, divorce, legitimacy, relationship by blood, adoption, or marriage, ancestry, or other similar *fact* of personal or family history." FED.R.EVID. 804(b)(4) (emphasis added).

148. And then, though it is not foundational element, the exception applies, by its own terms, "even though declarant had no means of acquiring personal knowledge of the matter stated." FED.R.EVID. 804(b)(4).

149. *See* note 144, just above.

C. Need + Reliability = 1

1. Need

Again, this is a Rule 804 exception, which means that the declarant's in-court testimony must be unavailable. Without this exception or the coincidence of some other, this declarant's evidence will be lost.

2. Reliability

These kinds of facts are so important within the family " 'and so interesting to the family in common that statements about them in the family' " are likely to be truthful and sincere.[150]

D. Use Note

1. The Relationship between This Exception and Rule 803(19), the Exception for Reputation Concerning Personal or Family History

There are two exceptions regarding personal or family history. This one, Rule 804(b)(4), applies to evidence of statements of personal or family history. The other one, Rule 803(19), applies to evidence of reputation concerning personal or family history. The two compliment each other. The former is an exception for statements of fact and, as an 804 exception, it applies only when the in-court testimony of the declarant is unavailable. The latter is an exception for statements of reputation and, as an 803 exception, the availability of the declarant's live testimony is irrelevant.

2. Admission of Evidence beyond the Fact of the Event or Relationship — the Details

This exception — Rule 804(b)(4) — allows statements of *fact* regarding birth, adoption, marriage, divorce or the like.[151] By its own terms it does not include

---

150. United States v. Carvalho, 742 F.2d 146, 151 (4th Cir. 1984) (quoting 11 MOORE'S FEDERAL PRACTICE § 804.07(4) (2d ed. 1982)).

151. By its own terms, the rule applies to statements concerning "birth, adoption, marriage, divorce ... or other similar *fact* of personal or family history." FED.R.EVID. 804(b)(4) (emphasis added). United States v. Pena-Gutierrez, 222 F.3d 1080, 1088 (9th Cir. 2000) (at defendant's prosecution for transporting illegal aliens, the prosecution must prove that the person transported was an illegal alien; the testimony of the person transported is unavailable, but he had told an INS agent that he was an illegal alien; an unavailable "declarant's 'state-

opinion evidence.[152] Further, it does not include statements about motives for entering into such relationships,[153] And it does not include statements about "events, activities, or emotional states occurring within [these] relationships."[154]

3. Competence, Double Hearsay, and This Exception

This exception specifically overrides Rule 602's requirement that witnesses have personal knowledge of the facts about which they testify.[155] So long as the declarant is the right person as defined in the rule, multiple levels of hearsay are not a problem. If a declarant makes an out-of-court statement about his place of birth (and if the other elements of the exception are satisfied), then the statement is admissible even if opposing counsel can show that declarant heard this from his aunt and uncle who raised him, who heard it from his late stepfather, who heard it from his late mother. If the chain of hearsay gets too long, there might be admissibility problems, but they will be relevance or Rule 403 problems, not hearsay problems.[156]

---

ment to immigration officers regarding his citizenship and alienage' " is admissible under this exception (citation omitted)), *but see* United States v. Medina-Gasca, 739 F.2d 1415, 1454 (9th Cir. 1984) (similar statement inadmissible "notwithstanding ... Rule 804(b)(4)"); Moore v. Goode, 375 S.E.2d 549, 562–63 (W. Va. 1988) (appellant's testimony that her grandmother had told her "that Isaac N. Morris was her father" should have been admitted under this exception); In re Egbert Estate, 306 N.W.2d 525, 527 (Mich. 1981) ("On the front of the postcard is a photograph of a young girl, who plaintiff alleges is herself. On the back is the alleged handwriting of the deceased stating: 'Ren Robinson, My Sister, Daughter, Age About 3, /s/ Ernest Egbert'." Properly authenticated, this exhibit was admissible under this exception.).

152. Though the line between fact and opinion is unclear to nonexistent, *see* Chapter 8(II)(B), below, the plain language of this exception requires that it be drawn.

153. United States v. Carvalho, 742 F.2d 146, 151 (4th Cir. 1984).

154. State v. Hester, 470 S.E.2d 25, 28 (N.C. 1996) (defendant claimed that he did not murder the victim, but that her husband did; regarding the proffered statement, only the fact of the marriage would have been admissible under this exception, not the details about the husbands abuse of his wife); People v. Raffaelli, 701 P.2d 881, 884 (Colo. 1985) ("[T]he fact that the baby died, the dates of her death and birth, and parentage are admissible under this hearsay exception. The statements relating to the condition of the baby, or the events and circumstances leading up to the death ... or the circumstances surrounding the birth, were not admissible under [this hearsay exception]."). The line between "facts relating to," on the one hand, and "events, activities, or emotional states occurring within," on the other, may be as difficult to draw as the line between fact and opinion. *See* note 149, above in this chapter, and the cross-reference therein.

155. In addition to the terms of the rule, see, for example, United States v. Hernandez, 105 F.3d 1330, 1332 (9th Cir. 1997) (this exception allows witnesses to testify to where they were born even though they do not—cannot—have personal knowledge of that fact).

156. *See particularly* Chapter 11(V), below. *See also* Chapter 12(II), below.

VII. Forfeiture by Wrongdoing Exception: Rule 804(b)(6)

A. Text of the Rule

(b) Hearsay exceptions. The following are not excluded by the hearsay rule if the declarant is unavailable as a witness:

****

(6) Forfeiture by wrongdoing. A statement offered against a party that has engaged or acquiesced in wrongdoing that was intended to, and did, procure the unavailability of the declarant as a witness.

B. Foundational Elements

1. A party engaged or acquiesced in wrongdoing that was intended to and did procure the unavailability[157] of the declarant as a testifying witness.

2. The out-of-court statement is offered against that party.

C. Need + Reliability = 1

1. Need

The need for this evidence is self-evident. The exception requires that "wrongdoing ... procure[d] the unavailability of the declarant as a witness."[158] The live testimony of the declarant is unavailable.

2. Reliability

The reliability of the evidence is less evident.[159] This hearsay exception does not really fit the mold of exceptions. It is more like a rule of forfeiture or a waiver than an exception. It is not based on reliability, but on the idea that

---

157. *See* part I of this chapter, above.

158. Fed.R.Evid. 804(b)(6). In addition, this is a Rule 804 exception, which, by itself, means that the in-court testimony of the out-of-court declarant must be unavailable.

159. One could argue, I suppose, that the wrongdoer would not have procured the witness' absence unless the witness was telling the truth, for there are less drastic ways of dealing with a lying witness.

one should not be allowed to profit from this kind of wrongdoing. Parties should not receive the benefit of an act as dastardly as, for example, murdering a witness to keep that witness from testifying.

D. Use Note

1. The Motivation behind Procuring Unavailability

The rule requires a finding that the defendant acted with the intention of making the declarant unavailable as a witness. It is enough, however, "that the evil doer was motivated in part by a desire to silence the witness; [this] need not be the actor's sole motivation."[160]

This exception is not dependent on there being a lawsuit on file at the time of the wrongdoing. To prevent a person from testifying a wrongdoer can kill that person before the lawsuit is filed, before an arrest warrant is issued, before the act that motivated the killer to murder the victim is even discovered.[161]

2. The Subject Matter of the Statement

The statement need not refer to the lawsuit that led the party to procure the declarant's unavailability. The statement can, for example, be offered at the party's trial for crimes committed in connection with the threats, violence, or murder that left the witness unavailable. Rule 804(b)(6) does not limit the subject matter of the statements it covers. Other than the requirement that the statement be offered against the party who procured the unavailability, Rule 804(b)(6) does not limit the nature of the proceeding in which the statement is offered. It simply establishes that if you wrongfully procure the declarant's

---

160. United States v. Houlihan, 92 F.3d 1271, 1279 (1st Cir. 1996) (quotation regards then-applicable law regarding waiver of confrontation right; rationale also applied to common-law waiver of hearsay objection). *Accord*, United States v. Gray, 405 F.3d 227, 241 (4th Cir. 2005) ("applies whenever the defendant's wrongdoing was intended to, and did, render the declarant unavailable as a witness against the defendant, without regard to the nature of the charges at the trial in which the declarant's statements are offered"); United States v. Dhinsa, 243 F.3d 635, 654 (2d Cir. 2001); United States v. Johnson, 219 F.3d 349, 355–56 (4th Cir. 2000); State v. Ivy, 188 S.W.2d 132, 147 (Tenn. 2006) (preventing testimony need not be the sole reason for the wrongdoing).

161. *E.g., Ivy*, 188 S.W.2d at 147 (an arrest warrant need not have been issued against the perpetrator of the wrongdoing).

absence, then you forfeit the hearsay objection to any of declarant's out-of-court statements.[162]

3. The Exception Is Not Available to the Wrongdoing Party

The party who procured the witness's absence may not use this exception. It can only be used by a party offering the statement against the wrongdoing party. First and foremost, this is so from the terms of the rule: For the out-of-court statement to fit under this exception, the statement must be offered against the party who wrongfully procured unavailability. Second, the whole point is that the wrongdoing party forfeits the protection of the hearsay rule; the non-wrongdoing party does not forfeit the protection of the hearsay rule. Third, this was the rule under the common-law waiver that was the predecessor to this exception.[163]

This means that the non-wrongdoing party can offer part of an out-of-court statement under this exception and can still make a hearsay objection if the wrongdoing party tries to offer more of the statement. Then the question becomes whether the wrongdoing party can get around the hearsay problem by offering other parts of the statement under Rule 106, the Rule of Completeness.[164] The circuits are split on the question of whether Rule 106 makes admissible parts of a document otherwise inadmissible under some other rule of evidence.[165]

4. Unavailability Procured by the Wrongdoing of a Coconspirator

This exception applies to one who "engaged or acquiesced" in wrongdoing. If one member of a conspiracy engages in wrongdoing that procures the unavailability of a declarant and does so in order to silence that declarant, can the

---

162. *Dhinsa*, 243 F.3d at 652–54 (citing many cases); United States v. Emery, 186 F.3d 921, 926 (8th Cir. 1999).

163. *E.g., Houlihan*, 92 F.3d at 1283 ("[A] homicidal defendant may by his misconduct waive his hearsay objections, but that waiver does not strip the government of its right to lodge hearsay objections. It is only the party who wrongfully procures a witness's absence who waives the right to object to the adverse party's introduction of the witness's prior out-of-court statement.")

164. "When a writing or recorded statement or part thereof is introduced by a party, an adverse party may require the introduction at that time of any other part of any other writing or recorded statement which ought in fairness to be considered contemporaneously with it." FED.R.EVID. 106.

165. Regarding the relationship between Rule 106 and the hearsay rule, *see* Chapter 9(III), below.

statements of the declarant be used against other members of the conspiracy? Can other members of the conspiracy be held to have "acquiesced" in the wrongdoing? This, of course, depends on how the courts define "acquiesced." As a general rule, under an agency theory of liability every conspirator is liable for the wrongdoing of every coconspirator so long as the act was a reasonably foreseeable part of the conspiracy.[166] The best way to resolve this question seems to be by asking whether the wrongdoing that procured the unavailability of the witness was an overt or a reasonably foreseeable part of the conspiracy.[167]

5. Arguing This Exception in the Hearing of the Jury

This exception poses particular problems when it is argued in the hearing of the jury. If the party offering the statement argues in front of the jury that the statement is admissible because the opposing party murdered the witness, the prejudice is pretty obvious. The prejudice is even greater if the jury hears the trial judge agree (implicitly or explicitly) that the party in question murdered the witness. This is what happened in *United States v. Peoples.*[168] The prosecutor offered an out-of-court statement; the defendant made a hearsay objection; the prosecutor responded that the defendant "had murdered the witness"[169] and, therefore, the statement was admissible under the forfeiture by wrongdoing exception. The trial court overruled the hearsay objection, allowed the statement into evidence, and "instructed the jury that the statement had been admitted conditionally and [the court's] ruling did not mean that [it] believed that the defendants had caused [the witness] to be murdered." The appellate court concluded that "the prosecutor's remark was not improper, because it merely reiterated the government's theory of the case and provided legal support for the admissibility of the proffered statement."[170] Furthermore, even if it were improper, the court's instruction to the jury cured "any potential unfair prejudice."[171]

---

166. United States v. Cherry, 217 F.3d 811, 815–21 (10th Cir. 2000) (analogizing this to the Confrontation Clause cases and discussing, among other cases, Pinkerton v. United States, 328 U.S. 640 (1946)).

167. This is really the functional equivalent of the findings the judge must make when applying the definitional exclusion for statements by coconspirators, Rule 801(d)(2)(E). *See* Chapter 2(III)(F)(3).

168. 250 F.3d 630 (8th Cir. 2001).

169. United States v. Peoples, 250 F.3d 630, 635 (8th Cir. 2001).

170. *Id.* The court went on to say that "even if the remark was improper … the court's instruction was sufficient to cure any potential unfair prejudice." *Id.*

171. *Id.* Regarding limiting jury instructions, *see* Chapter 8(I)(D)(4)(g) and Chapter 12(IV), below.

The defendant in *Peoples* was on trial for aiding and abetting the murder of a federal witness. The late federal witness in question was the very person who made the out-of-court statement that was the subject of this hearsay ruling. The prosecutor stated that he believed that the defendant had murdered a witness against him; the witness against him was the man the defendant was on trial for having murdered; therefore, the prosecutor stated that he believed that the defendant was guilty of murdering the man he was charged with murdering. It does not seem sufficient for the appellate court to state "that prosecutor's remark was not improper, because it merely reiterated the government's theory of the case and provided legal support for the admissibility of the proffered statement." Perhaps defense counsel should have taken steps to have this hearsay ruling made before the trial, or perhaps defense counsel should have asked to approach, even go into chambers, to get outside the hearing of the jury to make the objection and hear the response. Perhaps defense counsel bears some of the blame. Still, it does not seem sufficient simply to say that the "prosecutor's remark was not improper, because it merely reiterated the government's theory of the case and provided legal support for the admissibility of the proffered statement."[172]

---

172. In this particular situation, this statement by the prosecutor carries this additional prejudice. The prosecutor has said in open court that the statement is admissible because the defendant had the declarant murdered and then the judge admitted the statement. Even though the judge told the jury that this did not mean that he thought the defendant had killed the declarant, they may well see through that. Perhaps the best the defendant could hope for is that this would be considered judicial comment and, like other judicial comment, it must be considered in the context of the entire proceeding and is only grounds for mistrial in the trial court or reversal on appeal if it is so prejudicial as to amount to the denial of a fair trial. Allen v. Montgomery, 728 F.2d 1409, 1415–16 (11th Cir. 1984); United States v. Preston, 608 F.2d 626, 636 (5th Cir. 1979). If this is judicial comment, then, in the context of the *Peoples* case, it is comment on the ultimate issue—the defendant killed the witness he is on trial for killing. (Actually, it is comment very nearly on the ultimate issue. The evidentiary burden for application of the forfeiture by wrongdoing exception is preponderance of the evidence. The burden of proof on the issue of defendant's guilt is beyond a reasonable doubt. The jury, however, does not know that the evidentiary burden applied by the judge is different than the burden of proof applied by them.) If that is so, then this rule kicks in: "In the circumstances we think the trial judge erred in stating the opinion that the respondent was guilty beyond a reasonable doubt. A federal judge may analyze the evidence, comment upon it, and express his views with regard to the testimony of witnesses. He may advise the jury in respect of the facts, but the decision of issues of fact must be fairly left to the jury ..." United States v. Murdock, 290 U.S. 389, 394 (1933). *See also* United States v. Fuller, 162 F.3d 256, 259–60 (4th Cir. 1998). If the due process, fair trial standard is the one used, then it seems unlikely that the judge's ruling on the evidentiary issue will be grounds for mistrial or reversal unless there is some abuse in the form of, for example, comment by the prosecutor on the meaning of the judge's ruling.

6. Action Outside of the Rule As Literally Interpreted

a. *Action Other Than Wrongdoing*

By its terms, the rule applies to "wrongdoing that was intended to, and did, procure the unavailability of the declarant as a witness."[173] Prior to the adoption of this statutory exception, a number of courts created similar, though broader, common-law exceptions. The Eleventh Circuit, for example, had written: "[M]isconduct leading to the loss of confrontation rights also necessarily causes the defendant to forfeit hearsay objections."[174] To the extent that other kinds of misconduct lead to the loss of confrontation rights, other than wrongfully procuring the absence of the witness, this exception for misconduct may extend beyond the terms of Rule 804(b)(6). [175]

The forfeiture by wrongdoing exception only applies when a party engages in "wrongdoing." Perhaps "wrongdoing" and "misconduct" are synonymous. But perhaps they are not.[176] Say, for example, that before, but in anticipation of, his indictment, the defendant in a criminal action encountered a witness and said: "I've got a family—four young kids. If I'm convicted, I'll lose my job and I don't know what they'll do." The witness takes pity on the defendant and disappears into the mountains of Nepal to avoid testifying. The forfeiture by wrongdoing exception only applies when a party engages in "wrongdoing" intended to accomplish and in fact accomplishing the unavailability of the live testimony of a witness. This defendant had the necessary intent and he accomplished his goal, but he may not have engaged in any wrongdoing. What he did may have been misconduct, in the sense that it was indecorous, but it may not have been wrongdoing.[177]

---

173. Fed.R.Evid. 804(b)(6).

174. United States v. White, 116 F.3d 903, 912 (D.C. Cir. 1997) (citing cases).

175. Other courts had created common-law exceptions that would be subsumed into this forfeiture by wrongdoing exception. *See, e.g.,* G. Michael Fenner, *Law Professor Reveals Shocking Truth About Hearsay,* 62 UMKC L. Rev. 1, 41 (1993).

176. "[The Confrontation Clause grants the defendant] the privilege of being confronted with the witnesses against him; but if he voluntarily keeps the witnesses away, he cannot insist on his privilege. If, therefore, when absent by his procurement, their evidence is supplied in some lawful way, he is in no condition to assert that his constitutional rights have been violated." Reynolds v. United States, 98 U.S. 145, 158 (1878). My hypothetical defendant has "voluntarily [kept] the witness away" and the witness is "absent by his procurement." Regarding the Confrontation Clause, see Chapter 14, below.

177. In Steele v. Taylor, 684 F.2d 1193 (6th Cir. 1982) "the witness was under the control of the defendant who procured her refusal to testify." *Id.* at 1199. The court found that

There is an argument that by using the word "wrongdoing" Congress meant to exclude any other misconduct exceptions, including preexisting misconduct exceptions coterminous with loss of confrontation rights. Under this argument, Rule 804(b)(6) actually narrows the range of admissible hearsay. There are several reasons it does not seem that this interpretation will get very far. First, such a narrow interpretation would be inconsistent with the rule that the rules of evidence "shall be construed to secure ... promotion of growth and development of the law of evidence to the end that the truth may be ascertained and proceedings justly determined."[178] Second, to the extent that the federal rules of evidence catalogue the exceptions to the hearsay rule and that unlisted common-law exceptions do not survive codification, Rule 804(b)(6) really is not an exception to the hearsay rule. Conceptually it is a rule of forfeiture: by your conduct, you forfeit the right to take advantage of the hearsay rule. There is nothing to indicate that by including this single rule of forfeiture on a list of hearsay exceptions, Congress intended to catalogue all of the forfeitures by wrongdoing. Rather, this was simply an attempt to write down one of them. At most, this rule of forfeiture is now both a rule of forfeiture and a hearsay exception; specifying it and, among rules of forfeiture, it alone as a hearsay exception means that none of the other rules of forfeiture are hearsay exceptions; it does nothing to their status as rules of forfeiture.[179]

b. The Turncoat Witness—Wrongdoing That Does Not Result in the Testimony of the Witness Being Unavailable, but Results in the Witness Telling a Different Story

This is a Rule 804 exception. If the in-court testimony of the out-of-court declarant is available, then this exception does not apply. This exception applies when a witness is threatened and does not testify. If a witness is threatened and does testify but changes the facts so that they now favor the wrongdoing party, the prior statement will be admissible to impeach the witness's testimony. In addition, the statement may be admissible as substantive evidence under some other exception to the hearsay rule, including perhaps the residual exception.[180]

---

the defendant had waived his right to confrontation. Though the court does not discuss the hearsay rule, waiver of the confrontation right *a fortiori* waives the hearsay objection. *E.g.*, United States v. Mastrangelo, 693 F.2d 269, 272 (2d Cir. 1982). Exerting a controlling personality is not necessarily "wrongdoing."

178. Fed.R.Evid. 102.

179. *See* Diaz v. United States, 223 U.S. 442, 458 (1912) ("Neither in criminal nor in civil cases will the law allow a person to take advantage of his own wrong.").

180. This interpretation of the residual exception is discussed below at Chapter 5(V)(E)(2).

Similarly, if a witness takes the stand and testifies that his prior statements were lies and then refuses to testify any further (even after held in contempt), then two questions must be asked. The first question is whether the statement can come in around the hearsay rule? Is this witness's testimony is unavailable?[181] If so, and if the other foundational elements are present, then this exception applies. If not, then the question is whether some other exception apply? The second question is whether the Confrontation Clause bars admission of the statement.[182]

7. The Burden of Establishing that the Party Against Whom the Evidence Is Offered Engaged or Acquiesced in Wrongdoing

The party offering evidence under this exception must prove that the party against whom the evidence is offered "engaged or acquiesced in wrongdoing that was intended to and did procure the unavailability of the [out-of-court] declarant as [an in-court] witness."[183] The offering party's burden is to show this by a preponderance of the evidence.[184]

---

181. *See* part I of this chapter, above.

182. Regarding the Confrontation Clause, see Chapter 14, below.

183. Fed.R.Evid. 804(b)(6).

184. United States v. Rivera, 412 F.3d 562, 567 (4th Cir. 2005); United States v. Dhinsa, 243 F.3d 635, 653–54 (2d Cir. 2001) (this is so by the plain terms of the rule). As is the case with the foundational elements of all of the exceptions to the hearsay rule, the proponent of the statement need only prove by a preponderance of the evidence that the opponent of the evidence procured the absence of the declarant and did so to keep the declarant from testifying. United States v. Price, 265 F.3d 1097, 1103 (10th Cir. 2001). *See also* Chapter 3(I)(D), above; Bourjaily v. United States, 483 U.S. 171 (1987), discussed in part 2(I) of Chapter 2, above.

CHAPTER FIVE

THE RESIDUAL EXCEPTION — RULE 807

I. Know This If Nothing Else[1]

The residual exception is not available unless offering counsel gives opposing counsel advance notice of an intention to offer the evidence in question. By the terms of the rule, this notice must come in advance of the trial or hearing at which counsel is offering the out-of-court statement. The question of the timing of the notice is not, however, as simple as declared in the text of the rule. Some jurisdictions allow notice well into the trial or hearing. This is discussed in more detail later in this chapter.[2]

For now, the two most important things to say about this exception are these: First, check your jurisdiction's interpretative case law to determine when the required notice must be given. Second, if you have any doubt about the admissibility of possible hearsay evidence, preserve your opportunity to use the residual exception by giving timely notice of an intention to offer the evidence in question.

II. Text of Rule 807

A statement not specifically covered by Rule 803 or 804 but having equivalent circumstantial guarantees of trustworthiness, is not ex-

---

1. Some of this chapter originally appeared as G. Michael Fenner, *The Residual Exception to the Hearsay Rule: The Complete Treatment*, 33 CREIGHTON L. REV. 265 (2000).

The residual exception is also known as the catch-all exception. Prior to December 1, 1997, there were two residual exceptions, one at the end of Rule 803 and the other at the end of Rule 804. They were identical except that one in Rule 804 required that the out-of-court declarant's testimony be unavailable. What difference did that make, since there was also a residual exception at the end of Rule 803? Perhaps that it made no difference was the main reason to combine these two exceptions into one new rule. Effective December 1, 1997, the two residual exceptions were combined into one new rule, Rule 807.

2. *See* part V(C)(2) of this chapter, below.

cluded by the hearsay rule, if the court determines that (A) the statement is offered as evidence of a material fact; (B) the statement is more probative on the point for which it is offered than any other evidence which the proponent can procure through reasonable efforts; and (C) the general purposes of these rules and the interests of justice will best be served by admission of the statement into evidence. However, a statement may not be admitted under this exception unless the proponent of it makes known to the adverse party sufficiently in advance of the trial or hearing to provide the adverse party with a fair opportunity to prepare to meet it, the proponent's intention to offer the statement and the particulars of it, including the name and address of the declarant.[3]

III. Foundational Elements

A. Five Required Findings ...

According to the rule, use of the residual exception requires five findings on the part of the trial court.[4]

1. Trustworthiness.[5]

2. Relevance.[6]

3. The evidence in question must have more probative value on the point to which it is offered than does any other (admissible) evidence the proponent can procure through reasonable efforts.

4. Application of the exception will serve the general purposes of these rules and the interests of justice.[7]

---

3. FED.R.EVID. 807.

4. These findings should be made on the record. *See* the Use Note, below.

5. *See* part V(D) of this chapter, below.

6. The rule requires "that the statement be offered as evidence of a material fact, which we take to be a requirement of relevance." Huff v. White Motor Corp., 609 F.2d 286, 294 (7th Cir. 1979).

7. The rule states that admission of the statement should serve "the general purposes of these rules and the interests of justice." FED.R.EVID. 807. The latter seems subsumed by, if not redundant of, the former. The general purposes of a set of evidence rules written to be used in the courts in the United States should include service to the interests of justice. Perhaps Rule 807 separates the two concepts in order to emphasize the latter. Regarding the general purposes of these rules, *see* FED.R.EVID. 102.

5. Notice to opponent of the proponent's intention to use the evidence in question. (The rule states that the notice must be sufficiently in advance of the trial or hearing to prevent surprise and to allow the adverse party an opportunity to prepare a counter argument. Some courts take a more "flexible" approach and allow notice at any time, so long as it provides the opponent sufficient opportunity to prepare to counter the evidence.[8])

B. ... Reduced to Three Required Findings

The second foundational element on the above list, relevance, is always required before any evidence can be admitted. Additionally, it is subsumed by the third element on the list, for the statement does not have any probative value unless it is relevant. Listing it as a separate foundational element adds nothing. The fourth finding—truth and justice—adds nothing to the general rules regarding the application of these rules of evidence as a whole.[9] This means the list of foundational elements over and above what is required in any event, can be reduced to three:

1. Trustworthiness.

2. Relative probative value.

3. Notice.

IV. Need + Reliability = 1

A. The Need for, and the Reliability of, the Evidence

The need for and reliability of this evidence are written on the face of the rule.

1. The Need for the Evidence in Question

Need is found in the exceptions requirement that the statement be the most probative evidence reasonably available to the proponent.[10]

---

8. *See* part V(C) of this chapter, below.

9. *See* FED.R.EVID. 102.

10. The rule requires that the statement be "more probative on the point for which it is offered than any other evidence which the proponent can procure through reasonable efforts." FED.R.EVID. 807.

2. Reliability

The statement must "not specifically [be] covered by Rule 803 or 804 but [must have] equivalent circumstantial guarantees of trustworthiness." The evidence let in under the residual exception must somehow be as reliable as the evidence covered by Rules 803 and 804. The guarantee of reliability is not inherent in Rule 807, but is a matter of reference back to Rules 803 and 804.[11]

B. The Need for the Residual Exception Itself

The residual exception is an expression of the need for flexibility in the rules.[12] The statutory rules replaced the common law of evidence. Common law rules allow for judicial flexibility: Judges create the rules; when they need another rule, they create one. Many, including those who drafted the Federal Rules of Evidence, believed that the evidence code needed flexibility of its own. The drafters of the rules recognized that not even a group as distinguished as itself could anticipate every situation. "It would ... be presumptuous to assume that all possible desirable exceptions to the hearsay rule have been catalogued and to pass the hearsay rule to oncoming generations as a closed system."[13]

Presumptuous, and potentially disastrous. The lack of a residual exception would lead to tortured constructions of the specific exceptions. There would be situations where the hearsay rule stood in the way of the admission of evidence that the trial judge found to be reliable and essential if justice is to be done. Pressure for the admission of such evidence would build. Without a safety valve, sooner or later, and more or less frequently, but unavoidably, the pressure would build to the point that it would impair the rule. The pressure of justice against the rigidity of the specific rules would result in the rules giving way.[14] Some of the evidence will come in anyway, and bringing it in through a residual exception is a more honest way of doing it.

---

11. This is discussed below. *See* part V(D)(1) of this chapter.

12. One court has said that this "'exception is to be used only rarely, and in exceptional circumstances [when there are] exceptional guarantees of trustworthiness ... and ... a high degree of probativeness and necessity ...'" United States v. Lawrence, 349 F.3d 109, 117 (3d Cir. 2003).

13. FED.R.EVID. 803(24) advisory committee's note.

14. The first Justice Harlan recognized this general problem as long ago as 1877: "'[I]t is the duty of all courts of justice to take care, for the general good of the community, that hard cases do not make bad law.'" United States v. Clark, 96 U.S. 37, 49 (1877) (Harlan, J. dissenting). It is also the duty of the legislature, and as regards the hearsay rule the Con-

V. Use Note

A. Near-Miss Evidence—the Relationship between the Residual Exception and the Specific Exceptions of Rules 803 and 804

One of the important residual-exception questions has been this: Can the residual exception be used to admit a statement that almost qualifies under a specific exception, but falls just short regarding one foundational element? This is the "near miss" problem. The question is this: Is the residual exception available for "near miss" evidence?

■ It seems self-evident that a statement that just misses qualifying under one of the specific exceptions can still fit under another. No one would argue that an excited utterance could not fit under the excited utterance exception because it was almost a present sense impression. An employee-admission can fit under that exclusion even though it almost qualifies as a coconspirator-admission.[15] A statement about a pain the declarant is experiencing might fall

---

gress of the United States fulfilled this duty when it included the residual exception. Justice Holmes saw the problem too:

> Great cases, like hard cases, make bad law. For great cases are called great, not by reason of their real importance in shaping the law of the future, but because of some accident of immediate overwhelming interest which appeals to the feelings and distorts the judgment. These immediate interests exercise a kind of hydraulic pressure which makes what previously was clear seem doubtful, and before which even well settled principles of law will bend.

Northern Securities Co. v. United States, 193 U.S. 197, 400–01 (1904) (Holmes, J. dissenting).

The legislative history of the residual exception includes the Senate's conclusion "that, absent a residual exception, the categorical exceptions might become 'tortured beyond any reasonable circumstances which they were designed to include.'" State v. Walker, 691 A.2d 1341, 1351 (Md. 1996) (quoting Senate Judiciary Committee Report No. 93-1277, accompanying H.R. 5463, 1974 U.S. Code Cong. & Ad. News 7051, 7065).

"The facts of this case demonstrate the wisdom of including in our rules a residual hearsay exception such as that in [the federal rules]. Otherwise, we face distorting or expanding our exceptions to the hearsay rule in a manner inconsistent with the text of the rules and the rationales justifying them, or excluding otherwise trustworthy hearsay evidence which may make it impossible to best serve the interests of justice." W.C.L., Jr. v. People, 685 P.2d 176, 178 (Colo. 1984).

15. Just as no one would suggest that an employee's statement concerning a matter within the scope of his or her employment and offered against the employer does not fit under that exclusion because it is almost a statement by an agent specifically authorized to speak on the matter. See, e.g., Canatxx Gas Storage Ltd. v. Silverhawk Capital Partners, LLC, No.

one foundational element short of the medical diagnosis or treatment exception and still fit under the state of mind exception.[16] A business record can be admissible under the business record exception even though it falls only days— even minutes—short of being an ancient document.[17]

H-06-1330, 2008 WL 1999234, *15 (S.D. Tex. 2008) ("an agent may make vicarious admissions for his principal whether or not he is specifically authorized to speak on the subject"; declarant's "statements are statements by a party opponent, regardless of whether [the employer] specifically authorized them").

16. It is "[a] statement of declarant's then existing state of mind, emotion, sensation, or physical condition." FED.R.EVID. 803(3).

17. While on the First Circuit Court of Appeals, now-Justice Breyer recognized this point when he wrote that "the 'potential' availability of one kind of hearsay exception [does not] automatically rules out the use of another. After all, normally, hearsay testimony is admissible if it satisfies any one exception. A declaration against penal interest, for example, is no less admissible simply because the declarant made the statement while testifying as a witness at an earlier trial (and vice versa)." United States v. Donlon, 909 F.2d 650, 654 (1st Cir. 1990) (Breyer, C.J.), *questioned on other grounds*, United States v. Gomez, 939 F.2d 326, 333 (6th Cir. 1991). "[M]erely because a statement suffers some impediment under one hearsay exception does not preclude the proponent of the evidence from satisfying a court that a different, better-fitting exception fully applies." People v. Buie, 658 N.E.2d 192, 198 (N.Y. 1995). Each exception is "based on different rationales and there is nothing inherently inconsistent about the admission, under [one], of evidence ruled inadmissible under [another]." Parker v. Reda, 327 F.3d 211, 214 (2d Cir. 2003) (insufficiently trustworthy for admission as a business record; admissible as past recollection recorded). *See also, e.g.,* United States v. Firishchak, 468 F.3d 1015, 1022 (7th Cir. 2006) ("[T]he ancient documents rule and the business records exception are independent grounds for determining admissibility."); United States v. Pelullo, 964 F.2d 193, 202 (3d Cir. 1992) ("[T]he residual exception may not be used as a substitute for the business records exception when counsel has not complied with the requirements of 803(6) *unless* the requirements of [Rule 807] have been met.") (emphasis added); United States v. McPartlin, 595 F.2d 1321, 1350 (7th Cir. 1979) ("Where evidence complies with the spirit, if not the latter [sic], of several exceptions, admissibility is appropriate under the residual exception."); Garcia v. Portuondo, 459 F.Supp.2d 267, 283 n.84 (S.D. N.Y. 2006) ("If the foundational elements for the public records exception could not have been met, Guttlein might have succeeded in offering the documents as business records."); Sternhagen v. Dow Co., 108 F.Supp.2d 1113, 1119 n.5 (D. Mont. 1999) ("[I]if hearsay almost fits another exception, this fact cuts in favor of admission under the residual exception."); United States v. Grant, 38 M.J. 684, 693 (USAF Ct. Mil. Rev. 1993) ("The ... statement's very close resemblance to an excited utterance enhances its trustworthiness and admissibility under [the residual exception]."); People v. Katt, 662 N.W.2d 12, 21 (Mich. 2003) ("We agree with the majority of the federal courts and conclude that a hearsay statement is 'specifically covered' by another exception ... only when it is admissible under that exception. Therefore, we decline to adopt the near-miss theory as part of our method for determining when hearsay statements may be admissible under [our residual exception]."). *And see* Chapter 10(I), below.

In addition, it is appropriate for a court to find that the statement is admissible under more than one exception, and one of them can be the residual exception. Furthermore, an appellate court can find that the trial court erroneously admitted a statement under one exception but find that it is admissible under a different exception, one not mentioned at trial, and affirm.[18]

How is it that these things could be accepted truth for all exceptions but the residual? They are not. The residual exception and the other hearsay exceptions are not mutually exclusive.[19] The appropriate limitations for the residual exception are found in the residual exception, and not in the residual exception plus all of the others.

The residual exception was included in these rules for application in either of two situations. First: things change. The residual exception is available to deal with new situations and kinds of evidence, situations and kinds of evidence unanticipated at the time the rules were written.[20] Second: the lines drawn to create the categorical exceptions in Rules 803 and 804 are not perfect lines. There will be times when the imperfections of the lines drawn will exclude — sometimes only barely exclude — needed and reliable evidence. The residual exception recognizes the imperfection of this kind of categorizing and allows ad hoc decisions to ameliorate these imperfections. Excluding near-miss evidence from the residual exception would place the rules of evidence back in the straightjacket from which it was intended to free them.[21]

---

18. *See, e.g.,* United States v. Samaniego, 345 F.3d 1280, 1283 (11th Cir. 2003) (the evidence was improperly admitted under one exception but would properly have been admitted under another; the trial court reached the right result for the wrong reason and is affirmed); State v. Stephenson Oil Co., 128 S.W.3d 805, 815 (Ark. 2003); State v. Walker, 691 A.2d 1341, 1353 n.9 (Md. 1997).

19. Williamson v. United States, 512 U.S. 594, 604 n.* (1994) (when a narrative is both self-incriminating and non-self-incriminating, only the self-incriminating parts fit under the statement against interest exception, but the non-self-incriminating parts might fit under the residual exception); United States v. Wilson, 249 F.3d 366, 375 (5th Cir. 2001) ("Despite the 'statement not specifically covered by rule 803' language in Fed. R. Evid. 807, 807 'is not limited in availability as to types of evidence not addressed in other exceptions … [807] is also available when the proponent fails to meet the standards set forth in the other exceptions.'") (citation omitted).

20. MORRIS K. UDALL, ET AL., LAW OF EVIDENCE 556 (3d ed. 1991), found at State v. Luzanilla, 880 P. 2d 611, 617 (Ariz. 1994).

21. In re Japanese Elec. Products Antitrust Litigation, 723 F.2d 238, 301–03 (3d Cir. 1983), *rev'd and remanded sub non* Matsushita Elec. Indus. Co. v. Zenith Radio Corp., 475 U.S. 574 (1986).

Additionally, excluding near-miss evidence from the hearsay rule "promises much litigation over how close a statement can come," United States v. Clarke, 2 F.3d 81, 84 (4th

■ The other approach to the residual exception draws the line between Rules 803 and 804, on the one hand, and Rule 807, on the other, by quoting this part of Rule 807: The residual exception applies to "[a] statement not specifically covered by Rule 803 or 804." This approach argues that the near-miss statement is "specifically covered" (and specifically rejected) by the exception it nearly hits. This interpretation preserves the boundaries drawn by those who drafted the specific exceptions and by those who enacted them into law; allowing near-miss evidence to come in under the residual exception erodes the carefully drawn boundaries of the exception the evidence has narrowly missed.

This approach is consistent with position that the exception should be limited to new and unanticipated situations.[22] Upon review of specific types of statements, the drafters decided that certain elements must be met before those statements can be admitted under an exception. The proponent must establish each and every foundational element of a hearsay exception.[23] Four out of five is not good enough. Near miss situations, this argument states, are not new and were not unanticipated. When the lines were drawn, they were intentionally left out. Rather than being new and unanticipated, they were considered and rejected.

This approach is consistent with the drafter's admonition that the residual exception should be used rarely and only in exceptional circumstances.[24] If

---

Cir. 1993), to a specified exception before the residual exception is rendered inapplicable. "Both litigants and courts spend their time more productively in analyzing the trustworthiness of the particular statement, rather than debating the abstract question of "How close is too close?" to a specified hearsay exception." *Id.*

22. UDALL, LAW OF EVIDENCE, *supra* at 556.

23. *See* Chapter 2(I) (evidentiary burdens) and Chapter 3(I)(D) (evidentiary burdens and the need to prove each foundational element), above.

24. Senate Comm. on Judiciary, Fed.Rules of Evidence, S.Rep. No. 1277, 93d Cong., 2d Sess., p. 18 (1974) (often found accompanying FED.R.EVID. 803(24) advisory committee's note). *See also, e.g.,* United States v. Laster, 258 F.3d 525, 532–35 (6th Cir. 2001) (Moore, J. dissenting); Bohler-Uddeholm America, Inc. v. Ellwood Group, Inc., 247 F.3d 79, 112 (3d Cir. 2001); United States v. Mitchell, 145 F.3d 572, 578 (3d Cir. 1998); United States v. Washington, 106 F.3d 983, 1001–02 (D.C. Cir. 1997) (proponent bears a heavy burden); United States v. Bailey, 581 F.2d 341, 347 (3d Cir. 1978); Wezorek v. Allstate Ins. Co., 2007 U.S. Dist. LEXIS 45555, *4–5 (E.D. Pa. 2007); Brown v. Philip Morris, Inc., 228 F.Supp.2d 506, 511–12 (D. N.J. 2002); Russo v. Abington Mem. Hosp. Healthcare Plan, 1998 U.S. Dist. LEXIS 18598, *9 (E.D. Pa Nov. 18, 1998) ("A catch-all rule such as Rule 807 must be sparingly invoked, lest its potential breadth swallow the carefully crafted narrowness of the enumerated exceptions."); Zenith Radio Corp. v. Matsushita Elec. Indus. Co., 505 F.Supp. 1190, 1263 (E.D. Pa. 1980), *aff'd in part, rev'd in part, remanded, sub nom* In re Japanese Elec. Products Antitrust Litigation, 723 F.2d 238 (3rd Cir. 1983), *rev'd and remanded sub non* Matsushita Elec. Indus. Co. v. Zenith Radio Corp., 475 U.S. 574 (1986).

near-miss evidence can qualify as residual-exception evidence, the exception will be used way too frequently and in common circumstances.

■ The answer to the question of whether near-miss evidence can be admissible under the residual exception starts with the language of the residual exception itself. Rule 807 states that it applies to statements "not specifically covered by Rule 803 and 804." Perhaps, then, the resolution of the near-miss problem depends on what is meant by "specifically covered." That, in turn, depends on specific definitions and general approaches.

Definitions: "Specific" is defined as "**a** : constituting or falling into a specifiable category **b** : sharing or being those properties of something that allow it to be referred to a particular category."[25] "Specifically covered" by one of the exceptions in Rule 803 or 804, then, seems to mean falling within one of those exceptions. It does not seem to mean falling outside the exception. No matter how close it came, a miss is still a miss.[26] This seems to be the plain meaning of the rule, as written.

That is, each exception has certain foundational elements, and if there is sufficient evidence of each foundational element for any one exception then the statement is "specifically covered" by the exception. If it does not fit under a particular exception, then, no matter how close it comes, it is *not specifically covered*.[27] In fact, in this latter situation, the statement is *specifically not covered* by the barely missed exception.

Basic Approaches: The basic premise of these rules favors the admissibility of evidence that is relevant and competent. The general rule is that all relevant and competent evidence is admissible, unless there is a rule that keeps it out. When in doubt, then, the rules should be interpreted so as to admit relevant, competent evidence—let it in and trust the lawyers to explain it to the jury and trust the jury to get it right.[28]

---

25. Merriam-Webster's Collegiate Dictionary, CD rom (Zane Pub. Co. 1996).
26. And a near miss counts only in horseshoes and hand grenades, not hearsay exceptions.
27. *E.g.*, United States v. Earles, 113 F.3d 796, 800 (8th Cir. 1997) (when a statement does not meet the requirements for admission of a particular exception, then that statement is not "specifically covered" by that exception, and the residual exception may be considered); United States v. Clarke, 2 F.3d 81, 83 (4th Cir. 1993).
28. Regarding most hearsay decisions, Rule 403 and the due process clause serve as the ultimate backstop against the same evil as is addressed by the hearsay rule. *See* Chapter 1(I), above, "Introduction to Hearsay." These evils do not exist here, however. Rule 807 only applies when the judge finds the statement sufficiently reliable, finds that it has sufficient relative probative value, and finds that admitting the evidence serves the interest of justice.

Furthermore, Rule 102 states that "[t]hese rules shall be construed to secure … elimination of unjustifiable expense and delay, and promotion of growth and development of the law of evidence to the end that the truth may be ascertained and proceedings justly determined."[29] If the out-of-court statement is reliable and if it is the most probative evidence on point that is reasonably available, then admitting it is consistent with Rule 102's rule of interpretation.[30] If there is other probative evidence of the point, but obtaining that evidence is unreasonably expensive, then letting in reliable near-miss evidence does eliminate unjustifiable expense. If the other evidence is time-consumingly difficult to obtain, then letting in reliable near-miss evidence does eliminate unjustifiable delay. If the near-miss evidence is reliable and alternative methods of proof are either unavailable or unreasonably expensive and time-consuming to obtain, then letting in the reliable near-miss evidence does promote the "growth and development of the law of evidence to the end that the truth may be ascertained and proceedings justly determined."[31]

What, then, is meant by Rule 807's first clause defining its coverage in terms of "statement[s] not specifically covered by Rule 803 and 804"? " '[S]pecifically covered' means exactly what it says: if a statement does not meet all of the requirements for admissibility under at least one of the 803 or 804 exceptions, then it is not 'specifically covered.' "[32] It means that out-of-court statements specifically covered by the more specific exceptions should be admitted under those exceptions, and not the residual. It means that lawyers and judges should not turn to the residual exception first. It means this: Rely on the residual exception only when you cannot rely on any other.[33]

Evidence that satisfies those three requirements could not run afoul of either Rule 403 or the due process clause.

29. Fed.R.Evid. 102.

30. *See, e.g., Zenith Radio Corp.*, 505 F.Supp. at 1261; United States v. Sheets, 125 F.R.D. 172, 176–77 (D. Utah 1989); Cummins v. Mississippi, 515 So.2d 869, 875 (Miss. 1987), *overruled in part, on other grounds,* Morgan v. Mississippi, 703 So. 2d 832, 841 (Miss. 1997).

31. Fed.R.Evid. 102. "Admission of the evidence will best serve the interests of justice by increasing the likelihood that the jury will ascertain the truth about the cause of the accident." Huff v. White Motor Corp., 609 F.2d 286, 295 (7th Cir. 1979).

32. United States v. Clarke, 2 F.3d 81, 83 (4th Cir. 1993). *Accord, e.g.,* People v. Katt, 662 N.W.2d 12, 21 (Mich. 2003) ("We agree with the majority of the federal courts and conclude that a hearsay statement is 'specifically covered' by another exception … only when it is admissible under that exception. Therefore, we decline to adopt the near-miss theory as part of our method for determining when hearsay statements may be admissible under [our residual exception].")

33. United States v. Laster, 258 F.3d 525, 530 (6th Cir. 2001) (citing cases and citing 5 Jack B. Weinstein & Margaret A. Berger, Weinstein's Federal Evidence § 807.03(4) (2d ed.

B. Grand Jury Testimony

A common example of the near-miss problem involves the admissibility against a defendant of grand-jury testimony. Today many of these issues will be resolved under the constitutional law, and not the law of evidence. The defendant is not able to cross-examine grand jury witnesses; grand jury testimony is testimonial;[34] therefore, unless the defendant is able to cross-examine the grand-jury witness in some other forum—such as the trial—the grand-jury testimony is not admissible.[35] If, however, the defendant is able to cross-examine the grand-jury witness, then the problem is one for the law of evidence. The evidentiary problem involves the intersection of the former testimony exception and the residual exception. Because the defendant has no opportunity to examine witnesses before the grand jury, that testimony can never fit under the former testimony exception.[36] The question, then, is this: If the defendant has some other opportunity to cross-examine the witness and thereby avoid the bar of the Confrontation Clause, can grand jury testimony be considered under the residual exception?

Most courts say that grand-jury testimony can fit under the residual exception.[37] The argument against that majority position is the "near miss" ar-

---

2000).); United States v. Earles, 113 F.3d 796, 800 (8th Cir. 1997) ("'specifically covered' means only that if a statement is admissible under one of the ... [other] exceptions, such ... [other exception] should be relied upon instead of [the residual exception]."). *See also* Brown v. Crown Equip. Corp., 445 F.Supp.2d 59, 67 (D. Me. 2006) ("Here, where the plaintiff has invoked a subsection of Rule 803 but has not presented sufficient evidence to allow the court to determine whether it applies to each of the proffered reports, the court cannot proceed to consider Rule 807 until a decision has been made that the reports are "not specifically covered by Rule 803," as Rule 807 requires."). *See additionally* the discussion of the residual exception and the admissibility of grand jury testimony in the text immediately following this footnote, *i.e.*, part (V)(B) of this chapter, just below.

34. Crawford v. Washington, 541 U.S. 36, 68 (2004).

35. The Confrontation Clause, U.S. Constit. amend. VI. Regarding the Confrontation Clause, see Chapter 14, below.

36. Grand jury testimony *by a party*, offered *against the party*, is not hearsay in the first place. It is a nonhearsay admission. Fed.R.Evid. 801(d)(2)(A). *See* Chapter 2(III)(B), above.

37. *Laster*, 258 F.3d at 532–33 (Moore, J. dissenting) (canvassing cases); *Earles*, 113 F.3d at 800; United States v. Dent, 984 F.2d 1453, 1462–63 (7th Cir. 1993) (not specifically covered by former testimony exception; properly considered under residual exception); United States v. Donlon, 909 F.2d 650, 654 (1st Cir. 1990) (then-Chief Judge Breyer), *questioned on other grounds*, United States v. Gomez, 939 F.2d 326, 333 (6th Cir. 1991); United States v. Marchini, 797 F.2d 759, 763 (9th Cir. 1986) ("There appears to be general agreement" that grand jury testimony can be considered under the residual exception), *questioned on*

gument, which, in this context, sounds as follows: The former testimony exception covers former testimony offered at a subsequent hearing, and grand jury testimony offered at a trial is just that; the residual exception does not apply to statements covered by the former testimony exception (or any other Rule 803 or 804 exception); therefore, the residual exception does not apply to grand jury testimony offered at a trial.[38] This conclusion is supported by reference to the legislative history to the rules. The residual exception was included to "provide for treating new and presently unanticipated situations."[39] Offering grand jury testimony at trial was not a "new" situation. It was not "unanticipated" by the drafters of the rules.[40]

---

other grounds, *Gomez*, *supra*; United States v. Barlow, 693 F.2d 954, 960 (6th Cir. 1982) ("[T]here is general agreement" that grand jury testimony can be considered under the residual exception), *questioned on other grounds, Gomez, supra*.

Justice Breyer, while Chief Judge of the First Circuit Court of Appeals, wrote that the residual exception can apply to grand-jury testimony. He rejected the near-miss argument based on the former testimony exception. In the process, he wrote that the former testimony exception does not apply to grand jury testimony because that exception was written to apply to statements made in "those kinds of proceedings for which cross-examination was potentially available." *Donlon, supra*. At a grand jury proceeding, the fact is that cross-examination is potentially available to the prosecutor and, therefore, the former testimony exception can be used against the prosecutor; cross-examination is not available to the defendant and, therefore, the former testimony exception cannot be used against the defendant. United States v. Salerno, 505 U.S. 317 (1992). *See* Chapter 4(II)(E)(5), above.

38. And, since cross-examination is not allowed at the grand jury, grand-jury testimony offered against the defendant in a criminal trial cannot fit under the former testimony exception.

United States v. Nigoa, 656 F.Supp. 1499, 1503–06 (D. N.J. 1987), *aff'd*, 857 F.2d 1467 (3rd Cir. 1988) ("[A]dmission of grand jury testimony under [the residual exception] is a perversion of the Federal Rules of Evidence and should not be condoned." *Id.* at 1506).

39. Fed.R.Evid. 803(24) advisory committee's note.

40. The advisory committee that drafted the Federal Rules of Evidence and whose note is quoted in the text accompanying the previous footnote circulated its preliminary draft in 1969, 46 F.R.D. 161, and its revised draft in 1971, 51 F.R.D. 315. The many cases addressing the hearsay rule and grand jury testimony prior to those dates, include the following: United States v. Capaldo, 402 F.2d 821, 824 (2d Cir. 1968) (assuming arguendo that grand jury testimony can fit under the statement against interest exception, this grand jury testimony does not); Young v. United States 214 F.2d 232, 239 (D.C. Cir. 1954) (admission of grand jury testimony in this case "comes within no exception to the rule excluding hearsay"); United States v. Kelinson, 205 F.2d 600, 601 (2d Cir. 1953) (grand jury testimony here not admissible as coconspirator's statement); United States v. Freundlich, 95 F.2d 376, 379 (2d Cir. 1938) (L. Hand, J.) (use of grand jury testimony at trial "may amount in reality to its substitution for the witness's upon the stand, and…, while the hearsay rule remains, the error may be enough for reversal"); People v. Johnson, 441 P.2d 111, 116 (Ca. 1968) (grand

The logic seems to be this: Grand jury testimony surely is testimony; when it is subsequently offered at a trial, it surely is former testimony; therefore, outside of the Confrontation Clause, its admission is governed by the former testimony exception. If it is governed by the former testimony exception, then it cannot be admitted under the residual exception. Here is the problem with that syllogism. If that is true, then this is too: A witness in front of a Senate subcommittee gives testimony; when that is subsequently offered at a trial, it surely is former testimony; therefore, it is covered by the former testimony exception and cannot be admitted under the residual exception. In the context of the scope of the residual exception, there is no apparent reason to distinguish grand jury testimony from Senate subcommittee testimony. Black's law dictionary defines testimony as follows: "Evidence that a competent witness under oath or affirmation gives at trial or in an affidavit or deposition."[41] If Black's is to be trusted, then the same syllogism applies to affidavits.[42]

In fact, a person who makes a public declaration of a religious experience is giving testimony. If such a statement is subsequently offered at a trial, it is former testimony. It is former testimony of a different sort than that contemplated by the former testimony exception, but it helps make this point: "Former testimony" has a special and specific meaning under the rules of evidence. That meaning is quite different from the Webster's dictionary meaning of testimony and even quite different from the meaning in Black's law dictionary. Under the rules of evidence, the meaning of "former testimony" is found in the foundational elements of the exception. If the foundational elements of the former testimony exception are not present, then it is not "former testimony" as defined by the rules of evidence. The exception applies to testimony given in those kinds of proceedings where cross-examination is potentially available.[43] If it is not former testimony as it is defined by the rules of evidence, then it is not covered by the former testimony exception. If it is not covered by the for-

---

jury testimony inadmissible under former testimony exception); Hollingsworth v. State, 211 S.W. 454, 455 (Tex. Crim. App. 1919) ("Her testimony before the grand jury was hearsay and inadmissible."); State v. Patton, 164 S.W. 223, 225 (Mo. 1914) (admitting grand jury testimony violates hearsay rule).

41. BLACK'S LAW DICTIONARY (7th ed. 1999).

42. *See also* White v. Illinois, 502 U.S. 346, 364 (1992) (Thomas, J. concurring in part) (Justice Thomas refers to "in-court testimony or the functional equivalent, such as affidavits, depositions, or confessions that are made in contemplation of legal proceedings.").

43. *Donlon*, 909 F.2d at 654 (then-Chief Judge Breyer wrote that the former testimony exception was written to apply to statements made in "those kinds of proceedings for which cross-examination was potentially available") (regarding *Donlon, see also* note 37, just above). This excluded testimony in a subcommittee hearing room or a church.

mer testimony exception, then it is eligible for consideration under the residual exception. This is so whether it is grand jury testimony, deposition testimony, affidavit testimony, or spiritual testimony.

A statement in front of a grand jury could be a substantively admissible prior inconsistent statement,[44] a statement against interest,[45] an expression of a then existing physical condition or state of mind,[46] former testimony,[47] or a statement admissible under the residual exception.[48] The fact that testimony in front of a grand jury just misses any one of these exceptions does not disqualify it for consideration under any other. This is so whether the other exception is the exception for statements of personal or family history[49] or the residual exception. No one would argue that grand jury testimony must be considered under the former testimony exception only. It is clear that if a defendant has a grand jury witness killed to keep him from testifying at trial the grand jury testimony can be admitted under the forfeiture by wrongdoing exception.[50] Either near-miss evidence is disqualified from consideration under all other exceptions, or it is not disqualified from consideration under any of them.

The argument against admitting grand jury testimony against the defendant when there is an applicable hearsay exception and no Confrontation Clause bar ignores the prime directive of the rules: "These rules shall be construed to secure ... elimination of unjustifiable expense and delay, and promotion of growth and development of the law of evidence to the end that the truth may be ascertained and proceedings justly determined."[51]. Furthermore, the residual exception states that it applies to "statement[s] not specifically covered by Rule 803 and 804,"[52] and grand jury testimony is "not specifically covered" by the former testimony exception. If there is another exception that fits, then the hearsay rule should not bar the admission of grand jury testimony; the residual exception should be available when such testimony is offered against the defendant.

---

44. FED.R.EVID. 801(d)(1)(A), discussed at Chapter 2(II)(A), above; United States v. Mayberry, 540 F.3d 506, 515 (6th Cir. 2008).
45. FED.R.EVID. 804(b)(3), discussed at Chapter 4(IV), above.
46. FED.R.EVID. 803(3), discussed at Chapter 3(IV), above.
47. FED.R.EVID. 804(b)(1), discussed at Chapter 4(II), above.
48. In United States v. Gonzalez, 559 F.2d 1271 (5th Cir. 1997), the court considered grand jury testimony under the statement against interest exception, but found the testimony was in the declarant's interest, and under the residual exception, but found that on the facts of this case the testimony was not trustworthy, *id*. at 1273–74.
49. FED.R.EVID. 804(b)(4), discussed at Chapter 4(VI), above.
50. FED.R.EVID. 804(b)(6), discussed at Chapter 4(VII), above.
51. FED.R.EVID. 102.
52. FED.R.EVID. 807.

C. Notice—Use of the Residual Exception Requires Notice in Advance of the Trial or Hearing

The residual exception is not available unless offering counsel gives opposing counsel advance notice of the particulars of the statement and his or her intention to offer it into evidence.[53] The rule itself calls for notice in advance of the trial or hearing at which the statement will be offered. The question of the timing of the notice is not, however, as simple as the text of the rule declares. Some jurisdictions allow notice well into the trial or hearing.[54]

1. The Substance of the Notice That Must Be Given

Rule 807 does not require pretrial notice of an intention to use Rule 807. All that is required is notice of an intention to offer the particular statement.[55]

---

53. FED.R.EVID. 807. The notice must include the name and address of the declarant. *Id.*

54. This is discussed below at part V(C)(2) of this chapter.

55. The relevant part of the rule is written as follows: " ... unless the proponent of [the statement] makes known to the adverse party ... the proponent's intention to offer the statement ..." FED.R.EVID. 807. *See also, e.g.,* United States v. Peneaux, 432 F.3d 882, 892 (8th Cir. 2005) (adequate notice is not an issue because well before the trial the government filed notice of its intent to introduce the statements, and included "information about the nature of the statements or where they could be located, along with the names, addresses, and phone numbers of the witnesses."); Alexander v. Conveyors & Dumpsters, Inc. 731 F.2d 1221, 1229 (5th Cir. 1984) (notice requirement not a problem here "since the [statement] was listed as an exhibit in [the proponent's] pre-trial order"); United States v. One 1968 Piper Navajo Twin Engine Aircraft, 594 F.2d 1040, 1041 (5th Cir. 1979) (specific reference to the residual exception is the better practice, but is not required; here "fair notice was not given" because counsel made specific reference "to a different rule, one with a different purpose and effect"); Limone v. United States, 497 F.Supp.2d 143, 153 (D. Mass. 2007) (specific reference to Rule 807 is not required); Sanchez v. Brokop, 398 F.Supp.2d 1177, 1191 (D. N.M. 2005) (regarding the notice requirement, the court held that "there is no indication that Defendant was unaware of how Rebecca Sanchez would testify at trial. Her deposition was taken by Defendant on at least one occasion and [defense counsel] was advised in the Pre-Trial Order of the likely contents of her testimony.").

But see, Rowland v. American Gen. Fin., Inc., 340 F.3d 187, 195 (4th Cir. 2003) (stating that the exception is only available if proponent gives opponent notice of an intention to rely on the residual exception; citing Rule 807); Herrick v. Garvey, 298 F.3d 1184, 1192 n.6 (10th Cir. 2002) (similar to *Rowland*); Kirk v. Raymark Industries, Inc., 61 F.3d 147, 167 (3d Cir. 1995) (similar to *Rowland*). Rule 807, however, requires notice of the "proponent's intention to offer the statement," and not notice of an intention to offer the statement under Rule 807. These cases seem to be making imprecise and not well thought through state-

Notice must include the particulars of the statement and the name and address of the declarant. This precludes the use of this exception where the declarant's identity is unknown.[56] It does not preclude the use of this exception when the declarant is unavailable so long as the declarant's name and address are given. The declarant can even be dead; the address can be Shady Rest Cemetery; the residual exception has always been available for out-of-court declarations by unavailable declarants, including those unavailable by reason of death.[57]

2. The Timing of the Notice That Must Be Given

Some courts interpret the notice requirement more in accord with what they see as its spirit than with its letter. The rule states that the notice must be "sufficiently in advance of the trial or hearing to provide the adverse party with a fair opportunity to prepare to meet [the evidence]." Some courts stress the "fair opportunity" part of the notice requirement over the "in advance of the trial or hearing" part. One influential court has said that in cases where the need to use this exception does not become apparent until after the trial has begun, midtrial notice given enough in advance of the actual use of the evidence can satisfy the rule's pretrial notice requirement.[58] Variations of this flex-

---

ments about what the rule requires, which do achieve the right result on the facts of the cases at hand.

56. Though this is not necessarily true. United States v. Medico, 557 F.2d 309 (2d Cir. 1977), upholds admission under the residual exception of a statement by an unidentified bystander. *Id.* at 313–16.

57. Prior to the 1997 amendments to the rules of evidence, this residual exception appeared at the end of Rules 803 and 804. As Rule 804(b)(5), the residual exception applied to statements by declarants whose in-court testimony was unavailable and, under Rule 804(a)(4), one of the grounds of unavailability is death. Regarding declarants who have died, *see, e.g.*, Nowell v. Universal Elec. Co., 792 F.2d 1310, 1314–15 (5th Cir. 1986); Dartez v. Fibreboard Corp., 765 F.2d 456, 460–63 (5th Cir. 1985); United States v. West, 574 F.2d 1131, 1134–36 (4th Cir. 1978).

58. United States v. Iaconetti, 406 F.Supp. 554 (E.D.N.Y. 1976) (Weinstein, J.), *aff'd*, 540 F.2d 574 (2d Cir. 1976). *See also* United States v. Obayagbona, 627 F.Supp. 329, 340 (E.D.N.Y. 1985) (offer of continuance cures lack of pre-trial notice) (Weinstein, J.). While affirming *Iaconetti*, the Second Circuit softened Judge Weinstein's holding: "Our holding should in no way be construed as in general approving the waiver of [the rule's] notice requirements. Pre-trial notice should clearly be given if at all possible, and only in those situations where requiring pre-trial notice is wholly impracticable, as here, should flexibility be accorded." *Iaconetti*, 540 F.2d at 578 n.6. *See also*, G. Michael Fenner, *Law Professor Reveals Shocking Truth About Hearsay*, 62 UMKC L. Rev. 1, 41–44 (1993).

Even in the Second Circuit, the course has been a wavering one. *E.g.*, United States v. Oates, 560 F.2d 45, 72 n.30 (2d Cir. 1977) (no notice in advance of trial, through no fault of pro-

ible approach predominate,[59] even though they are not consistent with the plain meaning of the rule.[60]

The lesson here is that even though the rule requires pretrial or prehearing notice, many courts do not—particularly when the lack of pretrial notice was through no fault of the lawyer now offering the evidence. A lawyer who just learned of the evidence, whose next witness has just refused to testify, or who only just found herself in a position where she needs the evidence to rebut surprise evidence from the other side has a lot of case law supporting an argument that

---

ponent, and no notice during trial until authenticating witness called to stand; "the advance notice requirement leaves no doubt that it was the intention of Congress that the requirement be read strictly"; no mention of *Iaconetti*).

59. *E.g.*, United States v. Bachsian, 4 F.3d 796, 799 (9th Cir. 1993) ("[T]he government's failure to provide pretrial notice is excused.... [T]he adverse party had an opportunity to attack the trustworthiness of the evidence."); United States v. Baker, 985 F.2d 1248, 1253 (4th Cir. 1993) ("[P]retrial notice was wholly impracticable and thus, under the exceptional circumstances of this case, we uphold [the trial court's] grant of notice flexibility."); United States v. Benavente Gomez, 921 F.2d 378, 384 (1st Cir. 1990) (in criminal cases, the flexible approach is used only when pretrial notice "wholly impractical," proponent is not responsible for delay, and the adverse party has adequate opportunity to examine and respond to evidence in question); Furtado v. Bishop, 604 F.2d 80, 92–93 (1st Cir. 1979) (the evidence is admissible even though the plaintiffs never explained their failure to give pretrial notice because the record indicates that defense "counsel had prepared to meet the evidence in question"); United States v. Bailey, 581 F.2d 341, 348 (3rd Cir. 1978) (admitting statement where proponent was not at fault for failing to provide notice in advance of trial and a continuance was granted to allow opponent sufficient time to prepare to contest admission of the evidence); United States v. Carlson, 547 F.2d 1346 (8th Cir. 1976) (scheduled witness refused to testify on eve of trial; government allowed to use residual exception to introduce grand jury testimony); Hicks v. Charles Pfizer & Co., 466 F.Supp.2d 799, 810 (E.D. Tx. 2005) (discussing various circuit courts of appeals decisions upholding the flexible approach, including one holding that the notice requirement is satisfied if opposing party has sufficient opportunity to determine the statement's trustworthiness, three upholding the admission under this exception of statements by declarants who have died, and one upholding admission of statements by unidentified bystanders).

It does seem pretty clear, however, that, no matter how far you stretch it, pretrial notice is missing if counsel raises the residual exception for the first time on appeal. *See, e.g.,* United States v. Guevara, 598 F.2d 1094, 1100 (7th Cir. 1979). *See also* United States v. Williams, 272 F.3d 845, 857–58 (7th Cir. 2001) ("Williams did not raise [Rule 807] below, and thus has forfeited it.).

60. Though one does not turn to legislative history when text is clear, it can be argued that the legislative history supports reading the exception restrictively, rather than flexibly. The legislative history states that the residual exception is to "be used very rarely, and only in exceptional circumstances." Report of the Senate Committee on the Judiciary, S.Rep. No. 1277, 93d Cong., 2d Sess., p. 18 (1974).

pretrial notice is not required. Even a lawyer who has only just realized that the statute requires pretrial notice has *an argument* that the court need not require pretrial notice. On the other hand, lawyers who know of hearsay evidence that they may want to get it into evidence take a huge risk if they do not give pretrial notice of the evidence.

3. The Form of the Notice That Must Be Given

"There is no particular form of notice required under the rule. As long as the party against whom the document is offered has notice of its existence and the proponent's intention to introduce [the document]—and thus has an opportunity to counter it and protect himself against surprise—the rule's notice requirement is satisfied."[61] When the "pretrial" part of the notice requirement *is* enforced, the pretrial notice may be more formal or less so: It may be a document filed with the court and styled "Notice of Intention to Introduce Certain Evidence" or it may be a letter to opposing counsel stating an intention to introduce particular statements, and including the names and addresses of all witnesses to the statements.[62] Regarding a written out-of-court statement, just listing it as an exhibit in a pretrial order may satisfy the rule's notice requirement.[63] Upon retrial, notice may spring from the fact that the evidence in question was used against the defendant at the first trial.[64] In one case, one party filed a motion in limine requesting a ruling that certain statements were admissible; the court denied the motion; the party offered the statements again at trial and this time the court found the evidence to be admissible under the residual exception. The motion in limine provided the required pretrial notice.[65] In an-

---

61. United States v. Munoz, 16 F.3d 1116, 1122 (11th Cir. 1994).

62. United States v. Vretta, 790 F.2d 651, 660 (7th Cir. 1986) (a letter to opposing counsel stating the intention to introduce statements and the names and addresses of all witnesses to statements satisfied the notice requirement; interpreting former FED.R.EVID. 804(b)(5), which has been moved into and subsumed by Rule 807.).

63. Opposing counsel must, of course, have access to knowledge of the particulars of the statement, including the name and address of the out-of-court declarant. United States v. Hong, 545 F.Supp.2d 281, 287 (W.D. N.Y. 2008) (defendants moved for disclosure of government's Rule 807 statements; government responded that it would disclose in its pretrial memorandum; court held government's plan for notice was sufficient); Alexander v. Conveyors & Dumpers, Inc. 731 F.2d 1221, 1229 (5th Cir. 1984) (statement was listed as an exhibit in offering party's pretrial order).

64. State v. Robinson, 735 P.2d 801, 812 (Ariz. 1987) (defendant aware of evidence in question because it was used against him at first trial; defendant's attorney knew it would be used at second trial).

65. FTC v. Kitco of Nevada, Inc., 612 F.Supp. 1282, 1294 (D.C. Minn. 1985).

other, a party filed a pretrial motion to have certain evidence suppressed; the court said this indicated that he had sufficient pretrial notice to satisfy the residual exception.[66]

4. A Conclusion Regarding Notice

The Use Note is this: On the one hand, an attorney may be able to get away with not giving *pretrial* notice under Rule 807. On the other hand, any attorney who has important evidence that may be hearsay and may not fit under any of the specific exceptions, should give specific notice of an intention to offer the evidence and include the other identifying information required by the rule. This notice should be given unless there is some specific, overbearing reason not to do so. (Perhaps surprise is critical, and outweighs the risk that the residual exception will be needed and will not be available.) The "Notice of Intention ..." should become a standard part of the trial attorney's arsenal. That way, there is no question—and counsel avoids that embarrassing moment when the client reads the opinion saying that a key piece of evidence would have been admissible if only counsel had given pretrial notice.[67]

D. Trustworthiness

To fit under the residual exception, the out-of-court statement must have circumstantial guarantees of trustworthiness equivalent to those of the exceptions in Rules 803 and 804.

1. Trustworthiness As Measured Against the Other Exceptions

Some evidence let in under Rule 803 and 804 seems quite reliable: The former testimony exception, with its full opportunity for a well-motivated cross-examination, comes to mind. Some of the evidence let in under Rule 803 and 804 does not seem terribly reliable: The ancient documents exception, under which a newspaper article comes in if it is old enough and found where you

---

66. State v. McCafferty, 356 N.W.2d 159, 162 (S.D. 1984).

67. United States v. Davis, 571 F.2d 1354, 1360 n.11 (5th Cir. 1978) (stating that the only other exception conceivably available is the residual, but the government made no attempt to give the required pretrial notice). *Cf.* United States v. Benavente Gomez, 921 F.2d 378, 384 (1st Cir. 1990) (the court was unwilling to take a flexible approach to the pretrial notice requirement and apply the residual exception); Cummins v. Mississippi, 515 So.2d 869, 874 (Miss. 1987) ("One day before trial is not sufficient notice ..."), *overruled in part, on other grounds*, Morgan v. Mississippi, 703 So. 2d 832, 841 (Miss. 1997).

would expect to find it, comes to mind.[68] The reliability requirement of the residual exception does not seem to be saying "Pick the weakest, least reliable of the exceptions and use it as the standard." The standard here seems to be some sort of aggregate. It is one that relates to the exceptions as a whole rather than to any single exception, and is heavily dependent on the facts of the particular case at hand.[69] The requirement that there be circumstantial guarantees of trustworthiness equivalent to those of the exceptions in Rules 803 and 804 seems to be an admonition to consider the reliability of the out-of-court statement using the Rule 803 and 804 exceptions as a guide. More on that in a moment.

First, the logical place to start, when looking for trustworthiness, is with the indicia of untrustworthiness that led to the creation of the hearsay rule in the first place. Important guarantees of trustworthiness include appropriate cross-examination—well-motivated cross-examination of the declarant at the time the statement was made[70] (as with the former testimony exception), or cross-examination of the declarant as a witness when the statement is offered (as with the recorded recollection exception),[71] or anywhere in between. If the statement was made under oath, that would tend to guarantee its trustworthiness.[72] The declarant's ability to have perceived the facts presented in the

---

68. Whatever the document in question, whether reliable or not, if kept in the right place long enough, it becomes an ancient document. *See* Chapter 3(XI)(D)(2), above.

69. On the other hand, some courts make statements such at this:

In comparison to the potential for truthfulness inherent in evidence admissible under other hearsay exception requirements, the potential for truthfulness here is at least equally high. Certainly the video has more probative weight and credibility than that ensured by the ancient document rule (Fed. R. Evid. 803(16)) ... If this video were "ancient", it would not be more relevant nor persuasive than it is.

Gonzalez v. Digital Equip. Corp., 8 F.Supp.2d 194, 201 (E.D.N.Y. 1998).

70. *See particularly* Idaho v. Wright, 497 U.S. 805, 815 (1990) (regarding Confrontation Clause, statement bore sufficient indicia of reliability particularly because defendant had adequate opportunity to cross-examine declarant when statement made) (citing Mancusi v. Stubbs, 408 U.S. 204, 216 (1972)). *Accord, e.g.*, Sternhagen v. Dow Co., 108 F.Supp.2d 1113, 1119 (D. Mont. 1999) ("factors worthy of consideration include[] availability of the declarant for cross-examination") (citing cases).

71. Cross-examination of the out-of-court declarant in the trial where the out-of-court statement is offered also supplies some demeanor evidence. *See* Chapter 1(I), above.

72. E.g., In re Slatkin, 525 F.3d 805, 812 (9th Cir. 2008) (among other things, the statement "was made under oath with the advice of counsel ... [and] after [declarant] was advised of his constitutional rights"); FTC v. Amy Travel Serv., Inc. 875 F.2d 564, 576 (7th Cir. 1989) (oath as a guarantee of trustworthiness); *Sternhagen*, 108 F.Supp.2d at 1119 (listing

statement can be an important consideration, as can factors affecting the declarant's memory of the facts stated, factors such as the time between the event and the statement.[73] If the statement is recorded on a digital, visual CD or on videotape, then the trier of fact can observe the declarant's demeanor—another guarantee of reliability.[74] As discussed at the beginning of this book, these are all part of what makes hearsay categorically unreliable and, therefore, presumptively inadmissible in the first place.[75] Turn them over, and they tend to make the statement reliable.

The logical second step is this. Each of the exceptions in Rule 803 and 804 is based on some factors that tend to make that category of evidence reliable. Look at the things that led the drafters of the rules to conclude those kinds of statements were reliable enough to be admissible hearsay.[76] In addition to the factors just mentioned, this would include the following: spontaneity[77] (as with present sense impressions); lack of capacity to fabricate (as with excited utterances);[78] self-interest and other incentives to be accurate (as with statements for purposes of medical diagnosis or treatment, records of a regularly conducted activity, and statements against interest)[79]; pressures exerted at the

---

"[f]actors courts consider," including "whether the declarant[] was under oath," made the statement voluntarily, based the statement on personal knowledge, contradicted any previous statement, etc.) (citing cases). The oath alone, however, is not enough to guarantee residual-exception trustworthiness. United States v. Fernandez, 892 F.2d 976, 981 (11th Cir. 1989).

73. United States v. Vretta, 790 F.2d 651, 659 (7th Cir. 1986) (close proximity in time between event and statements about the event as evidence of trustworthiness); *Sternhagen*, 108 F.Supp.2d at 1119 (consider "whether the declarant's perception or memory was faulty.") (citing cases).

74. *Sternhagen*, 108 F.Supp.2d at 1119 ("consider ... whether the declarant ... had the statement preserved on videotape to afford the jury an opportunity to evaluate declarant's demeanor").

75. *See* Chapter 1(I), above.

76. United States v. Banks, 514 F.3d 769, 777 (8th Cir. 2008) ("One method of approaching this [trustworthiness] analysis is to 'compare the circumstances surrounding the statement to the closest hearsay exception.' 2 Kenneth S. Broun, McCormick on Evidence §324 (6th ed. 2006)).

77. *E.g.*, *Sternhagen*, 108 F.Supp.2d at 1119 (consider "the statement's proximity in time to the events it describes; ... the statement's spontaneity") (citing cases).

78. *See, e.g.*, United States v. Grant, 38 M.J. 684, 693 (USAF Ct. Mil. Rev. 1993) ("The instant case is one where the statement's very close resemblance to an excited utterance enhances its trustworthiness and admissibility under [the residual exception].").

79. In re Slatkin, 525 F.3d 805, 812–13 (9th Cir. 2008) (among other things, "the criminal consequences to [declarant] of making the admissions ... provide a sufficient circumstantial guarantee of trustworthiness").

time of the declaration that tend to make it more or less reliable (as with the pressure towards truth exerted by the knowledge death is imminent, or the pressure away from truth exerted by a suggestive interrogation of a child allegedly under the stress of a sexual assault); cultural factors inherent in the situation that tend to produce truthful statements (as with statements under belief of impending death).[80]

Courts have also considered other factors,[81] such as whether there have been inconsistencies in various retellings of the story[82] or whether the statement has been corroborated;[83] self-interest and other incentives to be inaccurate, such as the declarant's relationship with the parties; the character or mental state of the out-of-court declarant;[84] the fact that federal law requires that the records be kept;[85] the use of appropriate language, such as age-appropriate language in a statement by a child; influences exerted on the declarant, including, if the statement was a product of an interview, the suggestive manner of that interview, and more.[86]

If the testimony of the declarant is unavailable, the reason for this unavailability may be relevant to whether his or her statements are trustworthy.[87] For

---

80. In a broader sense, the Seventh Circuit Court of Appeals has stated the following: "Where evidence complies with the spirit if not the latter [sic] of several exceptions, admissibility is appropriate under the residual exception." United States v. McPartlin, 595 F.2d 1321, 1350 (7th Cir.).

81. E.g., United States v. Vretta, 790 F.2d 651, 659 (7th Cir. 1986) (the fact that declarant made the statement a number of times to a number of different disinterested people from whom he had nothing to gain by lying as evidence of trustworthiness).

82. E.g., Sternhagen, 108 F.Supp.2d at 1119 (consider "whether the declarant ... contradicted any previous statement").

83. E.g., Sternhagen, 108 F.Supp.2d at 1119 (consider "whether the statement has been corroborated") (citing cases).

84. E.g., United States v. Two Shields, 497 F.3d 789, 794 (8th Cir. 2007) (declarant was drunk and at times incoherent; at one point he stated he did not recall how he had been injured; his "statement" that defendant was not his attacker was in the form of an ambiguous head shake in response to leading questions); Sternhagen, 108 F.Supp.2d at 1119 (consider declarant's "motivation to fabricate") (citing cases).

85. Banks, 514 F.3d at 777 (record keeping required by federal law is inherently trustworthy).

86. In this regard, see also Chapter 3(III)(D)(9) (excited utterances and child witnesses).

87. In State v. Nichols, 365 S.E.2d 561 (N.C. 1988), the court stated that if the declarant "'[p]ersists in refusing to testify concerning the subject matter of his statement despite a court order to do so' the court might weigh this as a factor against admitting declarant's statement." Id. at 566 n.2. As argued in the text following this footnote, persistence in refusing to testify could also work the other way; in the right context it could weigh in favor of admission. This is further evidence that the "trustworthiness" determination is very fact specific, very much dependent upon context.

example, if it can be shown that the declarant and the party married just so the rule of spousal incompetence would keep the declarant from having to testify against the party, that might be evidence of trustworthiness. Or, in a jurisdiction that has not adopted the newer federal exception for statements offered against a party whose wrongdoing secured the unavailability of the declarant,[88] a showing that a party killed or threatened a witness into silence might be evidence that the declaration is trustworthy.[89] A court may conclude that if the evidence were not trustworthy, there would have been less severe ways of dealing with the evidence than killing or threatening the witness (cross-examination, for example). If this can be so, then evidence of threats can be evidence that the out-of-court statement is trustworthy. While unavailability *per se* does not indicate trustworthiness, the reasons behind the unavailability might.[90]

The reliability requirement seems to boil down to this: The trial judge must find—and the proponent must argue—that the evidence is reliable enough to allow the jury to hear it. One way to do this is to take the various guarantees of trustworthiness that apply to the Rule 803 and 804 exceptions and see which, if any, apply to the out-of-court statement in question. The standard seems to be an aggregate standard that sometimes is established by reference to particular specific exceptions. "[T]trustworthiness," as one court of appeals has said, "is analyzed under a broad totality of the circumstances test."[91]

2. Focus on the Statement, Not the Testifying Witness

The requirement that the statement have circumstantial guarantees of trustworthiness focuses on the out-of-court statement and the out-of-court de-

---

88. *See* Chapter 4(VII), above.

89. For example, United States v. Ruffin, 12 M.J. 952 (USAF Ct. Mil. Rev. 1981) involved a man convicted of sexually abusing his step-daughter. At trial, after the stepdaughter refused to testify, the prosecutor offered into evidence a statement she had given to the military police. It was received under the residual exception. The court's list of factors guaranteeing the trustworthiness of the statement ended as follows: "Lastly, we can only conclude that K. L. D.'s refusal to testify on behalf of the Government was motivated by a desire to help her step-father." *Id.* at 955.

90. The silence of unavailability results from such divergent things as senility, on the one hand, and threats, on the other.

91. *Two Shields*, 497 F.3d at 794. *See also, e.g., Sternhagen*, 108 F.Supp.2d at 1119 ("No mechanical test exists for determining the reliability of out-of-court statements; such determinations are made on a case-by-case basis.").

clarant—not on the trustworthiness of the witness who is testifying in court and subject to cross-examination.[92]

3. Focus on the Circumstances at the Time the Statement Was Made, Not Hindsight

The requirement that the statement have circumstantial guarantees of trustworthiness focuses on the circumstances that existed at the time the out-of-court statement was made. It does not take into account factors "that may be added by using hindsight."[93]

---

92. *E.g.*, Idaho v. Wright, 497 U.S. 805, 819, 820 (1990) ("[T]he relevant circumstances include only those that surround the making of the statement and that render the declarant particularly worthy of belief"; statement made in context of the hearsay rule and held to apply also to the Confrontation Clause); *Two Shields*, 497 F.3d at 794 ("the focus of the inquiry is" the "trustworthiness of declarant's statement, not [the] credibility of person who witnessed the statement"; paraphrasing United States v. Atkins, 558 F.2d 133, 135 (3d Cir. 1977)); United States v. Lawrence, 349 F.3d 109, 117 (3d Cir. 2003)(declarant's "blinks and nods … were simply too ambiguous to constitute a meaningful statement"); United States v. Juvenile NB, 59 F.3d 771, 776 (8th Cir. 1995) (citing cases).

Mashburn v. Wright, 420 S.E.2d 379 (Ga. Ct. App. 1992), was an action to recover the value of a certificate of deposit in the deceased's name and found among the deceased's possessions. Plaintiff testified that the deceased had handed him the certificate and stated "this is yours, I want you to have it," that "the certificate would mature in February" and the two of them would go to the bank then and have it signed over to Plaintiff, and that the deceased would keep the certificate until then because he had a safe place to do so. Under Georgia's residual exception, the court found the statements were needed because the declarant was dead, and were trustworthy because they were against the declarant's pecuniary interest. *Id.* at 380–81. That the statements were in the interest of the testifying witness is a credibility question for the jury, not an admissibility question for the judge. *Id.* at 381. Regarding admissibility versus credibility, *see particularly* Chapter 3(I)(D), above.

93. United States v. Tome, 61 F.3d 1446, 1452 (10th Cir. 1995). "When applying this exception, the circumstantial guarantees of trustworthiness that we consider '"are those that existed at the time the statement was made and do not include those that may be added by using hindsight."'" *Id.* (quoting Idaho v. Wright, 497 U.S. 805, 823 (1990) (in turn quoting Huff v. White Motor Corp., 609 F.2d 286, 292 (7th Cir. 1979))). An out-of-court statement that was self-serving when it was made may not be sufficiently trustworthy. *E.g.*, Hill v. Brown, 672 S.W.2d 330 (Ark. 1984) (discussing declarant's self-serving out-of-court statement concerning ownership of a disputed piece of property). An out-of court statement that is in the interest of the testifying witness but was against the interest of the declarant when made may well be sufficiently trustworthy. *Mashburn*, 420 S.E.2d at 382, discussed and quoted in note 91, above.

4. Independent Evidence of the Fact Asserted Is Not a Circumstantial Guarantee of Trustworthiness

The prevailing and preferred view is that other evidence of facts asserted in the out-of-court statement is not a "circumstantial guarantee[ ] of trustworthiness."[94] In fact, since residual-exception evidence must be more probative on its point than other reasonably available admissible evidence, the more of this kind of corroborating evidence there is, the less likely the residual exception will apply.[95]

5. The Trustworthiness of the Statement of an Incompetent Declarant

The fact that at the time the statement was made the declarant was incompetent may be relevant to whether the statement is trustworthy,[96] but it does not render the statement per se, or even presumptively, untrustworthy.[97]

---

94. Fed.R.Evid. 807. *Tome*, 61 F.3d at 1452 (citing *Idaho v. Wright*, 497 U.S.at 823). *But see, e.g.*, United States v. Bailey, 581 F.2d 341, 349 (3d Cir. 1978) (trustworthiness of statement offered under residual exception should not be judged *solely* on basis of corroboration of facts asserted in statement); United States v. Doerr, 886 F.2d 944, 956 (7th Cir. 1989) (when assessing trustworthiness of hearsay evidence, court can consider "the existence of corroborating evidence.").

95. *E.g.*, v. Bailey, 581 F.2d at 349.

This kind of corroborating evidence does play some role in Rule 807 analysis. The United States Supreme Court, in a closely related context, described that role thusly: "the presence of [this kind of] corroborating evidence more appropriately indicates that any error in admitting the statement might be harmless, rather than that any basis exists for presuming the declarant to be trustworthy." *Idaho v. Wright*, 497 U.S. at 823 (this statement was made in context of a Confrontation Clause objection to an out-of-court statement which, at the time, required the court to find that the statement possessed "adequate indicia of reliability").

There is a second kind of evidence that can be labeled as corroborating: evidence indicating that the declaration itself is trustworthy—that is, evidence that the declarant had the ability to perceive the facts recorded, unable to have engaged in deception, and the like. This kind of evidence is a circumstantial guarantee of trustworthiness. In fact, as noted above, in part (D)(1) of this chapter, this kind of evidence may be particularly important when looking for guarantees of trustworthiness. If we say that corroborating evidence is not a circumstantial guarantee of trustworthiness, we must be careful how we define "corroborating evidence."

96. *Idaho v. Wright*, 497 U.S. at 825.

97. *See generally* the discussion in Chapter 13, below. *See particularly* Idaho v. Wright, 497 U.S. at 824; Doe v. United States, 976 F.2d 1071, 1082 (7th Cir. 1992); State v. Wagoner, 506 S.E.2d 738, 742 (N.C. Ct. App. 1988) (under the residual exception, a statement does not automatically lack guarantees of trustworthiness just because the declarant was

It is not a new thing to use, for example, the excited utterance exception or the statements for purposes of medical diagnosis or treatment exception to admit into evidence statements that were made by children who are too young to be competent witnesses.[98] There is no reason why the residual exception should be treated any differently. *Incompetent is not synonymous with untrustworthy.* There is overlap: Some incompetencies render a statement untrustworthy and some untrustworthiness renders a witness incompetent, but the one does not necessarily follow from the other. To repeat, incompetence does not create per se or presumptive untrustworthiness.

E. Probative Value

1. Probative Value in General

The residual exception requires that the evidence offered thereunder be "more probative on the point for which it is offered than any other evidence which the proponent can procure through reasonable efforts."[99] In general, this is simply a matter of determining if there is other evidence, if the other evidence is reasonably available,[100] and if the proffered residual-exception evi-

---

and still is incompetent to testify); W.C.L., Jr. v. People, 685 P.2d 176, 178 (Colo. 1984) (even though declarant-child incompetent to testify because she did not know what it meant to tell the truth, her statements have circumstantial guarantees of trustworthiness equivalent to specific exceptions and would fit under residual exception had Colorado adopted residual exception).

The question raised here has to do with the competence of the declarant at the time the statement was made, not at the time of the trial or hearing. As regards the latter, the following is, of course, true: "[T]he determination as to whether the hearsay statements are trustworthy must focus on the circumstantial guarantees of reliability which surround the declarant at the time the statement was made and not on the witness' competence at the time of the hearing." State v. Holden, 416 S.E.2d 415, 420 (N.C. 1992).

98. *See* Chapter 13(II)(B), below.

99. FED.R.EVID. 807(B). United States v. Czachorowski, 66 M.J. 432, 436 (U.S. Armed Forces 2008) (uncorroborated assertions do not satisfy the proponent's burden of showing that more probative evidence is not reasonably available; " ... some specific evidence of reasonable efforts to obtain other probative evidence is ... required....") (citing and discussing cases).

100. *See, e.g.,* Barry v. Trustees of the Int'l Ass'n Full-Time Salaried Officers and Emps. of Outside Local and Dist. Counsel's (Iron Workers) Pension Plan, 467 F.Supp.2d 91, 103–04, 105 (D. D.C. 2006) ("Courts have interpreted the [probative value] requirement 'as providing a basis for a trial court to evaluate the need for the statement in the case as compared to the costs of obtaining alternative evidence,' or 'as imposing a requirement of diligence.' 2 McCormick On Evidence § 324." "[P]laintiff here has not shown that, 'through reasonable efforts,' he could not have otherwise obtained the information that he now seeks

dence is more probative on the point than the other available evidence. It is a function of the availability of other evidence, the cost of securing the other evidence (in time, money, and the emotional cost of forcing the declarant to take the stand), and the relative probative value of the other evidence. It is a cost-benefit analysis comparing the evidence offered under the hearsay rule with all other available evidence on the point.[101]

2. The Turncoat Witness—Using This Exception to Admit Prior Statements by Witnesses Who Take the Stand and Change Their Stories

Once again, the residual exception requires that the out-of-court statement be "more probative on the point for which it is offered than any other evidence which the proponent can procure through reasonable efforts." In *Lovejoy v. United States*[102] the out-of-court declarant testified at the trial. Her in-trial testimony contradicted her out-of-court statement. The court found that the out-of-court statement was more probative of the fact asserted than was her in-court statement. Relying on the residual exception, the court let the statement in as substantive evidence of the facts asserted.

Lovejoy was convicted of attempted sexual assault of his 13-year-old daughter. The jury accepted this version of the facts: The victim's mother (Lovejoy's common-law wife) interrupted the assault, got Lovejoy out of the room, and preserved the victim's clothing for evidence. The next day, the mother took the victim and the clothing to a nurse and told the nurse what had happened to her daughter.[103]

---

to introduce via [Rule 807]."); Phan v. Trinity Reg'l Hosp., 3 F. Supp.2d 1014, 1022 (N.D. Iowa 1998) (the out-of-court statement is more probative than other evidence plaintiff can procure through reasonable efforts; the only other evidence would be the testimony of the alleged wrongdoers and it is unlikely they will acknowledge their wrongdoing).

101. To repeat an example used above, in a civil action with a maximum value of $10,000, an out-of-court statement would be more probative on a point than any other evidence reasonably available if the only other evidence at all available is the live testimony of a person who could be brought into court at a cost $4,000 (from, say, the mountains of Nepal). *See* the discussion of unavailability at Chapter 4(I)(C), above. The added benefit of the live testimony instead of the out-of-court statement may be small, particularly when the cost of getting that witness into court will eat up nearly one-half of the maximum recovery; in the context of the $10,000 case, the cost of the live testimony certainly is high.

102. 92 F.3d 628 (8th Cir. 1996).

103. *Id.* at 630–32.

At Lovejoy's trial, the daughter was unable to testify. She was blind, could not speak more than a few words, and could not write. Lovejoy could not be made to testify. The victim's mother—defendant's wife—did testify, but she told an entirely different story from what she had told the nurse. She said it never happened.[104] The trial court allowed the nurse to tell the jury what the mother had told her—allowed the mother's out-of-court statement in for the truth of the matter asserted.[105] The Eighth Circuit Court of Appeals held that the nurse's testimony "was more probative on the conduct of Lovejoy than any other evidence because the mother testified differently at trial, the victim could not testify and no other person witnessed the attempted assault."[106] The mother's out-of-court statement was considered more probative than her in-court statement. (Not more trustworthy, though it may be that too, but more probative.)

How can it be that her out-of-court statement is "more probative on the point for which it [was] offered" than her in-court testimony? By saying that in all probability she was telling the truth then and is lying. But is that the kind of "more probative" analysis the rule contemplates? Everyone suspects that, for the most part, such a next-day statement is more credible than the later recanting testimony. But the exception calls for probative value, and aren't probative value and credibility two different things? Additionally, the residual exception requires an examination of the declaration's trustworthiness *and* its probative value. Does not credibility relate to trustworthiness, more than to probative value?

---

104. *Id.* at 632.

105. The nurse's testimony was substantively admissible under Rule 803(4), because the mother's statement was for purposes of medical treatment. Lovejoy v. United States, 92 F.3d 628, 632 (8th Cir. 1996). The part of the opinion authorizing use of the residual exception is dictum.

The nurse's testimony would have been admissible to impeach the mother's testimony, as a nonhearsay prior inconsistent statement. There are two problems with that approach, however. First, there was almost no other evidence of the crime and no other evidence of the identity of the perpetrator. The prosecutor needed this evidence as substantive evidence. Second, I have argued elsewhere that if a lawyer calls a witness knowing she is going to recant, has her recant, and then argues she is not telling the truth—when the lawyer calls the witness only to impeach her—the witness's testimony on direct examination is irrelevant and inadmissible. G. Michael Fenner, *Handling the Turncoat Witness Under the Federal Rules of Evidence*, 55 Notre Dame Lawyer 536 (1980).

Since the mother's statement to the nurse was not under oath, it is not a nonhearsay prior statement by a witness, under FED.R.EVID. 801(d)(1)(A). Part of the mother's statement may be nonhearsay as a statement of identification of a person made after perceiving that person, under FED.R.EVID. 801(d)(1)(C), but not all of it—not enough of it.

106. *Lovejoy*, 92 F.3d at 632.

Can the former statement be more probative because we suspect it is more credible? Professor Norman M. Garland suggested that we cannot. He stated that "[i]f the declarant is available to testify, the argument is that the declarant's live testimony is more probative than an out-of-court, hearsay statement."[107] The United States Court of Appeals for the Fifth Circuit seems to agree with him:

> The live testimony of the available witness, whose demeanor the jury would have been able to observe and whose testimony would have been subject to cross-examination, would have been of more probative value in establishing the truth than the [out-of-court statement].... Although [the residual exception] appears to dispense with availability, the condition re-enters the analysis of whether or not to admit statements into evidence ... because of the requirement that the proponent use reasonable efforts to procure the most probative evidence on the points sought to be proved.[108]

In a similar vein, the United States Court of Appeals for the Fourth Circuit stated that "as a general rule, the credibility of a witness has nothing to do with whether or not his testimony is probative with respect to the fact which it seeks to prove."[109]

Intuitively, it seems that the judge cannot say that the former statement is more probative just because the judge finds the former statement more credible. Instinctively, as lawyers, we distinguish probative value and credibility: The former is a question of law for the judge and the latter is a question of fact for the jury. On reflection, however, it seems that the Eighth Circuit Court of Appeals may have hit on something very important.

When Professor Garland and the Fourth and Fifth Circuits discussed this element of relative probative value, they equated probative value with testability. They are not concerned with whether the out-of-court statement is more probative because it is more likely true, but with whether it is more probative because it is more testable than the in-court statement.[110]

---

107. Norman M. Garland, *An Overview of Relevance and Hearsay: A Nine-Step Analytical Guide*, 22 Sw. U. L. Rev. 1039, 1066 (1993).

108. United States v. Mathis, 559 F.2d 294, 298–99 (5th Cir. 1977) (citations omitted).

109. United States v. Welsh, 774 F.2d 670, 672 (4th Cir. 1985).

110. In the case of the turncoat witness, the out-of-court declarant is on the stand, and telling a different story. There is demeanor evidence and there is plenty of opportunity for each side to examine the witness. As regards the hearsay rule's preference for live testimony, we have the live testimony of the declarant—live testimony that will include plenty of opportunity to explain any difference between the live testimony and the earlier statement.

If "[t]he probative value of testimony is determined upon the assumption that the testimony is true,"[111] and the judge assesses the probative value of the "true" live testimony and the "true," but contradictory, out-of-court statement, then which of these two "true," but contradictory, statements is more probative? Is it the one that is presented live in court, is not hearsay, and can be cross-examined? If so, then when the question is "Which statement is more probative?", the in-court statement always wins.

If this is the rule, then, when a witness takes the stand and lies—recanting her earlier truthful telling of the facts—her contradictory out-of-court statement will never be admissible under the residual exception. On the other hand, when a witness has no memory of the event,[112] or is too frightened to testify,[113] or when the witness's in-court testimony is unavailable, then the out-of-court statement may be admissible under the residual exception. It may be trustworthy and it may be more probative than other evidence reasonably available. The lie—taking the stand and telling a false version of the events on trial—takes the residual exception off of the table. The non-lie[114]—refusing to testify—leaves the residual exception on the table. Advantage to the lie.

These rules are to be interpreted "to secure fairness in administration ... and promotion of growth and development of the law of evidence to the end that the truth may be ascertained and proceedings justly determined."[115] Giving the greater advantage to the greater lie hardly seems to serve those goals. And there is no reason why we must give such a narrow reading to the residual exception.

There is another way to look at this issue. The dictionary definition of probative has nothing to do with whether the item is testable, but with whether the item contributes to testing the proposition to be proved. Probative is defined as "[h]aving the quality or function of proving or demonstrating; affording proof or evidence; demonstrative, evidential."[116] The probative value

---

111. Eleanor Swift, *A Response to the "Probative Value" Theory of Hearsay Suggested by Hearsay From a Layperson*, 14 Cardozo L. Rev. 103, 116 (1992).

112. United States v. Lyon, 567 F.2d 777, 783–84 (8th Cir. 1977).

113. *E.g.*, United States v. Dorian, 803 F.2d 1439, 1444–45 (8th Cir. 1986) (discussing that an out-of-court statement made by a 5 year-old victim of sexual abuse was unable to testify meaningfully because she was frightened) (decided prior to the Supreme Court's recent change in the law of the Confrontation Clause; regarding the Confrontation Clause, see Chapter 14).

114. Or the lesser lie, for a whole new story seems a greater lie than "I don't remember."

115. Fed.R.Evid. 102.

116. VIII The Oxford English Dictionary 1402 (1970).

of evidence, then, seems to have to do with both whether the evidence is testable and whether it is credible. The trial judge has to decide whether the out-of-court evidence is more probative than any other reasonably available evidence. This seems to allow room for the trial judge to consider, among other things, the relative credibility of the out-of-court evidence versus that of the other available evidence.

The interpretation that keeps this evidence out from under the residual exception focuses on credibility, and says that credibility is someone else's concern, not the judge's. The better interpretation focuses on probative value and recognizes that when the judge is called upon to assess relative probative value, that assessment includes many things—sometimes it includes an assessment of the credibility of the pieces of evidence in question. Credibility standing alone is for the trier of fact; probative value, including sometimes an element of credibility, is for the trier of law. Judges commonly make credibility decisions when deciding if evidence is admissible.[117]

The conditions of admission under the residual exception do not include an evaluation of credibility standing alone, in order to decide which witnesses to believe. Rather, they include an evaluation of credibility as one part of an eval-

---

117. At *Daubert* hearings, for example, judges often make decisions regarding the credibility of the evidence put forward as the basis for a proffered expert opinion. *E.g.*, Claar v. Burlington N. R.R. Co., 29 F.3d 499, 501 (9th Cir. 1994) ("It is true that, whenever a court rejects expert testimony because it is based on faulty methodology or reasoning, it follows implicitly that the expert's conclusions are not to be credited. But as long as the court's analysis focuses on the expert's methods and reasoning, and not on the expert's conclusions, its actions are proper."); National Bank of Commerce v. Dow Chem. Co., 965 F.Supp. 1490, 1516 (E.D. Ark. 1996) ("[I]n a *Daubert* hearing the expert's scientific credibility cannot be avoided."); Tucker v. Nike, Inc., 919 F.Supp. 1192, 1196 (N.D. Ind. 1995) (expert testimony "is not admissible unless the expert credibly links his or her testimony to an issue in the case."); Chapple v. Ganger, 851 F.Supp. 1481, 1496 (E.D. Wash. 1994) ("A credible link must be established between the reasoning and the conclusion.").

In the face of evidence to the contrary, the trial judge need not believe a putative expert's testimony that his tests had sufficient scientific rigor, that there is a sufficient link between his reasoning and his conclusion, or that his conclusions are supported by the scientific community. These are things the trial judge may find incredible. Not in service of finding the witness's ultimate conclusions incredible, but in service of finding the general scientific theory or the witness's particular methodology flawed. Otherwise, there is no stopping junk science: All witnesses have to do is to tell the trial judge "What I am doing is science, and it is not junk." Whether the judge phrases it as "I do not believe you," the judge has to have the power to refuse to believe the witness. *See* Kumho Tire Co., Ltd. v. Carmichael, 526 U.S. 137 (1999); Daubert v. Merrell Dow Pharms,, Inc., 509 U.S. 579 (1993).

uation of probative value, in order to decide whether to admit more evidence.[118] The judge is not encroaching upon, or in any way diminishing, the jury's role as the trier of fact—not taking any part of the jury's credibility decision from them. In fact, the judge is giving them additional information upon which they can base their credibility decision. The split between the functions of the trier of law and the trier of fact is preserved

This interpretation is in service of the guiding principles of the rules: "These rules shall be construed to secure fairness in administration, elimination of unjustifiable expense and delay, and *promotion of growth and development of the law of evidence to the end that the truth may be ascertained and proceedings justly determined.*"[119]

This approach does not destroy the hearsay rule by making all prior inconsistent statements admissible under the residual exception. It simply recognizes that each exception stands on its own foundational elements—the residual exception included. Some prior inconsistent statements will satisfy the foundational elements of the residual exception; principally, they will be sufficiently trustworthy and their relative probative value will be greater than that of other available evidence.

This is an approach that takes into account the following scenario: First, a young girl is assaulted by a man living with her and her mother, and the mother wants treatment for her injured daughter. This creates certain pressures to tell the truth. Second, as the daughter's condition improves, the initial pressure is relaxed. Third, the assailant begs the mother's forgiveness, promises to change, and threatens to leave. This creates a new and different pressure—pressure to lie. This approach to the residual exception recognizes not only that the first statement can be more trustworthy, but that it can have greater probative value than any other evidence reasonably obtainable.

This approach also recognizes that the out-of-court statement, can have less probative value than the in-court statement. Sometimes the first statement seems to be the lie. Staying with the situation in *Lovejoy*, sometimes the alle-

---

118. Perhaps Professor Eleanor Swift put her finger on the problem when she said that "the same term—probative value—should not be used to denote the different acts that are performed by the judge and by the jury." Swift, 14 Cardozo L. Rev. at 111. She would use probative value for "the mental operation and data that the judge uses" and persuasive value for "the mental operation and data that the jury—or any factfinder—uses...." *Id.* Still, that does not mean that "probative value" cannot sometimes contain an element of credibility.

Regarding admissibility versus credibility, *see particularly* Chapter 3(I)(D).

119. Fed.R.Evid. 102 (emphasis added).

gation of abuse is a lie, perhaps concocted out of revenge and designed to hurt its object or to win a custody battle. The judge decides relative probative value and if the judge believes one of the statements is credible and the other is not, the judge can consider that as part of this probative-value decision.

Take this situation. A gang member witnesses a shooting by a member of a rival gang. Originally, the witness provides a detailed, credible description of the shooter. At trial, the witness recants. He says that the shooter was some-one else, unknown to him, whose description he does not much remember, but it definitely was not the rival gang member he had originally implicated. He states that he had made up his original identification as a kind of "payback." The prosecution offers expert testimony discussing a gang phenomenon known as "ratting off." This part of the code of the gang requires that one gang mem-ber never implicate another in a crime—even when the other is a member of a rival gang.[120] And perhaps there is other evidence, such as a statement the wit-ness made to a friend or relative, saying, essentially, that he was afraid for his gang status or even his life if he testified against the shooter. Given these facts, the question is not so much, "Can we say that the earlier statement is more probative?" Rather, the question seems to be, "How can we possibly say that the first statement is not more probative?" The first statement can be more trustworthy and more probative; a judge can find it so; it can fit under the residual exception.

If the federal rules apply then all or part of the out-of-court statement I have just described will not be hearsay in the first place. "A statement is not hearsay if … the declarant testifies at the trial or hearing and is subject to cross-examination concerning the statement, and the statement is … one of identi-fication of a person made after perceiving the person."[121] Still, that definitional exclusion may not cover the entire statement and there are some jurisdictions that have not made this definitional exclusion part of their code.[122] In any

---

120. So far, these facts are based on People v. Cuevas, 906 P.2d 1290 (Cal. 1995).

121. FED.R.EVID. 801(d)(1)(C).

This recanted statement will not fit under the relatively new forfeiture by wrongdoing exception, FED.R.EVID. 804(b)(5), because that requires that the out-of-court declarant's in-court testimony be unavailable. Some of the kinds of statements I am talking about here will be "near miss" statements in that they will satisfy all but one of the foundational elements of the forfeiture by wrongdoing exception. The one they will not satisfy is unavailability. Other recanted statements will not involve any specific wrongdoing directed at silencing the wit-ness and therefore will not fall anywhere near forfeiture by wrongdoing.

122. For a discussion of the adoption of this definitional exclusion by state legislatures, as of 1994, see People v. Cuevas, 906 P.2d 1290, 1299 n.2 (Cal. 1995).

event, this scenario is not included here to show that the residual exception will be needed on these facts. Rather, it is included because it shows that a prior out-of-court statement can be more probative than a later, contrary statement made in court and subject to cross-examination:

> "[T]he earlier identification has *greater probative value* than an identification made in the courtroom after the suggestions of others and the circumstances of the trial may have intervened to create a fancied recognition in the witness' mind.... The failure of the witness to repeat the extrajudicial identification in court *does not destroy its probative value,* for such failure may be explained by loss of memory or other circumstances. The extrajudicial identification tends to connect the defendant with the crime, and the principal danger of admitting hearsay evidence is not present since the witness is available at the trial for cross-examination."[123]

A significant number of times the former statement is more probative of the truth, and the judge knows it, the parties know it, and everyone in the room knows it. I am suggesting that while Justice can be blind, it need not be ignorant.

The definition of "probative" espoused here has not gotten much attention, and most of the attention it has gotten is contrary. I believe, however, that the United States Court of Appeals for the Eighth Circuit got it right. When a witness makes an out-of-court statement, then takes the stand and recants, the out-of-court statement may be admissible under the residual exception—admissible as substantive evidence of the facts declared therein.[124] If this view of the residual exception is correct, it provides prosecutors with a terrific weapon to combat hearsay in the case of a witness who gives a statement and then takes the stand and testifies to a different version of events.[125] More than that, however, its ramifications are not limited to the turncoat witness. If it is appropriate to

---

123. Gilbert v. California, 388 U.S. 263, 273 n.3 (1967) (emphasis added) (quoting People v. Gould, 354 P.2d 865, 867 (Cal. 1960)).

124. It may also be that *Lovejoy* was bending the rules because of the nature of the case: child abuse. I discuss this phenomenon at parts V(F) & (G) of this chapter, below.

The Confrontation Clause will does not bar the statement because this situation does not arise unless the declarant is testifying and can be confronted. *See generally* Chapter 14, below.

125. It will be a powerful weapon in cases where the out-of-court statement is not barred by the Confrontation Clause. This should not be a problem when the out-of-court declarant testifies and recants because the declarant can be confronted, can be cross-examined. *See generally* Chapter 14, below.

assess the credibility of the out-of-court statement in the turncoat-witness cases, then it is appropriate to consider it in any residual exception case where credibility issues are apparent.[126]

F. Using the Residual Exception to Promote Social Agendas

"Each generation has its own set of cases where the rules of evidence do not accomplish what we want to accomplish—they don't favor the civil rights worker over the redneck city administration; they don't favor the government and the child over the one charged with beating, sexually abusing, or murdering the child."[127] When it is the hearsay rule that is standing in the way of what we want to accomplish, it is often the residual exception that is called into play.[128]

Most of the foundational elements of this exception are particularly flexible, if not amorphous: trustworthiness; relevance; probative value relative to other reasonably obtainable evidence; and service to justice. The most circumscribed foundational element is advance notice, but, as discussed above, even this element is not as circumscribed as it appears on its face. The more flexible the foundational elements, of course, the easier it is to find them in a given set of facts. This exception, then, is the perfect exception into which to fit a social agenda.

If, for example, we want to spare a witness from having to take the stand and we can find the right out-of-court statement, then we can give the requisite notice, argue that the evidence is trustworthy and more probative on the point than is any other evidence reasonably obtainable, and that its admission serves justice. This can get it around the hearsay rule. (In criminal cases, the Confrontation Clause presents a different set of problems.) In the case of victim witnesses such as abused children, battered spouses, or persons being intimidated

---

126. This is, in fact, just what the court did in Phan v. Trinity Reg'l Hosp., 3 F.Supp.2d 1014 (N.D. Iowa 1998). This is an employment case alleging race discrimination. Ruling on motions in limine, the court stated that an out-of-court statement evidencing the wrongdoing fit under the residual exception. The only other evidence on the point would be the testimony of agents of the defendant hospital and the person allegedly given a preference over the plaintiff. Regarding the relative probative value of the out-of-court statement, on the one hand, and the live testimony, on the other hand, the court stated that the extra-judicial statement is more probative "because of the unlikeliness that [the alleged wrongdoers] will now acknowledge [their wrongful acts]." Id. at 1022.

127. G. Michael Fenner, *Law Professor Reveals Shocking Truth About Hearsay*, 62 UMKC L. REV. 1, 64 (1993).

128. *See* part III(B) of this chapter, above.

by gangs, it should not be too difficult for a lawyer to argue, and for some judges to find, that this application of the exception is in the service of justice. It should also not be too difficult to argue and to find that the out-of-court statement is relevant, trustworthy, and more probative on the point for which it is offered than any other reasonably obtainable evidence.

When the rule states that this exception should be used in the interest of justice, it is not limited to justice for the accused, or even justice for the parties. The interest of justice also includes justice for the victim and for society in general.[129] Absent Confrontation Clause problems, it serves justice to admit the statement because it enables the proceeding to go forward without forcing the abused child or the battered spouse or the intimidated witness to take the stand and relive the trauma.[130]

Historically, this exception has been used to protect this Nation's powerless citizens, including its children, its battered spouses, its honest citizens intimidated by gangs of hoodlums. It has been used to relieve them from having to relive the abuse, the battering, the intimidation, most often in the presence of the abuser, batterer, or intimidator and at the hands of the perpetrator's attorney. The victim's interest in justice pulls one way; the defendant's interest in justice pulls the other way; society's interest in justice takes both of those competing interests into account. The weighing of the competing interests of the victim and the defendant comes up with justice for society.

This is not to say that it is right for courts to do this, or that it is wrong, but just to say that they do it.[131] When the subject is today's major societal con-

---

129. *E.g.*, United States v. DeNoyer, 811 F.2d 436, 438 (8th Cir. 1987) (administration of justice served by admission of statement of victim of child abuse and not live testimony); United States v. Cree, 778 F.2d 474, 478–79 (8th Cir. 1985) (allowing into evidence statement of extremely young victim of abuse, and not requiring victim to take the stand serves the interests of justice). The decision to allow the statement without the testimony of the child might be affected by today's Confrontation Clause jurisprudence (*see* Chapter 14, below), but their point about the interest of justice is not. *Cf.* Reno v. ACLU, 521 U.S. 844, 869 (1997) (discussing the "compelling interest in protecting the physical and psychological well-being of minors"); New York v. Ferber, 458 U.S. 747, 776 (1982) (discussing the state's special and compelling interest in protecting children); United States v. Rouse, 111 F.3d 561, 567 (8th Cir. 1997) ("the court must … protect the State's paramount interest in the welfare of the child"; the Sixth Amendment confrontation right "must accommodate the State's 'compelling' interest in 'the protection of minor victims of sex crimes from further trauma and embarrassment'") (citing Globe Newspaper Co. v. Superior Court, 457 U.S. 596, 607 (1982).

130. Fenner, 62 UMKC L. Rev. at 64.

131. This is not a new phenomenon. In another forum, I have argued that around mid-century, the victim was the government and the rules were bent to put Communists in jail; in

cern, very many courts find a way to enforce that concern, hearsay notwith-standing—and it is the residual exception that allows some judges the flexibility to do just that.

G. The Residual Exception in Child-Abuse Cases[132]

The residual exception has frequently been used to admit out-of-court statements made by children who are alleged to have been victims of child abuse and, when constitutionally permissible, to admit them in lieu of live testimony from the child.[133] Much of the discussion in these cases has had to do with the foundational element of trustworthiness. Courts have focused on the suggestiveness of leading questioning by parents or other authority figures, including whether the child has been prompted, coached, or manipulated by others;[134] the child's age as related to the child's ability to fabricate such a statement;[135]

----

the 60s, the victims were civil-rights workers and demonstrators and the rules were bent to keep them out of jail; in the 70s, the victims were anti-war demonstrators, and the rules were bent to keep them out of jail; in the 80s, the victims were drug users—"Just say 'No' "—and the rules were bent to put drug dealers in jail; and in the 90s, the victims include abused children, and the rules are bent to put child abusers in jail. *See* Fenner, 62 UMKC L. Rev. at 64.

132. If the statement of a child is used in a criminal prosecution against the child's alleged abuser and in lieu of the child's in-court testimony, as happened in the cases discussed in this section, the Court's modern Confrontation Clause jurisprudence may change the outcome, and certainly changes the analysis. Regarding the Confrontation Clause, see Chapter 14.

133. "The residual exception appears to find its greatest use in trials where children are the victims of alleged sexual abuse. It is axiomatic, of course, that society has a deep and compelling interest in protecting the welfare of its children." United States v. Barror, 20 M.J. 501, 503 (USAF Ct. Mil. Rev. 1985), *rev'd on other grounds*, 23 M.J. 370 (USAF Ct. Mil Rev. 1987). *See also, e.g.*, Truman v. Watts, 598 A.2d 713, 722 (Family Ct. Del. 1991) (citing cases).

The residual exception is not the only exception called into play to help put away child abusers. The excited utterance exception, for example, is sometimes stretched right up to (and even beyond) its breaking point in order to protect children and put child abusers away. *See* chapter 3(III)(D)(9), above. Some jurisdictions have created statutory exceptions for declarations by alleged child victims. *See*, Fla. Stat. §90.803(23) (2000).

See Chapter 14, and its discussion of the Confrontation Clause.

134. *E.g.*, United States v. Juvenile NB, 59 F.3d 771, 776–78 (8th Cir. 1995); United States v. Grooms, 978 F.2d 425, 427 (8th Cir. 1992); State v. Lonergan, 505 N.W.2d 349, 355 (Minn. Ct. App. 1993); Norris v. State, 788 S.W.2d 65, 70–72 (Tex. App. 1990); State v. Conklin, 444 N.W.2d 268, 276 (Minn. 1989).

135. *E.g.*, United States v. Cree, 778 F.2d 474 (8th Cir. 1985); *Norris*, 788 S.W.2d at 70–72.

the amount of time that passed between the alleged act and the making of the statement,[136] on spontaneity, and on consistent repetition;[137] the use of language appropriate to a child of the declarant's age;[138] the mental state of the out-of-court declarant and any motive the child might have either to tell the truth or to lie;[139] the special training and experience of the person to whom the child made the out-of-court statement.[140] In other words, they focus on all of the things they should focus on: anything that increases the trustworthiness of the statement, prominently including those things that go into making trustworthy the various evidence in the Rule 803 and 804 exceptions.

As with all statements evaluated for trustworthiness under the residual exception, the focus is not on the witness, but on the statement. The trustworthiness of the child out-of-court declarant may, of course, be relevant to the trustworthiness of the statement, but the latter is the key that unlocks this exception, not the former.

Beyond trustworthiness, admission of the statement in question must serve the interests of justice. Some courts have relied on the notion that it is questionable justice to force an extremely young victim of abuse to take the stand and relive the traumatic experience.[141] It is true that this serves the child's interest in justice.[142] It surely does not serve the defendant's interest in justice.[143] Society's interest in justice would combine the two, and how much weight is to be given to each of these competing interests—the child's and the defendant's—is one of the ways in which this residual exception is so flexible.[144]

---

136. *E.g., Juvenile NB*, 59 F.3d at 776, 777–78; People v. District Court of El Paso County, 776 P.2d 1083, 1089 (Colo. 1989).

137. *E.g., Lonergan*, 505 N.W.2d at 355; *Conklin*, 444 N.W.2d at 276.

138. *E.g., Juvenile NB*, 59 F.3d at 776, 777–78 ("age-appropriate language"); *Grooms*, 978 F.2d at 427 (8th Cir. 1992); United States v. Nick, 604 F.2d 1199, 1204 (9th Cir. 1979); *Lonergan*, 505 N.W.2d at 355.

139. *E.g., Conklin*, 444 N.W.2d at 276. *See also Grooms*, 978 F.2d at 427 ("[N]othing in the record to suggest they were likely to have fabricated their stories of abuse.").

140. *E.g., Juvenile NB*, 59 F.3d at 776, 777–78 (interviewers had extensive experience in interviewing abused children and were strangers who had no motive to manipulate the evidence); *Grooms*, 978 F.2d at 427.

141. *E.g., Cree*, 778 F.2d at 478–79.

142. *See, e.g., Cree*, 778 F.2d 478 n.7 ("[T]he rights of defenseless child abuse victims must be protected.").

143. And, of course, if the trial at hand is a criminal trial, the statement was testimonial, and the child does not testify, then the Confrontation Clause may bar admission of the hearsay statement.

144. *See* part (V)(F) of this chapter, above.

So, justice is a factor in the foundational elements of this particular rule. Perhaps we do serve the interests of justice when we help the child victim escape yet another traumatizing attack, this one in the courtroom, on the witness stand, by an agent of the defendant, and in front of any number of perfect strangers plus the defendant himself.

Beyond trustworthiness and the interests of justice, the out-of-court statement must have more probative value on the point in question than does any other evidence the proponent can procure through reasonable efforts. The theory for admission is that a reasonable effort to secure the evidence elsewhere does not require making the abused child take the stand and subjecting the child to yet another kind of abuse, this time in the presence of the alleged perpetrator of the initial abuse, and at the hands of a lawyer who is working for the alleged perpetrator. That is to say, if an "effort" involves subjecting a child-victim to further abuse in open court, then, in our society, it is not a "reasonable effort." Working the cost-benefit analysis, the cost to the child, and to society's interest in the child, is too high.

Having found the evidence trustworthy and more probative on the point than any other evidence obtainable through reasonable efforts, and having found its admission under the residual exception to serve justice, then there are only two residual-exception questions left. Is the evidence relevant (and we can assume it is; otherwise we would never get to the hearsay question) and was advance notice given?

H. Findings Made on the Record

The Senate Judiciary Committee stated that the trial court should state on the record "the special facts and circumstances" that indicate "that the statement has a sufficiently high degree of trustworthiness and necessity to justify its admission."[145] Cases have held and commentators have concluded that the trial court should make specific findings, on the record, of each of the foundational elements of this exception.[146] As a general rule, if the trial court admits a statement under the residual exception but does not make these specific findings, appellate courts will examine the record and make their own determination as to whether they find the foundational elements in the record.[147]

---

145. S.Rep. No. 93-1277, at 7066 (1974).
146. State v. Walker, 691 A.2d 1341, 1354–56 (Md. Ct. App. 1997) (lengthy discussion; citing, quoting, and discussing cases and commentary).
147. *Id.* at 1356 (citing cases).

I. Miscellaneous Uses of the Residual Exception

Various uses of the residual exception include the following:

■ The report of a deceased fingerprint-examiner to prove that the fingerprint on the marijuana bag was defendant's.[148]

■ A list of property taken in a burglary, compiled by the now-deceased victim, offered to prove what items were taken.[149]

■ Polls and surveys offered to prove the truth of the assertions of those polled or surveyed.[150]

■ Police reports offered to prove the truth of the facts recorded therein.[151]

■ A judgment in a civil action offered to prove the truth of the fact adjudicated.[152]

■ A postmark offered to prove that a letter was mailed from a particular place.[153]

■ A police officer's testimony as to what a sign-language interpreter told him the defendant was signing to the interpreter.[154]

---

148. State v. Best, 703 P.2d 548 (Ariz. Ct. App. 1985). The United States Supreme Court's subsequent reinterpretation of the Confrontation Clause may change this result but this is still valid as a matter of evidentiary law. Regarding the Confrontation Clause, see Chapter 14, below.

149. State v. Echeverria, 626 P.2d 897 (Or. Ct. App. 1981). Such evidence could be testimonial and barred by the Confrontation Clause or non-testimonial and not so barred. *See* Chapter 14, below.

150. Pittsburgh Press Club v. United States, 579 F.2d 751, 757–60 (3d Cir. 1978) (survey in question not trustworthy because not objective, scientific, or impartial; surveys generally fit residual exception when conducted in accordance with generally accepted survey principles and results used in statistically correct way).

151. *E.g.*, State v. Silva, 670 P.2d 737 (Ariz. 1983) (police report admitted to prove chain of custody of evidence as recorded therein).

Police reports are, of course, a kind of statement particularly open to double hearsay: Witness to police officer (oral statement), is one potential level; police officer to police report (written statement), is the other. If so, each level will have to be dealt with. *See generally* Chapter 11, below.

152. State v. Yelli, 530 N.W.2d 250 (Neb. 1995) (civil paternity judgment offered in criminal nonsupport case).

153. United States v. Cowley, 720 F.2d 1037, 1044–45 (9th Cir. 1983) (postmarks generally fall under residual exception; error to admit postmark here under residual exception because no advance notice; harmless error).

154. United States v. Cordero, 18 F.3d 1248, 1253 (5th Cir. 1994); United States v. Nazemian, 948 F.2d 522, 525–28 (9th Cir. 1991); United States v. Lopez, 937 F.2d 716, 724

■ A child's statement to a social worker regarding sexual abuse, offered to prove the truth of the facts asserted by the child.[155]

■ Statements in a diary offered to prove the truth of the facts recorded.[156]

■ A "day in the life" film showing the plaintiff performing daily activities and tests of his physical abilities.[157]

This kind of a list can, however, be misleading. The point here is not the kind of out-of-court statement involved, but whether the proponent has satisfied the foundational elements of the exception. This is, of course, the point with every one of the exceptions. Here, however, there is not even a categorical label that can be applied to the evidence covered, such as "excited utterance." It is that the circumstances surrounding the making and the offering into evidence of some out-of-court statements will satisfy the residual-exception foundation, no matter what kind of statement it is, or where it is found.

What is misleading about it is this. Let us say that you have a case that holds that statements in a diary, offered to prove the truth of the facts recorded therein, are admissible under the residual exception. This does not mean that diaries generally fit under the residual exception, the way the excited utterance exception means that excited utterances are generally admissible under that exception. It only means that the trial judge found that these particular diary entries were trustworthy and had high relative probative value, and that the required notice was given.[158]

(2d Cir. 1991); Barraza v. United States, 526 F.Supp.2d 637, 642 (W.D. Tex. 2007). The factors the court considers to determine whether or not a particular interpreter is just a language conduit are discussed in the cases cited. They include factors "such as which party supplied the interpreter, whether the interpreter had any motive to mislead or distort, the interpreter's qualifications and language skill, and whether actions taken subsequent to the conversation were consistent with the statements as translated." *Nazemian*, 948 F.2d at 527. *But see* State v. Rodriguez-Castillo, 188 P.3d 288, 272–73 (Or. 2008) (rejecting the "language conduit" argument).

155. *Juvenile NB*, 59 F.3d at 778.

156. United States v. Sheets, 125 F.R.D. 172, 178 (D. Utah 1989).

157. Grines v. Employers Mut. Liab. Ins. Co., 73 F.R.D. 607, 611 (D. Alaska 1977). To the extent that the film is edited, one can argue that the editing is an out-of-court statement: the editing is conduct intended to make an assertion—plaintiff's diminished abilities—and it is offered in evidence, to the issue of damages, to prove the truth of that assertion.

158. In the following cases, the residual exception did not apply to: a suicide note, State v. Brown, 752 P.2d 204 (Mont. 1988) (note implicated defendant in crime, offered to prove defendant committed crime; statement in note insufficiently probative of point to which offered); an affidavit, State v. Hughes, 584 P.2d 584 (Ariz. Ct. App. 1978) (affidavit claim-

There is nothing categorical about this exception, as there is with the exceptions in Rules 803 and 804. This exception is entirely ad hoc.

---

ing signatures on check were forgeries, offered to prove truth of fact asserted; not shown more probative than other evidence reasonably available and, as statement in favor of declarant's pecuniary interest, lacking guarantees of trustworthiness); a police officer's note on an envelope, State v. Garvey, 283 N.W.2d 153 (N.D. 1979) (undercover agent's note on outside of envelope that envelope contained marijuana, offered to prove truth of fact asserted; no pretrial notice and lacking guarantees of trustworthiness); a letter from a doctor, de Mars v. Equitable Life Assurance Society of the United States, 610 F.2d 55 (1st Cir. 1979); (letter from now-deceased doctor to plaintiff's attorney, concerning plaintiff's symptoms, offered to prove truth of doctor's statements; lacking guarantees of trustworthiness).

CHAPTER SIX

RULES OF CIVIL AND CRIMINAL PROCEDURE AS HEARSAY EXCEPTIONS

I. Rule 32 of the Federal Rules of Civil Procedure

A. Overview

Depositions are, of course, out-of-court statements. If deposition testimony is offered in court to prove the truth of facts asserted in the deposition[1] and does not fit under any of the definitional exclusions in Rule 801(d),[2] then it is hearsay. Rule 32 of the Federal Rules of Civil Procedure is a giant hearsay exception for deposition evidence offered in civil cases. Rule 32 is discussed in depth below but let me say these two things now: (1) Because this exception is not found within the Rules of Evidence it can be overlooked, which is a terrible mistake as it is an important exception. (2) Regarding depositions, Rule 32 creates a "101 miles from the courthouse" exception to the hearsay rule. Rule 32 allows the use of deposi-

---

1. Deposition testimony can also be offered, for example, as a prior inconsistent statement to impeach a testifying witness. In that case, the out-of-court statement is not offered to prove the truth of the matter asserted, but only to show that it was said, and it is not hearsay. *See* Chapter 2(II)(A)(4), above.

2. If one party offers all or part of the deposition of an opposing party, then it is a non-hearsay statement of a party offered against that party. FED.R.EVID. 801(d)(2)(A). *See* Chapter 2(III)(B), above. Likewise if a party offers all or part of the deposition of a person who, at the time of the deposition, was an employee of a party opponent, then anything in the deposition which concerns matters within the scope of declarant's employment are nonhearsay admissions of an employee of a party opponent. FED.R.EVID. 801(d)(2)(D). *See* Chapter 2(III)(C), above. *See additionally* FED.R.EVID. 801(d)(1)(A) regarding prior-inconsistent deposition statements by a testifying witness; *Chapter* 2(II)(B) regarding FED.R.EVID. 801(d)(1)(B) and prior-consistent deposition statements by a testifying witness; *Chapter* 2(II)(C) regarding FED.R.EVID. 801(d)(1)(C) and a testifying witness' prior statements of identification.

tion testimony from the same or certain related cases in lieu of live testimony whenever the deponent is more than 100 miles from the courthouse at the time the deposition is offered, so long as the party against whom the deposition is offered had a chance to be represented at the deposition and the deponent's absence was not "procure[d]" by the party offering the deposition. The deponent need not be unavailable in the traditional sense,[3] just more than 100 miles away.

The effect of this rule is to give the deposition voice as though the deponent were on the stand testifying.[4] As will be discussed in detail shortly, this exception is important to how we try our cases and how we take our depositions.

B. Text of the Rule

Rule 32. Using Depositions in Court Proceedings

(a) **Using Depositions.**

(1) *In General.* At a hearing or trial, all or part of a deposition may be used against a party on these conditions:

(A) the party was present or represented at the taking of the deposition or had reasonable notice of it;

(B) it is used to the extent it would be admissible under the Federal Rules of Evidence if the deponent were present and testifying; and

(C) the use is allowed by Rule 32(a)(2) through (8).

(2) *Impeachment and Other Uses.* Any party may use a deposition to contradict or impeach the testimony given by the deponent as a witness, or for any other purpose allowed by the Federal Rules of Evidence.

(3) *Deposition of Party, Agent, or Designee.* An adverse party may use for any purpose the deposition of a party or anyone who, when deposed, was the party's officer, director, managing agent, or designee under Rule 30(b)(6) or 31(a)(4).

(4) *Unavailable Witness. A party may use for any purpose the deposition of a witness, whether or not a party, if the court finds*:

(A) that the witness is dead;

---

3. *See* Chapter 4(I), above.

4. Opposing counsel still has to make the same objections he or she would make were the deponent called to the stand: competence, relevance, hearsay layered within the deposition, etc. "Evidence authorized by Rule 32(a) cannot be excluded as hearsay, unless it would be inadmissible even if delivered in court." Ueland v. United States, 291 F.3d 993, 996 (7th Cir. 2002).

(B) *that the witness is more than 100 miles from the place of hearing or trial or is outside the United States, unless it appears that the witness's absence was procured by the party offering deposition;*

(C) that the witness cannot attend or testify because of age, illness, infirmity, or imprisonment;

(D) that the party offering the deposition could not procure the witness's attendance by subpoena; or

(E) on motion and notice, that exceptional circumstances make it desirable—in the interest of justice and with due regard to the importance of live testimony in open court—to permit the deposition be used.

(5) *Limitations on Use.*

(A) *Deposition Taken on Short Notice.* A deposition must not be used against a party who, having received less than 11 days' notice of the deposition, promptly moved for a protective order under Rule 26(c)(1)(B) requesting that it not be taken or be taken at a different time or place – and this motion was still pending when the deposition was taken.

(B) *Unavailable Deponent; Party Could Not Obtain an Attorney.* A deposition taken without leave of court under the unavailability provision of Rule 30(a)(2)(A)(iii) must not be used against a party who shows that, when served with the notice, it could not, despite diligent efforts, obtain an attorney to represent it at the deposition.

(6) *Using Part of a Deposition.* If a party offers in evidence only part of a deposition, an adverse party may require the offeror to introduce other parts that in fairness should be considered with the part introduced, and any party may itself introduce any other parts.

(7) *Substituting a Party.* Substituting a party under Rule 25 does not affect the right to use a deposition previously taken.

(8) *Deposition Taken in an Earlier Action.* A deposition lawfully taken and, if required, filed in any federal- or state-court action may be used in a later action involving the same subject matter between the same parties, or their representatives or successors in interest, to the same extent as if taken in the later action. A deposition previously taken may also be used as allowed by the Federal Rules of Evidence.

(b) **Objections to Admissibility.** Subject to Rules 28(b) and 32(d)(3), an objection may be made at a hearing or trial to the admission of any deposition testimony that would be inadmissible if the witness were present and testifying.

＊＊＊＊5

C. Foundational Elements

1. The out-of-court statement is in the form of a deposition.

2. The deposition is offered into evidence in a trial or hearing in a civil case.

3. The deposition was taken in either the same case in which it is being offered or in another action involving the same subject matter and the same parties or their representatives or successors in interest.

4. Either:

   (a) The deponent is (1) more than 100 miles from the courthouse in which the deposition is being offered, (2) dead, (3) unavailable to testify in person because of illness, age, infirmity, or imprisonment, or (4) the proponent of the deposition has been unable to procure the attendance of the witness by subpoena, or,

   (b) upon application and notice, and "in the interest of justice and with due regard to the importance of live testimony in open court," the judge decides that "exceptional circumstances" make it desirable to use the deposition in place of live testimony.[6]

D. Need + Reliability = 1

1. Need

The Rule 32 exception for deposition testimony includes depositions of witnesses who, for any of the traditional reasons, are unavailable to testify at the trial: the deponent is dead, too ill to attend the hearing, or for various reasons cannot be made to attend. These are the traditional unavailabilities found in Rule 804 of the Rules of Evidence and the need for the evidence here is the same as the need for it there.[7]

---

5. Fed.R.Civ.P. 32 (excluding the emphasis in some headings, emphasis added).
6. Fed.R.Civ.P. 32(a)(4)(E).
7. *See* Chapter 4(II)(D)(1), above.

Rule 32, however, goes a great deal further than Rule 804. For one thing, it allows use of the deposition if the judge decides, upon application and notice, that the out-of-court statement should be used in lieu of live testimony. Presumably, the need for the evidence will weigh heavily into the judge's decision.

Rule 32 also allows the deposition to be used when the witness is over 100 miles away from the place of trial or hearing, or out of the country. This 100-mile provision is considerably different from anything in evidence Rule 804. There is no categorical need here, as there is under the unavailability provision in Rule 804. Sometimes there will be a need for some particular depositions where the deponent is over 100 miles away. Perhaps it would be too expensive or cause undue delay. Other times this is just a rule of convenience[8]—or, for counsel who overlooks Rule 32, a trap.

2. Reliability

The fact that a particular deposition may be used in lieu of live testimony should affect how counsel decodes what kind of—how thorough—a deposition to take. If the witness deposed lives and works in a distant state or is critically injured or ill, any lawyer aware of Rule 32 will have to take the deposition with one eye on the fact that if the case goes to trial it may be used in lieu of live testimony. To the extent that the attorneys anticipate that the deposition may be admissible in the place of live testimony, then the guarantee of reliability is similar to, even greater than, the guarantee of reliability in the former testimony exception.[9] Counsel will be motivated and will have the opportunity to conduct a thorough direct and cross-examination at the deposition.[10]

There are two situations in which the reliability of the out-of-court statement will be problematic. One is when new information comes to light between the time of the deposition and the time of the trial. Even then, if the declarant can be subpoenaed, then opposing counsel can require that the deponent come to

---

8. In some jurisdictions—I have in mind parts of the Great Plains, where I live and work—a witness over 100 miles away can get to the courthouse in two hours. This can be less time than it takes some witnesses in some jurisdictions to get to the courthouse from another part of the same large city.

9. *See* Chapter 4(II)(D)(1), above, and the cross-reference therein.

10. Counsel's motivation on cross-examination may be exactly the same at the deposition and the trial. There may, on the other hand, be reasons counsel would want to hold back at a deposition in ways counsel would not want to hold back at trial, so as, for example, not to reveal trial strategy, but the motivation for a thorough examination will be there. Counsel's motives may be mixed but whether counsel's motivation to conduct a thorough examination wins out or not, it will be present. This is discussed further at part I(E)(8) of this chapter, below.

court for live testimony or perhaps a second deposition can be taken or the new information can be used to impeach or bolster the deposition testimony.[11]

The other is when a lawyer does not anticipate that the witness will become unavailable. If the deposition was an exploratory deposition, or if the deposition was one at which counsel wanted to hold back certain information regarding substance or strategy, then the deposition may not have the kind of reliability sought under most hearsay exceptions. With this in mind, Rule 32 has to change how lawyers think about depositions: counsel must consider the possibility that it will be used at trial in lieu of the live testimony of the witness.[12]

E. Use Note

1. The Relationship between Federal Rule of Civil Procedure 32 and Federal Rule of Evidence 804

Rule 32 of the Federal Rules of Civil Procedure is a separate exception to the hearsay rule, one that operates totally independently of Rule 804 of the Federal Rules of Evidence.[13] These two exceptions "are cumulative. Thus, even though a deposition does not fall within the exceptions to the hearsay rule ... in Rule 804, ... it is admissible if it falls within the provisions of Rule 32(a)(3)."[14]

---

11. *See* part I(E)(8) of this chapter, below.

12. *See* part I(E)(8) of this chapter, below.
The main text above discusses reliability under subpart (a)(4) of Rule 32, the only part of the rule that really qualifies as its own exception to the hearsay rule. Rule 32(a)(1)(A) is the former testimony exception from Rule 804, and presents little or no hearsay problem. Rule 32(a)(1)(B) is traditional impeachment, and presents no hearsay problem. For the most part (if not in total) Rule 32(a)(1)(C) deals with admissions by party opponents and their agents, and, because of FED.R.EVID. 801(d)(2), it presents little or no hearsay problem.

13. FED.R.EVID. 802 advisory committee's note.

14. In re Bankers Trust Co., 752 F.2d 874, 888 n.17 (3d Cir. 1984) (the rule referenced herein has been renumbered; it is now Rule 32(a)(4)). *See also Ueland*, 291 F.3d at 996 (trial judge excluded deposition, citing Rule 804; appellate court held the judge should have admitted it under Rule 32, which is "a freestanding exception to the hearsay rule"); Angelo v. Armstrong World Indus., Inc., 11 F.3d 957, 963 (10th Cir. 1993) (Rule 32 and the rules of evidence operate "independently" of each other); United States v. Vespe, 868 F.3d 1328, 1339 (3d Cir. 1989) (vis-à-vis Rule 804, Rule 32 is an "independent exception"); Carey v. Bahama Cruise Lines, 864 F.2d 201, 204 n.2 (1st Cir. 1988) ("Rule 32(a)(3)(B) is more permissive than Federal Rule of Evidence 804(a)(5), which requires the party seeking to admit the deposition testimony to show that it was unable to procure the attendance of the defendant through 'process or other reasonable means.' "); In re Complaint of Bankers Trust Co., 752 F.2d 874, 888 (3d Cir. 1984) (exceptions in Rule 32 and in the Federal Rules of Evidence are cumulative; a deposition not falling within a rules-of-evidence exception is nonetheless admissible if it falls within Rule 32).

2. This Rule Applies in Civil Cases Only

Though brief and easy to state—and so painfully obvious there is a chance the point will be missed—this is a rule of "civil" procedure. It does not apply in criminal cases.[15]

3. Depositions Offered in Cases Other Than the Case in Which They Were Taken

Rule 32 is not exactly a model of clarity. Part (a)(1)(A), for example, provides that a deposition "may be used against any party who was present or represented at the taking of the deposition or who had reasonable notice thereof" if the deponent is more than 100 miles from the courthouse at the time the deposition is offered into evidence and the witness's absence was not procured by the party offering the deposition. There is nothing in part (1)(A) of the rule that requires that the deposition have been taken in connection with the case on trial. However, a complicated reading of various parts of Rule 32 establishes that the deposition must have been taken in the same case as the one where it is offered into evidence or a case between the same parties, their representatives, or their successors in interest, which involve the same subject matter as the case in which the deposition is offered.[16]

Rule 32 of the Nebraska Rules of Discovery is mostly identical in its text to Rule 32 of the Federal Rules of Civil Procedure. The significant difference is that Nebraska's Rule 32 is not a statute, but a rule of discovery, promulgated by the Nebraska Supreme Court; the statutory rule of evidence regarding former testimony and unavailability cannot be overridden by the court rule of discovery regarding depositions and the deponent who is more than 100 miles from the courthouse. For this reason, Nebraska's rule is a much less valuable hearsay exception: It is not enough to show, that deponent is over 100 miles from the place of the hearing; the proponent must also show that the deponent's live testimony is unavailable as described in Rule 804. Maresh v. State, 489 N.W.2d 298 (Neb. 1992).

15. The companion rule of criminal procedure is discussed in part II of this chapter.

16. By its terms, Rule 32 (a)(1)(A) applies to any deposition, taken in any case, so long as the party it is offered against was personally present at the deposition, was represented, or had sufficient notice that he or she could have attended. The second paragraph of the next part of the rule, part 32(a)(8), states "[a] deposition lawfully taken and, if required, filed in any federal- or state-court action may be used in a later action involving the same subject matter between the same parties, or their representatives or successors in interest, to the same extent as if taken in the later action." This modifies all of part (a) of the rule (including the over-100-miles-from-the-courthouse exception). Part (a)(8) of the rule is written as though it is intended to expand the coverage of parts (a)(1)-(4) of the rule. In truth, it contracts them. In light of part (a)(8), parts (a)(1)-(4) only apply to depositions taken in the case in which they are offered into evidence and related cases between the same parties.

Rule 32 also requires that the two suits—the one in which the deposition was taken and the one in which it is offered—have the same subject matter. Some courts have interpreted "same subject matter" to mean that there must be substantial identity of issues.[17]

Rule 32 requires that the parties in the second suit must be either the same as in the first suit or representatives or successors in interest of the parties in the first suit. Some courts have interpreted that to mean that there must have been someone in the first suit with a motive to cross-examine similar to that of the party against whom the deposition is now offered.[18] This means that neither the party offering the deposition nor anyone with a similar interest has to have been a party to the former case. It also means that the party against whom the deposition is offered need not have been a party to the earlier case so long as someone similarly motivated to cross-examine the deponent was a party. This is a substantial judicial rewrite of the rule.

4. Objections to Evidentiary Problems within the Deposition, Including Multiple Hearsay

The deposition may be used at the trial or hearing "to the extent it would be admissible under the Federal Rules of Evidence if the deponent were present and testifying," so long as the party against whom it is offered "was present or represented at the taking of the deposition or had reasonable notice of it."[19] In other words, the deposition is treated as though the deponent were saying these things live and in person, from the witness stand. Objections to

---

17. Hub v. Sun Valley Co., 682 F.2d 776, 777–78 (9th Cir. 1982) (the decision is vested in the court's sound discretion; the rule's requirements that the lawsuits involve the "same subject matter" and "the same parties or their representatives or successors in interest" are construed in light of the goals of fairness and efficiency) (citing cases); Acme Printing Ink Co. v. Menard, Inc., 812 F.Supp. 1498, 1523–24 (E.D. Wisc. 1992) (defining "representative" and "successor in interest'" noting that the deposition in question is inadmissible under "the narrow definitions'" citing *Hub, supra,* for the proposition that these words are to be broadly interpreted, adopting the twin test of "substantial identity of issues" and "an adversary with the same motive to cross-examine," and finding the deposition admissible against one party and not against another); Woodard v. Branch, 256 B.R. 341, 343 (M.D. Fla. 2000) (regarding "the same subject matter," the question is whether the prior examination would satisfy a reasonable party opposing admission in the present litigation, so courts require only substantial identity of issues).

This is very similar to what some courts have done to the former testimony exception to the hearsay rule, as discussed at Chapter 4(II)(E)(2) & (4), above.

18. *See* authorities cited in note 17, just above.

19. FED.R.CIV.P. 32(a)(1).

evidentiary problems within the deposition may be made when the deposition is offered.[20] Objections may also be made before trial, such as in a motion in limine. The objections will be those that would be made were the deponent saying these things live and in person, from the witness stand. Insofar as hearsay is concerned, there may be successful hearsay objections to a deponent's testimony in a deposition, but not to the Rule 32 deposition itself.

5. Against Whom the Deposition May Be Used

Rule 32 lists four parties against whom a deposition may be used. (1) It may be used against a party who "was present or represented at the taking of the deposition or [who] had reasonable notice of it."[21]

(2) It may be used against substituted parties to the same extent as it could be used against the original parties.[22]

(3) "A deposition lawfully taken and, if required, filed in any federal- or state-court action may be used in a later action involving the same subject matter between the same parties, or their representatives or successors in interest, to the same extent as if taken in the later action."[23]

(4) A deposition may be used against any party to the extent its use is permitted under the Federal Rules of Evidence.[24] Rule 32 specifically states this, but it would be true even if Rule 32 never mentioned it. Rule 32 and the Federal Rules of Evidence are separate and independent grounds for the admission of depositions.[25]

6. The Witness Who Is Over 100 Miles from the Courthouse

Rule 32 is a hearsay exception that allows a deposition to be used in lieu of live testimony when "the witness is at a greater distance than 100 miles from

---

20. FED.R.CIV.P. 32(b). In fact, like any other objection, if they are not made by then they are waived. FED.R.EVID. 103(a)(1) requires a timely and specific objection. An objection when the deposition is offered at trial would be a timely objection to all but form-of-the-question problems with the evidence in the deposition.

21. FED.R.CIV.P. 32(1)(a).

22. "Substituting a party under Rule 25 does not affect the right to use a deposition previously taken." Fed.R.Civ.P. 32(a)(7).

23. FED.R.CIV.P. 32(a)(8).

24. FED.R.CIV.P. 32(a)(2)(B).

25. See the cases cited in footnote 14, above.

the place of trial or hearing, or is out of the United States, unless it appears that the absence of the witness was procured by the party offering the deposition." The in-court testimony of the deponent need not be unavailable: "100 miles is a bright line."[26]

The 100 miles from the courthouse part of this hearsay exception is not available if the party offering the deposition "procured" the declarant's absence. "The plain meaning of 'procure' in Rule 32(a) is 'to bring about' or 'to cause to happen.'"[27] It is an active word, not passive. It requires more than failing to ask the witness to come or to subpoena the witness. For example, the fact that the declarant is employed by the party offering the deposition and is on the job over 100 miles away is not enough to make Rule 32(a)(3) inapplicable.[28] The proponent must have taken some active step to keep the declarant out of the courtroom — something more than failing to facilitate the declarant's presence.[29]

In one extreme case a plaintiff, residing in California, sued her ex-husband in New York City. At the time of the trial she was in California and, in lieu of

_____

26. *Ueland*, 291 F.3d at 996 (admissibility not conditioned on "the witness' inability to show up in court; 100 miles is a bright line."). *Accord* Daigle v. Maine Medical Ctr., Inc., 14 F.3d 684, 691–92 (1st Cir. 1994) ("Distance is the decisive criterion: so long as a witness is shown to be more than one hundred miles from the place of trial, the admissibility of [a deposition under Rule 32] ... is not contingent upon a showing that the witness is otherwise unavailable."); Houser v. Snap-On-Tools Corp, 202 F.Supp. 181, 189 (D. Md. 1962) ("[T]he party attempting to submit the deposition into evidence need not proffer an excuse for the failure of the deponent to appear in court.").
The 100 miles is measured from the courthouse, not from the borders of the district defining the court's jurisdiction. Tatam v. Collins, 938 F.2d 509, 511 (4th Cir. 1991) (discussing the issue and citing cases).

27. Garcia-Martinez v. City and County of Denver, 392 F.3d 1187, 1191 (10th Cir. 2004) (quoting Webster's Third New International Dictionary 1809 (Philip Babcock Gove, ed., 2002)) ("In applying the rule, we start with its plain meaning.").

28. Carey v. Bahama Cruise Lines, 864 F.2d 201, 204 (1st Cir. 1988).

29. 392 F.3d at 1193 (plaintiff, an illegal alien, left the country to avoid arrest and deportation; at trial, his attorney offered his deposition under Civil Procedure Rule 32 and Evidence Rule 804(b)(1), arguing that since "[h]is absence was due to exigent circumstances beyond his control, the court should find him 'unavailable'"; the court noted that "[t]he proponent of the deposition bears the burden of proving ...'he has not procured his own absence'" and this plaintiff procured his own absence when he voluntarily left the country; furthermore, he "made scant effort to make other arrangements to appear temporarily for trial or to make himself available for remote testimony"); Ueland, 291 F.3d at 996 ("The party offering the deposition is forbidden to procure the deponent's absence (or distance); this is a far cry from requiring the litigant to procure the deponent's presence.... Subsection (3)(B) ... does not condition admissibility on the witness' inability to show up in court; 100 miles is a bright line.") (paragraph break omitted); Houser v. Snap-On-Tools Corp,

live testimony, she offered her own deposition. She was more than 100 miles away from the courthouse and this was not an absence "procured by the party offering the deposition"; she simply took no affirmative steps to get to New York City for the trial.[30] At the other extreme, a court found that counsel "procured" the absence of his expert witness when he selected an expert from half a continent away.[31]

7. Old, Infirm, or in Prison and Unavailable

The rule provides that "the deposition of a witness, whether or not a party, may be used by any party for any purpose if the court finds ... that the witness is unable to attend or testify because of age, illness, infirmity, or imprisonment."[32] Unlike the 100-miles-from-the-courthouse provision, this part of the rule does have an unavailability requirement. Counsel is not allowed to use the deposition just because the declarant is old, ill, infirm, or in prison. Counsel must show that the declarant is one or more of those things and, as a result of that status, unable to testify.[33]

---

202 F.Supp. 181, 189 (D. Md. 1962) ("[P]rocuring absence and doing nothing to facilitate presence are quite different things ...").

30. Richmond v. Brooks, 227 F.2d 490, 493 (2d Cir. 1955) (the "unless procured" clause does not render this deposition inadmissible).

A party can use Rule 32 to admit his or her own deposition or that of its own employees. *Id. Accord* In re Complaint of Bankers Trust Co., 752 F.2d 874, 888 (3d Cir. 1984); Hoppe v. G.D. Searle & Co., 779 F. Supp. 1413, 1420 (S.D.N.Y. 1991).

31. Caron v. GMC, 643 N.E.2d 471, 474 (Mass. App. Ct. 1994) ("Unlike fact witnesses, who are determined by their personal knowledge of relevant facts, regardless of where they live or work, a party normally has broad latitude in selecting his expert witnesses. By selecting an expert from Arizona, the plaintiff's counsel 'procured' the absence of his expert from the Commonwealth in the sense that he voluntarily created a situation in which his expert would be out of the Commonwealth unless he should make arrangements for the expert's appearance at trial.").

32. FED.R.CIV.P. 32(a)(4)(C). Referring to the similarly worded unavailability requirement in Rule 804 of the Federal Rules of Evidence, one case held: "The fear, nervousness or excitement that renders the child unable to testify in court, though it may be quite normal for someone his age, may fall within the scope of the term 'mental ... infirmity' as that term is used in Rule 804(a)(4)." Virgin Islands v. Riley, 754 F.Supp. 61, 64 (D.V.I. 1991) (the court found the child's in-court testimony unavailable, applied the former testimony exception, and allowed his videotaped deposition to be used against the defendant in a murder trial).

33. Boca Investerings P'ship v. United States, 197 F.R.D. 18, 19–20 (D.C.D.C. 2000) ("[T]he Rule by its terms requires proof of a causal connection between age, illness, infirmity or imprisonment and the inability to attend or testify. [A] party [must] demonstrate that the attendance of the witness is not possible 'because of' one of several enumerated

8. Deposition Strategy

Attorneys should keep the following in mind every time they are involved in a deposition: If the witness dies or becomes sufficiently infirm between the time of the deposition and the hearing or trial, or if the witness is over 100 miles from the courthouse at the time of the hearing or trial, then the deposition may be used in lieu of live testimony.

This may affect the kind of questions counsel will ask of a witness who is seriously ill or injured, headed for prison, unable to be subpoenaed, or simply lives and works over 100 miles from the courthouse in which the case will be tried. With such a deponent, counsel taking the deposition must at least consider being thorough.

There may be good reasons to hold back during a deposition, but there is no good reason to do so without forethought. The danger in conducting less than a full and complete examination of the deponent is that this less than full and complete deposition will be used against you. For example, counsel who does not cross-examine at the deposition—waives cross-examination—runs the risk that the deposition will be admitted at trial and there will not be any chance for any cross-examination. Attorneys must consider whether they can afford to sit back, hold their cards close to their vests, and not ask any, or many, questions at a deposition.[34]

9. The Ability of the Opponent of the Deposition to Counteract a Rule 32 Use of Deposition

So that opposing counsel is not surprised by the use of a deposition in lieu of live testimony, Rule 26 of the Federal Rules of Civil Procedure requires that parties must disclose the identity of witnesses who will testify as experts, in-

---

reasons.... Surely a party cannot just cite a witness's age as a justification for nonattendance; the party must explain why in the circumstances the witness's age prevents that witness from attending or testifying. Neither can a party simply assert that a witness's sickness or infirmity prevents attendance; the party must describe the illness or infirmity and convince the Court that the illness or infirmity is a genuine obstacle to attendance or to testifying. Similarly, a party cannot claim that an imprisoned witness need not testify in person without explaining why such imprisonment prevents that witness from appearing in person to provide live testimony.") (footnote and paragraph break omitted).

34. Melore v. Great Lakes Dredge & Dock Co., 1996 WL 548142, *4 (E.D.Pa. Sept. 20, 1996) ("[C]ounsel are always on notice that a deposition may be used at trial in accordance with [Rule 32 of the] Federal Rules of Civil Procedure.").

cluding those whose testimony will be presented by deposition. Each party must also disclose a great deal of information about each such expert (qualifications, publications, compensation, and prior expert testimony), and about the opinions each will express, and the basis for each opinion.

If counsel gives notice of intent to offer a deposition in lieu of the live testimony of a deponent who is 100 miles from the courthouse and that deponent can be subpoenaed, nothing prevents opposing counsel from subpoenaing the witness. If opposing counsel subpoenas the deponent and gets him or her into the courtroom, then the deponent is no longer over 100 miles away; Rule 32 no longer applies; and the deposition cannot be used in lieu of live testimony. [35]

If new information has been uncovered between the date of the deposition and the trial, then, short of subpoenaing the deponent, opposing counsel can ask for a second deposition. Additionally, perhaps the new information can be used to impeach or bolster the deposition testimony.[36]

In some cases, then, there are ways in which opposing counsel can get around, or at least mitigate, any unfairness that might be caused by the 100 miles from the courthouse exception.

10. Error in Refusing to Allow the Use of a Deposition May Be Harmless Error

If the trial judge does not follow Rule 32 but forces the proponent of the deposition to call to the stand a witness who is more than 100 miles from the courthouse, and that witness does testify, then the Rule 32 error is harmless. This makes Rule 32 largely discretionary when the deponent can be made to appear and testify in person.[37]

---

35. Rule 32(a)(4) "does not allow a party to cumulate evidence by both testifying at the trial and offering his or her deposition." CHARLES ALAN WRIGHT, ARTHUR MILLER & RICHARD L. MARCUS, 8A FEDERAL PRACTICE AND PROCEDURE § 2147, at 182 (1994), citing R.B. Matthews, Inc. v. Transamerica Transp. Servs., Inc., 945 F.2d 269, 273 (9th Cir. 1991).
The trial judge has power to control this sort of thing under the provision in Federal Rule of Evidence 611(a) regarding judicial control over the mode and order of testimony, and perhaps under Federal Rule of Evidence 403's provision regarding cumulative evidence.

36. The advisory committee's note to Rule 806 makes it clear that "[t]he [out-of-court] declarant of a hearsay statement which is admitted into evidence is in effect a witness." FED.R.EVID. 806 advisory committee's note. The declarant (here the deponent) can be impeached and, if impeached, rehabilitated.

37. Dhyne v. Meiners Thriftway, Inc., 184 F.3d 983, 989–90 (8th Cir. 1999) ("Many trial judges require that a deposed witness testify live, if available.... [T]hough arguably inconsistent with the language of Rule 32(a)(2), precluding a party from reading the deposi-

11. Ex Parte Depositions

Rule 32 does not apply unless the opposing party was represented at or given sufficient notice of the deposition. The opposing party does not have to show up at the deposition. If the opposing party has sufficient notice but decides not to attend, this hearsay exception still applies.

12. The Evidentiary Burden

The evidentiary burden is, of course, on the party using Rule 32 to introduce a deposition.[38]

13. The Confrontation Clause

The Confrontation Clause applies only in criminal cases; Rule 32 applies only in civil cases; the Confrontation Clause does not apply to Rule 32 evidence.

14. Miscellaneous Points

It does not matter whether the deposition in question is designated a "discovery" as opposed to a "trial" deposition.[39]

---

tion testimony of an available adverse party witness is at worst harmless error.") (citations omitted). "Dhyne suggests the practice is reversible error in Missouri state courts ... However, federal law governs this procedural issue." *Id.* at 990.

On a somewhat related point, *see* Nichols v. American Risk Mgmt., Inc., 45 Fed.R.Serv.3d (Callaghan) 1311 (S.D.N.Y. 2000) ("[G]iven the historical preference for live testimony and the strategy of limiting aggressive examination of opposing experts at depositions, a judge would be warranted in requiring live expert testimony *despite* Rule 32(a)(3)(B) under appropriate circumstances. Norton, however, has not suggested that it withheld any cross-examination during Lenk's deposition or that any special circumstances exist here which require an exception to Rule 32(a)(3)(B).") (emphasis added; footnotes omitted).

38. *E.g., Garcia-Martinez,* 392 F.3d at 1193; Fairfield 274–278 Clarendon Trust v. Dwek, 970 F.2d 990, 995 (1st Cir. 1992) (proponent's burden to show that he did not procure deponent's absence). Regarding evidentiary burdens and hearsay exceptions and exclusions generally, see Chapter 2(I), above.

39. "Most of the courts which have addressed 'discovery depositions' *vis a vis* 'trial depositions' have concluded that the federal rules do not set forth any definitions or distinctions as between the two." Estenfelder v. Gates Corp., 199 F.R.D. 351, 353 (D. Colo. 2001) (however, a party may be allowed to take a deposition after the close of the time for discovery, if the deposition is for the purpose of preserving testimony for trial) (citing and discussing cases). *Accord, e.g.,* Battle v. Memorial Hosp. at Gulfport, 228 F.3d 544, 551 (5th Cir. 2000); Tatmahn v. Collins, 938 F.2d 509, 511 (4th Cir. 1991); United States v. IBM Corp., 90 F.R.D. 377, 381 n.7 (S.D.N.Y. 1981) (distinction deliberately eliminated from the rule).

In a diversity action, Rule 32 prevails over a state statute or rule to the contrary.[40]

II. Rule 15(e) of the Federal Rules of Criminal Procedure

A. Text of the Rule

Rule 15. Depositions

(a) **When Taken.** Whenever due to exceptional circumstances of the case it is in the interest of justice that the testimony of a prospective witness of a party be taken and preserved for use at trial, the court may upon motion of such party and notice to the parties order that the testimony of such witness be taken by deposition and that any designated book, paper, document, record, recording, or other material not privileged, be produced at the same time and place....

* * *

(e) **Use.** At the trial or upon any hearing, a part or all of a deposition, so far as otherwise admissible under the rules of evidence, may be used as substantive evidence if the witness is unavailable, as unavailability is defined in Rule 804(a) of the Federal Rules of Evidence, or the witness gives testimony at the trial or hearing inconsistent with that witness's deposition. Any deposition may also be used by any party for the purpose of contradiction or impeaching the testimony of the deponent as a witness. If only a part of a deposition is offered in evidence by a party, an adverse party may require the offering of all of it which is relevant to the part offered and any party may offer other parts.

(f) **Objections to Deposition Testimony.** Objections to deposition testimony or evidence or parts thereof and the grounds for the objection shall be stated at the time of the taking of the deposition.

(g) **Deposition by Agreement not Precluded.** Nothing in this rule shall preclude the taking of a deposition, orally or upon written questions, or the use of a deposition, by agreement of the parties with the consent of the court.

---

40. Frechette v. Welch, 621 F.2d 11, 14 (1st Cir. 1980); *Dhyne*, 184 F.3d at 990 ("Dhyne suggests the practice is reversible error in Missouri state courts ... However, federal law governs this procedural issue.").

B. Foundational Elements[41]

1. The out-of-court statement is in the form of a deposition.

2. The out-of-court statement is offered into evidence in a trial or hearing in a criminal case.

3. The in-court testimony of the deponent is either:

   (a) unavailable, as defined in Rule 804(a) of the Federal Rules of Evidence or

   (b) inconsistent with testimony in the deposition.

C. Need + Reliability = 1

1. Need

When the deposition is used in lieu of live testimony Rule 15 requires the exact same unavailability as Rule 804 of the Federal Rules of Evidence. The need for the evidence here is just the same as the need for the evidence there.[42] When the deposition is used to contradict deponent's live testimony Rule 15 simply requires that the testimony be inconsistent with that witness's deposition. The need here is that, without this rule the inconsistent testimony might only be useable as credibility evidence; with the rule it can be used as substantive evidence of the fact in question.

2. Reliability

The guarantee of reliability here is that the statement is a deposition. The opportunity to cross-examine was present. To the extent that the opposing party was motivated to cross-examine at the deposition, that motivation will

---

41. In addition to the foundational elements laid out here, the rule provides that "[a]ny deposition may also be used by any party for the purpose of contradiction or impeaching the testimony of the deponent as a witness." Insofar as this rule specifies use for impeachment, this is nothing new and is not dependent on this rule; whenever a testifying witness's prior inconsistent statement is used to impeach his or her testimony, it is not offered to prove the truth of the matter asserted and is never hearsay. *See* Chapter 2(II)(A)(4)(a), above. Insofar as this rule specifies use for "contradiction," it would be something new, but for the fact that it seems redundant of the provision in the sentence that precedes it in the rule, which allows the deposition to be used "when the witness gives testimony at the trial or hearing inconsistent with that witness's deposition."

42. *See* Chapter 4(II)(D)(1), above, and the cross-reference therein.

be similar at the trial. A Rule 15 deposition is not a discovery deposition. The rule allows depositions whenever "due to exceptional circumstances of the case it is in the interest of justice that the testimony of a prospective witness of a party be taken and preserved for use at trial."[43] Everyone participating in this deposition knows that it is being taken so that it may be used at trial, in lieu of live testimony. Awareness of the likelihood that it will be used at trial profoundly affects the motive to cross-examine.

There may be many reasons a defendant in a criminal case would rather not engage a deposition witness in a thorough cross-examination: The defendant may want to keep his or her evidence under wraps. The defendant may want to avoid giving away his or her defense strategy. Under Rule 15, however, all of that changes with the knowledge that the deposition is being taken to use at trial in the place of the witness's live testimony.[44]

Part of Rule 15 allows a deposition to be used as substantive evidence when the deposed witness testifies at the trial or hearing and gives testimony inconsistent with his or her deposition. The reliability here is great: The witness is there to be observed by the jury and cross-examined by the objecting lawyer.

D. Use Note

1. Cross-References

Depositions taken within the confines of Rule 15 are admissible as though the deponent were there, in court, testifying live. Regarding objections to the testimony within the deposition—as opposed to an objection to the deposition itself, see the Use Note accompanying the discussion of Rule 32 of the Federal Rules of Civil Procedure.[45] Regarding the nonexclusivity of this exception and the evidentiary burden of establishing its foundation, see that same Use Note.[46]

---

43. FED.R.CRIM.P. 15(a).

44. United States v. Marchese, 842 F.Supp. 1307, 1308 (D. Colo. 1994) ("[E]veryone was aware that the Canadian witnesses were being deposed to preserve their testimony for trial and, therefore, all of the parties had the incentive to develop the testimony fully.").

The rule does not preclude depositions taken by agreement of the parties. The same tendency for reliability would exist for this kind of deposition—everyone should be aware of the possibility that someone might try to use it at trial.

45. See part I(E)(4) of this chapter, above.

46. See, respectively, parts I(E)(1) and I(E)(13) of this chapter, above.

2. Application of the Rule

This is a rule of *criminal* procedure. It does not apply in civil cases.[47] This rule applies only to depositions taken in the case at trial or hearing. Depositions taken in connection with other lawsuits may be admissible,[48] but not under Rule 15 of the Federal Rules of Criminal Procedure.

As a general rule, Rule 15 kicks in after the eventual defendant has been indicted or charged, that is, it is not available as a way to preserve testimony until the defendant has been indicted or charged.[49] If, however, witnesses are about to become unavailable—perhaps they are dying or leaving the country—then, upon application, federal judges have deemed the government and the targets of the investigation to be "parties" for the purposes of complying with Rule 15, and have allowed pre-indictment or pre-charge Rule 15 depositions.[50]

---

47. FED.R.CIV.P 32, the relevant rule of civil procedure, is discussed just above, in part I of this chapter.

48. *See, e.g.*, Chapter 4(II) (the former testimony exception), and particularly Chapter 4(II)(E)(1) (discussing many ways to get prior testimony into evidence around the hearsay rule), both above.

49. Rule 15 depositions are not discovery depositions. *See, e.g.*, United States v. Hutchings, 751 F.2d 239, 236 (8th Cir.); United States v. Cooper, 91 F.Supp.2d 79, 87 (D.D.C. 2000) ("'The purpose of Rule 15(a) is to preserve testimony for trial, not to provide a method of pretrial discovery.'" (quoting United States v. Kelley, 36 F.3d 1118, 1124 (D.C. Cir. 1994) (omitting multiple quotation marks and citations)).

Indeed, the first sentence of the rule begins: "Whenever due to exceptional circumstances of the case it is in the interest of justice that the testimony of a prospective witness of a party be taken and preserved for use at trial...." FED.R.CRIM.P. 15(a). Whether or not exceptional circumstances exist is generally a function of three things: (1) Whether the in-court testimony of the witness will be unavailable at the trial. (2) Whether the testimony is material to the moving party's case. (3) Whether taking the deposition will result in an injustice to the nonmoving party. United States v. Ramos, 45 F.3d 1519, 1522–23 (11th Cir. 1995); United States v. Drogoul, 1 F.3d 1546, 1552 (11th Cir. 1993) ("a substantial likelihood ... that the proposed deponent will not testify at trial").

50. *See* United States v. Hayes, 190 F.3d 939, 945 n.2 (9th Cir. 1999) ("[Rule 15] seems to assume that depositions will only be taken after indictment, when there is a 'defendant.' No doubt this is the usual practice, but of course here, the government invoked Rule 15 and sought depositions because the students were about to leave the country. The magistrate judge's order permitting the depositions deemed the government and the targets to be 'parties' for purposes of complying with Rule 15. However, Hayes did (and does) not contest the depositions themselves. Therefore, whether this was a proper procedure is not before us."). *See also* United States v. Omene, 143 F.3d 1167, 1170 (9th Cir. 1998) (the showing need not be "conclusive"; the rule "only requires that the trial court find that due to exceptional circumstances it is in the interest of justice that the testimony of a prospective witness be taken or preserved for possible use at trial").

3. Use of Depositions in Criminal Trials Is Disfavored

Simply stated: "The use of deposition testimony in criminal trials is disfavored, largely because such evidence tends to diminish a defendant's Sixth Amendment confrontation rights."[51] On the other hand, Rule 15 is becoming more and more important. With modern communication and transportation, however, crime increasingly takes on an international character and more and more often key witnesses live abroad. "[B]ecause federal courts frequently lack the power to compel a foreign national's attendance at trial, Rule 15 may offer the only practicable means of procuring critical evidence."[52]

4. Rule 15's Requirement of Unavailability or Inconsistency

a. Unavailability

One of Rule 15's foundational elements for the use of a deposition in lieu of live testimony is that the in-court testimony of the out-of-court declarant (the deponent) must be either unavailable or inconsistent with the declarant's testimony at the deposition. Regarding unavailability, by its terms, Rule 15's unavailability requirement is co-extensive with unavailability as defined in Rule 804 of the hearsay rules.[53]

Some parts of Rule 32 of the Federal Rules of Civil Procedure do not require that the out-of-court declarant's in-court testimony be unavailable or inconsistent. The difference in the availability requirement of civil Rule 32, on the one hand, and criminal Rule 15, on the other, makes sense in light of the following two considerations.

■ As a general rule, our system prefers that testimony be presented live in front of the trier of fact. That preference is enforced more diligently in criminal cases, where the penalties include loss of liberty or life. It fits the relative strengths of the preference that the use of depositions as a substitute for live testimony is more restrictive under the rules of criminal procedure than under the rules of civil procedure.[54] There are also Confrontation Clause issues in criminal cases that do not apply to civil cases.

---

51. United States v. McKeeve, 131 F.3d 1, 8 (1st Cir. 1997). Regarding the Confrontation Clause, see part 5 of this Use Note and see Chapter 14, below.

52. *McKeeve*, 131 F.3d at 8. *Accord* United States v. Siddiqui, 235 F.3d 1318, 1323 (11th Cir. 2000).

53. Fed.R.Evid. 804(a), discussed at Chapter 4(I), above.

54. *See* part II(D)(3) of this chapter, above.

■ Unlike civil Rule 32, criminal Rule 15's purpose is not to provide pretrial discovery. Rule 15's purpose is the preservation of evidence for use at trial.[55] Its purpose is the preservation of evidence that might otherwise be lost or unavailable at the time of trial: lost, for example, because the witness dies, disappears, or refuses to testify out of fear; unavailable, for example, because the witness is physically too infirm to come to court or is a foreign national who is not subject to service of process and will not appear voluntarily.

If the testimony would be lost without the deposition, then the deposition may be used as though it were live testimony (subject to objections made during the deposition). If, on the other hand, the live testimony is available, then the deposition may not be used as a substitute and, absent inconsistent testimony, it may not be used as substantive evidence.

In the first sentence of Rule 15 of the Federal Rules of Criminal Procedure, where it describes when courts are to allow depositions in criminal cases, the purpose of the rule is expressed as follows: "Whenever due to exceptional circumstances of the case it is in the interest of justice that the testimony of a prospective witness of a party be taken and preserved for use at trial."[56] One of those "exceptional circumstances" is when unavailability is anticipated. This part of the rule requires that this expectation come to pass, that is, that when the deposition is offered the declarant's in-court testimony is unavailable.

In a rational system, it would come as no surprise that the scope of the rule is tied to its purpose.

This is consistent with (perhaps actually redundant of) Rule 804(b)(1) of the Federal Rules of Evidence, the former-testimony exception.

b. Inconsistent Testimony

As noted above, Rule 15 requires that the deponent's in-court testimony be either unavailable or inconsistent with the declarant's deposition. (As also noted, Rule 32 does not require either.) The judicial system we have adopted prefers that testimony be presented in person to the trier of fact, especially in criminal cases. It is, however, a preference, not an absolute rule. We do not allow a witness to take the stand and lie and then hide behind this preference for live testimony.[57]

---

55. *See* part II(C)(2) of this chapter, above.
56. FED.R.CRIM.P. 15(a).
57. Harris v. New York, 401 U.S. 222, 226 (1971) (even though defendant's un-Mirandized statement is inadmissible as substantive evidence, it can be used to impeach defendant's testimony).

With or without Rule 15, we allow inconsistent statements in the deposition to be used to impeach the witness's live testimony.[58] With Rule 15, we also allow inconsistent statements in the deposition to be used as substantive evidence.

5. The Confrontation Clause

Rule 15 applies in two ways. One, it can be used at a criminal trial to admit deponent's deposition testimony when it is inconsistent with deponent's trial testimony, and to admit it as substantive evidence of the inconsistent fact declared. The Confrontation Clause is not a problem here. The witness is testifying and can be confronted.

Two, the deposition can be offered at a criminal trial in lieu of live testimony. Whether the Confrontation Clause would override Rule 15 in this situation likely depends on whether the defendant had an opportunity to confront the witness at the deposition being offered into evidence—not whether the defendant actually confronted the witness, but whether the defendant had the opportunity to do so. The Constitution does not require defendants to confront witnesses against them; it just says that if they choose to do so, they have a right to do so.[59]

III. The Non-Exclusivity of These Rules

Using Rule 32 or Rule 15, is not the only way to get all or parts of a deposition around the hearsay rule. There are a number of other ways counsel may be able to get a Rule 32 or a Rule 15 deposition around the hearsay rule. Additionally, there are a number of other ways counsel may be able to get into evidence deposition testimony that does not fit under either Rule 32 or Rule 15. Even a deposition taken in a civil case may be admissible in a criminal case if there is an exclusion or an exception to get it around the hearsay rule.[60] That

---

58. *See* Chapter 2(II)(A), above. *See also* California v. Green, 399 U.S. 149 (1970) (upholding the constitutionality of a state statute providing that if, at some point during the trial, the out-of-court declarant is given an opportunity to explain or deny his or her prior inconsistent statement, then said statement is not made inadmissible by the hearsay rule).

59. Maryland v. Craig, 497 U.S. 836, 847 (1990) ("Although face to face confrontation forms the core of the Clause's values, it is not an indispensable element of the confrontation right.").

60. If there are evidentiary problems other than hearsay, then, of course, they will have to be dealt with, as will any Confrontation Clause problems.

is, Rules 32 and 15 are ways around the hearsay rule. They are not exclusive.[61] They are not needed if there are other ways around the hearsay rule.

Regarding other ways to get a deposition around the hearsay rule, the former testimony exception comes to mind immediately; the deposition may fulfill its foundational elements.[62] If it is the deposition of a party, offered against that party, then it is a nonhearsay admission.[63] Parts of the deposition may be nonhearsay prior inconsistent or consistent statements.[64] The deposition may be a statement under belief of impending death.[65] Counsel may take the deposition of a witness who is known to be dying so that the deposition can be used at trial, after the witness has died. It is possible that parts of the deposition would fit under any number of exceptions: state of mind[66] and statement against interest,[67] for example. There is no reason why an old enough deposition could not fit under the ancient documents exception.[68]

Furthermore, Rule 32 does not apply to a deposition that is used as an affidavit. In proceedings where affidavit evidence is admissible, then a deposition meeting the requirements of an affidavit, but not the requirements of Rule 32, may be used as an affidavit.[69]

---

61. *See* part I(E)(1) of this chapter, above.

62. *See* Chapter 4(II)(B), above; part I(E)(1) of this chapter, above.

63. *See* Chapter 2(III)(A), above.

64. *See* Chapter 2(II)(A) & (C), above.

65. *See* Chapter 4(III), above.

66. *See* Chapter 3(IV), above.

67. *See* Chapter 4(IV), above.

68. *See* Chapter 3(XI), above.

69. SEC v. Antar, 120 F. Supp.2d 431, 445–46 (D.N.J. 2000); KZK Livestock, Inc. v. Production Credit Servs. of W. Cent. Illinois, 221 B.R. 471, 474–75 (Bankr. C.D. Ill. 1998) (citing cases).

CHAPTER SEVEN

STATE-OF-MIND EVIDENCE

I. Introduction

State-of-mind evidence is worth special consideration. There are two main reasons why. First, it is so common. Every statement is evidence of someone or another's state of mind—every single one.[1] Second, there are so many dif-

---

1. *See* part III(D) of this chapter, below.

ferent ways of handling state-of-mind evidence. So far state-of-mind evidence has been considered as it has come up as part of the definition of hearsay and the various exceptions to the hearsay rule. This chapter puts together various ways of handling evidence of a person's state of mind.

II. Eight Ways of Handling State-of-Mind Evidence

A. Live, Firsthand Testimony: Nonhearsay

One kind of state-of-mind testimony is this: The testifying witness tells the trier of fact about his or her own state of mind—current state of mind, or state of mind at some time in the past. This includes testimony such as, "I am depressed" or "I was depressed." It includes: "I was afraid they would kill me if I didn't go along." "I am as happy as I have ever been," or "Before the wreck I was a happy person." "I was cold." "I fell in the grocery store and later that day had a horrible pain in my knee, and I still have that pain in my knee today." There is no hearsay problem with this kind of testimony because there is no out-of-court statement. All we have here is an in-court statement of a first-hand perception of the testifying witness.[2]

From a hearsay standpoint, this is no different than a witness who testifies: "Defendant's car ran the red light, hit the plaintiff's van and sent it rolling across the intersection." There is no out-of-court declarant, there is no out-of-court statement.

B. Verbal Acts: Nonhearsay[3]

A second kind of state-of-mind testimony is verbal-acts evidence: Here is an example of a "verbal act." Gary claims he owns a car. Bob claims Gary gave it to him as a gift. At trial, Bob calls a witness to testify as follows: "I saw Gary hand some keys to Bob and heard him say: 'Bob, I want you to have this car

---

2. In Ostad v. Oregon Health Sciences Univ., 327 F.3d 876, 886 (9th Cir. 2003), for example, the witness's testimony that he "had 'some concerns about billing irregularities in the department'" is not hearsay. To the hearsay rule, it does not matter what the issue is because there is no out-of-court statement. That his concerns were based on what he had been told by others does not change the fact that his testimony about his personally held beliefs is not an out-of-court statement. If his concerns are relevant and his testimony satisfies the opinion-evidence rules, it is likely admissible.

3. See also part III(A)(9) of Chapter 1, above.

as a gift.'" The in-court statement is, "I saw Gary hand some keys to Bob and heard him say...." The out-of-court statement is, "'Bob, I want you to have this car as a gift.'"[4] In the suit over the ownership of the car, this out-of-court statement, coupled with the handing over of the keys, is a nonhearsay verbal act. Speaking these words in this context has legal consequences. Just speaking them, in context, changes the legal relationship between Gary and Bob, it changes who owns the car.[5]

Perhaps Gary was lying or joking. It does not matter. There are no take-backs. The speaking of the words in this context completes the deal. Whether Gary meant it or not the gift was completed and ownership of the car changed hands. What do we want to know? Whether the words were spoken.[6] What did the testifying witness perceive? That the words were spoken. The testifying witness is a real witness to what we want to know.[7] The testifying witness is an original manufacturer of this evidence.[8] It is the testifying witness whose credibility is in question.[9]

In the hypothetical above, when Bob offers Gary's statement against Gary it is a party's own statement offered against him. It is, therefore, both a non-hearsay personal admission[10] and a nonhearsay verbal act. Change the hypothetical. The testimony is the same: "I saw Gary hand some keys to Bob and heard him say: 'Bob, I want you to have this car as a gift.'" Bob had a wreck while driving the car in question. Bob has no money, Gary does have money. The other driver has sued Gary, claiming that he negligently loaned his car to Bob. Among other things, Gary argues that the car was not his. Gary testifies that he had given the car to Bob. He also offers a witness's testimony that she saw Gary hand some keys to Bob and say "Bob, I want you to have this car as

---

4. The out-of-court part of the statement is an expression of Gary's state of mind: his desire to give Bob the car.

5. *See* approach # 9 (the verbal-acts approach) of The Top Ten Approaches to Hearsay, Chapter 1(III)(A)(10), above.

6. Of course we also need to know the context in which the statement was made. In the hypothetical, the witness also perceived the context. If the witness had not perceived the context but only heard the words, there would have to be other evidence of context to prove the point but, either way, the statement is not hearsay.

7. *See* approach # 3 (the real-witness approach) of The Top Ten Approaches to Hearsay, Chapter 1(III)(A)(3), above.

8. *See* approach # 2 (the manufactured-evidence approach) of The Top Ten Approaches to Hearsay, Chapter 1(III)(A)(2), above.

9. *See* approach # 7 (the credibility approach) of The Top Ten Approaches to Hearsay, Chapter 1(III)(A)(6), above.

10. FED.R.EVID. 801(d)(2)(A).

a gift." This no longer is a party's own statement offered *against* the party who made it, but rather a party's own statement offered *by* the party who made it. It is, however, still a nonhearsay verbal act.[11]

Nonhearsay verbal acts include the words of a contract, to prove the contract;[12] slanderous statements, to prove slander;[13] racist or sexist statements in

---

11. It is no defense to a written contract to say, "Yes, I signed the contract, but I did not mean it. I lied." Or, perhaps, "I was only joking." Likewise, it is no defense to an oral contract to say, "Yes, I said that, but I did not mean it."

> [C]ommunications between the parties to a contract that define the terms of a contract, or prove its content, are not hearsay, as they are verbal acts or legally operative facts. *See, e.g.,* Preferred Properties Inc. v. Indian River Estates Inc., 276 F.3d 790, 799 n. 5 (6th Cir. 2002) (verbal acts creating a contract are not hearsay); Kepner-Tregoe Inc. v. Leadership Software, 12 F.3d 527, 540 (5th Cir. 1994) (finding contract to be a signed writing of independent legal significance and therefore non-hearsay); Mueller v. Abdnor, 972 F.2d 931, 937 (8th Cir. 1992) (holding contracts and letters from attorney relating to the formation thereof are non-hearsay); United States v. Tann, 425 F. Supp. 2d 26, 29 (D.D.C. 2006) (finding negotiable instruments to be legally operative documents that do not constitute hearsay) ...

Lorraine v. Markel Am. Ins. Co., 241 F.R.D. 534, 566 (D. Md. 2007).

12. *E.g.,* Schindler v. Joseph C. Seiler & Synthes Spine Co., 474 F.3d 1008, 1010–11 (7th Cir. 2007) ("words of contract or slander") (see the next footnote for a more complete quotation); Cloverland-Green Spring Dairies, Inc. v. Pennsylvania Milk Mktg. Bd. 298 F.3d 201, 218 n.20 (3rd Cir. 2003) ("[A] statement offering to sell a product at a particular price is a 'verbal act,' not hearsay, because the statement itself has legal effect."); Preferred Props. v. Indian River Estates, 276 F.3d 790, 799 n.5 (6th Cir. 2002) ("The verbal acts doctrine applies where 'legal consequences flow from the fact that words were said, e.g. the words of offer and acceptance which create a contract.' Black's Law Dictionary ... 1558 [(6th ed. 1990)]...."); *Lorraine,* 241 F.R.D. at 566 (as quoted in note 11, above).

> [N]one of the excluded exhibits "brought the contract into being," "affected the legal rights of the parties," or had any legal consequences independent of its substantive content. *Compare* United States v. Montana, 199 F.3d 947, 950 (7th Cir. 1999) (explaining difference between verbal acts such as "a promise, offer, or demand," which "*commit* the speaker to a course of action," and hearsay statements, which "narrate, describe, or otherwise convey information, and so are judged by their truth value") (emphasis added), *and* Trepel v. Roadway Exp., Inc., 194 F.3d 708, 717 (6th Cir. 1999) (upholding exclusion of statement as hearsay where statement "was not an offer to sell" but rather, a declaration of the price range the owner "would be willing to take ... should someone make an offer to buy"); *with* Puma v. Sullivan, 746 A.2d 871, 874–76 (D.C. 2000) (holding that oral statement containing an offer, *which statement's proponents had accepted,* was admissible for consideration on summary judgment as a "verbal act").

Echo Acceptance Corp. v. Household Retail Servs., 267 F.3d 1068, 1088 (10th Cir. 2001).

13. Statements that constitute verbal acts (e.g., words of contract or slander) are not hearsay because they are not offered for their truth. *See* FED. R. EVID. 801(c)

the workplace, to prove workplace discrimination;[14] cancelled checks, to prove payment;[15] words that are an element of a crime, to prove the crime;[16] consent to a search, to prove the validity of the search,[17] criminal-activity statements

---

Advisory Committee Notes (noting that the Rule 801(c) excludes from the definition of hearsay "'verbal acts' and 'verbal parts of an act,' in which the statement itself affects the legal rights of the parties or is a circumstance bearing on conduct affecting their rights." [That situation must be distinguished from one] "[w]here a plaintiff attempts to introduce the testimony of an individual who did not personally witness the alleged defamatory statement but was later told by another that the statement was made, such testimony is rejected as hearsay. This is precisely what [this plaintiff] is attempting to do through his own testimony."
Schindler, 474 F.3d at 1010–11 (citations and paragraph break omitted). *See also, e.g.*, Anderson v. United States, 417 U.S. 221, 219–20 (1974) (statements admitted "to prove that the statements were made so as to establish a foundation for later showing ... they were false" are not offered to prove the truth of the matter asserted and, therefore, cannot be hearsay).

14. *E.g.*, Wilson v. City of Des Moines, 442 F.3d 637, (8th Cir. 2006) (plaintiff did not offer statement to prove she is a bitch or a slut but to demonstrate systematic discrimination; the words themselves are the discrimination); Noviello v. City of Boston, 398 F.3d 76, 85 (1st Cir. 2005) (coworkers' insults and taunts aimed at plaintiff were offered to prove sexual harassment and retaliation in the workplace; what matters regarding these statements is, first, that the words were said "and, thus, contributed to the hostile work environment" and, second, the effect they had on the plaintiff; the relationship between the statements and those issues does not depend on the truth of the taunts and insults); Talley v. Bravo Pitino Rest., Ltd., 61 F.3d 1241, 1249 (6th Cir. 1995) (to the issue of discrimination, racist comments were not offered to prove the truth of the statements but to demonstrate the racial attitudes of the declarants).

15. *E.g.*, United States v. Pang, 362 F.3d 1187, 1192 (9th Cir. 2004) (regarding the admissibility of cancelled checks: "[O]ut-of-court statements that are offered as evidence of legally operative verbal conduct are not hearsay. They are considered 'verbal acts.'"); Richter & Phillips Jewelers & Distribs., Inc. v. Dolly Toy Co., 31 Bankr. 512, 514 n.1 (Bankr. S.D. Ohio 1983) (to the issue of payment, a "Paid" stamp on the back of the check is not hearsay. "As proof of payment, [it] constitute[s] not secondary but primary evidence.").

16. This would include, "This is a holdup. Put your money in this bag." It often includes words spoken in the perpetration of crimes such as insurance or securities fraud. It can include any crime of solicitation, *e.g.*, United States v. Childs, 539 F.3d 552, 559 (6th Cir. 2008) ("'A witness who testifies at trial that [someone solicited them to commit a crime] is testifying to a verbal act of which the witness has direct knowledge: the extension of the invitation.'... It is the fact that the declaration was made, not the truth of the declaration, which is relevant."); United States v. Smith, 354 F.3d 390, 396 n.6 (5th Cir. 2003) ("solicitation of perjury [as] ... a verbal act"). Tompkins v. Cyr, 202 F.3d 770, 779 n.3 (5th Cir. 2000) (threats as verbal acts). Keep in mind here that if the words are those of the criminal defendant offered against the criminal defendant, then the statement is a nonhearsay statement by a party offered against the party. FED.R.EVID. 801(d)(2)(A).).

17. *E.g.*, United States v. Moreno, 233 F.3d 937, 940 (7th Cir. 2000) (consent to a search is a verbal act).

that led the police to investigate the crime on trial, to show why an investigation was begun (*e.g.*, to disprove an illicit motive for the investigation).[18] In these cases the utterance is the issue.[19]

C. Statements That Circumstantially Assert the State of Mind of the Speaker: Nonhearsay

A third kind of state-of-mind testimony is the out-of-court statement that circumstantially asserts the state of mind of the out-of-court declarant.[20]

---

18. *E.g.*, Fed.R.Evid. 801(c) advisory committee's note; United States v. Love, 521 F.3d 1007, 1009 (8th Cir. 2008) ("[A] statement is not hearsay if it is offered for the limited purpose of explaining why a police investigation was undertaken.") (multiple and internal quotation marks omitted); United States v. Tyler, 281 F.3d 84, 98 (3d Cir. 2002) (statements that "themselves 'affect[] the legal rights of the parties or [are] circumstances bearing on conduct affecting their rights'" are not hearsay; true or not, they "provided a jurisdictional basis for initiating a federal investigation into Tyler's activities ..."); United States v. Becker, 230 F.3d 1224, 1228–31 (10th Cir. 2000) (the statement was admissible nonhearsay evidence of the origin of the investigation and inadmissible hearsay evidence of the presence of drugs in the defendant's house); State v. Kemp, 948 A.2d 636, 648 (N.J. 2008) (a police officer's testimony that he acted "'upon information received,'" it is nonhearsay state-of-mind evidence "admissible ... to explain his subsequent conduct."); Chestnut v. Commonwealth, 250 S.W.3d 288, 294 (Ky. 2008) (when information furnished to the police is admitted solely because "'it tends to explain the action that was taken by the police ... as a result of this information *and* the taking of that action is an issue in the case,'" the statements are admissible nonhearsay verbal acts) (citation omitted).

19. Sometimes the words are *the* issue, sometimes *an* issue.

While verbal acts traditionally are words that have legal significance—words that alone or in context change a legal relationship—without regard to the declarant's intention to tell the truth, some courts simply refer to any out of court statement that is not an assertion as a verbal act. For example, in United States v. Manfre, 368 F.3d 832 (8th Cir. 2004), there was a nightclub explosion. A propane tank was found at the scene. Rush and Manfre were alleged coconspirators in this explosion. A witness' "testimony that he overheard Mr. Rush say 'propane tank'" is not hearsay. All that matters is that the words were spoken; from the fact that they were spoken the trier of fact could draw an inference connecting Rush "with a propane tank found at the scene ... This is ... a ... 'verbal act[.]' 'The hearsay rule excludes out-of-court assertions used to prove the truth of the facts asserted in them. Verbal acts, however, are not hearsay because they are not assertions and not adduced to prove the truth of the matter.'" *Id.* at 839 (quoting Mueller v. Abdnor, 972 F.2d 931, 937 (8th Cir. 1992)).

20. *Talley*, 61 F.3d at 1249 (*see* note 14, above); United States v. Hartmann, 958 F.2d 774 (7th Cir. 1991) (this case is discussed at Chapter 3(IV)(D)(2)(c), above); United States v. Williams, 697 A.2d 1244, 1248–49 (D.C. Ct. App. 1997) (Larson has been killed in his own apartment; the woman charged with the crime alleges Larson tried to molest her; the tes-

■ Here are two simple examples that will explain the principal: To the issue of Mr. Smith's mental state, a witness will testify: "When Mr. Smith told me that he was going to change his will to disinherit his son, I asked him why he would want to do something like that and he said: 'These shiny silver extra-terrestrials from Roswell impregnated my wife. The boy's not really mine. Let them take care of him. I'm not going to.'" To the issue of Mrs. Smith's mental state, a witness will testify: "Mrs. Smith stated: 'I am the Pope.'" While each of these statements was made out of court, neither is hearsay. The fact that these declarants *made* these statements is evidence of their state of mind — either it is evidence of their state of mind, or it is irrelevant. To state the obvious, neither of these statements is offered to prove the truth of the matter asserted.

Here is a more complicated example that can be understood in light of the simpler examples above. This is a custody case. At the time of the divorce, the mother was awarded custody. The mother remarried. At the time of the second marriage, the daughter in question was in foster care. When the foster mother mentioned her mother's new husband to the girl, the girl ran up to the foster mother, "put her arms around me and her head in my lap and started crying real bad and hard and said, 'He killed my brother and he'll kill my mommie too.'"[21] The father sued seeking to have custody awarded to him. In that suit, the foster mother's testimony regarding the girl's out-of-court statement is not hearsay. It is not offered to prove the truth of the matter asserted. It is offered as circumstantial evidence of the girl's state of mind. If the new husband had killed the boy, surely that would be relevant to who should have custody of the boy's sister, but that inference is not necessary to make the evidence relevant to the child custody action. The only inference that is necessary is that the girl has a horrible relationship with her mother's new husband and, consequently, the young girl would be better off with her father. Regarding the latter inference, the statement is not being used to prove the truth of the fact asserted, but instead to show the young girl's state of mind. There is no hearsay here, because the inference to be drawn is not dependent on the truth of the matter asserted in the statement.

---

timony of a man living in a neighboring apartment that Larson asked him to call the police if he heard any commotion from his apartment was offered as circumstantial evidence of Larson's state of mind; it is evidence that he was afraid that something might happen in his apartment and that he did not intend to molest or assault the defendant); State v. Martin, 458 So.2d 454 (La. 1984) (discussed at Chapter 3(IV)(D)(3), above).

21. Betts v. Betts, 473 P. 2d 403, 407 (Wash. Ct. App. 1970). This case is discussed at many places in this book, most completely at Chapter 1(IV)(F).

Here is why the first two examples—"extra-terrestrials impregnated my wife" and "I am the Pope"—are so easy to understand and the third example—"He killed my brother"—is so much more difficult. It is easy to see that the first two statements are not offered to prove the truth of the matters asserted since neither could possibly be true. It is more difficult to see that the third statement is not offered to prove the truth of the matter asserted because this statement could be true and in the right case with the right issue it would be offered to prove its truth. (It would, for example, be offered to prove its truth in the new husband's first-degree murder trial for killing the brother.)

■ There is a difference between an out-of-court statement that circumstantially asserts the declarant's state of mind and one that directly asserts the declarant's state of mind: The former is not offered to prove the truth of the matter asserted, while the latter is. Assume this is the issue: Did the out-of-court declarant dislike X? Consider two pieces of testimony: First, the testifying witness heard the out-of-court declarant say "X is a sniveling coward!" This is not offered to prove that X is a sniveling coward; therefore, it is not offered to prove the truth of the matter asserted; therefore, it is not hearsay. It is offered as circumstantial evidence of whether the out-of-court declarant disliked X. It is not hearsay and absent some other evidentiary problem, it is admissible.

Second, the testifying witness heard the out-of-court declarant say "I do not like X!" This is offered to prove that the declarant did not like X; therefore, it is offered to prove the truth of the matter asserted; therefore, unless Rule 801(d) excludes the statement from the hearsay definition, it is hearsay. It is relevant as direct evidence of whether the out-of-court declarant disliked X, but it is hearsay and unless a hearsay exception can be established it is not admissible.[22]

---

22. One court discussed this point as follows: If the issue is the out-of-court declarant's state of mind towards X, it is the difference between these two statements: First, "X threatened to kill me," which is circumstantial evidence of the speaker's state of mind regarding X. Second, "I hate X," which is a direct statement of the speaker's state of mind regarding X. The former is not hearsay because it is not offered to prove the truth of the matter asserted. The latter is hearsay because it is offered to prove the truth of the matter asserted. Rafanelli v. Dale, 924 P.2d 242, 253 (Mont. 1996). Declarant's statements that he was afraid of his wife were hearsay because they were offered to prove that he was afraid of his wife. The statements were, however, admissible under the state of mind exception. Id. at 254.

Judge Weinstein has demonstrated just how far this nonhearsay state-of-mind argument can go.

> Gollender was part of a conspiracy. The question was whether Muscato [was also]. Gollender *testified* that he'd put a label on a gun. There was evidence there had been a label on the gun found on Muscato. This arguably linked Muscato to Gollender, and, through Gollender, to the conspiracy on trial.

D. Statements Offered for Their Effect on Those Who Heard Them: Nonhearsay

A fourth kind of state-of-mind evidence is the out-of-court statement that is offered to show the effect it had on the state of mind of someone who heard it.[23]

> Gollender was impeached ... In response, the prosecutor called a special agent of the United States Treasury Department who testified that Gollender had made an out-of-court statement regarding the labeling of the gun, and had made the statement before there was any opportunity for anyone to have placed the suggestion in his mind. Judge Weinstein let this earlier statement in as non-hearsay under the theory that it is circumstantial evidence of Gollender's state of mind; it proves the existence of a memory in Gollender's mind at a relevant time past; and, in terms of whether this was in Gollender's mind on this date past, we can cross-examine a person who has first-hand knowledge ... "Who is the real witness?" as Professor McElhaney would ask. The treasury agent, and he is testifying.

Fenner, 62 UMKC L. REV., at 11–12 (footnotes omitted) (discussing United States v. Muscato, 534 F.Supp. 969 (E.D.N.Y 1982)). For other examples, *see* Fenner, 62 UMKC L. REV., at 10–21. Regarding this category, *i.e.*, statements that circumstantially assert the state of mind of the speaker, *see also* Chapter 3(IV)(D)(9).

23. "[T]he hearsay rule does not apply to statements that are offered to show what effect they produced on the actions of a listener." United States v. Meserve, 271 F.3d 314, 320 (1st Cir. 2001). In addition to cases cited elsewhere in this part of this chapter, see United States v. Harper, 463 F.3d 663, 668 (7th Cir. 2006) (defendant objected to the admission of a letter from the Federal Government to defendant's attorney stated that defendant had $23,535 in unreported income; eight days after his attorney received the letter defendant filed an overdue tax return and a few months later filed a second one; defendant is now charged with filing false income tax returns in connection with the unreported income; the letter was not admitted to prove the truth of the matter asserted but to show "its effect on Defendant — it spurred him to cover his tracks"); United States v. Rubin, 591 F.2d 278, 283 (5th Cir. 1979) (to the issue of criminal intent, the statements were not offered "to prove the truth of the matter asserted, but ... to prove that he had heard them and to establish their effect on his mind"); Tucker v. Housing Auth. of the Birmingham Dist., 507 F.Supp.2d 1240, 1269 (M.D. Ala. 2006) ("In this case, Plaintiff's testimony regarding Griffin's out-of-court statements was not offered to prove the truth of the matter asserted but merely the effect of those comments on Tucker's belief that he was the subject of discrimination."); Chapman v. Ford Motor Co., 245 S.W.3d 123, 130 (Ark. 2006) ("A statement is not hearsay if it is offered not for its truth, but merely to show the fact of the assertion, to explain someone's responsive actions, or, in this case, to support Ford's position that it did not act with malice."); Holland v. State, 713 A.2d 364, 371 (Md. 1997) (the statement was offered as circumstantial evidence of the collective state of mind of the declarant and those who heard it); Armstrong v. State, 826 P.2d 1106, 1116–20 (Wyo. 1992) (bartender's out of court declaration that the defendant had gone home to get a gun so he could come back and shoot the deceased was not offered to prove the truth of the facts asserted, but to show the state

■ A very common use of this effect-on-the-hearer evidence is to prove notice. Just after a rain, the plaintiff slipped and fell on the defendant's wet parking lot. In the subsequent negligence action, the plaintiff had to prove that the defendant knew or should have known of the dangerous condition of the parking lot when wet. The plaintiff offered the testimony of defendant's receptionist that on a number of occasions after a rain people had told her that the parking lot was slippery. This was not offered as evidence that the parking lot was slippery when wet but as evidence that the defendant was on notice that the lot was slippery when wet.[24] Depending on what the defendant admits and de-

---

of mind of the persons who heard him make the statement; this state of mind was relevant to the degree to which they were paying attention as subsequent events unfolded); In re Fromdahl, 840 P.2d 683, 690–91 (Or. 1991) (in a custody battle, Father alleged that Mother was mentally unfit, suffering from delusions that Father had sexually assaulted the children; Mother's testimony that the children and a police detective told her about this abuse, and that she had been told Father failed a lie detector test regarding the abuse was not offered for truth, but as circumstantial evidence of Mother's state of mind, *i.e.*, that her perceptions were rational and not delusional); State v. Eaton, 524 So.2d 1194, 1204 (La. 1988) (a statement "offered ... to show the effect it had on the mind of the person who heard it ... is not hearsay because its value does not lie in its truthfulness, ... [but] in the fact it was said"); State v. Irick, 231 S.E.2d 833, 844–45 (N.C. 1977) ("The declarations of one person are frequently admitted to evidence ... [the] state of mind of another person who heard or read them ... to explain [the latter's] subsequent conduct.") (multiple quotation marks and citation omitted); Commonwealth v. Fiore, 308 N.E.2d 902, 907 (Mass. 1974) (evidence of a group's state of mind). Regarding this category, *i.e.*, effect on the mind of the hearer, *see also* Chapter 3(IV)(D)(9).

24. Vinyard v. Vinyard Funeral Home, Inc., 435 S.W.2d 392, 396 (Mo. Ct. App. 1968). *Accord, e.g.*, Marseilles Hydro Power, LLC v. Marseilles Land and Water Co., 518 F.3d 459, 468 (7th Cir. 2008) ("[N]ot hearsay if it is used only to show notice."); United States v. Rettenberger, 344 F.3d 702, 707 (7th Cir. 2003) (defendant offered self-serving testimony about his statements to the Social Security Administration not for the truth of their assertions but to show the statements were made and the latter had the information, *i.e.*, was on notice); Crowley v. L.L. Bean, Inc., 303 F.3d 387, 408 (1st Cir. 2002) ("Juhl is her 'little stalker'" was not offered to prove the assertion but to show that defendant was on notice of Juhl's behavior); Martinez v. McCaughtry, 951 F.2d 130, 133 (7th Cir. 1991) ("'When a person's knowledge or state of mind is at issue, evidence that he has heard or read a statement may be relevant, and lies beyond reach of a hearsay objection.'" (citation omitted)); Clayton v. Fargason, 730 So.2d 160, 164 (Ala. 1999) (that defendant had been told that children had been hit in the area where the accident occurred was not offered for the truth of that assertion but as evidence defendant had notice of a dangerous condition, which is relevant to what kind of driving is reasonable; "'Where there is an attempt to prove out-of-court statements for the purpose of showing notice, knowledge or motive, or to show that information within the knowledge of a witness bore on his subsequent conduct, such proof does not constitute hearsay.'" (citations omitted)).

nies, these out-of-court statements are relevant to two issues in this case: Is the lot slippery when it is wet? Was the defendant on notice? To the first issue, these statements are hearsay. To the second, they are not hearsay. All the plaintiff needs to get over the bar of the hearsay rule is one winning argument that the statements are not hearsay.[25]

■ Another related common use is the evidence third-party statements used to prove motive—perhaps a criminal defendant's motive for committing the crime charged;[26] perhaps an employer's motive for having taken adverse employment against the plaintiff.[27]

■ Assume the charge is illegal possession of ammunition and the defense is duress. The defendant testifies that the people who he claims forced him to carry the ammunition said to him that they would kill him if he did not do what they told him. Defendant's testimony about what these people said to him is

---

25. In addition, of course, the nonhearsay use of the evidence must be relevant. And then the evidence must survive a Rule 403 balance weighing the probative value of the admissible use of the evidence against the danger of unfair prejudice from the inadmissible use. See part III(C) of this chapter, below.

26. United States v. Safavian, 435 F.Supp.2d 36, 45–46 (D.C. D.C. 2006) (defendant's emails "admissible because they might help to explain [the] motive and intent" for some of defendant's future actions, including representations he made to investigators; they are not admissible to prove the truth of the facts asserted; the jury must be instructed that these emails "may be considered only insofar as they may have had some impact on [defendant]'s state of mind or provided him with a motive to make false statements or obstruct justice");

27. E.g., McIntosh v. Partridge, 540 F.3d 325, 322 (5th Cir. 2008) ("The internal e-mail and ... audit go to show why [defendant] believed [plaintiff] was inadequately performing his duties..., which is relevant ... [to defendant]'s motivation for suspending [plaintiff]. Since each of the documents is admissible for a relevant purpose other than the truth of the statements contained within them, they are not inadmissible hearsay."); McInnis v. Fairfield Communities, Inc., 458 F.3d 1129, 1143 (10th Cir. 2006) (statements to an employer are nonhearsay "to show an employer's state of mind in making employment decisions" but not here, as there is no evidence that any termination decision-makers ever saw these email statements); Noviello, 398 F.3d at 85 (as quoted in footnote 14, above); Luckie v. Ameritech Corp., 389 F.3d 708, 716 (7th Cir. 2004) (plaintiff was fired after an investigation by and at the instance of defendant's Vice-President for Human Relations (VP); VP's evidence that she had been told plaintiff was having a "toxic effect" on the company was "not offered to prove the truth of the matter asserted[, but] to show [VP's] state of mind at the time she was evaluating [plaintiff's] performance"); Faulkner v. Super Valu Stores, Inc., 3 F.3d 1419, 1434–35 (10th Cir. 1993) (to the issue of why defendant did not hire employees from another particular store, testimony that defendant had heard talk of employee vandalism, food product damage, low morale, and animus towards the employer at that other store was offered to establish defendant's state of mind in making its hiring decisions, and not to prove the truth of the facts asserted).

not hearsay. It is not offered to prove they actually would have killed him, but only to show the effect these words had on his state of mind.[28] The defendant is a real witness to the fact that the words were said and he is the real witness to their effect on him. It is his credibility that matters.[29]

■ In a drug conspiracy case the defendant argued that he had not known that those he was working with were involved in such a conspiracy and he inferred that the government was acting in bad faith when they prosecuted him. That opened the door for the government to introduce a DEA agent's testimony that, while he was debriefing one of the leaders of the conspiracy, the leader told him that the defendant knew they were involved in drug trafficking. The government offered this evidence to rebut the inference that this was a bad faith prosecution. When used in this way, it does not matter whether the out-of-court statement was true; all that matters is that a member of the conspiracy said it to the agent and that the agent found it credible. If it was said to the agent and he believed it, then there was a good faith basis to pursue the prosecution. To this issue, the agent is the real witness, the agent is the manufacturer of this evidence.

This is evidence of the state of mind of the agent who pursued the case against the defendant.[30] The agent's state of mind is relevant because the de-

---

28. *See* Subramaniam v. Public Prosecutor, 100 Solicitor's Journal 566 (Judicial Committee of the Privy Council 1956), found in Jon R. Waltz & Roger C. Park, *Cases and Materials on Evidence* 97 (9th ed. 1999). Approach # 8 (the effect-on-the-mind-of-the-hearer approach) of The Top Ten Approaches to Hearsay, Chapter 1(III)(A)(8), above. *See also* approaches # 6 (the plain-fact-that-the-words-were-spoken approach); # 7 (the credibility approach); and # 10 (the verbal-acts approach).

29. *See also, e.g.,* People v. Goodman, 399 N.Y.S.2d 56, 57 (1977) ("[D]efendant presented a justification defense; it was his claim that he believed that the victim had been hired to kill him and that, at the time of the stabbing, the victim had been reaching for a gun." A witness's testimony that she had heard defendant being told that someone had been hired to burn his car was not hearsay. "The fact that the defendant had heard such a statement could circumstantially indicate his state of mind.").

30. United States v. Goosby, 523 F.3d 632, 638 (6th Cir. 2008) ("Background testimony" is not hearsay. We have allowed ... DEA agents ... to testify about information they received from an informant, which precipitated a controlled purchase of heroin from the defendant. 'The statements were not offered "for the truth of the matter asserted," ... but only to provide background information and to explain how and why the agents even came to be involved with this particular defendant.'") (one set of parenthesis omitted); United States v. Love, 521 F.3d 1007, 1009 (8th Cir. 2008) ("not hearsay if it is offered for the limited purpose of explaining why a police investigation was undertaken." (multiple and internal quotation marks omitted)); Jewett v. Anders, 521 F.3d 818, 827 (7th Cir. 2008) (officer's testimony about what he had been told was offered to show officer's state of mind as he encountered plaintiff and to explain why he detained plaintiff); United States v. Tyler, 281 F.3d 84, 98

fendant raised the issue of the agent's bad faith, and his state of mind is evidence of his good faith. The agent is the real witness to his own state of mind. Were this out-of-court statement offered to prove the defendant's guilt, then its value would depend on whether or not it was true. Where, however, it is offered to rebut the inference that this was a bad faith prosecution, then its value does not depend on whether it was true.

■ In the usual extortion case, the victim must have parted with something of value and done so under compulsion: no compulsion, no extortion. The state of mind of the victim is crucial. In such a case, any out-of-court statement made to the victim and relevant to this state of mind has at least one non-hearsay use.[31] It is not offered for the truth of the matter asserted, but only to show that it was said and the effect it had on the victim.[32]

(3d Cir. 2002) (statement not offered to prove the truth of its assertion but to "provide[ ] a jurisdictional basis for initiating a federal investigation into defendant's activities"); United States v. Posada-Rios, 158 F.3d 832, 870 (5th Cir. 1998) (statements to police regarding defendant's knowledge of specific crimes offered to refute defendant's inference that the government acted in bad faith by prosecuting someone it knew to be innocent); Torraco v. Port Authority of New York & New Jersey, 539 F.Supp.2d 632, 637 (E.D.N.Y. 2008) (not hearsay "on the issue of probable cause as they form a part of the information that [the officers] had in determining to make an arrest."); Chestnut v. Commonwealth, 250 S.W.2d 288, 294 (Ky. 2008) (statements to a police officer are not hearsay when offered "to explain the action that was taken by the police officer as a result of this information" and it is admissible when "the taking of that action is an issue in the case.'") (citation omitted); State v. Irick, 231 S.E.2d 833, 845 (N.C. 1977) (one officer's statements "were offered to explain [another officers'] subsequent conduct in pursuing the suspect vehicle and were admissible for this limited purpose. The[y] ... were not offered to establish the truth of any matter asserted [therein].").

See also the discussion of the *Hernandez* case in parts III(B) & (D) of this chapter, below.

31. See, e.g., United States v. Adcock, 558 F.2d 397, 403–04 (8th Cir.).

32. Anyone who heard the threatening statements, including the victim, is a real witness, has all of the first-hand knowledge we need, and provides opposing counsel with sufficient opportunity for cross-examination. "Thus it is no ground for objection that the third person making the statement to the victim is not produced as a witness or even that he is not named. The defendant's right of cross examination is preserved in that he can ask the witness whether he truly heard these fear-producing statements." *Adcock*, 558 F.2d 404. *Accord, e.g.,* United States v. Williams, 952 F.2d 1504, 1518 (6th Cir. 1991) (to the issue of the victim's state of mind in a trial for extortion, testimony by the victim or other witnesses regarding fear-producing statements to the victim are not offered to prove their truth, but just to show their effect, true or not, on the victim); United States v. Grassi, 783 F.2d 1572, 1578 (11th Cir. 1986) ("'The victim's fearful state of mind is a crucial element in proving extortion. The testimony of victims as to what others said to them, and the testimony of others as to what they said to victims is admitted not for the truth of the information in the

■ This kind of state-of-mind evidence can be admissible on behalf of criminal defendants who argue that they lacked specific intent to commit the crime charged because they believed they had permission to commit the act in question. In one case a defendant on trial for stealing the contents of a home testified that a man named Trott had told him that the owner of the house was his aunt, that the house was going to be torn down, that he (Trott) had permission to take some antiques from the house. Defendant testified he talked with Trott in the town of Dover or Dexter, he could not recall.

One of the elements of the crime "is that the accused entered a structure 'knowing that he [was] not licensed or privileged to do so.'"[33] "[T]he only seriously disputed issue at trial was whether Crocker had permission to enter and remove items from the ... house."[34] This evidence was not offered to prove the truth of the matter asserted, but to show the effect it had on Crocker, on his state of mind. The fact that the statement was made—if the jury chooses to believe that it was made—provides the factual basis for Crocker's state of mind. Defense counsel is not trying to prove that Crocker really did have permission—for, by now, everyone agrees that he did not—but that he believed he had permission.[35]

■ One party entered into a contract to buy a business from another. Before the deal was closed, the buyer backed out. The seller sued on the contract.

---

statements but for the fact that the victim heard them and that they would have tended to produce fear in his mind.'" (citation omitted)).

33. State v. Crocker, 435 A.2d 1109, 1111 (Me. 1981).

34. *Id.*

35. Who is the real witness? Crocker is one of them, and Trott, if he exists at all, is another. We would like to have Trott there to ask him if any of this is true, but there is no rule that says we must have all of the witnesses present and testifying (and if there were such a rule, it would not be the hearsay rule). Do we believe Crocker is telling the truth? No. His story is not credible. Credibility, however, is a question of fact, not a question of law. It is a question that must be decided by the trier of fact and cannot be decided by the trier or law. The trier of law is concerned with whether it is admissible, not whether it is believable. The prosecutor can impeach Crocker, pointing out that Crocker has no idea who or where this Trott might be, cannot recall what town he was in when he was told he could help himself to the antiques, and has no explanation for why this stranger was so generous. Regarding admissibility versus credibility, *see particularly* Chapter 3(I)(D), above. Regarding trustworthiness versus credibility, *see* Chapter 5(V)(E)(2), above; *see also* Chapter 3(VIII)(E)(4)(a), above.

Accord, e.g., State v. Getz, 830 P.2d 5, 10–11 (Kan. 1992) (evidence that a declarant told defendant she owned the horses and asked him to help sell them was not admitted for the truth of the assertion, but as evidence of defendant's state of mind, *i.e.,* that he thought he had permission to sell the horses).

At the trial, the buyer's attorney asked questions that elicited from the buyer certain things that he had been told by others. He claims that his having heard these things was the basis for his refusal to honor the contract. (Perhaps he heard the product was defective or the seller was a criminal or that the world was coming to an end. For the hearsay rule, it does not matter.) This is not hearsay. It is nonhearsay state-of-mind evidence. The judge will decide whether or not as a matter of law these things are enough to justify the buyer's breach of contract. The judge will decide as a matter of law whether these statements are relevant. The jury will decide as a matter of fact whether they believe that the buyer was in fact told these things. There may be problems with this evidence, but as offered here it is not hearsay, the problems are not hearsay problems.[36]

■ Take care with this particular effect-on-the-mind-of-the-hearer kind of nonhearsay. The effect the out-of-court statement has on the listener must truly be relevant in the case at trial. Statements admitted to show the effect of the words on the state of mind of the person hearing them are not offered to prove the truth of the matter asserted and, therefore, are not hearsay. If, however, the state of mind of the person hearing them is not at issue in the case, then this use of the statement is inadmissible as irrelevant.[37]

E. Statements That Directly Assert Declarant's Then-Existing Mental State: Hearsay

An out-of-court statement that directly asserts the declarant's mental state at the time he made the statement is hearsay when it is offered to prove the declarant's mental state at that time. An out-of-court statement such as "I am scared" offered to prove that, back when he made the statement, the declarant was scared. The out-of-court statement "I have a terrible pain in my chest" offered to prove that, at the time she made the statement, the declarant had a pain in her chest. The out-of-court statement "I am confused" offered to prove that, at the very moment he made the statement, the declarant was confused. Each of these statements is hearsay, but none is excluded by the hearsay rule. Let us look at each of these three statements. In each case, assume that the statement is relevant and that it is offered to prove the truth of the matter asserted.

■ "I am scared." This is hearsay, but if it does not violate any other rules, it is admissible. It fits under at least two, and perhaps three, exceptions: (1) It

---

36. *E.g.*, Beckman v. Carson, 372 N.W.2d 203, 209 (Iowa 1985).
37. *See* part III(B) of this chapter, below.

does fit under Rule 803(1), the present sense impression exception. (2) It does fit under Rule 803(3), the statements of then existing mental emotional or physical condition exception.[38] (3) It may fit under Rule 803(2), the excited utterance exception.

■ "I have a terrible pain in my chest." This fits under (1) the present sense impression exception; and (2) the exception for statements of then existing mental emotional or physical condition. (3) As above, it may fit under the excited utterance exception. (4) In addition, the statement may fit under Rule 803(4), the statement for purposes of medical diagnosis or treatment exception.

■ "I am confused." In a trade dress infringement case, regarding the likelihood of confusion between two products, we have the testimony by an officer of the company bringing the action that she had personally received complaints from customers that her company was selling its product to other retailers at a lower price. The truth, on investigation, was that it was the competitor's (defendant's) product that was being sold at the lower price. So far, this is not hearsay at all because it is not offered to prove the truth of the matter asserted: It is not offered to prove that the company bringing the action was selling to some retailers at a lower price. Rather, these are statements that circumstantially assert the state of mind of the declarants: the declarants are the customers, and the statements circumstantially assert their confusion between the two products.[39]

Change the facts and have the customer directly assert his confusion to the officer of the company. A customer said to the testifying witness "I am confused." This statement would be admissible hearsay under the exceptions in Rule 803(1), the present sense impression exception, and Rule 803(3), the state of mind exception.[40]

---

38. [An out-of-court declarant's] statements to a Naval Reserve officer that he thought his wife was going to kill him and that he was afraid of her were hearsay because they were introduced as direct evidence to prove that the declarant was afraid of his wife.... [T]he statements met the [state of mind] exception to the hearsay rule[, however,] because they were offered to show the declarant's state of mind at the time he sought to reenlist in the Navy.
Rafanelli, 924 P.2d at 254 (characterizing State v. Losson, 865 P.2d 255, 259 (Mont. 1993); also discussed at note 22, above).

39. *See* part V(C) of this chapter, above.

40. *See* Fun-Damental Too, Ltd. v. Gemmy Indus. Corp., 111 F.3d 993, 1003–04 (2d Cir. 1997).

F. Statements of Declarant's Intention Offered as Evidence That Declarant Did the Thing Intended: Hearsay

An out-of-court statement of intention is hearsay when it is offered to support an inference that the intention was carried through. Take this out-of-court statement: The statement is in a letter from Walters to his fiancée saying "I am going to be leaving Wichita and going to Crooked Creek with Mr. Hillmon." If Walters' statement is offered to prove that *Walters intended* to go to Crooked Creek, which makes it more likely he did so, then it is admissible hearsay. The part about what the declarant himself intends to do is hearsay, but it fits under the exception for then-existing mental, emotional, or physical conditions. If Walters' statement is offered to prove that *Hillmon intended* to go to Crooked Creek, which likewise makes it more likely Hillmon did so, then it is inadmissible hearsay. The part about what Hillmon intends to do is hearsay and does not fit under the exception for then-existing mental, emotional, or physical conditions. This exception covers evidence of the future conduct of the declarant (Walters), but not the future conduct of another (Hillmon).[41]

Change the example just a bit. What if the issue is Did *Walters intend* to travel with Hillmon and did *Walters intend* to travel to Crooked Creek? Now, the entire out-of-court statement is being offered to show Walters' intention, his then-existing mental, emotional, or physical condition. The whole thing is admissible hearsay.[42] (When the subject is hearsay, much depends on how the issues are framed.)

G. Statements of Declarant's Intention Offered to Prove What Someone Else Did: Hearsay

As a general proposition, an out-of-court statement of state of mind is inadmissible hearsay when it is offered to prove the future conduct of another person. Furthermore, there is no state of mind exception that applies here.

Take the example from just above and change the facts once more. What if there are three issues: Did Walters go to Crooked Creek (and this evidence is offered to show that he had intended to go, which makes it more likely that he did go)? Did Walters intend to go with Hillmon (and this evidence is offered to show that he had intended to go with Hillmon, which makes it more

---

41. Regarding this general point and specifically regarding the *Hillmon* case, *see* Chapter 3(IV)(D)(4) & (5), above.
42. *See* Chapter 3(IV)(D)(4) & (5), above.

likely that he did go with Hillmon)? And did Hillmon go to Crooked Creek (and this evidence is offered to show that Walters thought Hillmon intended to go, which makes it more likely that Hillmon did intend to go, which, in turn, makes it more likely that Hillmon in fact did go)? The out-of-court statement is admissible hearsay to the first two of these issues: Did Walters go and had he intended to go with Hillmon both fit under Rule 803(3). To the third issue, the statement about what Walters intended to do with Hillmon is a statement of Walters' present intention being used to prove Hillmon's future conduct and it does not fit under Rule 803(3).[43] Depending on other facts, however, there may be some other exception that will apply.[44] If there is no other exception that lets the statement in as evidence of Hillmon's future conduct, then the part of the statement that mentions Hillmon is admissible to one issue and inadmissible to another. When this happens, Rule 403 comes into play: probative value to the admissible issue versus unfair prejudice regarding the inadmissible issue.[45]

H. Statements Reflecting Back on a Past State of Mind, Offered to Prove State of Mind at That Time Past: Hearsay

As a general proposition, an out-of-court statement of a previous state of mind, that is, an out-of-court statement of a past feeling, a past emotion, a past mental or physical state, is inadmissible hearsay when it is offered to prove the

---

43. This is the general—but not exclusive—rule in federal court. The legislative history of the state of mind exception to the hearsay rule, that it, "the report of the House Judiciary Committee[,] states that it intended Rule 803(3) to 'be construed ... to render statements of intent by a declarant admissible only to prove his future conduct, not the future conduct of another person.' H.R. REP. NO. 93-650, at 13–14 (1973), *reprinted in* 1974 U.S.C.C.A.N. 7051, 7075, 7087." Coy v. Renico, 414 F.Supp.2d 744, 768 (E.D. Mich. 2006). Regarding this legislative history, see also part IV(D)(6) of Chapter 3.

Coy canvasses federal and state court decisions on this issue and draws the above conclusion regarding federal courts. *Coy* concludes that state courts are much more generous when it comes to admitting such a statement to prove a nondeclarant's future conduct. "[W]hether doing so explicitly or implicitly, the "overwhelming majority of [state-court] jurisdictions,"—at least 28—have allowed introduction of [such] statements to establish the future conduct of a nondeclarant under the state of mind exception. Only three [state-court] jurisdictions have reached the opposite conclusion that such statements are not admissible under the state of mind exception." *Coy*, 414 F.Supp.2d at 769–70 (citations and footnote omitted).

44. *See* Chapter 3(IV)(D)(6), above.

45. *See* Chapter 12, below.

truth of that state of mind. Example: "Boy, was I scared last week!" Example: "Holy cow, did my back ever hurt just after my fall." Offered to probe "scared" or "hurt" it is hearsay, and it is the kind of backward-looking, or reflective pronouncement does not fit under the state of mind exception.[46]

III. State-of-Mind Evidence and the Question of Relevance

A. Introduction

When dealing with state-of-mind evidence, the question "Is it relevant?" is just as important as the question "Is it hearsay?" Every statement is evidence of someone or another's state of mind. Every statement says something about the state of mind of the person who says it and has some effect on the state of mind of everyone who hears it. Because of this, there is a very real argument that every out-of-court statement is nonhearsay. The trick is to make that state of mind relevant.

B. Nonhearsay State-of-Mind Evidence That Is Irrelevant

In *United States v. Hernandez*,[47] Hernandez was convicted on two counts relating to possession and distribution of cocaine. At his trial, a Special Agent of the Drug Enforcement Agency was asked how Hernandez first came to the attention of the DEA. The judge overruled a hearsay objection and the Agent replied, "We received a referral by the U.S. Customs Service as Hernandez being a drug smuggler." On appeal, the government argued that this testimony was nonhearsay state-of-mind evidence. They argued it was evidence of the moti-

---

46. *See* Chapter 3(IV)(D)(3), above.

Such statements may, however, not be hearsay in the first place or may be admissible hearsay under another hearsay exception. In the context of particular litigation it might be excluded from the hearsay rule as an admission by a party opponent, Rule 801(d)(2)(A), or it might qualify under the exception for statements against interest, Rule 804(b)(3). Furthermore, if handing my watch to my brother today, while saying "Bob, I had meant to give this to you as a birthday present," constitutes a *present* gift, then, for purposes of whether there has been a gift, the statement is not hearsay in the first place. *See* approach # 9 (the verbal acts approach) of The Top Ten Approaches to Hearsay, Chapter 1(III)(A)(10), above. And, in that circumstance, the statement would not be backward looking and so, even if it were hearsay, it would fit under the state of mind exception.

47. 750 F.2d 1256 (5th Cir. 1985).

vation for the DEA's investigation of Hernandez. They are right, that is, when used as evidence of the DEA's motive, this evidence is not hearsay. Rather, it is offered only to show the effect it had on the mind of the person (or organization) who heard it. The problem with this analysis, as the court of appeals recognized, is that the DEA's motivation is irrelevant.[48] To the issue of Hernandez's guilt, the evidence is inadmissible hearsay. To the issue of the DEA's motivation, well, their motivation is not at issue in this case. The evidence is not hearsay, but it is not admissible either, because it is irrelevant.

Every statement is circumstantial evidence of the state of mind of the declarant and has an effect on the mind of everyone who hears it;[49] therefore, there is always an argument that a statement is nonhearsay state-of-mind evidence. This does not mean that every out-of-court statement is admissible, but that when it is offered as nonhearsay state-of-mind evidence and it is not admissible, it is some rule other than the hearsay rule that keeps it out. In the usual case, it is the rules regarding relevance: the state of mind of the speaker and the listener are irrelevant.[50]

---

48. *Id.* at 1257–58. *See additionally, e.g.,* United States v. Meserve, 271 F.3d 314, 320 (1st Cir. 2001) ("[T]he hearsay rule does not apply to statements that are offered to show what effect they produced on the actions of a listener." The government offered the statement made to the detective to show the detective's motivation for driving by the defendant's house. Since nothing of value to the case occurred during the drive by the defendant's house, the drive-by is irrelevant, as is the motivation for the drive-by. "In light of the government's baldly pretextual basis for the introduction of [the] out-of-court statement, this court is not prepared to say that the statement is admissible non-hearsay.")

49. Every statement heard impacts the mind of any person who hears it. It affects their state of mind. Every statement is in some way circumstantial evidence of the state of mind of the declarant. Even a statement that directly assert a state of mind is circumstantial evidence of some other state of mind. "I am cold" circumstantially asserts that the declarant is uncomfortable. Maybe I like it cold and I am comfortable; maybe I do not and I am uncomfortable. "Cold" does not prove discomfort, but the inference is reasonable. Circumstantial evidence is

> evidence that tends to prove a fact in issue by proving other events or circumstances which according to the common experience of mankind are usually or always attended by the fact in issue and that therefore affords a basis for a reasonable inference by the jury or court of the occurrence of the fact in issue[.]

"circumstantial evidence." Webster's Third New International Dictionary, Unabridged. Merriam-Webster, 2002. http://unabridged.merriam-webster.com (19 Sep. 2008).

50. All statements have an effect on the mind of the hearer, but not all statements having an effect on the mind of the hearer are relevant; therefore, not all are admissible. Were it otherwise, all kinds of extrajudicial statements would be admissible. For example, anything the police say to a suspect prior to the suspect's confession is relevant to the suspect's state of mind when he or she confesses. Whatever the police say to the suspect before the

C. Nonhearsay State-of-Mind Evidence That Is Inadmissible under Rule 403

In *Bridges v. State*,[51] a young girl had been a victim of a sexual assault. Her out-of-court statement to her mother and to a police officer described exterior and interior details of the house in which she had been assaulted. This

---

latter's confession is nonhearsay state-of-mind evidence—true, false, or endlessly debatable, it is not hearsay to the issue of the defendant's state of mind. But defendant's state of mind may very well be irrelevant. FED.R.EVID. 402 ("Evidence which is not relevant is not admissible."). *E.g.*, Shepard v. United States, 290 U.S. 96, 104 (1933) ("There are times when a state of mind, if relevant, may be proved by contemporaneous declarations of feeling or intent."); Rowland v. American Gen. Fin., Inc., 340 F.3d 187, 194 n.6 (4th Cir. 2003) ("If ... the district court did not admit the letter to prove the truth of the matter asserted, we fail to see its relevance. Even if the letter was somehow relevant," Rule 403 would keep it out.); United States v. Sesay, 313 F.3d 591, 599 (D.C. Cir. 2002) (the statement here "is not relevant for anything other than its truth."); United States v. Evans, 216 F.3d 80, 85 (D.C. Cir. 2000) (If the statement "did not go to the truth of [its] assertion, to what did it go? ... For testimony to be admissible for any purpose ... it must be relevant."); United States v. Harvey, 959 F.2d 1371, 1375 (7th Cir. 1992) (even if evidence falls under this exception, to be admissible it must be relevant to an issue in the case); United States v. Hedgcorth, 873 F.2d 1307, 1313 (9th Cir. 1989) ("[Declarant's] prior writings have no bearing on his state of mind during offenses committed years later."); United States v. Scirma, 819 F.2d 996, 1000 (11th Cir. 1987) (before a statement can be admitted to show declarant's state of mind, declarant's state of mind must be relevant); United States v. Udey, 748 F.2d 1231, 1243 (8th Cir. 1984) (if Gitner's statement were a post-arrest statement made regarding his pre-arrest state of mind, it would be backward looking and inadmissible by the terms of the state of mind exception; if it were a post-arrest statement regarding his state of mind on the day he made the statement, it would be irrelevant to his pre-arrest state of mind; either way, it is inadmissible); Prather v. Prather, 650 F.2d 88, 90 (5th Cir. 1981); State v. Fulminante, 975 P.2d 75, 85 (Ariz. 1999) (statement must be relevant to prove state of mind and state of mind must be relevant to an issue in the case); State v. Cook, 628 S.W.2d 657, 659–60 (Mo. 1982) (the interrogating police officer was asked what he told the defendant prior to the defendant's confession; the officer answered: "I advised him that we had received information, and he was involved in the robbery, and that his picture had been picked out by the two witnesses as a suspect who had committed the robbery," *id.* at 659; on appeal, the state argued that the statement was offered only to show that it was made—for the effect it had on defendant's state of mind; under this reasoning the evidence is not hearsay, but this reasoning does not work here because appellant's state of mind was not in issue—"... the state cannot make up an issue for the purpose of providing a basis for the admission of the hearsay," *id.* at 660).

For cases that are relevant and are nonhearsay state-of-mind evidence, *see* Chapter 3(IV)(D)(9), above.

51. 19 N.W.2d 529 (Wis. 1945).

description closely fit the defendant's home (and perhaps many others?). The mother and the police officer testified to the girl's description. The court held that this was not hearsay because it was only offered to show that these facts were in the little girl's mind. This seems a bit disingenuous, but the court held that the statement was not offered to prove its truth but only to show that the little girl had this information in her brain. I think the court was saying that this is nonhearsay state-of-mind evidence.

Here is how I would look at it: Major premise: "I was assaulted in a house that had features x, y, and z." Minor premise: The defendant lives in a house that has features x, y, and z. Conclusion: The assault occurred in the defendant's house. If this works at all, it only works if the major premise—the out-of-court statement—is true. The young girl's out-of-court statement is offered to prove the truth of the matter asserted and it does not fit under any of the exclusions in Rule 801(d).[52] Therefore it is hearsay. The original manufacturer of this evidence is the little girl, not her mother. The real witness is the little girl, not the police officer. And yet isn't the court right when it states that this out-of-court statement is relevant just because it was said, without regard to its truth? Isn't it relevant that the little girl could describe the interior of the defendant's home, just the fact that she could describe it? Isn't it relevant that the little girl had these facts in her head? Leaving aside any question of truth or non-truth, doesn't the fact that she could give this description advance this case?

In *Armstrong v. State*,[53] two men were involved in an argument in a bar. One of the two men, Armstrong, left the bar to get a gun. The bartender told the other man and other patrons in the bar that Armstrong had gone home to get a gun. He told the other man, the victim, that for his own safety he should leave. The victim did not leave. Armstrong returned with a gun and shot the victim dead. At his trial, Armstrong claimed that he killed the victim in self defense. The evidence in question here is the testimony by the other patrons in the bar about what the bartender told them, that is, that he told them Armstrong had gone home to get a gun. This evidence is important because evidence that Armstrong left the bar with the intention to go home and get a gun and then return to shoot the victim is evidence of premeditated murder, not self defense. The court let the testimony in as state-of-mind evidence. Here is the court's reasoning: The persons to whom the bartender made these statements were fact witnesses at the trial; once the bartender said these things to

---

52. *See* approach # 1 (the formula) of The Top Ten Approaches to Hearsay, Chapter 1(III)(A)(1), above.

53. 826 P.2d 1106 (Wyo. 1992).

these patrons, their state of mind is that Armstrong is going to get a gun and come back, and that means that when Armstrong did come back they were likely to be paying attention; that they were paying attention makes them more credible fact witnesses. A fact witness who was paying attention to what was going on is more credible than one who was not. Whether what the bartender said was true or not, it affected the state of mind of the patrons, caused them to pay attention, and is relevant to their credibility as fact witnesses.

Cases like these are right, in a way. All of this evidence is state-of-mind evidence and there are theories under which all of this state-of-mind evidence is relevant without regard to whether it is true. Mostly, however, they are wrong. First, they are wrong because if we look at hearsay this way then nothing is hearsay. Everything everyone says circumstantially indicates some state of mind on the part of the speaker and everything everyone says has some effect on the state of mind of the listener. The logic of these cases does away with the hearsay rule. Second, they are wrong because they do not seem to recognize that all of this evidence also has an important use that is dependent on its truth. All of it has an important use where it is hearsay. In the *Armstrong* case, the evidence is relevant to credibility without regard to its truth and it is relevant to premeditation only if it is true. It has two uses in the case: to one issue, credibility, the truth of what the bartender said does not matter; to another issue, premeditation, the truth of what the bartender said does matter. What we have in these cases is evidence that may be nonhearsay if we look at it one way, to one issue, but is hearsay if we look at it another way, to another issue. Is this evidence hearsay or not? Yes! It is hearsay and it is not hearsay. The question then becomes Is the evidence admissible?

If the evidence fits under a hearsay exception,[54] then it is nonhearsay to the issue of credibility and it is admissible hearsay to the issue of premeditation. If the evidence does not fit under an exception, then it is admissible nonhearsay to one issue and inadmissible hearsay to another issue. This is a Rule 403 problem.[55] The problem is one of probative value versus unfair prejudice. The danger of unfair prejudice in *Armstrong* is this: the evidence is prejudicial because it is evidence of premeditation, in opposition to Armstrong's claim of self defense; the prejudice is unfair because to this issue the evidence is inadmissible hearsay.[56]

---

54. Maybe the bartender's statements were excited utterances. Maybe not. Without more we cannot say for sure.

55. *See generally* Chapter 12, below, regarding hearsay and Rule 403.

56. *See also, e.g., Rowland,* 340 F.3d at 194 n.6 (as quoted in footnote 50, above); *Cook,* 628 S.W.2d at 659–60 (discussed in note 62, above); United States v. Muscato, 534 F.Supp. 969 (E.D.N.Y. 1982) (discussed at part I(C) of this chapter, above); Posner v. Dallas County Welfare, 784 S.W.2d 585 (Tex. App. 1990) (the county attempted to terminate parental

D. Conclusion

■ *All Hearsay Evidence Is Also Nonhearsay State-of-Mind Evidence, but Not All Hearsay Evidence Is Admissible:* Courts should begin recognizing that it is true that all hearsay evidence is also nonhearsay state-of-mind evidence. It either circumstantially indicates the state of mind of the declarant or affects the state of mind of those who heard it or both.

Sometimes—as in the *Hernandez* case[57]—a hearsay statement is also nonhearsay evidence of state of mind, but state of mind is not relevant. When state of mind is not relevant, then this way of looking at the evidence will not justify its admission and it will only be admissible if there is an exception to the hearsay rule. If there is no exception, then the evidence is irrelevant to one issue (the investigator's state of mind) and inadmissible hearsay to the other (defendant is a drug smuggler). Either way, it is inadmissible.

Other times, hearsay evidence is relevant to one issue as nonhearsay state-of-mind evidence and relevant to another issue as hearsay evidence, and it fits under an exception to the hearsay rule. When this is the case, then the evidence is admissible nonhearsay state-of-mind evidence and admissible hearsay evidence. It is admissible to both issues. Either way you look at it, the evidence is admissible.

At still other times—as in the *Armstrong* case[58]—hearsay evidence is relevant to one issue as nonhearsay state-of-mind evidence and relevant to another issue as hearsay evidence, but it does not fit under any exception to the hearsay rule. In this case, then it is admissible state-of-mind evidence to one issue and inadmissible hearsay to another issue. This situation—admissible to one issue, inadmissible to another—is resolved by applying Rule 403. Is the probative value of the evidence to the admissible issue substantially outweighed by the danger of unfair prejudice to the inadmissible issue?[59]

---

rights; while playing with a friend, the daughter said, "[G]ive me your doll and I'll show you with mine how daddies sex their little girls," *id.* at 587; over a hearsay objection, the court held that this statement was admissible nonhearsay state-of-mind evidence; what the court said, actually, is that the testimony was not offered to prove the truth of the matter asserted but only to show that the statement was made and so it falls under the state of mind exception, that is, the court said that this evidence was nonhearsay state-of-mind evidence that fit under the state of mind exception to the hearsay rule).

57. *See* part III(B) of this chapter, above
58. 826 P.2d 1106 (Wyo. 1992), discussed in detail at part III(C) of this chapter, above.
59. *See generally* Chapter 12, below.

■ *If You Are Having a Hearsay Problem, Always Consider Whether the Statement Is Admissible as State-of-Mind Evidence:* Every out-of-court statement is nonhearsay state-of-mind evidence. Not every out-of-court statement is admissible into evidence, however, because more often than not state of mind is irrelevant. Since every out-of-court statement is nonhearsay state-of-mind evidence, but much nonhearsay state-of-mind evidence is irrelevant, every hearsay question can be turned into a relevance question. If it suits counsel's purpose, every hearsay argument can be changed into a relevance argument.

CHAPTER EIGHT

Opinion Evidence as a Way around the Hearsay Rule

I. Expert Opinion

A. Text of Rules 702 and 703

Rule 702. Testimony by Experts.

If scientific, technical, or other specialized knowledge will assist the trier of fact to understand the evidence or to determine a fact in issue, a witness qualified as an expert by knowledge, skill, experience, training, or education, may testify thereto in the form of an opinion or otherwise, if (1) the testimony is based upon sufficient facts or data, (2) the testimony is the product of reliable principles and methods, and (3) the witness has applied the principals and methods reliably to the facts of the case.[1]

Rule 703. Bases of Opinion Testimony by Experts.

The facts or data in the particular case upon which an expert bases an opinion or inference may be those perceived by or made known to the expert at or before the hearing. If of a type reasonably relied upon by experts in the particular field in forming opinions or inferences upon the subject, the facts or data need not be admissible in evidence in order for the opinion or inference to be omitted. Facts or data that are otherwise inadmissible shall not be disclosed to the jury by the proponent of the opinion or inference unless the court determines that their probative value in assisting the jury to evaluate the expert's opinion substantially outweighs their prejudicial effect.[2]

B. "Foundational Elements"

The key to each hearsay exception is knowing its foundational elements— the proponent of the hearsay evidence must establish each element of at least one exception and the opponent must defeat at least one of the elements of each exception offered. Looking at Rules 702 and 703 together as exceptions to the hearsay rule,[3] these are the foundational elements:

1. The witness must be qualified as an expert in the relevant field of expertise.

2. The expert witness must be testifying to an opinion.

3. The expert witness will be basing this opinion on hearsay evidence that is itself inadmissible as substantive evidence.[4]

4. It must be shown that experts in the particular area of expertise involved reasonably rely on this kind of hearsay when forming their expert opinions.[5]

---

1. FED.R.EVID. 702.

2. FED.R.EVID. 703. The final sentence of this rule is an amendment that took effect December 1, 2000.

3. LaCombe v. A-T-O, Inc., 679 F.2d 431, 436 n.5 (5th Cir. 1982) ("Expert witness testimony is a widely-recognized exception to the rule against hearsay testimony.").

4. This is a discussion of using these rules to get around the bar of the hearsay rule. Hearsay is therefore the condition of inadmissibility stated in the foundational elements. It could, of course, be an evidentiary bar other than the hearsay rule. This technique can, of course, also be used to get around other evidentiary bars.

5. Items one, two, and four on the list are what can be called the foundational elements—

C. Need + Reliability

1. Need

Sometimes, without an expert, there is no *admissible* evidence of an essential element of a cause of action, an affirmative defense, a counterclaim—no admissible evidence of something one party or another must prove. Sometimes, for example, all other evidence of an essential element is inadmissible hearsay. Unless something is done, the party with the burden of production will lose. The cause of action, affirmative defense, etc. will not get past a motion to dismiss.

The solution to this problem may be expert-opinion testimony based on the inadmissible evidence. The Federal Rules of Evidence expressly sanction the admission of some expert-opinion testimony that is based on inadmissible evidence.[6] In circumstances discussed below, an expert opinion based on the inadmissible evidence can satisfy the burden of production and get the case to the jury.

2. Reliability

The reliability of the expert opinion based on inadmissible hearsay comes from a combination of these things. First, the witness must be an expert in a relevant, recognized field of expertise and it must be reasonable for experts in that field to form the kind of opinion at issue based on the kind of data (including the inadmissible hearsay) in question. Experts in the field treat this kind of opinion as reliable—sometimes reliable enough to support life or death decisions—even though the opinion is based on evidence inadmissible in a court of law.

Second, the expert expressing the opinion is in the courtroom, under oath, and subject to whatever truth-telling pressure that exerts. The jury can observe the expert's demeanor, and opposing counsel can test the expert's opinion on cross-examination.

Putting those indicia of reliability together, if the opinion is reliable enough for the experts, then, particularly with the added courtroom safeguards, it is reliable enough to be presented to the trier of fact.[7]

---

the things proponent must demonstrate. Item three limits the application of one, two, and four to the situation under discussion, *i.e.*, their use as an exception to the hearsay rule.

6. *LaCombe*, 679 F.2d at 436 n.5 ("It has long been the rule of evidence in the federal courts that an expert witness can express an opinion as to value even though his opinion is based in part or solely upon hearsay sources.")

7. *E.g.*, FED.R.EVID. 703 advisory committee's note ("[The expert's] validation, expertly performed and subject to cross-examination, ought to suffice for judicial purposes.");

D. Use Note

1. Identifying and Qualifying the Expert

A person who has specialized knowledge can be qualified as an expert. Expertise can come from "knowledge, skill, experience, training, or education."[8]

United States v. De La Cruz, 514 F.3d 121, 133 n.5 (1st Cir. 2008) ("a physician's reliance on reports prepared by other medical professionals is 'plainly justified in light of the custom and practice of the medical profession.'... [I]t is unrealistic to expect a physician, as a condition precedent to offering opinion testimony..., to have performed every test, procedure, and examination himself.'") (citation omitted); United States v. 14.38 Acres of Land, 80 F.3d 1074, 1077 (5th Cir. 1996) ("[I]n determining the admissibility of expert testimony, the district court should approach its task 'with proper deference to the jury's role as the arbiter of disputes between conflicting opinions. As a general rule, questions relating to the bases and sources of an expert's opinion affect the ... opinion['s weight] rather than its admissibility....'") (citation omitted); McCullock v. H.B. Fuller Co., 61 F.3d 1038, 1044 (2d Cir. 1995) (listing various quarrels with the expert testimony that go to weight, not admissibility); *LaCombe*, 679 F.2d at 436 n.5 ("[T]he expert, because of his professional knowledge and ability, is competent to judge for himself the reliability of the records and statements on which he bases his expert opinion. Moreover, the opinion of expert witnesses must invariably rest, at least in part, upon sources that can never be proven in court. An expert's opinion is derived not only from records and data but from education and from a lifetime of experience."); Utsey v. Olshan Found. Repair Co. of New Orleans, 2007 U.S. Dist. LEXIS 85918, *9 (E.D. La. Nov. 19, 2007) ("[V]igorous cross-examination and the presentation of contrary evidence"); In re Agent Orange Prod. Liab. Litig., 611 F. Supp. 1223, 1245 (E.D.N.Y. 1985) (Weinstein, J.) ("The guarantee of trustworthiness is that [the hearsay relied on must] be of the kind normally employed by experts in the field.").

This is similar to part of the guarantee of reliability for the business records exception, FED.R.EVID. 803(6), discussed at Chapter 3(VII)(D).

8. FED.R.EVID. 702. *Accord, e.g.*, United States v. Farmer, 543 F.3d 363, 370 (7th Cir. Sept. 9, 2008) (federal agent's experience investigating drug cases qualified him as an expert in the translation of narcotics code language); Castro-Pu v. Mukasey, 540 F.3d 864, 869 (8th Cir. Aug. 28, 2008) ("published works and frequent travels to Burma qualified [the witness] as an expert on current country conditions."); Mullins v. Crowell, 228 F.3d 1305, 1317 n.20 (11th Cir. 2000) (eleven years work experience as a general foreman and supervisor of craftworkers; expert regarding plaintiff's ability to perform craftwork); Sphere Drake Ins, PLC v. Trisko, 226 F.3d 951, 955 (8th Cir. 2000) (police detective experienced in the investigation of jewel thefts; expert on whether missing jewels were stolen) (case discussed at parts (I)(D)(2), (3), and (4)(a) & (g) of this chapter, below); United States v. Gomez, 67 F.3d 1515, 1525–26 (10th Cir. 1995) (a minor in Spanish and a 23-month religious mission in South America; expert in Spanish to English translation); Thomas v. Newton Int'l Enters., 42 F.3d 1266 (9th Cir. 1994) (twenty-nine years work experience as a longshoreman; expert on working conditions of longshoremen); United States v. Johnson, 28 F.3d 1487, 1492 (8th Cir. 1994) (gang membership; expert on gang activity); United

It can be knowledge however gained, so long as it is specialized—*i.e.*, beyond that of the ordinary lay person—and "reliable."[9] An expert can bring that specialized knowledge into the courtroom when it "will assist the trier of fact to understand the evidence or to determine a fact in issue."[10]

2. The Importance of Expert Witnesses to a Discussion of the Hearsay Rule

Counsel must introduce some evidence of each essential element of a cause of action, an affirmative defense, a counterclaim, or the like—or lose. Without at least some evidence of each essential element, that part of the case cannot get to the jury; it must be dismissed. Here is the syllogism: counsel can only win by introducing some evidence of each essential element of the cause

---

States v. Bagnell, 679 F.2d 826, 834 (11th Cir. 1982) (a pastor who was an advisor and counselor to a predominately homosexual congregation and familiar with the social and sexual mores of a large part of the city's homosexual population; expert on the issue of the obscenity of films of homosexual sex); United States v. Johnson, 575 F.2d 1347, 1360 (5th Cir. 1978) (one element of the crime charged was that the marijuana possessed had to be imported from a foreign country; prosecution's expert witness testified the marijuana in question came from Columbia; the witness "had no special training or education for such identification. Instead, his qualifications came entirely from 'the experience of being around a great deal and smoking it'"; expert in marijuana identification); State v. Briner, 255 N.W.2d 422, 423–24 (Neb. 1977) (retired burglar; expert in the identification of burglary tools).

On the other hand, see, *e.g.*, O'Conner v. Commonwealth Edison Co., 13 F.3d 1090, 1107 and n.19 (7th Cir. 1994) (a doctor was not allowed to testify that plaintiff's cataracts were radiation induced; his opinion was based on his "observation" of the cataracts; he claimed expertise based on his prior experience with radiation-induced cataracts, but had only treated five such patients in his 20 years of practice; this limited experience does not "qualif[y] as a basis for a scientifically sound opinion"); Delaney v. Merchants River Transp., 829 F.Supp. 186, 189–90 (W.D. La. 1993), *aff'd*, 16 F.3d 1214 (5th Cir. 1992) (having designed one barge does not make one a barge-design expert).

9. Kumho Tire Co. v. Carmichael, 526 U.S. 137, 147, 149, 158 (1999); Daubert v. Merrell Dow Pharm., Inc., 509 U.S. 579, 589, 597 (1993).

10. Fed.R.Evid. 702. Perhaps obviously, an attorney usually qualifies a witness as an expert by putting the witness on the stand and asking the questions that establish that the witness does in fact have specialized knowledge. An expert can also be qualified by stipulation to the witness's expertise or through a combination of questions and documentary evidence, such as a resume. If counsel is not allowed to qualify a witness as an expert, perhaps because the witness was not on a required pretrial list of expert witnesses, counsel may be able to get the same testimony out of the same witness as a lay witness. *See* part (II)(C) of this chapter, below.

of action; all of the evidence of one essential element is inadmissible hearsay; counsel cannot win. The expert witness may be a way to change the syllogism to the following: counsel can only win by introducing some evidence of each essential element of the cause of action; though all non-opinion evidence of one essential element is inadmissible hearsay, an expert witness can state an opinion that satisfies the need for evidence of this element; counsel can win.[11] This is why the admissibility of expert opinion based on inadmissible evidence is so important to a discussion of the hearsay rule.[12]

---

11. *See* the cases cited in notes 31 and 43, below and *Daubert*, 509 U.S. at 592 ("[A]n expert is permitted wide latitude to offer opinions, including those that are not based on firsthand knowledge or observation."); Conwood Co. v. U.S. Tobacco Co., 290 F.3d 768, 786 n.3 (6th Cir. 2002)(experts can "rely on documents ... that are otherwise inadmissible."); United States v. Locascio, 6 F.3d 924, 938 (2d Cir. 1993) ("[E]xpert witnesses can testify to opinions based on hearsay or other inadmissible evidence if experts in the field reasonably rely on such evidence in forming their opinions."); In re James Wilson Assoc'd, 965 F.2d 160, 172 (7th Cir. 1992) ("An expert is ... permitted to testify to an opinion formed on the basis of information that is handed to rather than developed by him—information of which he lacks first-hand knowledge and which might not be admissible in evidence no matter by whom presented."); LaCombe, 679 F.2d at 436 n.5 (5th Cir. 1982) ("Expert witness testimony is a widely-recognized exception to the rule against hearsay testimony. It has long been the rule of evidence in the federal courts that an expert witness can express an opinion ... even though [it] is based in part or solely upon hearsay sources.") (citing cases); Lilley v. Home Depot U.S.A., Inc., 2008 U.S. Dist. LEXIS 53903, *8 (S.D. Tex. July 15, 2008) (The doctor's opinion is not excludable just because it is "'based only on his patient's self-reported history.'"); Yamagiwa v. City of Half Moon Bay, 523 F.Supp.2d 1036, 1075 (N.D. Cal. 2007) ("The ... report was not admitted into evidence, as it was never properly authenticated and constituted hearsay. Hence, the report and statements within it cannot be used as substantive evidence. Nonetheless, ... [the expert] was still entitled to rely on the report as a basis for forming his expert opinions.") (footnote omitted); Velazquez v. State, 655 S.E.2d 806, 810 (Ga. 2008) ("Even when an expert's testimony is based on hearsay, the expert's lack of personal knowledge does not mandate the exclusion of the opinion but merely presents a jury question as to the weight which should be accorded the opinion.").

    In contrast to expert witnesses, lay witnesses may not base their opinions on indirect information such as hearsay. As discussed in part II of this Chapter, below, lay opinions must be based on the witness' own personal knowledge, not on second-hand knowledge.

12. There are, of course, other reasons an attorney might go to the trouble of finding and hiring an expert witness—other than to get around an evidentiary bar. The two most prominent are these. Sometimes there is an aspect of the case that is beyond the comprehension of lay persons—including the attorney. For example, if the function of a 406111 Center Section Casting is important to the case, counsel needs an expert to explain it. Sometimes counsel hires an expert for the bounce it can give the case, the bounce from having a witness who has a resume a mile long, including the best schools, the most prestigious professional honors and awards, and the premier position in his or her field, the bounce from an expert who will be more persuasive by reason of looks, attitude, demeanor, and the like.

■ In one such case, the State of Washington brought petitions against two men alleging that they should be civilly committed.[13] To succeed, the State had to prove that the two men were sexually violent predators—that is, the State had to prove their current mental state. The men in question refused to cooperate with the State's experts. The only available evidence of their current mental state was hearsay evidence contained in psychological reports and criminal histories. The State had two experts review these reports and histories. They formed the opinion that the men were sexually violent predators.

At trial, they were qualified as experts. They testified that they had diagnosed the two men. Each diagnosis was based on inadmissible hearsay from the reports and histories. These reports and histories "are the types of materials reasonably relied on to diagnose future dangerousness of sex offenders."[14] The experts testified that in their opinion the two men were sexually violent predators, and the men were committed.

■ In another such case, the defendant was on trial for "possession of a firearm by a convicted felon"[15]—this "firearm" was a bomb. The United States had to prove that the bomb in question had traveled in interstate commerce.[16] As its only evidence of this essential element of its case, two expert witnesses for the prosecution testified that component parts of the bomb had been manufactured outside the state where the bomb exploded. Therefore, assembled or unassembled, it necessarily traveled in interstate commerce. The experts based there opinions on hearsay: "discussions with the manufacturers, corporate literature and reference material maintained by the ATF, studies of distinctive markings on the products, and their personal experience in law enforcement."[17] The court found that experts in this particular field reasonably rely on this kind of hearsay to form this kind of opinion.[18] The experts opinions supplied

---

With occurrence witnesses, a party is stuck with the persons who witness the occurrence—no matter how nervous they appear on the stand, no matter how long their criminal record, no matter how they treat their mothers, small children, or animals. The party can choose an expert, however, who appears calm and confident, has an unblemished record, and treats all beings with the greatest respect, and deserves the same in return—in sum, an expert who not only is telling the truth, but also appears to be telling the truth.

13. In re Young, 857 P.2d 989 (Wash. 1993).

14. *Id.* at 1018.

15. United States v. Gresham, 118 F.3d 258, 259 (5th Cir. 1997).

16. *Id.* at 264-65.

17. *Id.* at 266.

18. *Id.*

the only substantive evidence of this essential element of the prosecution's case. The defendant was convicted.

■ A third case: A young girl was seriously and permanently injured.[19] The witness was an expert in rehabilitation counseling and, as such, in the preparation of life-care plans. She testified regarding damages: future health care and living expenses. She estimated the girl's future "medical needs, attendant care, special education, housing, nutrition, and transportation, among others."[20] In determining those needs, the expert had to make some assumptions regarding the girl's present and future medical needs. Appellants pointed out that this witness was not a medical doctor and that there was no medical evidence introduced through qualified medical experts to support the expert's testimony. They argued "that the court allowed [this expert], who is not a physician, to render medical opinions and other opinions based on hearsay," opinions regarding the severity of the girl's injuries and her prognosis.[21] The court of appeals held that though the expert's opinions were based in part on medical reports, they were not medical opinions. Her opinions on the future cost-of-care were adequately supported by the kind of evidence reasonably relied on by experts in her field.[22]

■ A fourth such case involves a defendant using an expert to plug a hole in his case.[23] Some insured jewelry went missing from a jeweler. Whether the insurance company paid on its policy depended on whether or not it was missing by reason of a "mysterious disappearance"[24] or a theft. The company, the plaintiff in this case, put on evidence that it was a "mysterious disappearance." The jeweler needed evidence that it was a theft or he would lose. All the jew-

---

19. Kent Village Assocs. Joint Venture v. Smith, 657 A.2d 330, 338 (Md. 1994).

20. *Id.*

21. *Id.*

22. This ruling makes a great deal of sense, assuming the trial judge did sufficient *Daubert* testing on the expert and her testimony: who better to testify to the cost of supporting this young girl for the rest of her life? An expert in the preparation of life care plans or a medical doctor? The medical-needs evidence was basis evidence. She was not testifying, after all, to proximate cause or to the nature and extent of the injuries, but just that this is her opinion as to what it is going to take to support a young girl with a certain set of particular injuries. And mustn't a rehabilitation counselor rely upon what she hears and reads from doctors regarding the client's condition, what she has heard and read about future inflation, and, in fact, hearsay of all sorts? If there is a problem with any of the information on which she is basing her opinion, medical or otherwise, then the defense can probe the problem on cross examination and call its own witnesses to point it out.

23. Sphere Drake Ins. PLC v. Trisko, 226 F.3d 951 (8th Cir. 2000). *See also* parts (I)(D)(3) and (4)(a) & (g) of this chapter, below.

24. *Sphere Drake Ins. PLC*, 226 F.3d at 955.

eler had was this: A police detective had been told by two informants "that two individuals had been paid $20,000 each to steal [the] jewelry."[25] This is evidence of theft, but it also is inadmissible hearsay. The detective was qualified as an expert and allowed to testify that in his opinion—based in large part on this informant hearsay-evidence—the "loss did not constitute a mysterious disappearance, but rather was likely a theft."[26] Without the expert's opinion, the main evidence of theft—perhaps the only evidence—was inadmissible hearsay. The jeweler had a hole in his case, and he filled it with an expert witness. The jury returned a verdict for the jeweler.

■ One more example, again a defendant using the expert testimony to plug a hole in its defense. The wife of a man who died in the crash of a small plane he was piloting brought suit against the plane's manufacturer, alleging the plane had a number of defects.[27] The defendant argued that the plane was not defective and that the cause of the crash was pilot error. Defendant's proximate cause argument was based on the testimony of an expert, "a physician trained in aeronautical psychology."[28] The expert made a study of the pilot's life. He interviewed many of the pilot's associates and co-workers and others, and concluded that the pilot "was under a great deal of stress in his personal life and … this stress caused him to lose the concentration necessary for flying."[29] Here we have a defense based on an expert opinion in turn based on what the expert had been told by a number of non-testifying lay persons.

If you have a burden of production or a burden of proof problem because all of the evidence of one essential element of your case is inadmissible, you may be able to satisfy that burden with an expert opinion based on that inadmissible evidence. An expert opinion based on inadmissible hearsay is yet one more way around the restrictions on the courtroom use of hearsay evidence.[30]

---

25. *Id.* at 954.

26. *Id.*

27. Stevens v. Cessna Aircraft Co., 634 F.Supp. 137 (E.D. Pa. 1986), *aff'd without opinion*, 806 F.2d 252 (3d Cir. 1986). The discussion at this point in the text is taken from G. Michael Fenner, *Law Professor Reveals Shocking Truth About Hearsay*, 62 UMKC L. REV. 1, 90–91 (1993).

28. *Stevens*, 634 F.Supp. at 140.

29. *Id.*

30. *See additionally* the Uniform Composite Reports as Evidence Act, which has to do with the admissibility of certain written reports of certain experts. "[W]hen testified to by" a person who made the report and "if, in the opinion of the court, no substantial injustice will be done the opposite party, the report "shall … be admissible" without calling the persons who furnished the information or producing the writings on which the report was based. The act has an adverse-party notice requirement, which can be waived if the court finds that no sub-

3. The Expert's Reliance upon Inadmissible Evidence Must Be Reasonable

An expert may testify to an opinion that is based on inadmissible evidence if, and only if, it is reasonable for experts in the particular field to rely upon this kind of evidence when forming opinions.[31] The other side of this coin is, of course, that an expert may not base an opinion on inadmissible evidence if it is not reasonable for this kind of expert to do so.[32]

---

stantial injustice would result. As of this writing, only two states have adopted this uniform act. Nebraska and South Dakota. See NEB. REV. STAT. §25-12,115 (Reissue 1995); 7A S.D. COD-IFIED LAWS §19-15-5.2 through 19-15-8 (Michie 1995). Ohio has enacted a similar statute, but does not refer to it by the uniform act's name. Ohio Rev. Code Ann. §2317.36 (West 2004).

On its face, the act allows the writing itself to be entered into evidence and, therefore, taken to the jury room, so long as "no substantial injustice will be done the opposite party." This is in contrast to the recorded recollection exception where the recollection is read into evidence and the physical record of the recollection is not allowed into evidence because letting the jury to take the document into the jury room gives it undue emphasis. See chapter 3(VI)(C), above.

31. See the cases cited in notes 11, above, and 43, infra; FED.R.EVID. 703; United States v. LeClair, 338 F.3d 882, 885 (8th Cir. 2003); Brennan v. Reinhart Inst'l Foods, 211 F.3d 449, 450–51 (8th Cir. 2000); United States v. Corey, 207 F.3d 84, 89 (1st Cir. 2000) (reasonable for ATF agent to base an opinion as to the state in which a shotgun was manufactured on telephone conversations with a gun historian and research into technical and reference manuals from the ATF research libraries); Scott v. Ross, 140 F.3d 1275 (9th Cir. 1998); United States v. Gresham, 118 F.3d 258, 266 (5th Cir. 1997) ("[I]t is axiomatic that expert opinions may be based on facts or data of a type reasonably relied upon by experts in a particular field, even if the sources are not admissible evidence."); United States v. Davis, 40 F.3d 1069, 1075 (10th Cir. 1994) (an expert may testify from another person's notes if this practice is accepted in the field); United States v. Locascio, 6 F.3d 924, 938 (2d Cir.1993); Ellipsis, Inc. v. Color Works, Inc. 428 F.Supp.2d 752, 760 (W.D. Tenn 2006); Remtech, Inc., v. Fireman's Fund Ins. Co., 2006 U.S. Dist. LEXIS 1145, *3 (E.D. Wash. Jan. 4, 2006) ("[A]ppraisers routinely and reasonably rely upon such hearsay in the course of their duties valuing property."); United States v. Stone, 222 F.R.D. 334, 340 (E.D. Tenn. 2004) ("'[T]he court must make an independent assessment, based on a factual showing, that the material in question is sufficiently reliable for experts in that field to rely on it.'" (quoting 4 Jack B. Weinstein & Margaret A. Berger, WEINSTEIN'S FEDERAL EVIDENCE, §703.04[2] (Joseph M. McLaughlin, ed., Matthew Bender 2d ed. 2004)); Thurman v. Missouri Gas Energy, 107 F.Supp.2d 1046 (W.D. Mo. 2000); Lai v. St. Peter, 869 P.2d 1352, 1362 (Haw. 1994) (experts reasonably rely on knowledge derived from lectures and conversations with colleagues; "'[I]t is by assimilation of hearsay ... that expert opinions are in fact, for the most part, made[.]'") (citation omitted).

32. FED.R.EVID. 703 advisory committee's note (it is not reasonable for an accident reconstruction expert to form an opinion on the point-of-impact rely based on eyewitness state-

■ Let us return to the case of the missing jewelry.[33] The insurance company paid out under a policy covering the jewelry if it was a theft, and not if it was a "mysterious disappearance."[34] A police detective was qualified as an expert witness and testified that in his opinion the "loss did not constitute a mysterious disappearance, but rather was likely a theft."[35] He based his opinion in large part on this inadmissible hearsay: two informants had told him that two people "had been paid $20,000 each to steal [the] jewelry."[36]

The detective was qualified as an expert on theft in the city where the jewelry went missing. "He investigated thefts in the area for several years, and has specialized knowledge of jewel thieves and their methods of operation."[37] He "testified that he regularly relied on the statements of informants as an investigating officer."[38] The officer testified that his reliance on this kind of inadmissible hearsay was reasonable for an expert such as himself, and there was no expert testimony to the contrary. He was allowed to rely on the statements of these informants "in forming the basis of his expert opinion," and was allowed to state his opinion to the jury.[39]

---

ments of their observations); Schafer v. Time, 142 F.3d 1361, 1374 (11th Cir. 1998) (testimony inadmissible because the hearsay document was "hardly the type … an expert might rely upon within the ordinary course of his or her profession"); Faries v. Atlas Truck Body Mfg. Co, 797 F.2d 619, 623 (8th Cir. 1986) (accident reconstruction testimony of state trooper excluded because its basis included what an eyewitness had told him about the occurrence); Kelley v. American Heyer-Schulte Corp., 957 F.Supp. 873, 877–78 (W.D. Tex. 1997) ("[C]onfronted with a proffer of expert testimony based upon particular studies, the Court must as an initial matter determine whether the studies could be reasonably relied upon by the expert."); Henry v. Hess Oil V. I. Corp., 163 F.R.D. 237 (D.V.I. 1995) (the underlying data was not the kind reasonably relied on by experts in the field); Wade-Greaux v. Whitehall Labs., Inc., 874 F.Supp. 1441, 1482–83 (D. V.I. 1994) (opinions that a particular drug caused a particular deformity were inadmissible because based on data not reasonably relied upon in the relevant scientific community); McLendon v. Georgia Kaolin Co., 841 F.Supp. 415, 419 (M.D. Ga. 1994) (unreasonable for an expert to rely on an opinion stated by an employee of the defendant without knowing that employee's occupation, training, or background, without knowing what data the employee used to form his opinion; counsel's argument that the opinion expressed by the employee is an admission does not change the fact that it is not the kind of evidence reasonably relied upon by scientific experts).

33. Sphere Drake Ins. PLC v. Trisko, 226 F.3d 951 (8th Cir. 2000). *See also* part (I)(D)(2) of this chapter, above, and part (I)(D)(4)(a) and (g) of this chapter, below.
34. *Sphere Drake Ins. PLC*, 226 F.3d at 955.
35. *Id.*
36. *Id.* at 954.
37. *Id.* at 955.
38. *Id.*
39. *Id.*

■ A second example: An expert-witness economist testified to his opinion of the present cash value of the plaintiff's future lost wages.[40] His opinions were based on interest and inflation rates taken from United States Government reports, but he had never seen these reports himself. He called the Government Records Department of the city library and got the information from them, over the phone. This is an opinion based on inadmissible hearsay—the telephone call. (There is double hearsay here: the government reports themselves and the librarian's statements over the telephone about what the reports said. The reports themselves, however, fit under an exception and are admissible hearsay. The telephone call does not fit under an exception and is inadmissible hearsay.)

Is this opinion admissible, based as it is on the inadmissible information obtained over the phone? We may not know the answer to the question, but we do know where to look for the answer. Is it reasonable for this kind of expert to rely upon this kind of inadmissible data? Is it reasonable for an economist who is an expert at determining present cash value to rely on numbers provided over the phone by the records department of the city library?

And, by the way, who will counsel ask if it is reasonable for this kind of expert to form this kind of opinion based on this kind of evidence? As a general rule, a witness qualified as an expert is competent to testify to what is a reasonable course of action for like experts. Counsel will ask the expert witness who is about to state the opinion. How likely is it that the expert will testify that what he or she did was not reasonable? Unless what the expert says about what is reasonable is patently wrong or opposing counsel puts on some evidence to the contrary, the point is made.

4. Basis Evidence

a. Defining the Problem

"Like a house built on sand, the expert's opinion is no better than the facts on which it is based."[41] The value of an opinion is not self-contained, and it is not just a product of expert's education, experience, and other qualifications. An expert's opinion is only as good as its basis—more convincing if it is based on a large

---

40. This is based on Drexler v. Seaboard Sys. R.R., 530 So.2d 754 (Ala. 1988). The court held that the expert's reliance on numbers "obtained from an out-of-court source not falling within any of the 'hearsay' exceptions" rendered his entire testimony on the subject inadmissible. Id. at 757. That is the wrong question, at least under the federal rules. The right question is this: Is it reasonable for experts in this field to rely on this kind of telephone communication when forming this kind of opinion?
41. Kennemur v. California, 133 Cal.App.3d 907, 923 (1982).

amount of high-quality information and less convincing if it is based on only a small amount of low-quality information. The most highly qualified expert in the world can form a barely credible opinion when it is based on too little information of low-quality and the most marginally qualified expert can form a highly credible opinion when it is based on a lot of high-quality information.

The trier of fact must decide how much, if any, weight to give to each expert's opinion. To make the best possible decision, the trier of fact must know the basis for each opinion. Quality in, quality out—the jury is entitled to know the quality of the data that went into the opinion. As one court has put it:

> To prevent the expert from [testifying to basis evidence] "places an unreal stricture on him and compels him to be not only less than frank with the jury but also ... to appear to base his diagnosis upon reasons which are flimsy and inconclusive when in fact they may not be." Absent a full explanation of the expert's reasons, including underlying facts and opinions, the jury has no way of evaluating the expert testimony and is therefore faced with a "meaningless conclusion" by the witness.[42]

As a general rule, then, counsel is allowed to question the expert about the basis for each and every opinion, to get the basis evidence into the record and in front of the jury.[43]

---

42. People v. Anderson, 495 N.E.2d 485, 489 (Ill. 1986) (citation omitted). "Absent a full explanation of an expert's reasons, including the underlying facts and opinions, the jury has no way of evaluating the expert testimony." People v. P.T., 599 N.E.2d 79, 83 (Ill. App. Ct. 1992).

43. "An expert is of course permitted to testify to an opinion [based on inadmissible hearsay.] And in explaining his opinion an expert witness normally is allowed to explain the facts underlying it, even if they would not be independently admissible.... The fact that inadmissible evidence is the (permissible) premise of the expert's opinion does not make that evidence admissible for other purposes, purposes independent of the opinion." In re James Wilson Assoc'd, 965 F.2d 160, 172–73 (7th Cir. 1992) (opinion by Posner, J.) (citation omitted). *Accord, e.g.*, some cases in notes 11 and 31, above, and Hartley v. Dillard's, Inc., 310 F.3d 1054, 1061 (8th Cir. 2002) ("As a general rule, the factual basis of an expert opinion goes to the credibility of the testimony ...") (citation and multiple quotation marks omitted); United States v. Williams, 212 F.3d 1305, 1310 (D.C. Cir. 2000) ("[T]rial judges generally rely on the structural check of cross-examination in permitting opinion testimony with a weak foundation"; denial of re-cross was error); Engebretsen v. Fairchild Aircraft Corp., 21 F.3d 721, 729 (6th Cir. 1994); United States v. L.E. Cooke Co., 991 F.2d 336, 342 (6th Cir. 1993) (when the factual basis for an expert's opinion is weak, "it is up to opposing counsel to inquire into [that] basis"); International Adhesive Coating Co. v. Bolton Emerson Int'l, 851 F.2d 540, 545 (1st Cir. 1988) ("[T]he fact that an expert's opinion may be tentative or even speculative does not mean that the testimony must be excluded so long as opposing counsel has an opportunity to attack the expert's credibility"); Fox v. Taylor

When the basis evidence is otherwise inadmissible, however, there are two sides to the coin. Assume that the trial court lets the expert testify to otherwise inadmissible basis evidence. In that case, the basis evidence is admissible for one thing (basis or credibility evidence) and inadmissible for another (substantive evidence of the facts declared in the basis evidence). Assume the basis evidence for expert's opinion is powerful (and otherwise inadmissible). When, on direct examination, the expert states the opinion and its basis, that benefits the proponent's case (the jury has more complete information about the quality of the opinion) and prejudices the opponent's (the jury hears the otherwise inadmissible evidence). If, on the other hand, the expert states the opinion but is not allowed to state its basis, that devalues the proponent's case (the expert's opinion appears weaker) and benefits the opponent's (the jury does not hear the otherwise inadmissible hearsay).[44]

Diving & Salvage Co., 694 F.2d 1349, 1356 (5th Cir. 1983) ("An expert is permitted to disclose hearsay for the limited purpose of explaining the basis for his expert opinion, Fed. R. Evid. 703, but not as general proof of the truth of the underlying matter, Fed. R. Evid. 802."); Bryan v. John Bean Div. of FMC Corp., 566 F.2d 541, 545 (5th Cir. 1978) (Basis evidence that is inadmissible hearsay is "as permissible on cross-examination as on direct.").

But see, e.g., Clearwater Corp. v. Lincoln, 301 N.W.2d 328 (Neb. 1981), which states that "[s]imply because such evidence is relied upon [by the expert] does not affect its admissibility." Id. at 330 (dictum). If the court really meant this, it must be wrong. Surely the fact that the expert relied on the evidence "affect[s]" it admissibility. Before the expert's reliance, there was only one use for the evidence—as substantive evidence of the fact stated—and that use is inadmissible hearsay. After the expert's reliance, there is a second use for the evidence—as the basis for the opinion—and to that use it is nonhearsay.

If the basis is strong, offering counsel will bring it out. If the basis is weak and offering counsel does not bring it out, opposing counsel will. Rule 26 of the Federal Rules of Civil Procedure enables the cross-examiner to make an intelligent decision as to whether to cross-examine on the basis of the expert's opinion. It requires that parties disclose to all other parties the identity of any person who may be called to testify as an expert, "all opinions to be expressed" by each expert, "and the basis and reasons therefor." FED.R.CIV.PRO. 26 (emphasis added). Failure to disclose basis evidence is sufficient reason for a court to exclude the opinion, and certainly sufficient reason to exclude the basis evidence. See, e.g., Cummins v. Lyle Indus., 93 F.3d 362, 371 (7th Cir. 1996) (some of the expert's opinion was excluded in part because plaintiff failed to disclose the basis evidence as required by Rule 26).

44. For an example, consider again Sphere Drake Ins. PLC v. Trisko, , 226 F.3d 951 (8th Cir. 2000), also discussed at parts (I)(D)(2), (3), and (4)(g) of this chapter, above. The insurance company paid if the missing jewelry was stolen; a police detective testified to his expert opinion that it had been stolen; this opinion was pretty much the jeweler's only evidence it was stolen. The jury must evaluate this opinion; there is no other legitimate way to determine who wins. To give the opinion whatever credit it deserves, the jury must know its basis. The question, then, is this: Will the expert be allowed to testify that he based it in large part on the fact that two informants told him that two people "had been paid $20,000

b. Resolving the Problem of Basis-Evidence Admissibility

Evidence admissible to one issue and inadmissible to another is not a new problem. Generally throughout the law of evidence, this is handled by applying Rule 403: Does the risk of unfair prejudice from admitting the evidence substantially outweigh the evidence's probative value? And this is how this basis evidence problem used to be handled in federal court—prior to the 2000 amendment to Rule 703—and is still handled in some state courts.

(1) Rule 703's *Ad Hoc* Resolution

As amended in 2000, Rule 703 states that otherwise inadmissible basis evidence "shall not be disclosed to the jury by the proponent of the opinion or inference unless the court determines that [its] probative value in assisting the jury to evaluate the expert's opinion substantially outweighs [its] prejudicial effect."[45] This is similar to Rule 403, but different in two ways, one of which is important.

■ The important difference: Under Rule 403, the danger of unfair prejudice must substantially outweigh probative value. Under Rule 703, the probative value must substantially outweigh the prejudice.[46] The balance is weighted quite differently. Rule 403 enacts a preference for the evidence—for letting it in. When the evidence is offered by the proponent of the opinion, Rule 703 enacts a preference against the evidence—for keeping it out.[47]

---

each to steal [the] jewelry"? To the issue of the weight and credibility of the expert opinion, the informant's statements are *admissible nonhearsay*—not offered to prove the truth of the matter asserted, but just to show that the expert heard them and factored them into his opinion. To the issue of whether the jewelry was stolen, they are *inadmissible hearsay*.

45. Fed.R.Evid. 703.

46. Fed.R.Evid. 703 (2000 amendment); United States v. Milkiewicz, 470 F.3d 390, 400 (1st Cir. 2006); Louis Vuitton Malletier v. Dooney & Bourke, Inc., 525 F.Supp.2d 576, 666 (S.D.N.Y. 2007); Sanchez v. Brokop, 398 F.Supp.2d 1177, 1192 (D.N.M. 2005); Bado-Santana v. Ford Motor Co., 364 F.Supp.2d 79, 102 (D.P.R. 2005); Rambus, Inc. v. Infineon Techs. AG, 222 F.R.D. 101, 111 (E.D. Va 2004).

47. Hynix Semiconductor, Inc. v. Rambus, Inc., 2008 U.S.Dist. LEXIS 10859, *20 (N.D. Cal. 2008) ("Rule 703 only prevents the proponent of the expert's opinion from disclosing the expert's otherwise-inadmissible basis for his opinion. By emphasizing the bar on the proponent, the rule implies that the opposing party may freely cross-examine an expert on the otherwise-inadmissible basis for his or her opinion. The advisory committee note further explains that '[n]othing in this Rule restricts the presentation of underlying expert facts or data when offered by an adverse party.' FRE 703, adv. committee note (2000)."); Rambus, Inc. v. Infineon Techs. AG, 222 F.R.D. 101, 111 (E.D. Va 2004) ("Rule 703 'provides a presumption against disclosure to the jury of [inadmissible] information used as the basis

■ The unimportant difference: Rule 403 does not bar the admission of the evidence unless it is *unfairly* prejudicial. Rule 703 speaks only of "prejudice," not "unfair prejudice." There is prejudice inherent in the introduction of most evidence. If, after all, it does not prejudice the other side, why offer it? There is great prejudice inherent in, for example, a lawfully obtained, admissible confession, but the prejudice is not unfair. Rule 403 requires the judge distinguish between prejudice and unfair prejudice; Rule 703 does not; this is a difference, but not a distinction.

The prejudice to the opponent that is inherent in allowing the proponent of opinion evidence to introduce otherwise inadmissible basis evidence is necessarily unfair. Unfair prejudice has to do with "an undue tendency to suggest decision on an improper basis, commonly, though not necessarily, an emotional one."[48] The danger of prejudice here is that the jury may use the otherwise inadmissible hearsay as substantive evidence of the facts stated in the evidence, making their decision in part on an improper basis—and that is necessarily unfair to the opposing side. Rule 403 refers to "unfair prejudice" to distinguish that from prejudice that is "fair"; Rule 703 only refers to prejudice and only applies to situations where the prejudice is unfair.[49]

---

for an expert's opinion ... when that information is offered by the proponent of the expert.' 4 Jack B. Weinstein & Margaret A. Berger, Weinstein's Federal Evidence § 703.05 (2d ed. 2003).").

48. FED.R.EVID. 403 advisory committee's note.

49. In the courts of a state that has adopted the rules like the Federal Rules of Evidence but has not adopted this amendment to Rule 703, then Rule 403 is used to decide the admissibility of otherwise inadmissible basis evidence. Likewise, 403 is the rule in pre-amendment cases. For example, one court stated that, "the case law of other jurisdictions is in general agreement that [on direct examination] an expert may discuss the underlying facts and data upon which he or she is relying..., even though hearsay may be involved." Tabieros v. Clark Equip. Co., 944 P.2d 1279, 1326 (Haw. 1997) (citing and discussing cases). Later in its opinion, the *Tabieros* court held that the particular hearsay basis-evidence there was inadmissible and stated that the need for judicial oversight is "particularly acute ... where the probative value of the testimony 'is substantially outweighed by the danger of unfair prejudice, confusion of the issues, or misleading the jury.'" *Id.* at 1330, citing Rule 403. *See also, e.g.,* Myers v. American Seating Co., 637 So.2d 771, 774 (La. Ct. App. 1994); Bong Jin Kim v. Nazarian, 576 N.E.2d 427, 434 (Ill. App. Ct. 1991).

Rule 403 was also the applicable rule in federal cases prior to the December 1, 2000 effective date of the amendment to Rule 703. *E.g.,* Nachtsheim v. Beech Aircraft Corp., 847 F.2d 1261, 1270–71 (7th Cir. 1988); Barrel of Fun, Inc. v. State Farm Fire & Cas. Co., 739 F.2d 1028, 1033 (5th Cir.1984); United States v. Neeley, 25 M.J. 105, 107 (U.S. C.M.A. 1987) (regarding the claim that an expert opinion "*smuggled*" hearsay into evidence, the "real question" is whether the opinion violated Rule 403).

Rule 403 is, of course, not the rule applicable in this situation in states that have adopted

Rule 703 applies in federal court and in any state court that has adopted the 2000 amendment to the federal rule. In those courts, the much less liberal provisions of Rule 703 are used to decide the admissibility of otherwise inadmissible basis evidence. Rule 403 applies in other jurisdictions. Whichever version of the balance applies, one of the questions to ask it this: How trustworthy is the basis evidence? It may be that like-experts reasonably rely upon the evidence in forming opinions but the evidence is not sufficiently trustworthy to come in as basis evidence. For example, courts should be wary of basis evidence furnished by biased witnesses.[50]

If this test comes out in favor of the admissibility of the basis evidence, the hearsay rule is not a problem. Evidence offered as basis evidence is not offered for the truth of its assertions, but only to show that the assertions were made and the expert relied upon them. It is not offered as substantive evidence of the facts asserted, but only as credibility evidence.[51] For exam-

---

the federal 2000 amendment. *E.g.*, Ward v. Dretke, 420 F.3d 479, 494 (5th Cir. 2005).

Finally, there are examples of federal courts that seem to have missed the 2000 amendment and continuing to apply Rule 403 rather than the newer version of Rule 703. *E.g.*, Williams v. Consol. City of Jacksonville, 2006 U.S. Dist. LEXIS 8257, * 24-25 (M.D. Fla. Feb. 8, 2006) (applying Rule 403 rather than the 2000 amendment to Rule 703).

Regarding Rule 403, *see also* Chapter 11(V) and Chapter 12(II), below.

50. *E.g.*, Gong v. Hirsch, 913 F.2d 1269, 1272-73 (7th Cir. 1990) (it was proper to allow the expert in this case to state an opinion based in part on the hearsay statement involved herein because, as required by Rule 703, it is reasonable for this kind of expert to rely on this kind of statement, however, because of the "obvious concern over the trustworthiness of [this] statement," it was not an abuse of discretion to prevent the expert from telling the jury that this hearsay was part of the basis for his opinion; the reasonable reliance Rule 703 demands before the evidence may be used as part of the basis for the expert's opinion is different from the trustworthiness required before the expert will be allowed to tell the jury that this evidence was part of the basis; reasonable reliance so the expert may use it and trustworthy so the jury may hear it are two different standards); Barrel of Fun, Inc. v. State Farm Fire & Cas. Co., 739 F.2d 1028, 1033 (5th Cir. 1984); Leake v. Burlington N. R.R., 892 S.W.2d 359 (Mo. Ct. App. 1995) (court seems concerned about motivation of the out-of-court declarant).

One court has gone so far as to say that "[i]f the underlying evidence is furnished by a biased witness, it probably will be excluded." Brunner v. Brown, 480 N.W.2d 33, 35 (Iowa 1992).

51. *E.g.*, Engebretsen v. Fairchild Aircraft Corp., 21 F.3d 721, 728-729 (6th Cir. 1994) (Rule 703 does not allow the admission of the otherwise inadmissible basis evidence to prove the truth of the matter asserted but it does allow it " 'to be admitted to explain the basis of the expert's opinion.' "); United States v. Ramos, 725 F.2d 1322, 1324 (11th Cir. 1984) ("[H]earsay ... admitted to show the basis of [the expert's] opinion ... and not for the truth of the assertions ... is admissible ..."); Celebrity Cruises, Inc. v. Essef Corp. 434 F.Supp.2d

ple, when a patient's statements to a medical expert are admitted as basis evidence only, then they are not admitted for their truth, but only to show what the doctor relied on in forming his or her expert opinion. Whether the statements were true or not, the doctor relied on them. In that use, they are not hearsay.

(2) Categorical Resolution

There some specific situations where basis evidence is categorically inadmissible. There is no test applied in the particular case. The evidence simply is not admissible. First, basis evidence is not admissible when the expert does not testify to an opinion for which it is the basis. Take this case of a plaintiff injured on the job.[52] The defendant-railroad's rehabilitation expert testified that he had contacted the rehabilitation officer at the railroad to get plaintiff's rehabilitation history and was told the plaintiff had refused their rehabilitation services. It is reasonable for this kind of expert to rely on this kind of data when forming opinions. Here, however, the expert "failed to advance any 'opinion' which was supported or formed using"[53] this hearsay statement.[54] He testified to the basis, if you will, but not the opinion. What the court is left with is a transparent use of the expert as a conduit for the admission of otherwise

---

169, 192 (S.D.N.Y. 2006) (characterizing the evidence as "background evidence underlying [the] opinion"); Remtech, Inc. v. Fireman's Fund Ins. Co., 2006 U.S. Dist. LEXIS 1145, *3 (E.D. Wash. Jan. 4, 2006) ("The Court considers such hearsay evidence solely as a basis for the expert opinion and not as substantive evidence."); Golob v. People, 180 P.3d 1006, 1010 (Colo. 2008) (Generally, "'expert witnesses may testify to the information upon which they have relied in reaching their conclusions.... When presented for this purpose, the statements are not evidence of the matters stated, and hence not hearsay, but are merely explanatory of the opinion, enabling the jury to weigh it in the light of its basis.'"); Bong Jin Kim v. Nazarian, 576 N.E.2d 427, 433 (Ill. App. Ct. 1991) ("[T]he underlying facts or data are admitted not for their truth, but for the limited purpose of explaining the basis of the expert's opinion.").

52. *Leake*, 892 S.W.2d 359.

53. *Id.* at 364.

54. Furthermore, though the expert testified that he routinely relies on this kind of information in his analysis, the appellate court seems to have found this particular reliance unreasonable because the defendant's expert was relying on a self-serving hearsay statement made by an employee of the defendant. The court seems to be hinting at a kind of Palmer v. Hoffman, 318 U.S. 109 (1943) trustworthiness problem involving concerns about the motivation of the out-of-court declarant. *See* Chapter 3(VII)(D)(5)(a), above. Add the fact that the problem was easy for the defendant to avoid—the railroad could simply have called the out-of-court declarant, *i.e.*, its rehabilitation officer, to the stand—and the evidence is inadmissible. *Leake*, 892 S.W.2d at 364.

inadmissible evidence—but only as a conduit.[55] Evidence is not basis evidence until there is an opinion based thereon.

A second situation, which may just be a variation of the first, is where basis evidence is not admissible unless the expert did actually rely on it in forming his or her opinion. Here, this otherwise inadmissible evidence is not admissible as basis evidence because it was not the basis for anything.[56]

Third, basis evidence is inadmissible when the expert is ready to state an opinion and then describe the inadmissible basis evidence, but the opinion itself is inadmissible. For example, an opinion *based on* inadmissible evidence may be admissible, but an opinion *about* inadmissible evidence is not admissible. An expert opinion about a defendant's mental state, based on reports from other doctors, may be admissible. An expert opinion about what an otherwise inadmissible report is saying about the defendant's mental state is not admissible. In terms of the hearsay rule, there is no difference between testifying, "Here is what my mother said about that accident she saw, about how it happened," and testifying, "Here is my expert opinion—and I've been her son and interpreting what she says for many years—as to what my mother's [inadmissible] statement about the accident means." Before basis evidence is admissible to explain an opinion, the opinion itself must be admissible.[57]

---

55. "[T]he judge must make sure that the expert isn't being used as a vehicle for circumventing the rules of evidence. The fact that inadmissible evidence is the (permissible) premise of the expert's opinion does not make that evidence admissible for other purposes, purposes independent of the opinion." In re James Wilson Assoc'd, 965 F.2d 160, 172–73 (7th Cir. 1992) (opinion by Posner, J.) (citation omitted). *See also, e.g.*, Dura Automotive Sys. v. CTS Corp., 285 F.3d 609, 613-14 (7th Cir. 2002) (Posner, J.) ("mouthpiece" expert); Engebretsen v. Fairchild Aircraft Corp., 21 F.3d 721, 729 (6th Cir. 1994); Fox v. Taylor Diving & Salvage Co., 694 F.2d 1349, 1356 (5th Cir. 1983); Louis Vuitton Malletier v. Dooney & Bourke, Inc., 525 F.Supp.2d 576, 664 (S.D. N.Y. 2007); United States v. Hernandez-Mejia, 2007 U.S. Dist. LEXIS 54792, *29 (D. N.M. April 30, 2007) (government cannot use an expert as a conduit for the admission of evidence in violation of the Confrontation Clause); Tucker v. Ohtsu Tire & Rubber Co., Ltd., 49 F.Supp.2d 456, 462 n.12 (D. Md. 1999) (basis evidence is not permitted as an "end run" around a party's inability to designate new experts because the time for so designating has passed); Cobb v. State, 658 S.E.2d 750, 752 (Ga. 2008); Linn v. Fossum, 946 So.2d 1032, 1035-39 (Fla. 2006); State v. DeShay, 669 N.W.2d 878, 886 (Minn. 2003) (cannot use expert opinion to "launder inadmissible hearsay evidence").

56. Tabieros v. Clark Equip. Co., 944 P.2d 1279, 1327-28 (Haw. 1997) (finding that the expert had not actually relied on part of the evidence offered as basis evidence and, therefore, it should not have been admitted).

57. "The expert opinion only helped the jury to understand the inadmissible document [on which it was based] rather than the evidence at trial." Riggins v. Mariner Boat Works,

Fourth, basis evidence is not admissible when it is not reasonable for this kind of expert to rely upon this kind of fact or data. If none of the facts or data are of the kind reasonably relied on by this kind of expert, then the opinion itself will not be admissible, and, therefore, neither will any of the basis evidence be admissible.[58] Sometimes the opinion and some, but not all, of the basis evidence will be admissible. Sometimes the basis evidence will include both of the following: (1) enough facts or data reasonably relied upon by experts in the field to support admitting the opinion into evidence; and (2) some facts or data that this expert relied on, but that are not reasonably relied on by like experts. In this case, the latter should be excluded.

Part of the point here is that if the basis evidence is coming in first, before the opinion, make sure that there will be an opinion and that it will be admissible.[59] Further, even though some of the basis evidence is coming in, that does not mean all of it must come in.

d. Corroborating Opinions Offered as Basis Evidence

A somewhat common situation involves the problem of corroborating opinions offered as basis evidence, that is, the expert who attempts to testify that other experts agree with his or her opinion. Sometimes an expert's opinion is based in part on the opinions of other experts.[60] Sometimes, however, the opinions of the other experts do not play a part in the formation of the testifying expert's opinion, or at least not enough of a part, but rather simply tend to confirm that opinion. The former may be admissible as basis evidence. The latter is not admissible as basis evidence.[61]

Inc., 545 So.2d 430, 432 (Fla. Dist. Ct. App. 1989). The opinion offered in *Riggins* was an opinion *about* inadmissible evidence, not an opinion *based on* inadmissible evidence. Rule 703 allows the admission of the latter, but not the former.

58. *See* part I(D)(3) of this chapter, above.

59. See FED.R.EVID. 705 regarding the possibility that the basis evidence comes in before the opinion itself.

60. In fact, nearly every expert's opinion is based to some degree or another on the opinions of other experts. All modern day expertise is built upon the investigations and opinions of predecessors. Experts make certain assumptions based on opinions formed by other experts. *See* part II(B) of this chapter, below.

61. Here is how one court suggests telling the difference. The opinions of the non-testifying experts truly are basis evidence when they serve as a somewhat narrower "premise supporting the testifying expert's opinion on a broader issue." Bong Jin Kim v. Nazarian, 576 N.E.2d 427, 434 (Ill. App. Ct. 1991). On the other hand, they are not basis evidence when they are offered only as "corroborating opinions on the same issue as that addressed by the testifying experts." *Id.* at 434.

Often, however, evidence will have elements of both reasonably-relied-upon basis evidence and corroborating-opinion evidence. What then? Under the post-December 1, 2000, version of the federal rules, the court applies Rule 703's balance. Ask this: Is the prejudice inherent in the evidence substantially outweighed by its probative value as basis evidence supporting the expert's credibility?[62]

Some courts deal with this problem way more rigidly. One court has said that, "[a] medical expert's recital of the confirming *opinion* of an absent physician is inadmissible hearsay."[63] Though part of the state's evidence statute authorizes the admission of basis evidence, "'the statute does not authorize the admission of any hearsay opinion on which the expert's opinion was based.'"[64] Whether the test is in Rule 703 or 403, this seems far too rigid and really at cross-purposes with the rest of Rule 703. It also seems to be at cross-purposes with the hearsay rule itself. Hearsay is inadmissible because it is unreliable. For categories of hearsay that seem reliable, we have created exceptions that allow those statements to be admitted into evidence. The fact that experts rely

---

If the expert's colleague merely corroborates the opinion independently arrived at by the expert, such corroboration might reinforce the expert's confidence in the opinion; the corroborative opinion, however is not the basis of the expert's opinion. Even if a colleague's "second opinion" brings to light a factor which the expert overlooked, it would presumably be the overlooked factor, not the second opinion itself, upon which any change in the expert's opinion would be based.

Id. Accord Golob v. People, 180 P.3d 1006, 1010 (Colo. 2008) ("'[T]he testifying expert did not use the peer's conclusions as a *basis* for her findings and opinions. The conclusions merely *bolstered* her findings and opinions.'").

On a related matter, basis evidence is not permitted as an "end run" around a party's inability to designate new experts because the time for such a designation has passed. Tucker v. Ohtsu Tire & Rubber Co., 49 F.Supp.2d 456, 462 n.12 (D. Md. 1999).

Even if the corroborating opinion is not admissible as basis evidence, it might, of course, be admissible in its own right. For example, if the corroborating opinion is in a learned treatise it may fit under the hearsay exception for learned treatises. FED.R.EVID. 803(18). *See* Chapter 3(XIII). The corroborating evidence under discussion in this part of the text is corroborating evidence that is inadmissible unless it is admissible as corroborating evidence.

62. In cases using Rule 403 — pre-amendment cases and cases in jurisdictions that adopted a version of the Federal Rules but did not adopt the 2000 amendment — testimony as to the basis of an expert's opinion need not be allowed if its probative value in explaining the expert's opinion is substantially outweighed by the likely prejudicial impact or the tendency to confuse the jury. The fact that a colleague agreed with the testifying expert's opinion is of dubious value in explaining the basis of the opinion. The party who is unable to cross-examine the corroborative opinion of the expert's colleague, on the other hand, will likely be prejudiced. *See* part (I)(D)(4)(b)(1) of this chapter, above.

63. CSX Trans. v. Casale, 441 S.E.2d 212, 214 (Va. 1994) (emphasis added).

64. *CSX Trans.*, 441 S.E.2d at 214.

upon a particular kind of hearsay statement when they form their expert opinions tends to make many such opinions reliable[65]—considerably more reliable than, say, newspaper articles that are over 20 years old.[66]

There are situations where out-of-court expert-opinion evidence is, and legitimately so, basis evidence for the expression of an in-court expert's opinion. Take the case where the issue is whether the defendant should be civilly committed as a sexually violent predator, and the defendant refuses to cooperate with the state's expert.[67] The state's expert's opinion may very well be based entirely on the hearsay statements of other doctors who have diagnosed the defendant in the past and others (lay witnesses) who have observed defendant's behavior. The opinions of these other experts may be *genuine* basis evidence. The approach that says that a hearsay *opinion* is never admissible as basis evidence seems far too rigid under either Rule 703 or 403.

Other courts make statements that seem to go too far the other way. One court has stated that it matters not whether the expert used the data to form an "opinion" or to "confirm" an opinion already reached. In truth, there is no difference between a new opinion that is the same as the old one but is based on both old and new data on the one hand, and an opinion confirmed by new data on the other.[68] There is, however, something to this latter view. The opinion's edifice is one that is constantly growing. From the time the matter is first considered until the time the opinion is expressed, the foundation is enlarged by all relevant information that comes the expert's way—including the opinions of other experts.

Much depends on how the lawyer asks the question, "have other experts agreed with your opinion?" versus "will you tell us, please, what things you have considered in forming the opinion you are expressing here today?" If the expert witness can state the corroborating opinion as a genuine part of the basis of his or her opinion, rather than as a kind of afterthought, then it should be treated as any other basis evidence.

e. Basis Evidence Alone Will Not Get a Cause of Action to the Jury

Otherwise inadmissible basis evidence only comes in as credibility evidence; it is not substantive evidence of the facts declared; it alone will not get a cause

---

65. *See* part I(c)(2) of this chapter, above.

66. *See* the ancient documents exception to the hearsay rule, FED.R.EVID. 803(16), discussed at part XI of Chapter 3.

67. *See* In re Young, 857 P.2d 989 (Wash. 1993), discussed at part I(D)(2) of this Chapter, above.

68. Blanks v. Murphy, 632 A.2d 1264, 1270 (N.J. Super. Ct. App. Div. 1993).

of action to the jury. But basis evidence is not admissible in the first place unless an opinion is expressed for which it is the basis.

f. One More Factor that may be Important on Appeal of the Basis Evidence Question

When an appellate court is considering whether or not the admission of otherwise inadmissible basis evidence was reversible error, it may take into account the extent to which the evidence was emphasized during the opening statement and the closing argument?[69]

g. Basis Evidence and Limiting Instructions

If the evidence is admissible only as basis evidence, the opposing party is entitled to a limiting instruction.[70] The judge will tell the jury that they may only consider the evidence to the extent it helps them decide what value, if any, to give to the opinion; they may not consider it as substantive evidence of the fact declared. In the jewelry theft case discussed above,[71] the question was whether certain jewelry was missing by reason of a "mysterious disappearance" or by reason of a theft. The expert-witness police detective testified that in his opinion the "loss did not constitute a mysterious disappearance, but rather was likely a theft."[72] The opinion was largely based on the fact that two informants had told him that two people "had been paid $20,000 each to steal [the] jewelry."[73] If he is allowed to state that inadmissible-hearsay basis for his

---

69. *See* In re James Wilson Assoc'd, 965 F.2d 160, 173 (7th Cir. 1992) (if an expert "(call him A) bases his opinion in part on [an otherwise inadmissible] fact (call it X) that the party's lawyer told him, the lawyer cannot in closing argument tell the jury, 'See, we proved X through our expert witness A.'") (Posner, J.); Bong Jin Kim v. Nazarian, 576 N.E.2d 427, 434 (Ill. App. Ct. 1991) (erroneous admission of basis evidence not harmless error in part because of the degree to which it was emphasized during opening statement and closing argument).

70. *E.g.*, United States v. 0.59 Acres of Land, 109 F.3d 1493, 1496 (9th Cir. 1997) ("When inadmissible evidence used by an expert is admitted to illustrate and explain the expert's opinion, however, it is 'necessary for the court to instruct the jury that the [otherwise inadmissible] evidence is to be considered solely as a basis for the expert opinion and not as substantive evidence.'"); Engebretsen v. Fairchild Aircraft Corp., 21 F.3d 721, 728-29 (6th Cir. 1994); Paddack v. Dave Christensen, Inc., 745 F.2d 1254, 1261–62 (9th Cir. 1984). Regarding limiting instructions, see particularly Chapter 12 (IV).

71. Sphere Drake Ins. PLC v. Trisko, 226 F.3d 951 (8th Cir. 2000), discussed above in parts I(D)(2), (3), and (4)(a) of this chapter.

72. *Sphere Drake Ins. PLC*, 226 F.3d at 954.

73. *Id.*

opinion, then opposing counsel is entitled to a jury instruction telling the jury that they can consider the testimony about what the informants said when they are deciding what weight, if any, to give the opinion of the detective, but they may not consider the testimony about what the informants said when they are deciding whether or not the jewelry is missing by reason of a "mysterious disappearance" or by reason of a theft.[74]

Whether the jury is able to follow such a limiting instruction—or whether the limiting instruction just reminds them of and highlights for them this other invalid, but logically relevant, use of the evidence—is debatable.[75] To some

---

74. Limiting instructions can be used to instruct jurors to disregard evidence entirely and they can be used to instruct jurors that they can use evidence for a certain purpose but not for others. Joel D. Lieberman and Jamie Arndt, *Understanding the Limits of Limiting Instructions*, 6 PSYCHOL. PUB. POL'Y & L. 677, 685 (2000). *See also* Chapter 12 (IV).

75. Most cases express the opinion that limiting instructions work. (And were they to say otherwise, how would we get our work done?) The United States Supreme Court has said this:

> [We have] tie[d] the [use of limiting instructions to] maintenance of the jury system. "Unless we proceed on the basis that the jury will follow the court's instructions where those instructions are clear and the circumstances are such that the jury can reasonably be expected to follow them, the jury system makes little sense." We agree that there are many circumstances in which this reliance is justified. Not every admission of inadmissible hearsay or other evidence can be considered to be reversible error unavoidable through limiting instructions; instances occur in almost every trial where inadmissible evidence creeps in, usually inadvertently. "A defendant is entitled to a fair trial but not a perfect one." It is not unreasonable to conclude that in many such cases the jury can and will follow the trial judge's instructions to disregard such information. Nevertheless, as [we have recognized], there are some contexts in which the risk that the jury will not, or cannot, follow instructions is so great, and the consequences of failure so vital to the defendant, that the practical and human limitations of the jury system cannot be ignored.

Bruton v. United States, 391 U.S. 123, 135 (1968) (citations omitted). *Accord, e.g.,* United States v. Caballero, 277 F.3d 1235, 1243 (10th Cir. 2002) ("We presume that jurors will follow clear instructions to disregard evidence 'unless there is an "overwhelming probability" that the jury will be unable to follow the court's instructions, and a strong likelihood that the effect of the evidence would be "devastating" to the defendant.'"); Kennon v. Slipstreamer, Inc., 794 F.2d 1067, 1078 (5th Cir. 1986) (Thornberry, J., dissenting) (had a limiting instruction been given, "I am confident that the jury would have done as the judge told them. I am not so naive [sic] as to believe that jurors can simply forget what they have heard, but I do believe that they generally make a conscientious effort to follow instructions."); United States v. Kilcullen, 546 F.2d 435, 447 (1st Cir. 1976) (perhaps limiting instructions cannot prevent a jury from consciously or unconsciously considering evidence for other than the limited purpose for which it was properly introduced; there is, however,

this kind of instruction seems akin to the judge telling the jury, "Don't think of a white horse." It is impossible.[76] What is not debatable is this: Some courts have held that failure to request a limiting instruction can constitute a waiver of the objection to the jury considering the evidence as more than just basis evidence, but as substantive evidence of the fact declared. If counsel objects to the admission of the basis evidence and the judge allows it in and counsel does not request a limiting instruction, counsel may be waiving the objection to the admission of the basis evidence.[77]

h. Summary

Sometimes using an expert witness allows counsel to take advantage of otherwise inadmissible evidence by getting an expert opinion that is based on the evidence. Sometimes using an expert witness allows counsel to get into evi-

---

"a strong presumption that proper limiting instructions will reduce the possibility of prejudice to an acceptable level."). *See also* Chapter 12 (IV).

76.   We do not pretend that a jury can keep one inference in mind without thinking about the other. An instruction told the jury to do this, but this is like telling someone not to think about a hippopotamus. To tell someone not to think about the beast is to assure at least a fleeting mental image. So it is here. Each juror must have had both the legitimate and the forbidden considerations somewhere in mind, if only in the subconscious.

United States v. DeCastris, 798 F.2d 261, 264–65 (7th Cir. 1986).

"With few exceptions, empirical research has repeatedly demonstrated that both types of limiting instructions are unsuccessful at controlling jurors' cognitive processes." *Lieberman, supra* note 75, at 686. Judges Learned Hand and Jerome Frank were particularly strong critics of limiting instructions. The *Bruton* Court quotes a number of harsh statements from those two judges about the inefficacy of limiting instructions and even the damage they do to the administration of justice. *Bruton*, 391 U.S. at 132-33 n.8. *Accord* United States v. DeCastris, 798 F.2d 261, 264–65 (7th Cir. 1986) (as quoted in the footnote following this one).

77.   There are not many of these cases, but they do exist. Sherman v. Burke Contracting, Inc., 891 F.2d 1527 (11th Cir. 1990) (defendant would have been entitled to a limiting instruction because the evidence in question was only admissible for a limited purpose — as substantive evidence it was inadmissible hearsay — but counsel did not request one; error in not giving a limiting instruction is cured by not requesting one, and the jury can consider the evidence for all purposes); United States v. Obayagbona, 627 F.Supp. 329, 337 (E.D.N.Y. 1985) (opinion denying motion for a new trial) ("Failure to request a more limited instruction after being invited to do so constituted a waiver of any objection to general admissibility.") (Judge Weinstein); Brunner v. Brown, 480 N.W.2d 33, 37 (Iowa 1992) (If there is no limiting instruction, "the jury may consider the [basis] evidence as substantive evidence. A limiting instruction, of course, should be requested.") (citations omitted).

dence not only the opinion based on the otherwise inadmissible evidence but also the otherwise inadmissible evidence itself.

The jury must assess the credibility of the opinion. The jury cannot fully assess the credibility of the opinion unless they are told what the opinion is based on. When the opinion is based in full or in part on otherwise inadmissible evidence, will the expert be allowed to describe to the jury the otherwise inadmissible evidence on which the opinion is based? Maybe so and maybe not. Under the Federal Rules of Evidence the answer is found by working the specific balancing test set out in Rule 703.[78]

II. Lay Opinion

A. Text of Rule 701

Rule 701. Opinion Testimony by Lay Witnesses

If the witness is not testifying as an expert, the witness' testimony in the form of opinions or inferences is limited to those opinions or inferences which are (a) rationally based on the perception of the witness, and (b) helpful to a clear understanding of the witness' testimony or the determination of a fact in issue, and (c) not based on scientific, technical, or other specialized knowledge within the scope of Rule 702.[79]

B. Lay Opinion Based on Hearsay

The lay-opinion rule itself states that lay opinions must be "rationally based on the perception of the witness."[80] Some see this as a bar against lay opinion testimony based on second-hand knowledge—on hearsay.[81] Most do not. There

---

78. In older federal cases and state cases that have adopted the federal rules generally, but not the 2000 amendment to Rule 703, the form of the balancing test to be applied is set out in Rule 403.

79. FED.R.EVID. 701. Part (c) was added by amendment, effective December 1, 2000.

80. FED.R.EVID. 701(a).

81. United States v. Kaplan, 490 F.3d 110, 119 (2d Cir. 2007); KW Plastics v. United States Can Co., 131 F.Supp.2d 1265, 1273 (M.D. Ala. 2001) ("'By restricting lay opinions to those based on the perception of the witness, the implication of Rule 701 is that lay opinion may not be based on hearsay.'") (citing cases); United States v. Garcia, 994 F.2d 1499, 1506 (10th Cir. 1993) ("In order for a lay opinion to be 'rationally based on the perception of the witness,' the witness must have 'first hand knowledge' of the events to which he is testifying."); Blakey v. Continental Airlines, 1997 U.S. Dist. LEXIS 22074, *13 (D.N.J. Sept.

are four reasons why this part of the rule does not mean that lay opinions must be based on firsthand knowledge.

First, lay persons routinely form opinions rationally based on their perceptions of second-hand knowledge. Employers (including employers who are not experts in personnel matters) make rational decisions about prospective employees based on what they hear from persons listed as recommendations. Homeowners make rational decisions about painters, carpenters, and plumbers based on what they hear from friends and neighbors. Prospective students often make decisions about which schools to attend, which are rationally based on second-, third-, and fourth hand information, and very little firsthand factual perception. Lay persons make all kinds of decisions that are rationally based on their perceptions of hearsay. Rule 701 states that lay opinions must be "rationally based on the perception of the witness." It seems clear that this "rationally based" language can include hearsay evidence that rationally forms part of the basis of a lay opinion.[82]

Second, hearsay evidence involves "the repetition of a statement made by someone else."[83] Opinion evidence involves taking in information, processing it, and making a judgment based on it. The hearsay objection applies to the former. The opinion objection applies to the latter. Regarding the latter, the question is not whether there was any hearsay that went into the formation of the opinion, but whether the opinion is rationally based on the perception of the witness. These are quite different questions.

Third, there really is no such thing as firsthand knowledge. Every opinion is based on second-hand knowledge. All of our knowledge is created by

---

9, 1997) (quoting C. WRIGHT & V. GOLD, FEDERAL PRACTICE AND PROCEDURE: EVIDENCE, § 6254 (1997)).

82.   Those items whose exclusion we especially question were statements by the plaintiff's expert witness and by Agfa's own board of directors regarding the quality of A-1. The principal grounds for exclusion was that these statements were based on what the expert and the directors had been told by customers and engineers and were therefore hearsay. We agree only up to "therefore." Business executives do not make assessments of a product's quality and marketability by inspecting the product at first hand. Their assessments are inferential, and as long as they are the sorts of inference that businessmen customarily draw they count as personal knowledge, not hearsay.

Agfa-Gevaert v. A.B. Dick Co., 879 F.2d 1518, 1523 (7th Cir. 1989) (citations omitted) (Posner, J.). In this regard, the Hawaii Supreme Court has stated something about expert witnesses that applies as well to lay opinions: "'[I]t is by assimilation of hearsay ... that expert opinions are in fact, for the most part, made[.]'" Lai v. St. Peter, 869 P.2d 1352, 1362 (Haw. 1994) (quoting Jefferis v. Marzano, 696 P.2d 1087, 1092 (Or. 1985)).

83. *Agfa-Gevaert*, 879 F.2d at 1523.

the "'assimilation of hearsay.'"[84] "He hid behind a lectern. How do I know it was a lectern, and not perhaps a podium? I looked it up in a book. The dictionary told me." There is no such thing as fact. Every thing is opinion. "She wore a green jacket. And how do I know what green is? Some told me. And if you do not agree with that and, instead, believe that green is an absolute, observable, primary fact, how do you account for the fact that my opinion of 'green' quite often differs from that of my wife?" ("Or was it chartreuse?") Was it really a boccie ball the witness saw flying through the air, or was it perhaps a croquet ball or a roundish cut of sirloin, and how does the witness know the difference between the boccie ball, the croquet ball, and the piece of meat? Should the witness be forced to testify that it was "a round or roundish body or mass: as … a spherical or ovoid body used in a game or sport?"[85]

The line between firsthand knowledge and second-hand knowledge may be "at best only one of degree," as Judge Learned Hand argued,[86] or it may not exist at all.[87] "All perception is inferential, and most knowledge social; since Kant we have known that there is no unmediated contact between nature and thought."[88]

Fourth, the line between lay witnesses and expert witnesses qualified by experience is anything but bright.[89] Historically the law did not allow opin-

---

84. Lai v. St. Peter, 869 P.2d 1352, 1362 (Haw. 1994) (quoting Jefferis v. Marzano, 696 P.2d 1087, 1092 (Or. 1985)).

"[M]ost knowledge is based, on information obtained from other people." Agfa- Gevaert, 879 F.2d at 1523. The most extreme example I have found is this: In The Queen v. Inhabitants of Lydeard St. Lawrence, 1 Gale & D. 191 (1841), a man was asked his birthplace. Lord Denman, C.J., sustained the objection that this evidence "is entirely hearsay." *See also* State v. Hyatt, 519 A.2d 612, 614 (Conn. Ct. App. 1987) ("Strictly speaking, when a person testifies regarding her age, that testimony is hearsay since one cannot exactly know her own age."). *See also* G. Michael Fenner, *Law Professor Reveals Shocking Truth About Hearsay*, 62 UMKC L. Rev. 1, 21–27 (1993).

85. Merrian Webster's Collegiate Dictionary (Zane Pub. Co. CD rom, 10th ed. 1997).

86. Central R.R. Co. v. Monahan, 11 F.2d 212, 214 (2d Cir. 1926).

87. James B. Thayer, A Preliminary Treatise on Evidence at the Common Law 524 (1898) ("In a sense all testimony to matter of fact is opinion evidence, *i.e.* it is a conclusion formed from phenomena and mental impressions.").

88. *Agfa-Gevaert*, 879 F.2d at 1523 (citations omitted). *See also* G. Michael Fenner, *Law Professor Reveals Shocking Truth About Hearsay*, 62 UMKC L. Rev. 1, 21–27 (1993).

89. *See, e.g.*, United States v. Hilario-Hilario, 529 F.3d 65, 72 (1st Cir. 2008)("[T]he same witness … may be qualified to 'provide both lay and expert testimony in a single case.'"); Farner v. Paccar, Inc., 562 F.2d 518, 529 (8th Cir. 1977) (a witness "who had been in the trucking business almost thirty years and who, at the time of trial, controlled twelve tractors, five of them Peterbilt tractors with air leaf suspension systems, could testify as to

ion evidence from lay witnesses. "At common law, witnesses not qualifying as experts were not permitted to [state opinions], but rather were required to limit their testimony to facts, those things 'they had seen, heard, felt, smelled, tasted, or done.'"[90] Because there is no such thing as firsthand knowledge, because it is so difficult to distinguish fact from opinion, the rule against lay opinion evidence began to break down.[91] This culminated in Rule 701, which puts to rest the rule against lay opinion. As the law began to take into account the difficulty with drawing the line between opinion and fact, it also began to notice the difficulty with drawing the line between expert witnesses and lay witnesses.[92] This rather slippery intersection between lay and expert witnesses is located at Rule 702, right where it states that a person may qualify as an expert based on "experience" or "knowledge" however obtained. When an experienced "lay witness" with an opinion based in part on inadmissible hearsay meets a judge who does not believe that lay witnesses can testify to opinions based on inadmissible hearsay, the witness can be re-presented as an experiential "expert witness."[93] (As noted in the advisory committee's

---

the simple use of the safety chains either as a lay witness speaking within his own knowledge and perception ... or as an expert qualified by knowledge, experience or skill").

90. Asplundh Mfg. Div. v. Benton Harbor Eng'g, 57 F.3d 1190, 1195 (3d Cir. 1995) (citation and paragraph break omitted), *superseded by statute*, Fed.R.Evid. 701, *as recognized in* Ex rel. Knoster v. Ford Motor Co., 200 Fed. Appx. 106, 111 n.3 (3d Cir. 2006).

91. *See Asplundh Mfg. Div.*, 57 F.3d at 1195 (the "rigid distinction between fact and opinion led to numerous appeals and pervasive criticism by commentators."); Teen-Ed, Inc. v. Kimball Int'l, Inc., 620 F.2d 399, 403 (3d Cir. 1980).

92. The difficulty with drawing this line is seen in the contrast between these cases. *See generally* the cases cited above in footnote 8 of this chapter, particularly United States v. Johnson, 28 F.3d 1487, 1492 (8th Cir. 1994); United States v. Johnson, 575 F.2d 1347, 1360 (5th Cir. 1978). *See additionally Asplundh Mfg. Div.*, 57 F.3d at 1199 (recognizing that lay opinion cases "have begun, in a subtle gradation, to permit lay witnesses to express their opinions in areas in which it would ordinarily be expected that only an expert qualified under Rule 702 could give such testimony") (citing cases); United States v. Westbrook, 896 F.2d 330, 335–36 (8th Cir. 1990) (two lay witnesses who were heavy amphetamine users were properly permitted to testify that a substance was amphetamine).

93. The other side of the discussion in the text *was* this: Just because a witness is offering an opinion that requires special knowledge or experience does not mean that the witness must be qualified as an expert. That is, there are situations where lay witnesses may state opinions that require special knowledge or experience. Just because an opinion involves special knowledge or experience does not mean that it may only be stated by one who is qualified as an expert witness. *Asplundh Mfg. Div.*, 57 F.3d at 1201. Part (c) of Rule 701 added in 2000. This amendment seems to have been designed to prevent future statements such as that just quoted from *Asplundh Manufacturing*. Fed.R.Evid. 701 advisory committee's note; Ex rel. Knoster v. Ford Motor Co., 200 Fed. Appx. 106, 111 n.3 (3d Cir. 2006).

note to Rule 701, because of the expert witness disclosure requirements in the federal rules of civil and criminal procedure, this must be done in advance of trial.[94])

Here, however, is the counter argument—the one that concludes that lay witnesses cannot testify to opinions that are based on second-hand knowledge. The main difference between expert and lay opinions is that the expert-opinion rules state that expert opinions may be based on "facts or data ... made known to the expert at or before the hearing" and upon facts or data that are not themselves admissible in evidence and the lay opinion rules do not.[95]

What then becomes of the argument that no opinion is based entirely on firsthand knowledge? What then becomes of the following truth? Witnesses constantly testify to lay opinions that are based on second-hand knowledge—however one interprets the rules, it is inescapable that they do so. Truth aside, how do we handle this problem under the Federal Rules of Evidence?

---

94. FED.R.EVID. 701 advisory committee's note (citing FED.R.CIV.P. 26; FED.R.CRIM.P. 16).

95. FED.R.EVID. 703. ("[O]nly an expert witness is permitted to rely upon hearsay evidence in formulating her opinions."). Ush Ventures v. Global Telesystems Group, Inc., 796 S.2d 7, 22 n.21 (Del. Super. Ct. 2000) ("[o]nly an expert witness is permitted to rely on hearsay evidence in formulating opinions.") (citing U.S. v. Elekwachi, 1997 U.S. App. LEXIS 6381, *9-10 (9th Cir. April 2, 1997)). *See also* FED.R.EVID. 701(c).

If Rule 701 is ambiguous about whether a law witness may testify to an opinion based on statements "made known to the expert at or before the hearing" or based on facts or data not themselves admissible in evidence, then perhaps the cannon of legislative construction *in pari materia* would lead to the conclusion that 701 does not allow such lay opinion evidence. *In pari materia* is the canon stating that "[w]hen a statute is ambiguous, its meaning may be determined in light of other statutes on the same subject matter." Wikipedia, http://en.wikipedia.org/wiki/Ejusdem_generis#Textual_canons (last visited Oct. 3, 2008). If we do not trust Wikipedia, Black's Law Dictionary defines this as the "canon of construction that ... inconsistencies in one statute may be resolved by looking at another statute on the same subject." Interpreting 701 (lay witnesses) in light of 703 (expert witnesses), we see that the latter specifically states that experts may testify to opinions based on "facts of data ... made known to the expert at or before the hearing" and on facts or data not themselves admissible in evidence, and the former does not. That it was left out of 701, the argument goes, must mean something and what it must mean is that the expert is allowed to testify to opinions formed on the basis of second-hand information and the lay witness is not.

Another canon of legislative construction, *expressio unius est exclusio alterius*, holds that "to express or include one thing implies the exclusion of the other, or the alternative." Black's Law Dictionary (8th ed. 2004). Rule 701 does not include the specific language found in Rule 703 that allows opinions based on evidence "made known to the expert at or before the hearing" and on facts or data not themselves admissible in evidence.

First, much lay opinion is based on hearsay but nobody notices it.[96] Second, if the opinion is based on admissible hearsay (as opposed to inadmissible hearsay) then courts tend to allow the opinion into evidence.[97] Third, much lay opinion is based on a combination of firsthand and second-hand knowledge. Courts tend to allow this kind of opinion, stating that the fact that there is second-hand knowledge in the mix goes to the weight of the evidence, not its admissibility.[98]

Fourth, like so much else in the law, the rules accommodate themselves to the real world. Is the opinion based on a shared common-knowledge? If so, then we consider it to be based on first-hand knowledge, even though that shared common-knowledge comes from others. My mother told me that a particular color was "chartreuse"; my wife's father told her that that same color was "green"; maybe someone else's mother or father told them that it was "yellow." What color was the room? In my opinion it was chartreuse, but that is based on what someone else told me about the particular color. Still, we consider a thing like this to be part of our shared common knowledge—even when someone else might disagree—and so we allow lay "opinion" on the matter.

"He was drunk." Once again, my definition of "drunk," passed down from my great aunt, is much different from that of my wife, passed down from her family. It is all based on a perception of the drunk or sober person in question, linked with what we were told as children and later about what it means to be drunk.

---

96. Over a half a century ago, addressing the testimony of expert witnesses based on second hand knowledge, Professor Maguire referred to "the diverse hearsay which escapes objection because it catches nobody's attention." JOHN MACARTHUR MAGUIRE, EVIDENCE: COMMON SENSE AND COMMON LAW, at 128 (1947).

97. *E.g.*, United States v. Leo, 941 F.2d 181, 193 (3d Cir. 1991) ("[L]ay opinion testimony can be based upon a witness's review of business records."); Burlington N. RR Co. v. Nebraska, 802 F.2d 994, 1004–05 (8th Cir. 1986) ("Personal knowledge or perception acquired through review of records prepared in the ordinary course of business … is a sufficient foundation for lay opinion testimony."); KW Plastics v. United States Can Co., 131 F.Supp.2d 1265, 1273 (M.D. Ala. 2001) ("[A] lay opinion 'based on hearsay is permitted under Rule 701 if the hearsay is admissible.'") (quoting 29 CHARLES ALAN WRIGHT & VICTOR JAMES GOLD, FEDERAL PRACTICE AND PROCEDURE §6254, at 130 (1997)); Neno v. Clinton, 772 A.2d 899, 904 (N.J. 2001) (lay opinion is not admissible when it is based primarily on *inadmissible* hearsay).

98. State v. Brainard, 968 S.W.2d 403, 412 (Tex. App. 1998) (an opinion based on both inadmissible hearsay and personal knowledge was admissible; the issue is not admissibility but weight), *aff'd in part, rev'd in part on other grounds,* Brainard v. State, 12 S.W.2d 6 (Tx. 1999). Regarding the weight of the evidence versus its admissibility, *see particularly* Chapter 3(I)(D), above. Regarding trustworthiness versus credibility, *see* Chapter 5(V)(E)(2), above; *see also* Chapter 3(VIII)(E)(4)(a), above.

May a witness testify that the person in question was drunk? Yes. Why? Because we believe we have a shared common knowledge regarding what it means to say one is drunk. We do not go to school to learn how to distinguish "drunk" from "not drunk" (though it did seem to be part of the curriculum where one of my children went to school).[99]

In this regard, we should be conscious of the difference between an opinion that simply vouches for someone else's opinion and an opinion that a witness has formed for him- or herself based on a combination of different pieces of information, some of which are themselves admissible in evidence and some not. "In my opinion, the driver was drunk," is not an admissible opinion if the answer to the next question would be, "I base my opinion on the fact that a bystander told me the driver was drunk." It is not rational to base such an opinion on such a shaky foundation, and it is not helpful to have the witness state such an opinion. Furthermore, the low probative value of such an opinion is substantially outweighed by the danger of unfair prejudice. There are plenty of reasons this opinion is not admissible but a general rule against lay opinions based on second-hand knowledge is not one of them.

Fifth, counsel may be able to make the problem go away by qualifying the witness as an expert.[100] Expertise can be based on experience. Many witnesses who might at first glance appear to be lay witnesses can be qualified as experts. Qualify the witness as an expert and the problem goes away.[101] (On the other

---

99. The advisory committee's note to Rule 701 refers to these things as "the 'prototypical example[s] of the type of evidence contemplated by the adoption of Rule 701 relat[ing] to the appearance of persons or things, identity, the manner of conduct, competency of a person, degrees of light or darkness, sound, size, weight, distance, and an endless number of items that cannot be described factually in words apart from inferences.' Asplundh Mfg. Div. v. Benton Harbor Eng'g, 57 F.3d 1190, 1196 (3d Cir. 1995)." FED.R.EVID. 701advisory committee's note.

100. The natural solution to this type of problem is to qualify your witness as an expert. Once the court recognizes your witness as such, the expert may then base his opinion on otherwise inadmissible hearsay. For example, in U.S. v. Elekwachi, 1997 U.S. App. LEXIS 6381 (9th Cir. April 2, 1997), the trial court allowed a lay witness to rely on otherwise inadmissible hearsay in formulating her opinion. On appeal, the 9th Circuit disagreed with the trial court, stating that "only an expert witness is permitted to rely upon hearsay evidence in formulating her opinions." Elekwachi, 1997 U.S. App. LEXIS 6381, at *3. The court noted that, had the prosecutor laid the proper foundation, the witness could have been qualified as an expert witness. As such, the expert's opinions based upon inadmissible hearsay would have been admissible.

101. In this regard, recall from above that this must be done in advance of trial in order to comply with the expert witness disclosure requirements in the rules of procedure. FED.R.EVID. 701 advisory committee's note (citing FED.R.CIV.P. 26; FED.R.CRIM.P. 16).

hand, sometimes the problem is that counsel is prevented from calling a witness as an expert because the court ordered the exchange of pretrial lists of expert witnesses and this person was not listed. Counsel's only recourse may be to call the witness as a lay witness.[102])

In the end, the problem, to me, is simply this: First, based on what the lay witness perceived, whether the perception was second hand or firsthand, does the trier of law believe that it was rational for this lay witness to form this opinion (and, of course, is the opinion helpful)?[103] Second, is the opinion inadmissible under Rule 403?[104] Can lay witnesses testify to opinions that are based on hearsay? Sometimes they can. A law witness may not simply repeat a statement made by someone else, but a lay witness may state an opinion that is partly based on things the witness was told by someone else. And it boils down to this: If lay witnesses cannot state opinions based on second-hand knowledge, then what opinions can they state? What is left?[105]

C. Situations in Which Counsel May Need to Have a Putative Expert Testify As a Lay Witness

Whether lay opinion may be based on inadmissible evidence, including inadmissible hearsay, is particularly important in the following three situations. First, sometimes there are times when counsel wants to call a witness as an expert but is not allowed to because the witness's name was not on a required

---

102. *See* part II(C) of this chapter, immediately below.

103. Fed.R.Evid. 701.

104. Fed.R.Evid. 403.

105. At least one court has come right out and said that "[l]ay witness opinion may be based on hearsay." Coker v. Burghardt, 833 S.W.2d 306, 310 (Tex. App. 1992). That said, the witness here did not state an opinion based on hearsay. The witness went to various automobile repair shops to familiarize himself with the cost of repairing his damaged car and, based on what he learned, testified to his opinion of the cost of repair. In this regard, the court stated that "[l]ay witness opinion may be based on hearsay." However, if a lay witness gets enough estimates of the cost of repair then this mass of estimates establishes the cost of repair without regard to whether any single estimate is somehow "true" or not. The amount of each estimate gathered by the witness is rationally based on the witness's perception and a critical mass of estimates is helpful to the determination of a fact in issue—the amount of damage done to the car. This was an opinion based on second-hand knowledge, but not one based on hearsay. In the alternative, this is not a lay opinion, but an expert opinion by one who became an expert through experience. Fed.R.Evid. 702 (a witness may be qualified as an expert by experience); Fed.R.Evid. 703 (expert opinion can be based on facts or data not themselves admissible in evidence so long as it is reasonable for this kind of expert to form this kind of opinion based on this kind of inadmissible evidence).

pretrial list of expert witnesses.[106] In this situation, counsel may be able to call the witness as a lay witness and get all she needs from the witness as a lay witness. Second, counsel may not be able to qualify the witness as an expert. Perhaps doing so is too expensive[107] or the trial court simply disagrees with counsel's presentation. Third, sometimes the appellate court holds that it was error for the trial court to have allowed a particular witness to have testified as an expert. Counsel can save the testimony—and perhaps the verdict—if the witness could have given the same testimony as a lay witness.[108]

---

106. Fed. R. Civ. Pro. 26(a). *E.g.*, Western Tenn. Ch. of Ass'd Builders & Contrs., Inc. v. City of Memphis, 219 F.R.D. 587, 589 (W.D. Tenn. 2004) ("'Defendant has not designated DJMA or any of its principles or employees as an expert. Because DJMA is not designated as an expert, DJMA is a lay witness....'").

107. *See* G. Michael Fenner, *The* Daubert *Handbook: The Case, Its Essential Dilemma, and Its Progeny*, 29 CREIGHTON L. REV. 939, 1031–32 (1996) (noting cases where it was argued that qualifying a witness as an expert is too expensive and beyond the financial ability of the party).

108. "[W]itnesses need not testify as experts simply because they are experts—the nature and object of their testimony determines whether the procedural protections of Rule 702 apply." United States v. Caballero, 277 F.3d 1235, 1247 (10th Cir. 2002). Rule 701(c) does not "preclude[] the use of lay opinion witnesses to testify to a topic merely because such testimony could also be introduced as expert testimony." United States v. Eiland, 71 Fed.R.Evid.Serv. (Callaghan) 455, n.8 (D.C.D.C. 2006). The rules "do[] not distinguish between expert and lay witnesses, but rather between expert and lay testimony." FED.R.EVID. 701 advisory committee's note (2000 amendment). *See, e.g.*, United States v. Munoz-Franco, 487 F.3d 24, 35 (1st Cir. 2007); United States v. Durham, 464 F.3d 976, 982 (9th Cir. 2006); United States v. Westbrook, 896 F.2d 330 (8th Cir. 1990) Teen-Ed, Inc. v. Kimball Int'l, Inc., 620 F.2d 399, 403 (3d Cir. 1980); Witherspoon v. Navajo Refining Co., 2005 U.S. Dist. LEXIS 46148, *3 (D. N.M. June 28, 2005).

Be aware, however, of the following statement made by the advisory committee in connection with a 2000 amendment to Rule 701: "Rule 701 has been amended to eliminate the risk that the reliability requirements set forth in Rule 702 [for expert witnesses] will be evaded through the simple expedient of proffering an expert in lay witness's clothing." FED.R.EVID. 701 advisory committee's note (2000 amendment). *See also* United States v. Garcia, 413 F.3d 201, 215-16 (2d Cir. 2005).

CHAPTER NINE

MISCELLANEOUS OTHER WAYS AROUND THE HEARSAY RULE

I. Trial to the Judge

Though the following is not a way to get hearsay into evidence, it is a way to get it in front of the trier of fact in a non-jury trial. In a trial to the judge it is not uncommon for the judge to respond to some objections with a version of the following: "I'll take it for what it's worth." This is the equivalent of saying: "I will go ahead and hear the evidence and, if in fact it is inadmissible, I will ignore it when making my decision and rendering my judgment."[1]

---

1. "In bench trials, judges routinely hear inadmissible evidence that they are presumed to ignore when making decisions." Harris v. Rivera, 454 U.S. 339, 346 (1981). *E.g.*, Stallings v. Bobby, 464 F.3d 576, 583–84 (6th Cir. 2006) (trial judges are presumed to consider only admissible evidence; where the judge affirmatively rules hearsay admissible, it strains the presumption; on the facts here it is unreasonable to assume that the trial judge did not consider the inadmissible hearsay); United States v. Cardenas, 9 F.3d 1139, 1154–55 (5th Cir. 1993) ("[A] trial judge is presumed to rest his verdict on admissible evidence and to disregard the inadmissible." In the joint trial of two defendants where hearsay is admissible against one and not the other the trial judge is presumed to have considered the evidence in support of the judgment against the one and not the other.); Shedd-Bartush Foods v. Commodity Credit Corp, 135 F.Supp. 78, 90 (D. Ill. 1955), *aff'd*, 231 F.2d 555 (7th Cir. 1956) ("While the depositions which the plaintiff took of its own officers are largely conclusionary, self-serving and hearsay, since the court is hearing the case without a jury their admission can do no harm. Accordingly, the depositions have been considered and given such weight as

The receipt of inadmissible evidence in a trial to the court is, of course, error — just as it would be in a trial to a jury.[2] The real question is whether it is reversible error. As a general rule, determining whether this error is reversible involves asking these two questions. First, was there sufficient admissible evidence to support the judgment? Here, the "No" answer is fatal: If there was not sufficient *admissible* evidence to support the judgment, then the receipt of the inadmissible evidence is reversible error. Second, did the inadmissible evidence induce the court to make an essential finding it would not otherwise have made? Here, the "Yes" answer is fatal: If the inadmissible evidence did induce the court to make an essential finding it would not otherwise have made, then the receipt of the inadmissible evidence is reversible error.[3]

II. Background Evidence

When out-of-court statements are offered as background evidence, offered to put admissible evidence in context, then they are not offered to prove the truth of the matter asserted and they are not hearsay.[4]

---

the nature of the testimony adduced warranted.")

And, of course, the truth is that judges often must first "hear" inadmissible evidence before they can decide that it is inadmissible.

2. The rules of evidence apply to courts. FED.R.EVID. 1101. That is, their application has nothing to do with whether the trial is to a judge or a jury. *Id.*

3. *E.g.,* Moore v. United States, 429 U.S. 20, 22–23 (1976) (per curiam) (trial judge relied on inadmissible hearsay in finding defendant guilty; remanded to court of appeals for determination of whether the error was harmless); Greater Kansas City Laborers Pension Fund v. Superior Gen. Contrs., 104 F.3d 1050, 1057 (8th Cir. 1997) (admission of inadmissible evidence in a bench trial is not grounds for reversal where there is sufficient admissible evidence to support the judgment and it does not appear that the inadmissible evidence induced the court to make essential findings it would not have made otherwise); Weber v. Weber, 512 N.W.2d 723, 728 (N.D. 1994) (generally it is not reversible error to have admitted inadmissible hearsay in a bench trial unless such evidence induced an improper finding). *See also* Harris v. Rivera, 454 U.S. 339, 346 (1981) (it is presumed that judges at bench trials ignore inadmissible evidence; author's note: if there is not sufficient admissible evidence to support the judgment, that presumption would be defeated).

4. United States v. Becker, 230 F.3d 1224, 1228 (10th Cir. 2000); United States v. Evans, 216 F.3d 80, 87 (D.C. Cir. 2000) ("Sometimes courts excuse the use of hearsay evidence for background purposes where the evidence is on an uncontroverted matter, where hearsay is the most efficient means of transmitting it, and where there is little chance of prejudice to the defendant"; to admit out-of-court statements as background evidence, background

The prosecutor, for example, need not pretend that a police officer just happened to stumble upon a scene where criminal activity was taking place. Take a case where an informant told an officer something that led the officer to go to a scene where he or she made the arrest that led to the trial at bar. If the officer tells the jury what the informant said and this out-of-court statement is offered as background evidence, to explain why the officer was at the scene, then the statement is not hearsay: It is not offered to prove the truth of the matter asserted but just to show the effect it had on the officer who heard it.[5]

Following that example, evidence of the origin of the investigation must be relevant. If the origin of the investigation is not relevant, then this non-hearsay use of the evidence is irrelevant and inadmissible.[6] If this evidence is admissible nonhearsay to one issue, *i.e.*, the origin of the investigation, and inadmissible hearsay to another issue, *e.g.*, whether the defendant committed the criminal act on trial, then turn to Rule 403 to decide if the evidence is admissible.[7]

---

must be relevant); United States v. Wilson, 107 F.3d 774, 780 (10th Cir. 1997) ("[T]estimony which is not offered to prove the truth of an out-of-court statement, but is offered instead for relevant context or background is not considered hearsay.").

5. *United States v. Evans, supra*; United States v. Running Horse, 175 F.3d 635, 638 (8th Cir. 1999) ("[T]he trial court did not admit the testimony for the truth of the matter asserted ... but ... as background information to assist the jury in understanding the origin of the investigation of [defendant]."); *United States v. Wilson, supra*; United States v. Love, 767 F.2d 1052, 1063 (4th Cir. 1985); United States v. Mancillas, 580 F.2d 1301, 1309–10 (7th Cir. 1978). Regarding origin-of-the-investigation evidence, see generally the discussion and cases in part II(D) of Chapter 8.

6. *United States v. Evans, supra*; *United States v. Wilson, supra*; *United States v. Mancillas, supra*.

7. *United States v. Mancillas, supra*, points out that even if the evidence cannot be received as substantive evidence, it can be offered as background evidence, "and it is by the offer that Rule 801(c) defines hearsay." When the statement is offered as background evidence, then the question is one of relevance and Rule 403 — is its probative value as origin-of-the-investigation evidence substantially outweighed by the danger that the jury will use the evidence for the purpose for which it is inadmissible — and not hearsay. (Since it is inadmissible to the other issue, its use to that issue is not just prejudicial, but unfairly prejudicial.) This is the subject of chapter 12, below. See also Becker, 230 F.3d at 1231 (the out-of-court statement was admissible nonhearsay evidence of the of the investigation and it was inadmissible hearsay evidence of the presence of drugs in the defendant's house; admission was error; in light of "the wealth of evidence presented by the government" and the limiting instruction given by the trial court, the error was harmless).

III. The Rule of Completeness as a Hearsay "Exception"

Rule 106, popularly known as the Rule of Completeness, states:

> When a writing or recorded statement or part thereof is introduced by a party, an adverse party may require the introduction at that time of any other part or any other writing or recorded statement which ought in fairness to be considered contemporaneously with it.[8]

The prevailing view seems to be that Rule 106 can provide a way around the exclusionary rules—including the hearsay rule. It can, in effect, serve as an exception to the hearsay rule. " ... Rule 106 can serve its proper function only if the trial court from time to time is prepared to permit the introduction of some otherwise inadmissible evidence."[9] The rule of completeness is only avail-

---

8. FED.R.EVID. 106 (titled "Remainder of or Related Writings or Recorded Statements").

9. United States v. Houlihan, 92 F.3d 1271, 1283 (1st Cir. 1996). *Accord* United States v. Bucci, 525 F.3d 116, 133 (1st Cir. 2008) ("[O]ur case law unambiguously establishes that the rule of completeness may be invoked to facilitate the introduction of otherwise inadmissible evidence.") (citing cases from the circuit and acknowledging that other circuits have held differently); United States v. Sutton, 801 F.2d 1346, 1368 (D.C. Cir. 1986) (discussing point and citing authorities); Meeker v. Vitt, 2006 U.S.Dist. LEXIS 15009, *10–11 (N.D. Ohio March 31, 2006) (citing United States v. Gallagher, 57 Fed. Appx. 622 (6th Cir. 2003) (unpublished disposition), as follows: "'Portions of a statement admitted under Rule 106 ... do not impact on the hearsay rule, because in effect, they are not offered for the truth. Their purpose ... is to put statements already admitted into the proper context.'").

But see United States v. Lentz, 524 F.3d 501, 526 (4th Cir. 2008) ("Rule 106 does not ... 'render admissible the evidence ... otherwise inadmissible under the hearsay rules.'") (*Lentz* quotes United States v. Wilkerson, 84 F.3d 692, 696 (4th Cir. 1996); *Wilkerson* makes the quoted statement about all hearsay statements and supports it with a citation to a case that only applies to "unrelated" hearsay statements—hearsay statements that would not fit under Rule 106 in the first place); United States v. Mitchell, 502 F.3d 931, 965 n.9 (9th Cir. 2007) (*Mitchell* cites United States v. Ortega, 203 F.3d 675 (9th Cir. 2000), which notes that Rule 106 only applies to written and recorded statements and, therefore, does not apply to the unrecorded oral statement at issue there and that even if Rule 106 applied it was still proper to exclude the statements because the "statements would still have constituted inadmissible hearsay." *Id.* at 682. *Ortega* does not state that these statements could not be admitted under Rule 106, but only that Rule 106 did not apply and, if it had, it would have been proper to exclude them.)

The case that plainly states that Rule 106 is not a vehicle for the admission of otherwise inadmissible hearsay is United States v. Collicott, 92 F.3d 973 (9th Cir. 1996). Because the statements in question "do not fall within an exception to the hearsay rule, they are inadmissible, regardless of Rule 106." *Id.* at 983. Also, "no writing or recorded statement was introduced by a party" and the completing statement did not correct a misleading impression from a statement already admitted. *Id.* In *Collicott*, counsel wanted to rehabilitate a wit-

able as a response to evidence introduced by an opponent.[10] "[It] does not allow a party to introduce otherwise inadmissible hearsay on the coattails of its own or stipulated evidence."[11] The rule only applies when the statement in question is either part of a larger statement, another part of which has already been admitted, or part of a statement related to one already admitted. The rule only applies when the statement in question is either written or recorded.[12]

---

ness who had been impeached with a prior inconsistent statement by introducing the rest of the prior statement. The statement was never offered to prove the truth of the matter asserted but just to show that the statement had been made; it was not hearsay in the first place. *Collicott*'s pronouncement on Rule 106 and the hearsay rule is dicta.

There are other cases that seem at first glance to stand for the proposition that otherwise inadmissible hearsay cannot be admitted under Rule 106. On closer examination, however, most really do not. One states that "'... Rule 106 ...' does not 'empower a court to admit *unrelated* hearsay ... [that] does not come within a defined hearsay exception.'" United States v. Ramos-Caraballo, 375 F.3d 797, 803 (8th Cir. 2004) (emphasis added) (citing United States v. Woolbright, 831 F.2d 1390, 1395 (8th Cir. 1987)). *Accord* United States v. Edwards, 159 F.3d 1117, 1127 n.6 (8th Cir. 1998). Rule 106, however, does not authorize the receipt of any *unrelated* evidence, hearsay or not.

Others affirm, stating that Rule 106 "does not *compel* admission of otherwise inadmissible hearsay evidence." United States Football League v. National Football League, 842 F.2d 1335, 1375–76 (2d Cir. 1988) (emphasis added). Many of the cases stating that it was not error to exclude evidence offered under Rule 106, are not stating that no other course would have been proper, but simply that keeping the evidence out was not an abuse of discretion.

Still others simply state the proposition and cite cases that do not support the proposition. United States v. Pendas-Martinez, 845 F.2d 938, 944 & n.10 (11th Cir. 1988), states that the rule in some circuits is that "Rule 106 addresses only an order of proof problem and does not make admissible what is otherwise inadmissible," and cites two cases, neither of which supports such a broad statement: The first, United States v. Burreson, 643 F.2d 1344, 1349 (9th Cir. 1981), upholds the exclusion of evidence offered under Rule 106 because it was irrelevant and inadmissible hearsay. Rule 106 applies to evidence that "ought in fairness to be considered contemporaneously"; all evidence that "ought in fairness to be considered contemporaneously" is relevant; Rule 106 does not apply to irrelevant evidence. The second, United States v. Costner, 684 F.2d 370, 373 (6th Cir. 1982), states that Rule 106 does not "make something admissible that should be excluded," (whatever exactly that means).

See also Echo Acceptance Corp. v. Household Retail Servs., 267 F.3d 1068, 1089 n.12 (10th Cir. 2001) ("[I]t is not clear whether the rule [of completeness] trumps the prohibition on hearsay statements." (citing Beech Aircraft Corp. v. Rainey, 488 U.S. 153, 178 n.18 (1988), as "avoiding the question")).

10. "When a writing or recorded statement or part thereof is introduced by a party, *an adverse party* may [take advantage of the rule of completeness]." FED.R.EVID. 106 (emphasis added).

11. *Echo Acceptance Corp.*, 267 F.3d at 1089.

12. FED.R.EVID. 106. United States v. Ortega, 203 F.3d 675, 682 (9th Cir. 2000); United States v. Bigelow, 914 F.2d 966, 972 (7th Cir. 1990) (responding to appellant's argument

Rule 106 can be a way for attorneys to use their opponents' evidence—to use their opponents' choice of what to introduce—as a way of getting in their own otherwise inadmissible evidence.[13]

IV. Judicial Notice

There is a famous story involving Abraham Lincoln as a trial lawyer. He was defending a man charged with murder. An eyewitness testified that he had seen Lincoln's client strike the fatal blow. He claimed to have seen the whole thing "by the light of a moon nearly overhead."[14] Lincoln "had sent out for an almanac."[15] When produced, it said that on the night in question the moon had nearly set by the time in question, so that the witness "couldn't have had much light from the sky ... to see by."[16] Lincoln offered and the judge received this evidence from the almanac. Lincoln's client was acquitted. What this judge really did was to take judicial notice of the truth of facts contained in an out-of-court statement. He took judicial notice of the accuracy of the facts contained in the almanac. Lincoln offered and the judge accepted judicial notice as a way around the hearsay rule.[17]

There are two kinds of judicial notice. One, called "resort to sources" judicial notice, requires the following: "A judicially noticed fact must be one not

---

that he should have been allowed to admit other parts of an oral statement under Rule 106, the court stated, "This rule, however, applies only to *written and recorded materials*.") (emphasis in original).

13. *See also* the Use Note to Rule 801(d)(1)(B) in part II(B) of Chapter 2, discussing the fact that impeaching a witness with parts of a statement may open the door for the admissibility of other parts of the same statement as nonhearsay substantive evidence of the facts declared.

Rule 106 is also used—improperly so, but nonetheless used—to justify ordering the parties in bankruptcy court to submit direct evidence in the form of affidavits. This is discussed at part V of this chapter, below.

14. Carl Sandburg, Abraham Lincoln The Prairie Years 55 (1926).

15. *Id.* at 56.

16. *Id.* at 57.

17. It is possible that the judge received this evidence under an exception to the hearsay rule, rather than taking judicial notice of the fact from the almanac; the record is not clear. Sometimes judicial notice and one or more exception to the hearsay rule both apply to the same evidence. For example, the National Automobile Dealers Association (NADA) guide to automobile prices, commonly called the "Blue Book," is admissible in two ways. First, the court may take judicial notice of the Blue Book. *E.g.*, In re Wierschem, 152 B.R. 345, 347 (Bankr. M.D. Fla. 1993). Second, the Blue Book fits under the market reports and compilations exception to the hearsay rule, Fed.R.Evid. 803(17). *E.g.*, In re Roberts, 210 B.R. 325, 330 (Bankr. N.D. Iowa 1997).

subject to reasonable dispute in that it is ... capable of accurate and ready determination by resort to sources whose accuracy cannot reasonably be questioned."[18] All "resort to sources" judicial notice is a way around the hearsay rule. It is a way to get an out-of-court statement into evidence to prove the truth of the facts asserted. Sometimes judicial notice does more than just get facts into evidence, but it always does at least that much, and every time it gets a fact into evidence to prove the truth of the fact, it is a way around the hearsay rule.[19]

---

18. FED.R.EVID. 201.

19. Ieradi v. Mylan Labs., Inc., 230 F.3d 594, 600 (3rd Cir. 2000) (judicial notice of opening and closing stock prices (*see also* FED.R.EVID. 803(17), the hearsay exception for market reports and commercial publications)); Long Trusts v. Atlantic Richfield Co., 893 S.W.2d 686, 688 (Tex. App. 1995) (appellant argued that the trial court committed error by basing part of the damage award on inadmissible hearsay; the court of appeals noted that the trial court took judicial notice of the fact in question and stated "[e]vidence that is judicially noticed does not constitute hearsay"). *But see* RWB Newton Assocs. v. Gunn, 541 A.2d 280 (N.J. Super. Ct. App. Div. 1988), where the court said that the judicial notice "rules may not be used to circumvent the rule against hearsay and thereby deprive a party of the right of cross-examination on a contested material issue of fact." *Id.* at 711. But of course the judicial notice rules may be used to do just that. That, in fact, is the point of the rules. What the appellate court should have said was that the accuracy of the sources resorted to here could reasonably be questioned and judicial notice was improper in this case.

On the other hand, there may still be hearsay problems in a judicial notice situation. A court may take judicial notice of an order or a judgment entered by another court, for example, but that does not mean it can take judicial notice of everything said in the order or opinion, including the repetition of hearsay allegations. It may be proper to take judicial notice of the fact that the order or judgment was issued because the accuracy of the order or judgment is "capable of accurate and ready determination by resort to sources whose accuracy cannot reasonably be questioned." FED.R.EVID. 201(b)(2). It may not be proper to take judicial notice of all of the facts stated within the order or opinion because the accuracy of every fact stated in the order or opinion is not "capable of accurate and ready determination by resort to sources whose accuracy cannot reasonably be questioned." FED.R.EVID. 201(b)(2). *Accord, e.g.,* Liberty Mut. Ins. Co. v. Rotches Pork Packers, Inc., 969 F.2d 1384, 1388–89 (2d Cir.1992) ("A court may take judicial notice of a document filed in another court 'not for the truth of the matters asserted in the other litigation, but rather to establish the fact of such litigation and related filings.'") (citing Kramer v. Time Warner Inc. 937 F.2d 767, 774 (2d Cir. 1991); United States v. New-Form Mfg. Co., 277 F.Supp. 2d 1313, 1325 n.14 (Ct. Int'l Trade 2003) ("[J]udicial notice of a sister court's records is taken for the limited purpose of recognizing that court's judicial acts. It does not recognize the sister court's findings of fact as true."); Ryan v. Commissioner, T.C. Memo 1998-331 (T.C. 1998).

In one case, United States v. Cowley, 720 F.2d 1037 (9th Cir. 1983), the court held that a postmark is hearsay when offered to prove the place from which the letter was mailed. "Although a machine affixes the mark, a postal official is responsible for setting the ma-

V. Trial by Affidavit in Bankruptcy Court

In bankruptcy courts across the land, there is a huge and largely undefended hearsay exception. It is common practice in bankruptcy court to receive evidence via affidavit. The rules vary from one district to the next, but typically provide that the court can order a witness's direct testimony to be entered into evidence via affidavit, even over objection by opposing counsel, so long as the witness is available for cross-examination by opposing counsel and redirect by offering counsel.[20]

The affidavit is, of course, an out-of-court statement. The kind of affidavit under discussion here is offered to prove the truth of the matter asserted.[21] It most certainly is hearsay.[22] Where the parties agree to submit testimony by affidavit, there is no error. Where evidence is submitted via affidavit and without objection, there is no reviewable error.[23] In bankruptcy court, however, it goes farther than this: Parties can be ordered to submit a witness's evidence via affidavit even over a timely and specific hearsay objection, and the judge can base the judgment on that affidavit. And bankruptcy judges typically do just that.

---

chine....." *Id.* at 1044. The court also found that a postmark would fit under the residual exception, but not in this case because the proponent did not provide the requisite pretrial notice. *Id.* at 1045. (Regarding pretrial notice and the residual exception, *see* Chapter 5(V)(C)). Assuming that a postmark is hearsay—and it may not be; see Chapter 1(II)(C)(1)—if counsel could produce the postmarked envelope, counsel could get the court to take judicial notice of the place from which the letter was mailed. The theory here is that a postmark is not reasonably subject to question.

20. If the witness is not available, then the affidavit is not admissible unless it fits into one of the definitional exclusions or exceptions to the hearsay rule. *E.g., Roberts*, 210 B.R. at 329.

21. It is offered to establish, through its truth, the essential elements of the party's case.

22. *E.g.,* Spivey v. United States, 912 F.2d 80 (4th Cir. 1990).

The affidavit offered to prove the truth of the assertions therein is hearsay, unless of course it is definitionally excluded by one of the provisions of part (d) of Rule 801. Rule 801(d), however, will not often, if ever, apply in the situation under discussion. An affidavit is not hearsay under 801(d), for example, if the affiant is a party and the affidavit is offered against the affiant. This is not be the case here because even if the affiant is a party, the affidavit is being offered by the party, in lieu of direct examination, and not against the party. For a second example, an affidavit is not hearsay if it is consistent with the affiant's testimony and offered to rebut an express or implied charge against the affiant of recent fabrication or improper influence or motive. This too will not be the case here because the affidavit under discussion is being used in lieu of testimony, not to rehabilitate testimony.

23. Absent, of course, plain error affecting substantial rights of a party. Fed.R.Evid. 103(d).

This is a clear violation of the hearsay rule, but it happens every day. This is a way around the hearsay rule in bankruptcy court. More than that, however, should this practice—this "rule"—continue to develop along current lines, should it be better defended or perhaps even affirmed by the Supreme Court, then there does not seem to be any logical reason this procedure cannot be extended to any bench trial. There is no reason for treating a trial to a bankruptcy judge any differently than a trial to any other federal judge—not so long as the same evidentiary rules apply in the courtroom of each.[24]

This issue is discussed at length elsewhere.[25]

VI. Opening Statements and the Hearsay Rule

At least one federal circuit court of appeals[26] and one state supreme court[27] have said that remarks during opening statements are not and cannot be hearsay.[28] The Sixth Circuit has defined hearsay as "testimony 'offered in evidence to prove the truth of the matter asserted,'"[29] noted that "opening statements are not evidence," and concluded: "Thus, by definition, the prosecutor's remarks [during opening statement] were not hearsay." In the Sixth Circuit, then, it seems that the hearsay rule does not apply during opening statement.[30]

---

24. "These rules apply to … United States bankruptcy judges…." FED.R.EVID. 1101.

25. G. Michael Fenner, *The Forced Use of Inadmissible Hearsay Evidence in Bankruptcy Court*, 8 AM. BANKR. INST. L. J. 453 (2000).

26. United States v. Levy, 904 F.2d 1026, 1030 (6th Cir. 1990).

27. Kroth v. Commonwealth, 737 S.W.2d 680, 681 (Ky. 1987) (opening statement not evidence). *Accord* Lillard v. State, 994 S.W.2d 747, 752 n.7 (Tex. App. 1999) ("The opening statement is not evidence; therefore, a hearsay objection is not applicable.");

28. *See additionally,* State v. Brooks, 618 S.W.2d 22, 24 (Mo. 1981) (limiting its ruling to statements that are "arguably admissible and … made in good faith with a reasonable expectation the evidence will be produced.").

29. *Levy*, 904 F.2d at 1030 (quoting FED.R.EVID. 801(c)).

30. The court went on to note that the defense had not made a contemporaneous objection, but the court's statement stands: "By definition, … remarks [during opening statement are] not hearsay." *Levy*, 904 F.2d at 1030. There are many appellate opinions that dispose of the claim that opposing counsel committed error by mentioning inadmissible hearsay during the opening statement by pointing out there was no objection during the opening statement—no timely objection.

On the other hand, "even if the statements were not hearsay, during opening statements prosecutors should avoid referring to evidence that is even of questionable admissibility." United States v. Adams, 74 F.3d 1093, 1097 (11th Cir. 1996). *See also* Hall v. Forest River, Inc., 2007 U.S. Dist. LEXIS 49376, *18 (N.D. Ind. July 5, 2007) ("'It is unethical to use an opening statement to discuss evidence where there is no reasonable basis for admissibil-

Under this kind, there are two other ways to deal with opening-statement mention of inadmissible hearsay. First, a Rule 403 objection may work: Discussion of inadmissible evidence is per se "unfair prejudice" and if it is inadmissible then it has no legitimate probative value. Under the Sixth Circuit's logic, however, this objection should not work any better than a hearsay objection: Rule 403 (like the hearsay rule) applies to the exclusion of "evidence,"[31] and the Sixth Circuit held that "opening statements are not evidence."[32]

Second, if counsel discusses inadmissible hearsay in an opening statement, opposing counsel may have a "good faith basis" objection. During the opening statement, attorneys tell the trier of fact what they expect the evidence will show. Counsel must have a good faith basis for believing that they will be able to introduce evidence of those facts during the trial. If it is clear that the evidence is inadmissible hearsay, then, the argument runs, there is no good faith basis.[33] This gets around the problem some courts find in the fact that "open-

---

ity.' ") (quoting Modern Trial Advocacy: Analysis and Practice, at 419 (2d ed. 1997).

When hearsay evidence is erroneously admitted during the trial, thing the appellate court will consider in deciding whether the error was harmless or reversible is whether the error or admission was compounded by the way the evidence was used during the opening statement, the closing argument, or both. *E.g.,* Peterkin v. Horn, 176 F.Supp. 2d 342, 362 (E.D. Pa. 2001); Oliver v. State, 783 A.2d 124, 124 (Del. 2001) ("[T]he prosecutor did not compound the problem by including the hearsay in his opening statement"); Blecha v. People, 962 P.2d 931, 943 (Colo. 1998) (prosecutor did not argue the inadmissible hearsay in opening statement, closing argument, or rebuttal argument; this suggests the statements "were of minimal importance to the prosecution's case"); People v. Reeves, 648 N.E.2d 278, 282 (Ill. App. Ct. 1995).

See United States v. Brassard, 212 F.3d 54, 57 (1st Cir. 2000) (prosecutor improperly referred to hearsay in the opening statement; the error was harmless as the offending remark was brief, the judge offered curative instruction, and it is likely that the remark, coming when it did, had little effect); Cargill v. Turpin, 120 F.3d 1366, 1381 (11th Cir. 1997) (mention of inadmissible hearsay during the opening and the closing was improper; however, "defense counsel failed to object … [,] both the prosecutor and defense counsel clearly and repeatedly stated that their opening and closing remarks did not constitute evidence[, and] … the trial court gave distinct instructions" that statements during the opening and closing were not evidence); State v. Allred, 505 S.E.2d 153, 156 (N.C. Ct. App. 1998) (counsel may not refer to inadmissible evidence during opening statement).

31. The rule provides that in certain situations "evidence may be excluded." Fed.R.Evid. 403.

32. *Levy,* 904 F.2d at1030.

33. State v. Smallwood, 594 N.W.2d 144, 150 (Minn. 1999) ("improper … to refer to evidence in an opening statement without a good-faith basis for believing the evidence is admissible."); Commonwealth v. Murray, 496 N.E.2d 179, 180 (Mass. App. Ct. 1986) ("Opening statements … are limited to outlining what counsel expects to prove or support

ing statements are not evidence." The "good faith basis" objection is not an objection to evidence, but an objection to counsel's bringing something up without a good faith basis for believing that he or she will be able to admit evidence of the thing in question.

_____

by relevant evidence. That expectation must have support in counsel's good faith belief that relevant evidence is admissible and available. Indeed, it is unprofessional conduct for defense counsel to allude to evidence in the absence of a reasonable, good faith basis that the evidence will be tendered.") (citations omitted); *Brooks*, 618 S.W.2d at 24 (counsel can use hearsay in opening if counsel has a good faith basis for believing it will be "produced" during trial).

CHAPTER TEN

HAVING FOUND ONE WAY AROUND THE HEARSAY RULE, KEEP LOOKING FOR OTHERS

I. Stack Up the Exceptions
II. Put on Evidence of All of the Foundational Elements for Each Exception in the Pile
III. Stacking Up the Exceptions, of Course, Does Not Always Work

I. Stack Up the Exceptions

Stack up the exceptions. *Ricciardi v. Children's Hospital Medical Center*[1] was a medical malpractice action. The plaintiff's medical chart contained a notation that there had been an accident during his surgery. It actually used the word accident. And this was the plaintiff's only evidence of negligence. If this notation on the chart is not admissible, not only does the plaintiff lose the verdict, the plaintiff loses the motion to dismiss at the conclusion of plaintiff's evidence. The physician who made the entry had no personal knowledge of the event and could not recall the source of his information. He knew nothing and he did not know anyone who did know anything.

Plaintiff offered the notation on the medical chart and he argued six ways to get the notation around the hearsay rule: (1) a nonhearsay adoptive admission;[2] (2) the exception for reports for purposes of medical diagnosis or treatment;[3] (3) the record of a regularly conducted activity exception;[4] (4) the

---

1. 811 F.2d 18 (1st Cir. 1987).
2. *See* Chapter 2(III)(E), above.
3. *See* Chapter 3(V), above.
4. *See* Chapter 3(VII), above.

471

recorded recollection exception;[5] (5) the residual exception;[6] and, finally, (6) the plaintiff hired an expert, had the expert look at the medical chart, and had the expert form an opinion based in part on what he saw on the chart.[7]

Here is the point: Stack up the exceptions. Or, at least this: just because you seem to have one good way around the bar of the hearsay rule, do not stop looking for others—especially if the evidence is important. One of the biggest problems students and young lawyers make is that they come up with one good idea and they let it go at that. Here are six good reasons that is a bad idea— six really good reasons to continue the search.

■ First, keep thinking, in case your first impression is not correct.[8] If you do not stack up the exceptions, you might miss the only exception or exclusion that truly does apply and instead rely on an exception that does not work. In *State v. Canady*,[9] the defendant was convicted of beating up his girlfriend. The police were called to the scene and found the victim injured, primarily about the face. The police called an ambulance, the victim was taken to the hospital, and the police followed and interviewed her there. Among other things, the police had a form to be filled out by victims of domestic abuse and the officer asked the victim the questions off of the form and wrote down her oral responses. The officer was allowed to testify as to what the victim said to him in his interview of her. The trial court allowed this under the state of mind exception. The prosecutor was allowed to introduce into evidence the police domestic-violence form. The trial court allowed this under the public records

---

5. *See* Chapter 3(VI), above.
6. *See* Chapter 5, above.
7. *See* Chapter 8, above.
8. *See, e.g.*, United States v. Firishchak, 468 F.3d 1015, 1022 (7th Cir. 2006) ("[T]he ancient documents rule and the business records exception are independent grounds for determining admissibility. Because the documents in question were admissible under the ancient documents rule, whether they were kept in the ordinary course of … business is irrelevant."); United States v. Samaniego, 345 F.3d 1280, 1283 (11th Cir. 2003) ("Our conclusion that [the] apology was not properly admitted under [the state of mind exception in Rule 803] does not end the matter." Though the trial court did not address alternative grounds for admissibility, the statement is admissible under the statement against interest exception in Rule 804. Though for the wrong reason, the trial court reached the right result and is affirmed); Parker v. Reda, 327 F.3d 211, 214 (2nd Cir. 2003) (evidence that lacked sufficient trustworthiness for admission as a business record was nonetheless admissible as past recollection recorded; each exception is "based on different rationales, and there is nothing inherently inconsistent about the admission, under [one], of evidence ruled inadmissible under [another]").
9. 911 P.2d 104 (Haw. Ct. App. 1996).

and reports exception. The appellate court found neither of these exceptions applicable—and quite rightly so. The conviction was reversed—perhaps not quite rightly so.[10]

No one ever argued the one exception that might have worked: the excited utterance exception. The victim had suffered a beating, surely an exciting event. She had been rushed to the hospital by ambulance and interviewed there. It seems likely from the record that she was still under the stress of the excitement of the beating. The out-of-court statements all concerned the startling event.

The appellate court vacated the judgment of conviction and remanded for a new trial. Though there could have been good reasons for not using the excited utterance exception, reasons not reflected in the opinion, it is also quite possible that the guilty verdict was lost solely for want of thinking it through to the correct exception.[11]

■ Second, keep thinking, in case your first argument is not the best one. Perhaps it is not the simplest solution, the easiest argument to make, the one a judge will most easily understand. Keep thinking in case there is a better solution.[12]

If you stop with the first exception that comes to mind, you might miss an exception that is much easier to establish. In *Reichhold Chemicals, Inc. v. Textron, Inc.*,[13] for example, the plaintiff offered into evidence writings produced by employees of the defendant in a "'house organ which detailed the activities of various plants and people of [the defendant corporation].'"[14] These docu-

---

10. As discussed below in this chapter, if the trial court makes the right ruling the appellate court will affirm even if the trial court's reasoning is wrong.

11. The point here is that if you do not stack up the exceptions and exclusions, then, while relying on exceptions that do not work, you might miss the one that does work. This almost happened in United States v. Ferber, 966 F.Supp. 90 (D. Mass. 1997). The prosecution argued that a statement was admissible both as a record of a regularly conducted activity, FED.R.EVID. 803(6), and as an excited utterance, FED.R.EVID. 803(2). The judge ruled against the government. "By the time this ruling was made, however, the government had come up with yet a third ground for admission," *id.* at 99, the present sense impression exception, FED.R.EVID. 803(1). In the nick of time, the prosecution argued the present sense impression exception and the judge admitted the statement.

12. *E.g., Firishchak,* 468 F.3d at 1022 (arguing that documents were not admissible under the business records exception, counsel argued there was insufficient evidence they were kept in the regular course of business; noting they were also offered under the ancient documents exception, the court concluded that, "[b]ecause the documents ... were admissible [as] ancient documents..., whether they were kept in the ordinary course of ... business is irrelevant.").

13. 888 F.Supp. 1116 (N.D. Fla. 1995).

14. *Id.* at 1130 n.15 (quoting witness's deposition).

ments were kept in the ordinary course of business and the first exception that comes to mind may be the exception for records of a regularly conducted activity.[15] In this particular case, however, it may be burdensome (or even impossible) to establish the other foundational elements of this exception. The writings were found in company files, and were dated from 1942, 1944, and 1945. They are old enough and they are authentic. With no trouble at all, they fit under the ancient documents exception.[16]

■ Third, keep thinking because there may be admissibility problems lurking behind your hearsay problem that are not immediately apparent and are not solved by your first argument. if you stop looking too soon, you might be stuck with a double hearsay problem that could have, but has not, been solved. In *Reichhold Chemicals*,[17] discussed just above, though the court did not mention it, it is also likely that these writings were statements by an agent of a party, offered against the party, and, therefore, were not hearsay in the first place.[18] This is the advantage of thinking this problem through to this next step: It is quite likely that these writings—" 'house organ which detailed the activities of various plants and people of U.S.I. Corp' "—were not based on the firsthand knowledge of whomever wrote them; it is quite likely that these writings presented multiple-level hearsay problems. In some courts, the definitional exclusion for admissions covers any and all preceding levels of hearsay.[19] The advantage of thinking this problem through to this definitional exclusion is that it may be a way to get around Rule 805 hearsay-within-hearsay problems. In any event, whether this exclusion applies in this case or not, with the addition of this nonhearsay-admission argument, there are now three good arguments around the hearsay objection.

■ Fourth, keep thinking because generally six good ideas are better than one. It is more difficult to ignore six good reasons than it to ignore just one. This

---

15. FED.R.EVID. 803(6), discussed above at Chapter 3(VII).

16. FED.R.EVID. 803(16), discussed above at Chapter 3(XI). "They may be admissible under the business records exception to the hearsay rule. F.R.E. 803(6). In any event, there is no question as to the authenticity of the documents and they are all at least fifty years old, so as to be admissible under the ancient documents exception. F.R.E. 803(16)." *Reichold Chemicals*, 888 F.Supp. at 1130 n.15 (citation omitted). They may also be nonhearsay admissions. This is discussed in the text following this footnote.

17. 888 F.Supp. 1116 (N.D. Fla. 1995).

18. FED.R.EVID. 801(d)(2)(D), discussed above at Chapter 2(III)(C). They are statements of employees of a party, made while they were employees of the party, offered against that party. If the statements were about matters within the scope of their employment—and it seems that they may have been—then they are nonhearsay Rule 801(d)(2)(D) admissions.

19. *See* Chapter 2(III)(G).

is true in any human endeavor, not just ruling on evidentiary objections. It is just human nature that a person—judge or otherwise—is more likely to be persuaded by six good reasons than by one.

■ Fifth, keep thinking even on appeal. Keep looking for new ways around the hearsay rule even if you won the point below. The appellate court may decide that the trial court erroneously applied a hearsay exception in your favor. You can save your judgment, however, if you can convince the appellate court that the trial court came to the right result, it just gave the wrong reason.[20] The right result, but for the wrong reason, will be affirmed on appeal if you give the appellate court the right reason. The court of appeals is, after all, engaged in the business of correcting incorrect results, not of correcting incorrect reasoning.[21]

■ Sixth—this is, in a way, the converse of number five—if you stop looking at the trial level, by the time of the appeal you may come up with an exception that should work, but be foreclosed from raising it. Appellate courts are in the business of reversing incorrect judgments, not incorrect rulings. If the trial judge gets the right result, but for the wrong reason, then the appellate court will cite the correct reason and affirm the judge's ruling.[22] However,

---

20. *E.g.*, United States v. Richards, 204 F.3d 177, 202 (5th Cir. 2000) (the exclusion used at trial (admission by an agent) was rejected on appeal but the government saved the conviction by its appellate reliance on a different exclusion (coconspirator's statement)); State v. McElrath, 366 S.E.2d 442, 450 (N.C. 1988) (the trial court admitted the hearsay under the residual exception; the appellate court found the evidence "admissible, not under [the residual exception], but rather under Rule 803(3) as a statement of intent to engage in a future act"). For additional discussion of appellate courts affirming a trial court by finding that, although the trial court gave the wrong reason, it came to the right result, *see* G. Michael Fenner, *Law Professor Reveals Shocking Truth About Hearsay*, 62 UMKC L. Rev. 1, 50–51 (1993).

21. "[O]ur power is to correct wrong judgments, not to revise opinions." Herb v. Pitcairn, 324 U.S. 117, 126 (1945).

22. United States v. Beckham, 968 F.2d 47, 52 (D.C. Cir. 1992) (citation omitted) states it as follows:

> Although the [appropriate way around the hearsay rule] was raised only tangentially before the district court ... we are entitled to consider it when raised by the government on appeal as part of the harmless error inquiry. Fed. R. Crim. P. 52(b) directs that "any error ... which does not affect substantial rights shall be disregarded." If evidence erroneously allowed in under one rule would nonetheless have been admissible under another, no substantial right of the defendant has been affected. Such an error cannot be used to reverse an otherwise valid conviction.

E.g., State v. Levan, 388 S.E.2d 429 (N.C. 1990) (statements by the victim admitted at trial under the residual exception; defendant was convicted of first-degree murder and appealed the admission of this evidence, arguing the statements did not fit under the residual ex-

if the trial judge gets it wrong and the right reason was never presented to the trial judge, then the appellate court may not listen to the right reason on appeal.[23] The trial judge gets the first shot at getting it right, and if the trial judge gets it right, whatever the judge's reasons, then so be it. If the trial judge gets it wrong, however, the correct approach must have been presented to the judge at trial: Absent plain error or constitutional error, it is only when the trial judge gets it wrong in the face of counsel presenting the correct approach that the trial judge will be reversed.[24]

In *Hewitt v. Grand Trunk Western Railroad Company*,[25] the question was whether the plaintiff's decedent's death was a result of an act of negligence on the part of the defendant or an act of suicide on the part of the decedent. A police officer investigated and took statements from eyewitnesses. The eyewitnesses did not testify. Instead, the railroad offered the officer's written report. The report was double hearsay: the eyewitnesses to the police officer; and the police officer to the report. The railroad argued the eyewitnesses' statements were admissible under the present sense impression exception and the excited

---

ception; the appellate court held that it did not have to decide whether they fit under the residual exception because they did fit under the statement against interest exception and the admission of the statements into evidence (and therefore the conviction) could be affirmed for that reason).

In an interesting variation on this particular issue, in Williams v. State, 413 S.E.2d 256 (Ga. Ct. App. 1991), a young man robbed an elderly man. Each made a statement. The victim was unable to testify at trial and the defendant could not be made to. The prosecutor offered the two statements. Over hearsay objections, the trial court excluded the victim's statement and received the defendant's statement. Defendant was convicted and appealed, arguing that he could not be convicted on his statement alone. The appellate court agreed that the evidence was insufficient but held that the exclusion of the victim's statement was error, and reversed and remanded for a new trial at which both statements would be admissible.

23. *E.g.*, Huff v. White Motor Corp., 609 F.2d 286 (7th Cir. 1979) (trial court excluded testimony as hearsay, rejecting defendant's argument that it was a nonhearsay admission or that it was admissible under the residual exception; on appeal, defendant argues both those theories plus one more—the statement against interest exception; the appellate court declined to hear the latter argument because it was not mentioned to the trial court as a basis for admitting the evidence).

24. Regarding plain error, *see* Rule 103. Regarding error that sinks to the level of a violation of the Constitution, *see, e.g.*, Chambers v. Mississippi, 410 U.S. 284 (1973) (state may impose voucher rule—counsel vouches for credibility of every witness he or she calls to stand; cannot impeach own witness—as a general rule; as applied here, however, voucher rule combined with certain application of hearsay rule, violates constitutional due-process right to fair trial).

25. 333 N.W.2d 264 (Mich. Ct. App. 1983).

utterance exception, and that the officer's report was admissible under the past recollection recorded exception. The trial court let the report in and the jury returned a verdict for the railroad. The "sole contention on appeal is that the officer's report was admitted in violation of the hearsay rule."[26] The court of appeals rejected the present sense impression exception because the eyewitnesses' statements to the officer were made up to 30 minutes after the incident; too much time had elapsed.[27] The court of appeals rejected the excited utterance exception because there was no showing the eyewitnesses were under the stress of excitement when he made the statement to the police officer.[28] The court of appeals rejected the recorded recollection exception because the officer's report, the paper being offered into evidence, was not based on the officer's personal knowledge.[29]

For the first time on appeal, the railroad contended that the reports were admissible under the exception for records of a regularly conducted activity and the exception for public records and reports. The court of appeals held that both of these arguments had been waived for purposes of appeal because they were not raised in the trial court.[30] "It is well settled that failure to raise an issue in the trial court waives the issue on appeal."[31] This is the risk a lawyer runs by not stacking up the exceptions: Having to go back to the client with an opinion that states that you may have had another argument, but you waived it by not making it at trial. Try going back to the client after the appeal is decided and explaining that the appellate court said the critical piece of evi-

---

26. *Id.*, at 266.

27. *See* Chapter 3(II).

28. *See* Chapter 3(III). "As the proponent of the evidence in question, it was incumbent upon defendant to establish the foundational elements of this hearsay exception." Hewitt v. Grand Trunk W.R., 333 N.W.2d 264, 268 (Mich. Ct. App. 1983). This defendant failed to establish that the declarants were under the stress of excitement when they made their statements to the officer.

29. *See* Chapter 3(VI).

30. Having stated that these "issues" were waived for purposes of appeal, the court went on to discuss both issues and to find that neither of these exceptions applied either. The court did not have to do that. The risk that it may not do that, leaving counsel with a statement from the court of appeals that there is another argument but the court of appeals will not address it because it was not brought up below.

31. *Id.* at 270. *Accord, e.g., Huff,* 609 F.2d at 290 (trial court excluded testimony as hearsay, rejecting defendant's argument that it was a nonhearsay admission or that it was admissible under the residual exception; on appeal, defendant argues both those theories plus one more— the statement against interest exception; the appellate court declined to hear the latter argument because it was not mentioned to the trial court as a basis for admitting the evidence).

dence—the one that might have gotten your client the win—may have been admissible at trial, if only you had made one additional argument, if only you had thought the problem through further.[32]

Back to *Ricciardi* in a moment, but, first, in *United States v. Young*,[33] a police officer continuously transmitted information to his dispatcher, including information that a man he had spotted had a gun and that, during a footchase, the man threw the gun into a stairwell. As is routinely the case, the officer's transmissions were tape-recorded. At trial, defense counsel asserted that after the officer found a gun in the stairwell he made up the story about having seen the gun on the defendant and having seen the defendant throw it into the stairwell. The court of appeals affirmed admission of the tape recording, finding sufficient foundation for the present sense impression exception and for the excited utterance exception. That court also found that the tape recording was a nonhearsay prior-consistent statement.[34] In addition, though the appellate court did not mention it, it is quite possible that the tape recording fit under the exception for records of a regularly conducted activity: The tape recording was an oral record made by the police officer in the regular course of a regularly conducted business activity.[35] It is also quite possible the tape fit under the exception for past recollection recorded: It is a record of a matter about which the officer once had personal knowledge but now has insufficient recollection to allow him to testify fully, it was made by him when the matter was fresh in his memory, and he can testify that it reflects his knowledge correctly.[36] It is likely, then, that this out-of-court statement, offered to prove the truth of the mat-

---

32. Regarding stacking up the exceptions or exclusions, *see also* Chapter 2(III)(F)(3)(g), above (discussing many ways to get statements by coconspirators into evidence around the hearsay rule); Chapter 3(III)(D)(8), above (discussing the close relationship between present sense impressions and excited utterances); Chapter 2(VIII)(E)(8), above (discussing documents that do not quite fit under the public records and reports exception, but do fit under another exception); Chapter 4(II)(E)(1), above (discussing many ways to get prior testimony into evidence around the hearsay rule); Chapter 5(V)(A), above (discussing the application of the residual exception to evidence that just misses fitting under one of the more specific exceptions); Chapter 6(I)(E)(12), above (discussing the non-exclusivity of FED.R.CIV.PRO. 32, which has to do with the admissibility of depositions); Chapter 7, above (this chapter on state of mind evidence collects various ways to get state of mind evidence around the hearsay rule, including hearsay exceptions and arguments that the statements are not hearsay in the first place).

33. 105 F.3d 1 (1st Cir. 1997).

34. FED.R.EVID. 801(d)(1)(B).

35. FED.R.EVID. 803(6). *See* Chapter 3(VII).

36. FED.R.EVID. 803(5). *See* Chapter 3(VI).

ter asserted, fits under one definitional exclusion and four exceptions.[37] Pretty soon, somewhere (and I think the magic moment is when you make your third good argument[38]) around reason number three, even a reluctant judge begins to believe that you have a point.

II. Put on Evidence of All of the Foundational Elements for Each Exception in the Pile

When stacking up the exceptions, do not forget to get all of the foundational elements into the pile. If you are arguing multiple exceptions, do what you can to lay the evidentiary foundation for each one. An exception does no good on appeal unless the foundation was laid at trial.[39]

III. Stacking Up the Exceptions, of Course, Does Not Always Work

Now back to *Ricciardi.* Plaintiff's lawyer argued six ways around the bar of the hearsay rule. In an excellent opinion, the court of appeals affirms the trial court and rejects all six arguments.[40] The evidence—plaintiff's only evidence of one essential element—was inadmissible and the appellate court affirmed the trial court's directed verdict for the defendants.

In *Meder v. Everest & Jennings, Inc.,*[41] the plaintiff fell out of his wheelchair and brought a products liability action against the chair's manufacturer. The defendant offered, and the trial court admitted, a critical piece of double hearsay: a police report prepared by the officer called to the scene, in all im-

---

37. It does not fit under the public records and reports exception. *See* FED.R.EVID. 803(8)(B), Chapter 3(VIII)(E).

38. I have no authority to cite for this. Still, I do believe it.

39. *E.g.,* Hynes v. Coughlin, 79 F.3d 285, 294–95 (2d Cir. 1996) (appellee argued the trial court's ruling was correct because the evidence in question was admissible under one or more of four exceptions; the Court of Appeals held that three of the exceptions clearly did not apply; the court stated that the record *suggests* that the fourth exception on counsel's list may apply, but the record *supports* only part of the foundation for that exception; counsel might have been able to lay the rest of the foundation, said the appellate court, but did not do so; because the judgment below was reversed and remanded for other reasons, this appellee gets another chance to lay this particular foundation).

40. 811 F.2d 18 (1st Cir. 1987). For the six arguments, see footnote 1 to this chapter.

41. 637 F.2d 1182 (8th Cir. 1981).

portant respects based entirely on what others told him. The plaintiff lost and appealed, and the appellate court reversed and remanded. On appeal, the defendant tried to save the verdict by arguing that the report itself was admissible as: (1) past recollection recorded; (2) expert opinion under Rule 702; or (3) lay opinion under Rule 701. Further, the defendant argued that the hearsay within the report was admissible as: (4) a party's own statement offered against the party who made it; (5) a present sense impression; (6) an excited utterance; (7) a record of a regularly conducted activity; or (8) a public record and report. In all, the defendant offered seven different ways around the hearsay rule, one of them twice (once for each level of hearsay). The appellate court discussed and rejected all eight arguments.[42]

Stacking up the exceptions does not always work.

---

42. Regarding the first exception in the above list, the recollections recorded were not the officer's own. Regarding each of the other proposed ways around the hearsay rule, the problem was that the officer had no recollection of how he gathered the data in his report— no recollection of who told him what, or of what it was his statements and conclusions were based on. That meant that regarding each argument one or more foundational element could not be established.

See also, e.g., Hewitt v. Grand Trunk W.R., 333 N.W.2d 264 (Mich. Ct. App. 1983), discussed above, text accompanying note 28, above in this chapter.

CHAPTER ELEVEN

Multiple Levels of Hearsay and Rule 805

I. Rule 805 and Multiple Levels of Hearsay

Rule 805 reads as follows: "Hearsay included within hearsay is not excluded under the hearsay rule if each part of the combined statements conforms with an exception to the hearsay rule provided in these rules."[1]

Hearsay often comes in layers. One hearsay statement often includes others within it. For example, if an employee makes a factual statement to her supervisor, and the supervisor, in turn, relates the statement to the plant safety manager, and at trial the plant safety manager is testifying to the fact in question, then there are two levels of hearsay—double hearsay. There are two out-of-court statements, each offered to prove the truth of the matter asserted: (1) employee to supervisor, (2) supervisor to plant safety manager.

If a witness tells his sister what he saw; and the sister tells a police officer; and the police officer writes it down in his police report, when the report is offered into evidence to prove what the witness saw, then there are three levels of hearsay—three out-of-court statements, each offered to prove the truth of

---

1. Fed.R.Evid. 805.

481

the matter asserted: (1) witness to sister, (2) sister to police officer, and (3) police officer to police report.

A wife tells her husband about an accident she had at work and then passes out; the husband calls an ambulance and tells an EMT what his wife told him about what happened; the EMT tells an emergency-room doctor; and the doctor writes it down in the hospital report. When the hospital report is offered into evidence to prove the nature of the accident at work—what the wife said about the accident—there are four levels of hearsay, four out of court statements, each offered to prove the truth of the facts asserted therein: (1) wife to husband, (2) husband to EMT, (3) EMT to doctor, and (4) doctor to hospital report.

And on and on. The possible length of a hypothetical chain of hearsay statements is limited only by the amount of time one is willing to devote to fantasizing links.

This is multiple hearsay, sometimes referred to as layered hearsay, and, when only two levels are involved, commonly called double hearsay.[2]

Levels of hearsay may be numbered from two different perspectives. Someone tells a newspaper reporter something; the reporter types it up, hits the send icon, and it ends up in the paper; the evidence offered in court is the newspaper. Numbering the levels chronologically, starting with the earliest in time, the first level of hearsay is what the source said to the reporter, and the second is what the reporter typed into the newspaper.[3] Numbering them archeologically, starting with the in-court evidence and peeling away layers, the first level is the newspaper article, the out-of-court statement by the reporter, and the second is what the reporter was told, the out-of-court statement by the source. Though perhaps obvious, this is mentioned because different writers number the levels from different directions. Keeping this in mind may help avoid confusion.

Layers of hearsay can be found in most any kind of out-of-court statement but look for it particularly where someone has recorded information gathered from or provided by another: records of a regularly conducted activity, public records and reports,[4] statements for purposes of medical diagnosis or treat-

---

2. In what might be a useful visualization, one court has referred to it as "totem-pole hearsay." United States v. Houlihan, 92 F.3d 1271, 1283 (1st Cir. 1996).

3. The old way, there might have been a third level: the typesetter. Today type is not set and under the modern assertion-based definition of hearsay the typesetter would not be making an assertion, but just setting type. *See* part II(C)(1) of Chapter 1.

4. There is a split of authority regarding whether statements incorporated into public records or reports do present traditional hearsay problems. This is discussed in part IV(B) of this chapter, below.

ment, transcripts of former testimony, depositions (where a court reporter is recording information provided by the deponent[5]) and other transcriptions, and the like. All that is required is in-court evidence that has been transmitted through two or more generations of out-of-court statements.

II. For Multiple Hearsay to Be Admissible, There Must Be an Exception or an Exclusion for Each Layer

When testimonial or documentary evidence is built upon multiple levels of hearsay, then, before the evidence will be admissible, there must be an exception for each level.[6] Ostensible multi-level hearsay problems can be solved with the application of an exception or a definitional exclusion to each layer. It can be the same exception or exclusion, applied once to each layer. It can be different exceptions or exclusions, one applied to each layer.[7] It can be the same exception or exclusion used more than once and in combination with other exceptions or exclusions.

A. Multiple Applications of Definitional Exclusions

Here is a simple example of multiple levels of out-of-court statements where the hearsay rule is no problem because each statement falls within a defini-

---

5. State v. Pinnell, 806 P.2d 110, 122 n.29 (Or. 1991).

6. *E.g.*, Regan-Touhy v. Walgreen Co., 526 F.3d 641, 650 (10th Cir. 2008) (witness testified that she heard the information in question from Mr. Abrams, who told her he had learned of it from Ms. Frazier, who had heard it from Ms. Whitlock; triple hearsay—Whitlock to Frazier; Frazier to Abrams; Abrams to witness; offering counsel must show an exclusion or exception for "each link of the chain" and has failed to do so); United States v. Payne, 437 F.3d 540, 547 (6th Cir. 2006) ("In order to admit an out-of-court statement that is nested within another, Rule 805 requires that *both* statements be admissible."); Clevenger v. CNH America, LLC, 76 Fed. R. Evid. Serv. 897, 903 (M.D. Pa. 208) ("A document containing multiple levels of hearsay is admissible only if each level of hearsay is independently admissible."). This is so with a few exceptions, discussed in part IV of this chapter, below. If there is not an exception, then there must be a definitional exclusion, but, of course, if any layer fits into a definitional exclusion, then that layer is not hearsay in the first place.

7. *E.g.*, Hoselton v. Metz Baking Co., 48 F.3d 1056, 1061 (8th Cir. 1995) (appellants' argument that each level of hearsay must satisfy requirements of business records exception for these business notes to be admissible, misstates law; "[t]he Federal Rules of Evidence do not require each level of hearsay to meet the requirements of the same exception").

tional exclusion. The defendant offers into evidence a memorandum written by a then-employee of the plaintiff about a matter within the scope of the author's employment. The memorandum includes a number of things its author was told by a number of other persons then-employed by the plaintiff, all speaking about matters within the scope of their employment.

There are two levels of potential hearsay here. The first level consists of each of the various statements the other employees made to the author. The second level is the author writing down the things he was told. It is the memorandum that is being offered into evidence. Every out-of-court statement involved here is a statement of an employee of a party, made during the existence of the employment relationship and about a matter that was within the scope of the employment of the declarant, and each is offered against that party-employer. Each level of potential hearsay actually is a nonhearsay admission by an employee of a party opponent.[8] The hearsay rule does not bar the receipt of this evidence.

B. Multiple Applications of Exceptions

■ Here is a simple example of multiple levels of out-of-court statements where the hearsay rule does not bar the receipt of the evidence because each statement falls within one exception or another. This involves the exception for former testimony offered at a subsequent trial.

The ultimate facts to be proved are those things stated by the witness who gave the former testimony. The evidence of those ultimate facts is the transcript of the testimony. There are two levels of hearsay: One level is the out-of-court statement made by the witness, and heard by the court reporter; and the other is the out-of-court statement made by the court reporter, i.e., the written transcript. In chronological order, the levels of hearsay are: (1) witness to court reporter (oral hearsay); (2) court reporter to transcript (written hearsay). There are two out-of-court declarants: the witness who testified at the former trial; and the court reporter who transcribed that testimony. The in-court "witness" is the transcript.

This kind of double hearsay problem can be quite easy to get around. The testimony at the first trial may well fit under the former testimony exception. The court reporter's transcript will likely fit under one or more of these ex-

---

8. Fed.R.Evid. 801(d)(2)(D); EEOC v. HBE Corp., 135 F.3d 543, 552 (8th Cir. 1998); Cooper Sportswear Mfg. Co. v. Hartford Cas. Ins. Co., 818 F.Supp. 721, 724 (D.N.J. 1993), aff'd, 16 F.3d 403 (3d Cir. 1993).

ceptions: present sense impression, past recollection recorded, business records, or public records and reports.[9]

In fact, one level of this kind of hearsay problem is so easy to get around — court reporter to transcript — that it is rare for an attorney to make an objection to this level of hearsay. To do so would be a waste of time, energy, and the judge's patience. Objection to this level is only made when there is some special problem with the transcript; when, for some reason out of the ordinary, there is reason to believe the objection might be successful.

■ Here is another example: A person with a medical problem makes a statement to a doctor hoping to have the medical problem diagnosed and treated. When this statement is offered to prove the truth of the things the patient said it is hearsay, but it fits under the medical diagnosis or treatment exception in Rule 803(4). All or part of it may also fit under the present sense impression exception in Rule 803(1), the state of mind exception in Rule 803(3), or a number of other exceptions.[10] The doctor to whom the statement was made writes it down in her medical report. When the report is offered to prove the truth of the things the patient said, it is hearsay — chronologically this is the second level of hearsay — but it may fit under the medical diagnosis or treatment exception in Rule 803(4) or the record of a regularly conducted activity exception in Rule 803(6).[11] Depending on the rest of the facts and how they fit with the foundational elements of the exceptions mentioned, there may well be a way to get each layer of hearsay around the bar of the hearsay rule.[12]

---

9. *See, e.g.,* State v. Pinnell, 806 P.2d 110, 122 (Or. 1991) (transcript of security release hearing testimony, double hearsay: words of event witness, offered to prove truth of what witness says he perceived, involves perception, recollection, narration, and sincerity of witness; transcript offered to prove what reporter heard witness say involves perception, recollection, narration, and sincerity of court reporter).

10. The patient's statement to the doctor may, for example, contain statements of personal or family history under Rule 804(b)(4). Depending on the rest of the story there could be lots of other ways parts of the patient's statement could get around the bar of the hearsay rule.

11. *E.g.,* Lewis v. Velez, 149 F.R.D. 474, 484 n.4 (S.D.N.Y 1993).

12. In McKenna v. St. Joseph Hosp., 557 A.2d 854 (R.I. 1989), an unidentified bystander made statements to rescue personnel who repeated the statements to hospital emergency room staff. "Rule 805 requires that we view each of the hearsay statements individually before ruling on the multiple hearsay. In this case both the unidentified bystanders' statements to the … rescue personnel and their restatement to the hospital staff constitute admissible hearsay." *Id.* at 858. Each statement fit under the exception for statements for purposes of medical diagnosis and treatment. *Id.*

C. Multiple Applications with a Mix of Exclusions and Exceptions

Here are some examples of multiple levels of out-of-court statements where the hearsay rule does not bar admission because each level is covered and, when taken together, they are covered by a mix of exceptions and definitional exclusions.

■ The defendant had a history of violent behavior against his wife. The wife and her father were walking when the defendant drove up and asked the wife to get in the car. She did so. The father saw the defendant lean towards his wife, and saw her begin to cry. The wife got out of the car and, "visibly scared, nervous, and shaking, related to her father that the defendant had told her he would kill her if she ever left him again."[13] The defendant is now on trial for the murder of his wife. There is evidence she was trying to leave him. The father took the stand to testify to what his daughter told him. His testimony was admissible over a hearsay objection. The first level of putative hearsay, what the defendant said to the deceased, is not hearsay at all. It is the defendant's own statement offered against him—a nonhearsay admission.[14] The second level, what the deceased said to her father, is hearsay, but is it admissible under the excited utterance exception.[15]

■ An employee stole from his company. The employer filed a claim under a policy insuring it against employee dishonesty. The policy had an exclusion regarding theft by employees when the employer had pre-policy knowledge of the employee's dishonesty. The insurance company refused to pay and the employer filed suit. The insurance company offered into evidence a memorandum prepared by a firm of private investigators. The memo quoted employees of the plaintiff and tended to show pre-policy knowledge of this employee's dishonesty. The out-of-court statements by the employees quoted in the memo are all employee-admissions under Rule 801(d)(2) and are not hearsay. The memo prepared by the investigator is a record of a regularly conducted activity under Rule 803(6). The memo is admissible over a hearsay objection.[16]

---

13. State v. Sutphin, 466 S.E.2d 402, 405 (W. Va. 1995).
14. Fed.R.Evid. 801(d)(2)(A).
15. Fed.R.Evid. 803(2).
16. *See also, e.g.,* United States v. Green, 258 F.3d 683, 690–91 (7th Cir. 2001) (defendants' statements to a police officer were nonhearsay admissions and the officer's written record of the statements fit under the past recollection recorded exception).

III. In Some Courts, Certain Exceptions or Exclusions Cleanse Preceding Levels of Hearsay

As a general rule, when an out-of-court statement is offered to prove the truth of its facts stated, then the out-of-court declarant must have personal knowledge of those facts. The advisory committee note to Rule 806 states that the out-of-court "declarant of a hearsay statement which is admitted in evidence is in effect a witness."[17] Rule 602 states that a witness cannot testify until it is shown that the witness bases his or her testimony on "personal knowledge."[18] And Rule 805 states that "[h]earsay included within hearsay is not excluded under the hearsay rule if each part of the combined statements conforms with an exception to the hearsay rule…."[19]

Out-of-court declarants must be shown to have personal knowledge. If there are multiple layers of hearsay, then there must be a way around the hearsay rule for each layer. That is the general rule. The courts of some federal and state jurisdictions, however, have held that various of the exclusions or exceptions are "excused" from this requirement.

■ *Admissions:* The premiere example is admissions. A number of courts have held that 801(d)(2) admissions cure all preceding levels of hearsay. Admissions need not be based on personal knowledge; admissions can be based on hearsay; proffering counsel does not have to deal with underlying levels of hearsay contained within the admission.[20]

Take nonhearsay employee admissions, for example. When an employee makes a statement concerning a matter within the scope of his or her employment, and that statement is subsequently offered into evidence against the employer, then the statement is not hearsay. Here is an example that involves an in-court declarant (the trial witness), an out-of-court declarant who makes a statement about a matter within the scope of his or her employment (the employee) and the company for which the employee works (the employer).

If the trial witness is to testify that he heard the employee say that the employer fired Jack Jones because of his race, then the general rule would require a showing that the employee had personal knowledge of that fact. In jurisdic-

---

17. FED.R.EVID. 805, advisory committee note.
18. FED.R.EVID. 602.
19. FED.R.EVID. 805.
20. This is discussed above, at Chapter 2(III)(G), along with the materials on admissions. It is also discussed below, at Chapter 13(II).

tions where admissions are exempt from the personal knowledge requirement, it does not matter whether the employee had personal knowledge of why Jones was fired. The employee could have been repeating rumors or office gossip. In these jurisdictions, it does not matter to the hearsay rule.

■ *Records of a Regularly Conducted Activity*: The Eighth Circuit Court of Appeals has written an opinion regarding the public records exception that has a great impact on the record of a regularly conducted activity exception. It wrote, in effect, that the trustworthiness clause in the public records exception assumes the admissibility of the public record or report unless the opponent of admission can "prove the report's untrustworthiness."[21] Hearsay statements within the report are admissible under this exception unless the opponent of admission can "prove the report's untrustworthiness." Layered hearsay is irrelevant except to the extent that they might be relevant to whether the judge finds the report untrustworthy.

As noted, this opinion has to do with the public records and reports exception. The logic of the opinion dictates that the rule applies to all exceptions containing a trustworthiness clause, including the record of a regularly conducted activity exception.

■ *Public Records and Reports*: In at least two circuits, it is the general rule that public records and reports cure preceding levels of hearsay—out-of-court statements incorporated into public records and reports are not excluded by the hearsay rule. The Seventh Circuit Court of Appeals held, essentially, that public employees generally do not have first-hand knowledge of the facts they record. If the proponent of a public record had to deal with layered hearsay problems the exception would be rendered largely useless. The Eighth Circuit held that the exception's trustworthiness clause excuses it from the operation of the general rules regarding hearsay within hearsay. The reasoning in each circuit is different, but the result is the same.[22]

■ *Ancient Documents*: There is an argument that Rule 805 and the multiple hearsay rule does not apply to ancient documents and, therefore, that out-

---

21. Amtrust, Inc. v. Larson, 388 F.3d 594, 599 (8th Cir. 2004). This is discussed further above at Chapter 3(VII)(D) & (VIII)(E), along with the materials on the record of a regularly conducted activity exception and the public records and reports exception, respectively.

22. Both opinions are discussed above, at Chapter 3(VIII)(E), along with the materials on the public records and reports exception, FED.R.EVID. 803(8). The second opinion is discussed there and in the text immediately preceding that to which this footnote is attached.

of-court statements incorporated into ancient documents are admissible around the hearsay rule just because they are in ancient documents.[23]

■ *Statements of Personal or Family History*: One exception to the hearsay rule states on its face that the declarant need not have personal knowledge of the fact declared. Multiple hearsay problems are written right out of Rule 804(b)(4), the exception for statements of personal or family history.[24]

IV. Multiple Hearsay and Rule 403

" '[W]ith every increased level of hearsay there is a corresponding decrease in reliability. Every level of hearsay provides another possibility that the facts were inaccurately reported by the declarant, … or misunderstood by the person to whom the statement was made.' "[25] At some point, the chain becomes so long that it is not reliable. There is no magic number: four layers, reliable, and five layers, not; eight, but not nine. It depends in part on the strength of each link of the particular chain.

When the chain of exceptions becomes so long that the evidence is unreliable, the evidence is still not excluded by the hearsay rule. So long as there is an exception that applies to each link, the hearsay rule does not keep it out. The rule that might keep it out, however, is Rule 403. The more links in the chain, the more likely the probative value of the evidence will be low, the evidence will present a danger of unfair prejudice, and the probative value of the evidence will be substantially outweighed by the dangers of unfair prejudice, undue repetition, or waste of time.[26] In other words, as you add links to the hearsay chain the more likely it becomes that the court will exclude the evidence under Rule 403.[27]

---

23. This is discussed above, at Chapter 3(XI)(D), along with the materials on the ancient documents exception, FED.R.EVID. 803(16).

24. This is discussed at Chapter 4(VI).

25. 4 JACK B. WEINSTEIN & MARGARET A. BERGER, WEINSTEIN'S EVIDENCE ¶ 805[01], at 805–7 (1996) (quoting Comment, *Hearsay Under the Proposed Federal Rules: A Discretionary Approach*, 15 WAYNE L. REV. 1077, 1231 (1969)). *Accord, e.g.*, United States v. Fernandez, 892 F.2d 976, 984 (11th Cir. 1989) ("[E]xperience suggests an inverse relationship between the reliability of a statement and the number of hearsay layers it contains."); Boren v. Sable, 887 F.2d 1032, 1036–37 (10th Cir. 1989).

26. FED.R.EVID. 403.

27. *See* Chapter 12(II), below. *See also* Chapter 8(I)(D)(4)(b), above.

CHAPTER TWELVE

A Statement that Is Inadmissible Hearsay to One Issue and Either Nonhearsay or Admissible Hearsay to Another

I. Introduction

Hearsay is defined by the issue to which the evidence is offered.[1] Take a lawsuit over a two-car collision at an intersection controlled by a traffic signal where liability turns on whether the plaintiff or the defendant had the green light. An occurrence witness *testifies* that the *defendant* had the green light. The same witness made an unsworn inconsistent pretrial statement that the *plaintiff* had the green light. The plaintiff offers the prior statement into evidence. This prior inconsistent statement has two possible uses in this case; it supports plaintiff's case in two different ways. First, credibility evidence: As a prior inconsistent statement it casts doubt on the credibility of the witness.

---

1. "[I]t is by the offer that Rule 801(c) defines hearsay." United States v. Mancillas, 580 F.2d 1301, 1309 (7th Cir. 1978). "'Hearsay' is a statement, other than one made by the declarant while testifying at the trial or hearing, offered in evidence to prove the truth of the matter asserted." FED.R.EVID. 801(c). This is discussed in detail throughout Chapter 1.

Because the witness has told contradictory versions of the event the witness' testimony is less credible. Second, substantive evidence: It is substantive evidence that in fact the plaintiff had the green light—had the right-of-way.

Again, hearsay is defined by the issue to which the evidence is offered. If the plaintiff offers the out-of-court statement to the issue of the witness' credibility—and only to that issue—it is not hearsay; the hearsay rule does not keep it out of evidence; unless there is some other rule that keeps it out, the statement is admissible. If, on the other hand, the plaintiff offers the prior statement as substantive evidence of which party had the green light, had the right-of-way, then the statement is offered to prove the truth of the fact asserted; it is hearsay;[2] and for purposes of this discussion we will assume that it does not fit under any exception.

The evidence is judged according to the issue to which it is offered. If the plaintiff offers the out-of-court green-light statement as an impeaching prior inconsistent statement it simply is not hearsay. This situation does, however, present this danger: If the jury hears this evidence they might consider it for its admissible use as impeachment evidence and for its inadmissible use as substantive evidence of right-of-way. The plaintiff has a permissible use for the prior statement, but there is also a danger that once it is in front of the jury they will consider it for its other, impermissible use. Since it has a relevant nonhearsay use, hearsay is the wrong objection; the evidence is coming in unless there is another objection. And, as we shall see, there is.

The dilemma discussed in this chapter is this: What to do when the same piece of evidence is admissible relevant nonhearsay to one issue in the case (the credibility of the witness) and relevant inadmissible hearsay to another issue in the case (the color of the light).[3]

When the same piece of evidence is both admissible and inadmissible the court should do the following, and in the following order. Step one: Redact the statement if possible. Step two: If redaction will not work, apply Rule 403. Step three: If Rule 403 does not bar admission of the multiple-use evidence, then, if requested to do so, grant a limiting instruction. And now, each of those steps discussed in sequence.

---

2. It is not a Rule 801 nonhearsay prior-inconsistent statement by a testifying witness because it "was [not] given under oath subject to the penalty of perjury at a trial, hearing, or other proceeding, or in a deposition." FED.R.EVID. 801(d)(1)(A).

3. *See, e.g.,* United States v. Becker, 230 F.3d 1224, 1230–31 (10th Cir. 2000); United States v. Harris, 942 F.2d 1125 (7th Cir. 1991) (discussed at length at Chapter 2(IV)(A), above); United States v. Brown, 490 F.2d 758, 763 (D.C. Cir. 1973).

II. Redact the Statement

The first thing to consider when a statement is admissible to one issue and inadmissible to another is whether the statement can be redacted. Sometimes an out-of-court statement can be broken apart. Sometimes the inadmissible parts can be removed, leaving only the admissible parts.[4] Problem solved: the admissible part comes in and the inadmissible part stays out.

Our witness testifies that the *defendant* had the green light. His prior inconsistent statement said this about the plaintiff: "That serial child abuser from America's Most Wanted—he had the green light." If the plaintiff offers this only for its impeachment value as a prior inconsistent statement, then the first part of the statement is irrelevant, inadmissible hearsay, or both; in any event, it is inadmissible. The final part, the inconsistent part, is not hearsay and, judged by the offer (impeachment evidence only), is admissible. Assuming that the inconsistent part is otherwise admissible,[5] then that part—"[The plaintiff] had the green light"—can and will be admitted, and the rest—"That serial child abuser from America's Most Wanted"—cannot and will not be admitted.

If the prior statement to be redacted is oral, the impeaching witness will be told what can be said and what cannot, and the witness can speak around the redacted part. The testimony will end up sounding like this: "I heard [the witness being impeached] say, "[The plaintiff] had the green light." If the prior statement to be redacted is one written by the witness to be impeached, the inadmissible parts will be blacked out and the description of the plaintiff will be altered, and the document will end up looking like this: "[The plaintiff] ~~That serial child abuser from America's Most Wanted~~ had the green light."[6]

III. Apply Rule 403

Sometimes the evidence cannot be redacted. Perhaps the admissible part of the statement does not make any sense without the inadmissible part. Perhaps every piece of the statement has both admissible and inadmissible values; the

---

4. *Brown*, 490 F.2d at 778; United States v. Marcy, 814 F.Supp. 670, 671–72 (N.D. Ill. 1992); State v. Roberts, 14 P.3d 713, 726–27 (Wash. 2001).

5. *See* part III of this chapter, below.

6. The brackets indicate that some descriptive term other than "serial child abuser from America's Most Wanted" will have to be inserted to designate the plaintiff.

statement cannot be divided because there are not discrete admissible and inadmissible parts of the statement. If the statement cannot be redacted, apply Rule 403.[7]

Continuing with the intersection collision example, two of the issues in the case are these: Who had the right-of-way? Are the witnesses credible? The out-of-court statement that "The plaintiff had the green light" is relevant to both of those issues: (1) right-of-way—as a statement of fact, it has substantive color-of-the-light value; (2) credibility—as a prior inconsistent statement, it has impeachment value. Inherent in this evidence is unfair prejudice to the party opposing its admission. The "prejudice" is that to one issue—the first listed above—it is relevant *inadmissible* hearsay that is damaging to the opposing party's case. If the evidence is let in as impeachment evidence, there is danger that the trier of fact will use it beyond just the issue of credibility and as substantive evidence of the color of the light. This prejudice is "unfair" because the evidence is inadmissible to the issue of the color of the light.

When the same statement is relevant to more than one issue and is admissible to one and inadmissible to another, apply Rule 403.[8] The judge must decide whether the probative value of the proper use of the evidence (its impeachment value) is substantially outweighed by the danger of unfair prejudice from its potential improper use (its color-of-the-light value). If the answer is yes, then the Rule 403 objection is sustained and the evidence does not come in at all, to either issue. If the answer is no, then the Rule 403 objection is overruled and the evidence does come in, but only to the issue of credibility, only for its impeachment value.[9]

---

7. FED.R.EVID. 403. *See* Chapter 11(V), above. *See also* Chapter 8(I)(D)(4)(b), above.

8. FED.R.EVID. 403. The prejudice here is necessarily unfair because the discussion assumes that the danger is that the trier of fact will use the evidence for an illegitimate purpose. Unfair prejudice, as used in Rule 403, "means an undue tendency to suggest decision on an improper basis, commonly, though not necessarily, an emotional one." FED.R.EVID. 403, advisory committee's note. The uncountenanced use of the evidence for its inadmissible hearsay purpose is the "improper basis" involved here. Unless there is enough other evidence of the point to which this evidence is inadmissible, then there is an "undue tendency to suggest [a right-of-way] decision" on the improper basis of this out-of-court statement. And there it is: unfair prejudice. *See* Nachtsheim v. Beech Aircraft Corp., 847 F.2d 1261, 1270–71 (7th Cir. 1988) (discussing Rule 403 in the context of an expert opinion and basis evidence that is hearsay as regards substantive issues and nonhearsay as regards the credibility of the expert's testimony); *Brown*, 490 F.2d at 763–82 (very good discussion of use of Rule 403 and in the context of state of mind evidence).

9. In the hypothetical in the main text, the Rule 403 argument most likely is a loser. This is the likely result because we do not like to allow witnesses to take the stand and change

In *United States v. Harris*,[10] there are out-of-court statements that are relevant to two different issues, each of which is relevant to the criminal prosecution at hand. Over the course of several years, Mr. Kritzik gave over a half a million dollars and some jewelry to Ms. Harris. Either Kritzik had to pay gift taxes on these transactions, or Harris had to pay income taxes. Neither paid either. Harris is on trial for willful evasion of her income tax obligation. Among other evidence, Harris offers several letters she received from Kritzik where he writes of his love for her and how much he enjoys giving her things. One issue in the trial is Harris' state of mind, her belief, relative to the things Kritzik had given her; to this issue, the out-of-court statements are admissible nonhearsay state of mind evidence. Another issue is Kritzik's intention when he gave her these things; to this issue, the statements are inadmissible hearsay. When evidence is admissible to one issue and inadmissible to another, and redaction is not possible, apply Rule 403.

Because the statements in question have an impact on a defense issue to which they are admissible (Harris' intent) and on a prosecution issue to which they are inadmissible (Kritzik's intent), we must consider the danger of unfair prejudice to the prosecution if the letters are allowed into evidence. "Prejudice" exists because as evidence of Kritzik's intent this evidence hurts the prosecution's case. The prejudice is "unfair" because as evidence of Kritzik's intent this evidence is inadmissible. The "danger" is that if we let the evidence in to the issue of Harris' intent, the jury might also consider it regarding the issue of Kritzik's intent.

The question to ask, then, is this: Is the probative value of this evidence to defendant-Harris (on the issue of her own intent) *substantially* outweighed by the danger of unfair prejudice to the prosecutor (on the issue of Kritzik's intent)? If not, and there is no other evidentiary problem, then it is admissible. If so, then it is inadmissible. The *Harris* court found the probative value of the evidence in its legitimate use to be high and not substantially outweighed by the danger of unfair prejudice in its illegitimate use.[11]

---

their stories about critical facts without being about to tell the trier of fact that the witness has done just that. Furthermore, this kind of prior inconsistent statement is quite probative of the witness' credibility and the witness is giving testimony on an essential element of a case. Add to that the feeling that, if the witness was called to the stand by defense counsel, it is inherently unfair to allow defense counsel to elicit testimony that defendant had the green light when he knows (or through discovery should have known) that the witness previously said that the plaintiff had the green light and then to let defense counsel get away with it by invoking Rule 403. Defense counsel's hands do not appear entirely clean.

10. 942 F.2d 1125 (7th Cir. 1991) (discussed in greater detail at Chapter 2(IV)(A), above).

11.   In this case … the letters were too important to Harris' defense to be excluded. Her belief … decides the issue of willfulness, which is an element of the

IV. Consider a Limiting Instruction

To recap, first consider redaction of the inadmissible part of the statement. If it cannot be redacted, consider Rule 403. If, after considering Rule 403, the statement comes in, consider a limiting instruction. The party prejudiced by the admission of the evidence has a right to a limiting instruction—if that party wants one. Upon request, the party who lost the Rule 403 battle is entitled to have the jury instructed that they may use the evidence for the one thing, but not for the other.[12]

In the green-light case, the limiting instruction would tell the jury that they could consider the witness' out-of-court statement when they are deciding how much weight, if any, to give that witness' testimony at the trial, but they cannot consider it when deciding which driver had the green light. Counsel opposing the admission of the prior statement is entitled to such a limiting instruction *upon request*.[13] If counsel would rather just let it go, that is counsel's right as well.[14]

---

offense, and she had no other objective means of proving that belief. True, admitting the letters would probably lead to some prejudice to the government's case. The jury would be hard pressed to consider the letters only for the permissible issue of what Harris thought of Kritzik's intent, and not for the impermissible issue of what Kritzik actually intended. The alternative, however, is to strip Harris of evidence that we believe was essential to a fair trial.

Harris, 942 F2d at 1131. *See also, e.g.,* United States v. Colon-Diaz, 521 F.3d 29, 33-34 (1st Cir. 2008) (discussion of limiting instructions applied to a number of statements admissible nonhearsay for some purposes and inadmissible hearsay if used for other purposes); *Becker*, 230 F.3d at 1230–31 (the out-of-court statement was admissible nonhearsay evidence of the origin of the investigation and it was inadmissible hearsay evidence of the presence of drugs in the defendant's house; admission was error; in light of "the wealth of evidence presented by the government" and the limiting instruction given by the trial court, the error was harmless).

12. *See* Joel D. Lieberman and Jamie Arndt, *Understanding the Limits of Limiting Instructions,* 6 Psychol. Pub. Pol'y & L. 677, 685 (2000) (limiting instructions can be used to instruct jurors to disregard evidence entirely and they can be used to instruct jurors that they can use evidence for a certain purpose but not for others).

13. The limiting instruction might be given as the evidence comes in or as part of the general post-trial instructions, or both. If both, the instruction during the trial, as the evidence comes in, might read like this: "Members of the jury, this out-of-court statement is being admitted solely for impeachment purposes. You may consider this statement when you are assessing how much weight, if any, you will give to this witness' testimony. You may consider the statement for that purpose only. You may not use this statement as evidence of the color of the light." Then the post-trial instruction might read something like this:

V. Four Sentence Summary of Chapter 12

When evidence is admissible to one issue in a case and inadmissible to another, follow these three steps as far as necessary to resolve the issue. First step: redact. If that is not possible, take the second step: apply Rule 403. If Rule 403 does not keep the evidence out, take the third step: give a limiting instruction, if one is requested.

"During the trial I called your attention to an out-of-court statement that was received in evidence only to aid you in deciding the credibility of a witness. Let me remind you that you must not consider that statement with regard to any issue other than the credibility of that witness. You must not consider it as evidence of the fact declared in that statement."

14. For cases and authorities on limiting instructions, including whether or not juries can actually follow such instructions, see part I(D)(4)(g) of Chapter 8.

CHAPTER THIRTEEN

COMPETENCY:
THE DECLARANT'S COMPETENCE
AND THE HEARSAY RULE

I. Competency as Another Way to Look at Many of the Hearsay Cases

A. Out-of-Court Declarant Must Have Personal Knowledge of the Facts Declared

In addition to everything else required of a hearsay statement, the out-of-court declarant must have been competent—the declarant must have had personal knowledge.[1] Rule 602 states that "[a] witness may not testify to a matter unless evi-

---

1. Brown v. Keane, 355 F.3d 82, 90 (2d Cir. 2004) ("It is one of the most basic requirements of the law of evidence that a witness's report may be admitted only where grounds exist for 'a finding that the witness has personal knowledge of the matter' to which the statement relates.... When ... the excited utterance exception ... permits the receipt of the out-of-court statement, ... the exception does not obviate the requirement that the declarant have personal knowledge of the subject of his report.") (citation omitted); Gross v. Burggraf Constr. Co., 53 F.3d 1531, 1541–43 (10th Cir. 1995) ("Rule 801(d)(2)(A) merely

dence is introduced sufficient to support a finding that the witness has personal knowledge of the matter." The advisory committee note to Rule 806 makes it clear that "[t]he [out-of-court] declarant of a hearsay statement which is admitted into evidence is in effect a witness." The advisory committee note to Rule 803 states that, "[i]n a hearsay situation, the declarant is, of course, a witness, and [these rules do not] dispense[] with the requirement of firsthand knowledge."

If there is a chain of hearsay, then the declarant who made the first statement in the chain must have had personal knowledge of the facts the statement is offered to prove and each subsequent declarant in the chain must have personal knowledge of the preceding out-of-court declaration.[2]

---

indicates that a party's own admission is not hearsay. It does not eliminate the requirement of Rule 602 of the Federal Rules of Evidence that '[a] witness may not testify to a matter unless evidence is introduced sufficient to support a finding that the witness has personal knowledge of the matter ...'"). *See also* Rule 806 which states that the credibility of the out-of-court declarant may be attacked and, if attacked, supported as though the declarant had testified in person; this includes attacking the declarant's competency even to the extent that the judge would have to find the declarant incompetent and, therefore, the statement inadmissible. FED.R.EVID. 806.

This is the general rule. Certain exclusions and exceptions have been held to do away with the personal knowledge requirement. They are discussed throughout as they come up. *See particularly, e.g.*, chapter 2(III)(G); chapter 3(VIII(E)(2) and XI(D)(7).

2. Declarant number 1 states a fact and must have personal knowledge of the fact. Declarant number 2 states that he or she heard number 1's out-of-court statement and must have personal knowledge of that statement (number 2 only claims that he or she heard the statement; number 2 does not claim personal knowledge of the statement's factual basis). And so on, to the end of the chain. The advisory committee's note to Rule 602, the rule requiring that witnesses have personal knowledge, states the following: "This rule does not govern the situation of a witness who testifies to a hearsay statement as such, if he has personal knowledge of the making of the statement." FED.R.EVID. 602 advisory committee's note. This is nothing novel. Insofar as the rules of competency are concerned, the original declarant in a chain of multiple hearsay must have personal knowledge of the fact stated. This advisory committee's note is simply recognizing that, insofar as competency is concerned, the second declarant need only have personal knowledge of what the first declarant said. The second declarant is competent to state what the first declarant said so long as the second declarant has personal knowledge of what the first declarant said. However many declarants there are after the original declarant, each of them need only have personal knowledge of the preceding statement in the hearsay chain. This advisory committee's note does not diminish the rule that the original declarant must have personal knowledge of the facts declared.

Consider the exception for statements for purposes of medical diagnosis or treatment. A child makes a statement to her father, expecting that he will use the information conveyed either to treat the problem or to see that someone else treats it. With the same expectation, the father repeats the statement to an EMT who arrives with the ambulance. Again with the same expectation, the EMT repeats the statement to the doctor. If the thrice repeated statement is the sort of thing that doctors reasonably rely upon when they diagnose or treat

The burden of establishing the declarant's personal knowledge is on the proponent of the evidence.[3] This burden is often satisfied by the following presumption: If a declarant makes a statement of fact, it is presumed that the declarant had personal knowledge of the fact stated.[4] This means that the declarant is presumed competent, presumed to have personal knowledge, until someone challenges his or her competence and presents enough evidence to over-

---

patients, then each out-of-court statement fits under this exception. The daughter has personal knowledge of what is wrong, the father has personal knowledge of what the daughter said, the EMT has personal knowledge of what the father said, and the doctor has personal knowledge of what the EMT said. At each step of the way, this is all of the personal knowledge that is required. There are three levels of hearsay—daughter to father; father to EMT; EMT to doctor—and each level fits under the hearsay exception for statements for purposes of medical diagnosis or treatment.

But see, Chapter 11(IV), below, and the cross-references therein.

3. "A witness may not testify to a matter unless evidence is introduced sufficient to support a finding that the witness has personal knowledge of the matter." FED.R.EVID. 602.

4. *E.g.,* Virgin Islands v. Joseph, 162 Fed. Appx. 175, 176 (3d Cir. 2006) ("Federal Rule of Evidence 601 presumes competency of a witness to testify."); United States v. Khoury, 901 F.2d 948, 966 (11th Cir. 1990); State v. Vondenkamp, 119 P.ed 653, 657 (Idaho Ct. App. 2005); Zimmer v. Peters, 861 P.2d 1188, 1193 (Ariz. Ct. App. 1993) ("The defendants suggest that the plaintiff did not testify from her own observations, but we do not find these suggestions sufficient to overcome the presumption favoring competency."). This is not a new presumption: *e.g.,* Alabama Gold Life Ins. Co. v. Sledge, 62 Ala. 566, 570 (1878) ("At common law the presumption was of the competency of witnesses....").

As discussed in the final section of this chapter, "[t]he rules reflect the modern trend which has converted questions of competency into questions of credibility ..." *See* part II(C) of this chapter, below.

See also M.B.A.F.B. Fed. Credit Union v. Cumis Ins. Soc., 681 F.2d 930, 932 (4th Cir. 1982) ("Rule 602 ... does not require that the witness' knowledge be positive or rise to the level of absolute certainty. Evidence is inadmissible under this rule only if in the proper exercise of the trial court's discretion it finds that the witness could not have actually perceived or observed that which he testifies to. 2 J. WIGMORE, EVIDENCE §658 (J. Chadbourn Rev. 1979); 3 J. Weinstein & M. Berger, Weinstein's Evidence, ¶602(02) (1981)."); United States v. Lanci, 669 F.2d 391, 394–95 (6th Cir. 1982) ("What a person who does not claim to know the facts may imagine or guess the facts to have been is never admissible.").

There are other statutory presumptions of competency, in addition to the one in Rule 601. For example, 18 U.S.C. §3509 enacts a presumption that children who have been "'[a] victim of a crime of physical abuse, sexual abuse, or exploitation' or who have witnessed a crime committed against another" are competent. United States v. Allen J., 127 F.3d 1292, 1294 n.1 (10th Cir. 1997). The statute further provides that the court may only hold a competency hearing regarding such a child witness upon written notice, 18 U.S.C. §3509(c)(3), and "only if the court determines, on the record, that compelling reasons exist" for having such a hearing, 18 U.S.C. §3509(c)(4).

come the presumption.[5] Then, and only then, must the proponent produce evidence that the declarant had personal knowledge—enough evidence "to support a finding that the witness [—here the out-of-court declarant—] has personal knowledge of the matter."[6]

B. Competency and the Hearsay Rule

Adding together the rule requiring that a witness have personal knowledge of the fact declared[7] and the fact that every out-of-court declarant is a witness[8] gives us another way to look at many hearsay cases. Many times when the problem seems to be hearsay it really is competence instead—or it really is both hearsay and competence. Too often, opponents of out-of-court statements miss the value of a competence objection.

Realizing that many hearsay problems are also—sometimes even primarily—competency problems, leads to this: the need to make both objections. The rules require a specific objection. The hearsay objection and the lack of personal knowledge objection are two separate objections, based on two separate rules, each of which must be considered separately. A hearsay objection does not raise (or preserve for appeal[9]) the issue of the incompetence of an out-of-court declarant.[10]

The personal knowledge requirement gives us another way to look at the *Shepard* case.[11] Dr. Shepard was on trial for the murder of his wife. His wife was the out-of-court declarant. The testifying witness, Mrs. Shepard's nurse, testified that Mrs. Shepard told her "Dr. Shepard has poisoned me."[12] The

---

5. As with most any problem of proof, the evidence that personal knowledge was lacking can be circumstantial or direct; it can be evidence from within the statement itself, the circumstances surrounding the making of the statement, or otherwise—any evidence that the declarant did not have personal knowledge.

6. Fed.R.Evid. 602.

7. *Id.*

8. Fed.R.Evid. 806 advisory committee's note.

9. Absent plain error, appellant cannot complain that evidence was erroneously admitted unless appellant lodged a specific objection with the trial court. Fed.R.Evid. 103(a)(1).

10. United States v. Nnanyererugo, 39 F.3d 1205, 1208 (D.C. Cir. 1994) ("[A]ppellant's contemporaneous hearsay objection at trial was insufficient to constitute an objection based on the witness' personal knowledge. These objections are denominated separately in the Federal Rules of Evidence.... We do not think that every hearsay objection ... logically implies an objection based on lack of personal knowledge...").

11. Shepard v. United States, 290 U.S. 96 (1933). This case is discussed at length at Chapter 1(IV)(A).

12. *Id.* at 98.

claim was that he had put poison in a bottle of whisky from which she'd drunk. The objection was hearsay and the argument whether or not Mrs. Shepard's statement fit under an exception to the hearsay rule. A second objection — one not made, but one every bit as good as the hearsay objection — would have been that the declarant was incompetent, that she lacked personal knowledge of two critical facts asserted in her out-of-court statement, *i.e.*, that there was poison in her whisky and, if there was, that Dr. Shepard had put it there.

First, was there a sufficient showing that she had personal knowledge that poison had been administered to her? Did she see the poison put into her drink? That seems unlikely for why, then, would she have drunk it? Did she taste poison in the drink? If so, how is it that she is qualified to identify poison by its taste?

Second, even if there was poison in the whisky, was there a sufficient showing that she had personal knowledge of who had administered the poison? There is circumstantial evidence that she did not see him put poison in her drink for, if she had, why would she have drunk it? If she did not see him add poison, then how would she know? Is she speculating based on motive or opportunity or her feelings about his feelings for her … based on what?

Insofar as the record discussed on appeal, there does not seem to have been any showing that Mrs. Shepard had personal knowledge of the thing of which she spoke. In fact, the circumstances seem to indicate that she did not.[13]

■ In *Betts v. Betts*,[14] a young girl said to her foster mother, about her natural mother's new husband, a man named Caporale, "He killed my brother and he'll kill my mommie too." Must there be some showing that the little girl has firsthand knowledge that Caporale killed her brother?

If the out-of-court statement is being offered in a homicide prosecution to prove that Caporale did kill the brother, then the answer is yes. If the out-of-

---

13. *See also* Horne v. Owens-Corning Fiberglass Corp., 4 F.3d 276, 283 (4th Cir. 1993) (using the ancient documents exception the court allowed into evidence an interoffice memorandum that seems to have been prepared by someone who lacked personal knowledge of the facts declared); Dallas County v. Commercial Union Assurance Co., 286 F.2d 388 (5th Cir. 1961) (a newspaper article stating that lightning struck a church steeple was admitted as an ancient document even though it appeared that the declarant (the reporter) lacked personal knowledge of the fact declared); EnergyNorth Natural Gas, Inc. v. UGI Utils., Inc., 2003 U.S. Dist. LEXIS 5681, at *3-4 (D.N.H. 2003); State v. Lawler, 1999 Ohio App. Lexis 5998 (1999) (a presentence investigation report was received as an ancient document even though it seemed that the declarant lacked personal knowledge of the facts declared).

14. 473 P.2d 403 (Wash. Ct. App. 1970). *Betts* is discussed at Chapter 1(IV)(F), above, and at other places throughout this book.

court statement is being offered in a custody proceeding and is nonhearsay evidence of the little girl's state of mind vis-à-vis Caporale, then the answer is no. In the latter situation, there is no need to show that the little girl had personal knowledge that Caporale killed her brother because whether he killed the boy is not the point. The point is her state of mind regarding Caporale; whether he actually killed the boy or not, this statement is circumstantial evidence of her state of mind regarding Caporale. State of mind has to do with what the out-of-court declarant believed or thought, not with whether that belief was based on personal knowledge or in any way rational. But if it is offered to prove the truth of the matter asserted, then it does have everything to do with whether the declarant's belief was based on personal knowledge. One could argue that the presumption of competency would be enough to get past the personal knowledge rule until someone puts on some evidence the child did not have personal knowledge, but I think one could argue the opposite as well. A competence objection would be worth the time here.

■ In one famous statement of the point being made here, Justice Cardozo said this: "To let the declaration in, the inference must be permissible that there was knowledge or the opportunity for knowledge as to the acts that are declared."[15]

II. Using Hearsay to Avoid Incompetence

A witness is incompetent if he or she lacks personal knowledge,[16] has no memory,[17] cannot communicate,[18] or is unwilling to take the oath or affirma-

---

15. Shepard v. United States, 290 U.S. 96, 101 (1933).

For other places in this book where this relationship between competence and hearsay is discussed, *see* Chapter 2(III)(G)(2) (discussing Rule 602 and personal knowledge, and the *Mahlandt* case; *Mahlandt* is also mentioned in Chapter 13(II)(A), just below); Chapter 4(III)(D) (discussing competence and confusion while in a state of impending death); Chapter 4(VI)(D) (discussing competence and double hearsay under the exception for statements of personal or family history).

16. Rule 602 requires that a witness have personal knowledge. FED.R.EVID. 602.

17. Rule 602 requires that a witness *have* personal knowledge. FED.R.EVID. 602 (emphasis added).

18. If a person cannot communicate, then that person is incompetent; even if one could argue that such a person is competent to be a witness (on the theory that the rules do not expressly make communication an element of competency), then the "nothing" that such a person has to say is irrelevant, FED.R.EVID. 401 & 402, and, if that is not enough, the probative value—even if it is not zero—would surely be substantially outweighed by the danger of unfair prejudice, confusion of the issues, and misleading the jury, FED.R.EVID. 403. Additionally, calling such a person to the stand would surely constitute the kind of "undue embarrassment" of that person that the judge is allowed to control under Rule 611, FED.R.EVID. 611.

tion.[19] Sometimes hearsay evidence can be used to avoid each of these incompetencies.

A. Getting Around the Out-of-Court Declarant's Lack of Personal Knowledge

The general rule is that if there are multiple levels of hearsay then the in-court testimony is not admissible unless there is an exception or exclusion for each layer.[20] Like every general rule, this one has its own exceptions: in some jurisdictions it is not applied to specific exceptions or exclusions. For example, this general rule does not apply to admissions by a party opponent, *i.e.*, to a party's own statement is offered against that party.[21] Two things flow from this exception to the general rule: The proponent of the evidence need not deal with underlying levels of hearsay and the proponent need not show that the declarant is competent, *i.e.*, that the declarant has personal knowledge of the facts in the out-of-court statement. When the general rules requiring multiple exceptions or exclusions for multiple-level hearsay is not applied, then too the general rule that the declarant must have personal knowledge of the facts declared is not applied.

The hearsay rule and the rule requiring competency are both about personal knowledge. Each asks for the real witness, the original manufacturer of the evidence, the person who knows firsthand what it is we are trying to prove. If multiple levels of hearsay precede a final out-of-court declaration that is a nonhearsay admission, and if the fact that it is an admission cures all of those preceding levels of hearsay, this means that we no longer care whether any of the out-of-court declarants in the chain have personal knowledge. Our witness need not have personal knowledge of the matter. In such a jurisdiction, we do not care whether the admission is based on hearsay, whether it is based on personal knowledge, whether it is based on pure speculation, or whether

---

19. "Before testifying, every witness shall be required to declare that the witness will testify truthfully, by oath or affirmation administered in a form calculated to awaken the witness' conscience and impress the witness' mind with the duty to do so." FED.R.EVID. 603.

20. This is the particular subject of Chapter 11 and is discussed elsewhere throughout this book.

21. United States v. Goins, 11 F.3d 441, 443 (4th Cir. 1993) puts it this way: "[T]he foundational requirements of Rule 602 do not apply to statements admissible as non-hearsay admissions under Rule 801(d)(2)." This case and others like it and disagreeing with it are discussed above, in Chapter 11, particularly in part IV, and the places cross-referenced therein.

it is based on someone's reading of his astrological charts. Except perhaps on the issue of the weight of the evidence, we simply choose not to look behind the admission.

In the *Mahlandt* case,[22] as part of his job Kenneth Poos handled a wolf named Sophie. Poos made an out-of-court statement that Sophie bit a child. That statement was admitted against Poos as a personal admission and admitted against his employer as an admission by an agent of a party opponent. Kenneth Poos was not there when the boy was injured and could not have firsthand knowledge of the fact declared, *i.e.*, that Sophie had bit a child. In spite of the fact that Poos had no personal knowledge of the fact, his out-of-court statement that Sophie bit a child was admitted to prove that Sophie did bite the child. Either Poos' out-of-court statement was part of a chain of hearsay (the testifying witness was testifying to what Poos told him and Poos was just repeating something that someone else told him) or Poos was incompetent (the testifying witness was testifying to what Poos told him and Poos was stating a fact about which he had no personal knowledge). The court found that the definitional exclusion for admissions cures all preceding levels of hearsay and that it does so without any need to show that Poos had any firsthand knowledge of whether or not Sophie bit the child.[23]

In a jurisdiction that follows the rule of the *Mahlandt* case, Kenneth Poos may be incompetent—if he took the stand and wanted to testify that Sophie bit a child, the rules requiring competency might prevent it—but whether he is incompetent or not his out-of-court statement is admissible as evidence against him and his employer.

Other examples of exceptions to the hearsay rule that can be used to admit statements even when the declarant lacks the personal knowledge usually required of competent witnesses are catalogued in Chapter 11, above.

B. Getting Around Other Incompetencies

The above discussion concerns the out-of-court declarant's personal knowledge of the facts stated. As discussed above, hearsay evidence can be a way around that kind of incompetence.

There are, in addition, other incompetencies, such as an unwillingness or inability to take an oath or affirmation and a lack of memory. The hearsay

---

22. Mahlandt v. Wild Canid Survival & Research Ctr., Inc., 588 F.2d 626 (8th Cir. 1978). This case is also discussed at Chapter 2(III)(G)(2), above.
23. *Mahlandt*, 588 F.2d at 630-31. *See* Chapter 11(IV).

rules may also provide ways around these incompetencies. An out-of-court statement may be admissible in place of the testimony of a witness who is incompetent to testify.

Some of what I am suggesting here is not novel. If the out-of-court declarant is incompetent due to death, serious illness, or loss of memory,[24] for example, then that declarant's out-of-court hearsay statement may be admissible under one or more of the hearsay exceptions. In other words, when a competent declarant makes an out-of-court statement and then becomes incompetent—dies; loses his or her memory; moves to the island of knights and knaves, where knights always tell the truth and knaves never tell the truth, and becomes a knave—the out-of-court statement may be admissible.

The somewhat novel use of the hearsay rules to avoid an incompetency that I want to address here involves this: When a declarant is incompetent when the statement is made and still incompetent at the time of the trial, is the statement admissible? A number of cases allow just that: They allow into evidence out-of-court statements made by declarants who were incompetent to be witnesses when they made the statements and who are incompetent to testify if they are called as witnesses.

This makes more sense than may at first seem. The out-of-court declarants in many (if not most) of these cases are children.[25] Though not always entirely

---

24. "A young child who lacks the capacity to remember from the time of event to the time of trial (often a period of months or years) may none-theless [sic] have had the capacity to remember from the time of event to the time of his or her hearsay statement (often a period of minutes or hours)." State v. Karpenski, 971 P.2d 553, 572-73 (Wash. Ct. App. 1999). This logic applies to any variety of witnesses who develop memory problems, not just children.

25. See, e.g., Morgan v. Foretich, 846 F.2d 941 (4th Cir. 1988) (youthful incompetence no bar to admission of child's excited utterances, id. at 946, or child's statements for purposes of medical treatment, id. at 949) (citing cases and authorities); United States v. Nick, 604 F.2d 1199, 1202 (9th Cir. 1979); State v. Wagoner, 506 S.E.2d 738, 742 (N.C. Ct. App. 1998) (residual-exception statements not necessarily inadmissible just because declarant was and is incompetent to testify); Virgin Islands v. Riley, 754 F.Supp. 61, 63 (D. V.I. 1991) (hearsay statements of a child witness to a murder admitted under the former testimony exception though the child was incompetent to testify in person because of the anxiety created by the courtroom atmosphere); State v. Lander, 644 S.E.2d 684, 691-93 (S.C. 2007) (statements of two-and-one-half-year old alleged victim of child abuse admitted as excited utterances; good discussion of the reasoning from other jurisdictions for allowing excited utterances to be admitted though the declarant is, by reason of youth, incompetent to testify); Oldsen v. People, 732 P.2d 1132, 1135 n.6 (Colo. 1986); State v. Galvan, 297 N.W.2d 344, 347 (Iowa 1980) (discussed in detail in a note in part III(D)(9) of Chapter 3, above).

clear, it appears that, to a child, they were incompetent to testify because they were too young: the incompetencies of youth. This means, it would seem, that they were too young to understand the oath, too young to understand about telling the truth and the need to do just that while testifying, or they were too young to get around an age-based state-rule of incompetence. The problem with these children as witnesses is that the guarantee of reliability of the oath is not present. Hearsay exceptions may take care of that. Part of the point of the hearsay rule is that we prefer evidence given under oath, but when the foundational elements of an exception are present we allow evidence given without the oath. When the foundational elements of an exception are present, there are guarantees of reliability that substitute for the oath.

United States v. Napier[26] involved an oath-based incompetency in an adult. The defendant was on trial for crimes in connection with having beaten a woman nearly to death. The beating left the victim unable to comprehend the significance of the oath and, therefore, incompetent to testify. Eight weeks after the beating, while under the incompetency, the woman saw a newspaper photo of the defendant and said, "He killed me, he killed me"[27] This was allowed in under a hearsay exception in spite of evidence that had she been called as a witness she would have been incompetent.[28]

What the cases say is that the hearsay exception supplies the trustworthiness, the absence of which renders the declarant incompetent to testify as a witness at trial. What most of the cases mean is that the hearsay exception supplies the trustworthiness missing from the inability to take or understand the oath. Surely, if the witness were incompetent because he had some neurological inability to process information correctly, the fact that he had made an excited utterance would not cure that incompetency.[29] And, if it may, then make

---

But see, e.g., State v. Karpenski, 971 P.2d 553 (Wash. Ct. App. 1999) (at the time of the trial the alleged-victim child was incompetent to testify because he was incapable of distinguishing truth from falsehood; his hearsay statements were likewise inadmissible because the evidence shows that he was incapable of distinguishing truth from falsehood at the time he made the out-of-court statements).

26. 518 F.2d 316 (9th Cir. 1975). This case is discussed in more detail at Chapter 3(III)(D)(4) & (7).

27. *Id.* at 317.

28. *Id.* at 317.

29. Look at the facts of State v. Chapin, 826 P.2d 194 (Wash. 1992). A resident in a nursing home made arguably-excited utterances about a nurse having raped him. Part of the reason that the court ruled the excited utterance exception did not apply was because the out-of-court declarant's "mental deterioration was severe." *Id.* at 199. He "was confused, prone to confabulation, subject to persecutory delusions, hostile to those who tried to di-

a Rule 403 objection and argue that the danger of unfair prejudice substantially outweighs any probative value the evidence may have.

The fact that an out-of-court declarant is incompetent to testify does not necessarily prevent the introduction into evidence of a prior statement made with personal knowledge, even when that statement was made during the incompetency. The hearsay exceptions may be a way to avoid the loss of an incompetent witness' evidence.

C. Modern Trend?

Perhaps all of this reflects "the modern trend which has converted questions of competency into questions of credibility while steadily moving towards a realization that judicial determination of the question of whether a witness should be heard at all should be abrogated in favor of hearing the testimony for what it is worth."[30] If this is so—and it seems it may well be—then one would expect that more and more hearsay exceptions, in more and more jurisdictions, will be used as ways to get around incompetencies.

---

rect his behavior, and hostile in particular to male attendants." *Id*. The court does not say that the declaration is inadmissible because the declarant was incompetent, though it would seem it could have. Rather the court uses this as evidence that one foundational element was lacking: the statement was not made while he was under the stress of excitement caused by the occurrence of a startling event.

30. State v. Cate, 683 A.2d 1010, 1015 (Vt. 1996) (multiple quotation marks omitted) (quoting 3 JACK B. WEINSTEIN & MARGARET A. BERGER, WEINSTEIN'S EVIDENCE ¶ 601[05], at 601–40 (1990) (in turn quoting Comment, *Witnesses Under Article VI of the Proposed Federal Rules of Evidence*, 15 WAYNE L. REV. 1236, 1250 (1969))). *Accord* United States v. Kelly, 436 F.3d 992, 996 (8th Cir. 2006) (regarding a child witness, defendant asked for a competency hearing; the court ruled that the issue was one of credibility, for the jury); United States v. Bedonie, 913 F.2d 782, 799-801 (10th Cir. 1990); United States v. Odom, 736 F.2d 104, 112 (4th Cir. 1984); United States v. Jones, 482 F.2d 747, 751–52 (D.C. Cir. 1973); State v. Baker, 2003 De. Super. LEXIS 286, *7 (Del. Super. Ct. Aug. 7, 2003) ("[F]ederal courts have … noted that 'because a witness's mental state during the period about which he proposes to testify is a matter which affects his credibility, it is a jury determination and thus not germane to competency to testify.'" (quoting United States v. Martino, 648 F.2d 367, 384 (5th Cir. 1981)).

CHAPTER FOURTEEN

THE CONFRONTATION CLAUSE

I. The Confrontation Clause

The Sixth Amendment to the United States Constitution states that, "[i]n all criminal prosecutions, the accused shall enjoy the right ... to be confronted with the witnesses against him."[1] This right has been incorporated into the Due Process Clause of the Fourteenth Amendment and, therefore, applies not just to federal prosecutions but to state and local prosecutions as well.[2]

---

1. U.S. CONST. AMEND. VI.
2. Pointer v. Texas, 380 U.S. 400, 403 (1965).

II. The Confrontation Clause and Hearsay

There is a close, and perhaps obvious, relationship between the Confrontation Clause and the hearsay rule. Each deals with the same problem — the testimonial infirmities attached to second-hand evidence.[3] Each bars the receipt of some second-hand evidence.

Exceptions to the bar of the hearsay rule are based on findings that particular categories of statements[4] or particular individual statements[5] tend to be reliable and, in some cases, that there is an unusual need for the evidence.[6] Hearsay reliability can be found in a number of ways: there was contemporaneous cross examination, the statement was made in the face of impending death or with the expectation that the it would lead to medical diagnosis or treatment, the time between the event and the statement was too short for the declarant to have fabricated a lie or have forgotten the relevant facts, and so forth.[7]

Exceptions to the bar of the Confrontation Clause also have to do with reliability, but here "reliability [must] be assessed in a particular manner: by testing in the crucible of cross-examination."[8] Where the confrontation right applies, the accused must have had or currently have an opportunity to confront the witness through cross-examination.[9]

---

3. Regarding the testimonial infirmities, see Chapter 1(I).

4. *See particularly* FED.R.EVID. 803 and 804.

5. *See particularly* FED.R.EVID. 807.

6. *See particularly* FED.R.EVID. 804 (declarant's in-court testimony must be unavailable) and 807 ("the statement [must be] more probative on the point for which it is offered than any other evidence ... the proponent can produce through reasonable efforts."

7. *See, e.g.,* and in the order in which they appear in the main text, the former testimony exception, above at Ch. 4(II)(D); the medical diagnosis or treatment exception, above at Ch. 3(V)(c); the present sense impression exception, above at Ch. 3(II)(C).

8. Crawford v. Washington, 541 U.S. 36, 61 (2004).

9. For years, Confrontation Clause jurisprudence more or less tracked the hearsay rule. The evidentiary rule and the constitutional clause dealt with the problem of the reliability of second-hand evidence in much the same way. The Confrontation Clause did "not bar admission of an unavailable witness's statement against a criminal defendant if the statement [bore] adequate indicia of reliability. To meet that test, evidence [had to] either fall within a firmly rooted hearsay exception or bear particularized guarantees of trustworthiness." *Crawford*, 541 U.S. at 40 (citations and internal quotation marks omitted) (describing the preexisting rule established in Ohio v. Roberts, 448 U.S. 56 (1980)). *Crawford* changed the preexisting rule. *See* State v. Buda, 949 A.2d 761, 774 (N.J. 2008) ("*Crawford* effected a fundamental shift in the constitutionality of evidence jurisprudence.").

"Dispensing with confrontation because testimony is obviously reliable is akin to dispensing with [a] jury trial because a defendant is obviously guilty." *Crawford*, 541 U.S. at 62. "Dis-

III. Use Note

In 2004, the Court stated these two important Confrontation Clause principles. First, the right to confront the declarant applies against out-of-court statements that are "testimonial," offered against the accused in a criminal prosecution, and offered to prove the truth of the matter asserted in the statement.[10] Second, introducing such a statement into evidence infringes the confrontation right of that accused unless the declarant's in-court testimony is unavailable and the accused had an opportunity to cross examine the declarant.[11]

A. The Right Attaches to Out-of-Court Statements That Are Testimonial, Offered Against the Accused in a Criminal Prosecution, and Offered to Prove the Truth of the Matter Asserted

1. Offered Against the Accused in a Criminal Prosecution

The right guaranteed by the Confrontation Clause is a right of "the accused."[12] The prosecution does not have an equivalent constitutional right to confront witnesses against the State. When offering a hearsay statement into

---

pensing with confrontation because testimony is obviously reliable" is a nice summary of the so-called *Roberts* rule, *i.e.*, the boundary of the right of confrontation that pre-existed *Crawford*.

See also Kentucky v. Stincer, 482 U.S. 730, 744 (1987) (not allowing the accused to be present at a hearing to determine the competency of two alleged-victim children does not violate the confrontation right; if the children are found competent and testify, the accused can cross-examine them).

10. *Crawford*, 541 U.S. at 59. Perhaps this is worth restating in the negative. The right to confront does not apply if the evidence is not an out-of-court statement; if it is not offered to prove the truth of the matter asserted; if it is not offered in a criminal prosecution against the accused; if it is not "testimonial;" or if the accused had a prior opportunity to cross-examine the declarant.

11. *Crawford*, 541 U.S. at 68 ("Where testimonial evidence is at issue ... the Sixth Amendment demands what the common law required: unavailability and a prior opportunity for cross-examination."). *Id.* at 53-54 ("[T]he Framers would not have allowed admission of testimonial statements of a witness who did not appear at trial unless he was unavailable to testify, and the defendant had had a prior opportunity for cross-examination."). *See also id.* at 59.

12. U.S. CONST. AMEND. VI.

evidence, the only rules the defendant must get past are the rules of evidence—not the rules of evidence plus the Confrontation Clause.

Furthermore, the right only applies "[i]n ... criminal prosecutions."[13] It does not apply in civil proceedings, even if they are quasi-criminal. It does not apply in criminal proceedings that are not "prosecutions."[14]

2. An Out-of-Court Statement Offered to Prove the Truth of the Matter Asserted

The evidence in question must be in the form of an out-of-court statement[15] that is offered to prove the truth of the matter asserted. If the evidence in question is straight-up in-court testimony regarding the witness's firsthand observations, then the accused can confront the real witness—the accuser.[16] If the statement is relevant in any of the non-truth ways discussed throughout this

---

13. *Id.*

14. This means, for example, that the right does not apply at a parole revocation hearing because it is not a criminal *prosecution*. United States v. Ray, 530 F.3d 666, 668 (8th Cir. 2008). The penalty stage of the proceeding is broken down into two parts, the eligibility stage and the selection stage. As of this writing, courts are unanimous that the right applies to the former and split on whether it applies to the latter. United States v. Concepcion Sablan, 555 F. Supp2d 1205, 1219 (D. Colo. 2007) (citing and discussing cases). *See also* Wolff v. McDonnell, 418 U.S. 539, 568 (1974) (Confrontation Clause does not apply to prison disciplinary hearings); United States v. Kelley, 446 F.3d 688, 689 (7th Cir. 2006) (Confrontation Clause does not apply to supervised release revocation hearings); Rosenthal v. Justices of Supreme Court, 910 F.2d 561 (9th Cir. Cal. 1990) (Confrontation Clause does not apply to state disbarment proceedings).

15. United States v. Lamons, 532 F.3d 1251, 1263 (11th Cir. 2008) (phone company billing data generated by computer does not implicate the confrontation right because " 'the Sixth Amendment provides the right to confront (human) "witnesses." ' ") (quoting United States v. Washington, 398 F.3d 225, 230 n.1 (4th Cir. 2007)); United States v. Mendez, 514 F.3d 1035, 1044 (10th Cir. 2008) (testimony that the witness searched a database and did not find an entry for the defendant did not violate the confrontation rights because there was no out-of-court statement). This same point is made in the context of hearsay exceptions in chapter 3, parts VII(D)(7) and IX(D).

16. *Crawford*, 541 U.S. at 59 n.9 ("[W]hen the declarant appears for cross-examination at trial, the Confrontation Clause places no constraints at all on the use of his prior testimonial statements.").

book, the clause does not apply.[17] Perhaps a statement offered for other than its truth cannot be testimonial.[18]

3. The Statement Must Be "Testimonial"

The confrontation right does not attach unless the statement is "testimonial."[19] Much of the litigation occurring as this is written involves this question

---

17. "The Clause also does not bar the use of testimonial statements for purposes other than establishing the truth of the matter asserted." *Crawford*, 541 U.S. at 59 n.9 (citing Tennessee v. Street, 471 U.S. 409, 414 (1985) (a statement not offered to prove the truth of its assertion "raises no Confirmation Clause concerns")). What is and is not offered for its truth is the subject of Chapter 1, above. Here are some cases specifically dealing with nonhearsay and the Confrontation Clause. State v. DeJesus, 947 A.2d 873, 882 (R.I. 2008) (context evidence offered to explain the defendant's responses is not offered to prove the truth of any assertions contained therein); Turner v. Commonwealth, 248 S.W.3d 543, 546–47 (Ky. 2008) (similar); Brunson v. State, 245 S.W.3d 132, 149 (Ark. 2006) (confrontation right does not attach to a statement offered as circumstantial evidence of the state of mind of the declarant).

Post-*Crawford* Confrontation Clause jurisprudence is based on the common law at the time of the ratification of the Constitution. Some courts have said that the Clause only applies when the evidence in question is hearsay. This is not exactly true. What is true is that the Clause only applies to evidence that was hearsay under the common-law definition. Under the common law, hearsay evidence is an out-of-court statement offered to prove the truth of the matter asserted. The federal-rules definition is somewhat different. *See generally* above, at Ch. 2. Thus, the Confrontation Clause sometimes applies to some few statements that were hearsay under the common law but are no longer hearsay under the Federal Rules of Evidence. These rules define certain prior consistent and inconsistent statements and statements of identification of a person as nonhearsay. FED.R.EVID. 801(d)(1). One of the foundational elements of these nonhearsay statements is that the declarant must be testifying and subject to cross-examination. Confrontation is available; there is no Confrontation Clause problem. These rules also define certain kinds of admissions, including admissions by an agent or a coconspirator, as nonhearsay. FED.R.EVID. 801(d)(2). The Confrontation Clause can apply to some of these nonhearsay statements because they were hearsay under preratification common law.

18. The Court has written that a statement made in the course of a police interrogation is testimonial when its "primary purpose ... is to establish or prove past events potentially relevant to later criminal prosecution." Davis v. Washington, 547 U.S. 813, 822 (2006). This, however, does not necessarily exhaust the field of testimonial statements.

19. "The text of the Confrontation Clause ... applies to 'witnesses' against the accused— in other words, those who 'bear testimony.'" *Crawford*, 541 U.S. at 51 (citations omitted). *Accord, e.g.*, State v. Cannon, 254 S.W.3d 287, 303 (Tenn. 2008) ("If the statement is nontestimonial, the Confrontation Clause does not apply, and the statement must be analyzed under the 'traditional limitations upon hearsay evidence.'") (quoting Davis v. Washington, 547 U.S. 813, 821 (2006)).

of what out-of-court statements are testimonial.[20] Because so much of the law of what is testimonial is currently up in the air, and because this is a more appropriate subject for a criminal procedure book, this discussion will highlight what is known so far and offer a suggestion or two.

a. The Relevance of the Identity of the Person Perceiving the Statement

Perhaps the first thing to know is that the identity of the person perceiving the statement, that is, the identity of the in-court declarant, is not the determining factor. Statements made to a police officer, a 911 operator, a doctor, or a family member can be testimonial or nontestimonial.[21] The key is the primary purpose of the statement as judged by the context in which the statement is made. The identity of the person to whom the statement was made is relevant insofar as it sheds light on the primary purpose of the statement.

b. The Primary Purpose Test

Perhaps the second thing to know is that the test for determining whether a statement is testimonial is a "primary purpose" test.[22]

> Statements are nontestimonial when made in the course of police interrogation under circumstances objectively indicating that *the primary purpose* of the interrogation is to enable police assistance to meet an ongoing emergency. They are testimonial when the circumstances objectively indicate that there is no such ongoing emergency, and that

---

20. There is a case awaiting decision in the United States Supreme Court as I write that has to do with the question of whether and perhaps when lab reports are testimonial. Commonwealth v. Melendez-Diaz, 870 N.E.2d 676 (Mass. 2007), *cert. granted*, Melendez-Diaz v. Massachusetts, 128 S.Ct. 1647 (2008).

21. Clarke v. United States, 943 A.2d 555, 557 (D.C. 2008) ("[T]hat a statement was made 'to someone other than law enforcement personnel,' does not—so far as *Crawford* and *Davis* teach—make it nontestimonial, for the Court left that issue open in both cases. Nevertheless, in a setting such as this one where [the person to whom declarant spoke, *i.e.*, his mother,] had no affiliation, even remote, with law enforcement and nothing in [declarant's] statement suggested that he meant her somehow to convey his utterance to the police, we think the fact that she was a lay person—indeed, a family member—must weigh against a finding that it was testimonial.") (citations omitted); *Cannon*, 254 S.W.3d at 305 (quoted below, in note 29); Garcia v. State, 246 S.W.3d 121, 133 (Tex. App. 2007) (statements to co-workers and friends, and to declarant's divorce attorney).

22. Davis v. Washington, 547 U.S. 813 (2006).

the primary purpose of the interrogation is to establish or prove past events potentially relevant to later criminal prosecution.[23]

"[N]ot all hearsay implicates the Sixth Amendment's core concerns."[24] Whether particular hearsay does or not depends on its primary purpose, which requires that the statement be judged in its context.[25] When investigating officers first arrive on the scene it is often the case that they need to assess the situation—the continuing danger, if any, to the victim, the officers themselves, and the public at large; the extent of the victim's injuries—and, in order to

---

23. *Davis*, 547 U.S. at 822 (emphasis added). *Accord, e.g.*, People v. Romero, 187 P.3d 56, 80 (Cal. 2008).

24. *Crawford*, 541 U.S. at 51.

25. "An accuser who makes a formal statement to government officers bears testimony in a sense that a person who makes a casual remark to an acquaintance does not." *Crawford*, 541 U.S. at 51. *Accord, e.g.*, *Davis*, 547 U.S. at 823-24; Commonwealth v. Nesbitt, 892 N.E.2d 299, 309 (Mass. 2008) (the dying victim's call to the 911 operator and her answers to the 911 operator's questions were clearly designed to get help for the victim and assess the danger the situation presented to the victim, first responders, and others; "As the 911 call revealed, [declarant] could barely talk at the time and was incapable of spelling her name or describing her injuries. She, like any person in that position, would have been consumed by the immediacy of the situation and was struggling to communicate. 'It is almost inconceivable that, moments after such an event, [someone in declarant's] condition—described as essentially frantic—could have spoken in contemplation of a future legal proceeding.' In these circumstances, her statement was plainly not testimonial."); Long v. United States, 940 A.2d 87, 94 n.6 (D.C. 2007) ("'[T]he Supreme Court has defined "testimonial" in functional rather than categorical terms.... [W]hile the purpose of any questioning is critical to the Court's analysis, the nature of the declarant's statement remains a significant factor.'... [T]he line between testimonial and non-testimonial statements will not always be clear,' and 'each victim statement thus must be assessed on its own terms and in its own context to determine on which side of the line it falls.'") (first quoting Thomas v. United States, 914 A.2d 1, 14 (D.C. 2006) and then United States v. Arnold, 486 F.3d 177, 189 (6th Cir. 2007) (en banc) (paragraph break omitted)).

"[S]tatements are not testimonial simply because they might reasonably be used in a later criminal trial. Rather, a critical consideration is the primary purpose of the police in eliciting the statements. Statements are testimonial if the primary purpose was to produce evidence for possible use at a criminal trial; they are nontestimonial if the primary purpose is to deal with a contemporaneous emergency such as assessing the situation, dealing with threats, or apprehending a perpetrator." People v. Romero, 187 P.3d 56, 81 (Cal. 2008) (citing cases). In *Romero*, officers responding to an emergency call "encountered an agitated victim of a serious assault, who described" his assailants and the attack. *Id.* His statements provided the officers "with information necessary for them to assess and deal with the situation, including taking steps to evaluate potential threats to others by the perpetrators, and to apprehend the perpetrators." *Id.* The primary purpose of the statements was not to produce evidence for a later trial, but "to determine whether the perpetrators had been apprehended and the emergency situation had ended or whether the perpetrators were still at large so as to pose an immediate threat."

do this, they often need to know who is doing what to whom. Statements to an officer in this context are nontestimonial.[26] On the other hand, the danger may have passed, the suspect may be in custody, and the primary purpose of the inquiry may be to collect and maintain evidence to use in the hoped for trial of the perpetrator. Statements obtained in this context are testimonial.[27]

And, of course, in some contexts statements to the police can slide from one primary purpose to another.[28] In *Davis v. Washington*,[29] the out-of-court declarant was the victim and the out-of-court statement was to a 911 opera-

---

26. *Continuing danger: Davis*, 547 U.S. at 831 (this "may *often* mean that 'initial inquiries' produce nontestimonial statements.") (emphasis in original); Long, 940 A.2d at 97-98 ("Under the circumstances Officer James' immediate task was not to investigate but to find out what had caused the injuries so that he could decide what, if any, action was necessary to prevent further harm. Asking [the victim] 'what happened' was a normal and appropriate way to begin that task.... Viewed objectively, [Officer James'] questions were designed to find out whether there was any continuing danger and to respond to the situation with which he was confronted." (citations and internal and multiple quotation marks omitted)).

Assessing the victim's injuries: State v. Warsame, 735 N.W.2d 684, 693 (Minn. 2007) (to assess a victim's injuries "officers must inevitably learn the circumstances by which the party was injured, and if the circumstances of the questions and answers objectively indicate that gaining such information is the primary purpose of the interrogation, then the party's statements are nontestimonial").

27. *E.g.*, Bobadilla v. Carlson, 570 F.Supp.2d 1098, 1111 (D. Minn. 2008) (five days after the sexual abuse of a child, after the police investigation had begun and a suspect had been identified, and the victim was not at imminent risk, the detective in charge initiated a formal interview with the victim, at police headquarters; the primary purpose of the statements was testimonial).

28. The interrogation can begin with the intent to get the situation under control and, once order is assured, can flow into one with the intent of gathering information to use in the prosecution of the perpetrator. *E.g.*, Long v. United States, 940 A.2d 87, 98 n.12 (D.C. 2007).

In State v. Cannon, 254 S.W.3d 287 (Tenn. 2008), the victim had been raped. She was treated by emergency-room medical professionals. Statements she made in the course of this treatment were nontestimonial. Later she was examined by a sexual-assault nurse examiner who was trained to examine suspected rape victims, who had been instructed by the police on how to ask questions and collect evidence, and who characterized her examination as an interrogation. By the time the victim talked with this nurse-examiner she had been treated and stabilized. Her statements to this nurse were testimonial. "[T]he primary purpose of th[is] interrogation was 'to establish or prove past events potentially relevant to later criminal prosecution.'" *Id.* at 305 (quoting *Davis*, 547 U.S. at 822). Moreover, the court recognized that its holding "should not be interpreted as a blanket rule characterizing as testimonial all the portions of all out-of-court statements given by sexual assault victims to sexual assault nurse examiners. As the Supreme Court in *Davis* recognized, statements may evolve from nontestimonial to testimonial." *Cannon*, 254 S.W.3d at 305 (citing *Davis*, 547 U.S. at 828).

29. 547 U.S. 813 (2006).

tor. The Court held that the "victim's statements to the 911 operator evolved from nontestimonial to testimonial at the point when the assailant drove away from the scene and the ongoing emergency ended."[30] If an assailant, who is not a danger to anyone other than the declarant, drives away, the declarant's statements may turn testimonial; if the assailant comes back, or even just seems to have come back, the statements may turn nontestimonial again.[31]

It is the same with out-of-court statements to family members or friends, to healthcare workers,[32] and to newspaper reporters. It is the same with spontaneous statements,[33] excited utterances,[34] recorded recollections, and public

---

30. *Cannon*, 254 S.W.3d at 305.

31. Smith v. State, 947 A.2d 1131, 1134 (D.C. 2008) ("[S]tatements about the forcible entry and physical attack upon complainant shortly before her call for help came well within the scope of nontestimonial circumstances because they objectively indicate that their main purpose was to summon help for an ongoing emergency.... In the circumstances here, it is undisputed that when complainant made the 911 call, she did not know appellant's location, could not know if the attack had ended, and feared he might return.").

32. When a victim is talking with medical professionals for the primary purpose of securing medical diagnosis and treatment, the victim's statements are nontestimonial. When the victim is talking with medical professionals for purposes of aiding the criminal investigation, the victim's statements are testimonial. State v. Buda, 949 A.2d 761, 778-79 (N.J. 2008) (a sobbing and emotional three-year-old child, in the hospital and likely to have been beaten, was questioned by a Division of Youth and Family Services (DYFS) worker about what had happened; the boy made statements implicating his father; the DYFS worker "was seeking information from a victim to determine how best to remove the very real threat of continued bodily harm and even death"; though the child's statements are certainly relevant to the investigation of the crime and the prosecution of the perpetrator that "did not convert it, in these circumstances, into a testimonial statement"); State v. Snowden, 867 A.2d 314, 329 (Md. 2005) ("The fact that there is a therapeutic element to the interviews does not eclipse the overriding fact that the interviews were designed to develop testimony that may be used at trial.").

33. *Buda*, 949 A.2d at 777-78 ("Because spontaneous statements do not bear the indicia of 'a formal statement to government officers' but instead are akin to 'a casual remark to an acquaintance[,]' we conclude ... that N.M.'s ... spontaneous and unprompted hearsay statement to his mother that 'Daddy beat me' is nontestimonial."); State v. Contreras, 979 So.2d 896, 903-04 (Fla. 2008) (canvassing cases where a child victim's "spontaneous statement to a friend or family member.... [or] to a medical professional" are not testimonial, and cases where "statements by child victims to police officers or members of child protection teams are testimonial in nature"); State v. Arroyo, 935 A.2d 975, 999 n.23 (Conn. 2007) (the social worker's primary purpose in taking the child victim's statements was to provide medical assistance; the statement was nontestimonial despite the fact that law enforcement personnel observed, and retained audiotapes of, the interview).

34. Long v. United States, 940 A.2d 87, 98 (D.C. 2007) ("As the trial court implicitly found when it admitted [the statements] as excited utterances, [declarant's] exclamations were not really responsive to [the officer's] questions. 'While the fact that [the] ... state-

records and reports. It is the same with lab reports,[35] test results, and other records of a regularly conducted activity.[36] It is the same with all out-of-court statements offered against the accused in a criminal prosecution.[37] In context, what was the primary purpose of the "conversation?" Was it sharing a confidence, seeking medical assistance, exclaiming out of shock or fear, or fulfilling a business duty, or was it developing evidence for use at trial? Or was it primarily some other purpose altogether?

---

ment was unprompted and thus not in response to police interrogation does not by itself answer the inquiry, [it] at least suggests that the statement was nontestimonial." (citations omitted)); United States v. Brito, 427 F.3d 53, 61 (1st Cir. 2005) (some courts hold that all excited utterances are nontestimonial and others hold that the excited nature of an utterance is irrelevant to whether it is testimonial; this court rejects both, holding that "the excited utterance and testimonial hearsay inquiries are separate, but related"—the former "focuses on whether the declarant was under the stress of a startling event" and the latter "focuses on whether a reasonable declarant, similarly situated (that it, excited by the stress of a startling event), would have had the capacity to appreciate the legal ramifications of her statement").

35. As I write this chapter, there is a case before the Supreme Court dealing with the Confrontation Clause and lab reports. Commonwealth v. Melendez-Diaz, 870 N.E.2d 676 (Mass. 2007), cert. granted, Melendez-Diaz v. Massachusetts, 128 S.Ct. 1647 (2008).

36. See the discussion of business records in the main text, a few paragraphs below this footnote.

37. There may be one exception to the general rule that testimonial hearsay statements offered against the accused in a criminal case are inadmissible unless the accused has, or has had, an opportunity to cross-examine the declarant, and that is when the statement fits under the hearsay exception for statements under belief of impending death. As explained in Crawford, the reasons for this are historical. The Confrontation Clause meant to constitutionalize the pre-ratification common law of confrontation, which included an exception for statements under belief of impending death. Crawford, 541 U.S. at 56. Accord, e.g., Commonwealth v. Nesbitt, 892 N.E.2d 299, 310-11 (Mass. 2008) "Although many dying declarations may not be testimonial, there is authority for admitting even those that clearly are. We need not decide in this case whether the Sixth Amendment incorporates an exception for testimonial dying declarations. If this exception must be accepted on historical grounds, it is sui generis." Crawford, 541 U.S. at 56 n.6 (citations omitted).

If this is accepted as an exception to the constitutional rule regarding confrontation, that leaves open this question: Does the confrontation exception only include statements covered by this hearsay exception as it existed pre-ratification, or does it include statements covered by post-ratification expansion of the hearsay exception? Did the Framers intend to allow statements under belief of impending death only to the extent they were allowed under the hearsay exception as it existed on the day of ratification or did they mean to allow for expansion or retraction of the exception? See Nesbitt, 892 N.E.2d at 311 ("Thus, in the unique instance of dying declarations, we ask only whether the statement is admissible as a common-law dying declaration, and not whether the statement is testimonial.").

To decide whether a statement is testimonial requires a thorough review of the context in which the statement was made, and, sometimes, because the primary purpose of a statement can change as the conversation progresses, a thorough review of the context in which various parts of the statement were made.

Regarding business records, *Crawford* states that, "by their nature [they are] not testimonial."[38] By nature they are not, but in context they can be. There are lots of business records that are specifically prepared to be used in criminal trials—to "testify" against the accused in an expected criminal trial. An example might be a report on the chemical analysis of the powder found on the defendant that is a necessary predicate to the decision to prosecute and then, at trial, stands as evidence (maybe the only evidence) of an essential element of the crime. This report is prepared in anticipation of the fact that, depending on the results of the test, the information in the report will be used to prosecute a defendant in a criminal case.[39] This business record is "a formal statement

---

38. *Crawford*, 541 U.S. at 56.
Just as business records are, by their nature, nontestimonial, statements by confidential informants may be, by their very nature, testimonial. United States v. Cromer, 389 F.3d 662, 670-71 (6th Cir. 2004); Turner v. Commonwealth, 248 S.W.3d 543, 545 (Ky. 2008) (citing United States v. Nettles, 476 F.3d 508, 517 (7th Cir. 2007); United States v. Hendircks, 395 F.3d 173, 181 (3d Cir. 2005)).

39. *Testimonial*: *E.g.*, State v. Belvin, 968 So.2d 516, 520 (Fla. 2008) (finding a "breath test affidavit" testimonial where "the sole purpose of [the] affidavit is to authenticate the results of the test for use at trial"); State v. Johnson, 982 So.2d 672, 678 (Fla. 2008) (finding a lab report from the Florida Department of Law Enforcement testimonial where it was prepared "in anticipation of the prosecution of the defendant" and "used by the State to prove that the seized substances were illegal drugs") (discussing cases); State v. March, 216 S.W.3d 663, 666 (Mo. 2007) (lab report "prepared solely for prosecution to prove an element of the crime charged is 'testimonial'"); State v. Caulfield, 722 N.W.2d 304, 309 (Minn. 2006) (lab report identifying seized substance as cocaine was prepared for litigation and was testimonial);

Not testimonial: United States v. Mendez, 514 F.3d 1035, 1043 (10th Cir. 2008) (ICE is a centralized database that archives records of documents granting entry into the United States; ICE was created and is maintained "in connection with ongoing regulatory functions independent of prosecution"; the primary purpose of the database is not testimonial) (citing many cases); Rockwell v. State, 176 P.3d 14, 26 (Alaska Ct. App. 2008) ("passport stamps and immigration card ... were not made and maintained for the primary purpose of criminal investigations, and the [Peruvian] government employees who stamped the documents preformed a ministerial duty that had nothing to do with prosecuting a particular person for criminal activity"; they "are not 'testimonial hearsay'"); Commonwealth v. Verde, 827 N.E.2d 701, 703-05 (Mass. 2005) (the lab reports here are "akin to ... business record[s] and the Confrontation Clause is not implicated by this type of evidence"; additionally, reports of chemical analysis "are neither discretionary nor based on opinion; rather,

to government officers."[40] Use as evidence may not be the report's primary purpose, but it is *a purpose* and in certain contexts it could be *the primary purpose* and, therefore, be testimonial.[41] (*Melendez-Diaz v. Massachusetts*, awaiting decision in the Supreme Court as this is written, may have answered this question already.[42])

While a record of the results of a breath test might be testimonial, as a general rule, a certificate of inspection regarding the breath-testing equipment should be nontestimonial. Depending on the facts, the former may have been recorded to be used in the potential criminal prosecution of the person whose breath was tested (or an attempt to get a dangerous driver off the road or, perhaps most likely, both), while the latter is a statement by an expert who has inspected a piece of equipment. The inspector's primary purpose is not preparing evidence to be used in a criminal prosecution but making sure that the machine is in proper working order and that those who will use it will know it is in proper working order. While the certificate may be used by the prosecutor in a criminal case, that use is not its primary purpose. Officers must know the machine works whether they will ever arrest anyone based on its results or not.[43]

---

they merely state the results of a well-recognized scientific test ... [and] are well within the public records exception to the confrontation clause [sic]").

40. *Crawford*, 541 U.S. at 51. *Johnson*, 982 So.2d at 677–78 ("[W]e find a distinction between records that are prepared as a routine part of a business's operation and records that are prepared and kept at the request of law enforcement agencies and for the purpose of criminal prosecution."); State v. Sweet, 949 A.2d 809, 819 (N.J. 2008) ("'A laboratory certificate in a drug case [setting forth that the substances at issue in that criminal case are, in fact, controlled dangerous substances] is not of the same ilk as other business records, such as an ordinary account ledger or office memorandum in a corporate-fraud case.'") (quoting State v. Simbara, 811 A.2d 448, 455 (2002)).

41. In United States v. Qualls, 553 F. Supp. 2d 241, 242 (E.D.N.Y. 2008), the court considered the admissibility of certifications authenticating foreign business records. The court stated that these "certifications are, at least superficially, statements attested to and 'produced through the involvement of government officers ... with an eye towards trial.'" *Id.* at 246. It concluded that Confrontation Clause issues arise with respect to the documents that were being introduced into evidence against accused, but not with the documents that were being used to authenticate the former. In part, the court relied upon the Supreme Court's statement in *Crawford* that business records "by their nature were not testimonial," *id.* at 246 (quoting *Crawford*, 541 U.S. at 56), and concluded that the documents used to authenticate those documents are not testimonial. *Qualls* makes too much of *Crawford*'s statement about business records. As discussed above, in the text, *Crawford* does not seem to mean that no business record can ever be testimonial. By the same reasoning it makes sense that while a lot of authenticating documents will not be testimonial, some may be.

42. Melendez-Diaz v. Massachusetts, 128 S.Ct. 1647 (2008) (order granting certiorari).

43. *See Sweet*, 949 A.2d at 819. One court argues that "§3505 certifications do not con-

The same kind of analysis can be applied to any number of other kinds of lab tests. Sometimes the results will be testimonial and sometimes not. Take the results of an autopsy. "Although any experienced [pathologist] is undoubtedly aware of the possibility that any information he gleans may ultimately become evidence, building a prosecution is not" necessarily the motivation for the pathologist's work.[44] An autopsy report can be testimonial or nontestimonial. A pathologist performing an autopsy, and creating a report, in a case where a death appears to be accidental, may uncover evidence of murder. While this may change the primary purpose for which the report is used, it does not seem to change the primary purpose for which the report was prepared. It is not likely to change the nature of the report from nontestimonial to testimonial.

An autopsy could be "in response to an emergency situation"[45] involving a possible epidemic, and being performed to get the situation under control, rather than to provide evidence. On the other hand, it could be an intentional gas attack and an autopsy with mixed motives: How do we help the affected survivors, and how do we convict those responsible? Just like statements by victims to investigating officers, lab work can evolve from nontestimonial to testimonial. And sometimes, when, for example, the police deliver a gunshot body and tell the pathologist, "There has been a murder, we have a suspect with a

---

tain any information about defendants, the relative merits of the charges against defendants, or any factual support for the charges. They simply attest to the reliability of 'the procedures necessary to create a business record.'" *Qualls*, 553 F.Supp.2d at 246 (quoting United States v. Ellis, 460 F.3d 920, 927 (7th Cir.2006)). The person whose job includes authenticating business or public records does so when called upon to do so. The authenticator can be called on by the police or a prosecutor who the authenticator knows wants the information to use in a criminal trial. Presumably, then, the Confrontation Clause can be an issue.

If the law focuses on the individual certificate of authentication, this last scenario seems to be a testimonial statement—a testimonial affidavit—made to be used in the prosecution of an accused. It is difficult to see how simply saying that the certificates "simply attest to the reliability of 'the procedures necessary to create a business record'" solves this problem. If the law focuses on the business of the person who prepares the certificates of authentication, then the answer depends on whether the authenticator primarily prepares certificates for police and prosecutors for use in criminal trials or, on the other hand, primarily prepares such certificates for a wide variety of people and organizations, for a wide variety of purposes. If the former, the defendant has a right to confront the authenticator at trial, unless the authenticator is unavailable and the defendant had the opportunity to cross-examine the authenticator. If the latter, then the Confrontation Clause does not bar receipt of the certificate.

44. Long v. United States, 940 A.2d 87, 97 (D.C. 2007) (substituting pathologist for police officer).

45. *Id.*

weapon, and we need to build a case," the work of the pathologist is to develop evidence for possible use at trial—the report is testimonial.[46]

In many cases, the lab technician is not going to remember the details or the results of any particular lab work, particularly lab work done months or years before the trial. In these situations, applying the Confrontation Clause would result in the lab technician having to be brought in to testify that he or she does not remember. Once this is done, the Confrontation Clause is not a problem because the out-of-court declarant is available and can be confronted, and the report can be entered into evidence under a hearsay exception.

c. Efficiency

Calling the expert who prepared a lab report that fits under an exception to the hearsay rule might be a significant waste of time and resources. However, efficiency is not the hallmark of individual rights. Most individual rights make government less efficient. A large part of the reason for individual-rights protection is to prevent government from taking the most efficient—the cheapest and easiest—approach when doing so infringes fundamental values.[47] An

---

46. Cases that say otherwise—cases that say that these kinds of reports are business records and therefore are never testimonial—seem to be incorrect. Take, for example, United States v. De La Cruz, 514 F.3d 121 (1st Cir. 2008), which states that, "[a]n autopsy report is made in the ordinary course of business by a medical examiner who is required by law to memorialize what he or she saw and did during an autopsy. An autopsy report thus involves, in principal part, a careful and contemporaneous reporting of a series of steps taken and facts found by a medical examiner during an autopsy. Such a report is, we conclude, in the nature of a business record, and business records are expressly excluded from the reach of Crawford." Id. at 133 (citing cases). Such a rigid rule is contrary to Davis' primary purpose test. It fails to recognize that the primary purpose of some lab tests (business records or not) is testimonial and the primary purpose of others is nontestimonial. The lesson from Davis surely is that each statement must be considered on its own facts and circumstances.

47. In Qualls, the court noted that in complex cases involving a lot of "business records from numerous sources, including foreign entities," it would be inefficient to have "to call a live witness or to accompany the defendant on a deposition abroad to lay the foundation for the business records of each foreign entity it sought to introduce." Qualls, 553 F.Supp.2d at 246. This, however, is a policy argument, not a constitutional argument. As noted in the main text, individual constitutional rights tend not to be efficient. The most efficient way of doing the government's business rarely needs protection. As with free speech, equal protection, and due process, there will be time when the exercise of the right to confront witnesses will be horribly inefficient. Efficiency is not the goal of constitutional rights. See Bowser v. Synar, 478 U.S. 714, 736 (1986) ("'Convenience and efficiency are not the primary objectives—or the hallmarks—of democratic government.'") (quoting INS v. Chadha,

approach to this problem that may be more efficient and still satisfy the confrontation right is to recognize that there is nothing in the Confrontation Clause that says that the out-of-court declarant has to be called to the stand by the prosecutor rather than the defendant. When the technician can be subpoenaed or will come into court voluntarily the prosecutor could offer the report and the defendant could call the technician as a witness if the defendant chooses to do so.[48]

In any event, calling a technician who does not remember details regarding the lab report in question is not necessarily a waste of time and resources. The technician will certainly have memory of how tests are generally conducted in the lab in question: chance of contamination, rate of error, expertise and experience of the technicians, quality of the equipment, standards controlling techniques, and other factors relevant to the credibility of and the proper weight to be given to the evidence.

In addition, if the technician who prepared the report is unavailable—dead, for example—then another expert could be brought in to form his or her own expert opinion based on the report. The rules of evidence allow experts to testify to opinions that are based on inadmissible evidence when it is reasonable for experts in the field to form such opinions based on such evidence.[49] Surely the Confrontation Clause does not mean that all expert testimony must be based on firsthand observation. Such a rule would do away with expert testimony in

---

462 U.S. 919, 944 (1983)). *See also Chadha*, 462 U.S. at 959 ("The choices … made in the Constitutional Convention impose burdens on governmental processes that often seem clumsy, inefficient, even unworkable, but those hard choices were consciously made by men who had lived under a form of government that permitted arbitrary governmental acts to go unchecked.")

48. Surely the right to confrontation is satisfied when the defendant calls and examines the witness. Why then wouldn't the defendant waive the right when he or she can call the witness and chooses not to do so?

One court has stated that *Crawford* announced "a *per se* rule: The Confrontation Clause bars the government from introducing testimonial statements at trial against a criminal defendant without calling the declarant to testify in person, unless the declarant is unavailable and the defendant had a prior opportunity to cross-examine the declarant." *Long*, 940 A.2d at 93 (quoting Thomas v. United States, 914 A.2d 1, 11 (D.C. 2006)). It seems to me that this is not entirely true. The government need not necessarily have called the declarant to the stand so long as the declarant is available for the defendant to call to the stand. All that is required is an opportunity to cross-examine the declarant at trial or unavailability and a prior opportunity to have cross-examined the declarant. *See Crawford*, 541 U.S. at 56 (regarding testimonial statements by an unavailable declarant the court writes of the necessity for a "prior *opportunity* to cross-examine.…" (emphasis added)).

49. *See* above, Chapter 8(I)(D)(3).

criminal trials, except, of course, for that offered by the defendant. All experts base opinions on what they have read, what they have been told, work that others have done. Experts base their opinions on the work of generations of experts who came before them. The expert to be confronted does not always have to be the exact same expert who did every piece of the leg work, who prepared every part of the report, and it needn't even be the one who prepared the report so long as the new expert has formed a relevant and independent conclusion. The testimony is the conclusion of the new expert; the new expert can be confronted. Just the same as expert opinion can be a "way around" the bar of the hearsay rule,[50] it can be a way to satisfy the demands of the Confrontation Clause.[51]

B. Forfeiture of the Confrontation Right

The right to confront witnesses is forfeited when the accused procures the unavailability of a witness and does so, in part at least, with the intent to make the witness unavailable.[52]

C. Situations Where the Right Attaches but Is Not Infringed

The right to confront witnesses is satisfied in either one of two ways. The right to confront witnesses is, of course, satisfied when the declarant is available to testify at the trial where the statement is offered. It is also satisfied where the accused had a prior opportunity to cross-examine the declarant about the statement and the state can show that the declarant is unavailable to testify in person.[53]

---

50. *Id.*

51. *See, e.g.,* United States v. Richardson, 537 F.3d 951, 960 (8th Cir. 2008) (a forensic scientist's opinion testimony about DNA evidence, based on the work of another forensic scientist in her office, "did not violate the Confrontation Clause"; she testified about "her independent conclusions derived from another scientist's test results" and she "was subject to cross-examination").

52. Giles v. California, 128 S.Ct. 2678, 2687 (2008) (the defendant's conduct must be "designed to prevent a witness's testimony."). *See also Crawford,* 541 U.S. at 62 ("[T]he rule of forfeiture by wrongdoing (which we accept) extinguishes confrontation claims on essentially equitable grounds."); Reynolds v. United States, 98 U.S. 145, 158 (1879) ("The Constitution does not guarantee an accused person against the legitimate consequences of his own wrongful acts.").

53. *See* State v. Cannon, 254 S.W.3d 287, 305 (Tenn. 2008) ("[U]navailability must be supported by proof, not by unsupported statements of counsel;" here, "the state offered no proof to establish unavailability," but only the Assistant District Attorney's "unsubstantiated assertion").

1. The Testifying Declarant

"The [Confrontation] Clause does not bar admission of a statement so long as the declarant is present at trial to defend or explain it."[54] It may be trite to say so but, if the defendant can confront the declarant at the criminal trial, then the defendant's right to confront the witness is not denied.

The right to confront the witness is satisfied if the accused has an *opportunity* to confront the witness. Actual confrontation is not required. This constitutional right is like all others in that the right-holder need not assert its protections.

Limiting or even denying cumulative re-cross-examination does not infringe the Confrontation Clause.[55] So long as the disallowed testimony is cumulative, the accused is not denied a full and fair opportunity to cross-examine the witness.

The declarant need not be cooperative. A hearsay declarant who takes the stand and denies any knowledge of the statement in question[56] or claims not to have any memory of the events in question[57] is available for cross examination. "The Confrontation Clause includes no guarantee that every witness called by the prosecu-

---

54. *Crawford*, 541 U.S. at 59 n.9. *See also, e.g.*, Kentucky v. Stincer, 428 U.S. 730, 744 (9187) (not allowing the accused to be present at a hearing to determine the competency of two alleged-victim children does not violate the confrontation right; if the children are found competent and testify, the accused can cross-examine them).

55. United States v. Perez-Ruiz, 353 F.3d 1, 10–11 (1st Cir. 2003).

56. *Crawford*, 541 U.S. at 59 ("[W]hen the declarant appears for cross-examination at trial, the Confrontation Clause places no constraints at all on the use of his prior testimonial statements."); State v. Simpson, 945 A.2d 449, 463 (Conn. 2008) (the right to confront the witness is satisfied if he or she "appears at trial, takes an oath to testify truthfully, and answers the questions put to him or her during cross-examination.") (citation omitted). *See also* United States v. Owens, 484 U.S. 554, 561 (1988) ("Ordinarily a witness is regarded as 'subject to cross-examination' when he is placed on the stand, under oath, and responds willingly to questions.").

57. *Crawford*, 541 U.S. at 53–54 ("[T]he Framers would not have allowed admission of testimonial statements of a witness who *did not appear at trial* unless he was unavailable to testify, and the defendant had had a prior opportunity for cross-examination.") (emphasis added); *Id.* at 59 n.9 ("[W]hen the declarant appears for cross-examination at trial, the Confrontation Clause places no constraints at all on the use of his prior testimonial statements."); *Owens*, 484 U.S. at 564 ("Admission of [a] statement of a [testifying] witness who is unable, because of memory loss, to testify concerning the basis for the [statement]" does not violate the Confrontation Clause) (pre-*Crawford*); State v. Holliday, 745 N.W.2d 556, 567 (Minn. 2008) (discussing the issue at length and citing numerous cases).

tion will refrain from giving testimony that is marred by forgetfulness, confusion, or evasion. To the contrary, the Confrontation Clause is generally satisfied when the defense is given a full and fair opportunity to probe and expose these infirmities through cross-examination, thereby calling to the attention of the factfinder the reasons for giving scant weight to the witness' testimony."[58]

2. A Pretrial Opportunity to Cross-Examine the Declarant

The right to confront witnesses is satisfied when the accused has an opportunity to cross-examine the accuser. That opportunity can come at the trial or prior to the trial. It is not enough, however, that the accused could have taken the deposition of the witness, but did not. For purposes of the Confrontation Clause, that does not count as an opportunity to cross-examine the declarant.[59] There must have actually been a trial, hearing, deposition, or other proceeding at which the accused had an opportunity to cross-examine the declarant.

3. The Declarant Who Is Present in the Courtroom but Invokes a Privilege or Otherwise Refuses to Testify

One particularly important Confrontation Clause question remaining to be answered concerns the declarant who is in the courtroom and can be put in the witness box but refuses to testify. The right to confront witnesses is the right to cross-examine them. Unlike a declarant who testifies but is uncooperative, a declarant who refuses to testify at all cannot be cross-examined. Therefore, if the out-of-court statement is testimonial and the accused did not have a prior opportunity to cross-examine the declarant (and unless the accused has forfeited the right to confront the witness[60]), then admitting the statement against the accused would seem to infringe his or her right to confront the witness.

4. The Child Victim Who Will be Further Traumatized if Made to Testify

Another important unanswered question is whether a child who has been a victim of abuse can ever be considered unavailable on account of the trauma the child would suffer if forced to testify.[61] Add up the majesty of some court-

---

58. Deleware v. Fensterer, 474 U.S. 15, 21–22 (1985).

59. *Johnson*, 982 So.2d at 681 n.6 ("[T]he opportunity to depose a declarant ... does not satisfy the opportunity for cross-examination required by the Confrontation Clause.").

60. *See* above, at part III(B) of this chapter.

61. *See generally, e.g.,* Robert P. Mosteller, *Testing the Testimonial Concept and Exceptions to Confrontation: "A Little Child Shall Lead Them,"* 82 IND. L.J. 917 (2007).

rooms, the solemnity of most court proceedings, the elevated bench with the black-robed gavel-wielding judge, the tables of lawyers facing the witness, the isolation and vulnerability one feels while sitting all alone in the witness box, and, in a jury trial, the strangers looking on from the jury box. On top of all of that, put the child in the witness box and the child's alleged victimizer a few feet out in front of the box, at a table with his defender armored in pin-stripes. If we did not know better, we might think that all of this was designed to traumatize the child further, and to leave the child afraid to testify. Can the trauma inflicted on the child-victim witness ever justify keeping the child off of the stand and entering into evidence the child's statement instead?

The first thing to be said here is that a lot of the trauma inducing circumstances can be avoided. The right to confront witnesses is the right to cross-examine them. It is not the right to get in their face, to bully or to instill fear in them. The child's testimony need not be taken in the courtroom or in any such solemn place. The judge need not be wearing a judicial robe (or even a suit and tie) or sitting behind an elevated bench (or even a desk), and there does not have to be a gavel anywhere in sight. The lawyers need not be lined up "across" from the child and the child need not be sitting all alone. And the judge can exercise control over the cross-examination of the child. Short of preventing a full and fair opportunity to cross-examine, the judge does have discretion to prevent cumulative questions, bullying, and the like. Creative ways of conducting this one part of the trial may reduce the trauma to an acceptable level.

In some cases, all, or some combination of the above can be an effective way to ameliorate the stress on the child to a point where there is no compelling reason to keep the child from testifying.

Furthermore, the jury may not even need to be present at the confrontation. Many a child sitting next to, even holding hands with, his or her mother, on a sofa in the judge's chambers, with the accused present, but not the jury, can be cross-examined. The child's in-chambers statement, including the cross-examination, can be recorded. With sufficient medical evidence that the presence of a "then existing physical or mental illness or infirmity"[62]—perhaps a physical or mental infirmity resulting from the abuse on trial—renders the child unavailable to testify, the recorded testimony, which the accused had an opportunity to cross-examine, can be introduced and played for the jury.[63]

---

62. Fed.R.Evid. 804(a)(4).
63. The defendant was able to cross-examine the unavailable witness, so the Confrontation Clause does not bar the evidence. The former testimony exception to the hearsay rule applies, so the hearsay rule does not bar the evidence.

The second thing to be said is that many out-of-court statements by the victim of child abuse are not "testimonial" and, therefore, the Confrontation Clause does not apply at all.[64] If they are not testimonial and either are not hearsay or fit under an exception to that rule, then the fact that the evidence is in the form of an out-of-court statement will not bar its admission.

In cases where none of the above works, what will happen seems to depend on whether the right to confront witnesses is an absolute right.[65] If it is absolute, then we are faced with three choices: find other evidence upon which to try the accused, force the child to suffer the trauma of facing the

---

For the majority in Coy v. Iowa, 487 U.S. 1012 (1988), Justice Scalia wrote that "'the right to *meet face to face*'" is the "irreducible literal meaning of the Clause." *Id.* at 1021 (quoting California v. Green, 399 U.S. 149, 175 (1970) (emphasis added in *Coy*). That can be accomplished in the less formal settings described.

64. Such statements are discussed throughout part III(A)(3) of this chapter.

65. Substantive constitutional rights are not absolute. If the state can show that the infringement is in service of a compelling state interest and is sufficiently narrowly tailored, it can infringe one's right to freedom of speech (*e.g.*, Osborne v. Ohio, 495 U.S. 103, 108 (1990) (finding a compelling state interest in "safeguarding the physical and psychological well-being of a minor") (internal quotation marks omitted)), freedom of expressive association (*e.g.*, Boy Scouts of America v. Dale, 530 U.S. 640, 648 (2000), equal protection of the law (*e.g.*, Parents Involved in Cmty. Schs. v. Seattle Sch. Dist. No. 1, 127 S.Ct. 2738, 2751–52 (2007); Johnson v. California, 543 U.S. 499, 505–14 (2005)), substantive due process (*e.g.*, Reno v. Flores, 507 U.S. 292, 301–02 (1993)), and perhaps the individual right to possess a useable firearm (District of Columbia v. Heller, 128 S. Ct. 2783, 2817–18 (2008))).

Unless this procedural right — confrontation — is absolute, then there will be situations where the state can satisfy the strict scrutiny test in the face of an assertion of the right to confront witnesses. *See* Coy v. Iowa, 487 U.S. 1012, 1022 (1988) (O'Connor, J., concurring) (Confrontation Clause rights "are not absolute but rather may give way in an appropriate case to other competing interests."); Illinois v. Allen, 397 U.S. 337, 343 (1970) (accused can lose the right to confront witnesses by his or her own "'misconduct'" during the trial; "It is essential to the proper administration of criminal justice that dignity, order, and decorum be the hallmarks of all court proceedings in our country."). Maryland v. Craig, 497 U.S. 836, 850 (1990) held that the accused's right to confrontation "may be satisfied absent a physical, face-to-face confrontation at trial only where denial of such confrontation is necessary to further an important public policy and only where the reliability of the testimony is otherwise assured." This pre-*Crawford* rule does not seem to satisfy *Crawford*'s holding that the Confrontation Clause calls for reliability to have been tested in one particular way: cross-examination. *See* part II of this Chapter, above. In addition, Justice Scalia's dissenting opinion in *Maryland v. Craig* states that the Confrontation Clause guarantees "face-to-face" confrontation "always and everywhere." *Id.* at 862 (Scalia, J., dissenting). Scalia seems to have won the point in his majority opinion in *Crawford*.

And see Johnson v. New Jersey, 384 U.S. 719, 734 (1966) (the suspect's "'absolute constitutional right to remain silent'"). *Compare* Boyd v. Dutton, 405 U.S. 1, 2 (1972) ("A per-

accused and being cross-examined in some format, whether in the court-room or not, or set the accused free. If it is not absolute but, like other con-stitutional rights, is subject to infringement when the state can prove that the infringement in question is a sufficiently narrowly tailored way of achiev-ing a compelling state interest,[66] then there will be cases where the out-of-court statement can be allowed into evidence and the available child be kept off the stand.[67]

---

son charged with a felony in a state court has an unconditional and absolute constitutional right to a lawyer."), *with* Wheat v. United States, 486 U.S. 153, 159, 160 (1988) (the Sixth Amendment "right to select and be represented by one's preferred attorney ... is circumscribed in several important respects," including "the institutional interest in the rendition of just verdicts in criminal cases...."") (paragraph breaks omitted).

66. Of all of the compelling state interests recognized by the courts, protecting children may be the most common. *E.g.*, Reno v. ACLU, 521 U.S. 844, 869 (1997) (the "compelling interest in protecting the ... well-being of minors" (internal quotation marks omitted); New York v. Ferber, 458 U.S. 747, 776 (1982) (the state's special and compelling interest in protecting children); United States v. Rouse, 111 F.3d 561, 567-68 (8th Cir. 1997) ("the court must ... protect the State's paramount interest in the welfare of the child;" the Sixth Amendment con-frontation right "must accommodate the State's 'compelling' interest in 'the protection of minor victims of sex crimes from further trauma and embarrassment") (pre-*Crawford*; cit-ing Globe Newspaper Co. v. Superior Court, 457 U.S. 596, 607 (1982); United States v. Bar-ror, 20 M.J. 501, 503 (A.F.C.M.R. 1985) (regarding the residual exception in child abuse cases: "[S]ociety has a deep and compelling interest in protecting the welfare of its children."). *See also* United States v. De Noyer, 811 F.2d 436, 438 (8th Cir. 1987) (admission of child-victim's statement rather than live testimony serves the interest of justice).

67. National security is another compelling state interest. Take a suspected terrorist who is an American citizen detained within the United States. Assume this person is put on trial—perhaps a full-blown criminal trial or some kind of newly created trial where pro-cedural and evidentiary rules are relaxed, but not the Constitution. Assume also that much of the persuasive evidence against the accused comes from the lips of a covert operative who is a foreign national living with family overseas. In any event, assume the trial of a ter-rorist where, if the confrontation right is absolute, there are these two choices: Make the op-erative testify at some kind of proceeding where the accused can confront the operative at great risk that secrets will be revealed and the operative and his or her family will be assas-sinated or dismiss the charges against the accused.

There can be national security cases where the state has a compelling interest in keep-ing secrets and protecting the lives of operatives and their families, and where keeping the operative off the stand (even if the operative is in physical and vocal disguise and the testi-mony is by deposition) is the least restrictive way of achieving either or both compelling interests. Just as there are terrorism cases where the government has a compelling interest and the lack of face-to-face confrontation is the least restrictive alternative, there are child-abuse cases where the same thing is true. If this right is not absolute, then, absent some other problem with the out-of-court statement, it can be used in lieu of live testimony.

D. *In Limine* Procedures

Because the resolution of these admissibility issues are so fact specific—particularly the issue of whether a statement is in whole or in part testimonial—"*in limine* procedure[s] are particularly important."[68] Courts should hold pretrial hearings to sort through the statement, to sort through the facts, and to decide what statements, or parts of statements, are testimonial and what statements are not. Statements should be redacted as necessary.[69]

E. Harmless Constitutional Error

A violation of the right of the accused to confront adverse witness is subject to harmless error review.[70] If the appellate court can say beyond a reasonable doubt that the verdict was not a product of the tainted evidence, then the error is harmless[71]. Errors of this class will not cause a conviction to be reversed.[72]

---

68. *Davis*, 547 U.S. at 829.

69. *Id.* In *Davis*, the Court related this to the procedure courts use to "redact or exclude the ... unduly prejudicial portions of otherwise admissible evidence." *Id.*

70. Some constitutional defects in trial procedure, called structural defects, are not subject to the harmless error rule. The damage done to the defendant when one of these defects if present cannot be apportioned against the rest of the evidence. United States v. Gonzalez-Lopez, 548 U.S. 140, 148 (2006); Duncan v. Louisiana, 391 U.S. 145 (1968); Tumey v. Ohio, 273 U.S. 510 (1927). Other constitutional defects can be measured, weighed against all of the other evidence admitted at the trial, and found "so unimportant and insignificant that they may, consistent with the Federal Constitution, be deemed harmless." Chapman v. California, 386 U.S. 18, 22 (1967). *Accord, e.g.*, Washington v. Recuenco, 548 U.S. 212, 218 (2006). *See also*, Fed. R. Crim. P. 52(a) ("Any error, defect, irregularity or variance that does not affect substantial rights must be disregarded.").

71. Mitchell v. Esparza, 540 U.S. 12, 17-18 (2003) ("A constitutional error is harmless when it appears beyond a reasonable doubt that the error complained of did not contribute to the verdict obtained.") (internal quotation marks omitted); Sullivan v. Louisiana, 508 U.S. 275, 279 (1993); State v. Gonzales Flores, 186 P.3d 1038 (Wash. 2008). The question is not whether the defendant would have been convicted "in a trial that occurred without the error ... That must be so, because to hypothesize a guilty verdict that was never in fact rendered—no matter how inescapable the findings to support that verdict might be—would violate the jury trial guarantee." *Sullivan*, 508 U.S. at 279.

72. *Chapman*, 386 U.S. at 24; United States v. Goldberg, 538 F.3d 280, 287 (3d Cir. 2008); United States v. Rittweger, 524 F.3d 171, 177 (2d Cir. 2008); United States v. Daulton, 266 Fed. Appx. 381, 387 (6th Cir. 2008); Schneble v. Florida, 405 U.S. 427 (1972); Smith v. State, 947 A.2d 1131, 1134 (D.C. 2008); Turner v. Commonwealth, 248 S.W.3d 543, 547 (Ky. 2008).

INDEX

MULTIPLE HEARSAY

See generally Chapter 11

Admissions May Cure Preceding Levels of Hearsay, 89–90, 109–120, 474, 487–489

Ancient Documents, *see* Ancient Documents Exception, this Index

Business Records, *see* Statement of a Regularly Conducted Activity Exception, this Index

Competence and Hearsay Contrasted, 505–506

Court Reporter Transcription, 483, 484–485

Depositions, *see* Depositions, this Index

Example Not Otherwise Indexed, 156–157

Expert Opinion Based on, *see* Opinion Evidence, this Index

Medical Diagnosis or Treatment Statements, 190–192

Personal Knowledge Required of Each Declarant in Chain of Hearsay, 499–500; *but see* Admissions; Personal or Family History Exception in Rule 804, No Personal Knowledge Required, this heading

Personal or Family History Exception in Rule 804, No Personal Knowledge Required, 319, 321, 489

Police Reports, 319, 321, 489

Public Records and Reports, *see* Public Records and Reports Exception, this Index

"Totem-Pole" Hearsay, 482

MUTUALITY OF INTEREST

See Former Testimony Exception, this Index

NEAR-MISS EVIDENCE

See generally 180, 336–341; *see also* the entry for the particular exception just missed

Grand Jury Testimony, *see* Grand Jury Testimony, this Index

OPENING STATEMENT

Basis-for-Opinion Evidence, Use of in Opening, 447

Good Faith Basis Objection, 467, 468–469

Harmless Error, Evidence Emphasized in Opening, 447, 468

Hearsay Objection, 467–469

Recent Fabrication or Improper Influence Suggested During Opening, 61

Rule 403 Objections, 468

OPINION EVIDENCE

See generally 425–458

Confrontation Clause, *see generally* Chapter 14

Expert Opinion,

See also Judicial Notice; Learned Treatises; Market Reports and Commercial Publications Exception; Medical Diagnosis and Treatment Exception; Public Records and Reports Exception; Record of a Regularly Conducted Activity Exception, this Index; Lay Opinion, this heading

Basis Evidence,

See generally 436–450

Amendment to Basis Evidence Rule Effective Dec. 1, 2000, 439–442

Categorically Inadmissible Basis Evidence, 442–444

Corroborating Opinions as Basis Evidence, 444–446

Limiting Instructions, 447–449

Prejudice and Unfair Prejudice (FED.R.EVID. 403 and FED.R.EVID. 703) compared, 439–441, 445–446

Relevant to Expert's Credibility, 437–439, 441, 445

Burden of Production Problems, *see* Hearsay Rule, Expert Opinion as a Way around the Barrier, this heading; Burdens, this Index

Burden of Proof Problems, *see* Hearsay Rule, Expert Opinion as a Way around the Barrier, this heading; Burdens, this Index

Expert Testifying As a Lay Witness, when Required, 457–458

"Foundation,"

See also Foundation, this Index
Burden, *see* Burdens, this Index
Foundational Elements, Expert Opinion Used as a Hearsay Exception, 426
Hearsay Rule, Expert Opinion as a Way around the Barrier, 427, 429–433, 471–472
Inadmissible Data,
  Opinion May Be Based on Inadmissible Data, 426, 427, 430–431, 433
  Reliance Must Be Reasonable, 426, 427, 434–436
Learned Treatises,
  See Learned Treatises, this Index
  Corroborating an Opinion with a Learned Treatise, 445
Limiting Instruction, 447–449, 496
Multiple Layers of Hearsay, Expert Opinion Based on, 436
Qualifying an Expert, 428–429
Uniform Composite Reports as Evidence Act, 433–434
First-Hand Knowledge Does Not Exist, 451–452
Lay Opinion,
  See also Personal or Family History Exceptions, this Index; Expert Opinion, this heading
  Expert Testifying As a Lay Witness, when Required, 457–458
  Lay Opinion Based on Hearsay, 430, 450–457
Line Between Lay and Expert Opinion, 430, 452–457
Personal or Family History Exception Excludes Opinion, 319, 321, 489
Prosecutor Stating Opinion Regarding Guilt, 326
Statement under Belief of Impending Death Exception, Foundational Elements and Opinion, 298
Trial Judge Stating Opinion Regarding Guilt, 326

PARTY'S OWN STATEMENT
See Statement by a Party Opponent, this Index

PAST RECOLLECTION RECORDED
See Recorded Recollection Exception, this Index

PERSONAL OR FAMILY HISTORY EXCEPTIONS
See generally 318–321; Table of Authorities under FED.R.EVID. 803(19) and 804(b)(4); *see also* cross-references under Records and Reports, this Index
Competence, 321, 504
Confrontation Clause, *see generally* Chapter 14
Evidentiary Burden, 134–136; *see also* Burdens, this Index
Factual Statements versus Opinions, 320–321
Foundation,
  See also, Foundation; Trustworthiness, this Index
  Burden, *see* Evidentiary Burden, this heading
  Elements of for Rule 804(b)(4), 319
Multiple Hearsay, 319, 321, 485, 489; *see generally* Chapter 11; *see additionally* Multiple Hearsay, this Index
Near-Miss Evidence, 345; *see generally* Near-Miss Evidence, this Index
Opinion Evidence of Family History, 320–321
Personal Knowledge Requirement, Specific Exemption, 319, 321, 489
Relationship between Rule 804(b)(4) and 803(19), 320, 485
Reputation evidence, 320
Stack up the Exceptions, 471–480
Unavailability,
  See also Unavailability, this Index
  Defined, 269–274
  Required, 269–274, 318, 319, 320

PREDECESSOR IN INTEREST
See Former Testimony Exception, this Index

PREJUDICE
See Unfair Prejudice, this Index

Foundation,
See also Foundation; Trustworthiness, this Index
Burden, *see* Burdens, this Index
Elements of, 78
Establishing with Statement Itself, 69–70, 81
Multiple Hearsay, 109–119; *see generally* Chapter 11; *see also* Multiple Hearsay, this Index
Personal Knowledge and Admissions, 109–119
Reliability, 68–69
Subsumed (Mostly) by Exclusion for Statement by Agent of a Party, 78–79

STATEMENT IN DOCUMENTS AF-FECTING AN INTEREST IN PROP-ERTY EXCEPTION
See generally 244–249; Table of Authorities under FED.R.EVID. 803(19) and 804(b)(4); *see also* Statement of Personal or Family History Exception; Property Interests, this Index
Evidentiary Burden, 134–136; *see also* Burdens, this Index
Foundation,
See also, Foundation; Trustworthiness, this Index
Burden, *see* Evidentiary Burden, this heading
Elements of, 245
Multiple Hearsay, *see generally* Chapter 11; *see additionally* Multiple Hearsay, this Index
Near-Miss Evidence, *see* Near-Miss Evidence, this Index
Stack up the Exceptions, 471–480

STATEMENT OF IDENTIFICATION OF A PERSON EXCLUSION
See generally 64–67; Table of Authorities under FED.R.EVID. 801(d)(1)(C)
Confrontation Clause, 67
Cross-Examination,
Declarant Must Be Testifying and Subject to, 67, 66–67

"Subject to" Defined, 66–67
Exclusion from Hearsay Rule, Not an Exception, 48–54
Foundation,
See also Foundation; Trustworthiness, this Index
Burden, *see* Burdens, this Index
Elements of, 64
Pretrial Identification of a Criminal Suspect, 65–66

STATEMENT OF PERSONAL OR FAM-ILY HISTORY EXCEPTION
See Personal or Family History Exceptions, this Index

STATEMENT UNDER BELIEF OF IM-PENDING DEATH EXCEPTION
See generally 270–274, 292–303; Table of Authorities under FED.R.EVID. 804(b)(2)
Competence of the Declarant, 300–303
Confrontation Clause, 303, 520; *see also* Chapter 14
Content of Statement, 299
Declarant Need Not Be Dead, 294–296
Deposition Anticipating Death, *see* Depositions, this Index
Evidentiary Burden, 134–136; *see also* Burdens, this Index
Foundation,
See also, Foundation; Trustworthiness, this Index
Burden, *see* Evidentiary Burden, this heading
Elements of, 292–293
Imminence of Expected Death, Declarant's Belief,
In general, 296–299
Question of Law, 136
Multiple Hearsay, *see generally* Chapter 11; *see additionally* Multiple Hearsay, this Index
Near-Miss Evidence, *see* Near-Miss Evidence, this Index
Other Evidentiary Problems Commonly Associated with These Statements, 300–303